THE GREAT JEWISH CITIES OF CENTRAL AND EASTERN EUROPE

A Travel Guide
and Resource Book
to Prague, Warsaw,
Crakow, and Budapest

ELI VALLEY

JASON ARONSON INC.
Northvale, New Jersey
Jerusalem

THE GREAT JEWISH CITIES OF CENTRAL AND EASTERN EUROPE

Bernard Kaplan

This book was set in 10 point Perpetua by Alpha Graphics of Pittsfield, New Hampshire and printed and bound by Book-mart Press, Inc. of North Bergen, New Jersey.

Copyright © 1999 by Eli Valley

10 9 8 7 6 5 4 3 2 1

All rights reserved. No part of this book may be used or reproduced in any manner whatsoever without written permission from Jason Aronson Inc. except in the case of brief quotations in reviews for inclusion in a magazine, newspaper, or broadcast.

Library of Congress Cataloging-in-Publication Data

Valley, Eli.
    The great Jewish cities of Eastern Europe / by Eli Valley.
       p. cm.
    Includes index.
    ISBN 0-7657-6000-2 (alk. paper)
    1. Jews—Czech Republic—Prague—History. 2. Prague (Czech Republic—Guidebooks. 3. Jews—Poland—Warsaw—History. 4. Warsaw (Poland)—Guidebooks. 5. Jews—Poland—Kraków—History. 6. Kraków (Poland)—Guidebooks. 7. Jews—Hungary—Budapest—History. 8. Budapest (Hungary)—Guidebooks. I. Title.
DS135.C96P846 1998
947—dc21   97-41373
                                                                          CIP

Printed in the United States of America on acid-free paper. For information and catalog write to Jason Aronson Inc., 230 Livingston Street, Northvale, NJ 07647-1726, or visit our website: www.aronson.com.

*Dedicated to my mother,
Marcia Steinbock,
and my father,
Noach Valley*

Contents

Acknowledgments	xv
Introduction: Peretz's Golem	xvii
A Note on the Term "Jewish Community"	xix

I   PRAGUE: CITY OF THE OLD AND THE NEW

INTRODUCTION	3
A HISTORY OF THE JEWS IN PRAGUE	5
In the Beginning	5
Servi Camerae Regiae	6
Oppression in the Fourteenth Century	7
Life among the Hussites	8
Persecution and Expulsion	9
The Renaissance and the Golden Age	10
The Seventeenth Century	12
Jewish Population Growth and the Familiants Laws	13
Expulsion: 1745–1748	14
The Edict of Tolerance	15
Enlightenment, Equality, Assimilation	17
The Holocaust	21
Postwar to Today	22
PRAGUE'S PHILOSOPHER KINGS	28
Tomas G. Masaryk	28
Vaclev Havel	30
SPOTLIGHT: RABBI JUDAH LOEW—THE "MAHARAL" (C. 1525–1609)	32
THE GOLEM OF PRAGUE	34
The Creation of the Golem	35
The Golem as Servant	37
The Golem as Savior	38
The End of Brother Thaddeus	40
The End of the Golem	41
THE GOLEM REDUX	44
Raba Bara Gavra	44
God's Golem	45
Golems in Jewish History	46
The Golem of Prague	48

VISITING PRAGUE: THE "JEWISH TOWN" TODAY	50
THE JURASSIC PARK OF JUDAISM	53
THE JEWISH ESSENTIALS	56
Praying in Prague	57
Mikveh	59
KEEPING KOSHER IN PRAGUE	60
Restaurant	60
Grocery Store	60
ORIENTATION AND SUGGESTED ITINERARY	61
The Altneuschul	64
The *Aron Hakodesh*	70
The *Amud*	72
The Women's Section	74
The *Bimah*	75
The Hebrew Inscriptions	76
The *Yahrzeit* Boards	77
The Banner	80
The High Synagogue	82
The Jewish Town Hall	85
The Pinchas Synagogue	88
The Old Jewish Cemetery	99
The Nefele Mound	116
The Ceremonial Hall	116
The Klausen Synagogue	121
The Maisel Synagogue	125
The Spanish Synagogue	129
ELSEWHERE IN PRAGUE	132
The Jerusalem Synagogue ("Jubilee")	132
The Old Olsany Cemetery	134
The New Olsany Cemetery	137
The Rudolfinum	140
The Statue of Rabbi Judah Loew (1910)	140
The Crucifix on Charles Bridge	141
Tyn Church	144
The Langweil Model of Prague	145

II WARSAW: CITY OF MONUMENTS

INTRODUCTION	149
A HISTORY OF THE JEWS IN WARSAW	150
The Earliest Jewish Community in Warsaw	150
Warsaw without Jews	150

The Rise of Praga	151
Partitioned Poland	152
Under Prussian Rule	153
The Duchy of Warsaw	155
St. Petersburg on the Vistula	155
Jewish Rebels	156
Jewish Life in the Nineteenth Century	158
Litvak Warsaw	159
The Jewish Utopias	160
Jewish Culture in Warsaw: The Triumph of Diaspora Jewry	161
Poland and the Jews between the Wars	163
The Holocaust	165
The Mass Deportations of July 22–September 21, 1942	170
The Warsaw Ghetto Uprising	171
The Generations After	173
SPOTLIGHT: EMMANUEL RINGELBLUM (1900–1944)	**177**
THE JEWISH ESSENTIALS	**179**
Praying in Warsaw	180
Mikveh	181
KEEPING KOSHER IN WARSAW	**182**
Restaurant	182
Buying Food	182
ORIENTATION AND SUGGESTED ITINERARY	**183**
The Jewish Cemetery in Warsaw	183
During the War	186
The Cemetery Today	187
The Memorial to Janusz Korczak	211
After the Cemetery: The Former Skra Stadium	213
The Memorial Route of Jewish Martyrdom and Struggle	214
Guide to the Monuments	216
The First Monument to the Warsaw Ghetto Uprising	217
The Warsaw Ghetto Monument	218
Elsewhere on the Monument Square	221
The Szmul Zygielbojm Memorial	222
Mila 18	225
Stawki 6/8	226
Umschlagplatz	228
The Umschlagplatz Square	229
The Monument	231
WARSAW: THE WALKING TOUR	**232**
Bohaterow Getta (Nalewki Street)	234
"Sony" Skyscraper (Tlomackie Street Synagogue)	237

The Jewish Historical Institute	238
Krochmalna Street	240
Plac Grzybowski	244
Prozna Street	244
The Street	245
The Buildings	247
Nine	247
Seven	247
Fourteen	248
Twelve	248
The Jewish Theater	249
The Nozyk Synagogue	249
ELSEWHERE IN WARSAW: PRAGA	**251**
A Brief History of Praga	251
Visiting Praga	252
Selected Highlights	253
The Praga Jewish Cemetery	253
Strezelecka Street 11/13	254
Stalowa Street 42	254
Mala Street	254
Klopotowskiego Street 31	255
Jagiellonska Street 8	255

III   CRACOW: CITY OF LEGENDS

INTRODUCTION	**259**
A HISTORY OF THE JEWS IN CRACOW	**261**
Life before Kazimierz	261
King Casimir the Great	262
The Dark Age of the Fifteenth Century	263
The Jews in Kazimierz	264
The Jewish Quarter of Kazimierz	265
The Kazimierz Ghetto?	267
The Golden Age	267
The Commercial Life of the Jews	269
Terrible Times	269
Into Modernity	270
The Holocaust	272
Postwar to Today	274
SPOTLIGHT: RABBI MOSES ISSERLES (1525 OR 1530–1572)	**275**
LEGENDS OF CRACOW	**278**
The Birth of the Rema	278

Yakov and the Heavenly Court	279
The Test	282
The *Cherem*	283
The Custom of the Wall	285
THE JEWISH ESSENTIALS	**287**
Praying in Cracow	288
Mikveh	289
KEEPING KOSHER IN CRACOW	**289**
ORIENTATION AND SUGGESTED ITINERARY	**291**
The Altschul	292
Old and Old New, Cracow and Prague	293
How Old Is Old?	294
The Twentieth Century and Beyond	295
The Vestibule	297
Entering the Main Sanctuary	298
The Main *Tzedekkah* Box	298
The Women's Sections	300
The *Bimah*	301
The *Aron Hakodesh*	302
The Museum Exhibit	303
Customs of the Altschul	304
The Rema Synagogue	307
The Old Jewish Cemetery of Cracow	310
History	312
Moses Isserles (1525 or 1530–1572): The *Rema*	315
Eliezer Ashkenazi (1512–1585)	318
Nathan Nata Spira (1585–1633): The *Megalleh Amukkot*	321
The Revealing of the Depths	322
The "Back" of the Cemetery: The Western Wall	326
Joel Sirkes (1561–1640): The *Bach*	326
Joshua ben Joseph (1578–1648): The *Meginnei Shlomo*	329
Abraham Joshua Heschel (d. 1663)	331
Michael Calahora (Late Seventeenth Century)	332
Isaac ben Mordechai Halevi (d. 1799)	333
Yomtov Lippman Heller (1579–1645): The *Tosefot Yomtov*	334
The Birth of a Legend	335
The Cemetery Square	337
The History	338
The Legend	338
The Original Story	339
Near the Cemetery Square	341
The Popper Synagogue	341

The High Synagogue	343
Nearby the High Synagogue	345
The Isaac Synagogue	346
The Legend of Reb Isaac Reb Jekeles	346
The Synagogue and Its Controversy	347
The Kupa Synagogue	350
Near the Kupa Synagogue	351
The Tempel	352
The New Jewish Cemetery	357
A Stroll through the New Jewish Cemetery	358
Elsewhere in Kazimierz	362
The Jewish Crafts School	362
Hebrew Grammar School	362
Plac Novy	363
Beit Midrash B'nei Emunah	363
Visniac's Gate	364
Beit Midrash Chevrah Tehilim	364
Corpus Christi Church	364
Kazimierz Town Hall	365
Bochenska Street	365
The Former Jewish Hospital	366
The Cracow Ghetto in Podgorze	366
History of the Cracow Ghetto	366
Selected Sites in the Former Ghetto	368

IV   BUDAPEST: CITY OF SYNAGOGUES

INTRODUCTION	375
A HISTORY OF THE JEWS IN BUDAPEST	376
The Magyars Arrive!	377
The Jewish Illiterate	378
The King's Favor, the Church's Rancor	378
Expulsion	379
The Law Book of Buda	380
The First Blood Libel of Hungary	381
The Jewish Prefect of Buda: King of the Jews	381
Among the Turks: Glory Days	382
The Obuda Century	384
Josef II	385
The Neolog Movement	387
Emancipation	389
World War I and the White Terror	389
The Holocaust	390
Postwar to Today	391

SPOTLIGHT: THEODOR HERZL (1860–1904)	396
THE JEWISH ESSENTIALS	399
Praying in Budapest	400
Mikveh	400
KEEPING KOSHER IN BUDAPEST	401
Restaurants	401
Butchers	402
Salami Store	402
Milk Store	402
Grocery Store	402
Patisserie	403
Hotel	403
ORIENTATION AND SUGGESTED ITINERARY	405
BUDA: JEWISH LIFE FROM THE MIDDLE AGES THROUGH THE TURKS	408
The Old Jewish District of Buda	408
The New Jewish District of Buda	411
The Mendel Houses	412
The Small Synagogue	414
The Star of David	414
The Arrow	415
Nearby the Small Synagogue	417
The Great Synagogue	417
The Churban of 1686	421
Megillat Buda	423
OBUDA: COUNT ZICHY'S JEWS IN THE EIGHTEENTH CENTURY	426
The Obuda Synagogue	428
PEST: THE JEW IN THE MODERN WORLD	431
The Hungarian Jewish Congress and the Three Synagogues of Pest	434
The Dohany Street Synagogue	436
Highlights of the Building	436
The Pulpits of Dohany	439
The *Aron Hakodesh*	439
The Dohany Organ	440
The Dohany Street Synagogue: A Legend!	441
Origins of the Dohany Street Synagogue	442
The Beginnings of the Synagogue	445
The Competition	447
The Opening of the Synagogue	448
The Dohany Temple of Solomon	450
The Dohany Street Church	451

The Hungarian Jewish Museum	452
The Martyrs' Cemetery	454
The Heroes' Temple	454
The Holocaust Memorial of Budapest	456
Nearby the Holocaust Memorial	457
The Rumbach Synagogue	458
History of the Rumbach Synagogue	460
The Rumbach and the Status Quo	462
The Status Quo Traditions of the Synagogue	463
The Rabbis of Rumbach	464
The Kazinczy Street Synagogue	465
ELSEWHERE IN BUDAPEST	**468**
Kozma Street Cemetery	468
Ohelim, Budapest Style	469
The World War I Memorial	470
The Holocaust Memorial	470
The Rabbinical Row	472
The Ujpest Synagogue	472
THE LIVING SYNAGOGUE: BUDAPEST'S SPECIAL TREASURE	**475**
The Dohany Street Synagogue	476
The Heroes' Temple	476
"Rumbach" Congregation	477
The Kazinczy Street Synagogue	477
The Rabbinical Seminary	478
Nagyfuvaros Synagogue	479
Bet Smuel ("Csaky")	480
Bet Aharon Synagogue	481
Dessewffy Street Synagogue	482
Bethlen Ter Synagogue	483
The Ujpest Synagogue	484
The Buda Synagogue	485
Teleki Ter Synagogue	486
Sasz Chevra	486
APPENDIX	**489**
Terezin	489
Treblinka	490
Auschwitz	492
GLOSSARY	**495**
BIBLIOGRAPHY	**501**
INDEX	**509**

Acknowledgments

It would not have been possible to write a book such as this without the generous cooperation of several people. I owe a sizeable chunk of gratitude to these individuals, spread throughout Europe, America, and Israel who assisted me while I was writing this book. I would like to take the space to thank them now.

Prague, of course, was my residence for years, and there is an unlimited number of individuals from that city whom I would like to thank. For assistance with this book, I'd like to thank Arno Parik, Alexandr Putik, Dani Ziss, Evan Lazar, Karel Cudlin, and, of course, Erika Borges for that first tour back in the old days of 1993.

In Warsaw, I am very grateful to the uncontested king of Warsaw Jewish history, Jan Jagielski, for accompanying me on practically every street of the city and for sharing his reservoir of knowledge. I would also like to thank Yale Reisner for his encyclopedic memory and his fortitude during my cosmic angst. Thank you also to Eleanora Bergman, Rabbi Chaskel Besser, Rabbi Michael Schudrich, Helena Datner, Helise Lieberman, Amos Levy, Kostek Gebert, Mateusz Kos, Krystoff Kononkowski, Ezra Mendelsohn, Sid Leiman, and Rabbi Dovid Goldwasser.

In Cracow, I would like to thank first and foremost Rabbi Lebovits, rebbe of the Nikolsberg *hasidim* in Spring Valley, New York. Rabbi Lebovits gave generously of his time and memory, inviting me into his home and sharing scores of legends, details, and nuances of Jewish civilization in Cracow. I am also greatly indebted to Henryk Halkowski, a wellspring of information who illuminated all corners of Cracow Jewish history. Thanks also to Henryk for helping me when I broke my ulna in the icy season. The volumes of the peerless Cracow historian Majer Balaban, written in Polish before the war, would have been all but inaccessible had it not been for the patient help of Anna Cichopek, a thoughtful guide with a big heart. Anna also assisted me in researching the wartime history of Cracow's Jews. I would like to thank Eugeniusz Duda for his endurance of my endless questions in a Czech masquerading as Polish, and for his keen insights into Cracow's Jewish history. Of course, I can't forget the Arielsters, especially Wojtek Olnat, for leisure time. Thanks also to Ivo Hribek for the pics, Jackie Cohen, the Sephardic limb therapist, for underwater aerobics, and my test-drive team of Hilary Soule and Laura Newmark for cutting through the jungle of early drafts.

In Budapest, I would like to thank Kinga Frojimovics, Zsuzsa Toronyi, and Tamas Szucs for pointing me to the right sources and for clarifying several aspects of Budapest's Jewish history. Rabbi Boruch Oberlander assisted me immeasurably, and I appreciate it. Erika Frohlich and her brother, Rabbi Robert, were very helpful as well. Thanks to the three generations of the Csillag family for hospitality, food, and games. Thanks also to Ilona Lukacs and the staff of the Jewish Theological Academy Library, and to Vera Szabo, Mark Lazar, Rabbi Laszlo Herczog, Rabbi Tamas Lowy, Rabbi Robert Deutsch, Aggie Peresztegi, Dora Niyari, Gabor Szanto, Zoltan Radnoti, David Ellenson, Tamas Kadar, and Judit and Zsuzsi Muller.

This book would not have been possible without the assistance of several polyglot friends who helped me navigate foreign language sources. These people asked for no further compensation than frequent pitstops at local pubs. For their generosity and kindness, I wish to express a heartfelt thanks: Ivo Hribek, Lisa Houghton, Manis Barash, Jonathan Terra, Helenka Roth, and Lukas Pribyl.

I am very grateful to the countless people I guided through Prague's Jewish quarter over the course of my years in Prague. It wasn't only an incomparable job, but each of those tours was an interactive mental draft of this book. Almost every one of my clients offered insights and analyses that I tried to include in some way in my writing. I would like to continue this tradition today—if you, ideal reader, have any comments or suggestions concerning your experiences, or recent changes to the sites included here, I would be eager to hear from you. I'd like to thank especially the several UCLA professors who turned a week-long conference in Prague into an unending interest and assistance in my work, particularly to David Myers, David Ellenson, and their extended families. I appreciate the help of Rabbi Chaim Rogoff and Shanna Koslowe. Rabbi Hershel Gluck, whose devotion to the Jewish communities of the region has not been matched anywhere, provided valuable assistance. In addition, I'd like to thank Jerold Goodman, a true philanthropist, and, of course, Adam Horovitz.

Naturally, thank you to my parents, to my big sister, Leah, for making me very proud, to Ray Rosenholtz for being a great person (and for the office 'n food), and to the rest of my family, especially the new additions, Ariel Kamen and Harrison Schiff, who entered this world while I was toiling over this book.

My biggest thanks to my friends, without whom I never would have remained in Prague. To name a few, in associative order: Dani Vesely, Patrik Vojtisek, Dasa Beran, Jiri Pospisil, Rudolf Kral, Petr Gyory, Renata Kabiljo, Mahulena and the Svoboda dynasty (including DJ Matej and Barnabas, but not Stalin & Benjy), Jajicek Porizova a nase krasny andely, Pinchas Mouric, Andrea Emyeiova, Martin Smok, Katka Ruzickova, Shoshi Janku, Sasa Braun, the blood of James Donahower, Martin Zemla, Pavel Kral, and Tomas Penicka. To those I may have forgotten, we'll do a rewrite. Thanks to the entire Prague Jewish Community, from my surrogate babicky to my teeny boppin' Jews. And to my little Slovak friends, too. Stateside, Andrea Kilpatrick, Jason Barr, and Jeff Fisher—I treasure the friendship.

I am thankful to Arthur Kurzweil for believing that this was a book that should be written, and for his continued support, guidance, and encouragement throughout the writing process. I am also very appreciative to Dana Salzman for her patient support during the editorial and production phases of this book.

❦ Introduction ❧
Peretz's Golem

One of the most mesmerizing visions of the Prague Golem, that superhuman anthropoid that shielded the Jews of the Ghetto, was written by the great Yiddish writer Y. L. Peretz. In just thirty-four lines, "The Golem" gives the briefest possible outline of the Golem's existence: the anti-Semitic attacks, Rabbi Loew's creation of the Golem, the Golem's superhuman work, and the Golem's ultimate demise. There are no details concerning the Golem's creation or activities. In fact, the story centers not on the Golem's life, but on its demise and storage in the attic of the Altneuschul of Prague. The story ends with a desperate proclamation:

> The *golem*, you see, has not been forgotten. It is still here! But the Name by which it could be called to life in a day of need, the Name has disappeared. And the cobwebs grow and grow, and no one may touch them.
>
> What are we to do?
>
> (Y. L. Peretz, "The Golem," in Irving Howe and Eliezer Greenberg, eds., *A Treasury of Yiddish Stories*)

In typical Peretz fashion the Golem is not simply a superhero of the Jews, but an entire culture and civilization that, by the beginning of the twentieth century, had become an afterthought to much of the Jewish world. The "Name" is more than God's Name; it is fervent belief, bound up in a culture where all of one's actions are determined by ancient tradition.

In Peretz's Europe, the birthplace and heart of much of this tradition, the Name had indeed been forgotten. So much the more so, then, is the case for American Jews, removed from the cradle of the Diaspora by thousands of miles and at least a century of isolation. When I worked as a tour guide for the Prague Jewish Community, what most surprised me was that the most secular and assimilated American Jews, who identified as Jews solely by culture, were literally starving for information about their roots and heritage. Secular Jews in America tend to identify most closely with the end of European Jewry: concentration on the Holocaust far exceeds that on any other period of world Jewish history. When Jews think of Central and Eastern Europe, the image that often comes to mind is a vast graveyard. Interest in the Holocaust is justified and necessary, but it has led to the unfortunate perception that Jews sprang up in Europe in the 1930s and died in the 1940s. Earlier periods of trial and triumph are simply a blur. And yet, I met thousands of Jews over the course of four years who were fascinated by the culture and nuance of Jewish history in life, not in death. Perhaps it was their trip to Europe that reminded them of the enormous span of pre-Holocaust Jewish life. It was like an entire unexplored world had been opened to them.

Now that the Iron Curtain has fallen and Jewish sites in Central and Eastern Europe are again the object of interest and delight, the slumbering giant of Jewish civilization is being awakened at last. It is the purpose of this book to remove as much of the cobwebs as possible, to restore at least some outline of the proverbial Name, and to bring the millennium-long culture of Central and Eastern European Jewry out of the attic and into life.

This book is part tour guide, part resource book. It is not written exclusively as a guide; only the most patient tourist can be expected to absorb a dozen pages while standing inside a synagogue packed with tourists. Instead, I advise you to read about the sites before you actually arrive at them. It is my intention to provide not only cursory dates and addresses, but also a comprehensive account of all aspects of Jewish life in these cities: from law to legend, from unique customs to architectural symbolism. It is meant to open up vistas of tangible Jewish history to any type of visitor. Secular Jews can learn about unique and rare traditions of their heritage, Orthodox Jews can learn about the multifaceted Jewish cultures that have always existed side-by-side with strict adherence to Jewish law, and Gentiles can gain a view into the Jewish world rarely seen by the outside Community. The book is meant to be enjoyed before, during, and after your visit to the region. It is my hope that, with this book, even the shortest visit to any of these cities will be an experience you will keep with you always.

This book is not meant to be geographically inclusive. Instead, its goal is to lift the veil of mystery surrounding the sites visited by tourists today. In order to delve as deeply as possible into these sites, the number of cities is necessarily limited. For example, Bratislava and Vilna, two of the more remarkable cities in the region, are not included. Vienna, which is farther east geographically than Prague, is also not included. In addition, hundreds of smaller towns in the region, which witnessed a development of Jewish life in many ways unique from the urban centers, are omitted. Why are only four cities included? Because this way, we can examine Jewish life in as much detail as possible in the places most tourists visit.

Why these four cities? Practically speaking, these cities are the most popular destinations among visitors to Central Eastern Europe today. But on another level, Prague, Warsaw, Cracow, and Budapest are a microcosm of practically every major trend in European Jewish history. Prague and Cracow, with their preserved synagogues from the Middle Ages and Renaissance, offer a view of seven hundred years of European Jewish civilization. All the nuances of a bygone life are there: incarceration in the ghetto, Church-inspired anti-Semitism, ancient synagogue symbolism, visionary legend and lore, prodigious philanthropy of court Jews, and the literary genius of rabbis. Warsaw and Budapest, whose sites derive mostly from the nineteenth and twentieth centuries, highlight an image of the European Jews as they entered the modern world. Here we have the quest for civil rights; the prosperity in secular arts, literature, and science; the problems of assimilation; the birthpangs of religious reform; the rise of modern Yiddish literature; the dreams of Jewish utopias in socialism, Zionism, and the Bund; and the transformation of anti-Semitism into a modern nationalist phenomenon. But this is not the only point of comparison. In the modern period alone, Prague and Budapest offer us a picture of Western European Jewry as it thrust itself away from tradition and into the modern world. Warsaw and Cracow, by contrast, draw a much different picture of Jews seeking to reconcile modernity with centuries-old Jewish traditions. In short, a visit to these four cities is perhaps the best education one can get in the full spectrum of Jewish civilization on the continent.

A NOTE ON THE TERM "JEWISH COMMUNITY"

The term "Jewish Community" appears repeatedly throughout this book. American visitors who associate the expression with Jewish Community Centers in the United States are often confounded by the term as it is used abroad. In Europe, the term refers to the independent communal authority (*kahal* in Hebrew) that collected taxes and administered all the affairs of the Jews in municipalities. The Jewish Community originated in the Middle Ages when the Church, the Crown, and the Jews themselves had vested interests in establishing a sovereign Jewish communal system that had full authority over Jewish tax collection and social services. Jewish Communities lost their authority in all but religious matters in the early nineteenth century, when European states began to integrate the Jews into secular society. Communities continued to exist as organized bodies, but with less control over Jewish life.

The Nazis transformed these pre-existing Jewish Community administrations into the *Judenrat*. After the war, the governments of communist countries reinvented the Jewish Community structure as a means to control and patrol the Jews. It is rare to find Jewish Community leaders during the communist era who were not forced to collaborate, in various ways, with state authorities. At the same time, Jewish Communities continued their age-old responsibilities such as allowing for some sort of religious life and providing social care for the elderly.

Today, Jewish Communities in Central and Eastern Europe continue to serve as the main administrative bodies for the Jews, but without interference from the state. These Jewish Communities handle religious affairs, officiate charity work, campaign for the restitution of Jewish property, plan social and cultural events, and represent the Jews before national and international bodies.

There is so much diversity in American Jewish life that Jews need not be members of official "Communities" to assert their Jewish identity. But in Central and Eastern Europe, where there are far fewer Jewish institutions than in America, the Jewish Community is often the only place one can express his or her Jewishness. Instead of belonging to a synagogue, as is commonplace among American Jews, European Jews belong, if anything, to the Jewish Community itself. With its long history, the Jewish Community continues to serve as the official structure of European Jewish life.

1

*Prague:
City of the
Old and the New*

Introduction

During the First World War, several young Jews in Prague published a small volume of essays, poems, and reflections entitled *Das judische Prag* (Jewish Prague). The book contained discussions of Prague's extensive Jewish history and included illustrations of tombstones in the Old Jewish Cemetery and the Altneuschul interspersed in the text. The writers were Jews living in Prague or those influenced by the city's charm.

What was fascinating about *Das judische Prag* was that it emerged in an era when Jewish tradition had been all but abandoned in Prague. An entire generation of Jews had been raised in an atmosphere of unprecedented assimilation into Czech society. Several Bohemian synagogues, kosher slaughterhouses, and *mikvehs* had shut down for lack of interest. Had it not been for an influx of Galician Jewish refugees at the beginning of the war, the decline of Czech Jewish life would have been seismic.

This is what made *Das judische Prag* remarkable. The book was revolutionary for Prague in that it marked an attempt by Jews to construct a new Jewish identity on the basis of Prague's old Jewish history. Robert Weltsch (1891–1984), an active Prague Zionist, wrote, "We know an old cemetery and a synagogue, which are shown to strangers, the last remains of a once living Jewish quarter. . . . The entire chain of events, sorrows, and excitement, of striving and of laughter—this whole history of living, Jewish Prague—we do not know. . . . The sons now know, however, that one thing is needed: the building of a new—to use an old Prague Jewish word—'old-new' society" (quoted in Hillel J. Kieval, *The Making of Czech Jewry: National Conflict and Jewish Society in Bohemia, 1870–1918*). It was as if the makers of the book, writing only a decade after the Jewish town of Prague was irretrievably altered by urban renewal, were attempting to locate a vestige of Jewishness in the remaining buildings and to expand this vestige into a defining new identity.

In the 1960s, a similar phenomenon could be seen in the former Jewish Town. Spurred by a political and cultural thaw in the communist system, several Czech Jews began to gather in the Jewish Town Hall, interested in learning about the history and lifeblood of past generations of Prague Jews. Although the interest waned during state oppression of the 1970s, the period marked the second time in the twentieth century in which old Jewish sites served as the inspiration for a new Jewish identity.

Today it's happening again. Many young Czech Jews, highly assimilated and usually born to only one Jewish parent or grandparent, have flocked to the old sites in the former Jewish Town the way Jews used to flock to synagogue services. Many of them have sought to build a new Jewish identity based on the old remnants of Jewish civilization in the city. Ironically, the interest is all the more intense among Jews who have no desire to maintain Jewish tradition today. Many more Jews in Prague work as tour guides in the Jewish Town than attend religious services. There is a thirst for knowledge and an emotional pride in the old sites and history that is so heartfelt it is sometimes a religion in itself. Often, one's Jewish identity consists exclusively of this pride.

Why does the old constantly enter the new in this city? One reason is the existence of several ancient synagogues in the heart of the Old Town. One cannot help but be reminded of his or her Judaism in this city. When the former ghetto was destroyed at the turn of the twentieth century, the historical landmarks that were spared instantly became shrines baring glimpses of a different world. Franz Kafka is said to have made a famous, cynical remark, "Our heart knows nothing of the slum clearance which has been achieved. The unhealthy old Jewish town within us is far more real than the new hygienic town around us. With our eyes open we walk through a dream: ourselves only a ghost of a vanished age" (Gustav Janouch, *Conversations with Kafka*).

This typically Prague blending of the old and the new is mirrored, of course, in the sites themselves. Everything in the quarter speaks to the intertwining of the past and the present. The most obvious example is the *Altneuschul* ("Old New Synagogue"), Prague's most famous Jewish archetype. But the old-new mystique is also more subtle. It can be found, for instance, in the fact that the newest synagogue in the area, the Spanish Synagogue, was built on the exact spot of the oldest synagogue, the Altschul.

The atmosphere of the former Jewish Town of Prague is summed up most concisely by the whimsical Hebrew clock on the Jewish Town Hall. Although it is connected to the same mechanism that operates the normal clock above it, the Hebrew clock has insisted on running backwards for centuries. In a new metropolis above the ancient ghetto, the time-chasing clock captivates Prague Jews and visitors alike. The Czech Jewish writer Viktor Fischl wrote a poem, "The Clock in the Ghetto," which concludes:

> Like that clock turning back,
> so you are pushed backward,
> beneath the sediments of rivers, beneath the lava of years,
> up to the place where first whispered a lip,
> when a bittersweet psalm dripped onto it.
>
> (Viktor Fischl, "Hodiny v ghettu")

A History of
the Jews in Prague

IN THE BEGINNING

In the 1970s, schoolchildren in Czechoslovakia were taught that as far back as the year 965, an itinerant Arab merchant recorded the existence of the city of Prague to the outside world.

Two things were left out of the lesson. First, the merchant, Ibrahim ibn Jakub, was an Arabian Jew. Second, ibn Jakub recorded the existence not only of the city itself, but also of Jewish merchants in Prague markets. From this we know that Jews had a part in Prague city life from its earliest origins.

According to one legend, when Prague's Founding Mother Libuse prophesied the establishment of the city, she had a vision that her descendants would encounter a nation from a faraway country, with a religion different from their own. Only if this nation was received in peace would Prague be blessed with prosperity. Sure enough, when the settlement around the Castle District was established, the Czechs welcomed the Jews to settle just below it.

There is some truth to the legend: There used to be a Jewish settlement in the Ujezd district of Mala Strana, comfortably located in the shadow of the Castle. In fact, between the tenth and twelfth centuries, Jewish settlements sprang up around all the major markets and trade routes of Prague: near the Castle, beneath the twelfth-century Castle at Vysehrad, and in the area of today's "Jewish Town." From the thirteenth century, there was even a Jewish cemetery in the New Town (Nove Mesto). Far from being confined to a single space, it is clear that at least in their early history, the Jews of Prague were free to settle in all the main districts of Prague.

Eventually, of course, the Jewish settlement in the Old Town gained ascendancy over the others. In another legend, it is said that the Jewish Town became the single Jewish settlement in Prague out of the twisted machinations of the First Crusade of 1096. The story has it that the Crusaders destroyed the Jewish settlements in Mala Strana and Vysehrad, but left the third settlement untouched. Apparently they feared that fires from the Jewish buildings would leap over and burn down the precious churches of the Old Town. In fact, although the Vysehrad settlement probably was destroyed during the pogroms of 1096, a settlement in Mala Strana continued into the twelfth century. Eventually, this settlement succumbed to the dominance of the Jewish Community located in the Old Town.

Even the "Jewish Town" in the Old Town did not begin as a single entity but evolved in three districts. One settlement, possibly the oldest, centered around the twelfth-century

Altschul, on the spot where the Spanish Synagogue stands today. Some contend that the Altschul settlement was home to Byzantine Jews who practiced the Sephardic rite. Another settlement arose by the banks of the river, where the Pinchas Synagogue was later built. This settlement stretched into the general area of today's Siroka Street, and was the commercial core of the Jewish Town. Finally, Jews settled the area around the Altneuschul and completed the tripartite Jewish settlement in the Old Town. Meanwhile, King Vaclav I created the Old Town as an official entity in the 1230s, including the Jewish Quarter within its walls. The Old Town became the main trade center of Prague, attracting merchants and craftsmen from throughout the region. The growth of the urban center was mirrored in the Jewish Town. By the end of the thirteenth century, the settlements by the Altneuschul and the later Pinchas Synagogue fused together, separated from the Altschul Community by Christian homes. The district of the Altschul eventually evolved into a mini-ghetto, since it was severed from the main area of the Jewish Town. A series of rules were later promulgated regarding the times and conditions Jews were permitted to pass from the large settlement to the smaller one. Within the larger area of the Jewish Town, it was the district of the Altneuschul that soon assumed chief importance as the spiritual, cultural, economic, and administrative center of the Jews.

The earliest stars in the constellation of Prague Jewish scholars appeared at this time. In the beginning of the thirteenth century, the Jewish Community was headed by Abraham ben Azriel, whose well-known work is *Arugat Ha'Bosem* ("The Garden Bed of Spices"). His pupil was Isaac ben Moses (c. 1180–1250), who passed his time in the Rhineland but always came back to Prague. He was known as the *Or Zaru'ah* ("The Sown Light") after the title of his most famous work, a commentary on the Talmud. From the writings of these men, which occasionally lapsed into Czech (written in Hebrew letters) to explain complicated concepts, we know that from at least the thirteenth century the Jews of Bohemia conversed in a Slavonic language.

SERVI CAMERAE REGIAE

As was the case throughout Europe, the position of Prague's Jews deteriorated considerably in the early thirteenth century. The year 1215 marked the convention of the Fourth Lateran Council hosted by Pope Innocent III. The Council decided that as punishment for the sin of Deicide, Jews were to be separated from Christian society and forced into a state of squalor. Almost all the anti-Semitic decrees that were used to persecute the Jews for over six hundred years were promulgated at this time. These included the prohibition from owning land, prohibitions from living among Christians, and exclusion from guilds and from public office. Jews were forced to wear identifying marks on their clothing, originally to help Christians avoid having sexual intercourse with them. Because Christians perceived money lending as usury, Jews were channelled into this profession, but the Council restricted the amount of interest Jews were permitted to charge. The theological basis for these laws was the collective guilt of the Jews, but on a propagandistic level the inferior Jewish status was designed to be a permanent reminder to Christians of God's wrath toward those who stray from Jesus. In Prague, what this meant was that the Jewish Town, which had been considered a section of the Old Town, was increasingly isolated from Christian parts of the city. In the span of roughly two centuries, the Jewish Town slowly evolved into an enclosed ghetto.

The laws of the Fourth Lateran Council posed a quandary for the kings of Europe. Because the Jews were almost totally disenfranchised from society, they could not pay taxes through the normal channels of the feudal system. In response to this, kings established royal charters with their Jewish communities, primarily to collect taxes from the Jews but also to install the Jews as the king's moneylenders or tax collectors. Jews were labelled *servi camerae regiae*, or "servants of the royal chamber," and granted numerous privileges and protection.

Following the model of Hungarian King Bela IV's Jewish laws of 1251, King Premysl Otakar II issued his Royal Charter for the Jews in 1254. The charter contained the usual business legalisms: The Jews were protected as money lenders and as servants of the king, and were required to pay high taxes as well as supply occasional loans to the royal treasury. But even more importantly in the face of increasing Christian anti-Semitism, the Royal Charter protected the Jews from persecution. It refuted the blood libel attack on the Jews; prohibited violence against Jews, their property, synagogues, and cemeteries; and outlawed all forced baptisms in the kingdom. The church was dismayed at this infringement on its jurisdiction, and issued complaints against King Otakar II. The king responded that the Jews, as official servants of his treasury, fell under his control and protection. Thus began a centuries-long balancing act between the castle's exploitation of Jewish finances, and the church's campaign against what it called "Jewish perfidy."

As a direct result of the Royal Charter, the Jewish Town became an autonomous district where Jews were permitted to govern most of their internal matters. The religious freedoms granted in the charter led to a flourishing of Jewish life, and settlement increased in the Jewish Town. The prosperity can be seen no better than in the building of the Altneuschul in about 1270. Jewish spiritual, cultural, and political life soon became centered around the twin-naved synagogue, which from the thirteenth century until today has served as the unifying symbol for all the Jews of Bohemia.

OPPRESSION IN THE FOURTEENTH CENTURY

Jewish life in Medieval Europe was never unequivocally good or bad for a long period of time. It was more like a roller coaster of fortune: sweeping privileges alternated with severe restriction, pogrom, and exile—sometimes in a matter of decades. Thus it was that after Jewish religious and economic privileges were strengthened during the middle of the thirteenth century, by the end of the century the Jewish Community had entered a period of instability. In 1296, King Vaclav II thought up the foolproof fundraising scheme of capturing Jews and holding them for ransom. John of Luxembourg and Vaclav IV followed suit in a similar fashion, actually arresting the leaders of the Jewish Community on a whim. King Charles IV, who endeared himself to the Jews with the banner he granted them in 1357, borrowed the Hungarian royal custom of cancelling all debts owed to Jews in order to appease the estates. Kings Charles IV and Vaclav IV allowed themselves to be heavily bribed by the nobility in return for such favors against the Jews.

One of the most prominent Jews in Prague at the time was a man by the name of Lazar. In recognition of Lazar's frequent loans to the royal treasury, he was given a tax amnesty in the years 1350 to 1352. The greatest mark of Lazar's influence, however, was his privilege of living outside the Jewish Town. From this we learn that in the fourteenth century the ghetto enclosure was not as strictly enforced as it was in later periods. After the death of Lazar, Charles IV claimed his home for one of the first sites of Charles University, the oldest university in Central Europe.

At the same time, religious anti-Semitism found fertile ground in fourteenth-century Bohemia after having been nurtured in the churches of Germany for several decades. Christian superstitions of the Blood Libel and the Desecration of the Host, in which Jews were accused of ritual murder and insidious plots against the Christian religion, became embedded in the Bohemian imagination like fairy tales of good versus evil. The atmosphere in Prague reached its nadir in 1389. In Easter of that year, which coincided with Passover, Jews were accused of vandalizing the eucharistic wafer. Throughout Prague, priests sermonized that Jews had tortured the Host just as they once tortured and killed Jesus. In the resulting pogrom, three thousand Jewish men, women, and children were murdered in the streets, homes, and especially the synagogues of the ghetto. Rabbi Avigdor Kara, who witnessed his own father murdered in the pogrom, wrote an elegy that is read every year in the Altneuschul on Yom Kippur:

> . . . For the glory of God we all had to die,
> For the mercy of God we only could cry.
> On the eve of the feast began their foul deed,
> When they grabbed every Jew they found in the street,
> And forcibly tried to make him give up,
> the creed of his fathers, his trust in our God . . .
> May the offering please God: be it lamb or sheep
> or the innocent children over whose suffering we
>   weep . . .
> O God, put an end to such murderous deed:
> it follows us everywhere, the thought makes us bleed,
> it made us a target of cruel contempt
> in the Land of Bohemia and wherever we went. . . .
>
> (Quoted in Hana Volavkova,
> *A Story of the Jewish Museum in Prague*)

After the pogrom had ended, many Jews fled the decimated ghetto for Poland and Hungary.

LIFE AMONG THE HUSSITES

The position of Prague's Jews fluctuated throughout the fifteenth century, but there was some reprieve from Catholic persecution during the era of the Hussites. The Hussites were Bohemian religious revolutionaries who followed the teachings of Jan Hus, a popular preacher who was burned at the stake in 1415 for his critique against the corrupt power of the Church. From 1419 to 1436, the Hussites waged war for sovereignty in the Kingdom of Bohemia. During their struggles, they lent support to the Jews against persecution by the Church. The Jews, for their part, helped the Hussites in their fortifications against Vysehrad in 1420.

The Hussites pioneered a uniquely Czech form of philo-Semitism, which was to find repeated expression in later centuries. This was the fascination, among a persecuted, dissident group, with the Jewish people and religion. Radical Hussites mined the Torah for inspiration and came to regard themselves as the People of the Book. Instead of claiming that they had supplanted the Jews (as the early Church had), the Hussites regarded the Jews as their natural allies. This was particularly resonant when they considered the suffering the Jews had undergone at the hands of the Church. In a bizarre prophecy of early twentieth-century Labor Zionism, the Hussites proclaimed that it was due to Christian anti-Semitism that the Jewish people had been wrenched from an agrarian lifestyle and forced into non-physical financial pursuits. In correcting this, the Hussites were perhaps the first religious group in Christian European history to argue against the ban on Jews in craftsmaking and farming. This undoubtedly had an effect on the economic and social life of the Jewish Town, but unfortunately the reign of the Hussites was short-lived.

Admittedly, life under the Hussites was not a utopia. It was during their tenure, for instance, that pogroms erupted in Prague in 1421 and 1422, causing many Jews to flee to Poland. Nevertheless, the Hussites were far more progressive than other Christian movements in their relations with the Jews. Unlike Martin Luther's similar program in the sixteenth century, the Hussite movement did not predicate its kindness to Jews on the condition that they would be baptized. The Hussites even derived some of their messianic furor from Rabbi Avigdor Kara himself, who sympathized with their struggle against Catholic domination. As mentioned, this was not the last time a Czech opposition movement would find strength in the Jewish religion. As recently as the 1970s and 1980s, several Gentile dissidents in Prague began meeting in the Jewish Community. Apparently they, too, identified with Judaism's perennial struggle in the face of hostile authority. Some of these dissidents even converted to Judaism.

In the early fifteenth century the most famous Prague Rabbi was Yomtov Lippmann Muhlhausen, author of *Sefer Nitzachon* (The Book of Victory), which argued against the theological tenets of Christianity. Rabbi Muhlhausen is today considered to be one of the greatest Jewish thinkers of the Middle Ages.

PERSECUTION AND EXPULSION

An unforeseen consequence of the Hussite wars was the weakening of royal power in favor of the nobility and estates in the countryside and towns. As a result, Jews in the fifteenth century could not be as certain of the king's power to protect them, and ended up paying tax money to as many as three different administrations. Soon enough, increased competition in the towns, combined with rousing anti-Semitic speeches, led to expulsions from all the royal cities of Moravia. Similar expulsions shook Bohemia at the turn of the sixteenth century. The situation was different in Prague, where the Old Town began to administer Jewish rights and taxes during the Hussite wars. As long as the tax revenues kept flowing, Jews were left in relative peace. It was at this time that a third synagogue was added to the Jewish Town. Built by the Horowitz family, it was a private prayer hall that later became one of the main synagogues of the ghetto, the Pinchas Synagogue. It was located on the grounds of one of the earliest Jewish settlements in the Jewish Town.

In 1501, King Vladislav Jagiello gave the Jews of Prague the usual offer they couldn't refuse: For an annual fee of thousands of silver coins, he promised to protect the Jews and to secure their right to live in Prague and elsewhere in Bohemia. The royal bribe was put to the test the following year, when Old Town burghers decided that tax revenues were not sufficient reason to keep the Jews in the city. They attempted to expel the Jews from Prague and even from the rest of Bohemia. In 1507 and 1509 they made similar attempts, but in 1510 the king lived up to his promise and issued the Edict of Olomouc, which reaffirmed the right of Jews to remain in Bohemia.

The situation changed after Bohemia became part of the Hapsburg Empire in 1526. Although the Jewish Town enjoyed the arrival of Renaissance culture and growth—between 1522 and 1541 the population of the Jewish Town doubled—King Ferdinand I succumbed to burgher pressure and expelled the Jews from Bohemia in 1541. After some postponements, almost all the Jews of Prague were forced to leave in 1543. Residency permits were issued only to the highest bidders and to a few Jewish administrators. In 1545 the Jews were permitted to return, but a decade later another expulsion order was issued, in 1557. After various extensions and postponements, the Prague Jewish printer Mardocai Zemah made a trip to Rome to entreat Pope Pius IV to call off the persecutions. The pope acquiesced and instructed King Ferdinand I that it was no longer necessary to expel the Jews. The expulsion order was cancelled in 1563.

THE RENAISSANCE AND THE GOLDEN AGE

In spite of these fluctuations of fortune, the Jewish Community of Prague plunged heartily into the Renaissance early in the sixteenth century. One of the finest examples of this was the celebrated Hebrew printing press established in 1512 in Prague. Emerging roughly forty years after the first such press was established in Rome in 1473, the Prague press is the oldest Hebrew press north of the Alps. One of the oldest existing products of this press is the *Seder Zemirot u'Birkat Ha'mazon*, an illustrated book of hymns, including the grace after meals, from 1514. The book was especially remarkable for its use of colored woodcuts. Other highlights of the press were the Pentateuch from 1518 and 1530, and the famous Prague Haggadah of 1526, which was the world's first Haggadah to be illustrated with woodcuts, including a rather surprising one of a naked female torso. These books were imitated throughout Europe for their innovative typographical and illustrative style. The leading Hebrew printer of the time was Gershon HaCohen and his sons, later known as the "Gersonide family," which dominated Hebrew printing in Prague until the end of the eighteenth century. In 1527 King Ferdinand I himself granted them an exclusive license to print Hebrew books in Prague. Perhaps in gratitude, the Gersonides designed a logo effusive with a love for Prague: it features Prague's coat of arms, consisting of the three towers of Prague, as well as the twin-tailed Bohemian lion.

It was in this period that the Prague ghetto was enlivened by the feisty Horowitz family, an irreverent clan of power brokers and mystics led by the inimitable Aaron Meshulam Horowitz. Aaron Meshulam Horowitz, a recalcitrant merchant with privileges granted by two kings, was the most powerful Jew in Prague in the first half of the sixteenth century. It was partly due to his efforts that the Jewish Community survived even during the repeated expulsion orders of the time. As a mark of his prosperity, Aaron Meshulam built the Pinchas Synagogue in 1535 for his family and friends.

But true prosperity could begin only after the death of the problematic King Ferdinand I in 1564. His successor, King Maximillan II, ushered in a heyday of cultural growth for the Jews. It is said that King Maximillan II's Protestant sympathies gave him the courage to resist traditional Church anti-Semitism. First he cancelled the expulsion order that had been a scourge on the Jews of Bohemia throughout Ferdinand's reign. In 1567, Maximillan II reconfirmed the right to life and religion for the Jews of Prague. He lifted the ban against Jews in trade, and in 1571 paid the Jewish Town a royal visit. It was King Maximillan II who provided the infrastructure of tolerance that blossomed into an unprecedented period of prosperity during the regime of his successor, Emperor Rudolf II. Reigning from 1576 to 1612, Rudolf II has been immortalized in Jewish history as ruler during the Golden Age of Prague Jewry.

Emperor Rudolf II certainly tolerated the Jews. Mad as a bat, Rudolf II tolerated just about anything, from alchemists to astrologers to pseudo-surrealist painters. In 1584, Emperor Rudolf II moved his imperial seat and residence to Prague, festooning the city with his trademark lunacy and giving the new capital an economic and population boom. The emperor spearheaded an irreverent foray into the arts and sciences, providing the substance for much of the "Magic Prague" mystique of future generations. It was in this electrified atmosphere that the Jews were permitted economic, religious, and cultural freedom. In the legal realm, Rudolf II extended Jewish privileges as soon as he was coronated. He promised Jews permanent safety in Prague and Bohemia, protecting them under his royal umbrella. He issued decrees protecting the Jews from the hostility of the Old Town burghers and guilds, permitted them to become craftsmen, and ensured that all disputes between Jews and Christians be judged by the royal court. In 1599 Rudolf II even exempted the Jews from all city taxes. It was due to these economic policies that the Jews of Prague were finally able to branch beyond moneylending and become shopkeepers and artisans.

What resulted was the Golden Age of Prague Jewish history, typically referred to as the period from 1570 to 1620. In numbers alone, the Community grew from practical obliteration in 1564 to over three thousand by the end of the century. Prague became a true Jewish melting pot, as enterprising Jews from all around the world came and settled in the Jewish Town. In this favorable climate, the Jews had the freedom to produce some of the most eminent personalities of the Diaspora. A brief glance at the Who's Who list reveals a cultural diversity rarely matched in Jewish history. There was, first and foremost, Rabbi Judah Loew, the charismatic iconoclast who is recognized as one of the greatest rabbis of all time for both his philosophy—an articulate blend of mystical and rationalist thought—and his Community ardor. It was Rabbi Loew, for instance, who established the guidelines for the first modern Jewish Burial Society in Prague and who revolutionized Jewish education by focusing on the ethical basis of Jewish law. There was the historian, mathematician, and astronomer David Gans, who discoursed with the likes of royal court astronomers Tycho Brahe and Johannes Kepler. Finally, and perhaps most importantly for the well-being of the Jewish Town, there was Mordechai Maisel, the first modern "court Jew" and a philanthropist of awe-inspiring magnitude. Mordechai Maisel built up the topography of the ghetto and made it a place where the average Jew could live in decency and respect. The mayor of the Jewish Town, Maisel built the High Synagogue, the Maisel Synagogue, the original Klausen buildings, a *mikveh*, an almshouse, a hospital, a cemetery extension, and the Jewish Town Hall. It was Maisel who covered the sand-swept and muddy paths of the ghetto with cobblestones. The face of the Jewish Town was fundamentally altered, reflecting the unprecedented prosperity of the day. As Hana Volavkova, former director of the Jewish Museum in Prague, put it, "Toward the end of the sixteenth century and at the beginning of the seventeenth century there cannot have been a more familiar sound in Prague Jewish Town than the noise of the builder's hammer, the stone-cutter's chisel, and the slap of the mason's trowel as he laid stone upon stone . . ." (Hana Volavkova, *The Pinkas Synagogue: A Memorial of the Past and of Our Days*).

THE SEVENTEENTH CENTURY

Not long after Maisel died, his role as benefactor was filled by Jacob Bashevi, who gave the Jewish Town yet another urgently needed face-lift. Bashevi was the first Jew in the Hapsburg monarchy to be knighted; his new name was Jacob Bashevi von Treuenberg. A "court Jew" like his predecessor, Bashevi built the High Court Synagogue (since destroyed) and orchestrated an unprecedented expansion of the Jewish Town by thirty-nine houses. It was largely due to Bashevi's influence that the Jewish Town was spared exile and pogrom during the Bohemian battles of the first half of the seventeenth century.

The year 1620 is ingrained on Czech consciousness as the defining moment of its modern history. In November of that year, the Czech anti-Catholic forces were defeated at the Battle of White Mountain, devastating Czech national sovereignty for two hundred years. According to a Czech tradition that has never been proven, the victorious Catholic Hapsburg gave the Protestants a choice: convert to Catholicism, convert to Judaism, or leave the country altogether. Perhaps at no other time in Europe's pogrom-laden history were people forced to become Jewish. If the tradition is true, there are no conversion statistics: it was such an embarrassment that no records were saved by either side. The numbers of converts, it should be noted, were relatively small. Nonetheless, many Czechs today trace their ancestry to that enforced conversion. One of them is the renowned writer Ivan Klima, who insists that although both his parents are Jewish, his mother's ancestors were among those to convert after White Mountain. It should be mentioned, however, that the White Mountain stories are told mostly by Czech Jews eager to shed all vestiges of their Jewishness. Thus it was that early in the twentieth century, many Jews insisted that their Slavic surnames indicated a Czech pedigree distorted after the Battle of White Mountain.

The devastation of the Thirty Years War (1618–1648) brought mixed fortune for the Jews of Prague. On the one hand, Emperor Ferdinand II, desperate for economic support in the war, took great pains to ensure the safety of the Jews. While his troops were ransacking Prague after the Battle of White Mountain, for instance, the emperor prohibited them from harming the Jewish Town. In 1623, the emperor confirmed the freedom of life, trade, and religion for the Jews of Prague and Bohemia. On the other hand, the fluctuations of the war forced the Jews into the unenviable position of having to balance their loyalties between two factions, either of which could devastate the Jewish Town if it suspected treachery. In addition, wartime taxes drained the Community of resources. It was these very tax burdens that in 1627 led the Jews of Prague to turn on their great Rabbi Yomtov Lippman Heller, who was forced out of Prague and eventually settled in Cracow [*see page 334*]. Despite these hardships, the Jewish Community of Prague continued to grow. In 1638, the first official census of Prague's Jews revealed that there were 7,815 Jews residing in the Jewish Town.

JEWISH POPULATION GROWTH AND THE FAMILIANTS LAWS

At the beginning and end of the 1680s two natural disasters almost wiped out the Jewish Town of Prague. The first struck in the form of the plague of 1680, which claimed three thousand Jews and led to the opening of a plague cemetery outside the Old Town. Then in 1689 a boundless fire ravaged the ghetto, killing several people and destroying 318 homes and eleven synagogues. Almost nothing in the Jewish Town was untouched by the fire, and the 1690s were spent in massive restorations of homes and synagogues.

Meanwhile, the Jews had to deal with constant Jesuit attacks against their religion and life. The Jesuits, housed in Prague's famous Klementinum, conducted regular show trials and open scenes of torture designed to frighten and amaze the illiterate masses of Bohemia into becoming devout Catholics. All prior sadism and ruthlessness of the Church was invested by the Jesuits with an imaginative, homey spin that included ripping people's tongues out, dismembering people alive in public, gouging out people's hearts and eyes, and burning people at the stake. Naturally, the Jews received the brunt of these "Bible sessions." The most notorious was the case of Lazar Abeles, who was tortured into suicide after being accused of killing his baptized son. Another case led to the imposition of the famous Hebrew prayer that adorns the statue of Jesus on Charles Bridge. In addition, Jewish books were regularly censored, and Jews were forced to attend proselytizing sermons.

Ideas for Jewish population control had been brewing in the Prague City Council as well as the entire empire for some time. The fire of 1689 gave these campaigns the force of urgency. Thus the Jews of Prague were attacked on both sides: They were not given enough land in which to live, and when the overcrowding resulted in fires, they were blamed for forcing too many people into the town. The City Council considered moving the ghetto outside the Old Town to the village of Liben or even to Stvanice Island in the Vltava! Thankfully, these proposals were abandoned and the Jews, through the help of Jewish communities throughout Europe, were able to remain and rebuild the Jewish Town in Prague.

The Jewish population in Prague continued to grow. At the beginning of the eighteenth century, there were approximately eleven thousand Jews in the ghetto. They comprised half the population of the Old Town, and twenty-eight percent of the total population of Prague. At this time, the Prague Jewish Community was the largest Jewish Community in the world, a rank it would never match again. Due to privileges granted throughout the seventeenth century, their economic life was not limited to moneylending: in the census of 1729, almost one-third of the twenty-three hundred "gainfully employed" Jews worked as artisans, including tailors, shoemakers, goldsmiths, and even musicians. In the second half of the seventeenth century, these artisans began to organize themselves into eclectic Jewish guilds, which imitated the Christian guilds of Prague from which Jews were prohibited. The growth of Jewish Prague mirrored the Jewish population growth throughout Bohemia and Moravia, due in part to the influx of Jewish refugees from Eastern Europe fleeing the Chmielnicki massacres of 1648.

In response to what he considered an intolerable growth of the Jewish population, Emperor Charles VI issued the *Familiants Laws* in 1726 and 1727. These were to have a devastating effect on Bohemian Jewry for the next 120 years. The *Familiants Laws* decreed that only 8,541 Jewish families would be tolerated in Bohemia, and 5,106 in Moravia. Only the eldest son in a Jewish family would be given the right to marry. All other sons were forced to emigrate, to marry illegally in the countryside or under the protection of nobility, or to die single. Such emasculating legislation remained in effect all the way up to the Revolution of 1848. It was the repeal of the *Familiants Laws*, in fact, that allowed Franz Kafka's grandfather Jakob to marry finally at the age of 34; before that, he had been prohibited from marrying because he had a stepbrother who was one year older.

EXPULSION: 1745–1748

The tenuous position of the Jews under Emperor Charles VI was made even worse when his daughter, Maria Theresa, became empress in 1740. An ardent Catholic who imbibed more than her share of Church anti-Semitism, Empress Maria Theresa accused the Jews of siding with the Prussians during her battles for the "Hapsburg Heritage." At her wit's end, the empress decreed the expulsion of the Jews from Bohemia in 1744 and from Moravia in 1745. Although the Prague City Council opposed the action, the Jews were forced out of Prague during a severe winter in January 1745. For a few years, they were to be permitted to remain in Bohemian villages at a distance of at least two days' journey from Prague. Afterwards, all of Bohemia and Moravia were to be off-limits for Jews.

But Empress Maria Theresa had not counted on the devastating effect a *Judenrein* Prague would have on the economy. Jews had been moneylenders, suppliers of raw materials, and reliable customers in Prague markets. Without the Jews, inflation shot up. At a hearing in 1747, most of the guilds in Prague lamented the loss of Jews in the economy. Meanwhile, officials from England, the Netherlands, and elsewhere expressed grave concern over the empress's treatment of Jews. Finally, in 1748, the empress rescinded her decree, and Jews were permitted to return to Prague. To avoid humiliation she imposed a severe annual "toleration tax" of 204,000 guldens that the Jews were required to pay to be tolerated and to prevent future expulsions. As usual in European society, the Jews were compelled to do whatever was necessary to remain in Empress Maria Theresa's favor. The Jewish Museum in Prague owns a fascinating book of benedictions written by Rabbi Ezekiel Landau (1713–1793), the famous anti-acculturation rabbi, filled with prayers for the recovery of the empress from illness.

By the autumn of 1749, 6,061 Jews had returned to the Jewish Town of Prague. During the banishment, the ghetto had become a slum for Prague's poor, and the area was badly in need of repair. But just as the Jews set out to rebuild their town, a devastating fire raged through the ghetto in 1754. After the blaze of 1689, this was the second worst fire in the cramped ghetto's history, destroying 190 houses and six synagogues. In all, two-thirds of the homes in the ghetto were destroyed. The reconstruction that followed, combined with the empress's continually increasing "toleration tax," sapped the Jewish Community of its previous economic strength.

By the time rebuilding was finished in 1765, the Jewish Town had acquired the early Classicist look it retained, in spite of later renovations, until the ghetto was destroyed at the turn of the twentieth century.

THE EDICT OF TOLERANCE

At the end of her life, Empress Maria Theresa was drawn into a debate with her son, Josef II, about what to do with the Jews. The empress was convinced that the Jewish question in the Hapsburg Monarchy could be solved only through forced conversion or expulsion. Josef II, by contrast, was determined to jump-start the monarchy from a feudal, agrarian system into a modern capitalist economy driven by autonomous individuals and guided by a centralized state. He felt that the age-old Christian disenfranchisement of the Jews was an anachronism that had to be discarded if the monarchy was to enter the modern era. Besides, Enlightenment thinking argued against religious fundamentalism in the economic and political spheres of society. Indeed, it was Josef II's plan to unyoke not only the Jews, but all non-Catholic denominations as part of his overall program to centralize authority in his empire. These debates took place against the backdrop of the first partition of Poland in 1772, which delivered the phenomenal figure of 250,000 Galician Jews into the domain of the Hapsburg monarchy.

As soon as his mother died in 1780, Emperor Josef II had free reign to implement his views. Almost at once, the debate on the "Jewish Question" hit the streets of Vienna and Prague. Anonymous pamphlets appeared extolling the industriousness of the Jews and testifying that this would only improve if they were given more rights. Opposition pamphlets painted the Jews as venal parasites who would destroy the monarchy from within. One memorandum repeated the blood libel accusation that Jews murdered Christians for ritualistic purposes. It went on to argue that Jews already owned one-third of the wealth of Bohemia, and even without equal rights they would control all the money in the monarchy within fifty years. Jews were depicted as devils, goats, and leeches. As was often the case, the anti-Semitic arguments drew a specter of Jewish vampirism when the real fear was of equal economic competition. Josef II listened to these arguments and ultimately modified his more ambitious plans. Even after he presented his compromise plan, the Bohemian government argued that instead of giving the Jews rights, the state should deport all but the richest Jews to the farthest reaches of the empire.

Nonetheless, in October 1781 Josef II issued the Edict of Tolerance for the Jews of Bohemia. Early in 1782, Moravian Jewry received a similar Edict. Although it was not a declaration of equal rights, the Edict of Tolerance did much to overhaul the structure of Jewish communal life and to give Jews their first opportunity to enter the larger world. In order to integrate the Jews into the economy of the state, the Edict forbade the use of Hebrew in all business documents and secular transactions. Jews were encouraged to abandon the *cheder*, or Jewish religious school, and to establish state-supervised elementary schools with secular curricula. By 1786, only graduates of these secular elementary schools would be permitted to marry. In small Jewish communities, the children would be permitted to attend Christian schools. The universities were opened up to Jews. In order to move Jews beyond moneylending, an occupation that had for centuries been encouraged openly by the king and tacitly by the clergy, all sorts of trades were made available to the Jews. That Jews had already been practicing trades for centuries might have escaped Josef's attention; perhaps the ruling was meant to encourage the habit in the countryside. Jews were also encouraged to start factories and to engage in agriculture, although they were still forbidden from owning land. In addition, anti-Semitic legislation requiring Jews to wear special identifying marks were declared null and void.

There are several points to stress about the Edict of Tolerance. This was not a Civil Rights Act by any means; nor was it a Patent of Citizenship, Decree of Equality, or Declaration of Love. Josef II boasted that his Edict granted the Jews "near-equality," but this was an exaggeration at best. The Edict upheld restrictions on Jewish settlement and on "tolerated Jews," continued to deny citizenship to the Jews, and forbade them from becoming master craftsmen. The Familiants Law was upheld. Jews continued to be confined to the ghetto until 1849, and complete emancipation would come only in 1867. The emperor was more candid when he conceded the purpose of the Edict was "to make [the Jews] useful to the state." Subsequent decrees furthered the cause. In 1783 and 1784, the authority of the *beit din*, or Jewish court of law, was abolished except in religious and marital matters; all other disputes were to be tried in secular courts. In 1787, Jews were required to adopt German surnames. With a changed language, education, commerce, communal authority, and even names, the Jews would indeed be more useful to the economy of the monarchy as it shifted its engines for the landscape of a modern state.

Ever since the earliest throes of emancipation, it has been hotly debated whether the reforms were healthy for the Jewish Community or the beginning of its destruction. On the one hand, the status quo of segregation and persecution had to be altered. On the other hand, once it was altered, Jewish autonomous integrity faced a schism from which it would never quite recover. Ironically, Jews had survived as a closely-knit entity through seventeen centuries of Diaspora largely due to state-sanctioned persecution. Once the legal barriers began to disappear, Jews found that the most successful way to enter the larger European society was to abandon any reminder of their Jewish heritage. This they did with a zest unparalleled in Jewish history, ushering in an age of almost mind-boggling assimilation in the nineteenth century. Needless to say, the same crisis and debate continues to rage, albeit in a much different environment, in the United States today.

Even in eighteenth-century Prague, the praises of emancipation were not sung in all circles. The greatest rabbi in Bohemia in the eighteenth century, Rabbi Ezekiel Landau (1713–1793), feared that the new measures would intrude overwhelmingly on Jewish observant life. Elected chief rabbi one year after the catastrophic fire of 1754, Rabbi Landau—known as the *Nodeh Bi'Yehudah* after his most famous work—succeeded in rebuilding the Prague Jewish Community into the most vibrant Jewish Community in Central Europe. Rabbi Landau feared that the Edict of Tolerance, along with the internal changes of the "Jewish Enlightenment," would lead the Jews on a path away from Torah law. Nonetheless, even such a staunch critic as Rabbi Landau had to compromise in the face of the monarchy's steadfast determination to "educate" the Jews. After being given a role in planning the schools, and after being assured that the most radical plans would not be implemented, Rabbi Landau gave the schools his tacit approval.

In Prague alone, approximately 17,800 students—or forty percent of Jewish school-age children—passed through the newly ordained Jewish school between 1790 and 1831.

ENLIGHTENMENT, EQUALITY, ASSIMILATION

Two major trends marked the Prague Jewish Community in the nineteenth century. On the one hand, the Jews made enormous strides in the economic and cultural life of Czech society as discrimination laws were abolished. On the other hand, it was these years that saw the near-total erosion of Jewish religious life in Bohemia. As a result of nineteenth century emancipation, the autonomous Jewish Community structure, which had defined Jewish life for over half a millennium, was dismantled everywhere as Jews were integrated into the secular state. Soon enough, Jewish communities all over Europe were powerless to stop the high rate of withdrawal from Jewish tradition.

But in Prague, the movement away from Judaism came particularly early, and was all the more severe. This fact is often overlooked by visitors, who assume that the plethora of synagogues in the Old Town alone indicates a vibrant Jewish religious Community that was destroyed only in the Holocaust. In reality, Jewish tradition in Bohemia had become so desolate that in 1924, Rabbi Gustav Sicher rang a desperate note in the *Zidovsky kalendar* (Jewish Almanac): "In Bohemia, there is an immense decline of Judaism, of Jewish life, of Jewishness, in scholarship, religion, and ritual. . . . Does anyone need to be told that ritual Judaism is almost dead? . . . Today if they are not empty or used for entertainment, our synagogues have become rooms for a mute Community, ignoring the appeals of the cantors. How wretched the figures that have to be looked for and paid to make up a *minyan* . . ." (excerpted in Wilma Abeles Iggers, *The Jews of Bohemia and Moravia: A Historical Reader*). Even the population eventually stagnated. There were 27,000 Jews in Prague in 1890. This number increased to only 31,751 in 1921.

What were the reasons for the unparalleled exodus away from Jewish tradition? First, of course, was the Edict of Tolerance and the comprehensive education transformation among the Jews. Young Jews raised in the German language and secular subjects had little incentive to pursue a traditional Jewish education, which offered little practical preparation for the modern world. The second factor to influence assimilation came in the form of laws passed in the middle of the nineteenth century. These led to the full emancipation of the Jews: In 1841, Jews were permitted to own property; in 1849, they were released from the ghetto; finally, in 1867, Jews were given full emancipation with the creation of the Dual Austria-Hungarian Monarchy. In appreciation for these rights and in eagerness to assimilate, Prague Jews embraced German language and culture wholeheartedly as they entered the urban bourgeois class. They dropped Yiddish from the vernacular, considering it a vestige of the ghettoes from which they had struggled so arduously to escape.

Other reasons for the decline of Jewish tradition were more complex. In the nineteenth century, Prague lacked an Orthodox rabbinical heavyweight comparable Bratislava's Rabbi Moses Sofer, known as the "Chatam Sofer" (1762–1839), who headed a yeshivah that was a beacon of Jewish tradition throughout Central Eastern Europe. Although Prague's venerable Rabbi Solomon Judah Rapoport (1790–1867) was a crucial figure in Enlightenment circles, he did not work to provide a bulwark against rampant assimilation. After Rabbi Rapoport, there have been no rabbis of great magnitude in Prague to this day. There was no rabbinical seminary in the Czech lands. In the nineteenth century, in fact, many of Prague's rabbis came from abroad. As for the tradition itself, Jews who became disenchanted with Orthodoxy found little desire for Reform Judaism. Instead, Prague's Jews generally avoided all expression of Jewish practice by the end of the nineteenth century. It is possible that the secular bent of Czech Jews was partly the influence of larger Czech society, whose anti-clerical tradition had made Czechs skeptical of the Church for centuries.

Another factor in the massive assimilation was demographics. When the Jews were permitted freedom of movement in 1848, they began moving in large numbers from the countryside to towns and cities. This in turn led to a weakening of the strong Jewish family traditions that had once been the norm in the countryside. Jews who came to urban centers such as Prague were often too preoccupied with survival in the city to be able to continue the ancient practices of their parents. Such was the case for Hermann Kafka, who owned a dry goods store. His son, Franz Kafka (1883–1924), perhaps the most searingly perceptive writer of the twentieth century, summed up the demographic shift in an anguished letter addressed to his father in 1919:

> You really had brought some traces of Judaism with you from the ghetto-like village Community; it was not much and it dwindled a little more in the city and during your military service; but still, the impressions and memories of your youth did just about suffice for some sort of Jewish life . . . Basically the faith that ruled your life consisted in your believing in the unconditional rightness of the opinions of a certain class of Jewish society . . . Even in this there was still Judaism enough, but it was too little to be handed on to the child; it all dribbled away while you were passing it on. . . . The whole thing is, of course, no isolated phenomenon. It was much the same with a large section of this transitional generation of Jews, which had migrated from the still comparatively devout countryside to the cities.
>
> Franz Kafka, "Letter to His Father," in *The Sons*

To this day, the transformation of Jewish life in the nineteenth century continues to be felt among Prague's Jews, who are as resistant to Jewish tradition as their great-grandparents once were.

But Jewish fondness for the culture and language of the Hapsburgs was not without its price. It is an irony of history that just as the Jews began to orient themselves toward German culture, the Czech national movement was born. Czech nationalists saw the Hapsburg Monarchy as their oppressors. It seemed the next logical step to view the Jews, as cogs in the Hapsburg wheel of domination, as their adversaries. Beginning in the 1870s, many Czechs protested against the preponderance of German-language schools in Bohemia, and blamed the Jews for being the schools' most avid supporters.

At first, Jews responded to Czech nationalist anti-Semitism by embracing German culture more fully. But toward the close of the nineteenth century, the German minority in Prague became more stridently nationalistic and anti-Semitic. Jews responded by trying to adopt Czech culture instead. The Czech-Jewish movement was born, with its aim the full integration of the Jewish people into an independent Czech state. In 1890, seventy-four percent of Jews in Prague claimed German as their first language. By 1900, the proportion had shrunk to forty-five percent. The Czech-Jewish journal *Rozvoj* appeared in 1904 with its aim the further assimilation of Jews into Czech society. Jewish students increasingly attended Czech-language schools. But despite their drive for acceptance among the Czechs, Jews continued to be considered either an instrument of the Hapsburgs or as an entirely foreign entity. One example of this was the rioting of November 1920, during which Czechs broke into the Jewish Town Hall, destroyed archives, and burned Hebrew manuscripts. To quell the rioting, the American embassy flew the American flag over the Jewish Town Hall, protecting the people within.

Thus it was that no group would accept the Jews as a member: the Germans felt the Jew was racially unacceptable, and the Czechs felt the Jew was too German. It was a classic vise in which the Jews had been caught time and again in the Diaspora. Young Jews often castigated their parents for the expedient alliances the latter formed, volleying between the Germans and the Czechs. Kafka wrote to his father, "You were capable, for instance, of running down the Czechs, and then the Germans, and then the Jews, and what is more, not only selectively but in every respect, and finally nobody was left except yourself" (Franz Kafka, "Letter to His Father," in *The Sons*).

As the nineteenth century drew to a close, many younger Jews sought a new path away from the competing nationalisms of Germans and Czechs. There was also the age-old issue of fathers and sons. The Jewish men and women who had poured into Prague in the middle of the nineteenth century had to grapple each day to survive the competitive urban metropolis. Not so their children, who came of age after their parents had achieved some measure of stability. After studying a wide range of subjects in German schools, the children formed the first generation of Prague Jewish intellectuals in the modern period. These Jews, already excluded from both Czech and German society, faced an additional burden: they were repelled by the commercial lifestyles of their parents. In addition, some of these Jews reproached their parents for having brought so little Jewish spirituality and tradition with them from the countryside. A very similar conflict would later arise in the United

States between uneducated Jewish immigrants and their intellectually ambitious children. In Prague in the late nineteenth century, young Jews often felt a longing to return to their roots, but they disagreed with the tenets of Orthodox Judaism. As the Prague writer Otokar Fischer put it as late as the 1920s, "A wayfaring half-breed whose psyche is transitional, / I am too alienated for values that are traditional. / I am different from those whose song I air, / A renegade to those whose blood I share" (excerpted in Wilma Abeles Iggers, *The Jews of Bohemia and Moravia: A Historical Reader*). Young Jews were truly afloat, both nationally, spiritually, and professionally.

It was the convergence of all these pressures and confrontations that compelled Jews to redefine their very identity at the end of the nineteenth century. The result often produced the great Jewish geniuses of the modern age. In addition to Franz Kafka, Sigmund Freud and Gustav Mahler were born in Bohemia and Moravia to typical Jewish parents of the time. Of course, every Jew in fin de siecle Prague was not, as some scholars have suggested, writing the Great Jewish Novel or redefining the destiny of the Jewish people. Most Jews chose lifestyles as conservative, pragmatic, and assimilated as those of their parents. But the minority of Jews that sought an alternative to the status quo was so prolific in its activities that one can almost point to a Renaissance of Jewish culture in the early twentieth century.

One way of filling the national and spiritual void was to plunge headlong into Prague's cultural scene. To name but a few writers, Max Brod (1884–1968), Franz Werfel (1890–1945), Karel Polacek (1892–1944), Frantisek Langer (1888–1965), Oskar Baum (1883–1941), and Egon Erwin Kisch (1885–1948) virtually defined the atmosphere of fin de siecle Prague. Other Jews sought strength in a campaign for national Jewish rebirth. In 1899, the Zionist *Bar Kochba* society provided an intellectual student forum in Prague for the issue of Jewish rejuvenation in Palestine. The *Bar Kochba* society was concerned not only with Zionism but with all aspects of modern Jewish identity. Still others (admittedly a small minority) walked the streets of Prague's dissolving Jewish Town and found inspiration in the Jewish past.

None of these paths constituted a return to traditional Jewish life but rather an attempt to find a replacement for the quintessential Jewish sense of spiritual and communal vertigo in modern Europe. In fact, only one Jew in Prague became famous for a total return to Jewish tradition and life. This was Jiri Langer (1894–1943), the iconoclastic younger brother of the famed Czech playwright Frantisek Langer. Tellingly, Jiri Langer did not find his Jewish roots in Prague itself. Instead, he left Prague entirely and headed East to Galicia, where Jewish life was still untrammeled by massive assimilation. There he met and studied in the Belz hasidic court. After he returned to Prague, Langer became, to the shock and horror of his family, the only homegrown *hasid* in Prague in the twentieth century. Franz Kafka, who learned a little Hebrew from Langer, also found his greatest Jewish fulfillment not in Prague but among Jews from Eastern Europe: among his friends in a travelling Yiddish theater from Lvov, at the court of a visiting hasidic Rebbe, and among Galician refugees in the First World War.

The Czechoslovak state created in 1918 revealed much of the demographics of European Jewry in microcosm: From the widespread assimilation of Bohemian Jews in the far west to the strict adherence to centuries-old tradition of Sub-Carpathian Ruthenian Jews in the far east, the integrated Jewish communities of the new state had little in common. But the structure of the state looked good for the Jews: it was a democracy and Jews were given minority rights. The president, Tomas G. Masaryk, was one of Europe's most amicable leaders toward the Jews. The stable democracy of Czechoslovakia promised great opportunities for the Jews of Prague. In 1930, there were 35,463 Jews living in Prague. This number would increase to nearly 55,000 in 1940, partly due to the influx of refugees from the Sudetenland, Austria, and elsewhere.

THE HOLOCAUST

With the Munich Agreement of September 30, 1938, Great Britain effectively handed Czechoslovakia to the Germans under the pretext of "appeasement." On March 15, 1939, the Germans occupied Prague and created the Protectorate of Bohemia and Moravia. Throughout the Czech lands, synagogues were burned and pogroms unleashed against the Jews. Fascists tried to blow up the Altneuschul twice in 1939, but both attempts failed. In June, Jews were expelled from all facets of the economy. Jews who ceded their property and belongings to German banks were permitted to leave the country. Adolf Eichmann originally tried to concentrate all the Jews in Bohemia and Moravia into a Prague ghetto, but this plan was abandoned.

When war officially began in September 1939, the situation became much worse. Anti-Semitic legislation was repeatedly passed, denying the Jews everything from free movement to war rations. Schools, trams, parks, and restaurants were only some of the places from which Jews were forbidden. Beginning in September 1941, all Jews wore yellow Stars of David labelled "Jude." At this time, there were 46,801 Jews registered in Prague. One month later, five thousand Jews were transported to the Lodz ghetto. Only 260 people survived.

Reinhard Heydrich became Acting Reich Protector on September 27, 1941. He soon convened a meeting of top Nazi officials in Prague Castle to decide on methods of achieving the "final solution" to the Jewish question. Terezin was chosen as a temporary camp where the Jews would be incarcerated; those who did not die there would be shipped to Auschwitz. The Jewish Community was informed of the deportations to Terezin, but was told that it would simply be a "labor ghetto."

At each deportation, the deportees were marched at night to wooden shacks on the Veletrzni grounds in Holesovice. There they slept on the floor of the shacks while administrative details—signing over all personal belongings—were worked out. Usually within three days, they were shipped to Terezin.

Terezin, which had room for approximately seventeen thousand people, was overcrowded with as many as sixty thousand Jews at any moment after the full-scale deportations began. People died of hunger, disease, and especially deportations to death camps in the east. Of the 45,500 Prague Jews deported to Terezin, only seventy-five hundred survived the war.

Czechs generally pride themselves on being innocent bystanders who did not harm the Jews during the Holocaust. This was decidedly not the case. Although the Czechs were far less vociferous in disposing of their Jewish population than were their Slovak neighbors, they also offered virtually no help to the Jews being taken away. There was complete silence and indifference to the Jewish transports throughout Bohemia and Moravia. Instances of Jews being assisted by Czechs were almost nonexistent. Instead, Czechs in general waited silently for their Jewish neighbors to be deported, after which they raided the vacated apartments for furniture and valuables. This behavior was not unique; it is borne out in countless survivors' testimonies, and in several stories and novels written about the Holocaust. In *Life with a Star*, Jiri Weil's nightmarish account of Jewish life in Nazi-occupied Prague, the author paints an expressionistic picture of Czechs visiting their Jewish neighbors before the latter are deported. Perhaps more than anywhere else, the scene summarizes Czech moral lethargy during the Holocaust:

> They didn't say a word. They didn't look at us; they pretended not to see us at all. I remained sitting at the table, and in my embarrassment I began to stir the tea I had drunk long before. They only looked at the objects in the room. They caressed the furniture, took the pewter mugs in their hands, felt the upholstery on the sofas. They calculated loudly between them the quality and sturdiness of various objects; they discussed how they would move the furniture around. We were already dead. They had come to claim their inheritance. . . . Only when they left did they look at us, but I noticed that they were actually looking at the teacups, spoons, and sugar bowl.
>
> Jiri Weil, *Life with a Star*

POSTWAR TO TODAY

After the war, about twenty thousand Jews came to Bohemia and Moravia, one-third of whom originated in the easternmost fringe of Czechoslovakia, or Sub-Carpathian Ruthenia. Prague was a center of Jewish life until a large wave of emigration to Israel began in 1948.

It is important to remember that almost all the Jews who renewed religious communal life after the war were transplants from the East. They came from villages in Sub-Carpathian Ruthenia, a part of Czechoslovakia (today the Ukraine) that had experienced centuries of traditional Jewish life almost completely shielded from Western European currents of Enlightenment and assimilation. Without them, Jewish communal life in Prague might have been erased completely in the Holocaust. Even today, the situation is much the same. If you come to pray in the Altneuschul, you will find that practically all the elderly worshippers who are not tourists are from Eastern Slovakia or Sub-Carpathian Ruthenia.

In 1948, Czechoslovakia was the only country to offer a steady supply of arms and military training to the newborn state of Israel. In the same year, the Communists gained power, and in the next two years twenty-six thousand Jews left Czechoslovakia, most of them heading to Israel. The country's Jewish population was thus reduced by more than half.

In 1950, the Jewish Community in Prague and in all of Czechoslovakia entered yet another era of trial and torture. Rudolf Slansky, a Jew who was the general secretary of the Czechoslovak Communist Party, was accused of plotting against the government. Suddenly, reports circulated about a "cosmopolitan Zionist conspiracy" to subvert the Czechoslovak state. A total of fourteen leading Communist officials, including eleven Jews, were tried in the so-called "Slansky Trial," the first government-orchestrated show trials in the communist world. The Jewish roots of most of the accused were not merely hinted at: they were made the focus of attention in the most iniquitous anti-Semitic propaganda campaign since that waged by Germany in the previous decade. The trial turned into a farcical crusade against the Jewish state and all of its "covert emissaries"—i.e., Jews—living in Czechoslovakia. Eleven of the accused were executed; three were given life imprisonment. The communist newspaper *Rude Pravo* wrote, "May the dogs die a dog's death—the Jews a Jew's death" (excerpted in Wilma Abeles Iggers, *The Jews of Bohemia and Moravia: A Historical Reader*).

The Slansky trial did not end with the sentences passed. Jews throughout Czechoslovak society were forced out of their jobs and even the most assimilated Jews, eager to erase all remnants of their Jewish pasts, were branded as Zionist conspirators. The campaign was orchestrated by the state but permeated all aspects of Czechoslovak society, from employment to education to social discourse. In the 1990s it was revealed that the Czechoslovak secret police had been compiling lists of "Zionists" (Jews) in the event of the need for scapegoats in the future.

The political and social thaw in the 1960s, culminating in Dubcek's "Prague Spring," unleashed a surprising amount of interest in things Jewish. Books were published on Jewish themes including the Holocaust, and many Czechs who weren't Jewish began to feel solidarity with the Jewish people. But with increasing Soviet hostility to Israel after the Six Day War of 1967, followed by the crushing of Prague Spring by Warsaw Pact troops in 1968, the situation for Prague's Jews became more difficult. Throughout the 1970s and 1980s, there were not-so-secret police officers stationed at Prague's Altneuschul, noting the identities of those who attended services. Even the rabbi was forced into collaborating with the authorities; if he hadn't, there probably would have been no Jewish worship at all during those years. Nonetheless, it is a mistake to describe the 1970s and 1980s as a desert of Jewish life. Communal institutions carried on, but in a more cautious manner.

In Prague, as in each of the other cities discussed in this book, the generation of Jews born soon after the Holocaust has come to be known as the "missing generation." Survivors of the Holocaust who remained in Central Eastern Europe discouraged their children, either subtly or quite openly, from expressing any form of Jewish identity. This changed during the thaw of the 1960s, when many Jews began to meet socially in the Jewish Town Hall, but in the repression of the 1970s, old habits of nonexpression returned.

It was during this time that Jewish life exerted an exotic pull on many Czech dissidents and others who resented the totalitarianism of the regime. Judaism was seen as the ultimate dissident religion, and during the 1980s several dissidents met under the auspices of the Jewish Community or in private homes. Some even converted to Judaism.

After the change of government in 1989, Judaism became fashionable among the general populace. A Gentile pop group drew inspiration from Jewish themes and became famous; Gentile teenage girls were known to sport Stars of David on their necks and ears; Gentile Czechs claimed, in ridiculous numbers, to have Jewish ancestry. It was as if the populace was so eager to forget the past—or, in the case of the older generations, their complicity in that past—that they identified with a religion and culture that was free of the sins of the past half-century.

In the 1990s, when a new generation of Czech Jews took a more active interest in its roots, it was often done in a vacuum. So few parents had maintained contact with Jewish tradition and Community that young Jews had to build an identity practically out of scratch. On a very minor scale, this mirrored the search for roots seen among many Jews in Prague in the early twentieth century. In both eras, young Jews were rebelling against the assimilation of their parents. In both eras, young Jews often came to identify not with local Czech tradition, which had atrophied, but with Jewish life as practiced in areas to the East. In the 1990s, for example, many young Jews saw "true" Judaism not among Prague's native Jews but among postwar Jewish immigrants from Sub-Carpathian Ruthenia who continued to live in Prague. The legacy of the fierce assimilation of nineteenth century Prague has made it even more difficult today for young Jews to locate themselves in a continuum of Jewish life. A Czech Jewish friend once complained to me, "What can Czech Jews do? We can return to the tradition of no tradition!"

As for the general situation in the Prague Jewish Community following the fall of communism, there are two American myths that are extremely widespread. The first, popular among tourists, is that not a single Jew is left in Prague. The second, popular in the American media, is that recent years have witnessed a phoenix-like rebirth of Jewish life in the city.

The reality of the situation is far less dramatic than either scenario. Prague is by no means absent of Jews. Unfortunately, though, the great opportunity for a rebirth of Jewish life was never seized in the 1990s. There are several reasons for this. First, though, the statistics: there are 1,350 people registered in the Jewish Community of Prague, half of whom are over the age of seventy. This number represents only the active members of the Jewish Community; unofficial estimates of Prague Jews range from ten to twenty thousand. Unlike the case in America or Israel, where a plurality of Jewish life implies a diverse range of outlets for Jewish expression, the structure in most European countries—particularly in the aftermath of the Holocaust—is that of a single Jewish communal structure that oversees both the religious and social affairs of the Jews.

There are various reasons why thousands of Jews in Prague do not affiliate with the Jewish Community. The first is the most obvious: For the older generations, open identification as Jews exposed them to the horrors of the Nazi era. The first thing the Germans did when they entered the Jewish Town Hall was demand a list of all registered Jews in Czechoslovakia. Later, in the 1950s and again in the '70s and '80s, state-sponsored anti-Semitism forced most Jews to hide all traces of their Jewish past. Such experiences have convinced many Jews that it is wiser to remain unaffiliated. Indeed, those Jews who did not leave the country after the Holocaust were, in most cases, people who wished to begin life anew as Czechs, without any connection to their stigmatized religion. These attitudes toward Jewish identity have been passed, usually in subtle ways, to subsequent generations. The effect is so strong that even today, most young Czech Jews are aware of their ancestry but feel no reason to openly identify as Jews. Finally, even before the Holocaust, Czech Jews were among the most assimilated in Europe. Today's trend of disassociation is certainly extreme, but it is by no means an anomaly in modern Czech Jewish history.

But perhaps the most tragic aspect to the Community's paltry membership is that the fault lies largely with the Jewish Community leadership itself. In the entire decade following the return to democracy in Prague, the leadership of the Jewish Community has not shown itself open to new members. The attitude of the Jewish Community is no better expressed than by the Jewish Town Hall. The building, since the sixteenth century the primary symbol of Prague Jewish autonomy, is today a barricaded fortress. Visitors to Prague are often shocked when they encounter the guards—referred to in the Community as "cowboys"—who smoke cigarettes outside the building. They seem to be less interested in fending off skinheads than in protecting the building from Jews. This is not a joke. For anyone who has worked in the Prague Jewish Community, the stories are endless: Every week, varying numbers of young Jews in Prague approach the Jewish Town Hall for the first time in their lives. After being harassed by the guards, they flee from the quarter, never to return.

This might seem like an irrelevant example, but it's indicative of the Community's attitude toward Jews in Prague. Since 1989, there has not been a single outreach effort launched by the Prague Jewish Community. There has not been a single public advertisement for a Jewish event to appeal to families who fled their Jewish pasts after the Holocaust. One can explain this through recent history: The Jewish Community is run by people who were all but broken by the communist system. Whether as participants or as dissidents, the leadership was molded by an era in which Jewish life was best experienced in discretion. To these individuals, the concept of publicly promoting Judaism is akin to self-destruction. When I was organizing a Hanukkah party in 1995, I spent hours bargaining with the leaders of the Community, who insisted that there not be a single public advertisement for the event anywhere in Prague. When I pointed out the absurdity of their position, the president exclaimed, "You don't know what it was like to have 40 years of communism!" This is the paradox of the Prague Jewish Community: The horrors of the past are used not as a pivot for change in the current climate of freedom, but as a justification for apathy and neglect.

One of the only people in the Jewish Community who has struggled to prepare for the future is Chief Rabbi Karol Sidon. Rabbi Sidon labors to supply Prague with the essentials of Jewish infrastructure: a *mikveh*, kosher food, and, if his dream comes true, a Jewish day school. Unfortunately, practically all his projects are met with resistance by the bureaucrats of the Community. In addition, Rabbi Sidon himself is not an administrator. His brainchild, a Jewish day school, was surrounded by confusion from the moment it was launched in 1997. Even the teachers did not know who was in charge. Ultimately the venerable Ronald S. Lauder Foundation stepped in to provide backing. It is hoped that with Lauder assistance, the school will come to resemble its fine counterparts elsewhere in the region. More than financial assistance, though, the Community desperately needs educational and administrative advisors. At its opening ceremony, there were ten students in the first grade; Rabbi Sidon's plan is to add a new grade in each subsequent year. It remains to be seen whether the school will actually blossom into a real Jewish day school.

In the west, Rabbi Sidon has become well known for his dissident past: A signatory of the famed "Charter 77" manifesto of dissent, Rabbi Sidon was formerly a renowned Czech novelist who was persecuted under the communist regime. Comparisons with Vaclav Havel, the playwright-president, are too tempting to avoid: Rabbi Sidon appeared to be a novelist-rabbi. But this, too, is an exaggeration. Rabbi Sidon returned to Judaism in the 1980s after studying in Heidelberg and Jerusalem. During this time, he was persuaded that the only viable expression of Jewishness was Orthodoxy. After assuming the Prague rabbinical post in 1992, Rabbi Sidon forbade religious services that are not Orthodox, and he has refused to allow the formation of non-Orthodox groups within the Prague Jewish Community. The problem is that in Prague, the majority of Jews have opted away from Orthodoxy for 150 years. Before the war, it was non-Orthodox synagogues that attracted most of Prague's affiliated Jews. In effect, the current policy prohibits the most natural form of religious expression for Czech Jews. The absurd result is that Prague has several synagogues that remain neglected and abandoned, forbidden from being used for worship.

There are those who explain this intransigence as the influence of Rabbi Sidon's former teachers in Jerusalem, who are waging a similar war against non-Orthodox Jewishness in the Jewish State. Unfortunately, the policy has had a negative effect on Prague Jewish life: the overwhelming majority of Prague's Jews are turned off by the intense Orthodoxy as practiced in the Altneuschul. The only people who attend services are a smattering of recent converts and elderly Jews from Sub-Carpathian Ruthenia. Among the worshippers in the Altneuschul on Shabbat, there is practically not a single person who was born Jewish in Prague.

In the midst of all this, the Jewish Community of Prague has silently become one of the wealthiest Jewish communities in all of Europe. Through a combination of restituted properties and tourist revenues, the Community is today a multi-million dollar enterprise. The enormous amount of capital flowing into the Community has created unprecedented opportunities for corruption and mismanagement. It is an open secret in the Jewish Community that millions of Czech crowns disappear every year. The question remains as to how many individuals are involved in the "disappearance." No matter how much clamor is raised for an independent audit of Community finances, the leadership refuses to open its books to the public. Unfortunately, members of the Jewish Community haven't campaigned vehemently enough for action; they seem more content to gossip in outrage than to change the situation. Meanwhile, unfathomable amounts of cash are disappearing while scores of Czech Holocaust survivors subsist in poverty.

If this were the whole story, the prognosis would be bleak. By the middle of the twenty-first century, Prague Judaism would be a lucrative business enterprise without any Jews. However, various new groups have emerged in the 1990s to fill the gap left by the Jewish Community. One of the first alternative communities was *Bejt Simcha* ("House of Happiness"), which styled itself as a Reform group. *Bejt Simcha* became unpopular among some Jews when it was noticed that many, if not most, of its members were not Jewish. However, the group has sometimes served as a launching board for Jews just discovering their

Jewish roots. *Bejt Simcha* continues to meet today and forms an important part of Prague Jewish life outside the Jewish Community. A larger, independent organization that caters to Jews was formed in 1995. Known as *Bejt Praha* ("House of Prague"), the organization was formed by a mixture of American and Czech Jews frustrated by the Community's stagnation and eager for an alternative to Rabbi Sidon's Orthodoxy. Calling itself the "Open Jewish Community of Prague," *Bejt Praha* has already made its presence felt with weekly Kabbalat Shabbat meetings (Rabbi Sidon has forbidden use of the word "service" because women sit with men), services on the major holidays, as well as social events throughout the year. At first, the organization was perceived as the Jewish arm of American cultural imperialism in Prague. However, after two years it became clear that *Bejt Praha* was a viable organization that would benefit Czechs as well as expatriates. Besides, even Rabbi Sidon has confessed that the future of Prague Jewish life depends on foreign expatriates. If *Bejt Praha* continues to orient itself to Prague's local Jews, it might very well become the catalyst for a renewal of Jewish life in the city. Their work is cut out for them. With the absence of a single traditional Jewish family in Prague and with a lack of Community cohesion, most Czech Jews who wish to raise Jewish families have already emigrated to Israel or to America.

Prague's Philosopher Kings

Czechs can take pride in the fact that two of Europe's greatest leaders toward the Jews emerged from their country. Of course, given Europe's bloody history, the few rulers who treated Jews benevolently naturally stand out. These Czech leaders were not just relatively superior, however. They each possessed an integrity that elevated their stature into the realm of ethical transcendence. The first such man was Tomas G. Masaryk, who led the nascent state of Czechoslovakia from its inception in 1918 until 1935. The second is Vaclav Havel, the first president of post-communist Czechoslovakia, and the current president of the independent Czech Republic.

TOMAS G. MASARYK

Well before he served at the helm of the independent First Republic, Tomas Masaryk distinguished himself with his humanitarianism and integrity. While serving as professor of philosophy at Charles University, Masaryk was active in Czech nationalist circles as leader of the progressive Realist movement.

Oddly enough, it was Masaryk's involvement in Czech nationalism that gave him a profound respect for Jewish ethnic and cultural renewal. Masaryk became such an impassioned supporter of Jewish national rights that he was actually an embarrassment to Jews who were determined to assimilate. What were the Jews to make of this philosophizing troublemaker, who was more of a Jewish nationalist than the Jews themselves? Masaryk even criticized Jews for not being Jewish enough! In the *Zidovsky kalendar* (*Jewish Almanac*) of 1929–1930, Masaryk is quoted, "I am not in favor of the Jews becoming Czechs. . . . I am not for mechanical means, I do not believe that they can become Czech through a declaration . . ." (excerpted in Wilma Abeles Iggers, *The Jews of Bohemia and Moravia: A Historical Reader*).

At first glance the comment seems exclusivist and anti-Semitic, but in fact Masaryk held too much respect for the Jews as a nation to submit to their disappearance in a dominant Czech culture. He had little patience for the "Czech-Jewish" assimilationists, not because he didn't believe in equal rights but because he believed those Jews were selling themselves short. In Masaryk's progressive view, only when the Jewish people were seen as a distinct nation could there be true rapprochement between Jews and Gentiles. In this regard, Masaryk identified with Jewish national renewal and saw in it parallels to the resurgence of Czech national identity.

Masaryk is perhaps the only European leader who ever heard of—let alone read—the great cultural Zionist Ahad Ha'am. Ha'am's influence on Masaryk's developing concept of cultural integrity was enormous. "In a word," Masaryk wrote, "Ahad Ha'am points to the improvement of Jewry through a spiritual and religious awakening" (quoted in Hillel J. Kieval, *The Making of Czech Jewry: National Conflict and Jewish Society in Bohemia, 1870–1918*). Masaryk viewed this Jewish "awakening" as a source of inspiration in his own quest for Czech cultural rebirth.

Nowhere else did Masaryk display his courage and integrity more than he did in the notorious blood libel trial known as the "Hilsner Affair." In 1899, a nineteen-year-old dressmaker was found dead in the Bohemian town of Polna. Since the body was found in the impoverished Jewish quarter, the stage was set for the accusation of ritual murder. The blood libel superstition, in which Jews are accused of murdering Christian virgins or babies and using the blood in Passover matzoh, had been employed in Europe since at least the twelfth century as a pretext for pogrom. Few people realize, however, that in this part of the world there were more blood libel accusations in the supposedly enlightened nineteenth century than in any previous era. Immediately, a vagabond Jew named Leopold Hilsner was picked up and charged with the murder. Amid nationwide hysteria demonizing the Jews, Hilsner was found guilty and sentenced to death by hanging. Masaryk, risking both his academic and political careers, stepped into the fray at once to defend Hilsner. He published a brochure as well as several articles calling on his countrymen to resist anti-Semitism. Referring to the demagogic prosecutors, he wrote, "People who pretend to save the Czech nation actually poison it with base, incongruent lies and ignorance. . . . Shame!"

It is important to remember Masaryk's action in the context of the tumult surrounding the case. As a politician, he did the unthinkable: He stood up for a despised minority during an age of racist nationalism. Another thing to note is that many people erroneously cite Masaryk's stance as a symbol of Czech sympathy toward the Jews. This fails to acknowledge the euphoric cheers all over the country when Hilsner was sentenced to death; the popular backlash against Masaryk; the vicious behavior of the right-wing press, in which Masaryk was mockingly compared to the Dreyfus defender Emile Zola; and, most tellingly, the grass-roots popularity of the prosecutor in the case, a certain Karel Baxa, who later became mayor of Prague. Masaryk represented nothing but the high ethics that were almost totally absent from Europe in this century.

Hilsner's death sentence was eventually commuted to life imprisonment, and in 1918 he was pardoned. But Masaryk's stance did not go unpunished. During the furor, he was put on an enforced leave from Charles University, and condemned in chauvinist demonstrations—all as a result of his unremitting pursuit of truth and rationality. Ultimately, a combination of student support and liberal activism allowed Masaryk to return to popularity, and he became President in 1918. Even then he continued his progressive attitude toward the Jews. In 1927 he became the first European leader to visit the Jewish pioneer settlements in Palestine. He gave private donations to the establishment of Hebrew high schools in Sub-Carpathian Ruthenia, and was an avid supporter of Jewish national causes throughout his tenure.

VACLAV HAVEL

Although it is still too early in Vaclav Havel's political career to make any sweeping assessments, Havel has already begun to emulate the example of his enlightened predecessor. Like Masaryk, Havel has shown a respect for Jews and Judaism that is grounded in a universalist sense of ethics. Masaryk's legacy of tolerance has not been lost on the new leader. "As President," Havel has said, "I am full of admiration for the sense of justice, humanism, and objectivity of my great predecessor, Tomas G. Masaryk. . . . He had but one goal in mind: to find the truth. . . . 'Anti-Semitism,' [Masaryk] wrote, 'is in my opinion a blow to ourselves and, in fact, only to ourselves. It damages us, coarsens us, and degrades us.'" In Havel's deliberate following of the footsteps of Masaryk, there is a sense of symmetric harmony: Masaryk began the democratic tradition with an appeal to reason and morality, and Havel continues this noble tradition in the new democracy today.

The most poignant example of Havel's humanity toward Jews is his impetus in the reconstruction of the Pinchas Synagogue Holocaust Memorial, which had been destroyed by the previous regime under the flimsy pretext of "water leakage." For several years before 1989, the communist government had made frequent pledges to restore to the Pinchas Synagogue's walls the names of 77,297 Czech Jews murdered in the Holocaust. In 1990 Havel declared, "Our first priority will be to renovate this memorial." This declaration, as much as anything else, demonstrated how easily the previous regime could have restored the Memorial if only it had had the will to do so.

His years as a dissident sensitized Havel to oppressed people in general and to Jews in particular, as several of his co-dissidents had Jewish roots. Even more, the dissident years honed Havel's view of the existential basis of humanity and justice. "As a dissident," he said in 1990, "I lived for many years in something of a ghetto and I learned what irrational injustice can mean. I learned that it can only be resisted by maintaining that sense of personal freedom which is impervious to external oppression."

Just as Masaryk's sympathy for the Jews came out of a strong sense of Czech nationhood, Havel also views Jewish destiny as a parallel to the history of the Czechs. Soon after becoming President, he expanded upon this:

> I often think about what the history of the Czechs and the history of the Jews had in common. We were both small nations whose existence could never be taken for granted. An unceasing fight for survival, a feeling that our very existence was always being called into question, was projected into the cultural and behavioral patterns of both nations. Writers and philosophers took the burden of politics on themselves. Both nations revered the written word and those works which kept their language and traditions alive. . . . Czechs and Jews have always looked to their past, seeking in it a source of strength and solace. . . . Political reality made us both withdraw into the family, into privacy, and engendered in us traits like skepticism, a distrust of power, a disdain for the so-called public interest. At the same time, it sharpened our sense of humor and restrained us from ever taking ourselves too seriously.

(Havel passages from Natalia Berger,
Where Cultures Meet: The Story of the Jews of Czechoslovakia)

Such thoughtful insights on the Jews and the Czechs reveal the President's humble urge to govern not from strength but from mutual understanding. Just as important, he possesses unique bravery in tackling the question of Jewish existence beyond the post-Holocaust cliches of suffering.

When he does speak of the Holocaust, Havel shows genuine candor and empathy not often heard in Europe. In a speech before a concert in memory of Czechoslovak victims of the Holocaust in 1991, Havel confessed that he felt "strangely paralyzed" and "desperately speechless." "I am ashamed," he declared, "if I may put it this way, of the human race. I feel that this is man's crime and man's disgrace, and therefore it is my crime and my disgrace, too." (Vaclav Havel, *Toward a Civil Society: Selected Speeches and Writings 1990–1994*). Havel's comments are nothing less than revolutionary in the European discourse of blame and counter-blame for the extermination of its Jews. What other contemporary European leader takes upon himself *personal blame* for the Holocaust? Ruminating on the meaning of the phrase "Chosen People," Havel considered that Jews are chosen by narrow-minded man as a scapegoat for his insufficiencies. Havel took it one step further in light of the Holocaust. In the same address, Havel states, "They were chosen by fate for the horrible task of confronting modern man, through their suffering, with his global responsibility, to cast him down to the depth of his true metaphysical self-awareness. A look at the atrocities he is capable of committing awakens him—through shame—to an increased sense of responsibility for the conduct of the whole human Community." It seems to be no accident that Masaryk and Havel, calling their countrymen to task for the horrors they commit through anti-Semitism, both focus on a single, spiritually probing word: "Shame."

A charming example of Havel's respect not only for Jewish people but also for their customs and traditions occurred in 1994. An Australian benefactor had donated money to restore an ancient Torah in the Altneuschul. Havel was a guest at the Torah rededication ceremony. Where else in the world can one imagine a head of state joining Jews in rededicating a Torah? The President accompanied Jewish locals and visiting Israeli scribes as the Jews danced down Maiselova Street, carrying the Torah in their arms.

When the entourage came to the Altneuschul, the lady at the door handed Havel a *kippah*, or Jewish head covering. The President politely refused it. Immediately, there were shocked whispers from the crowd. How could the President refuse the *kippah*? At risk was a potentially embarrassing diplomatic faux pas. It is forbidden to enter a house of Jewish worship without one's head covered; all the same, this *was* the President of their country. All eyes were on the cloth *kippah* dangling from the doorwoman's hand. What should be done?

Just then, Havel smiled. He reached into his pocket and pulled out a beautiful embroidered *kippah* the color of gold. "I came prepared," he said, and entered the synagogue amid sounds of relieved laughter.

SPOTLIGHT:
Rabbi Judah Loew—The "Maharal" (c. 1525–1609)

It is only fitting that a description of Rabbi Judah Loew should begin with the legend of his birth. It was the first evening of Passover. Rabbi Loew's father, Rabbi Bezalel, was one of the most distinguished Jews in the city of Posen. As such, he opened his home to all the poor Jews of the city, so that they might partake of the seder with him. Toward the end of the seder, Rabbi Bezalel opened the door for the prophet Elijah, as is the custom throughout the world on Passover. Just at that moment, his wife went into labor. The guests immediately streamed out the opened door, shouting in panic for help. Just outside the house, they saw a man and ran to him. The man turned on his heels and ran away. A policeman saw him and, thinking the crowd was pursuing a criminal, stopped the man and brought him to the stationhouse. Upon inspection, it turned out that the man was hiding not a stolen valuable, but the corpse of a baby. He was about to enter the cellar of Rabbi Bezalel's house, where he had intended to hide the baby, when the crowd burst out the front door. The man had been hired by Christians to frame Rabbi Bezalel in the age-old ritual murder accusation called the "blood libel." The man and his accomplices were thrown in jail. Rabbi Bezalel, in celebration of the redemption, declared, "This child will redeem us from the evils of our oppression!" The child was named Judah Loew [German for "lion"], after the passage in the Bible, "Judah is a lion's whelp; On prey, my son, have you grown" (Genesis 49:9).

The story sheds light on the reverence shown for Rabbi Loew to this day for his protection of Prague's Jews from annihilation, particularly from the notorious blood libel accusation. The most famous example of Rabbi Loew's care for his fellow Jews is the story of the Golem (*see page 35*). But in spite of these tales, there was no blood libel accusation that we know of during Rabbi Loew's tenure in Prague. Instead of being a physical redeemer of the Jewish people, Rabbi Loew was actually a passionate intellectual and moral redeemer who elevated the spiritual life of Prague's Jews to a level that has probably never been matched.

Born about 1525 in Poznan (Posen), Rabbi Loew began his rabbinical career in 1553 as the chief rabbi of Moravia, based in Mikulov (Nikolsberg). In 1564, he penned all the rules of the Prague *Chevrah Kaddishah*, or Jewish Burial Society, which had been established by Rabbi Eliezer Ashkenazi. It was the first modern *Chevrah Kaddishah*. In 1573 he came to Prague itself, where his wife's family resided, though he did not yet serve officially as the chief rabbi of the city. Instead, he began teaching in the newly constructed *klausen yeshivah* built by his friend Mordechai Maisel. Rabbi Loew's *yeshivah* became famous almost immediately. He abandoned the popular method of talmudic instruction known as *pilpul*, a dialectical mind game involving the analysis and comparison of detailed talmudic tracts. Rabbi Loew argued that such an approach lost sight of the ethics behind the arguments. He refrained from teaching young children the *Gemarah* until they had already learned the Bible itself. In his *yeshivah*, the Torah was taught for its own sake.

Rabbi Loew instantly became known for his fierce independence of thought and character. In 1584, when he was given the opportunity to become chief rabbi of Prague, he refused to ingratiate himself with the leaders of the Prague Jewish Community, whom he believed were corrupt and selfish. He gave a sermon in the Altneuschul in which he fervently argued for upright moral conduct, even going so far as to excommunicate members of the Community who were guilty of slander! Naturally, the leaders of the Prague Jewish Community felt threatened by Rabbi Loew, and they did not elect him to the chief rabbinical position.

Rabbi Loew then left Prague, returning either to Moravia or to Posen, but came back in 1588. In February 1592 he was invited to Prague Castle for an audience with Emperor Rudolf II, a meeting that has become legendary. In that same year, Rabbi Loew was again passed over as chief rabbi of Prague. He left again, becoming chief rabbi of Posen. It was only in 1598 that Rabbi Loew finally became chief rabbi of his beloved Prague.

Rabbi Loew's contribution to Jewish philosophy was enormous. In works such as *Netivot Olam* (The Ways of the World) and *Tiferet Yisrael* (The Glory of Israel), he contemplated themes ranging from human ethics to the destiny of Israel. Although the Golem legend is the most well-known output of Rabbi Loew's talent, his writing has little to do with pursuits in the practical *Kabbalah*. Nonetheless, Rabbi Loew's remarkable synthesis of mystical and rationalistic concepts made him one of the main precursors of the hasidic movement, which began over a century after his death. Rabbi Loew's meditations on the uniqueness of Israel and the unnatural condition of Exile have also been a source of inspiration to religious Zionists to this day.

The Golem of Prague

The first thing many Jews think of at the mention of Prague is the Golem, the superanthropoid created by Rabbi Judah Loew, who protected the Jews until he was destroyed and buried in the attic of the Altneuschul. The legend is so enduring that on any given day, scores of tourists can be found whimpering at the doors of the Jewish Town Hall, begging anybody they find for keys to the synagogue attic. "Have you ever been up there?" they ask, their eyes opened wide at the greatest of mysteries in Prague Jewish history. When they are told that it is forbidden even for the Chief Rabbi to ascend the steps to the attic, they stand spent and dejected as if their entire journey to Prague has been in vain.

Unfortunately, the significance of this pivotal archetype in the Jewish imagination is often forgotten. In order to clear these cobwebs from the attic, so to speak, I include here the story of the Golem in its fullest detail: his creation, his activities on behalf of the Jews, and, finally, his destruction. This is followed by a special section that explains what it is about the Golem that makes it a uniquely Jewish concept. With such folkloric material firmly in hand, I am convinced that one's visit to Jewish Prague will be all the more rich and rewarding.

Not a generation passed when European Jewish communities were not subjected to the infamous "blood libel" accusation. The Christian superstition claimed that Jews murdered Christian virgins or babies in order to use the blood in food and wine. Such accusations reached a crescendo every Passover, when Christians, propelled into a frenzy by the vicious sermons preached during Eastertime, claimed that the Jews used blood in Passover matzoh. All over Europe, priests asserted that human blood made the dough bind better, and that Jews relished the taste all the more when they knew they were eating innocent Christians. The blood libel superstition was so recurrent that it is as inseparable from European culture and society as is the feudal system. These teachings of the church led inevitably to the violence and murder known to the modern world as pogroms.

In the legends of the Prague Golem, such anti-Semitic hysteria was conveniently located in a legendary man known as "Friar" or "Brother" Thaddeus. Brother Thaddeus, a well-respected member of the Dominican Monastery, delivered sermons in all the magnificent churches of Prague. Raising his fist in the air, he condemned the Jews for killing Jesus, chastised the Jews for worshipping the Devil, accused the Jews of murdering Christian virgins and babies for their blood, damned the Jews to eternal torment in Hell, and goaded his fellow Christians to send them to the next world as swiftly as possible. Whenever Thaddeus preached—and hardly a week went by when he did not ascend a pulpit somewhere in Prague—the city became a volcano bursting with racial hatred. Prague's citizens were livid that there should be even a single Jew residing in their midst.

THE CREATION OF THE GOLEM

The Jews in the ghetto watched in alarm as Thaddeus's popularity continued to rise. It was only a matter of time before the Christians launched a savage pogrom. Some even feared expulsion from the Bohemian kingdom.

Amid the panic and confusion, the Jews could at least take solace in their rabbi, the shining star of the Diaspora, the High Rabbi Judah Loew, the Maharal, protector of the Jews. Rabbi Loew vowed to find a way to protect his people from the assaults of anti-Semites. He decided that prayer was not enough; the only way to combat the murderers was to seize destiny in his own hands. And the most profound way to do this was, of course, to ascend the emerald staircase of Jewish mysticism, the *Kabbalah*.

One night, the rabbi placed a clean sheet of paper underneath his pillow. He then recited a kabbalistic "dream question," directed to Heaven, asking for advice on how he might battle Brother Thaddeus. When he awoke the next morning, his prayer had been answered. On the sheet of paper was scrawled, in the most exotic of inks, the following ten words, corresponding to the first ten letters of the Hebrew alphabet:

Atah B'ra Golem Devuk Ha'chomer Vi'tigzar Zeidim Chevel Torfei Yisrael.

("You create a Golem stuck together out of clay and cut off the evil ones, those who would prey on Israel.")

He summoned his son-in-law, Isaac ben Shimshon Katz, and his best pupil, Jacob Sasson, to his private study. Bleary-eyed, the two men sat bewildered as Rabbi Loew launched into a discussion of the *Sefer Yetzirah* ("Book of Formations"), the ancient kabbalistic recipe-book for creating a Golem. Rabbi Loew then confided his intentions: "In order to protect the Jews of Prague, I have decided to embark on the creation of a Golem. But I will need your help. There are four elements to the universe: fire, water, air, and earth. You, Reb Isaac, are a Cohen, and you embody the element of fire. You, Reb Jacob, are a Levi, and you embody the element of water. I myself embody air, and together we will transform the fourth element, earth, into a living Golem."

During the next seven days, Rabbi Loew, Rabbi Katz, and Rabbi Sasson prayed and meditated with greater devotion than ever before. None of them told their wives the reason for their behavior, as the creation and existence of a Golem must be kept a secret. On the seventh day, they immersed themselves repeatedly in the *mikveh*, or ritual bath. In the middle of the night, Rabbi Katz and Rabbi Sasson followed the Maharal's broad, sure strides outside the ghetto gate toward the outskirts of the city. Before long, they left Prague and entered a densely wooded forest.

They stopped at the banks of the Vltava River. Rabbi Loew donned his *kittel*, the white gown worn customarily on Yom Kippur. Rabbis Katz and Sasson lit torches and chanted psalms as the Maharal pulled mud from the ground and began forming it into the figure of a six-foot-tall man lying on his back. Rabbi Loew did not omit a single organ as he sculpted and then carved into the clay. With its gaze turned upward, the supine sculpture resembled a darkened human corpse. Then the Maharal positioned his two assistants by the clay figure's feet, and instructed each of them in a special combination of the Divine Names. Rabbi Katz then proceeded to walk in a counterclockwise direction around the figure while reciting his combination of Names. As he did so, the figure became bright red, as if it were filled with burning coals. After Rabbi Katz finished his seventh circuit, the Maharal instructed Rabbi Sasson to circle the figure. It was during these rounds that the figure became filled with flowing water. When this was over, the three rabbis witnessed hair sprout on its body and nails grow on its fingers and toes. Then the Maharal began his rounds. The night, which had hitherto been balmy, suddenly hosted a fierce wind that shook the trees and made the river lurch with waves. When the Maharal finished his seventh round, he carved with his cane the Hebrew word *Emmet*, "Truth," onto the figure's forehead. Then he placed a parchment containing the four-letter *Shem Hamefurash*, the unpronounceable Name of God, underneath the tongue of the Golem. All three men then bowed to the North, South, East, and West while reciting the following verse from Genesis 2:7: "He blew into his nostrils the breath of life, and man became a living being."

The figure—the Golem—opened its eyes.

"Rise!" commanded Rabbi Loew. The Golem immediately stood up. Rabbi Loew's two assistants dressed the Golem in the humble clothes of a *shamash*, or sexton. As the sun began to rise, the men—no longer three, but four—exited the forest and headed back to Prague. The word *Emmet* on the Golem's forehead was invisible to the naked eye; he was completely indistinguishable from normal men.

On the way, Rabbi Loew addressed the Golem: "I have created you to protect the Jews from persecution. You are obligated to obey everything I command you, even if it entails walking through fire, diving into the sea, charging at a drawn sword, or jumping from a great height. Whenever a single Jewish life is in danger, you are obligated to rescue him or her."

"He looks like an ordinary man," the Maharal then told his two human companions, "Nobody will know he was created through artifice. The only difference between the Golem and Divinely created humans is the capacity for speech: the Golem is completely mute. This reflects the main difference between animals and men. In this way, we have not created a human soul—that is absolutely forbidden—but something like an automaton. Everything I say, he will do. But unlike other servants, the Golem is indestructible. Specifically, he is like Yossef Sheida, the being that assisted our talmudic sages whenever there was danger."

Turning to the Golem, the Maharal said, "Being that you are endowed with the spirit of Yossef Sheida, we shall call you Yossef."

When the three rabbis reached Prague, each returned to his own home, vowing never to reveal the secret of what had transpired on the banks of the Vltava. The Golem went to the guest room of Rabbi Loew, and prepared himself for his first orders.

THE GOLEM AS SERVANT

The Golem's tasks ranged from the mundane to the profound. Every day he could be found in the Altneuschul or in one of the sundry study halls in the ghetto. He performed menial tasks in the prayer halls, such as sweeping the floors and carrying books, and made sure that the synagogue was tidy and prepared for every Shabbat. Rabbi Loew gave the Golem meticulous instructions concerning all his duties. Indeed, it was in his capacity as *shamash* that the tall and speechless Yossef—called "Yossele the Mute"—was known throughout the ghetto. Had Rabbi Loew not given the Golem a daily occupation, people would have become suspicious of the large, jobless man. Rabbi Loew told his family that he had found Yossele wandering the streets, and had taken pity on the poor mute. The Golem slept on a cot in the Maharal's own home.

Rabbi Loew, aware that the Golem could not reason and would follow even the most foolish instructions, forbade anyone other than himself from giving Yossele orders, and absolutely prohibited the use of Yossele for private errands. There are many humorous Golem anecdotes that concern the breaking of this very rule. In one story, Rabbi Loew's wife, Pearl, asked Yossele to go to a well to fetch water to fill up two large barrels in her home. Hours later, water began to pour into all the rooms of Rabbi Loew's house. People ran to and fro trying to find the source of the flood. Finally they saw the Golem standing next to the two barrels, obediently pouring extra pails of water into the overflowing containers. The entire household broke into laughter as Yossele ran back to the well to fetch more water. Rabbi Loew chided to his wife, "You should have told him to stop when the barrels were full!" Then he shouted to the Golem, "Enough!" and the Golem dropped his pails. From then on, the Jews of Prague knew better than to send Yossele the Mute on private errands.

On another occasion, Prague was subject to a terrible storm before the holiday of Rosh Hashanah. No fishermen dared to venture out in such weather, and as a result there was not a fish to be found in all the markets of Prague. Rabbi Loew, who wanted to fulfill the custom of eating fish on the holiday, gave the Golem a net and a sack and explained how to catch fish in the river. Undaunted by the storm, the Golem set off. While he was gone, it happened that a man from outside Prague brought the rabbi a fish, and as a result the rabbi forgot about the Golem's errand. Several hours later, Rabbi Loew recalled that the Golem was still fishing in the river. He immediately sent a messenger to tell Yossele to come back at once; if Yossele had still not caught a fish, the messenger was to say, "The rabbi doesn't care about the fish anymore!" The messenger went to the river and, sure enough, there he found Yossele standing in the water preparing to drop the net again. The messenger called out, "It's time to come home!" Yossele indicated with his half-full bag that he wasn't yet finished. The messenger then called, "The rabbi doesn't care about the fish anymore!" Without a second's hesitation, the Golem turned his sack upside down and poured dozens of fish back into the water. Then he ran back to the side of Rabbi Loew. When the rabbi heard what the Golem had done, he saw that Yossele was truly incapable of independent reason, and would have to be used only in sacred and emergency situations.

THE GOLEM AS SAVIOR

It is these sacred situations that form the core of almost all the tales of the Golem of Prague. Every night, the Golem would be posted on guard duty, patrolling the streets of the ghetto in search of suspicious-looking characters. Sometimes he dressed up as a Christian porter, so as to mingle among the populace and listen for any potential plots against the Jews. When the situation warranted it, Rabbi Loew provided the Golem with a kabbalistic amulet that made him invisible. During the Passover season, the Golem was even more vigilant in his activities to protect the Jews.

One Passover, a Christian butcher in Prague attempted to spark a blood libel against the Jews. In particular, he wanted to frame Mordechai Maisel, the wealthy financier, because he owed the latter five thousand gulden and was unable to pay. Late one night, the butcher went into a Christian cemetery and exhumed the body of a boy who had just died. He carried the body to the slaughterhouse, which was located at the border of the Jewish ghetto. The butcher took out his knife and slit the corpse's throat, to make it appear that he had been killed in a ritualistic ceremony. (Incidentally, the association of Jews with vampires is never far from any blood libel accusation.) Then he wrapped the boy in a *tallis* that he had pilfered from a nearby Jewish prayer hall. Snatching a pig from a nearby pen, the butcher slaughtered it, opened its stomach, and hid the boy inside so that nobody would know he was carrying a dead boy in his wagon. The butcher then drove toward the home of Mordechai Maisel. Suddenly, he saw the figure of a man standing in the middle of the street. The butcher increased his gallop, hoping to frighten the man away, but the figure stood like a piece of the earth itself.

It was . . . yes, the Golem! Raising his arms, the Golem caught the horses by their ears and pulled them to a stop. He jumped into the back of the wagon and groped about. Yossele was always ready to inspect mysterious parcels entering the ghetto. When he found the slaughtered pig, he felt its underside and pulled out the corpse of the boy. Meanwhile the butcher, a giant of a man himself, had snuck up behind the Golem. Taking out his knife, he tried to give the Golem the same incision he had given the dead boy. The Golem, endowed with superhuman instincts, grabbed the butcher's wrists and flung him over onto his back. Violence ensued. When the butcher regained consciousness, he found himself bloodied, bruised, and tied to the corpse of the slaughtered pig. Meanwhile, the Golem was in the driver's seat, riding the frenzied horses to the police station. When they heard the noise of galloping horses, the city policemen ran from their offices to investigate the commotion. They found the butcher and the pig with a dead baby in place of entrails. The butcher confessed his crime, although heatedly denying he had murdered the boy. The Golem, meanwhile, had long disappeared. The Jews were saved from yet another blood libel.

Indeed, most of the Prague Golem stories involve some threat of annihilation posed against the Jews. The man most often behind such plots is the arch nemesis of the Jewish people, Brother Thaddeus.

On another Passover, Thaddeus summoned to his church two Christian handymen who worked in the Jewish ghetto. He gave them a filled vial and said, "Get work with the wine seller and pour a couple drops of this liquid into each of the barrels. You will be doing the work of our Savior, and you will be handsomely rewarded." When the handymen explained that only Jews are permitted to work on kosher wine, Thaddeus was undaunted. "Then get some work in their matzoh factory," he said, replacing the vial with a box of powder. "Pour this into the flour, and make sure it's the flour for Rabbi Loew's matzoh!" Racked by guilt, and unwilling to slay all the Jews who had employed them for years, the handymen poured only half the poison into the flour. "Maybe they'll just get bellyaches," they reasoned.

On the eve of Passover, when Rabbi Loew was praying with the Community in the Altneuschul, he made a startling error in the liturgy. Instead of reciting "*umachalif et hazmanim*" ("and He changes the seasons"), he said "*umachamitz et hazmanim*" ("and He sours the seasons"). Rabbi Loew stopped the prayer. He knew immediately that a grave threat was posed against the Jews. His mistake was nothing less than a warning from the Heavenly Sphere. He told the congregation to continue the service, but to not leave the Altneuschul until he gave word. A similar message was posted to all the synagogues of Prague.

Meanwhile, it occurred to Rabbi Loew that the word *umachamitz*—which shares the root of *chometz*, leavened bread—concerned the purity of the Passover matzoh. He summoned the Golem and ordered him to fetch two samples of his matzoh—one ordinary piece, and one piece of *shemurah* matzoh, specially guarded matzoh made in the Prague matzoh factory. When the Golem returned, Rabbi Loew commanded him to taste the ordinary matzoh. The Golem ate the entire matzoh in an instant, joyfully licking his lips when he finished. Then the Maharal ordered him to taste the *shemurah* matzoh. As soon as the Golem bit into it, he winced, changed color, and frantically clawed at his throat. Rabbi Loew had to clasp the Golem's body in order to draw away the pain. The rabbi spoke to the matzoh makers and learned that on the last day of baking, the two Christian handymen had assisted in making lines in the dough. A *shamash* was immediately dispatched to all the synagogues in Prague, prohibiting anyone from eating matzoh made on the day before Passover.

Then the Maharal gave the Golem a kabbalistic amulet that rendered the wearer invisible, and ordered him to search the home of the handymen for any poison. The Golem found the half-empty box and brought it back to Rabbi Loew. When the rabbi sniffed the powder, he recognized the smell from the poisoned *shemurah* matzoh. He ordered the Golem to return the box to the home of the two handymen, and retreated at once to the chief of police. The two handymen were arrested, and the Jews of Prague celebrated the Passover holiday with more festivity than ever before. Thaddeus, however—who denied any involvement in the scheme, and against whom the police had no direct evidence—was still free to terrorize the Jews.

Terror was Brother Thaddeus' most practiced art. In one story, Thaddeus employed his power of spiritual seduction to lure an innocent Jewish girl into the catacombs of his church. On the eve of her baptism, the girl became despondent and longed for the comfort of her people and for her parents' home. Thaddeus, unwilling to pass up the prospect of a young Jewish convert, locked her in her room and posted a guard at the door. It was only the Golem, armed with his invisibility amulet, who was able to rescue the girl from Thaddeus's grip.

THE END OF BROTHER THADDEUS

Finally at his wit's end, Thaddeus decided that the only way to secure a successful blood libel against the Jews was to do it himself. He waited patiently until another Passover arrived, and then set a trap sure to destroy the Jews once and for all. First he lured his servant's six-year-old child into his study. Enraptured by the promise of Paradise, he slit the boy's throat and diligently collected the blood in thirty glass vials. On each of the vials he printed the name of one of the Prague Jewish Community's prominent members. Rabbi Loew's name was printed largest of all. He then carried the body and the vials through a secret tunnel leading from his church to the ancient ruins of the "Palace Five," and hid them in a chest there. The "Palace Five" was so named because it was situated at the intersection of five streets and because it had five sides, each of whose sides had five columns. It also happened to be situated almost directly opposite the Altneuschul.

Rabbi Loew, meanwhile, was busy cleaning his home of every last morsel of *chometz*, or leavened bread, before the holiday. It came time to recite a passage concerning any bread he might not have spotted. Although Rabbi Loew knew all the prayers by heart, he made it a point to read out of the prayerbook. He motioned for his sexton to raise the torch over the prayerbook, and commenced reading. As soon as he opened his mouth, though, the torch went out. The sexton relit the torch, but again the light disappeared. When this happened a third and a fourth time, the Maharal knew that something was wrong. Refusing to give up, he ordered the sexton to stand by the wall lamp and to read the prayer aloud. The passage begins, "*Kol chamira vachamia de-ika birshuti*" ("Any leaven that is in my possession"), but when the sexton read the passage, he uttered, "*Kol chamira vachamia de-ika bechamishi*" ("Any leaven that is in *the fifth*"). Rabbi Loew exclaimed, "What did you say? Read it again!" But once again, the sexton made the same mistake. Then the Rabbi understood the threat against the Jews. "There is leaven in the Fifth," he cried to his confidantes. "It threatens to extinguish the light of our people!"

The rabbi related a dream he had had on *Shabbat Hagadol*, the "Great Shabbat" that precedes Passover. "There was a fire in the Palace Five that burst through its windows and leapt to the Altneuschul across the street. All of its worshippers were consumed in the blaze!"

"What does it mean?" asked his loyal sexton.

"There must be some *chometz* in the Palace Five that threatens to destroy the Jews! We must check it at once!"

Of course, that was easier said than done. The Palace Five was the most frightful structure in all Prague, a haunted building said to have been built during pagan times as a shrine for the Sun-god. It was said that after nightfall, demons, spirits, and ghostly goats stampeded through the building. But the Maharal insisted that the danger posed against the Jews was too great for them to wait until morning. Naturally, he brought along the Golem.

Just after midnight, Rabbi Loew, his sexton, and Yossele the Mute entered the dilapidated Palace Five. Carrying torches, they descended a winding staircase until they reached the cellar door. The Maharal ordered the Golem to open the door, which the latter did, practically ripping it from its hinges. At once they were accosted by a wail that was like a combination of screaming children, agitated dogs, and the roar of a lion. A wind rose and extinguished their torches. "Recite Psalm 91, and all will be well," intoned the staid Rabbi Loew. "O you who dwell in the shelter of the Most High . . ." the rabbi and sexton proclaimed in unison. When they had recited the psalm a third time, the wind and wailing ceased, and they relit their torches. But as soon as they entered the cellar, stones and boulders began to fall from the ceiling. "Yossele," the rabbi commanded, "you must go down yourself. If you find anything suspicious, bring it back to me here."

The Golem descended into the darkest reaches of the cellar, and five minutes later returned with the body of the murdered child wrapped in a *tallis* and a picnic basket filled with thirty vials of blood. The Maharal grimaced when he saw what Thaddeus had done. "An innocent baby!" he mourned. He emptied the basket of its blood-vials and ordered the Golem to place the baby inside. "Now go back down to the cellar and follow the stairs on the other side. They lead directly to the cellar of Thaddeus's church, where he keeps his wine barrels. Hide the basket there, and then return to me."

When the Golem returned, Rabbi Loew ordered him to dig a hole. There they smashed and buried the bottles of blood. Afterwards, they exited the cellar and the Palace Five forever.

Meanwhile, Brother Thaddeus had convinced his servant to tell the police that he suspected the Jews of kidnapping and even killing his son. On the morning before the first Passover seder, a contingent of policemen and soldiers, accompanied by the evil Thaddeus, laid siege to the Jewish ghetto. The chief of police announced to Rabbi Loew that, with the disappearance of a child and the suspicion of a ritual murder, he had a warrant to search every Jewish home in the ghetto.

The search, of course, turned up fruitless. But as they were passing the Palace Five, Thaddeus mentioned, as if to himself, "Now wouldn't that be an ideal place to conceal a corpse!" The police charged into the building at once, descending its weather-beaten stairs into the cellar. Thaddeus walked straight up to the sealed chest and stood triumphantly as the police pried it open. When he saw that it was empty, his expression turned to absolute horror.

The Jews celebrated their Passover with more joy than ever before. At seders throughout the ghetto, Jews told not only of their redemption from slavery in Egypt, but of their liberation from the blood libel of the evil Thaddeus.

As for Thaddeus himself, he slithered dejectedly back to his church. When Easter arrived, he ordered his servant to count his bottles of wine, to make sure they had enough for the ceremonies. In the middle of his task, the servant came upon the basket. When he opened it, he almost fainted. It was the corpse of his murdered boy. He went straight to the police, who arrested Thaddeus on the spot. Thaddeus was sentenced to ten years' imprisonment and was stripped of his priestly rights. At long last, the Jews of Prague were freed from the tyranny of their most vicious foe.

THE END OF THE GOLEM

Just as Jews are not permitted to work on Shabbat, so their servants and appliances may not work. The Golem, a combination servant-and-appliance, had to be shut down before every Shabbat began. Thus, every Friday afternoon Rabbi Loew would remove the four-letter *Shem Hamefurash* from underneath the tongue of the Golem. This caused the Golem to freeze for the duration of the Holy Sabbath. The Community assumed that Yossele the Mute, who was so busy running errands during the week, was utterly exhausted and slept through the day every Saturday. At the end of Shabbat, the Rabbi would return the *Shem Hamefurash*—really, like the battery of the Golem—and the Golem would awaken refreshed.

One Friday, the Maharal forgot this most crucial of chores. According to one account, which reveals the compassion of the great rabbi, the Maharal was too busy tending to his ill granddaughter to seek out the Golem. As a result, when Shabbat began the Golem went berserk. Overworked after a long week, and without any orders for the next day, he entered a manic rage in his desperate search for chores. Mimicking the rabbi's wife, whom he had seen baking challah for Shabbat, the Golem threw dough into the oven and made a giant fireball with all the wood he could find. The fire spread through the kitchen, but luckily the *rebbetzin* put it out with a blanket. Then the Golem ran into the streets, seeking more and more work. He uprooted any tree he could find (and in the ghetto, trees were a rarity!) and hurled people as far as ten feet if they dared to step in his way. The Jews ran in panic as the Golem sprinted down the ghetto streets, slaughtering a chicken here, pulling down a doorway there, destroying everything but the earth itself.

The message was obvious: Although Rabbi Loew was careful not to create a true human being, he was still dipping into the Promethean fire of creation. Another moral—because all tales have morals—is that the Jews had become overly dependent on the Golem, and were allowing their destiny to be guided by something outside their individual control.

In the midst of the chaos, Rabbi Loew was busy praying in the Altneuschul. The congregation was in the middle of the *Kabbalat Shabbat* ("Welcoming in Shabbat") service when some men ran down the steps to the synagogue and shouted, "Yossele the Mute has run amok!"

Rabbi Loew now remembered that he had forgotten to stop the Golem. But what was he to do? Shabbat was beginning; if he stopped the Golem on Shabbat, he would be desecrating the holy day. On the other hand, if he allowed the Golem to continue his mischief, who knew how much damage he would wreak? Perhaps all of Europe would be laid waste!

But the great rabbi had an idea. The congregation was about to pray "*Mizmor shir liyom ha'Shabbat*" ("A psalm, a song for the Sabbath day"). This psalm (Psalms 92), and the psalm that immediately follows it, occur just before the *Barchu* prayer, which marks the official onset of Shabbat. Rabbi Loew ordered his congregation to pray both prayers twice. This would give him time to stop the Golem before Shabbat really began, and then return to the synagogue for the Shabbat evening services. The congregation would, in effect, be prolonging the Friday afternoon before the beginning of Shabbat.

Running out into the ghetto streets, the Maharal followed the mixed sounds of panicked crying and the Golem's peculiar groan. When he spotted his creation, he shouted, "Yossele, enough! Stop where you are!" The Golem dropped the tree trunk and pet poodle that he had been waving, and froze in his tracks. Rabbi Loew stood before the Golem and carefully removed the *Shem Hamefurash* from underneath the Golem's tongue. Then, with some regret, the rabbi caused the word *Emmet*, "Truth," to emerge from its camouflage on

Yossele's forehead. There was a blinding ray of light as Rabbi Loew adroitly removed the *Aleph* from the word, so that it read only *Met*, "Death."

Yossele the Mute returned to lifeless clay, and crumbled in a great heap to the ground.

The rabbi ran back to the Altneuschul, where the congregation was just finishing its first rendition of Psalms 93. "Everything is fine," he assured the worshippers, and launched into the second reading of Psalms 92. When he reached the verse reading, "For you have gladdened me, God, with Your deeds; at the works of Your Hands I sing glad song," Rabbi Loew sang with more exhilaration than he had ever sung before.

When Shabbat had finished, Rabbi Loew decided that the Golem had already served his purpose. He called his two trusted helpers to his side. "Because he was used for sacred purposes," the rabbi told them, "even his clay remains are holy, and must not be destroyed. We must bury them in the attic of the synagogue, which will be their resting place for all eternity." The Golem was brought up to the attic of the Altneuschul, where he remains to this day.

It is said that the famed eighteenth-century Rabbi Ezekiel Landau fasted for a week, purified himself in the *mikveh*, and uttered psalms as he climbed the stairs to the attic of the Altneuschul. Several minutes later he returned, white as a ghost and shaking all over. "Nobody must ever go up there!" He warned. "Nobody evermore!"

Egon Erwin Kisch, Prague's legendary roving Jewish reporter, bribed his way into possession of the keys to the attic at the turn of the twentieth century. He put a ladder against the eastern facade of the synagogue, climbed up to the fire escape ladder spokes, and ascended to the door with the large Star of David on it. He opened the door, rummaged around inside, and later reported that there was nothing to report. Of course, he was a rationalist journalist, so that is to be expected.

The most intriguing aspect to the legend of the Prague Golem is its longevity. To this day, the Friday evening worshippers in the Altneuschul chant Psalms 92 and 93 two times, to commemorate the stopping of the Golem in the sixteenth century. This is the only synagogue in the world that observes such a custom. It is a unique example of legend entering the liturgy of the Jewish people.

The Golem Redux

"Is it, then, any wonder that Man should try to do in his own small way what God did in the beginning?"

—Gershom Scholem

The Golem of Prague is by no means the only Golem in Jewish lore. Just like the ghostly *Dybbuk*, the man-made anthropoid has arisen whenever the mystical needs of the Community have warranted it. A glimpse at other Golems in Jewish history will give us a better idea of what exactly a Golem is and, in so doing, reveal why the Golem of Prague is so unique.

RABA BARA GAVRA

The most famous of the ancient Golem stories is contained in the Talmud itself. In Sanhedrin 65b, it is recorded that Raba, a Jewish sage in fourth-century Babylon, played a little joke on his friends by sending them a creature of his own making. He was trying to explain the verse in Isaiah "Your iniquities have been a barrier between you and your God" (Isaiah 59:2) and reasoned that if a person does not sin even once, he will be no different from God. With a gleam in his eye, Raba told his fellow scholars, "If the righteous would so desire, they would be able to create the entire world!" Needless to say, his friends were unconvinced, so Raba decided to prove his point. The three rhyming words etched eternally into Golem lore are "*Raba bara gavra*"—"Raba created a man." Raba sent his Golem over to Rab Zera and waited to see what would happen. Rab Zera greeted his guest: "What's your name? Where are you from?" But when the Golem gave no response, Rab Zera saw through his friend's ploy. "You were sent by Raba, weren't you?" Rab Zera smiled. "Go back to your dust." And the Golem shrank away into nothingness.

The point was that the Golem had an essential flaw that separated him from man. Speech, which signifies a soul, can only be conferred by one who is completely without impurities. Thus even Raba himself, who extolled the possibilities of human perfection, could not create a real person. No human being is so flawless that he is indistinguishable from God and His power of absolute creation. In Jewish thought, this idea is supported by Psalms 8:6, which states that man was created only a "little less than divine." Because the most fundamental difference between animals and people is the capacity for speech, Golems cannot speak. Because of this difference, the mystic is not creating a true human but something like an animal. In the Israeli town of Tsfat—the kabbalistic center of the universe—I heard an ingenious take on the speaking prohibition in the six rhyming syllables of Raba. The *gematriah*—the numerical sum of all the letters—of *Raba bara gavrah* is 612, a number memorable only because it is one less than 613, which is the total number of commandments incumbent upon the Jews. Because the *gematriah* of *Raba bara gavrah* is less than 613, the phrase is somehow less than perfect. But, if you take the word *gavrah*, man, and change the Hebrew letter *gimel* to a *daled*, you arrive at a sum of 613, symbolizing completeness and harmony. And what does the sentence mean with a *daled*? *Raba bara davrah*, Raba created a *speaker*.

GOD'S GOLEM

In Jewish tradition, speech is at the center of all things creative. It is not only that the soulful quality of speech is denied the Golem. Speech is the tool used in the very creation of the Golem, as the mystic-creator recites a combination of names in order to achieve his goal. The verse itself, *Raba bara gavrah*, expresses this in its wordplay: It is a rhyming, repetitive reversal of three basic letters.

The power of words, and particularly the oral recitation of words, is of the highest mystical significance in Judaism. The entire universe was created through fiat, God's spoken breath. "God said, 'Let there be light'" (Genesis 1:3). Tradition has it that the world was created through Divine combinations of the Hebrew alphabet, particularly through permutations of God's unpronounceable Name. In one *midrash*, it is said that God deliberately arranged the sections of the Torah out of their natural order, because if they had been placed in perfect harmony, all who read it would be empowered to raise the dead and create the world.

The creation of a Golem thus has antecedents as far back as the creation of the universe. When a mystic endeavors to create a man, he is mimicking the most marvelled authority of God Himself. Indeed, many *midrashim* refer to Adam himself as the quintessential Golem ("nipped from clay" in Job 33:6), created by God from the dust of the earth. In this vein, the earth itself has within it the power of human life: "Let the earth bring forth every kind of living creature" (Genesis 1:24). The phonetic relation of the words Adam and *adamah*, earth, was a favorite topic among ancient biblical commentators.

Then, of course, there's the classic example from the Psalms, which contains the only occurrence of the word *Golem* in the Bible:

> My frame was not concealed from You when I was shaped in a hidden place, knit together in the recesses of the earth. Your eyes saw my Golem; it was all recorded in Your book; in due time they were formed, to the very last one of them. (Psalms 139:15–16)

Tradition has it that these psalms were uttered by Adam himself. "Golem" thus originally means "unformed." (In modern Hebrew, a larva is referred to as *golem*.) After Adam-Golem came to life, God gave him the selfless gift of a soul, and the Golem became human. In one *midrash*, the creation of Adam actually preceded that of the world itself. God was about to give him a soul, but then had second thoughts: "If I give him a soul now, everybody will consider him a partner in Creation. That would cause idolatry. So I'll keep him in a Golem state until the world is finished." God waited, created the world, and only then breathed a soul into Adam, who was now ready to be set into Eden. In the second and third centuries, a tradition arose in which Adam, in his Golemesque unformed state, was shown the history of Creation and civilization, with each generation passing before his (as yet unformed) eyes in quick succession. The size of Adam-Golem was infinite: He stretched, according to the sources, from one end of the world to the other. Only when he was given a soul did he shrink to human size. In yet another tradition, God symbolically married the earth itself, and created Adam as the "eternal symbol" of their love.

GOLEMS IN JEWISH HISTORY

Before Yossele the Mute arose from the dank banks of the Vltava River, Golems had nothing to do with the threat of a blood libel, and never served the function of savior. Indeed, nowhere is it even written that a Golem need resemble a man. The Talmud speaks of two sages, Rab Chanina and Rab Oshayah, who used to sit together just before Shabbat, absorbed in the *Sefer Yetzirah*, the "Book of Formations." Together, they would create a succulent three-year-old calf and then eat it on Shabbat afternoon. In a medieval legend, it is said that the two sages sat together to fathom the awesome *Sefer Yetzirah*. The book was so complex that it took them three years to understand it; just then, a calf was created. To celebrate their conclusion of the book, they slaughtered the calf. But just as the calf was slaughtered, the sages forgot everything they had learned. So they sat back down for another three years, until a second calf materialized. Although the two sages-cum-chefs undoubtedly made the calf into a hearty *cholent*, there would have been no prohibition against eating it live: Since they created the animal themselves, they did not need to follow the normal dietary laws.

Perhaps the oldest story of a man-made anthropoid concerns one of Adam's own grandchildren, Enosh. When Enosh's father sat down with his son and told him about the "birds and bees," Enosh asked if Grandpa Adam was created in the same way. Shrugging his shoulders, his father explained that the family tree extended no further than three generations. "What happened before that?" asked an astonished Enosh. His father told him the irrefutable truth: "Grandpa Adam was created by God out of the earth itself." Enosh was amazed and decided to give it a try. He dug up a mound of earth and formed from it the image of a man. But the sculpture remained inanimate. Enosh returned dejected to his father and asked what he had done wrong. "When God created grandpa," his father explained, "he blew the breath of life into his nostrils." Enosh, vexed that he hadn't thought of it himself, returned to his sculpture and began mouth-to-nose resuscitation (or "suscitation," as it were). Satan decided to play a trick on Enosh; he entered the sculpture and made its limbs move so that it appeared alive. The Golem came to be worshipped as a deity, and this is how idolatry entered the world. The message is clear: When man attempts to mimic God's singular power of creation, he risks destroying the foundations of monotheism itself.

Then there was Abraham, the father of monotheism. It is said that Abraham was the first person to utilize the combination of letters laid out in the *Sefer Yetzirah*, the "Book of Formations," (which, tradition has it, he scribed himself) to create a living being. His purpose was not to *mimic* the majestic power of God, as Enosh did, but rather to *demonstrate* the truth of monotheism. Evidence is cited from Genesis 12:5, in which Abraham and Sarah took out "the souls they had made in Haran." Haran was known as a depraved slough of idolatry. One interpretation of the verse is that the new "souls" were converts to Judaism. A more esoteric explanation is that Abraham created Golems in order to impress upon the heathens the power of God.

The prophet Jeremiah was said to have assisted his son in the creation of a Golem. After three years' recitation of holy words, Jeremiah and his son finished their Golem, which was decorated with the word *Emmet*, Truth, on its forehead. According to the Talmud, "Truth" is the seal of God. Suddenly, in a startling departure from Golem tradition, their figure began to speak. "Destroy me!" he said. "The Lord alone possesses the power of Creation. Remove the *aleph* from my forehead, lest the entire world regresses into idolatry!" Such a speech, of course—in which the Golem commands his own destruction—was not the result of independent thought but of Divine channelling; the Golem was simply a medium for the message. Father and son then recited the holy words in reverse and removed the *aleph* from the Golem's forehead. The Golem returned to dust.

Mystics are equal opportunity employers, so there are female Golems as well as male. The use of a female Golem was once met with outrage by the authorities. It happened in the eleventh century, when the philosopher and poet Solomon ibn Gabirol created a Golem that raised a few eyebrows. Ibn Gabirol suffered from a skin disease that was so contagious he was forced into complete isolation. The unbearable loneliness ultimately drove him to fashion a female Golem for himself. An account of this woman is recorded in the book *Mazref le-Chochmah* by the famous Renaissance Jew Joseph Shelomo del Medigo, who happens to be buried in the Old Jewish Cemetery of Prague (though unfortunately, his grave lies outside the current tourist walkway). The account reads as follows:

> It is also related of Solomon ibn Gabirol that he created a woman who waited on him. When he was denounced to the government, he proved that she was not a real, whole creature, but consisted only of pieces of wood and hinges, and reduced her to her original components. And there are many such legends that are told by all, especially in Germany.
>
> Quoted in Gershom Scholem's *On the Kabbalah and Its Symbolism*

There are those who believe this "Golemette" was created for romantic purposes (but the splinters . . . !); others claim the relationship was innocent and that the wooden woman simply performed household chores. Whether the authorities were concerned over Ibn Gabirol's forays with magic or forays with a wooden woman is still unclear.

In the twelfth century, the great commentator Ibn Ezra created a Golem in order to show just how much energy was contained in God's holy letters. Elsewhere, Rabbi Shmuel Hatzadik embarked upon so many extended journeys into Germany and France that he is said to have built a Golem as an ideal travelling companion. Since Golems cannot speak, his fellow voyager would have been the perfect listener as they rode from country to country.

In the case of the sixteenth-century Rabbi Elijah Baal Shem of Chelm, a direct contemporary of Rabbi Loew, the Golem was not a faithful servant but a destructive force. Rabbi Elijah evidently created a Golem with the Name of God fastened to his forehead. The Name was so powerful that the Golem grew and grew. Eventually the rabbi feared his creation would destroy the entire world. Seizing just the right opportunity, Rabbi Elijah tore the parchment from the Golem's forehead. The Golem collapsed onto Rabbi Elijah, scratching the latter's face. In a non-Jewish version of the same legend, the Golem actually crushed the rabbi to death as it fell back to clay. The message is obvious: When one tries to scale the heights of God's domain, only disaster can result.

Indeed, throughout the Golem stories there is a certain grave danger: By involving himself in creation, the mystic is risking both his life and the precious balance of the universe. In one story, the creators circle the Golem in the wrong direction and end up waist-deep in the earth. In another story—a version of the Jeremiah Golem—the creature had the words "God the Lord" next to *Emmet* on its forehead. When the *aleph* was removed from the forehead and only *met* (death) remained, the implication was the death of God Himself! Since there is room for only one God in Judaism, the Golem maker risks usurping the highest authority in the universe. This is why the Enosh Golem story, in which the Golem introduces idolatry to the world, is perhaps the most emblematic of all Golem lessons. The Golem exists in a precarious zone in which the abyss between man and God is suddenly and swiftly destroyed. For some, this is a glorious goal; for others, it is as unspeakable as death itself.

In none of these tales and legends is the Golem a superhero designed to protect the Jews, and there isn't a common denominator in the creation of these Golems. Sometimes the mystic wished to seize the power of God; sometimes he endeavored only to *prove* the power of God. Sometimes the Golem was a symbol of a transcendent mystical experience; other times he was nothing more than a dutiful servant. Only in the case of Rabbi Elijah did the Golem assume such menacing proportions that he threatened to destroy the earth itself.

THE GOLEM OF PRAGUE

The Golem of Prague differs from his predecessors in that he was created distinctly to protect the Jews from persecution, specifically from accusations of ritual murder. In this manner, the servant became a savior.

It was not until the beginning of the nineteenth century that the Golem of Prague entered Jewish literature. This has led many scholars to debunk the legend of the Prague Golem; others, in defending the Maharal's power, claim that the Golem never entered the history books because Christian chroniclers were horrified by the implications of the Maharal's ability.

The most famous account of the Prague Golem was brought to the world's attention in 1909 by a Polish rabbi named Judel Rosenberg. Rabbi Rosenberg issued a book, *Nifla'ot Maharal* ("Wonders of the Maharal"), that he claimed was written by the Maharal's son-in-law, Rabbi Isaac ben Shimshon Katz. Allegedly copied from a manuscript in the since-destroyed Library of Metz, *Nifla'ot Maharal* was an eyewitness account of the creation of the Golem and of the Golem's activities in Prague. Scholars have convincingly shown that the manuscript was a forgery. Nonetheless, Rabbi Rosenberg was so steeped in kabbalistic learning that he was able to relate the Golem story in all its mystical glory. The result was an engaging work that became the source of most later treatments of the Golem throughout the twentieth century. One of the classic renditions was Chayim Bloch's 1920 volume *The Golem: Mystical Tales from the Ghetto of Prague*, whose stories form the basis of the Golem legend in the present book.

The Prague Golem has entered the mythology of Bohemia and, indeed, of all Europe. Jakob Grimm and Johann Wolfgang von Goethe both drew inspiration from the legend of a man-made automaton. There is some belief (although not entirely credible) that Mary Shelley was aware of the legend when she sat down to write *Frankenstein*. Gustav Meyrink's classic work *The Golem* became inseparable from the mystique of Prague's former ghetto for generations, although it has little to do with Jewish tradition or legend. Josef Capek was undoubtedly inspired by the Golem when he wrote *R.U.R*, the play that introduced the word "Robot" to the world's languages. In the Jewish world, aside from the oral versions of the tale, we have Golem visions from such diverse Jewish writers as Y. L. Peretz, Jorge Luis Borges, Cynthia Ozick, and Franz Kafka, who penned a diary vignette relating the creation of the Golem to the creation of art.

Present-day versions of the Golem legend often involve biotechnology or the nuclear or digital age, reflecting humankind's recent fear that its creations will eventually take over and destroy. As early as 1965, when Israel built its first supercomputer, the historian Gershom Scholem was asked to dedicate the computer. He named the computer "Golem Alef," stating, ". . . I resign myself and say to the Golem and its creator: develop peacefully and don't destroy the world. *Shalom*" (Gershom Scholem, *The Messianic Idea in Judaism*).

Visiting Prague:
The "Jewish Town" Today

Prague's Josefov district is often touted as the "Jewish Quarter" or even as the "Jewish Ghetto" of Prague. As a result, millions of tourists each year stand gaping at Josefov's buildings, wondering how such an exquisite environment could ever have brought the Jews pain. Unfortunately, the modern "Jewish Ghetto" of Prague has become one of the most misunderstood phenomena of modern Czech history.

Since the second half of the twelfth century, Jews lived in this district in an autonomous "Jewish Town." Over the years, so many houses were built that a natural enclosure was formed. Six gates were constructed not for the purpose of imprisonment, but actually to protect the Jews from the threat of pogrom. There was no wall surrounding the Jewish Town; houses were packed densely together and small fences spackled the spaces between them.

By the end of the sixteenth century, the Jewish Town had become a densely populated ghetto. One street ran into a second street; narrow alleys twisted to and fro; courtyards were continuously subdivided to make room for more living space. Even the cemetery had become a twisting, cluttered mass of layered graves. In spite of these living conditions, the ghetto maintained a sense of Community and public order well into the nineteenth century.

Then in 1849 the Jews were finally released from the ghetto. Wealthier Jews had been trickling out of the ghetto for almost a century, but after 1849 the dam burst. A massive exodus began, with Jews moving to the Prague equivalents of the Upper West Side, Great Neck, and Rockland County. As a matter of fact, the situation was very similar to Jewish migration in the United States, where Jews left the urban ghetto as soon as they had the means to leave. The main difference was that in Prague Jewish confinement to the ghetto had been legalized, whereas in America it was due to economic circumstance. In the second half of the nineteenth century, Jews streamed out of the former ghetto to finer areas of the Old Town, as well as to the New Town and to the suburban district of Vinohrady. Their vacated tenements were filled by poor Praguers and by villagers looking for an opportunity in the capital.

During the next fifty years, the same phenomenon occurred in Prague as would later occur throughout the Jewish immigrant ghettoes of America. Deprived of the Community cohesion of the Jews, the overcrowded streets rapidly declined and formed a modern-day slum. The population density of the ghetto was three times the Prague average. Every conceivable urban vice bred and multiplied in the seedy corners of Josefov. Taverns, brothels, casinos, gangs, garbage, rats, typhus, flooding, crime, booze, and drugs lurked in the dilapidated ghetto. Buildings could not be repaired because the question of ownership was tangled and obscure. The terrible sewage system and lack of potable water made hygiene an unheard-of luxury. Jewish writer Leo Perutz, a luminary of Kafka's generation, recorded his impressions of the ghetto at the turn of the century:

> . . . tumbledown houses huddled together, sagging with age and in the last stages of dilapidation and decay, with extensions and shorings up that blocked the narrow streets, those winding, crooked streets in the maze of which I could easily get lost if I did not take care. Dark passages, gloomy courtyards, holes in the wall and cave-like vaults in which hawkers offered their wares. Wells and cisterns, the water of which was contaminated by the Prague disease, typhus, and at every hole and corner a den in which the Prague underworld forgathered.
>
> Leo Perutz, *By Night under the Stone Bridge*

There were still Jews there—many Orthodox Jews did not wish to leave, and the poorest Jews had no means to escape—but ninety percent of the residents were, by this time, poor Gentiles.

Toward the end of the century, the question loomed: Should one of the glorious gems of the Hapsburg Empire—the city of Prague—be permitted to wither into a cauldron of disease and decay? In 1893, Emperor Franz Josef and the Prague municipal authorities opted for urban renewal. They passed a sanitation bill to rebuild not only the ghetto but other parts of the Old Town and New Town. Most of the work, though, was centered around slum clearance in Josefov. After the necessary real estate was acquired, the former Jewish ghetto was destroyed between 1897 and 1917.

Over the course of twenty years, some three hundred buildings were razed, replaced by just eighty-three. The twelve passageways in the ghetto were totally eliminated, and the thirty-one narrow streets reduced to ten. The streets you see today might appear narrow, but by European old town standards, they're relatively wide. The new buildings became choice real estate in Prague in the early twentieth century.

After the destruction of three Baroque synagogues, Czech historical preservation societies fought for the protection of Jewish landmarks. As a result, the six remaining synagogues, the Jewish Town Hall, and most of the cemetery were preserved. Since the Altneuschul and the adjacent Jewish Town Hall were not torn down, the narrow alley between them, Cervena Street, can give you some idea of the size of the ghetto's former streets. Also, a quick look at the overcrowded cemetery, with its winding paths and thousands of graves stretching from the Klausen Synagogue to the Pinchas Synagogue, gives a picture in microcosm of how the ghetto looked.

Everywhere else, though, the "Jewish Town" is really a twentieth-century city. Parizska Street, named in honor of the early twentieth-century Parisian architecture that inspired its buildings, stretches from the Old Town Square to the Vltava River and is indeed the antithesis of a ghetto: Storefronts can cost upwards of two thousand dollars a month. The avenue covers up Wood Square, which once stood in front of the Altneuschul and allowed sunlight into its windows in the early morning. The Zigeuner Synagogue, where Franz Kafka celebrated his Bar Mitzvah, was situated on the site of today's Intercontinental Hotel parking lot. Had the Intercontinental stood there at the time, Kafka could have had his reception inside! Other priceless buildings now lost include the Renaissance palace of Jacob Bashevi, the first Hapsburg Jew ever to be ennobled.

The slum clearance begot a century of wavering reflection: Were the city planners insensitive to the ghetto's original flavor? Were certain buildings unnecessarily destroyed? Did the gentrification destroy a vital piece of Prague's history? On the other hand, wasn't the clearance necessary to stop the spread of disease?

For the purposes of this book, the slum clearance is important because the area is no longer either a "Jewish Ghetto" or a "Jewish Town." The few Jews who remain in Prague are now spread throughout the city. All we have in Josefov today are isolated islands of a Jewish past: the island of thirteenth-century Jewish life as seen in the Altneuschul, the island of sixteenth-century Jewish life as seen in the Maisel Synagogue, and so forth. The rest is the twentieth century. Today we can walk the geography of the ghetto, but the topography has vanished forever.

> NOTE: Diehard visitors who seek a true picture of the ghetto in the early nineteenth century are advised to visit the Prague Municipal Museum, which houses an awe-inspiring scale model of Prague from that era. [See page 145.]

The Jurassic Park of Judaism

> Mass murder constitutes the background of this museum, and the collections are by no means a symbol, but a very real document of the totality of human carnage.
>
> Hana Volavkova, *A Story of the Jewish Museum in Prague*

Today's visitor to Prague encounters one of the richest Jewish museum collections on the entire continent. No less than three synagogues and a ceremonial hall have been converted into sprawling showcases of objects depicting Jewish history and tradition.

Because of the enormity of the exhibition, one is tempted to credit the museum's origins to Jewish prosperity in Bohemia or to the charity of a great philanthropist. In fact, almost all the collections of the Jewish Museum in Prague were assembled from 1942–43 by the infamous "Museum of an Extinct Race," administered by the Nazis. This is why Prague's former Jewish Town escaped destruction during the war. It was to be both playground and exhibition center of the museum envisioned by the Nazis. Thus while the Nazis destroyed the physical landmarks of Judaism throughout Europe, they actively guarded the synagogues and cemetery in the Josefov district of Prague. Due to their methodology, the sites, if not the people, were to be protected and saved in Jewish Prague.

The "Museum of an Extinct Race," as it was later called, has been blanketed in mystery since its origin. There has been no definitive history written on the topic. However, the major outlines of this most bizarre period in Prague Jewish history are known. When large scale transports to death camps began in 1942, a wealth of Jewish property was left behind. It occurred to several Jewish scholars to save all specifically Jewish objects from theft or destruction through the creation of a special museum in Prague. The new museum would continue the work of the original Jewish Museum founded in Prague in 1906. Of course, operating as it was in the eye of the Holocaust, the museum's priorities were unique: It would focus on collecting and cataloging the sediments of Jewish life. It thus became the mandate of the wartime museum to preserve as much as possible of Jewish civilization even as that civilization was being destroyed.

It was when the scholars presented their idea to the Nazis that the Jewish Museum became a perverse partner to genocide. The Nazis accepted the proposal, on the condition that they would dictate the orientation of the museum. They had no intention of creating a memorial to Jewish life, but rather an exhibition to justify genocide: After the war, the collections of Judaica culled from Bohemia, Moravia, Slovakia, and elsewhere would form the core of a museum that would illustrate the supposed barbarism of the Jewish people. Here the visitors would silently rejoice over the progress of civilization. The Czech Jewish writer Jiri Weil, who worked for a short time in the wartime museum, later described it as follows: "The museum was supposed to be a victory memorial, for the objects displayed here belonged to a race scheduled for annihilation. Nothing would remain of that race but these dead things" (Jiri Weil, *Mendelssohn Is on the Roof*). The exhibits would be situated in the former synagogues in Prague, thus maximizing the contextual experience intended for the visitors.

As envisioned by the Nazis, the Museum would work like this: Aryan tourists, on vacation in Prague, would be able to step into the world of a long-exterminated people. From the ancient Jewish cemetery to the sundry synagogues in Prague, the visitors would wander through a caricatured microcosm of that which had been destroyed. The streets of Josefov would be converted, once again, into a teeming "Jewish Town" that would feature tourist entertainment mixed with historical artifact. In this way it would resemble the colonial village at Williamsburg, Virginia, or an Epcot Center of Jews, or—more precisely, since the Jews would be extinct—the Jurassic Park of Judaism. According to one account, the Nazis even planned to hire Czechs to dress up as hasidic Jews and to walk the streets of Jewish Town *à la* Mickey Mouse, making the experience all the more tangible for European tourists whose only glimpse of Jews would be in picture books.

These were not merely the pipe dreams of the Gestapo. The "Central Jewish Museum in Prague," as the Nazi-era museum was known, planned and executed several exhibitions in Prague's synagogues even while the war was waging. The Nazis actually paid for the restoration of these synagogues so that they would be suitable museum sites. Thus, in 1942, an exhibition of rare Hebrew books was installed in the High Synagogue. The women's section of the Altneuschul hosted a photographic exhibition detailing the building's early Gothic history. The Ceremonial Hall became a "Museum of the Prague Ghetto," and the Klausen Synagogue featured an exhibition on "Jewish Life from the Cradle to the Grave." In each of the exhibitions, the museum curators attempted to depict Judaism in a warm and humane light, offering Jewish values as a telling contrast to the barbarity of Nazi ideology. The Nazis, meanwhile, repeatedly ordered changes in the exhibits to focus more brazenly on the atavistic characteristics of a savage people. They insisted, for instance, on featuring pseudo-vampiric models depicting kosher slaughter and circumcision, two Jewish customs vilified by the Nazis.

As more and more Jewish homes and synagogues were emptied of their inhabitants, the collections of the Central Museum flourished. Even after most of the curators were murdered toward the end of the war, thousands of ritual objects continued to flow into the Central Jewish Museum. By the end of the war the Museum had expanded from one Jewish Community building to eight. It housed more than 30,000 objects and over 100,000 books from all over Europe, but particularly from the 153 decimated Czech-Jewish communities. More than 50 warehouses were filled with the inanimate objects of Judaism.

In 1950, the Jewish Museum was nationalized; it was only restituted to the Jews in 1994. Nonetheless, the museum continues to be haunted by its past legacy. Today, the Jewish

Museum possesses six priceless Torah curtains for every registered Jew in Prague. The overwhelming majority of these objects were literally stolen from people who were murdered; each item should be seen to represent one of the 153 Czech Jewish Communities destroyed in the Holocaust. Indeed, the objects would not be here today had it not been for the Nazi scheme to make a theme park out of genocide. As you walk through today's synagogue-museums in Prague, it is important to keep in mind the tainted origin of the otherwise luxurious items. The dual-perspective of this museum—on the one hand, the objects are treasures; on the other hand, they are stained with blood—creates a murky trial for today's visitor to Jewish Prague. Where relevant, I have given a brief account of each synagogue's wartime exhibition.

Finally, as you amble through the streets of the former Jewish Town, you might be startled by the masses of European Gentile tourists crowding into the Jewish sites. In the years following the demise of Communism, Prague's Jewish Quarter has become one of the city's most popular tourist attractions. One wonders why these tourists seem starved for a glimpse of Jewish civilization. Perhaps the visitors come from cities whose Jewish quarters have long since been destroyed; perhaps they are moved by guilt pangs for the crimes of an earlier generation. Regardless of the reason, it has become a bizarre irony of history that the "Museum of an Extinct Race" is flourishing today. Officially only 1,350 Jews live in Prague, but each year the Jewish Quarter is swamped with millions of tourists who hail from countries that, not too long ago, were complicitous in genocide. (A cynic might remark that they have replaced their machine guns with camcorders.) It is chilling that the Nazi dream of a Jewish fairy land without Jews has become, essentially, a reality.

The Jewish Essentials

The Jewish Community of Prague
Maiselova Street 18
Telephone (42–02) 231 9002

Most of the religious, cultural and administrative organizations are located here. If you plan to spend a considerable amount of time in Prague, you might wish to join the Jewish Community. Because the Community is extremely insular, and as a response to the high rate of Gentile Czechs fascinated with Judaism in recent years, the Community requires a letter, signed by a rabbi, that certifies that one is halachically Jewish. Many visitors, as well as Czechs, are put off by having to supply this "letter of authenticity." However, if one wishes to take advantage of the benefits of Community membership—which mainly consist of lunch discounts at the kosher restaurant—I advise you to procure this letter before you leave the United States. Annual membership charges hover around ten dollars, but administrative officers sometimes attempt to charge high fees to Americans. Don't allow yourself to be taken advantage of.

The Jewish Museum in Prague
Jachymova Street 3

This address is the administrative center of the museum. It is not the site of any exhibitions. All exhibitions are located in the synagogues (*see Orientation*).

Chabad House
Bilkova Street 14
Telephone (42–02) 2320 896

Chabad Lubavitch opened a Chabad House in 1996. The center is operated by Manis and Nechamah Dinah Barash, a young American-South African family that offers assistance, in the English language, for all religious needs.

PRAYING IN PRAGUE

The Altneuschul
Cervena Street, between Maiselova and Parizska

> *Kabbalat Shabbat:* According to sunset, but no later than 8:00 P.M. in the summertime.
> *Shabbat* and Holiday Mornings: 9:00 A.M.
> *Shabbat Minchah:* One hour and a half before the end of Shabbat.
> Weekday *Shacharit:* 8:00 A.M.
> Weekday *Minchah:* 2:00 P.M., only in the summer season.

Note: The Weekday Minchah *service is held in the High Synagogue, across Cervena Street from the Altneuschul. The service convenes when there is a* minyan *available. The High Synagogue is accessed through the Jewish Town Hall at Maiselova Street 18.*

The Altneuschul is the only place in Europe where one can pray in a synagogue used since the thirteenth century. For many visitors, a *Shabbat* in the Altneuschul is the highlight of their visit to Europe.

Women are advised that the women's section in the Altneuschul is the same as it was in the seventeenth century: behind a meter-thick wall, with slit windows looking into the main sanctuary. This has discouraged some female visitors from attending services here. Men are advised that in the main sanctuary, the area near the *aron hakodesh* is usually reserved seating. Generally, the closer the seat is to the eastern wall, the more likely the seat is reserved.

Aside from tourists who pack the synagogue full in the summer season, the congregants in the Altneuschul are a mixture of young *ba'alei teshuvah* (returnees to the faith) and elderly immigrants from Sub-Carpathian Ruthenia.

On Friday evening, many visitors are nonplussed when they hear the congregation reciting Psalms 92 and 93 two times. This is a unique custom in the Altneuschul. It commemorates the day when Rabbi Judah Loew, the "Maharal," put a final stop to the Golem of Prague. According to legend, he asked the congregation in the Altneuschul to pray Psalms 92 and 93 two times, to give him time to stop the Golem before the official onset of Shabbat. To this day, the Altneuschul continues the custom in a fascinating example of the interplay of legend and liturgy in Jewish life.

Detailed information about all aspects of the Altneuschul begins on page 64.

The Jerusalem Synagogue
Jeruzalemska Street 7

> *Kabbalat Shabbat:* According to sunset, but no later than 8:00 P.M. in the summertime.
> *Shabbat* and Holiday Mornings: 8:45 A.M. (High Holidays 8:00 A.M.)

The Jerusalem Synagogue does not have *Shabbat* afternoon services or *Shacharit* services on weekdays.

Shabbat services in the Jerusalem Synagogue are not held in the main sanctuary but in a smaller room upstairs. Services here have a much more homey flavor than those in the ancient Altneuschul. The humble chapel is filled with a small but devoted group of Czech Jews who warmly welcome visitors. The liturgy is Orthodox. Women sit in a separate room, but it is relatively easy for them to follow the service through an open doorway. Women often prefer the Jerusalem Synagogue's seating arrangement to the Altneuschul's.

One unique custom of the Jerusalem Synagogue is that on *Shabbat* morning, Psalms 92 is read after the *kaddish* following the *Amidah*.

After the Friday evening service, a *kiddush* including wine and challah is held in an adjacent room.

Bejt Praha
Telephone 2481–4162
Fax 2481–4164

Kabbalat Shabbat: 6:00 P.M.

Bejt Praha, a Jewish religious and cultural Community established in 1995, holds weekly *Kabbalat Shabbat* services and discussion groups inside the Jewish Town Hall on Maiselova 18. The group is a diverse mix of Czech, American, and Israeli Jews. Women and men sit together at Bejt Praha's meetings and services, although the group has resisted labels like Reform or Conservative. Instead, the organization calls itself "The Open Jewish Community of Prague."

Bejt Praha also organizes services and programs for each Jewish holiday as well as lectures, parties, carnivals, and instruction in Israeli folk dance, although the locations vary. Sometimes events are planned in partnership with the Prague Jewish Community. Please telephone them for an up-to-date schedule.

Bejt Simcha
Telephone 251–235 or 2481–2325, or Mobile Telephone 0603–426–564

Bejt Simcha styles itself as a "Reform Chevrah," although it is unclear whether the group is actually connected with the American Reform movement. American tourists mix with locals, many if not most of whom are Gentile Czechs in search of meaning, at *Kabbalat Shabbat* gatherings and programs for the Jewish holidays. The group often invites rabbis and lecturers from England and America. Bejt Simcha's religious orientation is progressive.

Bejt Simcha has recently changed locations in order to be able to meet in the Josefov district. Please telephone them to find out the current address and times of services.

MIKVEH

A modern *mikveh* is located next door to the Pinchas Synagogue. It is open one hour before the *minchah* service on Friday afternoons. At other times, it can be used by appointment with the Religious Association of the Jewish Community at Maiselova 18, telephone (42–02) 2310 909. As not everyone there speaks English, it might be easier to telephone Manis and Nechamah Dinah Barash at the Chabad House, telephone (42–02) 2320 896, who can open the *mikveh* for you.

Keeping Kosher in Prague

RESTAURANT

There is currently one kosher restaurant in Prague.

Shalom Restaurant
Maiselova 18, inside the Jewish Town Hall
Open daily, 11:30 A.M.–2:00 P.M.

This Jewish Community restaurant is renowned not for its culinary feats but for its place at the heart of the contemporary Prague Jewish experience. The auditorium of the Jewish Town Hall has become the primary stage where the tragicomedy of Prague Jewish life in the 1990s is acted out. At this writing, it is the closest thing to a social center for the Jews, and as such it attracts mostly elderly kaffeeklatschers supplemented by a tightly knit clique of younger Jews. It is often in the Shalom Restaurant that young Jews make their first appearance in the Community. A meal here offers a glimpse at the Community rarely seen elsewhere in the city. Remember to look but not touch: Prague Jews often feel like they're in a fishbowl as it is. Appearing in countless tourist photographs only exacerbates this feeling.

Only lunches are served at the restaurant, with the exception of Friday dinners. Shalom provides a set menu that can be changed only through Divine intervention. It's best to see what's on the day's menu before buying. Tickets are purchased not in the Jewish Town Hall but across the street, at the Matana Travel Office on Maiselova 15. For the same day's lunch, they sell tickets only until 1:30 pm. For Friday dinner and Shabbat lunch, you must pay in advance. Be sure to reserve an exact number of beverages, as once the reservations have been made the restaurant is powerless to change them. Many tourists have complained that their cups were decidedly not overflowing, so reserve all extra drinks in advance. Keep in mind also that Shabbat dinner is served after the Friday evening service in the Altneuschul. In the summer, this can be as late as 9:30 pm.

If you intend to spend a reasonable amount of time in Prague, you can eat very cheaply at Shalom. The Community subsidizes meals for its members (*see page 56*).

GROCERY STORE

The Kosher Shop
Brehova Street 10, around the corner from the Old Jewish Cemetery

The Kosher Shop provides a selection of foods, mostly of the Osem variety, imported from Israel. There is also a short-order cafe/restaurant, but it is not strictly kosher.

Orientation and Suggested Itinerary

For centuries, Jews were confined to a ghetto on the northwestern edge of the Old Town. The district is known as "Jewish Town" or "Josefov," after a visit made by Emperor Josef II. The Jews were released from the ghetto in 1849, and in 1861 the area officially became the "fifth quarter" of Prague. Although Josefov continued to be the Jewish communal center, in the nineteenth century Jews poured out of Josefov at such a rate that the district began to lose its specifically Jewish qualities. After the Holocaust, there were too few Jews in Prague to constitute a definable "Jewish Quarter." Today, with very few exceptions, the residents of the former Jewish Town are not Jewish. The area is still known as the Jewish District or Jewish Quarter, but the name refers to sites, not people.

But the sites are a treasure. Seven centuries of Jewish settlement left a sediment of six synagogues and a cemetery in an area of a couple of blocks. Most of the buildings are recent (*see page 50*), but in isolated spots we can explore the trends of Jewish life in each of the important epochs. The heart of the quarter is on Maiselova Street, by the Altneuschul and the Jewish Town Hall.

Today, all the sites in Jewish Town, with the exception of the Altneuschul, the High Synagogue, and the Jewish Town Hall, are owned and managed by the Jewish Museum in Prague. The Jewish Museum includes the Old Jewish Cemetery; the Ceremonial Hall; and the Pinchas, Klausen, Maisel, and Spanish Synagogues. The other sites are run by the Jewish Community in Prague. The two organizations are related, but not entirely interconnected.

Jewish Prague is managed like an efficient business, which is convenient for the visitor: Like Disneyland, everything is coordinated into a single ticket. This is the "Combination" ticket, which includes all the sites of the Jewish Museum, plus the Altneuschul run by the Jewish Community. Make sure your ticket includes all the sites.

Following are the public hours of the sites, year-round:

April–October
    Jewish Museum 9:00 A.M.–6:00 P.M.
    Altneuschul 9:00 A.M.–6:00 P.M. (Fridays 9:00 A.M.–5:00 P.M.)

November–March
    Jewish Museum 9:00 A.M.–4:30 P.M.
    Altneuschul 9:00 A.M.–5:00 P.M. (Fridays 9:00 A.M.–2:00 P.M.)

The Jewish Town of Prague

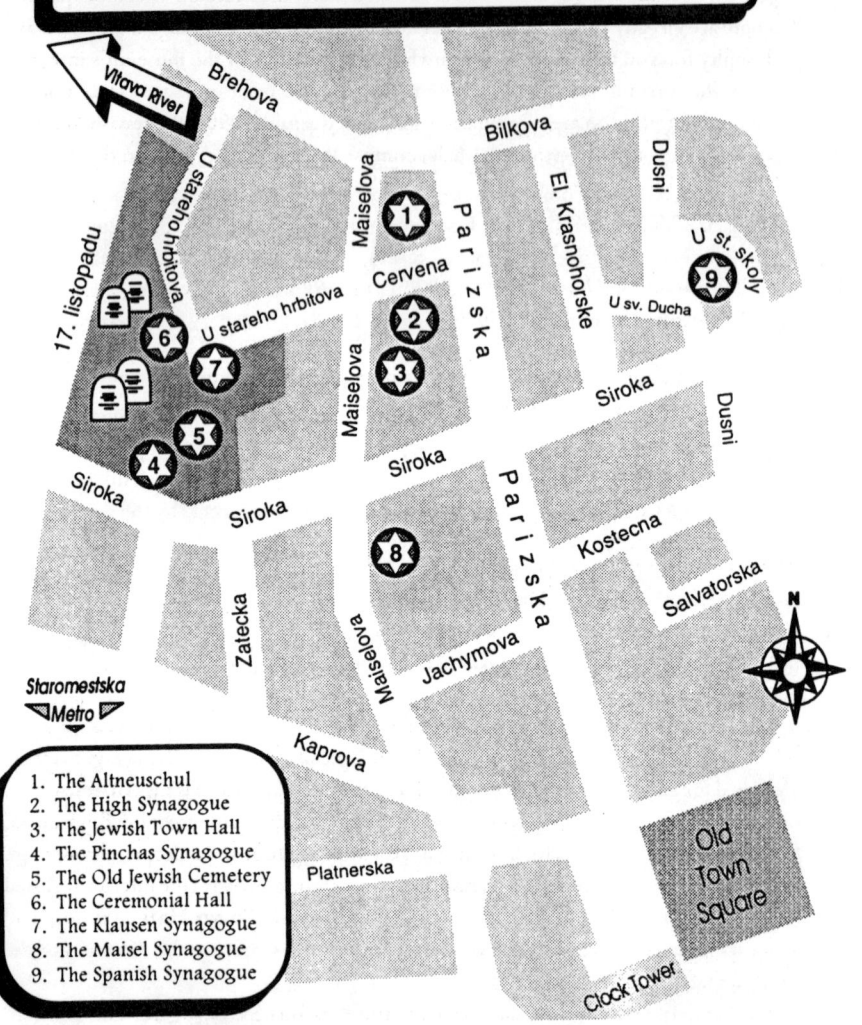

1. The Altneuschul
2. The High Synagogue
3. The Jewish Town Hall
4. The Pinchas Synagogue
5. The Old Jewish Cemetery
6. The Ceremonial Hall
7. The Klausen Synagogue
8. The Maisel Synagogue
9. The Spanish Synagogue

Ticket prices have been a source of acrimony in recent years. When the Jewish Museum was restituted to the Jews, ticket prices shot up exponentially almost overnight. The Jewish Community then increased prices for the Altneuschul. For its part, the Jewish Museum contends that since it is no longer state-run, it does not receive any state subsidies. Because it must outlay enormous amounts of money reconstructing the synagogues, it needed to raise prices. When confronted with the fact that visitors complain that churches in Prague are free while synagogues cost over fifteen dollars, the Museum director explained that if people are already anti-Semitic there is nothing one can do to change them. I'll leave that philosophy for you to mull over. Meanwhile, the true test of the museum's integrity will be after the Spanish Synagogue, whose restoration costs an estimated forty million crowns, is completed. In an average summer season in the mid-1990s, the Jewish Museum grossed this amount in only two-and-a-half months. If the prices do not go down soon, there will be cause for suspicion.

At this writing, the prices are:

Jewish Museum: 250 Crowns (students 190)
Altneuschul: 200 Crowns (students 140)

The "Combination Ticket" does not give a discount, but is simply the sum of the two numbers. It is equivalent to about fifteen dollars.

Places to Buy Tickets
There are four ticket offices:

Matana Travel Office on Maiselova Street 15
Inside the entrance to the Maisel Synagogue
Adjacent to the entrance to the Pinchas Synagogue
Adjacent to the entrance to the Klausen Synagogue

The last one usually has the shortest lines. It closes for a half-hour around lunch time.

The following recommended route is chronologically, thematically, and geographically designed for an optimal visit. Without a doubt the first place to go is the **Altneuschul**. The oldest continuously used synagogue on the continent, the Altneuschul will introduce you to customs you never dreamed of. It will also start the tour in its proper chronology. From there, take a look at the **High Synagogue** across the alleyway (the interior is closed to tourists as of this writing). Then stop by the pink **Jewish Town Hall** next door and check out its famous Hebrew clock (visible further up the street, in the direction of the Intercontinental).

Next, head down Maiselova and Siroka to the **Pinchas Synagogue**. This is where the cemetery begins, so it's best to visit the Pinchas Synagogue first. This synagogue is the second-oldest synagogue remaining in Prague. From the Pinchas Synagogue, visit the **Old Jewish Cemetery**. After the cemetery, stop by the cemetery exit in the **Ceremonial Hall**, which features a display of customs of the Jewish Burial Society, and then visit the **Klausen Synagogue**, whose exhibition concentrates on Jewish life cycle and traditions.

Afterwards, there are two magnificent synagogues that feature parts I and II of an exhibition of Jewish history in Bohemia and Moravia. The first is the **Maisel Synagogue**: head up Maisel Street; it's on the left side. Then head up Siroka Street a few blocks to the **Spanish Synagogue**, which is hidden perpendicular to the street on the left side, just after a church.

If time permits, I recommend you visit as much of the "Elsewhere" sites as possible. Many of them, such as the statue of Rabbi Loew, are close by. In addition, you'll inevitably walk across the Charles Bridge sometime during your trip; read up on the Crucifix there before you go.

THE ALTNEUSCHUL

Address: Cervena Street, between Maiselova Street and Parizska Street
Opening Hours: See page 61

It is fitting that your tour begins at the focal point of Bohemian Jewry. This synagogue has been the center of Prague's Jewish spiritual life for seven hundred years, and it's easy to see why. Located next to the Jewish Town Hall, the Altneuschul hosted Rabbi Avigdor Kara in the fifteenth century, Rabbi Judah Loew in the sixteenth, and Rabbi Ezekiel Landau in the eighteenth.

In the entire city of Prague, the Altneuschul is the only building that can truly call itself Gothic. All the rest of Prague's Gothic edifices experienced overhauling face-lifts in the Renaissance and Baroque periods (a notable example is the Tyn Church on Old Town Square, whose Gothic facade belies a largely Baroque interior). The Altneuschul, to be sure, has undergone various renovations since its construction in the thirteenth century, but none of these projects has altered the purity and integrity of its Gothic style. Thus the Altneuschul is one of the most precious relics of Prague's architectural history. In addition, the Altneuschul is the world's only extant example of a purely Gothic twin-naved synagogue. In the Gothic era, an even pair of naves was nothing short of revolution. Gothic buildings were normally constructed with three to seventeen naves, which were specially structured to support the daunting main nave. A Gothic church's main nave could thus stretch as high to the sky as possible, and make the worshippers feel as tiny as possible before God. Such a pulpit-oriented show of grandeur was decidedly absent from Jewish worship until the nineteenth century.

From the perspective of Jewish history, the Altneuschul is no less remarkable. It is the oldest continuously-used synagogue in all of Europe (the older ones, in Toledo, Worms, and Regensburg, were either destroyed or converted into museums or churches). Prague's most notorious pogrom took place within its walls. The first use of a Magen David as a heraldic symbol for the Jews is found on a giant banner hoisted inside. It is in the attic of the Altneuschul that the remains of the Golem have found their eternal rest.

The synagogue is so important to Prague's Jews that, at one time, it was the only building in the ghetto permitted to breathe. Elsewhere in the ghetto every square meter was used to maximum advantage; only in front of this synagogue was it deemed permissible to preserve a public square. Adjoining the eastern facade, "Wood Square" served for six hundred years as the economic and social center of the ghetto. It was to this square that the Maharal would step every Friday at sundown, raising a special banner high into the sky to inform the other synagogues that the Altneuschul had just lit its Shabbat candles, and that they were now free to light their own as well. Wood Square was demolished at the turn of the twentieth century.

The Main Legend

Everything harks back to the origins of Exile. It is said that when the Romans pillaged and destroyed the Second Temple in the year 70 C.E.—and sent the Jews into the Diaspora—two enterprising angels lifted a rock from the rubble and carried it directly from Jerusalem to Prague, the exact center of Europe. Twelve hundred years later, when Jews in the Old Town were searching for a spot to found a new synagogue, they saw the rock embedded in the earth and used it as a cornerstone for construction. On the day the Messiah appears, the two angels will lift up the rock again and take it back to Jerusalem for use in the Third Temple. Until that time, the angels stand above the doorway (some accounts have them transformed into doves), flapping their wings ever so gently to create a current of air that rings the synagogue and protects it from disaster.

The legend may sound schmaltzy, but on the 3rd of Tammuz 1689, a "flood of fire" swept through the ghetto and destroyed nearly everything in its wake, including the Jewish Town Hall only meters away from the Altneuschul. The Altneuschul itself was one of the only buildings still standing when the fire finally died.

The Name

There are three explanations for the peculiar dualism of the synagogue's name. "Altneu" is German for "Old-New." One theory states that the Altneuschul is composed of two synagogues built at different times: the Romanesque antechamber, built in 1270, and the Gothic interior, built in 1290. This theory has led many to interpret the low and unordained ceiling, the lack of a pointed arch in the vaults, and the thick white walls of the antechamber as indicative of late Romanesque architecture. However, almost all art historians dispute this theory, saying instead that the antechamber was actually built later than the interior.

The more accepted view is that the Altneuschul was originally called the Neuschul in order to differentiate it from an older synagogue called, not too surprisingly, the Altschul. (The Altschul was torn down in 1867 and the Spanish Synagogue was built in its place.) During the Golden Age of Prague Jewish history, between 1570 and 1620, so many synagogues were built in the ghetto that it became necessary to differentiate the Neuschul from the *truly* new *schuls*. So it became the Altneuschul.

The final explanation is the most poetic: "Alt-Neu" might be German for "Old-New," but "*Al Tenai*" is Hebrew for "On Condition." While the Jews are confined to Exile, all of their houses of worship are considered temporary structures in use for a limited period of time. This is the special condition under which they are built. When the Messiah comes, the synagogues will no longer be necessary, as the Jews will return en masse to the land of Israel. And when they return, two angels will be flying overhead, carrying between them the temporary rock of the Altneuschul.

The History

The institutionalization of anti-Semitism in Europe began between the years 1179 and 1215, when the Catholic Church convened the Third and Fourth Lateran Councils and announced that Jews were to live in separation and squalor as punishment for the sin of Deicide. The days of economic and social mobility Jews had hitherto enjoyed in European society ended. They were confined to ghettos, forbidden from owning land, forced to wear special identifying marks, outlawed from all guilds, and subjected to periodic pogrom and exile. Because the Christians deemed moneylending to be the sin of usury, they forbade themselves from practicing it and established it as the only permissible pursuit for the Jews.

The result of these decrees was that Jews were effectively disenfranchised from European society. This was all well and good for the Christian magistrates, but the kings soon found that because the Jews were not part of the feudal system, there was no way of collecting tax revenues from their communities. Thus began the practice of the "Special Charter" between kings and Jews. Jews would pay taxes directly to the kings, and in return would receive "protection" as special subjects of the crown. This protection was often not extended, but the Jews had no option to complain; it was an offer they couldn't refuse.

In Prague, although Jews were not yet officially incarcerated in an enclosed area, King Premysl Otakar II issued the Royal Charter in 1254. Jews became *"servi camerae regiae,"* or direct subjects of the Royal Court. All the external affairs of the Jewish Community would ultimately be decided by the king. It was in this charter that King Otakar II gave the Jews religious freedom and the permission to build a new synagogue, which was built in about 1270 and later called the Altneuschul. However, the king decreed that the synagogue must be lower in height than the lowest church in Prague, in order to represent the inferior status of the Jews. This—and, later, the raised street level due to river flooding—explains the stairs next to the entrances. In order to obtain the high Gothic ceilings in the interior, the Jews built the synagogue underground—an early example of finding loopholes in a law.

The Antechamber

> Note: Renovations on the eastern side of the antechamber in 1997 added an entrance that resembles an earlier entrance from at least the nineteenth century. At this writing, it is unknown which doors will be entranceways and which will be exits.

This initial room is the antechamber considered by some to be the "Old" part of the synagogue. According to this theory, the original *aron hakodesh*, or holy ark, would have been placed against the eastern wall where the doorway stands today. Even if this wasn't the "Old" synagogue, however, it's possible that the room once had its own *aron hakodesh* for early or later *minyans*. When the main sanctuary served its other uses as *yeshivah* or *beit din* (courthouse), the antechamber could be used as a small *shtiebel* by those who simply wanted to pray. The antechamber would have lost this function by at least the nineteenth century, when an entranceway much like the current one was added to the eastern wall.

Toward the eastern side of the antechamber is a meter-long rock.

> Note: During recent renovations this rock might be moved to a museum exhibit.

The rock, most likely from the seventeenth century, comes from another synagogue. If you look at the surface of the rock, you'll see the Hebrew letters *Shin* and *Tzadik*, initials for *Shaliach Tzibur*, or "Messenger of the Community," the common designation of the cantor. The cantor would place his *siddur* on the rock and pray while facing toward Jerusalem. In bygone days, when not all Jews knew how to read Hebrew, the custom developed in which the cantor repeated the blessings of the congregation. Thus he served as the prayer "messenger" for those congregants who would simply respond "Amen." The book holder is also called an *amud*, which means "stand."

On the north wall are two large stone vaults with thick wooden doors.

From the Royal Charter of 1254 onward, the Jews were required to pay taxes directly to Prague Castle. These two vaults were built in the late Renaissance and early Baroque periods to collect the mass amounts of gold and silver coins retrieved by royal emissaries during periodic visits to the ghetto. At one point, one vault was used for the king and the other for taxes collected by the Jewish communal authority itself.

At another time in history, the vaults were most likely used as overnight jails administered by the Jewish Community. That a jail would be located in a synagogue might seem peculiar, but it is difficult otherwise to explain the prison bars on the side of the far vault. Keep in mind that the Altneuschul was considered the safest place in the Jewish Town, where the Jews sought refuge during pogrom and where the most valuable items in the Community were kept. On the rare occasions of Jewish crime in the ghetto, the Jewish Community was afraid to hand over the criminal to the often-brutal Christian police. Thus the vault nearest the eastern wall was used as a detainment cell for Jewish offenders. Similar cells existed in contemporary synagogues in Cracow and Budapest. What is interesting here is that there is a hole in the wall inside the main sanctuary, in the same area as the vault. This has led experts to believe that the prisoner would be included in the Altneuschul's *minyan*, and would be encouraged to pray himself.

Still later, both vaults were used like a *genizah*, a chest that holds old Torahs and manuscripts on which are inscribed God's name. Because Jewish law forbids destruction of God's name, *genizahs* would be filled up and then their contents would be buried in the cemetery. Today the two vaults are empty.

To the right of the entrance to the main sanctuary is a series of clocks.

Because Jews pray according to sunrise and sunset, service times are modified according to the season. This series of clocks, called *Z'Manei Ha'Tfilot*, or "Times of Prayer," were once adjusted every week to alert synagogue-goers when prayers would begin. The clocks aren't real; they are simply service indicators. Each clock refers to a different service, including morning, afternoon, and Shabbat prayers. The set hasn't been used for years. Today, no longer in the age of aesthetics, the Community posts a typewritten page nearby to state the times of prayer.

Above the clocks is a seventeenth-century Hebrew inscription of the last line from Ecclesiastes. It reads, "God you shall fear, and His Commandments you shall keep, because this is all of mankind."

The doorway to the main sanctuary stands humbly below a thirteenth-century stone portal, one of the oldest Gothic portals in Bohemia. The exquisite relief, carved out of a single stone, is full of Judaic symbolism. Most obviously, it is the *Eitz Chaiim*, or Tree of Life from the Garden of Eden. The twelve roots of the tree symbolize the twelve tribes of Israel. The grapes are considered a symbol of life to Jews. There are thirteen bunches of grapes. Some art historians believe one of the original grape bunches has broken off in the course of the years; according to this view, the original fourteen bunches referred to the twelve tribes plus Ephraim and Menasheh. The four vines on the tympanum symbolize the four rivers of creation flowing from the Garden of Eden: the Pishon, Gihon, Tigris, and Euphrates (Genesis 2:10–14). Finally, the three basic sections of the portal correspond to the three continents known in the thirteenth century. World maps from the Middle Ages depict the universe with a cloverleaf design, with Europe on top and Africa and Asia below it. In the center of these three continents lay Jerusalem, considered the eye of the universe to Jews as well as Christians. The design of this portal also reflects this clover shape. The Western Hemisphere was as yet a cartographer's dream.

The Main Sanctuary

There are additional steps leading down to the main sanctuary, so that the arching Gothic vaults inside will not stretch too high into the sky. Some associate this enforced dwarfishness with the claustrophobia of ghetto life or with the European humiliation of the Jews. Others prefer to see it as a metaphor for the silent, introspective yearning of Jewish prayer. In marked contrast to the pomp of a Gothic church, which is determined to dazzle with the glory of God, the Altneuschul remarks upon the quiet humility of man.

Technically, Jews weren't allowed to build the synagogue. In accordance with the Third and Fourth Lateran Councils, in which Jews were forbidden from guilds, Jews could not become stone masons or architects. Realizing this, King Otakar II allowed the Jews to employ his royal stonemasons, who came from France to build the Convent of St. Agnes, about half a mile away from the Altneuschul. The masons were virtuosos in the use of light, and they designed the twelve windows in the Altneuschul to spin shafts of sunlight around the synagogue at various times of the day.

Because the synagogue was built by Christians, it bears certain resemblances to a Gothic church. But the Jews, who were paying for the construction, established certain rules to ensure the synagogue didn't become The Altneu of Our Lady Mary. First, a twin-nave design was chosen, in order to eliminate the reference to the Trinity commonly associated with triple-nave structures. That makes the Altneuschul the only Gothic twin-naved synagogue still standing in the world. Second, if you look at the ceiling you'll see five ribs descending from each of the six vaults. In a Gothic structure, four ribs are all that is needed to support the ceiling. But because the four resemble a cross, the fifth rib was added. You can see that the fifth rib is asymmetrical and that it hangs as a limp decoration without any structural bearing for the synagogue. Finally, it was a custom to decorate the walls of churches with images of saints and angels. In Judaism this is considered *avodah zarah*, or idol-worshipping. In order to make a synagogue aesthetically pleasing without transgressing the prohibition against images, it was customary to decorate it with leaves of the *Shivat Ha Minim*, or "Seven Species," which you can see adorning the spherical surfaces at the ends of the ribs. The Species ornamentation repeats throughout the synagogue, as there are more than seven spheres. The Seven Species are mentioned in the Torah as existing eternally in the Land of Israel. They are wheat, barley, grape, fig, pomegranate, olive, and date (Deuteronomy 8:8)—typical Israeli foodstuffs. (It should be mentioned that certain botanist myth-breakers have insisted they see chestnut leaves up there. "Alternative" travellers have claimed to see cannabis leaves. These are decidedly not among the "Seven Species." Nevertheless, the above explanation is included because it is simply too romantic to omit.)

More than halfway up the right aisle, there is an unfinished, broken-looking rock on the right-hand wall.

Unlike the rest of the rocks, this one has no species decorating its surface. This is not due to any carelessness on the part of the stonemasons. It is called *Zecher Ha'Churban*, or "Memory of the Destruction." Every Orthodox home and synagogue is required to have a little piece left unfinished as a reminder, like the broken glass at a wedding, of the destruction of the Second Temple in the year 70 C.E. It is a quintessentially Jewish concept to place a piece of sadness in the midst of celebration. The unfinished rock also serves to remind us that Exile is a transient state; one day the Messiah will come, and then the synagogues will no longer be used. Everything in the Diaspora is temporary. Because of this ephemeral state, it is a tradition among Jews to leave homes and synagogues slightly incomplete, lest they send a signal to God that they are not awaiting Redemption. Like the legend of the foundation stone, like the name "*Al Tenai*," and like the unfinished rock, the theology of Exile is one of conditional expectation.

Against the walls are a series of mirror-like surfaces.

The synagogue was originally illuminated with reflective surfaces similar to these. The surfaces were shined so industriously that two candles placed in the holders would reflect light all around. Again you can see the Seven Species decoration, which also coincides with certain Bohemian folk designs.

The hanging chandeliers were each donated between the fifteenth and the nineteenth centuries. The oldest ones are the smallest, on either side of the *bimah*. The reason each chandelier looks different is because it was a Jewish custom in Europe to send emissaries from one ghetto to another. These messengers would engage in trade as well as exchange information about the spiritual, social, and economic life of their ghettos. It was considered appropriate for the messenger to present the Community leaders with some kind of gift. Thus each of the chandeliers here originates from a different Jewish ghetto in Europe. Each looks different because each absorbed the different cultural motifs of the Community from which it sprang. For instance, the chandelier on the eastern wall to the right of the Ark comes from Vienna or Budapest or thereabouts. We know this because it is decorated with a double-headed eagle, the symbol of the Austro-Hungarian Empire. Noticeably absent are the cross-adorned crowns that normally adorn the Austro-Hungarian eagles; these were removed because of their obvious Christian symbolism. In fact, it is peculiar to find any sort of image in a synagogue. But because the eagle has two heads, it isn't a depiction of one of God's true creations. Yes, it's one more example of the Jewish loophole in the law.

Underneath the chandelier to the right of the aron hakodesh *is a large wooden seat with a wooden Star of David above it.*

This chair is commonly referred to as the *Kisei Ha'Maharal,* or Chair of the Maharal, the famous Rabbi Loew. Although the spot was indeed where Rabbi Loew sat, the wooden seat was added, along with all the other wooden seats in the synagogue, in the early nineteenth century. Before that, it had been the custom to sit on stone seats and pillows. But because this was his sacred place, nobody has sat in this spot since the Maharal died in 1609. The only people who try are Israeli tourists eager to have their picture taken in the spot of sanctity. A fragile chain today guards the seat and preserves its honor.

The seat to the left of the Maharal's was the chair of the eighteenth-century Rabbi Ezekiel Landau, commonly known as the *Nodeh Bi'Yehudah*. To the right of the Maharal's chair are seats reserved for the president of the Prague Jewish Community and the ambassador from Israel. Today's rabbi sits on the other side of the *aron hakodesh*, in order to show deference to the historical and spiritual greatness of Rabbi Loew.

THE *ARON HAKODESH*

In the center of the east wall is the aron hakodesh.

The *aron hakodesh*, or "holy ark" where the Torahs are kept, faces east, traditionally regarded as the direction of Jerusalem. The *aron hakodesh* steers the Altneuschul slightly off its Gothic course, since the decorated Renaissance columns of the ark were built in the sixteenth century.

The *aron hakodesh* is not simply an ark, but a metaphorical reminder of the Old Temple of Jerusalem. Synagogues in the Diaspora are painstakingly designed to recall the collective prayer ceremonies at the Old Temple; for this reason, a synagogue is often referred to as a *mikdash mi'at*, or "little temple." The *aron hakodesh* represents the Holy of Holies in the Old

Temple, which contained the Ark of the Covenant and the Tablets of the Ten Commandments. The Holy of Holies was separated from the outside by a curtain known as a *parochet*. In the Torah, the *parochet* is described as blue, purple, and crimson and made of fine twisted linen—the same materials used in the sacred vestments of Aaron, the first High Priest (Exodus 26:31–33; 39:1). In all active synagogues, the *parochet* from the Old Temple is recalled through a curtain, also called *parochet*, suspended over the doors of the ark.

The *parochet* in the Altneuschul is changed regularly, but normally it is not more than a century old. The more exquisite and antique *parochets* in the collection of the Jewish Museum are too fragile to be used today. During the Holocaust, the Jewish Museum was busy salvaging *parochets* from destroyed communities throughout Bohemia and Moravia. Today, there are literally thousands of these synagogal remnants, stored away in warehouses in Prague. One of the oldest *parochets* owned by the museum comes from the Altneuschul. It is a multicolored, quilted *parochet* from the year 1592, and it is displayed today on the right side of the *aron hakodesh* in the Maisel Synagogue. On Rosh Hashanah and Yom Kippur, a white *parochet* is used in order to symbolize the purity of atonement and the Day of Judgement.

The Ark in Jerusalem's Old Temple was covered by a dazzling golden ornament known as a *kapporet*. The *kapporet*, related to the Hebrew word *kapparah*, or "atonement," served as a metaphorical vehicle for the atonement of Israel. The renowned seventeenth-century Prague Rabbi Shelomo Ephraim Luntschitz (the *"Klei Yakar"*) interpreted the *kapporet* as a covering vital for containing the secrets of the Torah, which should not be revealed to everybody. The *kapporet* was adorned by two *cherubim* hammered out of gold and facing each other. The Torah prescribes the exact form: "The *cherubim* shall have their wings spread out above, shielding the cover with their wings. They shall confront each other, the faces of the *cherubim* being turned toward the cover" (Exodus 25:20). According to one *midrash*, the heads of these *cherubim* looked down in shame when the people of Israel sinned against each other. When all was well, the *cherubim* stared ahead with bright and shiny faces.

This *kapporet* is symbolized in the synagogue by a narrow, identically named *kapporet* curtain that stands above the *parochet*. The *kapporet* used in the Altneuschul is much older than the *parochet*. It dates from the early eighteenth century. Sometimes a *kapporet* will be fashioned out of wood, plaster, or stucco, as is the case in the Maisel Synagogue. In the Altneuschul, the first thing to notice on the *kapporet* are the two *cherubim*, their heads hidden (out of shame, or out of protection against graven images?) inside the Crown of the Torah. These *cherubim* stand in the center of the *kapporet*. On the far left and far right sides, you'll find additional wings inexplicably covering up more graphic depictions of *cherubim* situated on wooden planks. If you look closely, you can see parts of these *cherubim* peaking out.

The main series of images on the *kapporet* refers to the sacrifices in the Old Temple in Jerusalem. Ancient sacrifices are a central theme in Jewish liturgy because of their once-dominant position in Old Temple prayer worship. Thousands of years ago, it was a common ritual of Middle Eastern religions to sacrifice a virgin or firstborn baby to the gods. Of course, the Hebrews—progressive from the beginning—considered such practices somewhat antisocial. So in an early Jewish campaign for human rights, they initiated the radical practice of sacrificing animals or crops, instead of human beings, to God. The biblical precedent for this was set when Abraham was ordered not to sacrifice his son Isaac, and sacrificed instead a ram that appeared for him. In the synagogue and service, there is much metaphorical value attached to the sacrificial ceremonies from the Old Temple. For example, the afternoon *minchah* service cannot commence before 12:30 P.M., because that is when the afternoon sacrifice was offered at the Temple. The idea is that during the period of Exile, prayer is a substitute for sacrifice. The prophet Hosea put it most succinctly: "Instead of bulls we will pay the offering of our lips" (Hosea 14:3). Again, the spiritual present is linked to the material past. The *kapporet* becomes a velvet chronicle of this past, boasting images of the instruments used during sacrifices. From left to right, these images are: the traditional Levite pitcher of water, the headdress worn on the forehead of the High Priest, the copper laver of water, the wood and gold table containing the so-called "Bread of Display," the Two Tablets of the Law, the menorah, the altar for the burnt offering, the twelve–stoned *choshen* (breastplate) of the High Priest, and another Levite pitcher.

In front of the *kapporet* hangs another symbol of the Old Temple. This is the *ner tamid*, or everlasting light, a symbol of the constant flame ascending to Heaven from such sacrifices in the Jerusalem Temple. According to other opinions, the *ner tamid* is a reminder of the constantly burning olive oil lamp in the Old Temple: "It shall be a due from the Israelites for all time, throughout the ages" (Exodus 27:21). For this reason, the *ner tamid* must always be lit, electrically or otherwise.

THE *AMUD*

To the right of the stairs leading up to the *aron hakodesh* stands the cantor's pulpit, or *amud*. The cantor stands in front of the *amud* in a lowered groove a couple of feet wide. This refers to Psalms 130:1, "*Mima'amakim kara'ticha Hashem*," "From out of the depths I call to you God." Everything spiritual in Judaism has a counterpart in the physical realm. Just as the unfinished rock is the physical representation of exile, this lowered area is the physical representation of the depths of the soul.

While he is praying from his *siddur* on the *amud*, the cantor occasionally looks up in front of him at the shield inscribed with Hebrew letters known as a "*Sh'viti* Tablet." These have been customary since the sixteenth century in Jewish communities from Central Europe to Palestine. The four large letters on the tablet spell out God's holy and unpronounceable Name, the *Shem Hamiforash* or tetragrammaton. Surrounding the name are the words of Psalms 16:8: "*Sh'viti Hashem l'negdi tamid*," or "I place God in front of me always." Throughout the tablet are a series of permutations of God's name in mystical form. Jewish mysticism often utilizes the *gematriah*, or numerical equivalents of Hebrew letters that, when added a certain way, allude to various teachings or symbols. Thus when the cantor looks up, quite literally, at God's name spelled out before him, he can achieve a heightened state of mystical devotion, known in Hebrew as *kavanah*. *Sh'viti* tablets were directly influenced by the Jewish mystical revival known as Lurianic *Kabbalah*, named after the sixteenth-century Tsfat kabbalist Isaac Luriah. Because they could be found in Central European synagogues that did not have a strong kabbalistic tradition, they serve as remarkable evidence of the once-common cross-fertilization of mystical and rationalistic elements in Judaism.

> "I place God in front of me always."
>
> The verse from Psalms 16:8 that decorates the *Sh'viti* tablet (and that is abbreviated on the upper left side of the eastern wall) has always been a source of inspiration to the Jews. The importance and symbolic value of the verse was once explained by Rabbi Abraham Danzig of Vilna (1748–1820):
>
> "The verse *I place God in front of me always* (Psalms 16:8) conveys a high religious-ethical principle. When a man is alone in the house he does not act as if he were in the presence of a great king; his manner of speech is not among his own relatives and friends what it might be in the company of a king. Hence, when a man realizes that the supreme King, whose glory fills the whole universe, is always near him, marking all his actions, he is bound to be inspired with reverence and humility."
>
> (Quoted in Philip Birnbaum, *Encyclopedia of Jewish Concepts*)

An interesting side note is that the two Shabbat candles attached to the *Shi'viti* tablet were originally situated in a lower position. However, when the candles were lit, smoke from the flames circled in front of God's name and blotted it out—a major transgression in Judaism. So the candle holders had to be raised in order to preserve the holy name of God.

On the left side of the stairs are two seats. On one of the seats there used to be a pillow inscribed with the Hebrew inscription, "This is the chair of Elijah." During a circumcision (*bris*), it is the custom to reserve a special chair for the prophet Elijah to come and bless the child. Thus the *sandek* or grandfather would sit in one of the seats with the eight-day-old baby in his arms, the *mohel* would stand above them, and the second seat would be left empty throughout the ceremony for the visiting prophet.

Toward the ceiling of the eastern wall, between the two circular windows, there is an oblong window carved into the wall with a yellow glass placed in its interior. You might have to step back a few feet to see the yellow glass.

This hole in the wall faces east and was once used to indicate when to begin the *Shacharit*, or morning service. As soon as the sunlight entered the hole, the service could begin. Remember that the synagogue is underground and that the hole in the wall is not as high as it appears. Remember also that the synagogue used to be bordered on its eastern facade by a large square. The sun rose over this square and shined immediately into the synagogue. When the city authorities destroyed the square as part of the ghetto renovation at the turn of the century, Parizska Street was built in its place. Today, the buildings of Parizska block out the sunlight in the morning. But fortunately we have watches. When it was built, though, the royal stonemasons were such virtuosos that they were able to design the entire Gothic synagogue around the rising of the morning sun.

Other explanations for the hole in the wall are more creative. One has it that the hole allowed the cantor to see when three stars had risen in the sky. On Friday evenings, this would indicate when Shabbat was to begin. A corollary account has it that the hole reminds the cantor when the afternoon service should end and the evening service begin. The wildest explanation has it that every Shavuot, a single beam of light pierces the yellow window and hits the outstretched Torah while it is being read on the *bimah*. The ray illuminates a single series of words concerning the holiday.

THE WOMEN'S SECTION

There are narrow window slits above the chairs on the northern and western walls. These windows are the single controversial feature of the Altneuschul. Even the most Orthodox Jewish women visiting the synagogue are shocked when they learn that on the other side of these meter-thick walls lies the *ezrat nashim*, or women's section. The western annex was built first, in the sixteenth or seventeenth century. Later, the northern annex was added; it was rebuilt in the first half of the eighteenth century. Together, the two rooms twist along the sides of the main sanctuary and serve to this day as the prayer room for women, who peek through the fortress-like window slits at their husbands, brothers, and sons praying inside.

Although the *ezrat nashim* appears provocative when considered as separate from the main sanctuary, it should be kept in mind that it has its own *aron hakodesh* in order to make it a sacred place of worship equal to the men's section on the interior. In this way, it was not so much a women's section but a distinctly separate *schul*. It is possible that women didn't follow the men's service but rather conducted their own simultaneous service. Some historians even think that the women customarily had their own rabbis, albeit without *semichah*, who would lead the women in the separate service.

The books that line the walls remind us that the room is still used in its dual function as a *cheder*, or study hall. In addition, the morning *minyan* prays here because there are not enough men in the morning to fill up the main sanctuary. It is joked that during these morning *minyans* the women have to stand outside. (This isn't true; they sit in the back.)

The *ezrat nashim* in the Altneuschul logged its own bizarre history during the German occupation of Prague. In 1943 it became one of several exhibition halls of the Museum of an Extinct Race. Jewish curators of the museum set up a photographic exhibit documenting the early history of the Altneuschul, complete with analogies to similar Gothic structures of the time. The only contemporary Gothic structures in Bohemia and Moravia, though, were monasteries. When the exhibit was opened, the Germans were infuriated. The exhibit had documented the influence of Gothic churches on the Altneuschul, including the Convent of St. Agnes in Prague as well as other edifices with octagonal pillars. The Nazis were intent on showing that Judaism, even in its architecture, was an aberration in European history; any evidence of cooperation between the two religions, even architecturally, was considered outrageous and offensive. The exhibit was closed almost as soon as it was begun.

There are two large pillars on either side of the bimah.

According to legend, the pillars refer to the two pillars in the Old Temple of Jerusalem, Jachin and Boaz (see I Kings 7:21). At first glance, it appears that the pillars would obstruct the congregants' view. But, as mentioned earlier, Judaism is not a spectator sport. Before the nineteenth century, Jewish services were never focused on a magnificent main nave or on an awe-inspiring pulpit, but on individual and collective prayer.

If you look to the top of each of the pillars, you'll see again the seven species decorated on shields. Two of the shields are left smooth and unadorned. This is not another memory of the destruction of the Temple. There are eight sides to the pillar; eight minus two is six. Six adorned shields on each of the two pillars makes a total of twelve, symbolizing the twelve tribes of Israel. Similarly, there are twelve windows symbolizing the tribes, with an additional two added to the eastern wall in the fourteenth century.

THE *BIMAH*

In the center of the synagogue is the bimah.

The *bimah* is the raised and caged area for the reading of the Torah. Its central location allows the words of the Torah to spread out to the surrounding worshippers.

Many people assume the synagogue is Sephardic, because of the central location of the *bimah*. In reality, though, there has never been a sizeable Sephardic Community in Prague. Originally, synagogues all over the Jewish world were designed with the *bimah* in the center. The reason for this is that the *aron hakodesh* represents the Holy of Holies in the Old Temple while the *bimah* represents the sacrifices; if the two are placed too close to each other, the Ten Commandments would symbolically be incinerated! It was only in the nineteenth century that Ashkenazic Jews, starting in Germany, moved the *bimah* to the front. Jews were assimilating and converting at such a drastic rate during the period of Enlightenment and Emancipation that rabbis, particularly in the nascent Reform movement, began to ponder how to keep Jews coming to synagogue. It was taken for granted that Jews associated the synagogue with an ancient, bizarre, even occultist tradition. Churches, on the other hand, were seen as acceptable because they belonged to the coveted majority. So Ashkenazic Jews moved the *bimah* to the front of the synagogue to mimic the priest's pulpit. Other contemporary examples of Jews mimicking their neighbors include the introduction of the sermon into the liturgy and the praying in the vernacular, both rites already institutionalized in the Church. In the Sephardic world, there was a higher level of tolerance between the Jewish and Islamic peoples and therefore little of the uniquely European, internalized self-hatred that drove entire Jewish communities to adopt the manners and customs of their tormentors. Although the Altneuschul is Ashkenazic, it was built in the thirteenth century, at a time when not only was it not the custom to mimic churches, but when Jews would do everything in their power—including adding a fifth rib to the ceiling vaults—to distinguish themselves from other nations.

The fifteenth-century iron grillwork surrounding the *bimah* is intended to symbolize a throne. Indeed, one walks up a couple stairs to the *bimah* as if he were ascending a throne, and the term for being called to the Torah is *aliyah*, "to go up." Jews were always seeking the most lofty physical symbolism to represent the spiritual, and the ancient kingdom of Israel provided a wellspring of metaphors and images of inspiration. The idea is that the Torah is the highest spiritual object, and thus equivalent to a king. In addition, the Torah is to be obeyed as if it is a king. The ornate crowns designed to decorate the Torah enhance this imagery; a Jew himself was never permitted to wear a crown, because this would lead to idolatry. The crowns were preserved for the real majesty, King Torah.

In addition to being a throne for the Torah, the caging around the *bimah* recalls the *sukkot*, or tabernacles, Jews built in the wilderness before receiving the Torah. On the holiday of Shavuot the caging is decorated in green branches to represent the verdant Mount Sinai and the agricultural aspect of the traditional Shavuot wheat harvest. The tradition is followed with such zest that entering the synagogue during Shavuot services is something like wading through a tropical rain forest. On Simchat Torah the caging is hung with myriad party decorations to symbolize the rejoicing over the Torah. Finally, the caging has traditionally been used during wedding ceremonies to hold the *chupah*, or wedding canopy. Attached to the top of the caging itself, the *chupah* hovers above almost the entire *bimah* while the bride ritually circles the groom in order to make sure he is the correct choice. The double-seated chair on the rear side of the *bimah* is the place where the bride and groom sit together for the first time during the marriage ceremony.

The circular container decorated with a Moravian rosette, hanging at the front and left side of the *bimah*, was once traditionally used as the centerpiece of the *eruv*. An *eruv* is a designated area in Jewish communities under which people can carry items on Shabbat. The use of the *eruv* makes it possible to bring things like *tallitot* and *siddurs* to synagogue without violating the prohibition against transporting items on the day of rest. *Eruvs* still function in religious Jewish communities today. Usually they are delineated by a rope or wire that encircles the Community. It was a custom for members of the Community to contribute food to a central location as a way of symbolizing their unity within the boundary. Often this food was a piece of challah or Passover matzoh placed in a central location. According to another theory, Jews are permitted to carry things on Shabbat inside their homes; because the defining characteristic of a home is the existence of bread, the placement of bread within the synagogue turns the edifice into a home where carrying is possible.

In the Altneuschul there is a unique tradition regarding the *eruv*. Every year on the last day of Passover, a piece of round *shemurah matzoh* (painstakingly guarded kosher matzoh) is placed into this container. The matzoh is not removed until just before the next year's Passover, on the day when homes are cleaned of bread. According to this tradition, as long as the matzoh remains in the synagogue the Community is united together and protected from harm. Although there is no longer an *eruv* in Prague today, if you look through the holes in the container, you'll see the whites of a matzoh sitting within, harking back to a time when an action as seemingly cursory as carrying a book carried the most profound implications.

Perhaps most importantly, the *eruv* symbolized the closeness and unity of the Jewish Community, bound together by a common piece of bread as if the entire Quarter was a single home.

THE HEBREW INSCRIPTIONS

Hebrew letters are inscribed near the top of all the walls in the synagogue.

The mysterious letters are *rashei tevot*, or Hebrew abbreviations of various inspirational messages. They were added to the synagogue in the early seventeenth century.

On the eastern wall, above the *aron ha'kodesh*, are two abbreviations. On the right side is abbreviated: *Sh'viti Hashem l'negdi tamid*, "I place God in front of me always." As on the *Sh'viti* tablet, this is a reference to Psalms 16:8. On the left side is abbreviated: *Da lifnei mi atah omed*, "Know before Whom you stand" (Babylonian Talmud, *Berakhot* 28b). If a person's mind begins to wander during the service, he can look up at the tops of the walls and concentrate his mind on devotion and the purpose of prayer.

On the western wall are three inscriptions (the first one is divided into two parts). Beginning from the right side, they are: *Gadol ha'oneh amen yoter min hamevarech*, "Greater is he who answers amen than he who makes the blessing." This is also from *Berakhot*, and its purpose is to encourage everybody to contribute to the service. This is related to the concept of the cantor as the "messenger of the Community," discussed earlier in the antechamber. Those who couldn't read Hebrew would simply say "amen" to the cantor's benedictions, thus counting as if they had said the prayer themselves. In addition, the concept served to unify the Community as a single, indivisible entity during prayer.

Sur me'rah v'aseh tov, "Shun evil and do good" (Psalms 37:27).

And *Ach tov l'Yisrael selah*, "Thus He will be good to Israel forever."

The northern side contains the following inscription:

Ha'Shem echad u'Shmo echad,
"God is one and His name one." (Zechariah 13:9)

The letters topped by circles have a *gematriah* (numerical sum) that indicates the date, in the early seventeenth century, when the synagogue underwent renovations.

On the southern side is written:

Ki bachar Ha'Shem bi'zion ivah le'moshav,
"For the Lord has chosen Zion; He has desired it for His seat." (Psalms 132:13)

Again, the letters marked by circles add up to a date in the early seventeenth century when the walls were whitewashed (the word *nitlaven*, which precedes the quotation, refers to whitewashing). Evidently, the walls of the synagogue were once covered by a painted floral design. In the early seventeenth century, it was removed.

THE *YAHRZEIT* BOARDS

On the western wall of the synagogue are situated two metal boards, each resembling the Two Tablets of the Law. Inside the glass, there are several rows of names placed alongside electric bulbs.

These are the *yahrzeit* boards of the Altneuschul. A *yahrzeit* is the death anniversary of one's parent. Every year, on the eve of a *yahrzeit* in the Hebrew calendar, a deceased person's children will light what is called a *"yahrzeit* candle." This is in keeping with Proverbs 20:27, which attests that "The lifebreath of man is the lamp of the Lord . . ." The candle is lit on the death anniversary because only at the end of one's life can one be fully evaluated. It remains burning for 24 hours. In many synagogues, particularly in the modern era, a *yahrzeit* board shows the *yahrzeit* dates of many members of the Community. Often these boards are designed in the shape of the Tree of Life, with names on each of its leaves. In recent times, electric bulbs are lit as symbols of the *yahrzeit* candle, as is the case with the *yahrzeit* boards in the Altneuschul.

These electric boards are two of the most recent furnishings in the Altneuschul. Instead of the Tree of Life, these represent the Two Tablets of the Law. The board on the right side was installed first. The two Hebrew words on its top mean "In Memory of Souls." Members of the Jewish Community can insert the names of loved ones and every year during the *yahrzeit*, a corresponding bulb will be lit. In 1996, the additional board on the left side was added. Contrary to popular rumor, the numbers on the tablets are used strictly for administrative purposes and have no bearing on the seat numbers in the synagogue.

The paper names in these *yahrzeit* boards change from time to time, as succeeding generations install new names to remember their parents. The top row of names in the right-hand board, however, remains fixed and permanent. These are some of the most famous rabbis in Prague Jewish history. From 1439 to 1986, the row of rabbinical greats is a testament to the awe-inspiring continuity of the Altneuschul.

The oldest name is found in the upper right-hand corner. This is the *yahrzeit* date of Avigdor Kara, who died in 1439 and whose grave is the oldest that has been identified in the Old Jewish Cemetery. Rabbi Kara gained renown not only as a rabbi, but also as a doctor and poet. His most famous poem, entitled "All of the Hardships That Befell Us," is an elegy written about the Easter pogrom of 1389. This pogrom was the most devastating carnage wreaked on Prague's Jews in all the centuries preceding the Holocaust [*see below*]. In fact, much of the pogrom occurred within the walls of the Altneuschul. For this reason, Rabbi Kara's *kinah*, or elegy, is read in the Altneuschul every year on Yom Kippur. The intent is to beseech God to send the messiah in light of the terrible suffering of the Jews. As Rabbi Kara pleaded near the end of his elegy, "Let come, O Lord, finally the day of Thy hope!"

If you find a *machzor*, or High Holiday prayer book, printed in Prague or for the Prague Jewish Community, you'll find Rabbi Kara's complete elegy inside.

The Easter Pogrom and Rabbi Kara's Elegy

In addition to the so-called "Blood Libels," in which Jews were falsely accused of murdering innocent Christian virgins and babies, Jews were also accused of the infamous "Desecration of the Host." According to the latter superstition, Jews stole into churches and practiced sorcery on the Host, the eucharistic wafer eaten during Mass as a symbol of the body of Jesus. There exist scores of Christian manuscripts, from the Middle Ages to the Enlightenment, that describe in minute detail Jews poking the Host with razor-sharp needles, after which the Host allegedly cries out like a lamb or begins to bleed. These superstitions were fed by the dogma that Jews were collectively guilty for the sin of Deicide. As such, they reached their peak during the holiday of Easter. The rationale, simply put, was: Jews killed our God, and now they're mutilating His body. Since Easter often falls on or near the Jewish holiday of Passover, the normally joyous Jewish celebration of liberation would often turn into a week of panic and terror.

So it was in Prague in 1389. The Easter holiday fell on the last day of Passover, and King Wenceslas IV was absent from Prague. Several priests used the opportunity to deliver incendiary sermons on Easter Sunday, demonizing the Jews and claiming that they had desecrated the Host. Specifically, they charged, Jews had thrown stones at a priest carrying the Host to a dying Christian nearby the Jewish Town. That evening, an enraged crowd gathered on Old Town Square and then burst into the ghetto. In the ensuing carnage, over three thousand Jews were murdered with axes and knives; women and girls were raped in the streets; scores of homes were burnt down with their tenants inside; and almost all valuables in the ghetto were pillaged. Many Jews committed suicide rather than submit to forced baptisms. Days later, bodies were still burning in the streets of the ghetto. Rabbi Kara, who witnessed his own father's murder during the pogrom, recorded the bloodshed:

> Without any reason they drew their knives
> and slaughtered our men, children, and wives.
> Our homes, our precious homes, they burned,
> together with all our dear ones within . . .
> With axes and other weapons of dread
> our brothers' and sisters' blood was shed.
> They smashed in our doors,
> they tore down our walls . . .
> For the glory of God we all had to die,
> For the mercy of God we only could cry . . .
> So sad is my heart when I think of the dead,
> the good, learned men—how much wisdom they had!
> (Quoted in Hana Volavkova,
> *A Story of the Jewish Museum in Prague*)

The bloodshed in the streets was so great that many Jews ran to the two synagogues, the Altschul and the Neuschul (today's Altneuschul), which were considered the safest and most fortified locations in the ghetto. But the Christians, far superior in numbers, broke down the doors and slaughtered all the people within. The Altschul was almost completely destroyed by fire. In the Neuschul, the walls became completely red from the carnage.

There are various Altneuschul traditions regarding the blood that once stained its walls. One account states that the red was left on the walls for centuries after the event as a reminder of the catastrophe. In another version, no matter how many times the Jews had the walls repainted, the red would return in the morning. A final version has it that whenever and wherever there is Jewish suffering in the world, the walls become red again. Jiri Weil, the great Czech Jewish writer who survived the Holocaust in hiding, refers to the Altneuschul walls in his masterpiece, *Life with a Star*. In this book, Weil recounts that at one point during the war, the Altneuschul became a "valley of death" as it was used as a temporary center to announce deportees. The Nazis set up a table and chair by the Altneuschul's *aron hakodesh*, and read off lists of Jews who were to be deported.

> The names dripped slowly. Out of the depths we cry to Thee, O Lord, from the depths of pain and despair. . . . It was impossible to tell whether those called were present—there were too many people in the sanctuary. There were no children there, though the names of children were also called. Women mingled with men in this sanctuary, even though a special gallery was set aside for them. There were bloodstains on the walls, which it was forbidden to whitewash. The blood on the walls of this sanctuary had never dried—sometimes it turned black while at other times, when things were very bad, it turned red again. Names continued to fall into the darkness and shadows.

> The wall was covered by people's backs; nobody could see whether the wall was bloody. . . . It was a good thing the wall with the bloodstains was behind me so I couldn't see them. I looked only at the man reading the names. . . . I listened as the names changed into the words of the prayer for martyrs.
>
> <div align="right">Jiri Weil, <i>Life with a Star</i></div>

With harrowing, laconic lyricism, Weil links the horrors of the Holocaust into the continuum of the age-old European slaughter of Jews.

Rabbi Kara's own elegy is like a diminutive prophecy of what would occur in the twentieth century. He writes of book burnings: "In the Old [synagogue] and the New one asunder they tore / our most sacred books, and the scrolls of the Torah." He writes of how even the clothes of the dead were stripped and stolen. The mob even stormed the Jewish cemetery and dug up graves in order to pick gold teeth and other treasures. All of these atrocities would become everyday occurrences in Nazi-occupied Europe.

This is important to remember because, especially in America, we often think of anti-Semitism as a phenomenon that began in the nineteenth century and culminated in the Holocaust. But even a cursory glance at European history shows that from century to century, Jews were systematically dehumanized to such a degree that even their skeletons could be defiled with impunity. In such a culture, it is no wonder that by the twentieth century, so few European states attempted to stop the Nazi genocide. Another point to mention is that the Nazis were not pioneers; they simply employed earlier methods of organized bloodshed that had been the norm in Europe for centuries. These methods were promulgated by the Church as early as the twelfth and thirteenth centuries. The ghettoization, the Jewish laws, the Jewish badges, the theft, the murder, and even the disrespect for the dead all had precedent in Europe's relationship to the Jews. The only original aspects of Nazi anti-Semitism were the racial fixation and the transformation of temporary solutions to an extreme and final solution. Rabbi Avigdor Kara's verses can be applied to almost any generation in European history, from the centuries of Church-inspired hatred all the way up through the Holocaust:

> Plundering they shouted, "Outlaws are all Jews—
> Go, take their belongings, their silver, their dues.
> Ours will be what's left when the last Jew is dead!"
> And afterwards, of course, clean hands they had.

THE BANNER

Above the bimah *hangs a large red banner.*

The Jews were given the privilege of hoisting a flag by Charles IV in 1357. Many people point to this as a symbol of Jewish sovereign rights in Prague, but considering that Prague's most notorious pogrom was perpetrated only three decades after the flag was made, it reveals more the roller coaster history of Jewish existence in Europe. Eight men were required to lift the flag—you can see the eight poles extending from the initial pole, decorated in the orange and black of the Hapsburg regime. The flag was reconstructed in 1716—the Hebrew year "*Tikkun*," which means "to mend" (that the year is spelled with a *kaf*, not a *kuf*, is a minor point). Apparently, the banner badly needed alterations; when it had reached such a deteriorated state, the state actually fined the Jews for not taking better care of it.

On the interior of the banner is a Jewish Star with a hat inside. The Jewish Star was added sometime before 1527, and Jewish historian Gershom Scholem points to this flag as the first use of a Jewish Star as a heraldic emblem for a Jewish Community. Thus, the Altneuschul boasts yet another trophy of Jewish history. Before the Prague banner, the pentagram alternated with a hexagram as decoration for synagogues and churches. From the banner of Jewish Prague, however, it spread east and west until it eventually became the unrivaled symbol of the Jews.

The hat inside the Jewish star is a unique symbol of the Prague Jewish Community. It originated sometime in the seventeenth century. Everywhere in the ghetto you will see this symbol, from portals to tombstones to books to Torah curtains. There are two explanations for the hat, one highly imaginative and one highly reasonable.

The imaginative explanation is that in 1648, at the end of the Thirty Years' War, the Swedes tried to capture the Jewish ghetto because of its strategic location on the riverbed. As a result, the Jews were forced to fight the Swedes and eventually succeeded in throwing them off Charles Bridge. The King, as a token of his gratitude, gave the Jews the Swedish warrior helmet as a sort of trophy. This story is apocryphal because the Jews in ghettoized Europe weren't exactly known for their warrior abilities. Perhaps they assisted in the form of a fire brigade or through some financial help, but the Charles Bridge flourish is pure legend.

A more logical scenario is that during the Middle Ages, certain Jews were entitled to visit the Castle during special hours in order to do business in the Royal Court. In order to signify their inferior status as Jews, they were forced to wear a yellow hat. In other parts of Europe, the yellow badge on the chest or sleeve was used; in Prague it was the so-called "Hat of Shame." But because only the most wealthy Jews were permitted to leave the ghetto, they considered it less a hat of shame than a symbol of privilege and entitlement. Inside the ghetto, the dunce cap became a Versace. And so they incorporated it into the Jewish Star as a symbol of their hierarchy as leaders of the ghetto.

Next to the door of the main sanctuary is a box for tzedakkah, *or charity.*

The box is adorned with the simple Hebrew word, "*mavi*" (the bringer). This refers to the bringer of charity, but it is also an abbreviation for "*Matan biseter yichapeh af*," "A gift in secret subdues anger" (Proverbs 21:14). The anger in question is the anger of God. The idea borrows from Maimonides's teaching that one of the highest forms of charity is that in which the donor is anonymous to the recipient, and vice versa. In this way, the donor is not motivated by the expectation of accolade. By the same token, the recipient of charity is less humiliated when he or she does not feel indebted to the benefactor.

THE HIGH SYNAGOGUE

Address: Cervena ulice, across from the Altneuschul

The High Synagogue is closed to visitors at this writing, but *minchah* (the afternoon service) is usually held here weekdays at 2:00 P.M. (especially in the summertime). Entrance to *minchah* is through the passageway in the Jewish Town Hall.

There is practically no site remaining from the former Jewish ghetto that does not owe its existence to the largess of Mordechai Maisel. This is especially the case with the High Synagogue, which Maisel built next to the Jewish Town Hall in 1568. According to the contemporary historian David Gans, Maisel lavished the new synagogue with several Torahs decorated with handmade breastplates and *rimonim* of silver and gold. Like the similar High Synagogue in Cracow, the name derives, quite simply, from the location of the sanctuary on the second floor. The synagogue was one of a gaggle of buildings erected during the Golden Age of Prague Jewry (1570–1620). Unlike the other buildings of the Jewish Town, which burnt to their foundations in the fire of 1689, the High Synagogue was damaged but never destroyed. In addition, its style remained essentially unchanged throughout the centuries. For this reason, the High Synagogue is the purest example of Renaissance architecture extant in the Jewish Town.

The Italian master builder Pancratius Roder was called in from Venice to supervise construction. He might have been thinking of Venice when he designed the sanctuary on the second floor. In addition, Roder introduced Prague to an innovative architectural approach he imported from Italy: Religious buildings should be styled no differently from secular buildings. For this reason, the High Synagogue has come to symbolize the cross-fertilization of religious and secular thought in Rudolfine Prague. The space of the synagogue, with its Renaissance vaulting and lunettes, could easily pass for a hall in a wealthy burgher's home. In a similar manner, the most famous Prague Jews of the Renaissance also utilized the fruits of the secular world: David Gans studied Copernicus; Rabbi Eliezer Ashkenazi was also a doctor; Joseph Shlomo Delmedigo was a polyglot who studied Greek and Roman philosophy; Rabbi Judah Loew was well acquainted with contemporary philosophers.

The most memorable feature of the synagogue is its entrance. Originally, the synagogue was accessed through a special passageway leading directly from the Chief Rabbi's office in the Town Hall. In fact, scholars believe the High Synagogue was once the private prayer hall of Jewish Town administrators. This explains why it was built in tandem with the Jewish Town Hall. Maisel himself became mayor of the Jewish Town soon after 1576. In this light, the High Synagogue reveals the once-common intermingling of Jewish spiritual life with Jewish communal governance. In fact, the Chief Rabbi could just step out of his office to hold brief services or meetings of the *beit din*, or religious court, in the High Synagogue. The passageway was blocked during reconstruction at the end of the nineteenth century, but a century later, in 1996, it was reinstated and once again the High Synagogue is inexorably linked to the administration of the Jewish Town in Prague.

The interior of the synagogue is a nearly perfect square with a centrally designed Renaissance ceiling overlooking the *bimah*. The plasterwork on the ceiling is said to be a reference to molded Gothic ribs. On the north side, three windows offer a lovely view of the attic of the Altneuschul and perchance a glimpse of the slumbering Golem therein. Originally, there were similar windows on either side of the *aron hakodesh*, but these were removed when a new building blocked the eastern facade in 1907.

The High Synagogue was one of the few buildings not destroyed in the fire of 1689. Nonetheless, it was damaged and during its restoration a much larger *aron hakodesh* was added in the Baroque style in 1691. The color was a rich, reddish brown imitating marble from the nearby quarries of Slivinec—the same marble used for tombstones in the Old Jewish Cemetery since the seventeenth century. During reconstruction of the synagogue in 1883, the *aron hakodesh* was redecorated and became a garish white structure with gold designs. Only during restoration in 1982 was the original brownish hue revealed and preserved. The *aron hakodesh* from 1691 has become the highlight and focal point of the synagogue. The inscription below the tympanum reads, "Moses charged us with the Teaching as the heritage of the congregation of Jacob" (Deuteronomy 33:4). The final two words read "*aron kodesh.*" The letters indicated with dots add up to form the year, 1691, in which the ark was constructed.

Below this, a newly furnished *kapporet* was added to the *aron hakodesh* in 1883. It is the only part of the 1883 refurnishing that was left intact during restoration of the synagogue in 1995–96. Stripped of the other 1883 adjustments, the *kapporet* serves as an exquisite crown for the *parochet*. According to tradition, the *kapporet* is decorated with various symbols from the Jerusalem Temple. From left to right, there is the table containing the "bread of display"; the copper laver of water; the 12-stoned *choshen*, or breastplate, of the High Priest; the burning incense; and the menorah. Note the golden wings of the *cherubim*, which were attached to the *kapporet* in the Old Temple to guard the Ark of the Covenant (*see page 71*).

The 1883 *kapporet* actually covers some important inscriptions and decorations on the *aron hakodesh*. For instance, behind the *kapporet* there is a crown surrounded by the words *keter Torah*, or "Torah crown." Above the right pair of pillars, there is an abbreviation of Psalms 16:8, "I place God in front of me always." On the left side, there is an abbreviation of the famous sentence in the Talmud "Know before Whom you stand" (Babylonian Talmud, *Berakhot* 28b). Both abbreviations are paeans to the Altneuschul across the street, which has the same inscriptions on its eastern wall. On either side of the *aron hakodesh* are grooved platforms for candlesticks or candelabras. They were built around 1800.

It was most likely during or after the reconstruction of the synagogue in 1690–91 that the women's gallery was built on the southern side. Before that there was no women's section, since the synagogue had been used primarily by Jewish Community officials. The women's gallery was accessed by a special door on the eastern side of the synagogue, later blocked by a building erected on the site in 1907.

Extensive reconstruction in 1883 blocked off the passageway to the Jewish Town Hall, refurbished the women's gallery, and added a staircase that extended from the ground floor to the attic. In 1907, when a modern building was erected on the eastern side of the synagogue, the entrances to the men's and women's sections were blocked. This was when the entranceway opposite the Altneuschul was built.

It was in the High Synagogue that the Nazi "Museum of an Extinct Race" organized its first exhibition. One year after services in the synagogue had been prohibited, an exhibition of Hebrew books and manuscripts was opened in autumn of 1942. It consisted of many priceless books that had come into the hands of the Museum from Jews deported to their deaths. The exhibit documented Jewish literature from the Renaissance right up until the eve of the Nazi occupation, including works from seventy-four different Hebrew printing presses. In the process of setting up the exhibit, the High Synagogue was restored at a cost of 208,162 crowns, half of which was spent on display cases. All the work was performed in the midst of systematic deportations of Jews. When winter came in 1942, an entourage of high Nazi officials from Berlin came to visit the High Synagogue Museum. All documents indicate that the Germans enjoyed the exhibit immensely.

After the Holocaust, services resumed in the High Synagogue for a short time. In 1950, the High Synagogue became part of the State Jewish Museum. Various exhibits were held, ranging in theme from Jewish folk art to children's drawings from Terezin. The most recent exhibit, from 1982 to 1993, featured a sample of the enormous collection of synagogue textiles from Jewish Communities that were annihilated in the Holocaust.

In 1994, when the Jewish Museum was restituted to the Jews, the High Synagogue once again became the property of the Jewish Community and in 1995–96, the synagogue underwent fundamental restorations. Recognizing the cultural importance of the building, donors ranged from the City of Prague and the Czech Ministry of Culture all the way to the European Union in Brussels. The hope was that once again the High Synagogue would be used by an active congregation in the former Jewish Town. A new, wooden *bimah* was installed in the middle of the synagogue, directly below a luxurious gold-plated chandelier that had been added to the synagogue in the nineteenth century. In the women's gallery, a *beit midrash* and library were added. The most fun part of the synagogue is upstairs in the attic, where a moveable wooden roof allows the attic to be used as an uncommon *sukkah* during the holiday of Sukkot. The attic doubles as a classroom for the afternoon Jewish school started in 1996. It is filled with construction paper cutouts, Hebrew words and phrases, and children's games.

When the synagogue was reopened for a *Kabbalat Shabbat* service in 1996, it was a watershed moment in contemporary Prague Jewish history. This was the first additional synagogue to be opened for regular services in nearly fifty years. At last, the Altneuschul and Jerusalem Synagogue would be complemented by a third congregation. It was the wish of Karol Sidon, Chief Rabbi of the Czech Republic, to establish "Beginner Services" in the High Synagogue. These would be designed for the hundreds of Jews in Prague who feel alienated by the stern and insular atmosphere of Altneuschul services. The *Kabbalat Shabbat* service in the High Synagogue fulfilled these expectations. The synagogue was filled with people who had earlier tried services in the Altneuschul only to be befuddled by the ritual and frightened by the unwelcoming ambiance. The rabbi explained various parts of the service in Czech, and the congregation was urged to participate together. It was the most emotional Shabbat service in years. There was a heady feeling that Jewish services in Prague finally would serve the Community in the truest sense of the word.

Unfortunately, no other evening services were planned in the following half year. The synagogue began to be used on weekday afternoons, but this fact is misleading: It is the exact same *minyan* that used to meet in the Altneuschul for *minchah*. Young people who are active in the Jewish Community began to view the High Synagogue with a feeling of betrayal, as if it had teased them only to close its doors again. On top of all that, many Jews in Prague wished to use the High Synagogue for services, but the Rabbinate would not permit them, fearing a rebirth of non-Orthodox Judaism in Prague. Thus *Bejt Praha*, a nascent Jewish organization in Prague, was not permitted to meet for *Kabbalat Shabbat* in the synagogue. The consensus both inside and outside the Jewish Community was that the Rabbinate would actually lock up the High Synagogue rather than open it to a non-Orthodox service. In fact, the vast majority of Prague's Jews are far from Orthodox, but they lack the legal strength to win a synagogue from the Rabbinate. The ultimate catch-22 was that even while it forbade progressive services, the Rabbinate was too disorganized to prepare the much-needed "Beginner" services it had spoken of for years. It seems ridiculous, but the High Synagogue was actually used to blot out a resurgence of worship among hundreds of disenchanted Jews in Prague. The synagogue—ready for services but closed to worshippers—became hostage to inane factional wars over Jewish worship.

Finally, in the summer of 1997, evening services were again scheduled for the High Synagogue. It is unclear whether this is an earnest attempt to launch a new "Beginners" *minyan* in Prague, or whether it is a pragmatic wish to provide more prayer space for the droves of tourists in the summer. At this writing, one cannot yet say; we have to watch the synagogue in the coming winters, when tourists are few, to see if indeed it becomes a regular house of worship. Sometime in the future, the High Synagogue will be the yardstick by which to measure the Prague Jewish Community's resurgence or demise.

THE JEWISH TOWN HALL

Address: Maiselova Street 18

The Jewish Town Hall is the administrative center of the Jewish Community of Prague, and is not open to tourists. However, the Jewish Community restaurant ("Shalom Restaurant") is situated in the ceremonial room inside the building. Lunches are served daily from 11:30 A.M.– 2:00 P.M. Shabbat dinners are served after services Friday evening. You can buy lunch tickets at the Matana travel office across the street on Maiselova 15. For the same day's meal, tickets must be purchased no later than 1:30 P.M. For Shabbat meals, tickets must be paid for in advance.

The classic image of Jewish Prague, captured in countless engravings, paintings, and postcards in the nineteenth and twentieth centuries, is the Altneuschul backed by the Jewish Town Hall. Aside from the aesthetic juxtaposition of Gothic greys and Baroque pinks, the image depicts the interdependence of the spiritual and the pragmatic in Jewish life. In the Altneuschul, one's thoughts are directed toward God; in the Jewish Town Hall, they are directed toward the day-to-day administration of the ghetto.

Ever since it was built in about 1568, the Jewish Town Hall has been the chief symbol of Jewish communal autonomy in the Jewish Town of Prague. Built by Mordechai Maisel simultaneously with the High Synagogue, the building was meant to serve the Council of Elders who collected taxes, administered public works, and provided for the residents of the ghetto. This original mandate continues to this day: The Jewish Town Hall is the cultural, financial, administrative, and social center for the Jewish Community of Prague.

Even before this Town Hall was built in the 1560's, an earlier Town Hall existed on the site from at least 1541. One year after Emperor Maximilian II granted the Jews freedom of life and religion in 1567, Mordechai Maisel set out to reconstruct the Town Hall. Pancratius Roder, who built the High Synagogue, was commissioned to build the Jewish Town Hall as well. Pieces of the sixteenth-century Renaissance structure are maintained in bricks and vaulting in the northern part of the cellar. It is also possible that an even earlier Jewish Town Hall stood here from the thirteenth or fourteenth century. A small room in today's cellar has a five-ribbed Gothic vault that dates back to that time. Thus, almost from the beginning of Jewish settlement in this part of the Old Town, a Town Hall has stood side-by-side with the Altneuschul as the focus point of the Jewish Town.

In the "flood of fire" that ravaged the ghetto in 1689, the Jewish Town Hall burned down. In the same year, however, it was rebuilt in the Baroque style. In another fire in 1754, it burned down again, and in 1763–65, the Jewish Town Hall was rebuilt in the late Baroque style you see today.

During this reconstruction, the famous Hebrew clock was added to the northern side of the building below the bell tower clock (it is best seen up Maiselova Street, by the Altneuschul). The Hebrew clock runs counterclockwise in a whimsical reminder that Hebrew text is read from right to left. Both the Roman and the Hebrew clocks are operated by a single machine designed by the watchmaker of the Royal Court in 1764. The time is usually right; if you imagine it reversed or through a vertical mirror, it shows normal time. The Hebrew clock itself is one of the better-known symbols of Jewish Prague. It has been variously interpreted as the alien existence of the Jews in Europe, as the Jewish urge to recall the past, as a commentary on old Jewish buildings amidst new apartment houses, as the cessation of time in Jewish Prague, or simply as the quirky, inexplicable magic associated with the erstwhile ghetto. Its most famous incarnation was in a poem by Guillaume Apollinaire. The renowned Czech-Israeli writer Viktor Fischl (aka Avigdor Dagan) wrote an ode to the clock as well (see page 4).

During the destruction of the ghetto at the turn of the twentieth century, the Jewish Community used a new plot to add substantial space to the Jewish Town Hall. Looking at the building from Maiselova Street, the expanded wing can be seen on the far right. Without this addition, the Jewish Town Hall resumes the symmetrical appearance it had until the beginning of the twentieth century. Above the main entrance to the Jewish Town Hall, the date 1908 refers to the date of this expansion of the building. The date on the door to the left, 1765, refers to the earlier reconstruction of the Town Hall. This date is depicted around the symbol of the Jews of Prague—the Star of David enclosing a hat (see page 81).

An auditorium was built on the ground and first floor of the new addition. Today this is the site of the kosher restaurant Shalom, which provides subsidized meals for members of the Jewish Community. The Community's social life revolves around this auditorium. Not only is it the site of daily intrigues, gossip, and companionship, but each of the Jewish

Community's social functions convenes there as well—all the holiday celebrations and even some rituals, such as the Community's Passover seders. In addition, the auditorium hosts concerts, meetings, and the occasional wedding reception. It's always been this way.

⋘⋙

It was in the auditorium of the Jewish Town Hall that Franz Kafka (1883–1924) had some of his most moving Jewish experiences. Tellingly, his encounters had little to do with the Jews of Prague but rather with Jews from farther east. One evening at the end of the summer of 1920, Kafka observed over one hundred Russian Jews who were being temporarily housed in the auditorium. The next day he wrote, ". . . If someone had told me last night I could be whatever I wanted, I would have chosen to be a small Jewish boy from the East, standing there in the corner without a trace of worry . . . they are all one people . . ." (Franz Kafka, *Letters to Milena*).

Even before that moment, Kafka's embrace of an Eastern European Judaism he considered to be pure and untrammelled was acted out in the auditorium.

On February 18, 1912, an evening of Yiddish drama was organized in the auditorium by none other than Franz Kafka himself. In the most public cultural role Kafka would ever fill, Kafka printed the program and tickets, reserved the auditorium, numbered the seats, assembled the stage, requisitioned costumes, sold the tickets, put ads in newspapers, and submitted the program to both the police and the Rabbinate in the Jewish Town Hall. All this was so that his friend, the terrible twenty-four-year-old actor Yitzchak Levi, could deliver monologues from Yiddish plays. Kafka was well aware that the assimilated Jews of his parents' generation considered Yiddish a backward language reeking of the "ghetto." Kafka, by contrast, saw in the Yiddish theater a living image of a Judaism in which a Community of people were bound together. His encounters with Eastern European Jews, in fact, ultimately led Kafka to his most stirring spiritual yearnings. It also led him to open confrontation with the Prague Jewish bourgeois, whom he regarded as cold, overly assimilated, hostile toward Jewish spiritual life, and lacking any sense of Community bonds.

As it turned out, Kafka considered his Yiddish talk the most pivotal public speaking engagement of his life. Standing in an auditorium packed with Jews who had long rejected Yiddish as a degenerated symbol of the lifestyle they or their parents had abandoned, he embraced the pariah tongue. He used the Yiddish language itself as a jury to condemn the Jews of Prague for their lifestyle and habits. "Our Western European conditions, if we glance at them only in a deliberately superficial way, appear so well ordered; everything takes its quiet course. We live in positively cheerful concord, understanding each other whenever necessary, getting along without each other whenever it suits us and understanding each other even then. From within such an order of things who could possibly understand the tangle of Yiddish—indeed, who would even care to do so?" (Franz Kafka, "An Introductory Talk on the Yiddish Language," in Mark Anderson, *Reading Kafka: Prague, Politics, and the Fin de Siecle*).

At the end of his lecture, Kafka abandoned the confrontational mode and reached out to the audience in a final gesture of hope: If Prague's Jews would only open themselves up to it, Eastern Jewish life could liberate them from the cold sterility that defined their Prague Jewish existence, an existence Kafka publicly declaimed a thing to be feared. ". . . Once Yiddish has taken hold of you and moved you—and Yiddish is everything, the words, the hasidic melody, and the essential character of this East European Jewish actor himself—you will have forgotten your former reserve. Then you will come to feel the true unity of Yiddish, and so strongly that it will frighten you, yet it will no longer be fear of Yiddish but of yourselves."

THE PINCHAS SYNAGOGUE

Address: Siroka Street, opposite the end of Valentinska Street

> *Note: I recommend that you read the following general history before entering the synagogue itself—on a nice day, for instance, in the courtyard in front of the entrance. Once inside, it is hard to think of anything else except the Holocaust memorial, which is explained afterwards.*

For several reasons, the Pinchas Synagogue is one of the most integral pieces of the mosaic of Jewish Prague. First is its antiquity: It stands in the area of one of the oldest Jewish settlements in Prague. Architectural excavations in the 1950s exposed parts of the walls of an eleventh-century Romanesque synagogue on the site. The synagogue was dismantled and rebuilt so many times that today's building is a veritable time capsule from every period of Jewish history in the Old Town. Even without its earlier histories, today's Pinchas Synagogue is the third oldest monument in the former Ghetto, after the Altneuschul and the Old Jewish Cemetery. The building is a landmark of the Prague Jewish Community as it stood on the brink of the Renaissance.

But that's only part of the Pinchas Synagogue's uniqueness. Along with the Klausen Synagogue, it is one of the rare examples of a synagogue in the Czech Republic that lies adjacent to a cemetery (the other example is in the Moravian town of Straznice). In contrast to the Christian custom of churchyard graves, Jewish cemeteries are customarily placed at a distance from synagogues in order to keep the impurities in a graveyard from grazing the holiness of the house of prayer. The problem in Prague, though, was a simple matter of space. After using up all the area in what was to become the ghetto, the Jews had no alternative but to stretch their cemetery all the way to the synagogue wall. It reaches not only the Pinchas Synagogue, but the Klausen Synagogue on the other side as well.

The name "Pinchas" remains a mystery. Various Pinchases have been associated with the site since the late fifteenth century. Rabbi Israel Pinchas owned a building and prayer hall on the site as early as 1492. Eventually it becomes clear that the synagogue was owned by the Horowitz family, but that doesn't help matters. In the sixteenth century, there were so many Pinchas Horowitzes in Prague that the two names were almost interchangeable. It is most likely, though, that the Pinchas in question was the famous merchant Rabbi Pinchas Horowitz of Cracow, one of the grandsons of the current building's founder in the sixteenth century. This Pinchas, known as "Pinchas the Doctor," gained international renown for his influence in Polish Jewish life. It was about this time that the name "Pinchas" stuck to the synagogue. Whether the Pinchas from Cracow is indeed the namesake of this synagogue, the synagogue's name has achieved everlasting prominence through one of Prague's most charming Jewish legends, told on page 97.

History

As mentioned, there was a private prayer hall on this site in 1492. It was owned by the powerful Horowitz family of Prague, an irrepressible clan of printers, musicians, financiers, and mystics with origins in the Bohemian town of Horovice. In Israel today there is a Horowitz Society whose members can trace their ancestry to Bohemia. That an entire synagogue was built for a single family shows just how large Jewish families once were. Of course, other people came to pray as well, and after a couple of generations it became one of many small public synagogues in the ghetto. If you didn't like the rabbi in the Altneuschul, you'd cross the street to the High Synagogue. If you preferred the prayer rites in the Pinchas Synagogue, you'd amble on over there. One of the first things Prague visitors mention is the diminutive size of these synagogues. It should be remembered that unlike in America, where there are large tracts of suburban space to build synagogues, the Jews in the ghetto were constantly grappling with an economy of space. This explains the concentration of eight synagogues in a span of about three blocks. By the time of the expansive Spanish and Vinohrady Synagogues (the latter was destroyed during the war), Prague's Jews had already been released from the ghetto.

In 1535, a man by the name of Aaron Meshulam Horowitz built a lavish synagogue on the site of the family's earlier *schul*. His building is the main part of the synagogue today. Aaron Meshulam Horowitz was probably the most prestigious Bohemian Jew in the first half of the sixteenth century. The richest Jew in Prague, he obtained special privileges from the king for his entire family. Among these privileges were two permanent seats in the Community leadership for members of the Horowitz family and the power to choose one of Prague's rabbis. Aaron was one of the more feisty characters in sixteenth-century Jewish Prague. His quarrels with the Community reached such explosive proportions that eventually the rabbis of Poland and Germany sent an emissary to settle matters. Although four hundred Jews signed a treaty to resolve the hostilities, Aaron Meshulam Horowitz was intransigent. He threatened the peacemaking rabbi so excessively that on three occasions the rabbi fled across Charles Bridge and sought refuge in Prague Castle.

The Horowitz clan was even better known for its starry-eyed mysticism. In the 1520s, a young Marrano in Lisbon named Diogo Pires was so eager to return to the faith of his forefathers that he took out a knife and performed autocircumcision. Perhaps as a result of the trauma this produced, Pires went overboard. He changed his name to Shlomo Molcho and began to tour Europe as, rather immodestly, the Messiah. In Prague, the inimitable Horowitzes became so convinced he was the true Redeemer that some of the family accompanied him on his mission to the king in Germany. After Molcho was burned at the stake in 1532 by the Inquisition, the Horowitzes managed to procure not only Molcho's banner but even his embroidered robe, which they boldly exhibited in the Pinchas Synagogue for centuries after the false messiah's death.

Of course, there were also more mainstream mystical strains of the Horowitz line. Aaron Meshulam's younger brother, Shabbatai, was a well-known kabbalist in early seventeenth-century Prague who explicated the teachings of Yitzchak Luria, also known as the "*Arizal*." Shabbatai's grandson, Rabbi Isaiah ben Abraham Horowitz, was the chief rabbi of Prague from 1614 to 1621. He wrote the famous kabbalistic tract entitled *Shnei Luchot Ha'brit*, or "The Two Tablets of the Law." In 1621 he left for the true home of *Kabbalah*, Tsfat in Israel.

Another unique fact of the Pinchas Synagogue is that its Renaissance renovations were performed by one of the few Jewish architects of the time. Between 1607 and 1620, Judah Goldschmied—also known as Judah Tsoref de Herz—built the women's aisle and the women's gallery above it, as well as vestibules on the southern side. Goldschmied was also known for his work on the Maisel Synagogue. When you stand outside the Pinchas Synagogue's main entrance, you'll see the miniature Renaissance courtyard Goldschmied built, complete with circular and rectangular windows; it was surrounded by houses until the ghetto was destroyed.

Floods in the eighteenth and nineteenth centuries necessitated further renovations and adjustments to the interior. As a result, it is difficult to point to a single architectural style; more often, one sees a hodgepodge of styles in a single setting. Thus there are the restored remains of an early Renaissance portal, a Baroque *bimah*, and a Rococo grille round the *bimah*. Even the floor is not what it used to be: After a flood in 1860, the floor was raised one and a half meters. For this reason, the ceiling appears lower today, and the lower women's gallery is on practically the same level as the main sanctuary. But today the synagogue is vital not for its style but for the countless names written on its interior walls (*see page 91*).

During the war, the Pinchas Synagogue at first served as a collection depot for the objects of the Museum of an Extinct Race. After some time, it was decided to turn the synagogue into an exhibition hall, like most of the other synagogues in the Jewish Town. In May 1943, the idea for a "Ghetto Exhibit" emerged, to trace the history of the Jews of Bohemia and Moravia up to the end of the nineteenth century. Everything from maps of Jewish streets in the countryside to royal edicts concerning the Jews would be displayed.

Given the mass murders being committed at the time, the intended exhibition was terrifying. In the gallery of the Pinchas Synagogue, the exhibition would begin with a re-creation of a typical medieval street of the Prague Jewish Town. Thus the Disneyland-type atmosphere of the Museum would reach its climax. Next to this would be a mock-up of a typical *cheder*, or Jewish elementary school, as well as a model of a talmudic scholar's study. Downstairs, a display on Jewish firefighters of the Middle Ages would be situated next to an exhibit on the history of the Pinchas Synagogue. The main hall would chart the history of Czech Jews through various eras.

The war ended before the Nazis could transform the Pinchas Synagogue into such a Jewish Park. Instead of a museum, the synagogue became a living parchment testifying to one of the most horrendous periods of human history.

The Holocaust Memorial

> What can one say about this Synagogue?
> That it is a structure dating from approximately the year 1536, or that it is the last, final outcry of the Old Prague Ghetto?
> Now it is something else.
> It is a tomb.
>
> from Arnost Lustig, "The Wall," in Hana Volavkova, *A Story of the Jewish Museum in Prague*

From 1955 to 1959, the Pinchas Synagogue became a house of remembered tragedy. The names of all 77,297 Czech Jews who were murdered in the Holocaust were inscribed on the walls. This includes Jews from Bohemia, Moravia, and part of Silesia. Slovak names were not inscribed on the walls for a number of reasons, even though Czechoslovakia was united at the time. First of all, Slovakia was an independent fascist state during the war, disposing of its Jewish population with an enthusiasm almost unmatched during the Holocaust. After the war they had their own, separate atoning to do. Secondly and more pragmatically, there simply wasn't enough interior space to include the roughly one hundred thousand Slovak Jews murdered.

Then, in the late 1960s, two things happened. First, Israel defeated its Arab neighbors with a stunning victory in the Six Day War in June 1967. The Soviet Union, which had allied itself with the Arabs, instantly broke all ties with Israel. With the notable exception of Romania, all countries behind the so-called Iron Curtain recalled their ambassadors from Israel. The war affected not only international relations, but the position of Jews within most of the communist countries as well. Suddenly, Jews who had no connection to their religion were labelled by the state as "Zionist conspirators," a recent spin on the term "dirty Jew."

Second, in the 1960s Czechoslovakia experienced a political, cultural, and economic liberalization that culminated in Alexander Dubcek's "Prague Spring." It all was destroyed when Warsaw Pact troops entered Prague on August 21, 1968, crushing the "Prague Spring" and ushering in an oppressive period of normalization. The Jewish Community experienced this more acutely than did the general population; just as a political thaw under totalitarianism meant good news for the Jews, a political frost spelled extra repression toward the Jews. Eventually, secret lists of "Zionist spies" were drawn up. Zionists were said to have collaborated with the Nazis, and Jewish suffering in the Holocaust was claimed to have been exaggerated.

What these events amounted to was that in 1968, only one year after a Czechoslovak postage stamp featuring the Pinchas Synagogue Memorial had been issued, the synagogue was closed under the pretext of restoration. It was kept closed for the next twenty years. During this time, the names of the Jewish martyrs were silently whitewashed off the walls.

It is still unclear whether the whitewashing was a direct act of provocation or not. The authorities claimed that water leakage had necessitated the procedure, but this does not explain why for twenty years the names were not rewritten. Today, employees of the Jewish Museum downplay the malicious motives of the government, but it is preposterous to say that anti-Semitism played no part in the decision to destroy the memorial. It is most likely that the act was not intended as direct provocation but was another example of the brute vulgarity and insensitivity of the communist regime toward Jews. To blame it on communism is also deceptive: After 1968 in Prague, there were few ideological communists in the Party, only self-serving opportunists. And the word "communist" deflects responsibility from the Czechs in the same way that the word "Nazi" obfuscates the German people's responsibility for genocide. The destruction of the memorial proceeded from the simple rationale that Jewish memory, as well as Jewish life, were unnecessary to preserve.

Only after the transformations of 1989 did it become a priority to renew the memorial. Vaclav Havel, one of the greatest European rulers toward the Jews in recent memory (not a very difficult role to fill, considering European history), placed immediate emphasis on the reinscription of the names when he was elected president in December 1989. In 1990, Havel wrote:

> As a human being and as a Czech citizen, I can only express my deep sorrow over the fate of the Jews in the Czech lands, particularly with regard to those who were the victims of genocide. The scope of this tragedy can be perceived in the Pinchas Synagogue in Prague where the names of all the Jews known to have perished in the concentration camps and gas chambers have been inscribed on the walls. Our first priority will be to renovate this memorial.
>
> excerpted from Natalia Berger, *Where Cultures Meet: The Story of the Jews of Czechoslovakia*

From 1992 to 1996, scaffolding sprawled throughout the interior of the synagogue as graphic design students painstakingly inscribed, for the second time in half a century, the names of 77,297 Jewish martyrs on the walls. On April 16, 1996—that year's *Yom Ha'Shoah*, or Holocaust Remembrance Day—the cantor from the Altneuschul chanted the *kaddish* inside the Pinchas Synagogue as the memorial was opened again.

One final note: Due to its antiquity, the Pinchas Synagogue is a symbol of Prague Jewish ghetto life. But today it is also a living monument to the tragic history of modern Jewish Prague and a symbol of Jewish life in all of Central and Eastern Europe in the twentieth century. As a record of the Holocaust, it reminds us of the destruction of European Jews. As a destroyed memorial, it reflects the annihilation of Jewish memory under communist regimes. And as a renewed memorial today, it reflects both the possibility of tolerance at last, and the rebirth in Prague of the collective memory of the Jews.

Explanation of the Memorial

The Holocaust Memorial begins in the antechamber of the synagogue. It continues in the main sanctuary and the women's section and gallery. In the main sanctuary, on both sides of the *aron hakodesh*, there is a list of ghettoes, concentration camps, and death camps where the people were killed. The names are written in the language of the country (e.g., Oswiecim is Polish for Auschwitz).

The lists of names are catalogued in three colors:

Yellow is used for listing the town the person came from. All the towns and cities are listed alphabetically, and sheer placards in front of the walls act as keys to the index. It should be noted that the main sanctuary of the synagogue is reserved exclusively for Prague, as that was the largest Jewish Community in the Czech lands. All other cities in the Czech Republic are grouped alphabetically in the antechamber, the women's section, and the women's gallery upstairs.

Red refers to the family name of the individual. There is not enough wall space to print each person's first and last name, so first names are grouped under common surnames. The individuals listed under common surnames are therefore not necessarily related to each other. It should be noted that many of the names will sound familiar. This is because in 1787, Emperor Josef II had the Jews adopt German first names and surnames as part of his efforts to integrate the Jews into the larger society and economy. For this reason, many Czech Jews have names (Birnstein, Fischer, Friedman) identical to those of many American Jews.

Black lists the first names, dates of birth, and dates of deportation or arrest. The Nazis were meticulous in making lists of deportations. These lists were collected after the war and served as a reference for the Memorial. Since the Nazis tried to destroy evidence of genocide, the dates of actual murder are more difficult to ascertain with certainty. However, every individual listed on the wall was murdered during the Holocaust.

Question marks, often in place of birth dates, indicate that this information is not known.

The name of the Pinchas Synagogue is often spelled "Pinkas." Although this undoubtedly represents varying transliterations of the Hebrew, the secondary spelling has begotten a recent explanation. "Pinkas" in Hebrew means a "ledger." The Pinchas Synagogue has become an enormous ledger of the Czech Holocaust.

With its list of dates, the Holocaust Memorial delineates the ages of each of the martyred Jews from the Czech lands; subtracting the first date from the second date gives the age of each when deported. Thus there are six-year-olds remembered as well as eighty-five-year-olds, women of thirty-eight, men of forty-three, babies, infants, teenagers, adults, and the elderly.

It is important to not underestimate the uniqueness of this memorial in Europe. Elsewhere on the continent, Holocaust memorials come as either abstract sculptures or representative figures that recall, rather grudgingly, an untidy period in the nation's past. In scores of memorials, the tragedy of Europe is put out of focus through visual ambiguity and textual platitude. To use an extreme example, in Harburg, a suburb of Hanover, there's even a monument against fascism that was deliberately sunk into the ground, apparently intended as an avant garde commentary on the act of monument building itself. Eventually, the monument is supposed to disappear forever. This German monument casts a light on European Holocaust memorials in ways it was probably never intended to do. On the continent where the Holocaust was perpetrated, memorials tend to gentrify and to anaesthetize rather than remember the unspeakable.

Not so the Pinchas Synagogue Memorial. Here, the Holocaust is not a blur tidily telescoped into a generalized form. It is not an anonymous figure sanitizing the erasure of an entire civilization. Instead, the Pinchas Synagogue Memorial reminds us of what the Holocaust really was: an act of murder committed, in the case of the Czech lands, 77,297 times on 77,297 individuals. The victims are not generalized: each had a name, age, and place of birth. It should be pointed out that the original memorial in the Pinchas Synagogue preceded the Vietnam War Memorial in Washington, D.C., by over two decades. It is this personalization of the suffering of the Holocaust that makes the Pinchas Synagogue Memorial an act of monumental art: No matter how much one tries to brush by the fact, the 77,297 names remain to alert the world of the brutality and horror of Europe in the twentieth century.

Inside the Synagogue

The first thing to notice inside the synagogue is the stone memorial plaque on the left side of the entranceway. Originally situated on the western facade of the synagogue, it was installed either when the synagogue was erected or during a later restoration. If the former is true, then it is one of the oldest remaining parts of the building. In soaring terms, it refers to Aaron Meshulam Horowitz, who built the synagogue in 1535: "And a man came from the House of Levi and his name was Aaron Meshulam, and he mounted the ladder of the bountiful spirit, following the steps of his fathers, princes and leaders, and he built this synagogue, the splendor of buildings . . ." The appearance, style, and content of the plaque imitate the style of cemetery tombstones, which draw from a broad range of scriptural sources to extol an individual's lofty qualities. In this case, the first line alone plays off the first line of the Book of Ruth, which reads, ". . . And a man came from Bethlehem [*Bet lechem* in Hebrew]." *Bet lechem* is changed to read *Bet Levi*, or "House of Levi," because Aaron Meshulam was a Levite. The reference to princely fathers is not literal, of course, but serves to highlight Aaron Meshulam's importance in the Community.

After passing through the entrance vestibule and antechamber, you enter the main sanctuary of the synagogue. Looking back, you'll find the reconstructed Renaissance portal to the synagogue. The portal features the symbol of Jewish Prague: a shield of David with a hat in the middle. In addition, there are two Levite's pitchers, referring to the Levite pedigree of Aaron Meshulam Horowitz and his sons. The Hebrew letters on the portal are an abbreviation for the customary inscription on the door to a synagogue: "This is the gateway to God, righteous people enter here," but there is something strange about this portal. Normally the inscription stands above the doorway as you enter the synagogue or main sanctuary (as is the case, for instance, with the Klausen Synagogue). Here, though, the portal is reversed, with its inscription facing the main sanctuary itself. This is a mystery that has confounded scholars. Surely the synagogue was not situated in the antechamber. Some assert that when the portal was reinstalled after a fire, it was accidentally reversed—but that's quite a profound error. The mystery remains unsolved today. All we can say for sure is that it's another backwards sight, like the Hebrew clock on the Jewish Town Hall, that typifies Jewish Prague.

But, like the dualism of Pinchas and Pinkas, there is a way to view the reversed portal in the context of the Holocaust memorial. According to Jewish tradition, every person who dies through *kiddush ha-Shem*, or the sanctification of God's Name, gains instant access to the "World to Come." By twisting itself around to face the walls, the portal is staring at the mass of names and attesting that each of them is a righteous person who, on grounds of his or her martyrdom, has entered into Heaven.

The names written on the main sanctuary walls are exclusively from Prague. They begin alphabetically in the northwest corner, and run clockwise around the periphery of the room. At the end of the list on the western wall, there is a small list headed by the yellow word *dodatky*, or "additions." These are names that had not been included, for various reasons, in the original memorial.

On the northern wall, you'll find a Hebrew letter at the top of each of the floor panels. Read from right to left, the letters are *Taf*, *nun*, *tzaddik*, *bet*, *heh*. It is a Jewish custom to place these letters on tombstones. Taken together, they are an abbreviation for "May their soul be bound in the bundle of life" (*inspired by I Samuel 25:29*). By placing the tombstone inscription on the walls of the Pinchas Synagogue, the memorial attempts to give a traditional Jewish burial to the thousands of unmarked graves. Interestingly, the Old Jewish Cemetery is located on the other side of the wall. The layers of graves in the cemetery actually rise in tandem with the rows of names on the wall. In this way as well, the martyrs receive an implied Jewish burial. Finally, the shape of the wall panels bears an uncanny—and unplanned—resemblance to tombstones in Jewish cemeteries.

As mentioned earlier, the floor level of the synagogue was raised one and a half meters after flooding in 1860. As a result, the intricate late-Gothic-cum-Renaissance vaulting of the ceiling does not appear as high as it once was. The *bimah* stands slightly off center in order to make more room in the back of the main sanctuary for the entranceway. Following a devastating flood in 1771, the *bimah* was reconstructed in Baroque style in 1775. At this time, the stonework of the *bimah* was removed in favor of red-painted stucco. The Rococo iron grill around the *bimah* was donated by the nobleman Joachim Popper in 1793. Note the four Jewish stars with hats in the middle, the Prague Jewish symbol that crops up at almost every site in the quarter. As for the *aron hakodesh*, none of the tapestries remain here. The *aron hakodesh* was rebuilt in 1775 and again in 1862. In 1838, a new cabinet for the Torahs was added, but only a part of it remains today. A photograph from the early twentieth century shows plants in vases adorning the top of the *aron hakodesh*.

It is interesting that the area in front of the *aron hakodesh* follows the same tradition as that in the Altneuschul. Thus the cantor reads from the lectern in a lowered area, according to Psalms 130:1: "From out of the depths I call to you God." There once stood a *Sh'viti* tablet in front of the lectern, filled with kabbalistic permutations of God's name to inspire the cantor to more devotion during the service. Left of the lectern, the bench was used for the *brit milah*, or circumcision. A special seat was set aside for the prophet Elijah to visit the ceremony.

Against the southern wall of the synagogue lies the women's section and, above it, the women's gallery. You'll find faintly legible Hebrew lettering on the walls of the main sanctuary that connect to the women's section. This is one of the most fascinating recent finds in the synagogue. When initial restorations were begun in the early 1950s, soundings were taken on the walls. They found eight layers of paint so old and worn that it was impossible to preserve the original text completely. The inscriptions found on the southern wall, along with a floral design partly revealed today, are thought to have been added in the nineteenth century. The inscriptions are common prayers: "O God, our King, who sits on the throne of mercy," "Praised and blessed be the divine name," "I am thine and my dreams are thine. May the one whose meaning I do not comprehend lead to good."

Inside the lower women's section there are obstructed inscriptions of an entirely different nature. Here the Jewish Museum decided to preserve a piece of the original memorial, complete with the marks of the whitewashing. From this we can point out two things: First, the whitewashing was indeed haphazard and provocative; second, the Jewish Museum succeeded in recreating the original memorial perfectly, down to the original typeset of the letters. The names in these preserved sections were repainted in the new parts of the memorial.

Today the synagogue is bare of its pre-war furnishings. It is difficult to imagine the richly decorated interior as it appeared before the war. It used to be crowded to overflowing with the objects of Jewish prayer. Chandeliers hung throughout, the *bimah* and *aron hakodesh* were richly decorated with fabrics, and the synagogue was filled with long wooden pews added in the 1840s (before that, all the seats were arranged to face the *bimah* on all sides). Aside from the inspirationals on the side walls, there was a giant inscription high above the *aron hakodesh*, written above the circular window in a curved arch and reading, "Know before whom you stand" (Babylonian Talmud, *Berakhot* 28b). The window itself was designed as a giant rosette Jewish star.

> Note: Upstairs in the Pinchas Synagogue, a special room has been set aside for a permanent exhibition of children's drawings from the Terezin concentration camp.

Nearby the Pinchas Synagogue

As you exit the courtyard of the Pinchas Synagogue and head toward the cemetery, you'll pass a complex of small buildings. During reconstruction work in the 1970s, underground rooms were discovered below the complex. Included in the discoveries was a fifteenth-century *mikveh*, or Jewish ritual bath. *Mikvehs* must contain water from a natural spring or river. In this case, it is so close to the Vltava that the river literally flowed through it.

There is a modern, quasi-apocryphal tale that when Jewish Museum officials discovered the *mikveh* in the 1970s, they had no idea what it was. Only when an American Jewish visitor proved through measurements and explanations what it was did the incredulous museum workers agree.

In 1993, the Jewish Community of Prague wished to reopen the *mikveh* for contemporary use. However, it had become old and fragile, and the only way to make it fit for use would be to severely alter the landmark. So they decided to build a new *mikveh* next to the old one. Today the upstairs part of the complex houses a modern, tiled *mikveh*. Thus it is that Prague has an Altneu-*mikveh*.

> Note: Because of the cramped space in the underground rooms, the ancient mikveh is not open to the public.

The Legend of Pinchas

The name "Pinchas" most likely comes from Rabbi Pinchas Horowitz, a grandson of Aaron Meshulam Horowitz. Pinchas himself is a nebulous figure in Prague Jewish history—there were several Pinchases in the Horowitz clan. However, there is a Prague Jewish tale about how the synagogue's namesake amassed his wealth, and it's such a gem that it almost doesn't matter if this Pinchas, like so many other Prague characters, never existed.

The legend:

In the fifteenth century there lived a poor, honest Jew named Pinchas. During the day he walked the streets of the ghetto with a torn bag, buying and selling old clothes from his sack. He spent all of his nights studying the *Gemarah*.

Pinchas was so poor that his entire family would have starved were it not for the benevolence of a kindly Bohemian Count. He admired Pinchas's honest and devout nature, and so every Friday afternoon he gave Pinchas enough money to purchase Shabbat candles and challah. The Count gave an extra bonus before each holiday, so that Pinchas could properly celebrate Jewish customs and tradition.

But something bothered the Count. Each time he gave Pinchas holiday coins, he longed to hear Pinchas praise his good name. But each time it was the same. Pinchas would stretch his hands to heaven and exclaim, "Almighty God, who never leaves his children in need or distress, I thank you for your help!"

This annoyed the Count. It was he, not God, who was assisting Pinchas. Shouldn't he receive at least a token of thanks for his magnanimous deeds? So the Count decided to put the devout Pinchas to a test. When the holiday of Pesach came, the Count would not give Pinchas a thing. If it really was God who aided Pinchas, then Pinchas would not be abandoned on the holiday of Pesach.

Pesach came around. Pinchas made his usual trip to the Count's palace and asked for assistance.

"Oh dear, it's been such a trying season," said the Count. "My tenants haven't paid their rents on time, you know how it is. I can't afford to give you a thing. But don't worry; as you always say, your God will help you." The Count could barely suppress a smirk.

Pinchas grimaced. But he believed; he had faith. "I have absolute faith that God will help me," he said.

When Pinchas came home, his wife and children were waiting eagerly by the door. What kinds of Pesach goodies would they be able to buy with this year's bonus? "*Nu?*" said his wife. "What did the Count give you?"

"Absolutely nothing," Pinchas responded, and pulled two pieces of dust from his empty pockets.

Immediately the uproar began. His wife cried, "Who will feed the children? What will we do for Pesach?"

But it was time for evening prayers and Pinchas, who had had a tough day already, headed for his tiny study hall and shut the door.

He remained there until after midnight, studying the tracts of the Talmud dealing with the Pesach holiday. He didn't even take a bite to eat, so caught up was he in his studies.

Suddenly he heard a crash. He looked up—was he dreaming?—and at the window he saw a huge form, sillouhetted in black, moving toward him. Terrified, Pinchas held up his Talmud as a shield. The form fell to the ground and lay there, stiff.

After a long silence, Pinchas got up and slowly approached the body.

When he lifted the head, he saw that it was not a human but a monkey. And it was dead.

Now, Pinchas knew monkeys. He knew that it was a custom among the rich to domesticate these animals and keep them as pets. But what was this monkey doing in his home?

His wife knocked on the door. "What's all that noise?" she asked. Pinchas let her in and showed her the dead monkey. "Oy vey!" his wife cried. "It's another blood libel!" In the blood libel accusation, Jews were falsely accused of murdering Christian virgins or babies and using the blood in Passover matzohs. Pinchas's wife continued, "Easter is near, they want to try you for ritual murder, only this time they're using a monkey and not a baby!"

"So what do we do?" asked Pinchas, nearing his wit's end.

"We'll have to destroy the animal before the Christians come to arrest you! Bring it to the kitchen—we'll have to burn it!"

Pinchas began to drag the monkey across the floor when a gold coin fell out of the monkey's mouth. He noticed that the monkey was extremely heavy. "Bring me a knife," he asked his wife. Pinchas then cut open the belly of the monkey and removed its large, bulbous stomach. He cut open the stomach and out poured over a hundred gold coins.

Pinchas shouted for joy, quoting from Psalms 37:35, "I've been young and I have grown old, but I have never seen a righteous man forsaken, or his children seeking bread."

The next day, during the Pesach seder—the most exquisite seder the Pinchas family had experienced—a knock was heard at the door. Pinchas, hoping it was the prophet Elijah who is said to visit each seder, opened the door. It was the Count.

When the Count saw the fresh foods on the table, the decorations on the walls, and the children's new clothes, he was astonished. "Where did you get the money for this?" he asked.

Pinchas told him the whole story. "That's funny," mused the Count. "My monkey Theodore has been missing for two days now. Tell me, what did he look like?" Pinchas described the monkey, who apparently had distinguishable birthmarks, and the Count was convinced it was Theodore.

"And I know how the gold coins got in his stomach," claimed the Count, proud of his perspicacity. "I always test my gold coins by biting them. Theodore, who loves to mimic, must have thought I was eating the coins, and he did the same!"

It turned out that the Count's porter wanted to play a joke on Pinchas, and he threw the monkey through the window. The porter was sent to jail. Pinchas, honest as ever, tried to return the gold coins to the Count. But the Count refused to accept them, maintaining that it was all part of God's plan, for he now saw that God did not abandon his beloved Pinchas. "The gold coins were a gift from God," said the Count, and he sat down in humble awe to watch the Jewish feast.

With the stomachful of gold coins, Pinchas became one of the most skilled and honest merchants in the ghetto. In gratitude for his fortune, he built the Pinchas Synagogue for his entire family and for the rest of Prague's Jews.

THE OLD JEWISH CEMETERY
Address: Siroka Street, entrance through the Pinchas Synagogue entrance

The Dates

The Old Jewish Cemetery was used from the early fifteenth century until 1787, when Josef II forbade any further burials in what had become, over the course of the centuries, a massive hill of human bodies. The oldest known grave here is that of Rabbi Avigdor Kara (*see page 78*). Unfortunately, his grave is inaccessible from the current tourist walkway. But the tombstone itself, which has vastly deteriorated, is now on display in the Maisel Synagogue. A replica was placed by Rabbi Kara's grave in 1981.

As with most things in Prague, old does not mean oldest: Two other Prague Jewish cemeteries predate the Old Jewish Cemetery. The oldest, which most likely dates back to the eleventh century, lay on the other side of the river by the former Jewish settlement in Mala Strana. No trace of it remains. Another cemetery was used in the so-called "New Town," or Nove Mesto, at the site of today's Vladislavova Street, from the thirteenth century until 1478. Traces of tombstones from this cemetery were unearthed during building excavations in 1866; the fragments were brought to the Old Jewish Cemetery and embedded in a wall adjacent to the Klausen Synagogue (*see map on page 104*. Unfortunately, today's path through the cemetery does not include this section).

After 1787, two main cemeteries came into use in other parts of Prague, far from the human congestion of the ghetto. One is on Fibichova Street (*see page 134*), and the other, the New Cemetery, is adjacent to the Olsany Cemetery (*see page 137*).

The Big Picture

There is no site in Jewish Prague more frequented than the Old Jewish Cemetery. As soon as you climb the entrance stairway, you'll see why: The jilted crosscurrents of tombstones groping one atop the next creates the impression as much of life as of death. Each stone is slightly different, askew in its own way. As such, the kaleidoscope of graves, a testament to four hundred years of Jewish history, almost resembles a coliseum of conversing souls. Anybody who has ever attended a Jewish conference will understand this effect immediately. That each tombstone has sunk its own distance into the teeming soil adds to this image. It looks as much like a rising, a stretching up to the surface, as it does a sinking down into the ground. And each stone tells its own story. The Hebrew texts match with adorning images to describe the individual's life, attributes, accomplishments, and sometimes—as in the case of victims of pogroms—death. In this way the cemetery is like a holy scroll outstretched to reveal, in word and picture, the story of the Jews of Prague.

The serenity of the cemetery finds a special harmony in each of the seasons. Springtime brings a cacophony of crows, more crows than can be found anywhere in Prague, nesting in the trees sprouting from the graves. Summertime adds a helter-skelter crisscross of shadows to the already angled tombstones. When autumn comes the tombstones are draped in leaves as if awaiting a celebration or judgment. Winter is a time of monochromatic tranquility.

Perhaps it is these qualities that draw the massive numbers of tourists—predominately European Gentiles—from all over the world to this cemetery. Interpretations of this fascination include the cynical (if the most-visited area of the ghetto is a cemetery, then this is indeed a Museum of an Extinct Race), the thoughtful (it is guilt that drives them here), the pragmatic (they no longer have Jewish communities in their midst, so they come here to see it), the more cynical (Jews control the world—let's see what they're like!), and finally the obvious (it really is an unforgettable place). This last explanation gains weight when we consider that last century, during the Czech National Revival movement, which sought to express Czech autonomy through language, education, and culture, a startling number of poets and painters came to the cemetery for inspiration. Easels cropped up all over the twisting paths, and the spindly stew of tombstones found its way onto sundry canvasses. The great Bohemian landscape painter Antonin Manes was the first; his watercolors and etchings in 1830 set the form for an artistic flood pouring from the cemetery every season. This romanticism of Jewish past—particularly Jewish death—continues today as millions of tourists leave coins or wistful notes on the densely packed gravestones. (It should be noted that this is not a Jewish custom; only in the case of known sages is there a practice of leaving a *kvittel*, or note.) It is as if they are paying homage to the mysterious beauty and exoticism of the ghetto—but it's important to remember that this cemetery derives its exaggerated appearance not through any form of Jewish aesthetics, but because of anti-Semitism.

The Building of the Cemetery

The ghetto dehumanized the Jews in death as well as in life. Although the Jewish Community succeeded, at various times, in adding small amounts of adjoining land to the graveyard, it was unable to add sufficient space because to do so would require stretching outside the demarcations of the ghetto. Because the Prague authorities refused to grant the Jews more land for a cemetery (the cemeteries in the Mala Strana and Vysehrad regions had by this time already been destroyed), and because Jewish law forbids disinterring a body from the ground once it's been placed there, the Jews of Prague were left with no alternative but to bury people on top of one another. The original tombstone would be removed, the new body would be placed on top of the old grave, soil from another part of the ghetto would be placed on top, and the original tombstone would be returned, along with a second one for the new grave.

This happened over and over again, so that what resulted is a hill of human bodies twelve layers deep at its greatest depth and five or six layers deep in general. If you measure out a human form amidst the tombstones, and then count the tombstones in that area, you can arrive at a rough estimation of the number of bodies layered in that area. The term "deep" is misleading, because the digging stopped after the first layer of bodies; afterwards, burial here amounted to the construction of a hill. This explains the steps you ascend as you enter. It is interesting that in the Altneuschul you step down to enter, but in the Old Jewish Cemetery you step up. You'll also see that the high windows of the Pinchas Synagogue come up to your waist here. The names lining the Pinchas Synagogue's walls actually rise in tandem with the layers of buried bodies. It is two eras of Jewish existence and death meeting in the same place.

There are twelve thousand visible tombstones in the cemetery. Estimates of the total number of tombstones, however, reach as high as one hundred thousand. This means that the vast majority of tombstones have sunk all the way into the soil. Most of the visible tombstones are themselves well along the journey back to the ground. Often what looks like a rock jutting out of the earth is actually the last speck of a drowned tombstone.

One thing to keep in mind when walking through the cemetery is that this is the single place in the former ghetto that was largely exempted from urban renewal at the turn of the century. As such, it is the one area where we can witness the topography of the medieval ghetto. Looking at the paths crisscrossing the cemetery, you gain an idea of the claustrophobia, congestion, and paranoia of ghetto life. (The confined paths on which you walk were designed for tourist control.) Just as the original paths wind almost randomly, so the streets of the ghetto became helter-skelter shards. Similarly, people lived just as they were buried here: like the tombstones clustered next to each other, one home was built right into another because of lack of space.

The Three Pillars of the Golden Age

There generally are three pillars necessary to underpin any Golden Age in Jewish history: the cultural, the financial, and the spiritual. If just one of these interrelated elements is missing, prosperity will not burst into a true Golden Age. In the Old Jewish Cemetery, you will find the graves of three individuals, each of whom embodied one of these pillars of prosperity and together united the cultural, financial, and spiritual realms in a critical mass that erupted into the famous Golden Age of Prague Jewish history from 1570 to 1620.

The Cultural:

The cultural realm is consummately personified by **David Gans** (1541–1613), whose grave is the first to see when you enter the cemetery. The famous "Renaissance Jew," David Gans spearheaded an intellectual and cultural explosion in the ghetto with his forays into astronomy, mathematics, and history.

The Financial:

Farther on lies the grave of the great financier **Mordechai Maisel** (1528–1601). Maisel, one of the wealthiest men in Europe, used his mass riches to rebuild the entire ghetto. Every public works project of the time, from the lowliest cobblestone in the street to the most ornate house of prayer, owes its existence to him.

The Spiritual:

Nearby lies the grave of Rabbi **Judah Loew** (1525–1609). Rabbi Loew, one of the greatest rabbis in all Jewish history, was a bedrock of spiritual wisdom and intellectual independence. It was Rabbi Loew's *yeshivah* that turned out some of the most broadly educated rabbis of the time. His teachings and writings concerning God, Israel, Exile, and Redemption continue to inspire generations of Jews to this day.

These three people reached the peak of their extraordinary activities toward the close of the sixteenth century. The Golden Age of Jewish Prague could never have stood without each of these foundational pillars. But the cultural, financial, and spiritual pillars are not enough to maintain prosperity. The fourth pillar, which might be considered a "hidden pillar," stands outside the Jewish Community in the person of a king or ruler who does not foment anti-Semitism and who loosens the bridle on Jewish restrictions. In Prague, this "hidden pillar" was Emperor Rudolf II. The emperor entered Czech history and legend as an eccentric, hallucinating king who forever searched for the elixir of youth, everlasting life, and alchemical gold. Many of the legends concerning the Golden Age of Jewish Prague feature this benevolent but slightly insane emperor.

Why did Rudolf II tolerate the Jews? It is possible his eccentricity prompted him to it. Christian anti-Semitism saw the Jews as a sinister lot, practicing witchcraft and courting evil in an effort to subvert good in the universe. For an eccentric delving into the mysteries of life, it was quite possible to flip to the other side of this superstition. Certainly the Jews are evil, but might not their supernatural powers give them the secret I so desperately seek? Thus Rudolf II actually fetishized the ghetto as a mysterious place of wisdom. Without his tacit approval, the Golden Age could never have occurred.

Individual Graves: A Walking Tour

> Note: The following route begins at the **Pinchas Synagogue** entrance to the Jewish Cemetery. From the courtyard next to the Pinchas Synagogue, head straight up the steps in the back.

After you walk up the entrance steps to the cemetery, the first grave you'll come to is that of the historian and astronomer David Gans. His tombstone is roughly opposite the cemetery entrance.

David Gans (1541–1613)

David Gans's grave is marked by a simple marble stone right by the tourist walkway. If you look closely, you'll see depicted on the top of the tombstone a bird standing atop a Star of David. An image on a tombstone refers to the individual's name, occupation, or notable qualities. In this case, "David" is represented by the star, and "Gans"—German for "goose"—is represented by the bird. Another reason for the emblem is that Gans's last work, a book on astronomy written for his sons and printed in 1612, was called *Magen David*, or Shield of David. The star is one of the rare examples of a Star of David in this cemetery.

Astronomer, mathematician, historian, and geographer, David Gans was the first man who could be considered a true "Renaissance Jew," meaning he was the first Jew to be engaged in a wide variety of intellectual and cultural pursuits outside the study of Talmud. This is not to be confused with the secular Jews who charged upon the world scene in the nineteenth century. Whereas secular Jews departed from the observance of Jewish law, David Gans continued attending religious services even when he was theorizing about the moon's path around the earth. Although he considered Copernicus the greatest scholar of his time, he did not feel obliged either to accept or to rationalize Copernicus's heliocentric view of the universe, which ran counter to the Jewish idea of the earth as center of all matter. Indeed, even his geometry books he penned in the holy tongue of Hebrew, and on his tombstone he is immortalized, lest anyone should beg to differ, as *Ha'hasid*, or "the devout one."

Born in Germany, Gans studied in Cracow under the great Rabbi Moses Isserles (*see page 275*) who, according to tradition, advised Gans to learn mathematics and astronomy. Gans moved to Prague at the age of twenty-three, where he became such a well-known intellectual that he was seen browsing the heavens with the likes of imperial astronomers Tycho Brahe and Johannes Kepler. Gans is most famous today for his chronicle of Jewish and world history, *Tzemah David*, or "Offshoot of David" (another of the double entendres of which Jewish writers were so enamored). Published in 1592, the work is considered an invaluable chronicle of the Prague ghetto at the end of the sixteenth century, and has led many to consider Gans the first Hebrew historian of Central Europe.

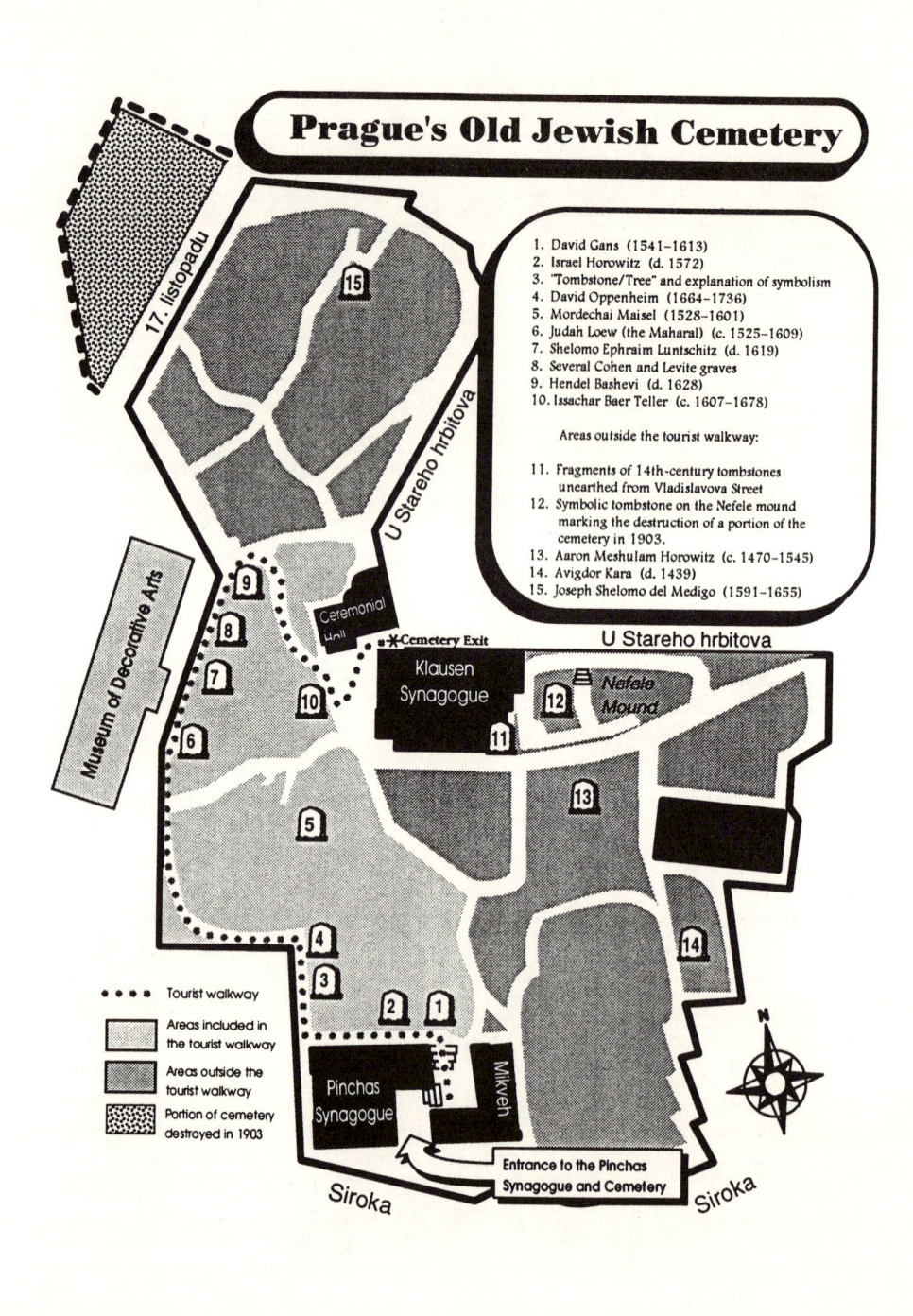

Prague's Old Jewish Cemetery

1. David Gans (1541–1613)
2. Israel Horowitz (d. 1572)
3. "Tombstone/Tree" and explanation of symbolism
4. David Oppenheim (1664–1736)
5. Mordechai Maisel (1528–1601)
6. Judah Loew (the Maharal) (c. 1525–1609)
7. Shelomo Ephraim Luntschitz (d. 1619)
8. Several Cohen and Levite graves
9. Hendel Bashevi (d. 1628)
10. Issachar Baer Teller (c. 1607–1678)

Areas outside the tourist walkway:

11. Fragments of 14th-century tombstones unearthed from Vladislavova Street
12. Symbolic tombstone on the Nefele mound marking the destruction of a portion of the cemetery in 1903.
13. Aaron Meshulam Horowitz (c. 1470–1545)
14. Avigdor Kara (d. 1439)
15. Joseph Shelomo del Medigo (1591–1655)

- - - - Tourist walkway
- Areas included in the tourist walkway
- Areas outside the tourist walkway
- Portion of cemetery destroyed in 1903

David Gans's Historic Omission

In David Gans's masterpiece, *Tzemah David*, the author mentions the single recorded instance of a meeting between Rabbi Loew and Emperor Rudolf II. According to Gans, the meeting was so secret and sacred that he was unable to reveal what transpired between the men. Ironically, Gans's glaring omission in the text engenders many of the most famous legends of Jewish Prague. If he couldn't reveal it, what could those two have been up to? Raising the dead? Sharing secrets of the Golem? Aligning the stars? Here is just one of many legends as to why the two men met:

Emperor Rudolf II was about to sign a decree expelling the Jews from Prague. The Maharal became aware of this and, in order to save his fellow Jews, waited until the Emperor was asleep in the Castle and then caused him to have a dream.

In the dream, Rudolf II was on a hunting expedition. After a long while of hiking through the woods, he grew very weary. Suddenly he came to a large lake and said, "Wouldn't that be refreshing!" Stripping off his clothes, the Emperor dove in. Later, when he came back to shore, he found his clothes had disappeared. He began walking until, exhausted and hungry, he arrived at a village. He knocked on the first door. The man inside chased him away as he would a scavenging hobo. "But I'm the Emperor!" exclaimed the naked Rudolf, to no avail. The same happened at the second door, then at the third, fourth, and so on. Finally, devoid of any remaining strength, he arrived at the final door. Inside was a man who invited the Emperor in, gave him food, bathed him, clothed him, cut his hair, even sheared his nails for him. The Emperor was so grateful, he said, "You will be rewarded justly for your kindness. Ask me for anything and it is yours." The man replied at once, "Rip up the proclamation expelling the Jews." Then the Emperor awoke. "Just a dream!" he sighed in relief. Then, turning to his bedside table, he gasped in horror. There, on a silver platter, lay his shorn hair and fingernails! The Emperor immediately sent for his couriers. "Who is the most important Jew in the ghetto?" he asked, terrified. "That would be Rabbi Loew, the Maharal," they said. "Bring him to me at once!" the Emperor demanded.

When Rabbi Loew arrived at the Castle, Rudolf II saw that the Maharal was identical to the man in his dream. It was during this meeting that Rudolf II agreed to spare the Jews of Prague, on the condition that the Rabbi would give the Emperor his blessing. Naturally, the Emperor did not want the public to hear of such a humbling experience. So David Gans was forbidden from revealing the background and contents of the royal encounter.

Originally, the tombstones in the Old Jewish Cemetery were made from fine sandstone. Then, from the sixteenth century onward, tombstones were often made from marble brought from a quarry in nearby Slivenec. Because of the harsh treatment of the elements, the sandstone today appears grey or black and the marble has changed from its original color of reddish-brown to a faint and sun-bleached pink.

There are two types of inscriptions on the tombstones. The oldest inscriptions are chiselled into the stone. This type of tombstone can be seen on graves to the right of the grave of David Gans. These engravings were replaced in the mid-sixteenth century with the embossed technique, in which the sculptor carved around each of the letters in the text to create a raised impression. Such a technique was considered more elaborate and was naturally more expensive to commission. It is ironic that over the course of the centuries, rain and snow slowly marred the text on many of the more elaborate tombstones, whereas the older, chiselled technique was better preserved from the elements. Religious Jews claim that the chiselled technique is more in keeping with Jewish tradition, which discourages the creation of embossed lettering. In fact, there is a kabbalistic teaching that raised letters on one's tombstone is actually a guarantee of being forgotten.

In the text on the stones, the deceased are remembered through their place in the Community, their employment, and their good deeds. Often, passages from the *Tanach* will be cited to refer to the individual's particular characteristics. This can be seen most exquisitely in the case of Israel Horowitz, whose grave lies about ten feet beyond David Gans's on the walkway.

Israel Horowitz (d. 1572)

Israel Horowitz was the oldest son of the eminent Aaron Meshulam Horowitz, the founder of the Pinchas Synagogue adjacent to Israel Horowitz's grave. (The grave of Aaron Meshulam Horowitz himself is outside the area of the current tourist walkway.) Israel Horowitz was granted the same royal privileges his father had received earlier, including the right to choose one of Prague's rabbis.

The text on his tombstone combines both the engraved and embossed techniques, and perhaps for this reason it is among the most readable tombstones in the cemetery. The first line of description, "My father, my father, the chariots of Israel," is from II Kings 2:12, when Elijah is carried to heaven on a flaming chariot.

There are many interlocking reasons for this passage on the tombstone. First, it poetically—and literally—tells of the ascent to heaven of the deceased. But the "my father" speaks specifically of Israel's father Aaron, one of the most prestigious personalities in the ghetto in the first half of the sixteenth century. By referring to Aaron throughout the text, the passages praise Israel for being his father's son, or a member of such a noble family in the ghetto. Finally, the passage makes a double entendre of the name "Israel." Throughout the tombstone, there are references to the "rock of Israel," the "people of Israel," the "generations of Israel," and the "house of Israel." Through this wordplay, the text cleverly refers to Israel Horowitz's devout nature, his important position in the Community, and the exalted status of his fellow Jews by repeated references to his name.

Walk up the path until you turn the corner. You will see many tombstones almost completely sunk into the earth. After you pass several tombstones, you'll come to a tree next to the path.

This site is not a tombstone but a tree. We point out this spot purely for the photo opportunity; it is a sight in the Old Jewish Cemetery that shouldn't be missed. The tree is actually growing around a number of tombstones. Look to the left of the tree: there is a tombstone partially inside the tree itself. At one point a tiny sapling grew adjacent to a grave, and over the course of the generations the tree grew into and around the tombstone until the tree finally overtook it—or perhaps the process was the reverse, with the tombstone growing into the tree. Judaism, it should be noted, has nothing against the concept of reincarnation (known as *gilgul*).

Directly to the left of the "tree-stone" is a recently reconstructed tombstone, and therefore a good spot to explain the general symbolism of the stones.

Just as synagogues in the Diaspora contain a great deal of symbolism from the Old Temple in Jerusalem, so do the tombstones in Jewish cemeteries. The significance is that when the Messiah comes, the dead will rise to life and return to Israel—in some accounts, through underground passages leading straight to Jerusalem—where they will partake in ceremonies at the rebuilt Third Temple. Thus the tombstones are a recollection of the earlier Temples as well as a barely concealed yearning for the revival of life in the Messianic Age.

On the tombstone, you can see two pillars that represent the two copper columns, designed by the coppersmith Hiram, that stood at the portico of the Great Hall of King Solomon's Temple. The one on the right is called "Jachin" and the one on the left "Boaz" (I Kings 7:13–22). The slender curled motifs refer to the trumpets blown by the *Cohanim* during Temple ceremonies. During the dedication of Solomon's Temple, 120 *Cohanim* blew trumpets at such a feverish pitch that they actually created a cloud that interfered with the service until some worshippers had to leave (II Chronicles 5:12–14). In the midst of Second Temple rites, as many as 120 trumpeters served as a backup orchestra for the Levite singers. Usually the trumpets on a tombstone are designed in symmetrical pairs; these refer to the two silver trumpets constructed by Moses that were displayed in the Temple. The Arch of Titus recalls the Romans removing from the Temple not only the Menorah, but the two silver trumpets as well. The tightly spiralling circular motifs on many tombstones refer not to trumpets but to the rams' horns, or *shofarim*, blown during Rosh Hashanah ceremonies in the Temple. You can find these on either side of the shell at the top of the tombstone. Finally, the shell itself alludes to the shell given by the Queen of Sheba to Solomon, which he installed in the Temple.

Keep walking along the path until you arrive the grave of David Oppenheim on the corner. Opposite his grave is a plaque bearing his name and years of life.

David Oppenheim (1664–1736)

Rabbi David Oppenheim was the first man to hold the modern office of chief rabbi of Bohemia.

In the late seventeenth century, with the increase in the rural population of Jews, the Bohemian rabbinate splintered into four chief rabbis: two presided over Prague and two presided over the rest of Bohemia. Everybody, it seemed, was a chief rabbi. It should be kept in mind that in the days of ghetto incarceration, the chief rabbi was not only the spiritual but in many ways the judicial, political, and financial director of the Community. As a result, the cloning of the chief rabbinate became an administrative nightmare that threatened to critically fragmentize Bohemian Jewry.

Out of the chaos emerged the figure of David Oppenheim. Oppenheim, born in Worms, was made chief rabbi of Prague in 1702 after serving as the chief rabbi of Moravia since 1689. In the first quarter of the eighteenth century he was able to unify the Bohemian Rabbinate. In 1713 and 1715 he assumed the Bohemian rabbinical posts, and in 1718 he scooped up the remaining Prague position. Thus, the multitude of chief rabbinates were assumed by the single Oppenheim, who became the effective chief rabbi of all Bohemia. Thirteen years after Oppenheim's death, the state finally abolished the system of "Lands rabbi" and made the chief rabbi of Prague the rabbi of all Bohemia as well.

But Rabbi Oppenheim's everlasting fame has little to do with the bureaucratic tangles of eighteenth-century Jewry. Perhaps in compensation for his own rather sparse output of writings, Oppenheim was an avid collector of Hebrew books. "Avid" is putting it rather mildly. Using the massive inheritance he had received from his uncle, the great Viennese financier Samuel Oppenheim (*see page 122*), David was able to feed his book habit to such a meticulous degree that at its height his collection numbered six thousand printed books and one thousand manuscripts. Meanwhile, he was forced into a religious dispute with the local Parson Franciscus Haselbauer. Fearing that the Jesuits would burn his library, Rabbi Oppenheim sent it for safekeeping to Hanover. In 1829, the entire collection was bought by Oxford University, and today it forms the core of Oxford's Bodleian Library. The library is one of the most priceless collections of Jewish books in the world.

Oddly enough, a similar course was taken by another Prague Jew, two centuries and three years after Oppenheim's death. When the Nazis occupied Prague in 1939, Max Brod smuggled out a suitcase filled with the bulk of Franz Kafka's manuscripts. After various adventures, these works were ultimately acquired by Oxford University's Bodleian Library. Today, most of Kafka's manuscripts, with the exception of *The Trial*, sit in the same library as the books of David Oppenheim. The similarities are uncanny: In both instances, Prague Jewish books were sneaked out of the country to protect them from imminent destruction. By a bizarre twist of fate, these same books converged in the same location in England. This is how Prague's latter-day sage has been united with his predecessor of two hundred years before.

It should be added that in the case of his own writing, Oppenheim shared another similarity with his literary descendent. His main work, a topographical dictionary of the Talmud, was left unfinished at his death.

Atop the tombstone of Rabbi Oppenheim is one of the rare images of a Shield of David in the cemetery, used in this case to represent his name. Also note the spiralling *shofars* depicted on the tombstone.

You can also see that Oppenheim's tombstone is among the largest in the cemetery. It was a custom to design these sarcophagus-like tombstones beginning in the early seventeenth century. This shift in gravestone style was a reflection of the relative prosperity the Jewish Community experienced during its Golden Age from 1570 to 1620. During this time the buildings, the streets, and even the tombstones of the ghetto were improved. It was then that marble began to replace sandstone gravestones and the text shifted from engraved to embossed relief. Perhaps the most noticeable change in the cemetery was the introduction of sarcophagi. Of course, the grave is not really a sarcophagus. In keeping with the biblical verse, "For dust you are and to dust you shall return" (Genesis 3:19), Jews are forbidden from being buried in anything but the earth itself. Thus the large tombstones do not contain the bodies but instead allow more space for elaborate text and decorative reliefs on their surfaces. In Hebrew they are called *ohelim*, or "tents," which symbolize the booth-like homes of ancient Israel. There are more than 20 *ohelim* placed atop the graves of wealthy benefactors, learned men, and prominent rabbis in the ghetto.

To the right of Oppenheim's grave is a tombstone with a wolf depicted on its top. This is the grave of **Ze'ev Auerbach** (d. 1632), another chief rabbi of Prague. *Ze'ev* is Hebrew for "wolf."

The Stones on the Tombstones

Tour guides in Prague often instruct their groups to leave notes or written wishes on the tombstones. This bizarre practice turns the cemetery into a field of paper in the summertime. Just like Emperor Rudolf II, it seems that many Gentile European tourists attribute the Jews—at least deceased Jews—with mysterious powers. A typical note, from the mid-1990s, read, "2 Rolls Royces and a Mercedes." It is almost certain that the paucity of Jews in Europe after the Holocaust has led to this fetishism of Jewish "powers." Although it is a Jewish custom to leave *kvittels*, or written requests, on the graves of righteous individuals, there is no custom to leave notes on random graves. The cemetery has also become a wishing well, with coins of every European currency often left on the tombstones.

It is a Jewish custom, though, to leave a small pebble on a gravestone as a sign that you have visited the grave. Most Jews, however, are unaware of the roots and reasons for this tradition. As with all folk traditions, the explanations are as varied as the experiences of the Jews in Exile. Following are a few interpretations—in some cases *bubbe meises*—that shed light on a quintessentially Jewish concept.

Life and Death

Jewish tradition does not support the custom of leaving flowers in a cemetery. Flowers are a symbol of life, and only God has the power to bring life into the realm of death. Therefore, in order to signify that we are not trying to mimic God's majesty inanimate rocks are preferred to plants or flowers.

Humility

A more specific reason to forbid flowers is that ostentation goes against the grain of Jewish tradition. The Talmud reports that during the Babylonian exile, King Nebuchadnezzar was informed that Jewish tombstones exceeded his own palaces in their majesty (see Babylonian Talmud, *Sanhedrin* 86b). As a result, the rabbis forbade floral decorations. In addition, lavish floral arrangements place a wedge between the rich and the poor, who cannot afford such grand displays on their tombstones.

History

When the Jews were wandering in the desert for forty years after being freed from slavery in Egypt, there was no soil for burial. As a result, they had to cover their dead with large rocks in order to protect the bodies from birds or animals of prey. (A variation is that soil did exist, but wild animals were able to dig up the dead after the burial.) Whenever they passed one of these piles of rocks (and they passed each one repeatedly, wandering as they were for two generations), they placed another rock atop the pile. This would remind people that the area was a holy burial ground, lest the pile of rocks should sink into the sand and disappear altogether.

Sentiment

A tombstone is almost always designed with perfect symmetry. When you place a pebble on one side of the tombstone, you take away from the balance. It is a personal way of saying that without your loved one, the world has lost its sense of harmony.

Spiritual

Rocks are said to be neutral in terms of spiritual properties. It is said that evil spirits descend on cemeteries at night in order to harass and bother the souls resting there. The pebble, because it is neutral, acts as an amulet atop the tombstone and repels the spirits from the person buried there.

Goodly Deeds

This is the kind of *mitzvah* that everybody can do. When you put a pebble on a tombstone, it is as if you symbolically take part in the burial itself. Burial is one of the highest *mitzvot*, considered *Hesed shel emmet*, or "Lovingkindness of truth," because one cannot expect the deceased to repay the good deed. Putting a pebble on the tombstone allows everybody to take part in this *mitzvah*. There is the added view that because the deceased can no longer perform *mitzvot*, you do this *mitzvah* for their benefit as well.

Humorous

It acts as a weight to prevent the person from coming back. (One of my tourists told me this; it's just a joke!)

Keep walking the path, following it as it turns right. Some meters after the path turns right, you will see a blocked-off path that cuts right into the graveyard. If you stand a few steps before the path and look straight into the cemetery you will see, almost all the way on the other side, a reddish-brown tombstone situated to the right of a sapling. Atop the tombstone is a hand-sized, nondescript pedestal. If you look carefully, you can see a plaque standing to the right of the tombstone, identifying it.

Mordechai Maisel (1528–1601)

Mordechai Maisel was the richest man in all of Prague at the end of the sixteenth century. It is not known how Maisel became so wealthy, but legends abound as to his financial acumen. In one legend, Emperor Rudolf II unknowingly gave the young Maisel his first coin. Maisel used this coin as the foundation of his business empire. It is true that Maisel became the banker of Rudolf II. Some consider him the first modern Court Jew; others consider him the first Jewish capitalist. There is a joke that Emperor Rudolf II, who poured so much energy into the alchemical sciences, found his true alchemist in the person of Mordechai Maisel, who could turn anything into gold. Both emperor and empress borrowed money from Maisel whenever they needed it.

Maisel was a legend even during his own lifetime for his philanthropy. A leading figure of the Golden Age of Prague Jewish history (*see page 101*), Maisel singlehandedly built up the entire ghetto. He built the High Synagogue, the Jewish Town Hall, the Maisel Synagogue, the original Klausen buildings, an expansion to the cemetery, a poorhouse, and a *mikveh*. People joked that he was throwing his money into the streets when he paved the entire ghetto in cobblestones. It is said that Maisel was so wealthy, he could spread sugar on his honey. He gave of his wealth to almost anybody who needed it. Widows and orphans relied on Maisel for subsistence. On Hanukkah he clothed all the poor of the ghetto. Every year he paid the dowries for two destitute girls chosen at random. He donated Torah scrolls to synagogues in Prague, Cracow, Posen, and Jerusalem. He even helped Christian charities and donated a great deal of money for the completion of a Prague church.

Maisel was so influential that in 1598 the emperor gave him the unique privilege to dispose freely of his wealth. For a Jew, this was a precious honor; European rulers considered Jews to be chattel of the royal treasury. Thus if a Jew had no heirs—Maisel had no children from either of his two marriages—his property would legally be "returned" to the king. But Maisel, the living legend, was different. On March 1, 1601, Maisel wrote out his will in the presence of no less an authority than Rabbi Judah Loew himself, leaving his enormous estate to various relatives including his two nephews. His funeral two weeks later was a day of ghetto-wide mourning. Emperor Rudolf II sent an emissary to the Jewish Cemetery to pay his royal respects. But while Maisel's grave was still fresh, Bohemian bailiffs knocked on his wife's door and demanded all his property. Emperor Rudolf II actually revoked his own decree regarding Maisel's will. Apparently the emperor, for all his benevolence to the Jews, couldn't live without Maisel's wealth in the royal treasury. A visitor passing by the ghetto that day would have been treated to an unforgettable sight, something like the spectacle of fifty clowns emerging from a tiny car in a circus: servants of His Majesty were seen removing from a ghetto home precious gems, silver objects, exquisite fabrics, and wheelbarrowful after wheelbarrowful of gold coins. The emperor even had one of the heirs tortured into revealing any hidden treasure. The total estate amounted to the mind-boggling sum of half a million guldens—a number roughly equivalent to the emperor's annual budget. Maisel's wife and nephews protested the decision, which amounted to grand theft, but they had no power against the Bohemian authorities.

There is a legend that before the emperor succeeded in removing all of Maisel's property, his wife hid a portion of it somewhere in the ghetto. There have been various mythic expeditions through the streets of the Jewish Town, in search of Maisel's hidden treasure. Would Frumet have stown the valuables in such an obvious place as the *ohel* atop her husband's grave? On his *ohel* it is written that the tomb was restored three times, including once after the expulsion of Jews from Prague in the eighteenth century. This would indicate, perhaps, that when Prague was free of Jews, even some Christians in the city ran to the cemetery, hoping to find a secret treasure atop a Jewish grave.

A final story has it that when the Jewish Town was destroyed at the turn of the century, the smoke that arose from the demolished buildings was the final embodiment of Maisel's wealth, vanishing forever.

Maisel's tombstone was the first *ohel* in the cemetery. Maisel, who himself purchased additional land for the cemetery, was so wealthy that he could easily have afforded a tombstone the size of the large white building you can see in the background. (It is the Klausen Synagogue, the original of which Maisel built himself.) But because Jewish law emphasizes humility in life as well as in death, Maisel's tomb remains within the limits of decency.

Continue on the path another 5 meters. Adjacent to the path is the most famous grave in the cemetery, that of Rabbi Judah Loew. It is identified on the wall opposite by a plaque bearing his full name: "Jehudah Liva ben Becalel."

Judah Loew—The "Maharal" (c. 1525–1609)

The grave of Rabbi Loew (the "Maharal") is by far the most visited site in the cemetery (*see Spotlight, page 102*). Jews from all over the world come to pay their respects at his grave, and Gentiles crowd around the tombstone as well, having heard of the rabbi's awesome powers of the spirit. Half the legends of Jewish Prague touch on Rabbi Loew somehow; the most famous is the story of the Golem (*see pages 34–43*).

The tombstone is topped by a stylized cluster of grapes, which repeat in more literal form on the lower part of the tombstone. Grapes are a symbol of life, fertility, and redemption, as well as a symbol of the tribe of Judah: "He washes his garment in wine, his robe in blood of grapes" (Genesis 49:11). There is also a lion depicted near the top of the tombstone. The tribe of Judah was symbolized by a lion while "Low" and "lev" mean "lion" in German and Czech, respectively. Rabbi Loew's wife, Pearl (d. 1609), is buried next to him. Whenever a tombstone is divided down the middle like this one is, the sides refer to husband and wife. In this case, Pearl Loew's inscription is on the right, Rabbi Loew's is on the left.

One more legend about Rabbi Loew: Originally, the entire tombstone was situated slightly to the left, more parallel with today's walkway. But before Rabbi Loew's grandson Samuel died in 1655, he wished to be buried next to his eminent grandfather. The rabbis didn't know what to do. Rabbi Loew's plot was congested with his family and students; there was simply no room right next to the great rabbi. And to raise the earth and bury over Rabbi Loew was simply out of the question.

All night, the *Chevrah Kaddishah*, or Jewish Burial Society, met in their offices to decide what to do. When the sun rose the next morning, they still had not found a solution. Dejected, they returned to the cemetery with a meterstick, hoping there might be some space, perhaps in the far corner, that they hadn't noticed before.

When they arrived, they were dumbfounded. Rabbi Loew's tombstone had moved, on its own accord, half a meter to the right. Apparently Rabbi Loew himself adjusted his position for his beloved grandson. Samuel was buried in the new space to the left of Rabbi Loew, where you can still see his angled tombstone today.

Continue up the path. You will soon see a grave decorated by a fish (it's recessed two or three rows). If you can read Hebrew and it's a sunny day out, you'll see the third line from the bottom reveals his name: Israel Karpeles. In reference to his name, the tombstone is adorned by a carp.

To the left of Karpeles is the grave of Rabbi Shelomo Ephraim Luntschitz. The site is marked on the opposite wall by a plaque.

Shelomo Ephraim Luntschitz (d. 1619)

Rabbi Luntschitz was asked to assist Rabbi Loew in 1604, when the latter became too infirm to lead the Prague rabbinate. Rabbi Luntschitz himself became the chief rabbi, but he remained in close contact with Rabbi Loew and was very much influenced by Rabbi Loew's ideas. For example, Rabbi Luntschitz supported Rabbi Loew's innovations in teaching as well as his critique against corruption in the Jewish Community.

Rabbi Luntschitz is also known as the *Klei Yakar*, or "Precious Vessel," after the title of his best-known work. *Klei Yakar* is a commentary on the Bible that is included in all annotated editions of the *Chumash*, or Hebrew Bible, to this day.

Farther down the path, you will see several graves decorated with two hands. These are graves of *Cohanim* (plural of *Cohen*), or priests. For purposes of worship in the Old Temple, Jews fell into three distinct groups: Cohen, Levite (Levi), and Israelite.

Back in the days of the Old Temple, the *Cohanim* used to perform the Priestly Benediction with their hands raised and joined in a shape resembling the Hebrew letter *shin*. *Shin* stands for *Shaddai*, one of the Divine Names for God. Even though the Temple in Jerusalem no longer exists, Jews who are patrilineally descended from priests are still considered *Cohanim*. On the High Holidays, they recite the Priestly Benediction as the last vestige of the service in the Old Temple. All the tombstones decorated by hands indicate *Cohanim* buried beneath.

It is possible, in fact, that this was once the Cohen section of the cemetery. *Cohanim* are forbidden from entering cemeteries, where *teumah*, or impurity, is said to lie. *Cohanim* must preserve their special spiritual cleanliness for when the Messiah comes and they resume their functions at the rebuilt Temple. For this reason, Jewish cemeteries throughout the world reserve special areas, often by the cemetery gate, where only *Cohanim* are buried. In this way, *Cohanim* are able to visit their loved ones without actually stepping foot inside the cemetery. It is possible that one gate to the cemetery once stood nearby. The neo-Renaissance Ceremonial Hall, for instance, was built only in the twentieth century. Centuries ago, there might have been a gate at that exact spot. At any rate, today you can find *Cohanim* spread throughout the cemetery. This is most likely because the area here became too congested, and the Jews had no choice but to bury *Cohanim* elsewhere.

The Vulcan High Priests

It is a little-known fact that the Vulcan hand symbol on *Star Trek* comes straight out of Jewish religious history.

Leonard Nimoy of *Star Trek* fame tells a story of attending High Holiday services at his synagogue when he was a child. During the ceremony of the Priestly Benediction, which recalls the ceremonies of the High Priests in the Old Temple, the *Cohanim* in the synagogue go to the *aron hakodesh*, drape *tallises* over their heads, and bless the congregation with outstretched arms. One isn't supposed to look at the *Cohanim* during this ceremony, but young Nimoy couldn't resist and took a quick peek at the shrouded men on the *bimah*.

That night, he was terrified that perhaps he had cursed himself by glimpsing the holy *Cohanim*. And yet he was mystified by the way they had spread their fingers, and began practicing it himself. After a couple of months, he became an expert.

Years later, when filming the *Star Trek* scene where the Vulcan Queen first appears, Nimoy suggested to the director the pose of the High Priests. The director, who had no idea what went on in Jerusalem's Old Temple, thought it was a nifty idea. Mr. Spock adopted the greeting himself, and the rest is interplanetary history. One can only guess that somewhere, in a dingy bar, sleazy characters are whispering, "Even the Vulcans are Jews!"

Some tombstones along the path are decorated by pitchers (look closely; the elements have weathered many images away). The pitchers can be found toward the top of the tombstones. These are symbols of Levites. In the Old Temple, Levites would wash the hands of the *Cohanim* before the latter would begin the Priestly Benediction. The pitchers of water indicate that Levites are buried here. Levites today are patrilineal descendants of the Levites of ancient Israel.

The long path makes a u-turn around the dazzling tombstone of Hendel Bashevi.

Hendel Bashevi (d. 1628)

The grave of the wealthy philanthropist Hendel Bashevi is the only large, *ohel*-style tombstone for a woman in the cemetery. Usually if women are buried in such elaborate tombstones, they are buried together with their husbands, as is the case of Pearl, wife of Rabbi Loew (*see page 112*). Otherwise, unmarried women are buried in more humble graves, usually out of financial constraints.

But finances were not a problem for Hendel Bashevi. Her husband, Jacob Bashevi (1580–1634), was the first Jew in the entire Hapsburg Empire to be given the title of nobility. It was in 1622 that Emperor Ferdinand II knighted Bashevi as "von Treuenberg." You can see his coat of arms decorated on both long sides of Hendel's tombstone. Interestingly, it is adorned by three stars, but they are not Stars of David.

Jacob Bashevi was a Court Jew whose privileges were enormous: He could trade and purchase property throughout the empire and he could go anywhere without the Jewish "Hat of Shame." As mayor of Jewish Town, Bashevi was able to enlarge the ghetto with new, desperately needed space. He added several public works to the ghetto, and built a lavish synagogue and three-story palace that were destroyed during the sanitation project at the turn of the twentieth century.

Bashevi was certainly one of the more colorful characters of seventeenth-century Jewry. In 1622, he became involved in a minting consortium that provided silver coins for much of the empire. In this he worked closely with the legendary general Albrecht Waldstein (1581–1634). Soon enough, the coins became worthless, and Emperor Ferdinand II, who had knighted Bashevi a decade earlier, threw him in prison in 1631. Bashevi escaped to Waldstein's estate, but died after Waldstein was assassinated in 1634. Bashevi is buried in Mlada Boleslav.

But his wife was clean of these intrigues. As the wife of a nobleman, she was permitted to move freely throughout Prague. She used her wealth and power to build philanthropic institutions not only in the ghetto, but in Christian Prague as well. In Jewish Prague, she became a legend for her generosity. She oversaw the creation of an orphanage and spearheaded social welfare programs for the poor. On her tombstone, the text describes her virtue at length, comparing her in one section to the biblical judge Deborah.

The lions on the tombstone, a repetition of the lions found on Bashevi's coat of arms, are a symbol of nobility as well as of the Bohemian lion. (Look on any Czech coin and you'll find the same two-tailed lion.) A three-dimensional image pushes the limits of the prohibition against graven images, but Hendel is safe: a two-tailed lion isn't really one of God's creatures, and therefore it is not a real animal depicted on the stone.

Over the years, many Czechs found it shocking that a woman should be buried with such high honor. A legend developed that this was secretly the grave of a Polish queen who, snubbed by the king, came to Prague where she wished to die in anonymity. That's why she came to the Jewish cemetery, a place where nobody would ever find her amid the Jewish tombstones. Some accounts have her converting to Judaism before she died.

Follow the path around the tombstones to the end. When you exit the path, instead of leaving the cemetery, go to the open space to the right. On the right side, a few graves in, you'll find a large tombstone decorated by a lion, and to its right a smaller tombstone decorated by a bear.

Issachar Baer Teller (c. 1607–1678)

The tombstone with a bear belongs to the remarkable Prague doctor Issachar Baer Teller. The bear, an image of his Yiddish middle name, is sometimes hard to see, depending on the sunlight. It is on all fours, in profile, and facing the left. In its grasp is a lancet, a symbol of the medical profession.

Dr. Teller is best known today for his work *Be'er Mayim Chayim* ("Wellspring of Living Water"). The *be'er* of the title, Hebrew for "well," is a play on Dr. Teller's name. The book offers a series of home remedies to various ailments, so that Jews in the ghetto would be able to administer first aid and the like without having to go to the hospital at every emergency. It is a vital document of the social life of the Jews in the seventeenth century. What's more, the book, written in Yiddish, offers evidence that as late as the seventeenth century, the Jews of Bohemia continued to speak that language.

To his left is his son, *Judah Loew Teller* (d. 1697), who followed his father's footsteps in the medical profession. Judah's tombstone is decorated by a lion, representing the tribe of Judah. Like the bear next door, the lion is holding a lancet.

In the open area in front of the white building, there is a small marble platform.

This platform, with its Baroque shape, was built in the seventeenth or eighteenth century. It was originally used as part a table for the *taharah*, or ritual cleansing of the body before the funeral. Later the platform was probably brought here, where it would hold the coffin during the rabbi's eulogy. The nearby grey Ceremonial Hall was also used for the funeral. After it was built in 1908, the rabbi stood from its balcony to deliver the eulogy in front of family and friends *(see page 116).*

Outside the Tourist Walkway

The oldest grave in the cemetery, that of Avigdor Kara (d. 1439), is located in an area that is off limits to visitors. However, his original tombstone can be seen in the Maisel Synagogue museum. Other graves that fall outside the current walkway include those of Aaron Meshulam Horowitz (c. 1470–1545), the builder of the Pinchas Synagogue, and the famed Renaissance polyglot scholar Joseph Shelomo del Medigo (1591–1655), who studied under Galileo himself.

On the other side of the white Klausen Synagogue, also off limits to visitors, there is what is called the *Nefele* mound.

THE NEFELE MOUND

Originally, this was the site of a hospital built by Mordechai Maisel in the late sixteenth century. A little over a decade after the hospital burned down in the fire of 1689, the area became the *Nefele* mound, used to bury miscarriages and very young babies, who are traditionally buried in more common graves. The word *Nefele* in old Hebrew can be used to connotate a miscarriage.

During the sanitation project at the turn of the century (*see page 50*), a part of the cemetery containing some two thousand tombstones was demolished to build the street today called 17. listopadu Street. Much of the grounds of the destroyed area were placed in the *Nefele* mound, and many of the tombstones were embedded in its wall. The large, *ohel*-style tombstone on the mound was put up by the *Chevrah Kaddishah*, or Jewish Burial Society, in 1903. It describes the destruction and movement of part of the cemetery and it is shocking for its seething invective. According to the inscription, the *Chevrah Kaddishah* was left in the dark during negotiations between the Jewish Community and the City of Prague. It refers to the negotiators "sitting secretly" and making "a verdict that could not be overturned." There was supposed to be a *beit midrash*, or study house, built on public property, perhaps as a means of compensating the religious Community, but apparently it was never built. Nearby, seven symbolic tombstones mark the area where the exhumed bones were placed.

THE CEREMONIAL HALL

Address: U stareho hrbitova, to the right of the cemetery exit

The building that adjoins today's cemetery exit seems to be the oldest structure in the quarter, older than the Altneuschul itself. But nothing is what it seems in Jewish Prague, where clocks run backwards and the "ghetto" is the newest part of town.

In fact, the Ceremonial Hall is the most recently built Jewish communal structure in Josefov. It was the only religious edifice built during the slum clearance at the turn of the twentieth century. As if to memorialize the past that was being razed in their midst, the Jews erected this Ceremonial Hall in Neo-Romanesque style in 1906–08. Intent on historical perfection, they even used the same building materials that had been used in medieval Prague.

It was to be the hall of the *Chevrah Kaddishah*, or Burial Society, which met for services just next door in the Klausen Synagogue. Above the doorway, the inscription reads, "*Chevrah Kaddishah Gomlei Chasidim*" (Holy Society for Deeds of Lovingkindness). Inside the Ceremonial Hall, there was a mortuary, a room for *taharah*, or ritual cleansing of the dead, and offices. The Hall stands on the site of an earlier mortuary that was demolished when the new structure was built. Of course, it would seem impractical to build a new mortuary on the grounds of a cemetery that had not been in use since 1787. Jewish funerals throughout the twentieth century took place in cemeteries far from the historic Jewish Quarter, mainly in the New Jewish Cemetery in Strasnice. But even though Jews were spread throughout Prague, Josefov continued to be regarded as the city's core of Jewish history and roots—especially the Old Jewish Cemetery, where some of the greatest personalities in Prague Jewish history were buried. For this reason, funerals would begin at the Ceremonial Hall and proceed on horse and buggy all the way to the New Olsany Cemetery, miles away from Josefov. At the beginning of the funeral, the rabbi would deliver his eulogy from the balcony of the Ceremonial Hall to the gathered mourners. The balcony, situated above the *lavabo* for washing hands, faces the cemetery and is best seen as you head out of the cemetery itself. It's worth seeing, since it contains a Hebrew passage from the Book of Ecclesiastes designed to solace the mourners:

> A good name is better than fragrant oil, and the day of death than the day of birth. It is better to go to a house of mourning than to a house of feasting; for that is the end of every man . . .
> (Ecclesiastes 7:1–2)

The opening idiom in the passage is often inscribed on Jewish tombstones. It is difficult to appreciate the pyramidal poetry of the verse in English; the Hebrew reads, "*Tov shem mi'shemen tov.*" It means that one's reputation, built by good deeds in this world, is more important than the finest riches. The passage goes on to extol the day of death over the day of birth, for a person's goodness can be evaluated only after he or she has died.

After less than two decades of use, the Ceremonial Hall was closed in the 1920s. The municipal authorities argued that it was unhygienic to carry the dead through the congested Old Town several times a week. Perhaps they also shuddered at the remnants of ghetto life visible in the newly built metropolis. At any rate, the Ceremonial Hall was rented to the Prague Jewish Museum as its main exhibition hall in 1926.

During World War II, the Ceremonial Hall became an exhibition grounds for the grotesque Central Jewish Museum dictated by the Nazis. At the same time that Prague's Jews were being deported to their deaths, the Ceremonial Hall of the *Chevrah Kaddishah* was turned into a "Museum of the Prague Ghetto." One section focused on the early history of Jews in Prague, complete with maps and photographs and even the "Hat of Shame" the Jews were forced to wear in medieval times. The next section unfolded the history of Prague synagogues, with their most priceless artifacts on display. The Maisel Synagogue was represented by Maisel's banner and the exquisite Renaissance *parochet* and Torah mantle that are now displayed in the Maisel Synagogue itself. The Pinchas Synagogue was symbolized by eighteenth- and nineteenth-century silver objects and by the cherished vestments of Shlomo Molcho, the false messiah of the sixteenth century. Finally, there was the room of rabbis, squeezed into the small space in front of the stairs and containing portraits and documents pertaining to Rabbi Judah Loew, Rabbi David Oppenheim, and Rabbi Shlomo Rapoport.

After the war, the Ceremonial Hall became part of the State Jewish Museum. In 1961, the first exhibition in Czechoslovakia that concerned the Holocaust was opened in the building. Later, the Ceremonial Hall housed the collection of drawings from the Terezin ghetto (a more recent exhibition of these drawings is today on display upstairs in the Pinchas Synagogue).

In April of 1998, a new exhibition opens in the Ceremonial Hall, focusing on the cemetery and the activities of the Prague *Chevrah Kaddishah*, or Burial Society. After a visit to the Old Jewish Cemetery, a glimpse into the life of the *Chevrah Kaddishah* will not only animate the former ghetto of Prague, but also reveal one of the most important aspects of Jewish life throughout the world. It should be added that Prague's most famous rabbi, Rabbi Judah Loew, helped to establish Prague's *Chevrah Kaddishah*, the first modern society of its kind, in 1564. It also happens that today, one of the great highlights of the Jewish Museum in Prague is its priceless collection of instruments, combs, mugs, and paintings from the *Chevrah Kaddishah*.

To be in a *Chevrah Kaddishah* was considered the greatest honor for a Jew, and only the most prestigious members of the Community served in it. It is deemed the highest form of charity to prepare a body for burial, because once a man has died he cannot repay the favor. As if to reinforce this idea, Burial Societies were forbidden from being for-profit enterprises. Thus service in the Society was referred to as *Hesed shel emett*, or "Lovingkindness of Truth."

As evidence of the high stature of members of the Society, you'll see on display the ornately illustrated pitchers and mugs used during the Society's annual banquets, traditionally held on the seventh day of the Hebrew month of Adar, the anniversary of Moses' death, after a fast observed to memorialize the dead. During these banquets, it was a custom for the leader of the Society to drink wine out of a jug and then pass it around the table to each member. The rite expressed both the fraternal bonds of the Society and their lofty stature in the Community. In Bohemia and Moravia, these beakers were unique. Whereas silver was the material of choice for Burial Society beakers throughout Europe, Jewish communities in Bohemia used Bohemian glass, and those in Moravia used painted porcelain. Often you will see women depicted behind the men on the glass. This is because women formed their own separate Society for the burial of women.

You'll also see the charity boxes used during funerals. The Hebrew expression is "Charity saves from death" (Proverbs 10:2). During a funeral the mourners would give charity to the Society for its operations. Not only would the Society clean and bury the dead, but, because it was the foremost philanthropic society in the Community, it would also care for the sick and poor of the ghetto. Other items on display include inscribed silver utensils used for cleansing the body—combs; picks to clean the fluids from nails, ears, and nose; and purifying water plates—and a ballot box for the election of members and officers of the Society, traditionally held during the annual banquet dinner.

The Chevrah Kaddishah *Paintings*

The series of paintings of the Burial Society are perhaps the most fascinating exhibit of the Jewish Museum of Prague, giving us an otherwise unknown glimpse into both the activities of the Prague Jewish Burial Society and the landscape of the ghetto before it was destroyed. Commissioned by the Society in 1780, they originally hung in the ceremonial hall used during the annual banquet. This is the only Jewish version of the guild paintings that were so common in the

Christian world. The paintings are precious today also because they can be seen as a storybook of the eighteenth-century ghetto. Unfortunately, the artist of the paintings is unknown.

The series begins with a doctor visiting a sick man. The doctor is Jonas Jeitteles (1735–1806), one of the most distinguished personalities of the ghetto. During the Enlightenment he was renowned for his campaign for inoculation against smallpox. He was so well-respected that Emperor Josef II met with him in 1784 and granted him authorization to treat Gentile patients. Note the glass vial in Dr. Jeitteles's hands. It looks like a bottle of medicine or an infusion of some sort. It is also possible that the vial was used as an amulet to ward off the *Malach Mavet*, or Angel of Death. The feather on top of the vial was placed under the patient's nose to gauge his breath. When he has died, the feather will stop its fluttering. You can see by the furnishings, particularly in the back room, that the sick man comes from a well-to-do family.

In the second picture, the man has already died. Note the *tzizit* placed on his body. The Society is reciting prayers in a night vigil around the body. Many people find it odd that there are only nine men surrounding the body, and not the traditional ten men *minyan* required for prayer. If you look on the left side of the painting, though, you can see the small boy being held away from the body by his mother. This boy is most likely the deceased man's son. He has already reached the age of 13, so he is included in the *minyan*, but because Jewish law forbids looking at the corpse of a relative (hence no tradition of an open wake in Jewish funerals) the boy cannot stand in close proximity to his father's body. The rooms in the first and second pictures are slightly different, but the general shapes—perhaps a generic stock of the artist—are identical. Take a close look at the back room in the first and second pictures. You'll see that the mirror in the first painting has been replaced by a chandelier in the second. It is probable that the artist was instructed not to paint a mirror in the second room. The depiction of mirrors, far from uncommon in paintings of interiors, was inappropriate because in a Jewish house of mourning all the mirrors are covered or removed.

The third painting features the Burial Society taking custody of the dead man and preparing to bring the body to the hall of the Society for ritual cleansing.

In the fourth painting you can see the sewing of the shroud. Because of the biblical verse "For dust you are and to dust you shall return" (Genesis 3:19), it was the custom to bury only in a shroud, in order to have as little impediment as possible for the return to the soil. Eventually, European authorities became convinced that the bodies were somehow contaminating the water supply, and so the Jews were forced to begin using pine cabinets in burial. In the State of Israel today, though, Jews are once again buried according to the custom of a simple shroud. The only exception to this rule is in the case of soldiers, who are buried more ceremoniously in coffins.

The fifth picture is perhaps the most exciting in terms of its glimpse into the internal life of the Jewish Community. Here we can see the members of the Burial Society, dressed in black, actually cleansing the corpse with the utensils of the Burial Society displayed here in the Ceremonial Hall. The body has already been rinsed in water, and the man in the middle of the picture is drying it. The two men at the front of the body are cleaning the ears with a pick and combing the hair with an egg and vinegar solution. Note that the double-edged comb is dangling from the fingers of the elderly man. Three holes were often punched into these combs, and small chains ran from the holes to a ring worn by the person cleansing the body. In this way he could dangle the comb from his hand while using another utensil. On the right side of the painting, members are reciting psalms. Note the *tallit* (prayer shawl) held by the man outside the door. It is the *tallit* of the deceased man; when he is buried, it will be placed on top of his shroud.

The subsequent pictures depict the process of carrying the body from the house to the grave, including the collection of charity, the digging of the grave, the entrance into the cemetery, the recitation of the rabbi's eulogy, and the lowering of the body into the earth. Note that the faces of these people are not generically painted. Each one represents an individual in the Society, and each repeats itself throughout the series. For instance, the man holding the charity tin is identical in each picture. The faces are based on the artist's earlier paintings of individual members of the society. (It is unclear at this writing if these earlier, individual portraits will be on display as well. If not, a couple will be on display in the Klausen Synagogue, a couple in the Maisel Synagogue.) Thus we can see the way prestigious Jews looked and dressed at the end of the eighteenth century. In the painting of the mourners, you can see the same child as was depicted in the *second* painting, supporting the theory that he is the deceased man's son.

In the next-to-last painting in the cemetery cycle, there is depicted the custom of washing one's hands upon leaving a cemetery. Although widespread tradition says that the hands should not be dried, you can see two of the members hunching over towels. The Reform movement was not to begin for several decades, but perhaps these two were pioneers of change.

The final painting in the series is a group portrait of members of the Burial Society. You can see by their proud stances; their distinguished costumes including hats, wigs, and frock coats; and Napoleonic gestures that they really are the cream of the Jewish crop. The hands inside the coats actually show that the individual belonged to a certain Jewish organization, such as B'nai B'rith. How the fingers were concealed or revealed, as well as the rings on the fingers, were signs of particular club members.

An additional four paintings were commissioned later, around 1830, to accompany the original fifteen pictures. In the depiction of the Burial Society banquet, you can see again how distinguished were the members of the Society. The banquet fittingly takes place on the anniversary of Moses' death. Note the rabbi drinking out of the communal beaker before passing it around to the others. The banqueters may appear tipsy; that's because the Burial Society underwent a fast before every annual dinner in order to atone for mistakes made during the previous year. Above the scene of revelry are the fifteen pictures from the eighteenth century, adorning the Ceremonial Hall of the Society.

Based on the picture of prayers at the grave of Rabbi Loew, one might wonder if Jews were so short a mere one hundred and fifty years ago. But if you look at the tombstone, you'll see thirteen lines of text where today there are roughly seven lines. When we stand at the tombstone today, our heads are naturally higher above it. The painting is excellent documentary evidence for the sinking of the tombstones. In only one hundred and fifty years, six lines of text have disappeared into the earth—more: the snow in the painting conceals even more lines on the tombstone.

THE KLAUSEN SYNAGOGUE

Address: U stareho hrbitova. The Klausen Synagogue is the white building next to the exit of the Old Jewish Cemetery.

Mordechai Maisel, the tireless benefactor of Prague's Jewish Town, purchased various plots of land on the outskirts of the ghetto in 1564. He used some of these plots for a much-needed expansion of the Old Jewish Cemetery. On the other plots he built a Jewish hospital and, on the site of today's Klausen Synagogue, three additional buildings. They were built to honor Emperor Maximilian II's visit to the Jewish Town in 1573. One of the buildings housed a *mikveh*, another a *yeshivah*, and the third a small synagogue. In German, *klaus* refers to a small building; these three structures were collectively known by the diminutive *klausen*.

The *klausen* buildings, later destroyed in the "flood of fire" of 1689, are important to us today because this was where the great Rabbi Judah Loew, the Maharal, taught in *yeshivah*. Mordechai Maisel first invited Rabbi Loew to Prague in 1573, after the latter had already served in Mikulov as Chief Rabbi of Moravia for twenty years. Rabbi Loew was not yet the Chief Rabbi of Prague, and so he could not officiate in the Altneuschul down the street. But because Maisel revered the wisdom of Rabbi Loew, he suggested to his friend that he teach in the new *klausen yeshivah*.

This *yeshivah* soon became the talk of the Jewish world. Here was a "rabbi without portfolio" who had given up a vaunted position in Moravia in order to teach students for free—and students studying in a *yeshivah* that had no authority to ordain them as rabbis. Everything was done purely for the joy of learning. Obviously, there was something unique about Rabbi Loew's *yeshivah* that made it the most popular place of study in all Bohemia, attracting such star pupils as David Gans *(see page 103)* and Yomtov Lippman Heller *(see page 334)*.

In the *klausen yeshivah*, Rabbi Loew pioneered the concept of studying Torah for its own sake. He used the *yeshivah* as a laboratory for new teaching methods that he himself had developed. For example, Rabbi Loew abolished the hair-splitting instructional method known as *pilpul*, in which dialectical sophistry was extolled at the expense of the ethics behind the arguments. Rabbi Loew also insisted that the complex books of the *Gemarah* not be opened until the Bible itself was understood. These ideas were unheard of at the time, particularly in Prague, which had only recently become a bastion of the *pilpul* method. The *klausen yeshivah* soon became the most radical Jewish school in Prague.

But it wasn't only *pilpul* that Rabbi Loew laid waste in his *yeshivah*. He used the *klaus* as a podium to condemn what he perceived as the corruption, selfishness, and immorality of the lay leaders of the Prague Jewish Community. As Rabbi Loew wrote, and presumably preached in the *klaus*, "It is indeed more difficult to bear [the Community leaders'] yoke than the yoke of the Gentiles. For when they sense that there be one who does not respect them and does not want to recognize their authority, they seek to subdue and oppress and persecute him with every kind of persecution" (quoted in Ben Zion Bokser, *The*

Maharal: The Mystical Philosophy of Rabbi Judah Loew of Prague). Officials from the Jewish Town Hall watched in horror as their foibles were exposed in the *klaus*. Meanwhile, down the street in the Altneuschul, the conformist Chief Rabbi Isaac Melling was unable to attract the devoted following that surrounded Rabbi Loew. Since the Altneuschul was founded, this was the first time another synagogue had gained ascendence in the popular imagination. And it was only an unassuming *klausen*! Needless to say, when Rabbi Loew was finally permitted into the Altneuschul for a "sample sermon" in 1584, the lay leaders of the Jewish Community were too frightened to elect him as Chief Rabbi. Only after waiting fourteen years more, and serving as Chief Rabbi of Poland, was Rabbi Loew elected Chief Rabbi of Prague.

The original *klausen* on this site are important to us for another reason. In Yiddish slang, *klaus* refers to a synagogue used by a small segment of the Jewish Community. For instance, the Society for Visiting the Sick would pray in their own *klaus*. In the case of the *klaus* in Prague, there is reason to believe it served the functions of the Prague *Chevrah Kaddishah*, or Jewish Burial Society.

Why the Burial Society? There are three reasons. First, Mordechai Maisel bought the land for the *klausen* in 1564, the same year he was instrumental in founding the Prague *Chevrah Kaddishah*. Second, the two men who supported Maisel when he built the *klausen*, Rabbi Loew and Rabbi Eliezer Ashkenazi, were the same men who built the *Chevrah Kaddishah* that year. Finally, when the new Klausen Synagogue was built in the 1690s, it was known as *the* synagogue of the *Chevrah Kaddishah*. This is all the more important when we consider that the *Chevrah Kaddishah* in Prague has gained worldwide fame as the first modern organization of its type. So the original *klausen* here were unique for two reasons: This was the spot where Rabbi Loew reinvented Jewish learning, and this was the spot where Prague reorganized the rules for burying the dead.

The *klausen* buildings served their historic function in the Jewish Town until June 21, 1689. On that day, a terrible "flood of fire" ripped through the ghetto, tearing down 318 homes and almost all the synagogues. All three *klausen* buildings burned to the ground. During the reconstruction that followed, the current Klausen Synagogue was built. It was named Klausen because it stood on the exact spot of the three previous buildings. As mentioned, this new synagogue was used as the seat of the Prague *Chevrah Kaddishah*.

Finished in 1694, the Klausen Synagogue was second in importance only to the Altneuschul. At the time, it was the largest synagogue in Prague. Wedged as it is into the Old Jewish Cemetery, the synagogue is unique in that almost all its windows look out on gravestones. In 1696, the famed Viennese merchant Samuel Oppenheim financed the construction of the *aron hakodesh* in the Klausen Synagogue. Built in three parts in the style of Early Baroque, the *aron hakodesh* is considered by many to be the highlight of the synagogue.

The inscription on the *aron hakodesh* contains verses recited during the Torah reading ceremony on Shabbat. The highest panel reads, "When the Ark was to set out, Moses would say: 'Advance, O Lord! May Your enemies be scattered, and may Your foes flee before

You! For instruction shall come forth from Zion, the word of the Lord from Jerusalem'" (Numbers 10:35 and Isaiah 2:3). The middle panel reads, "Moses charged us with the Teaching as the heritage of the congregation of Jacob" (Deuteronomy 33:4). The last inscription, above the opening for the Torah, refers to the generosity of "Our leader, ruler and teacher Samuel Oppenheim."

Originally, the *bimah* stood in the center, surrounded by men's pews. Women sat in galleries on the northern and western sides before the balconies were built. In 1883–84, the synagogue was reconstructed: Its western side was extended, the western women's gallery was raised, and the balcony was added to the northern and western sides. A new facade was added to the building as well. Around this time, the *bimah* was moved to the front as part of the changes introduced by the Reform movement in Judaism. Another telltale sign that this became a Reform synagogue is God's name spelled out in the window high above the *aron hakodesh*. Orthodox Jews prohibit the placement of God's name in any vulnerable location, such as glass.

Of all the Baroque synagogues built in the seventeenth century, the Klausen Synagogue was the only one spared during the slum clearance at the turn of the twentieth century.

Above the entranceway there is the common synagogal inscription: "This is the gateway to God; righteous people enter here."

In 1943, the Klausen Synagogue entered a macabre era as the centerpiece exhibition of the Nazi Museum of an Extinct Race. The exhibition was titled "Jewish Life from the Cradle to the Grave," a title whose irony was not lost on the occupying Germans, who were busy orchestrating deportations of the Jews to their deaths. It was a top secret exhibit, opened only to SS personnel, and intended as a prototype of a planned permanent exhibition. As such, the Klausen Synagogue became a battleground on which the German directors and Jewish curators clashed over their conceptions of Jewish life.

The Germans wanted the exhibition to focus on what they considered to be the obscenity of the Jews. Borrowing from the Christian conception of the Jew as vampire, the Nazis sought to portray such Jewish rituals as circumcision and kosher slaughter as barbaric bloodletting.

The Jewish curators, on the other hand, had a different idea. They used the exhibition to portray Judaism in all its humanism and richness. In this way, they would subvert not only Nazi designs for the museum, but Nazi theology against the Jews.

Thus the Baroque charity box in the vestibule of the synagogue was supplemented by other charity boxes. Their inscriptions spelled out the Hebrew Proverb 21:14: "A gift in secret subdues anger." The inscription alludes to the Jewish teaching that acts of loving-kindness should be performed for their own sake, and not with the expectation of reward. Inside the synagogue, the first exhibit depicted birth and circumcision. It was decorated with joyous folk art and draperies, including swaddling cloths used during the child's circumcision, *bar mitzvah*, and wedding. Wooden objects, such as a nineteenth-century cradle and the traditional "Chair of Elijah" used during circumcisions, were added to give the exhibit immediacy and life. The scene focused on family love; there was not a single reference to barbaric bloodletting, as the Germans had intended. The next exhibit, focusing on marriage, was equally festive. *Kettubot*, or marriage contracts, were displayed next to *chupot*, or marriage canopies, along with intricate wedding veils and rings that had recently been delivered to the Jewish Museum from throughout Bohemia and Moravia. Other booths focused on holidays of the Jewish calendar: Shabbat, Rosh Hashanah, Yom Kippur, Passover, Shavuot, Purim, Sukkot, and Chanukkah. Again, these exhibits focused on communal celebration. There were also clearly subversive aspects: In the case of Passover and Purim, the exhibits were centered around the deliverance of the Jews from earlier genocide, first from the hands of Pharaoh and then from Haman.

The secret exhibition was opened in March 1943, exclusively for SS personnel. Around the holiday of Passover, *Sturmbannfuhrer* Hans Gunther paid the Museum a visit. When he saw the humanistic spin the curators had achieved, he was infuriated. The Germans ordered all Hebrew passages translated into German. They ordered that mannequins of Jews be added to the exhibition. They insisted that the section on *kashrut*, or Jewish dietary laws, be supplemented by a vulgar demonstration of kosher slaughtering. They made it clear that they would not tolerate any museum exhibit that portrayed Jewish customs in a positive light.

It is ironic that as recently as 1992 the State Jewish Museum unveiled an exhibition in the Klausen Synagogue having the exact same focus as the Nazi exhibition. It could even be argued that the exhibition in 1943 was more respectful of Jewish ritual and practice than the one in 1992. Unlike the exhibition planned by Jewish curators in 1943, in 1992 all the objects were either sanitized behind glass or otherwise removed from their real contexts. One might think the objects were wrestled from the grip of Icelandic Man. The explanations, too, often reeked of atavism, of the implied assumption that this was not a museum of continuity but a museum of the past. The overall effect of the exhibit was to inspire fascination in an ancient and dead civilization.

It is with this museum history in mind that we should look at the current exhibition. The second synagogue to be restored after the Prague Jewish Museum was restituted to the Jewish Community in 1994, the Klausen Synagogue opened a new permanent exhibition in April 1996. It is somewhat eerie that the focus is, once again, "Jewish Traditions and Customs." However, the current one is a breath of fresh air compared to past exhibitions in this synagogue. True, all the items are placed behind glass, some objects are thrown together randomly, and there are still no Hebrew explanations at this writing. But the explanations are generally well done, especially for the majority of tourists who know little about Jewish history and religion.

The exhibition offers only a tiny glimpse at the colossal treasures of the Prague Jewish Museum. Highlights include a small box-calendar for counting the *omer* (between the holidays of Passover and Shavuot); a Viennese seder plate from the year 1900 that gained fame when it was duplicated and sold as souvenirs during the 1980s' "Precious Legacy" exhibition in North America; a funky charity box with an extended hand to appeal to children; a *haggadah* translated into Czech during the nineteenth-century Czech-Jewish movement;

and one of the earliest examples of the world famous Prague Hebrew printing press: the illustrated Book of Hymns from the year 1514.

In the former women's gallery, there are preparations for additional exhibits of the "life cycle." Included here will be a unique double-seated chair used during circumcision (*see page 73*) and a collection of priceless swaddling cloths. On each cloth is written in Hebrew, "He will grow up to Torah, *chupah*, and good deeds." These cloths were woven for baby boys, who would be wrapped in them during their circumcisions. Thirteen years later, during the boy's *bar mitzvah* ceremony ("Torah" in the inscription), the cloth would be tied around the Torah. During his marriage, the cloth would be tied into the *chupah*, or wedding canopy. Each cloth bears its own unique style, complete with interwoven objects symbolizing the boy's name, hobby, or character. The swaddling cloths are among the most exquisite objects in the Museum precisely because they are a testament to the cycle of life. The Museum possesses hundreds of such cloths, each with its own folk style.

During restoration work on the synagogue in 1996, some original paving stones were found around the area of the original *bimah*. These are preserved beneath glass windows on the floor in front of the central display.

THE MAISEL SYNAGOGUE

Address: Maiselova Street 10

> The synagogue is slightly withdrawn so that, undisturbed, it can dream in the most hallowed serenity a charming vision of its mighty benefactor, and plunge into memories of ancient and awesome events that wildly descended, ever so often, on its noble, fair crown . . .
> —Czech historian and legendmeister V. V. Tomek
> in his *Prazske Zidovske Povesti a Legendy* in 1932

If Mordechai Maisel is the legendary wonder-merchant and mayor of the Golden Age of Prague Jewish history, then the Maisel Synagogue is his most opulent legacy. "It was so magnificent that there was no example of its grandeur in all the Diaspora of Israel," wrote Maisel's contemporary, David Gans (David Gans, *Tzemach David*). The synagogue—originally one-third longer than its present size—was widely considered a symbol of Jewish prosperity in Prague.

According to tradition, the Maisel Synagogue was the only self-indulgence that its namesake permitted himself. Decades earlier, he had built the High Synagogue, the Jewish Town Hall, a school, a *mikveh*, and a poorhouse for the Jewish Community; he had acquired extra land for the Old Jewish Cemetery; he had had cobblestones placed in the ghetto. All of his prior projects had been for public benefit. Finally, at the age of 62, the childless Mordechai Maisel felt it was time to build a synagogue for himself and his family. In 1590, a foundation stone was planted in what was then the southern reaches of the ghetto. Rabbi Jacob Segre, an Italian contemporary of Maisel's, composed a poem for the occasion, which was placed on the foundation stone:

> . . . Thus the Lord's temple grows from the noble hands of Mordechai Maisel,
> This is his shield, his token of redemption,
> Of his eternal memory pledge and peace onto the soul,
> A song in praise of the Almighty,
> Played on the joyful harp and the enchanted lyre. . . ."
>
> (excerpted in Hana Volavkova, *A Story of the Jewish Museum in Prague*)

Emperor Rudolf II made an exception to the ban on private synagogues and granted Maisel a building permit in 1591, a year after construction had begun. Maisel chose one of the few Jewish architects of his time, Judah Tsoref de Herz, to design the synagogue. Afterwards, de Herz continued working in the ghetto and later redesigned the Pinchas Synagogue. In 1592, Maisel's building was complete. Like everything else connected to the Maisel Synagogue, its year of construction is surrounded by joy: The Hebrew year, 5353, is numerically equivalent to the Hebrew word *simchah*, meaning "happiness." For this reason, the synagogue was opened on the holiday of Simchat Torah, "Rejoicing over the Torah." According to one account, a poem was inscribed on the interior, but much of it was destroyed in the fire of 1689. The surviving parts allegedly spoke of the philanthropy of Maisel and his wife, ending with the line, "May this synagogue never be destroyed!"

All told, the Maisel Synagogue cost ten thousand *thalers* to build. As a symbol of Mordechai Maisel's stature in Prague, his synagogue was entitled to certain privileges. First, it was forever exempted from any kind of taxation. Secondly, no police officers were permitted to enter the building. Finally, Emperor Rudolf II gave Maisel the privilege, on the opening of his synagogue, to construct his own banner similar to the one in the Altneuschul. A painted image of the banner can be seen in the vestibule to the left of the *aron hakodesh*. The pictured men are not running around a maypole, but lifting the banner by its six poles. Mordechai Maisel and his wife, Frumet, also had a lavish *parochet* and Torah mantel prepared for the synagogue's opening in 1592. These priceless textiles, in which hundreds of pearls and several garnets are woven into Hebrew letters, are on display to the left of the *aron hakodesh* in the synagogue.

Originally, the Maisel Synagogue boasted twenty pillars. In the "flood of fire" that ravaged the ghetto in 1689, the Maisel Synagogue was mostly destroyed. When the damage was assessed, all that remained standing were the synagogue's outer walls and the twenty charred pillars. Because of cost concerns in building an entirely new vault, these twenty were reduced to fourteen when the synagogue was restored in the 1690s, shortening the length of the synagogue by one-third. Today it is difficult to imagine that when it was built, the Maisel Synagogue was the most capacious synagogue in the ghetto. During the reconstruction, the women's sections that had stood on either side of the main nave were rebuilt and supplemented by side galleries.

The most fundamental change in the Maisel Synagogue's appearance occurred from 1892 to 1905, during the urban renewal of the ghetto. Originally, the entrance to the Maisel Synagogue faced the east. One entered the synagogue by one of the side vestibules beneath the balconies. When the ghetto was destroyed, the street named after Mordechai Maisel was removed to make room for the new buildings of Parizska Street and a new Maiselova Street was built one block west of the original. As a result, the entrance to the synagogue was effectively flipped over from the eastern to the western side. To spruce up the synagogue's new front, a neo-Gothic facade was built, together with a vestibule through which you enter the synagogue today.

The neo-Gothic theme continued on interior furnishings and design. False ribs were added to the ceiling, the *aron hakodesh* was rebuilt, and tripartite windows were added throughout. You can still see the *kapporet* above the *aron hakodesh*, incorporated in neo-Gothic style. Representing the *kapporet* that covered the Ark of the Covenant in the Old Temple in Jerusalem, this *kapporet* features various images of sacrifices in the Temple: from left to right, there is the table containing the "Bread of Display," the copper laver of water, the twelve-stoned breastplate of the High Priest, the altar for the burnt offering, and the menorah.

The western gallery was also added during these renovations. The neo-Gothic elements cloak the erstwhile Renaissance edifice almost completely. However, you can see traces of its former design in the side vestibules and women's galleries, which hark back to the 1690s reconstruction. As for the original, eastern facade of the synagogue, read on for a secret, contemporary passageway into the depths of Prague's Jewish past.

By this time, the synagogue had already been used for some decades by Prague's Reform Jews. The *bimah* was moved to the front of the synagogue in the nineteenth century. (Today's central *bimah* was built in 1995 for display purposes.) There are two other telling signs that this was a Reform synagogue in the mid-nineteenth century. First, in the window high above the *aron hakodesh*, you'll find the *shem hamefurash*, or Holy Name of God. Orthodox Jews would never place the unpronounceable Name in a place where it could be destroyed. Secondly, in the Ten Commandments that adorn the facade of the synagogue, the numbers are written not in Hebrew letters beginning on the right-hand tablet, but in Roman numerals beginning on the left side. This acculturation to non-Hebrew languages is another sign of nineteenth-century Reform.

The organ is another matter entirely. Attached to the gallery to the left of the *aron hakodesh*, the balcony that once held the organ appears to be the most characteristically Reform element in the synagogue. However, professors have pointed out that the Maisel Synagogue contained this organ as early as the eighteenth century, long before the Reform movement spread about. This would seem to contradict the common association of the organ with religious reform. Initially, however, an organ was not considered unacceptable in the synagogue, as long as it was not played on Shabbat. Engravings and illuminations throughout the centuries have depicted Jews at prayer with organs. Some scholars believe that the Altneuschul itself once contained an organ. In the nineteenth century, however, Orthodox rabbis wished to distance themselves as far as possible from the Reform movement. As a result, they forbade any use of the organ in the synagogue.

⋘⋙

The Maisel Synagogue became a warehouse during the Nazi occupation. It was intended that it would be part of the Museum of an Extinct Race (*see page 53*), but the war ended before such plans were executed.

In 1965, the State Jewish Museum in Prague opened a permanent exhibit in the Maisel Synagogue to display the Museum's silver objects. Dozens of Torah crowns, spice boxes,

and candelabras were displayed in makeshift glass booths. There was little explanation. Dust collected through the holes in the booths. It looked more like a warehouse than a museum, and it was difficult to imagine that the objects were once used in the context of everyday Jewish life. The display of *yadayim*, shaped like miniature arms and used to follow the text of the Torah, became a symbol of Nazi intentions and communist insensitivity toward the Jews. In the Maisel Synagogue, the *yadayim* were arranged side by side, hanging pointed-down from racks. The overwhelming impression was of carcasses in a butcher's shop. In a way this was fitting, for each pointer represented an entire region of Jews annihilated during the Holocaust. But the manner in which they hung—sterile, rigid, lacking any contextual explanation—seemed to be the exact way the Nazis would have organized their museum.

The Maisel Synagogue was the first synagogue restored after the Jewish Museum in Prague was returned to the Jews in October 1994. The first permanent exhibit of the newly restituted museum was opened here in May 1995.

At long last, the permanent exhibition in the Maisel Synagogue was executed with finesse. The Prague Jewish Museum has come under fire in recent years for an exponential increase in ticket prices, but the permanent exhibition here seems worth it. New cabinets have been installed, the explanations are thorough and accurate, and the building feels like a synagogue, not a warehouse. The only thing missing today are Hebrew explanations—not a small mistake considering that the Nazis had abolished all Hebrew in their exhibits and ordered everything translated into German.

The permanent exhibition features Part I of "The History of the Jews in Bohemia and Moravia." It chronicles the history of Czech Jews from their origins in the tenth century until the brink of Emancipation in the late eighteenth century. Part II of the exhibition is situated in the Spanish Synagogue.

Highlights of the exhibition include the original tombstone of Avigdor Kara, whose 1439 grave is the oldest in the Old Jewish Cemetery. Because of deterioration, a replica tombstone was placed over his grave in 1981; it is outside the current cemetery walkway, however. You'll also find one of the last remaining relics from the Zigeuner Synagogue: a piece of the *bimah* grillwork. The Zigeuner Synagogue was destroyed during the slum clearance almost immediately after Franz Kafka celebrated his *bar mitzvah* there. Nearby is a replica of the flag once used by Shlomo Molcho, the famous false messiah of the sixteenth century. Molcho's banner and robe were once proudly displayed in the Pinchas Synagogue by the kabbalistically inclined Horowitz magnates. To the left of the *aron hakodesh* are displayed the *parochet* and Torah mantle donated by Maisel and his wife to the synagogue. These, along with the *parochet* to the right of the *aron hakodesh*, which was donated to the Altneuschul in 1592, are among the oldest and most precious items owned by the Prague Jewish Museum. Also on display are manuscripts by David Gans, a handwritten eulogy by Ezekiel Landau, a replica of the yellow "Hat of Shame" the Jews were forced to wear in Prague, a *kiddush* cup purportedly owned by Rabbi Judah Loew, and a rather shocking depiction of Josef II—the famed "Emancipator" of the Jews—inside a Hanukkah menorah. Evidently, Jews were so heady with Josef II's reforms that they abrogated the usual prohibition against graven images.

was built one block west of the original. As a result, the entrance to the synagogue was effectively flipped over from the eastern to the western side. To spruce up the synagogue's new front, a neo-Gothic facade was built, together with a vestibule through which you enter the synagogue today.

The neo-Gothic theme continued on interior furnishings and design. False ribs were added to the ceiling, the *aron hakodesh* was rebuilt, and tripartite windows were added throughout. You can still see the *kapporet* above the *aron hakodesh*, incorporated in neo-Gothic style. Representing the *kapporet* that covered the Ark of the Covenant in the Old Temple in Jerusalem, this *kapporet* features various images of sacrifices in the Temple: from left to right, there is the table containing the "Bread of Display," the copper laver of water, the twelve-stoned breastplate of the High Priest, the altar for the burnt offering, and the menorah.

The western gallery was also added during these renovations. The neo-Gothic elements cloak the erstwhile Renaissance edifice almost completely. However, you can see traces of its former design in the side vestibules and women's galleries, which hark back to the 1690s reconstruction. As for the original, eastern facade of the synagogue, read on for a secret, contemporary passageway into the depths of Prague's Jewish past.

By this time, the synagogue had already been used for some decades by Prague's Reform Jews. The *bimah* was moved to the front of the synagogue in the nineteenth century. (Today's central *bimah* was built in 1995 for display purposes.) There are two other telling signs that this was a Reform synagogue in the mid-nineteenth century. First, in the window high above the *aron hakodesh*, you'll find the *shem hamefurash*, or Holy Name of God. Orthodox Jews would never place the unpronounceable Name in a place where it could be destroyed. Secondly, in the Ten Commandments that adorn the facade of the synagogue, the numbers are written not in Hebrew letters beginning on the right-hand tablet, but in Roman numerals beginning on the left side. This acculturation to non-Hebrew languages is another sign of nineteenth-century Reform.

The organ is another matter entirely. Attached to the gallery to the left of the *aron hakodesh*, the balcony that once held the organ appears to be the most characteristically Reform element in the synagogue. However, professors have pointed out that the Maisel Synagogue contained this organ as early as the eighteenth century, long before the Reform movement spread about. This would seem to contradict the common association of the organ with religious reform. Initially, however, an organ was not considered unacceptable in the synagogue, as long as it was not played on Shabbat. Engravings and illuminations throughout the centuries have depicted Jews at prayer with organs. Some scholars believe that the Altneuschul itself once contained an organ. In the nineteenth century, however, Orthodox rabbis wished to distance themselves as far as possible from the Reform movement. As a result, they forbade any use of the organ in the synagogue.

The Maisel Synagogue became a warehouse during the Nazi occupation. It was intended that it would be part of the Museum of an Extinct Race (*see page 53*), but the war ended before such plans were executed.

In 1965, the State Jewish Museum in Prague opened a permanent exhibit in the Maisel Synagogue to display the Museum's silver objects. Dozens of Torah crowns, spice boxes,

synagogue today.

The neo-Gothic theme continued on interior furnishings and design. False ribs were added to the ceiling, the *aron hakodesh* was rebuilt, and tripartite windows were added throughout. You can still see the *kapporet* above the *aron hakodesh*, incorporated in neo-Gothic style. Representing the *kapporet* that covered the Ark of the Covenant in the Old Temple in Jerusalem, this *kapporet* features various images of sacrifices in the Temple: from left to right, there is the table containing the "Bread of Display," the copper laver of water, the twelve-stoned breastplate of the High Priest, the altar for the burnt offering, and the menorah.

The western gallery was also added during these renovations. The neo-Gothic elements cloak the erstwhile Renaissance edifice almost completely. However, you can see traces of its former design in the side vestibules and women's galleries, which hark back to the 1690s reconstruction. As for the original, eastern facade of the synagogue, read on for a secret, contemporary passageway into the depths of Prague's Jewish past.

By this time, the synagogue had already been used for some decades by Prague's Reform Jews. The *bimah* was moved to the front of the synagogue in the nineteenth century. (Today's central *bimah* was built in 1995 for display purposes.) There are two other telling signs that this was a Reform synagogue in the mid-nineteenth century. First, in the window high above the *aron hakodesh*, you'll find the *shem hamefurash*, or Holy Name of God. Orthodox Jews would never place the unpronounceable Name in a place where it could be destroyed. Secondly, in the Ten Commandments that adorn the facade of the synagogue, the numbers are written not in Hebrew letters beginning on the right-hand tablet, but in Roman numerals beginning on the left side. This acculturation to non-Hebrew languages is another sign of nineteenth-century Reform.

The organ is another matter entirely. Attached to the gallery to the left of the *aron hakodesh*, the balcony that once held the organ appears to be the most characteristically Reform element in the synagogue. However, professors have pointed out that the Maisel Synagogue contained this organ as early as the eighteenth century, long before the Reform movement spread about. This would seem to contradict the common association of the organ with religious reform. Initially, however, an organ was not considered unacceptable in the synagogue, as long as it was not played on Shabbat. Engravings and illuminations throughout the centuries have depicted Jews at prayer with organs. Some scholars believe that the Altneuschul itself once contained an organ. In the nineteenth century, however, Orthodox rabbis wished to distance themselves as far as possible from the Reform movement. As a result, they forbade any use of the organ in the synagogue.

∞

The Maisel Synagogue became a warehouse during the Nazi occupation. It was intended that it would be part of the Museum of an Extinct Race (*see page 53*), but the war ended before such plans were executed.

In 1965, the State Jewish Museum in Prague opened a permanent exhibit in the Maisel Synagogue to display the Museum's silver objects. Dozens of Torah crowns, spice boxes,

The Glass Stairway to Heaven

When the former Jewish Town was destroyed at the turn of the century, the original eastern facade of the Maisel synagogue was covered up by apartment blocks. Today's western entrance to the Maisel Synagogue has been in use only since 1904.

It's almost impossible for visitors to catch a glimpse of the original facade of the synagogue—impossible, that is, until today: Walk around the block from today's entrance, to Parizska Street number 11. The door is often locked, but a diehard traveller is always prepared for snags. Wait for someone to come out: best times are before 9 A.M. or soon after 5 P.M., when people enter and exit the building's offices. (If you want to take a photograph, do not come after 5 P.M., when the sun will be in your eyes.) Ask the people politely if you can see the building's renovations. Once inside, take the glass elevator in the back to the top.

As you rise inside the futuristic glass bubble, the former facade of the Maisel Synagogue will materialize before your eyes. It is like an ancient fossil discovered between modern tenements. On its top is a simple Jewish Star and on its bottom is the original entrance to the synagogue.

This surreal journey, a typical Jewish Prague synthesis of the old and the new, takes you to one of the most secret treasures in all of Josefov.

THE SPANISH SYNAGOGUE

Address: The corner of Dusni Street and Vezenska Street

Only in the Jewish Town of Prague, where clocks run backwards and the old collides irretrievably into the new, could the area's most ancient synagogue also be its newest. Such is the case with the Spanish Synagogue, built in 1868 on the site of the oldest known synagogue in Prague.

The old synagogue was called, quite fittingly, the Altschul. It dates back to the eleventh or twelfth century and was associated with what was most likely the oldest Jewish settlement in the Old Town. According to some theories, it was Byzantine Jews who arrived from the east and originally settled the area. Others have it that when the Jews were expelled from Spain and Portugal in the late fifteenth century, some refugees arrived in Prague and settled around the Altschul, rebuilding it in 1503. What is certain is that at some point in its history, the prayers in the Altschul followed the Sephardic rite. In 1605, for instance, a special prayer book was printed in Prague, which contained the Sephardic prayers used in the Altschul.

Another interesting thing about the Altschul was that it stood as a solitary island outside the main body of the ghetto. This smaller settlement, probably the oldest Jewish settlement in the Old Town, had been separated from the main Jewish ghetto from the time it was founded. The situation was exacerbated when the Church of the Holy Spirit was built between the two quarters in the thirteenth century. Special regulations evolved to dictate the hours and ways in which Jews were permitted to cross from the larger ghetto into the sister Community.

In the Easter Pogrom of 1389, Jews were murdered in the Altschul as well as the Altneuschul (then known as the Neuschul). The Altschul suffered more than the Altneuschul: It was burned to the ground, together with the Jews who had sought refuge inside. Rabbi Avigdor Kara chronicled the carnage in his elegy written after the pogrom (*see page 78*):

> Those who were living near the Old Synagogue
> were hiding inside, thinking there to be safe.
> But with swords they were killed by the brutal rogues,
> or as victims of fire they found there their grave.
>
> quoted in Hana Volavkova, *A Story
> of the Jewish Museum in Prague*

The synagogue remained idle for over a hundred years and, as mentioned, was only restored when an influx of Spanish and Portugese Jewish refugees rebuilt the synagogue in 1503. In subsequent centuries it underwent further restorations. Like the Altneuschul, the Altschul was spared the massive fire of 1689 because of its stone construction. Nonetheless, the city slated the Altschul for destruction as part of its efforts to contain the Jewish Town following the fire. Only a twenty thousand-guilder gift to the king spared the Altschul from demolition. Then the Archbishop of Prague argued that the Altschul had to be further isolated in order to prevent it from contaminating the Church of the Holy Spirit. According to his orders, the entrance was moved to the far side of the synagogue, away from the church; two windows were boarded up; and a wall that already surrounded the synagogue was made even higher, particularly on the side that faced the church. When the Jews returned from the expulsion of 1745–48, the synagogue was reopened for prayer. In the fire of 1754 it was badly damaged, but post-fire repairs maintained the synagogue's medieval character.

In 1837, the Altschul became the Temple—or the first Reform synagogue in Prague. The *bimah* was pushed to the front, an organ was added to the interior, the *aron hakodesh* and other furnishings were soon redone in neo-Gothic style, and German-language sermons became the highlight of the service. Its most eminent speaker was the brilliant, shrewd, and sarcastic Leopold Zunz, who escaped groveling destitution with his role as preacher here. A founder of the school of historiography known as the "Science of Judaism," Zunz achieved fame in the Jewish world for his analyses of post-biblical Jewish writing as not merely theological philosophy but literary genius. His synagogue preaching was a side gambit to earn him a living, but he took it seriously. When the Prussian government outlawed Reform Judaism's innovation of the sermon, Zunz penned the *History of the Jewish Sermon*, which clocked the history of Jewish preaching all the way back to the earliest synagogues. In a single stroke, Zunz recorded a vital piece of history while also justifying his means of subsistence.

The Altschul's first organist in the nineteenth century was memorable: Frantisek Skroup, the Czech composer who wrote the first Czech opera as well as the national anthem, wrote liturgical scores and drummed the keys here from 1836 to 1845.

The year 1867 was a turning point in Central European history for both Jew and Gentile. With the formation of the dual Austro-Hungarian monarchy, Jews were finally given the full emancipation they had actively sought for a century.

The historian Hillel J. Kieval has pointed out the ironic coincidence that in the same year, 1867, the Altschul was torn down and construction of the Spanish Synagogue was begun in its place. When you think about it, there is not a more searing symbol of the Jewish urge to live up to the dream of emancipation than this event. The Altschul, in spite of its recent Reform history, was a symbol of ancient religious orthodoxy as well as Christian anti-Semitism as witnessed in the Easter Pogrom of 1389. It was also a reminder of Jewish isolation in Europe. The synagogue itself experienced multiple layers of segregation: It was literally a walled-in satellite of the main ghetto, separated by a nearby church. As if impatient to discard all shreds of the ghetto past, the Jews destroyed the Altschul all the way down to its foundations, leaving not even a trace of the priceless historical landmark.

The new building, by contrast, was meant to be an expansive symbol of the hope and promise of emancipation. The Spanish Synagogue was built on the exact spot of the Altschul, as if recalling the end of one era and the start of another. The Reform congregation had grown by this time, and its wealthy members wanted a synagogue that reflected their prosperity. The size of the Spanish Synagogue, however, should not mislead you as to the extent of Reform Judaism in Prague. Prague Reform did not adopt the radical Reform movement of Germany but rather the more moderate Viennese Reform. In other words, the liturgy itself was conducted mostly in Hebrew, though the sermon was delivered in German. The Spanish Synagogue was not the site of a new religious movement so much as a symbol of Jewish prosperity and, as time went on, assimilation.

Completed in 1868, the building's exterior employed a neo-Romanesque style influenced by some Moorish details. From the outside, you cannot see the spectacular dome that rises above the center of the synagogue. Interesting to note on the facade are the Two Tablets of the Law, which are depicted backwards. Apparently the congregation was so enamored of emancipation that they eliminated both the Hebrew letters and the traditional right-to-left ordering of the Tablets. In this way, the icon is a counterpoint to the impishly backward Hebrew clock on the Jewish Town Hall. The interior, decorated from 1882 to 1893 in polychromatic stucco arabesques, went strictly the Moorish route. Although this was the style for progressive synagogues of the time, it is also possible that Moorish was chosen as a reminder of the Spanish and Portugese Jews who once prayed in the Altschul. In any event, the name of the synagogue refers to its Moorish inspiration.

During the war, the Spanish Synagogue was one of the main warehouses holding Jewish household objects and the growing collection of the Nazi Museum of an Extinct Race. After the war, the synagogue became part of the State Jewish Museum, which housed a synagogal textile exhibition here during the 1960s and 1970s. At other times it was used as a warehouse for these textiles, collected during the war from Jewish communities throughout Bohemia and Moravia. A total of twenty-eight hundred *parochets* dating from 1592 to 1939, as well as over forty-eight hundred Torah mantles, approximately two thousand Torah draperies, and over eighteen hundred synagogal cushions were left to wither in the synagogue, which had become completely closed to outsiders. As for the building itself, from the 1960s until the early 1990s it was left in an increasingly deteriorating condition. The facade became weatherbeaten and the arabesques began to chip off the walls.

The reconstruction of the Spanish Synagogue was the most ambitious and expensive project undertaken by the Jewish Museum in Prague after it was restituted to the Jews in 1994. According to the Museum's own estimates, total reconstruction would cost forty million Czech crowns. By the end of 1995, the roof had been repaired at a cost of around 3.5 million crowns. The Museum planned to reopen the synagogue in 1998, on the 130th anniversary of the construction of the synagogue. This is one reason why ticket prices are so high at the Jewish Museum in Prague. Because the Museum does not receive funding from the state, it raises revenues primarily through admission costs. It remains to be seen whether the prices will return to more reasonable levels once the period of construction is finished.

The new exhibition in the Spanish Synagogue, slated to open in 1998, is intended as Part II of the Jewish History in Bohemia and Moravia cycle that begins in the Maisel Synagogue. Specifically, the exhibition will chronicle Jewish history in the region from the beginnings of Emancipation in the late eighteenth century until the end of the Holocaust. In this case, form and function are cleverly matched, as the Spanish Synagogue itself is a symbol of the Age of Emancipation and Jewish prosperity in the nineteenth and early twentieth centuries.

Apparently, post-Holocaust Jewish life was not to be documented, but at this writing the exhibition had not yet been opened.

ELSEWHERE IN PRAGUE

Although the Jewish Town has the greatest concentration of Jewish sites in all of Prague, there are some priceless things to see outside the area as well. Some of them are located in the Old Town; others are spread out throughout Prague. What follows is a list of some interesting sites, many of which you might happen upon accidentally on your travels through the city.

After the Jubilee Synagogue and the cemeteries, the sites are an eclectic mix. Not all of them are particularly Jewish sites—included here, for instance, are a concert hall, a church, and a crucifix—but each has an anecdote, a legend, or even a grave that is part of the tapestry of Jewish life in Prague.

The Jerusalem Synagogue ("Jubilee")

7 Jeruzalemska Street
Jeruzalemska Street is located in the center of Prague. It runs northwest from the area of the Main Train Station (Hlavni Nadrazi) in Prague 1.
Opening Hours:
1:00 P.M.–5:00 P.M. Sunday through Friday

The Jerusalem Synagogue is open only during the summertime. The season begins around the end of March and continues until the end of the High Holidays. Admission, as of this writing, is 30 Crowns (15 Crowns students). Your ticket to the Altneuschul is valid here as well, providing that you come on the same day.

When the former Jewish ghetto was destroyed in the slum clearance at the turn of the century, three Baroque synagogues were demolished. Only afterwards did the Czech cultural Community argue for the preservation of Jewish landmarks in the area, but for the three synagogues, it was too late; they were lost forever. The synagogues were the Zigeuner Synagogue, founded in 1613; the Great Court Synagogue, founded in 1626; and the New Synagogue, founded as early as 1595. By the turn of this century, the synagogues—which had undergone several eras of reconstruction—hosted three rather diverse congregations, ranging from Orthodox to Reform. Franz Kafka, for instance, celebrated his *bar mitzvah* service in 1896 in the Zigeuner Synagogue, which had assumed the Reform rite, together with a choir, since the year he was born.

Although the synagogues followed varying rites, all three congregations decided in 1898 to unite and build a common synagogue to replace those that were slated for demolition. In 1905–06, just as their synagogues were being knocked down, the congregations built an extravagant new synagogue well outside the area of the slum clearance. It was named "Jubilee" because it was prepared for 1908, the year in which Franz Josef celebrated his sixtieth Jubilee Anniversary as emperor of Austria. Jews in the Austro-Hungarian Empire revered Franz Josef as their secular savior, as he was the ruler who granted them legal equality with Christians as well as the opportunity for massive assimilation. Kafka himself was named after the emperor. The bulk of Prague's Jews showed up at synagogue four times a year: on the three days of the High Holidays and on Franz Josef's birthday. Even more importantly, at the turn of the century Franz Josef represented a beacon of stability in the face of increasingly nationalistic—and anti-Semitic—fragmentation. This could be seen most clearly on the sixtieth anniversary itself. In the same year that Prague's more prosperous Jews honored Franz Josef with the Jubilee Synagogue, the Czech National Socialists stormed the streets in anti-Austrian violence; the Austrian reaction was martial law and a suspension of the Czech parliament and constitution.

The name "Jubilee" stuck until the First World War, when it was unfashionable, to say the least, to be a Monarchist. The Austro-Hungarian Empire fell into oblivion, replaced by a smattering of nation-states, including Czechoslovakia. The Jews of the Czech lands tried to assert their Czech patriotism, disposing of all vestiges of the Hapsburg reign. It was then, in fact, that Kafka's street-savvy father changed his name from "Herrrmann" to "Hermann," so that Czechs wouldn't think he was a German. At the same time, the atavistic title "Jubilee" was swept under the carpet and the neutral name "The Great Temple in Jerusalem Street" was born. The judicious congregation used the new name, along with the simpler "Jerusalem Synagogue," throughout the interwar years. According to the synagogue's worshippers today, the name "Jubilee" was forgotten after the Holocaust, except by a single elderly eccentric who was entranced by the bygone days of the Monarchy. Today, when so few people recall the reason for the name "Jubilee," the synagogue has attained the undisputed title of "Jerusalem."

It should be noted that the street was named Jerusalem not for the synagogue but for a nearby church. Two hundred fifty years before the synagogue was built, the nearby Church of Saint Jindrich was adjoined by a graveyard and a Baroque chapel shaped like Jesus' traditional grave in Jerusalem. In the seventeenth century, the street was given the name Jerusalem since it ran alongside the chapel. Both the chapel and cemetery were demolished during the reign of Josef II, but the name Jeruzalemska Street continues to the present day.

The Jubilee Synagogue is one of the world's most playful houses of prayer. Designed by the Austrian architect Wilhelm Stiassny, the building mixes Art Nouveau with Moorish styles and features an unabashed, even exuberant facade. With its red, yellow, and blue strips, its impishly gaping ovals, and its zigzag of triangles cut into the facade, one expects to find a circus master at the door or funhouse mirrors inside. Instead, one finds more of the same: a carnival of blues, reds, golds, flowers, glass, and metal. One exits the synagogue with a head filled with buzzing extravaganza. Whether or not the original name has been lost to history, the synagogue parlays an aura that is nothing less than jubilant.

Toward the top of the facade, there is the customary synagogue inscription, "This is the gateway to God, righteous people enter here."

In the interior of the synagogue there are various Hebrew inspirationals painted in gold and lining the balconies along the periphery of the sanctuary. The text is actually a conglomeration of several psalms designed to guide one's thoughts toward prayer. Facing the *aron hakodesh* and starting from the left, the text reads:

> Pray for the well-being of Jerusalem. May there be well-being within your ramparts, peace in your citadels. As for me, may my prayer come to You, O Lord, at a favorable moment; O God, in Your abundant faithfulness, answer me with Your sure deliverance. O Lord, set a guard over my mouth, a watch at the door of my lips. I call You, O Lord, hasten to me; give ear to my cry when I call You.
>
> (The text is from the following Psalms, in this order: 122:6–7; 69:14; 141:3; 141:1.)

The synagogue holds fifteen hundred worshippers. Along with the Altneuschul, it is one of the two Prague synagogues still in use today (*see page 59*). The congregation prays in a small chapel located upstairs.

The Old Olsany Cemetery

Fibichova Street and the park known as "Mahlerovy Sady"

From the metro station Jiriho z Podebrad, walk to the gigantic television tower, a metal structure visible from all over Prague. The remains of the cemetery are located next to the tower.

The cemetery is usually locked, although some enterprising visitors have found holes in the gate. In order to visit the cemetery, you must make an appointment at the office of the Rabbinate in the Jewish Town Hall on Maiselova 18. The cantor will send somebody to open and close the cemetery for you. It is appropriate to give this messenger something for his or her time.

The Old Olsany Cemetery once sprawled throughout the area now occupied by the television tower and park. Most of the cemetery was destroyed in 1960 at the behest of the communist authorities. The remaining part on the north—which happens to be the oldest section—is still an enriching trip through nineteenth-century Jewish history, and the ancient Hebrew inscriptions, juxtaposed against the ridiculous television tower in the background, make for some memorable photos.

In 1680, a catastrophic plague immobilized the Jewish ghetto. By the time the epidemic ended, it had taken approximately three thousand lives. For sanitary reasons, it was too hazardous to bury the exponential number of plagued bodies in the cramped confines of the ghetto. The bodies were instead carried outside the then-limits of Prague and buried in a new plague cemetery in Olsany. Burials in the cemetery resumed during the plague of 1713. When Maria Theresa expelled the Jews from Bohemia in 1745, this cemetery was used by the transient Jews on their way out of the country. In 1748, when the expulsion order was repealed, Jews returned to the ghetto and ceased burials in this suburban cemetery.

It was only in 1787 that the Old Olsany Cemetery began to be used as a regular burial grounds, when the Old Jewish Cemetery in the ghetto was closed due to overcrowding. Throughout the nineteenth century, until the cemetery was closed due to the expansion of Zizkov in 1890, this was the main cemetery of the Prague Jewish Community. All told, some thirty-seven hundred people were buried in the Old Olsany Cemetery. After 1890, the New Olsany Cemetery was established further out in the suburbs (*see page 137*). In 1948, 180 damaged Torah scrolls that had been taken by the Nazis from Holland were buried in the cemetery.

In 1960, the Jewish Community was pressured into relinquishing most of the cemetery grounds to the Prague municipal authorities. The authorities insisted that a park was necessary for the district, and promised not to build anything offensive on the grounds. The Jewish Community, reeling from state-sponsored show trials of the 1950s, had no choice but to acquiesce. Most of the tombstones were buried and a park—named, perhaps ironically, after the Jewish composer Gustav Mahler—was erected. Only the oldest part of the cemetery was spared. True to form, the authorities broke their promise of tastefulness and in 1986 commenced construction on the greatest eyesore ever to blight the skyline of Prague: the metallic, triple-pillar television transmitter visible today from all parts of the city. Modern Prague legend has it that the transmitter, completed in 1989, is emitting radiation that is poisoning the people living in its direct vicinity. This is said to be the revenge of the Jewish dead whose graves were defiled when the park and transmitter were built.

What is left of the cemetery today are some of the oldest, most exquisite graves from the late eighteenth and nineteenth centuries. It was in these very years that the Jewish Community underwent fundamental changes as it stood on the threshold of modernity. This is the chief reason the Old Olsany Cemetery is so fascinating to visit. A walk through the cemetery bears witness to this momentous transition, chronicling the lives of Orthodox rabbis, progressive educators, and industrialists who changed Jewish life in the nineteenth century.

By far the most famous individual buried here is Ezekiel Landau (1713–1793), the vanguard of Bohemian Orthodoxy also known as the *Nodah Bi'Yehudah*, after the title of his most famous collection of responsa. Rabbi Landau was the last fierce opponent of the *Haskalah*, or Jewish Enlightenment, fighting against radical changes in education and insisting that Jews resist the nascent assimilationist movement. During an era when the state was increasingly involving itself in internal Jewish matters, Rabbi Landau tried to keep the government out of Jewish life and education. A tribute to Rabbi Landau's continued influence on Jewish life was seen as recently as 1993.

In the early 1990's, Rabbi Landau's descendants from Brooklyn, New York, financed the restoration of his tombstone and those of close family members. For this reason, Rabbi Landau's tombstone is impossible to miss: It's the incredibly spruced-up one with its inscription enhanced by black paint. There is also a large explanatory board put up by his descendants. The tombstone itself is topped by a shell containing two lions guarding a water pitcher and basin, symbolizing Rabbi Landau's status as a Levite. In 1993, on the bicentennial anniversary of Rabbi Landau's death, hundreds of Orthodox Jews from all over the globe came to Prague for the rededication ceremony. Many were direct descendants; others had come because they had studied Rabbi Landau's teachings their entire lives. There was no greater testament to Rabbi Landau's enduring legacy in the Orthodox world. It was a rather jarring site: Underneath a communist TV transmission tower, surrounded by bemused residents, hundreds of Orthodox Jews set up a podium and microphone for the largest outdoor Jewish celebration Prague had seen in fifty years. Several rabbis spoke about Rabbi Landau's merits, and then the visitors filed past the newly refurbished tombstones. Many of the visitors remained for a few days, catching the traditional Jewish sites in Josefov. At the time, other tourists gaped: Was there truly such a thriving Jewish presence in a city decimated by the Holocaust? But when the week was over, Rabbi Landau's descendants left and Jewish Prague returned to its rather grim 1990s reality.

After Rabbi Landau died in 1793, the Jews of Bohemia embarked on a zealous path of religious and cultural reform that left its mark on Jewish life for the next century. A symbol of this transition was Rabbi Landau's own grandson Moshe Israel Landau (1788–1852), also buried in this cemetery. Moshe Landau ran a printing house that published traditional Jewish texts as well as popular books and the works of contemporary *Haskalah*, or Enlightenment, thinkers. Among other Enlightenment leaders buried in the cemetery, one of the most important is Peter Beer (1758–1839). Beer was an active instructor in the new German-Jewish schools of the Enlightenment, using his post to redefine his pupils' attitudes toward religion.

The Old Olsany Cemetery also contains two of Rabbi Landau's successors who typified the nineteenth-century change in Jewish life. Rabbi Eleazar Fleckeles (1754–1826), a pupil of Rabbi Landau, was an outspoken opponent of Prague's Sabbatian movement, a radical reform tendency in Judaism influenced by the same spiritual dissatisfaction that later inspired the *Haskalah* and nineteenth-century Reform. Rabbi Shlomo Jehudah Rapoport (1790–1867) was arguably the last truly extraordinary Jewish spiritual leader of Bohemia. His activities in Jewish historicism, the revival of Hebrew, and religious reform left an abiding imprint on Czech Jewish life into the twentieth century.

Alongside the rabbis, educators, scientists, and publishers of the nineteenth century are the graves of some of the earliest Jewish industrialists in Bohemia. These individuals used their financial clout to escape from the Prague ghetto even before it was opened up in the middle of the nineteenth century; their burial all the way out in Zizkov is a fitting symbol of the urge to fly the nets of ghetto indigence. Perhaps the most remarkable nineteenth-century Jewish industrialist was Leopold Porges von Portheim (1781–1870). Leopold and his brother Moses established a cotton printery in the Prague district of Smichov that was the first such mechanical factory in the Austro-Hungarian empire. The Emperor himself visited the factory in 1833 and was so delighted that he granted both brothers the title of nobility. Within ten years, the Smichov factory was the third largest in Bohemia, employing seven hundred workers. Savvy tourists might wish to check out the Portheimka building, located near their factory on Stefanikova Street in the Smichov district. The Porgeses bought this famous Baroque building for their residence; today it houses a gallery, cafe, and classical music radio station.

The New Olsany Cemetery

The Corner of Jana Zelivskeho and Izraelska Streets

The cemetery is located at the Zelivskeho metro stop.
Opening Hours: 9:00 A.M.–4:00 P.M. daily except Saturday
In the winter, the cemetery closes two hours before sunset on Fridays.

The New Olsany Cemetery, established in 1890, replaced the Old Olsany Cemetery as the main site of burial for the Prague Jewish Community. Over the course of the following fifty years, the cemetery reflected the wide cultural diversity the Jews in Prague experienced in the early twentieth century. There were about fifteen thousand burials in the New Olsany Cemetery up until the Holocaust. Many of the tombstones, utilizing styles ranging from neo-Classicist and neo-Gothic to Art Nouveau and Cubist, are exquisite works of art. A stroll through the cemetery is highly recommended as a modern, gentrified counterpoint to the Old Jewish Cemetery in Prague.

During the early years of the Nazi occupation, some Jews were able to procure jobs in the cemetery and thus defer deportation. The experiences of one of these workers is chronicled in Jiri Weil's *Life with a Star*.

Today the New Olsany Cemetery is the single Jewish cemetery in use in Prague.

The neo-Renaissance Ceremonial Hall, built in the early 1890s, contains an inscription from Ecclesiastes that is often written on tombstones: "A good name is better than fragrant oil, and the day of death than the day of birth" (Ecclesiastes 7:1). The passage teaches that one's reputation supersedes his or her riches, and that only after a person has died can his or her merits be properly judged.

By far the most famous individual buried in the New Olsany Cemetery, and by many accounts the most famous Jew in Prague's millennium-long Jewish history, is Franz Kafka (1883–1924). His grave is in Plot 21, along the main avenue extending to the right off the cemetery entrance.

Although there is practically no "ism" in the world that has not claimed Franz Kafka as its patron saint, Judaism has legitimate rights here. Much of Kafka's writing is a symbolic labyrinth in which he pursues the meaning of Jewish law, thought, and commentary, or offers an elaborate metaphor exploring the condition of the Jew in the modern world. In all his fiction, there is only one fleeting mention of Jews: The implication of pogroms in Russia in the short story "The Judgment." But his diary is so crammed with explorations of Jewishness that one can hardly read ten pages without happening upon profound insights into the contemporary Jewish condition. Evidently, while Kafka gave free rein to Jewishness in his diaries, his fiction deliberately explored the issues in cryptic form. Thus "A Report to an Academy" is an allegory of the Jew released from the ghetto; " "Josephine the Singer" is a metaphor of the Jewish Diaspora; *The Trial* is a parable of Jewish law and the struggle of the mystic to comprehend it.

Kafka's father, like so many others in his generation, abandoned the traditional Jewish lifestyle of the Bohemian countryside when he left home and arrived eventually in Prague. Franz Kafka viewed the few practices his father continued to keep as meaningless.

> How one could do anything better with that material than get rid of it as fast as possible, I could not understand; precisely the getting rid of it seemed to me to be the devoutest action. (Franz Kafka, "Letter to His Father" in *The Sons*)

Later, Kafka developed a profound relation to Judaism that had roots in his deep need for a sense of Community. Interestingly, his flight from Judaism and his burgeoning interest in Jewish life both sprang from a feeling of dissatisfaction with the lack of spiritual sustenance in the Prague Jewish Community. It should be mentioned that Prague's Jews were not only a highly assimilated western-type Community, but were extremely skeptical of all forms of religious fervor. Thus it was that Hasidism never had a strong following in Prague. Even the Jewish tradition that was maintained in Prague turned Kafka off by its cold, spiritless edges. In one of his most glaring indictments of Western Jewish practice, Kafka chastised the vacuity and decay of Prague religious rite, which had removed itself from any context of a living Jewish Community. Thus it was that after his baby nephew's circumcision in December 1911, Kafka wrote,

> Today when I heard the *mohel*'s assistant say the grace after meals and those present, aside from the two grandfathers, spent the time in dreams or boredom with a complete lack of understanding of the prayer, I saw Western European Judaism before me in a transition whose end is clearly unpredictable. . . . (Franz Kafka, *Diaries*)

On October 4, 1911, a couple of months before he attended his nephew's circumcision, Kafka's thoughts on Judaism began to change when he accompanied his friend Max Brod to the Cafe Savoy to watch a Yiddish theater troupe from Lvov. Kafka was entranced. It wasn't the production itself that attracted him; he saw through the cliched melodrama and the horrendous acting. Rather, Kafka was mesmerized by the portrayal of a world in which a Community was connected and defined by a common culture and faith. The next day, he wrote that the characters were "people who are Jews in an especially pure form because they live only in the religion, but live in it without effort, understanding, or distress" (Franz Kafka, *Diaries*). Over the course of the four months the Yiddish troupe played in Prague, Kafka attended over 20 performances and blanketed over 100 pages of his diaries with observations of the shows and the actors. On January 6, 1912, he wrote perhaps the most telling entry in his diary regarding the Yiddish troupe:

> When I saw the first plays it was possible for me to think that I had come upon a Judaism on which the beginnings of my own rested, a Judaism that was developing in my direction and so would enlighten and carry me farther along in my own clumsy Judaism, instead, it moves farther away from me the more I hear of it. The people remain, of course, and I hold fast to them.
> (Franz Kafka, *Diaries*)

When Kafka saw the Yiddish theater troupe, he realized that it was still possible for him to experience the sense of a Jewish collective. He began to scour the Eastern European actors for information and anecdotes about a Jewish world that was diametrically opposed to the stoicism of Prague Jewish life. He meticulously recorded in his diary accounts of wonder rabbis, talmudic discussions, rabbinical law, and Jewish communal activities. That which he had been missing in Prague he found in the traditional life of East European Jews. When thousands of Galician Jewish refugees flooded into Prague at the beginning of the First World War, Kafka loitered around refugee centers to observe what he considered to be an untainted form of Judaism in practice. He visited the Belz Rebbe when the latter was vacationing with his followers in Marianske Lazne (Marienbad). He devoured hasidic stories—not the anaesthetized Martin Buber versions, but basic folk tales devoid of artifice and conceit.

Kafka's fascination with Judaism was certainly a son's rebellion against assimilated parents. But it was also a uniquely Prague story: Kafka courted a "pure" form of Eastern European Jewishness for the simple reason that there was practically nothing in Prague, among any generation in Kafka's time, that could satisfy his abiding thirst for Jewish Community as expressed in daily life. For Kafka, the Jews of Eastern Europe symbolized the unity of the Jewish people as bound up in a collective. As he once allegedly remarked, "Jewry is not merely a question of faith, it is above all a question of the practice of a way of life in a Community conditioned by faith" (Gustav Janouch, *Conversations with Kafka*).

In his stories as in his life, Kafka attempted to locate the moment at which God was known to man, and in which the Jewish people were not an aggregation of individuals but a unity of one. Each time, he was disappointed in his search. Eventually, when Kafka was forty years old and very ill with tuberculosis, he fell in love with Dora Diamant, the nineteen-year-old daughter of hasidic Jews who had left the ways of her parents and moved to Berlin. Although Dora was no longer hasidic, Kafka was intrigued by her background—the languages, experiences, and traditions of a completely different world. In his ultimate attempt to transform a vision of Jewish completeness into reality, Kafka planned to move to Tel Aviv with Dora, where they would open a restaurant. He wrote to Dora's father, asking for her hand in marriage. Her father passed the letter on to his rebbe, who refused the match because Kafka was a "Western" Jew. Less than nine months later Kafka died.

The Rudolfinum

namesti Jana Palacha, on the riverside west of the Old Jewish Cemetery

The Rudolfinum is a nineteenth-century Czech concert hall that served as the first Czechoslovak Parliament building from 1918 to 1938. When the Germans occupied Prague, they changed the Rudolfinum into a German concert hall and renamed it the German House of Art. Reinhard Heydrich, the acting Reich Protector in Bohemia and Moravia, was a music lover eager to inaugurate the German House of Art with the bellowing sounds of a German symphony. While admiring the sculptures adorning the roof of the Rudolfinum, Heydrich was revolted to find a statue of Felix Mendelssohn, the nineteenth-century German composer who had Jewish roots. Infuriated, Heydrich ordered the statue toppled at once. Within hours, two Czech underlings found themselves on the roof of the Rudolfinum, searching for the statue of the Jew. Since neither knew which statue was Mendelssohn, the workers decided to measure the noses of each of the statues. The one with the biggest nose, they decided, had to be the Jew. After locating the largest nosed statue, they put a rope around its neck and toppled it to the ground.

On the opening night of the German House of Art, Heydrich looked up to the statues and nearly fainted on the spot. The statue that had been destroyed was that of Richard Wagner.

This semi-apocryphal tale is often related in Prague as a proud example, in pure Hasek fashion, of moral victory in the face of occupation. Jiri Weil spun a transcendent version in his novel *Mendelssohn Is on the Roof*. The novel, which examines almost every conceivable angle of the Nazi extermination of Prague's Jews, places statues—and not only Mendelssohn's—at the heart of its chronicle of genocide.

The Statue of Rabbi Judah Loew (1910)

Marianske namesti, one block west of Old Town Square. The statue stands on the right side of the Town Hall, just opposite the Klementinum building.

> *Note:* Contrary to rumor, this statue does not stand in or near the Jewish Town Hall. In fact, it is located a couple blocks south of the Jewish Quarter.

During the destruction of the old Jewish Town at the turn of the century, Prague's municipal authorities asked the famed sculptor Ladislav Saloun to design two figures representing Prague history and legend. The figures were to adorn the new Town Hall of Prague, which was simultaneously being built. On the left side of the building, Saloun depicted the "Iron Man," a figure out of medieval Czech mythology. (This statue is not, as some books claim, the Prague Golem.) On the right side of the building, Saloun erected a statue in honor and memory of Rabbi Judah Loew, the most magnificent rabbi in the history of Prague. Since Jews do not normally erect statues of people, this is the only statue of Rabbi Loew that exists in the world. The choice of a Jewish figure to adorn the secular Town Hall reveals how much the rabbi is revered even by non-Jewish Czechs. The statue has become a true symbol of the cross-fertilization of Jewish and Bohemian history and culture.

Saloun was quite the Art Nouveau romantic. His statue of Jan Hus on Old Town Square transmogrified the short, bald, Christian renegade into a towering figure of defiance. In the case of Rabbi Loew, however, Saloun didn't have to exaggerate. By all accounts, much of Rabbi Loew's charisma derived from his impressive height, which topped six feet. As for the young woman by his side, that's where Saloun let his romanticism reign. The woman's painstakingly rendered nudity would surely have raised the eyebrows of the Orthodox.

The sculpture refers to one of several legends about Rabbi Loew's death. The rabbi had such control over the temporal and supernatural worlds that he anticipated the arrival of Death itself. Because tradition teaches that one cannot die while studying the Torah, Rabbi Loew immersed himself, night and day, in learning. He took only one break: to accept a rose given to him by his innocent granddaughter. Death saw this as the perfect opportunity, and stole into the rose. When Rabbi Loew lovingly inhaled the flower, Death entered him and he died. The statue depicts Rabbi Loew just after inhaling the scent of the rose. The rose has fallen to his feet; his granddaughter clings to him, realizing what has happened, but it is too late. The great rabbi is on the verge of death. Saloun also depicted the Jews of Prague represented by an emaciated dog terrified by the passing of its master.

Saloun used the legend of Rabbi Loew's death to offer a rather subversive view of the destruction of the ghetto. According to him, the image of Rabbi Loew represented the ancient wisdom that coarsed through the ghetto streets. The young granddaughter, on the other hand, represented the dawn of a new age. Even in her form, the woman was a symbol of the luxurious and indulgent architecture that had come to replace the dilapidated buildings. In this way, the sculpture laments the destruction of a vital piece of Prague history.

The Crucifix on Charles Bridge
On the north side of Charles Bridge, the third statue from the right

This Crucifix is one of the greatest mysteries of Prague. Surrounding the figure of Jesus—usually presumed a Christian symbol—are the Hebrew words *Kadosh, Kadosh, Kadosh, Adoshem Tziva'ot*, or "Holy, Holy, Holy, the Lord of Hosts!" (Isaiah 6:3). The Hebrew text is found in one of Judaism's most sacred prayers, the *Amidah*. The image of Jesus surrounded by Hebrew has been paraded throughout the Prague tourist industry as a sublime symbol of Prague's cultural cross-fertilization. Apparently, Prague's promoters have no idea that putting Hebrew on a Crucifix is considered by Jews to be a profanity and a sign of religious oppression. In this case, the Hebrew text has been removed from a holy Jewish prayer and made a symbol of Christian intolerance: on the Crucifix, the text proclaims that Jesus is the king of the Jews.

On the base of the Crucifix are the bare facts of the case, inscribed in Latin, Czech, and German. It reveals that on September 14, 1696, the gold letters were erected as punishment imposed on a Jew who had blasphemed the Cross. The laconic inscription led to several legends regarding the details of the "crime." It was only in 1997 that the legends were debunked by Dr. Alexandr Putik of the Jewish Museum in Prague. What follows is the famous legend and, afterwards, the less-pretty picture of truth.

The Legend

In 1696, a Jew was making his way back across Charles Bridge after a particularly grueling day of business at the royal court. He had been repeatedly insulted, and his business had suffered as a result of the constant taunts and jeers.

When he passed the Crucifix, he felt so enraged at his inferior status that he spat out at it. Then, realizing he had committed a capital offense punishable by death, he hurried quickly back to the ghetto, where he hid in his home.

Meanwhile, two passersby had seen what had happened. They couldn't make out the face of the man who had desecrated the Cross; all they saw was his yellow hat. It was the "Hat of Shame," obligatory on all Jews. They alerted their friends, and before long a crowd of people, including two bailiffs from the court, marched into the Jewish ghetto.

Entering the Jewish Town Hall, they shouted, "Hand over the Jew! We saw him defile the Cross!"

But the leaders of the Jewish Community wouldn't budge. They had heard rumors of the Charles Bridge incident, but they knew that if they turned over the guilty party, he'd certainly be tortured and executed.

The crowd grew enraged. "If you don't hand over the Jew at once," someone shouted, "We'll lay your entire ghetto to waste!"

"Let's compromise!" pleaded the leader of the Jewish Community. "We'll do anything you want! You name the punishment!"

And so the crowd decided that as just punishment, the Jewish Community as a whole would pay for the gold letters on the Crucifix in retribution for the profanity.

In other versions of the legend, the guilty Jew refused to remove his hat, or uttered blasphemy, when passing the Crucifix.

The Real Story

The true story is even more tragic, particularly because of the damning light it sheds on Jewish personalities of the seventeenth century. Even more than a symbol of Christian persecution, the Hebrew Crucifix unmasks a labyrinthine trail of Jewish treachery against other Jews.

One of the greatest power feuds in Bohemian Jewish history centered around the so-called "Land's Jewry," the Jewish tax collection and distribution authority outside of Prague. The organization naturally attracted the most powerful Jews of Bohemia to its board of deputies. In 1674, Abraham Aron Lichtenstadt became the exclusive leader of the Land's Jewry. Lichtenstadt was extremely ambitious; he would stop at nothing to eliminate his adversaries. His chief antagonist was Elias Backoffen, an outspoken troublemaker who refused to tolerate Lichtenstadt's arrogance. After a decade of accusation and counter-accusation, Lichtenstadt devised a plan to ruin his adversary for good.

In the spring of 1693, Lichtenstadt intercepted a secret letter that Backoffen had written to an ally in Vienna. The letter contained either confidential business information or conspirational plans against Lichtenstadt; it was written in a top-secret code. The inscrutable letter was perfect for Lichtenstadt's plans. He marched at once to the Bohemian authorities and claimed that the letter blasphemed against Jesus and the Holy Cross as well as threatened baptized Jews. The accusation was nonsense, but the Court was eager for such reports. During the Jesuit reign over Bohemia, such a crime was a capital offense. Convicted blasphemers were publicly executed by having their tongues cut out and being left to bleed to death on Old Town Square: always a propaganda coup for the church. Even though it was obvious that Lichtenstadt was railroading his enemy, the Court accepted his accusations at face value. Both Backoffen and the addressee of the letter were arrested and thrown into prison.

Meanwhile, the Court could not decode the letter—both Backoffen and his ally had burnt the code key before their arrest. At the Court's request, Backoffen translated the letter according to his memory of the code key, but the Court insisted his translation was incomplete. In fact, the Court blindly accepted Lichtenstadt's "translation" of the cryptogram even though Lichtenstadt himself did not know the code key. Lichtenstadt even urged the Court to torture his adversaries, but the Court had its limits. In the end, no guilt of blasphemy was ever proved.

Nonetheless, after a year of being thrown in and out of prison, sometimes in shackles and fetters, Elias Backoffen was found guilty of blasphemy and intimidation on March 18, 1694, and sentenced to be pilloried and then expelled from Bohemia. Two days later, the sentence was reduced to a fine of one thousand gold florins, payable to charity. This "charity" became the gold letters placed on the Crucifix on September 13, 1696, and unveiled to pomp and ceremony the next day.

With such a verdict, Lichtenstadt destroyed the careers of his greatest enemies. What was most insidious about Lichtenstadt's scheme was that by framing a Jew for blasphemy, he tarnished all of Bohemian Jewry and exposed them to further suspicion, ridicule, and hatred.

You will notice that the letter *alef* of the last word, *tzva'ot*, is actually upside down. This has engendered a new story, which, like many things in Prague, is semi-apocryphal:

When the Nazis occupied Prague, they noticed the Crucifix on Charles Bridge and were horrified. The Nazis were opposed to all symbols of Judaism in the capital and assumed the statue pointed to a rapprochement between Judaism and Christianity in Bohemia. That wouldn't do. They ordered all the gold letters removed from the cross.

After the war, the Czechs, eager to restore monuments that had been destroyed under the Nazis, returned the Hebrew to the Cross. But because the Czechs knew so little about Judaism, they didn't know in what order the letters should be arranged. After consulting several scholars, they got the order right—but erred on a single *alef*. The Hebrew letters today reveal the use and appropriation of a misunderstood Jewish culture in the Czech Republic.

Tyn Church

Tynska Street, off the Old Town Square

It might seem peculiar to include a Christian site in a Jewish travel book, but considering the grim history of the Church's persecution of Jews, it should be no surprise that many Christian sites recall horrifying tales in the form of legends about the "perfidious Jews." Such is the case in the Corpus Christi Church in Cracow (*see page 364*), and likewise in the enormous Tyn Church just off Prague's Old Town Square.

A tomb within the Tyn Church reveals the extent of Christian-Jewish acrimony during the Jesuit era in Bohemia. The tomb is for Simon Abeles; it is found on the left side of the church, near the tomb of Tycho Brahe. The tomb is made of red marble, with an inscription in Latin. In the story of Simon Abeles, one can see the perilous position of Jews in seventeenth-century Europe.

Simon Abeles, a twelve-year-old Jewish boy, decided to convert to Christianity in September 1693. He ran away from the Jewish ghetto and sought shelter, prior to his baptism, in the Jesuit College in the Klementinum. It should be noted that after the catastrophic fire in the Jewish Town in 1689, most of Prague's Jews were housed temporarily in Christian households until their homes could be rebuilt. There they were able to experience, for a short time, a relatively comfortable life outside the dank and oppressed walls of the Jewish Town. For some, life among the Christians was too alluring to pass up. The young Simon Abeles was probably swayed to convert during this taste of freedom outside the ghetto.

The Jesuits returned young Simon to his parents. Less than six months later, the body of Simon Abeles was found buried in the Old Jewish Cemetery. Immediately, a show trial was staged in which Simon's father, Lazar Abeles, and a relative, Lobl Kurtzhandl, were accused of murdering the boy. Abeles underwent severe torture in the Old Town jail until he finally confessed. Fearing further torture, he committed suicide by hanging himself on his belt. The Court passed a guilty verdict and ordered that the sentence—torture to death—be performed on the corpse itself. The executioner threw the body from the prison window, after which it was dragged outside the city gate and then drawn and quartered. After this, the executioner cut out Abeles's heart, slapped it over the corpse's face in front of a wild throng, and then crushed it to a pulp. A month later, Kurtzhandl was found guilty and was tortured under a wheel until all his bones were broken. During this punishment, he accepted Jesus as his Savior and begged to be baptized. In gratitude, the authorities gave him a quick death instead of the intended slow torture of being hung inside the wheel above the hysterical crowd.

Egon Erwin Kisch, the roving reporter of turn-of-the-century Prague, examined the proceedings and claimed that the entire case was a setup orchestrated by the Jesuit propaganda machine. Kisch claimed not only that the men were innocent of murder, but that Lazar Abeles's suicide was staged. Kisch found it quite suspicious that a man in shackles and fetters could succeed in hoisting his body to hang himself.

A more moderate view is that Abeles, trying to teach his son never to abandon home again, beat him. During this beating, he acted too roughly and accidentally killed his son.

This view, which rejects both the original story and Kisch's interpretation, finds Lazar Abeles guilty of accidental homicide.

But to get a clear picture of the Jesuit relationship to the Jews, we need only glimpse the legends that surrounded the body of Simon Abeles after he was exhumed from the Old Jewish Cemetery. The memorial stone in the Tyn Church proclaims that after six days, the body had its natural color and no foul odor, and that the skin was soft and smelled of rose oil. The body was placed on display in the Old Town Hall, where every day thousands of people came to dip their hands in the pink blood that spurted continuously from his wounds. Two weeks after the "execution" of Lazar Abeles's corpse, a majestic procession of clergy, nobility, and ordinary people carried the body of Simon Abeles from the Old Town Hall to the Tyn Church, where he was buried amid the clanging of all the church bells in Prague.

The story of Simon Abeles's martyrdom was spread throughout Europe as an example of Christian grace and Jewish damnation. It became a morality tale that found its most graphic expression in a series of woodcuts and texts after Simon was buried in Tyn Church in 1694.

The Langweil Model of Prague

Prague Municipal Museum (*Museum hlavniho mesta Prahy*)

> Take the Metro to the Florenc station, and head to the McDonald's (just don't go in!). The Prague Municipal Museum is located next door to McDonald's.

Ever since the destruction of the former ghetto at the turn of the twentieth century, both locals and visitors have missed out on viewing the streets of Jewish Prague the way they once looked. All we have are some photographs and paintings—and a model. Antonin Langweil (1791–1837), an artist and lithographer, designed a scale representation of the city of Prague in the 1820s and 1830s. Over five meters long, the model includes everything in old Prague, including all the nooks and crannies in the destroyed Jewish Quarter. The only thing Langweil left out were all the tombstones in the cemetery.

Langweil's model is truly a gem. It is our best evidence of what the Jewish Town looked like in the nineteenth century. It was still a ghetto; Jews would be confined to the area northwest of Old Town Square for several more years. The model shows us that even though the ghetto was congested, it was not yet a slum. It was only in the second half of the nineteenth century, after Jews had left the ghetto in large waves, that the district became run down and impoverished.

Protected by a glass booth, the model can be illuminated by pressing buttons on the side. It's fascinating, good fun: Locate the Altneuschul, and note the square that once stood in front of it; then trace the narrow path on the other side leading to the cemetery. Or find the cemetery first, probably the easiest site to spot in the Jewish Town. See the Klausen Synagogue and the Pinchas Synagogue on either sides of the cemetery. Try to find the Maisel Synagogue; back then, it opened onto a different street. Spot the synagogues that were destroyed during urban renewal. Find the Altschul, the oldest synagogue in the area, demolished only decades after the model was built.

II

*Warsaw:
City of Monuments*

Introduction

In the fall of 1996, Jewish communal institutions on Twarda Street 6, Warsaw, decided to add some green to an otherwise dreary landscape. When construction workers began digging in the earth, they happened upon a chilling find: a human anklebone. Earlier, during renovations of the attic of the same building, workers lifted the floorboards and found manuscripts left by a family that had hidden there during the war.

Both of these incidents reveal Warsaw as a badly bandaged wound half a century after the war—and they are not unique. All over Warsaw, there are periodic, unbidden eruptions of the past into the present. After the Germans destroyed almost the entire capital in 1944, the city was determined to rebuild. Because the population could not clear away all the debris from the war, it simply built over what was there. Today's Warsaw is a single sprawling monument over what is in fact an expansive cemetery. Human life and human history are buried deep beneath the strata of postwar Warsaw.

From the Jewish point of view, Warsaw is especially marked by its monuments. The only site that gives one an inkling of the prewar Jewish presence is the cemetery. Elsewhere, there are just more monuments: to the Warsaw Ghetto Uprising, to the human hell of Umschlagplatz. Imagine visiting Jerusalem in the year 130 C.E., three generations after the Jews had been violently exiled from ancient Israel. Or Madrid in 1550. Because of its concentration of monuments, it is difficult to imagine what thrived here before the Holocaust.

Before the war, with its close to four hundred thousand Jews, Warsaw was the second-largest Jewish Community in the world, after New York. Jews accounted for one-third of the population. There were 230 Jewish periodicals, in Yiddish, Hebrew, and Polish, in Poland, many of which were based in Warsaw. There were about three hundred *shtiebels*, or Jewish prayer halls, in the capital. Warsaw wasn't only the second-largest Jewish Community in the world. It was also undeniably the capital of world Yiddishkeit. Yiddishkeit means Jewishness, and there was nothing anywhere like the Jewishness of Warsaw. Forget New York. The Jews of Warsaw built a Community, created an atmosphere, and embodied a mentality that stood for an entire spectrum of Jewish feeling. It wasn't only in the religious sphere. Sure, there were hundreds of *shtiebels* dotted throughout the city—on some streets up to thirty—but even the assimilated Jews expressed a Jewishness in their day-to-day life. Warsaw was the land of Yiddish theater, of Zionism, of the Bund—of social action motivated by the most Jewish of utopian ideals.

Although the postwar landscape has changed irreversibly from its earliest incarnation, it is important to remember that this city was once the wellspring of the Diaspora as it experienced some of its most lofty moments. Beneath each of the tombstones, monuments, and altered streets in Warsaw lies the sediment of the most vibrant Community in Jewish history.

A History of the Jews in Warsaw

THE EARLIEST JEWISH COMMUNITY IN WARSAW

For all its unrivaled prewar glory, the Warsaw Jewish Community developed fairly late on the European stage. Both numerically and culturally, the early Warsaw Jewish Community could not compete with Prague, Cracow, the Buda section of Budapest, or dozens of other cities where Jewish life thrived from the early Middle Ages or earlier. Our information about Jews in medieval Warsaw is therefore relatively scant.

Jews are thought to have settled in the Old Town of Warsaw in the late fourteenth century, but the first archival mention of a Jew comes in 1414. The Jew, a certain Eliezer, had a dispute with a Warsaw resident and brought him to court. If nothing else, the record shows that early in the fifteenth century, Jews had certain legal rights in the city. Tax records in 1423 counted ten taxpaying Jewish families and about ten families exempted. According to one estimate, this amounted to approximately 180 Jews in the city. The Warsaw Jewish Community was first mentioned in records of 1428. By 1460, we know of Warsaw rabbis, but all we have are their names: Rabbi David, Rabbi Aharon, and Rabbi Moshe.

As in other cities in the medieval era, Jews were concentrated on a certain "Jewish Street," of which no trace remained even before the Second World War. It stretched between the streets Waski Dunaj and Piekarska, which still exist today. Jews were not confined to Jewish Street, and settled in the area bordered by Waski Dunaj, Rycerska, Piekarska, and Piwna streets. On the corner of Jewish Street and Waski Dunaj stood the synagogue; nearby stood a *mikveh*; and south of the Old Town limits stood the Jewish cemetery, possibly around the area of the Hotel Bristol.

As in Prague, Budapest, and Cracow, the more the Jewish population increased in the city, the louder came the calls among the citizenry to curtail their rights or to throw them out entirely. Economic competition was often the primary cause for this xenophobia. Throughout Poland, larger towns such as Posen, Cracow, and Lvov severely curtailed Jewish trade rights. In 1483, the Jews were expelled from residence in Warsaw; even visiting merchants had to confine their business to the main trade fairs. Eventually some returned, but for the most part they settled in the suburbs outside the Old Town.

WARSAW WITHOUT JEWS

In 1525, Jews were again forbidden to reside in Warsaw or to conduct business there. Apparently the decree had little effect, and two years later King Sigismund I gave the city the official privilege *de non tolerandis Judaeis*. This was the law that sealed off Warsaw from the Jews for the next two-and-a-half centuries. The edict forbade Jews from spending the night in Old or New Warsaw or from owning flats there. As a result, many Jews settled just outside the city walls, in order to trade near the city without violating the prohibition.

King Sigismund Augustus responded with an even more restrictive edict in 1570. This is puzzling, given that this particular king was known for his religious tolerance and benevolence toward the Jews of Cracow. At any rate, his edict stated: "The Jews shall have no right to reside on any grounds, or to trade or ply their handicrafts, within a radius of two miles from Warsaw on either bank of the Vistula, under penalty of confiscation."

However, the edict did allow Jews to conduct business in Warsaw when the Diet met there. Later, Jews were permitted to enter the city for two weeks before and after Diets. They constantly faced the rivalry of the city burghers, guilds, and merchants, who did everything in their power to close the gates of Warsaw completely. In 1691, for instance, Warsaw merchants paid a bribe of ten silver thalers and 54 Polish gulden worth of lemons and oranges in order to keep Jewish merchants out of the city.

Because of the bustling markets, Jews were eager to live nearby, and soon they found ways around the restrictions. The ban concerned the municipality of Warsaw; however, there were several estates outside the city owned by magnates. These districts were called *jurydyka*; the king and Diet had permitted these areas to fall under the sole supervision of nobles. As was the case in the Obuda district of Budapest, these noblemen often welcomed Jews for the economic benefits and trade the latter brought. The noblemen protected the Jews from the hostility of city burghers as well as the Church. Thus began the centuries-long era of Jewish settlement in suburban pockets outside the Old and New Towns of Warsaw. This is difficult to picture today, since the former suburbs are parts of today's central Warsaw. Back then, though, the walls of the Old and New Towns defined the city's boundaries.

Thus Jewish settlements arose on several estates outside the Old Town. For instance, there was an estate around today's Tlomackie Street, which used to open onto a large square, as well around today's Al. Solidarnosci and today's plac Grzybowski. There were over thirty such estates outside Warsaw's city limits. Jewish residence in the vicinity of Warsaw continued to be confined almost entirely to the outlying estates through the eighteenth century. In 1765, there were 2,615 Jews in greater Warsaw.

A famous estate stood around today's plac Artura Zawiszy. Set up by Prince August Sulkowski, it was composed solely of Jews and acquired the name "New Jerusalem." A road leading from the estate was called "Aleje Jerozolimski." This road, in altered form, still exists today. But envious merchants argued against the existence of New Jerusalem from its very inception. Sulkowski was able to enlist the protection of the Russian army, but the City Council was unrelenting in its drive to destroy the estate. Finally, on January 22, 1775, armed guards invaded the district and destroyed all the Jewish homes, marking the end of Jewish settlement there.

THE RISE OF PRAGA

Another area of Jewish settlement was in the city of Praga on the other side of the Vistula River. At the time, Praga was a separate city. Although Praga was also technically a district *de non tolerandis Judaeis*, it was much more lenient and Jews found they could settle there in the eighteenth century without great opposition. Throughout the 1770s and 1780s, expulsion edicts and street riots in Warsaw proper led to an increase in the Jewish population of Praga. By 1787, Jews accounted for twenty percent of Praga's population. The bedrock of the Praga Community was formed by *Shmuel Zbitkower* (1730s–1801), a banker and merchant who was involved in the lumber trade and salt mines as well as smaller industries. Older inhabitants of Praga still refer to one section of town as "Szmulewizna," named after Zbitkower. In the late nineteenth century, Zbitkower was the chief benefactor of the Jews of Praga, establishing a cemetery and synagogue and becoming the Community's chief *parnas* in 1788. Even today, the Jews of Warsaw continue to marvel at Zbitkower's abilities. He was the official supplier of the Russian army, which in the end owed him seven thousand ducats, as well as the supplier of the Polish revolutionary army.

More Jews crossed the river in 1790, when the anti-Semitic tension in Warsaw bubbled into open conflagration. In that year, Warsaw merchants demanded that the Diet completely expel Jews from Warsaw. The Diet expelled all Jewish traders and craftsmen. When these Jews returned in a few weeks' time, the Christians organized a pogrom. Apparently a Christian tailor ran into a Jewish tailor and tried to grab the latter's cloth from him. The Jewish tailor ran away and, with the help of several other Jews, had the Christian placed under arrest. Then the Christian's employees spread the rumor that their boss had been killed by the Jews. In the ensuing riot, all Jewish shops were pillaged and burned. The riot ended only after state troops were sent in.

Meanwhile, a new method for Jews to enter Warsaw had developed. Jews were permitted to purchase tickets to enter the city for a specified number of days. If Jews were caught in Warsaw with an expired ticket, there were often severe punishments. The city earned as much as two hundred thousand Polish gulden annually from the sale of these tickets.

During the first half of the eighteenth century, armed peasants and Cossacks known as the Haidamaks assaulted, kidnapped, robbed, and murdered Jews in eastern Poland and Ukraine. The pogroms culminated in 1768, when the Haidamaks murdered thousands of Jews in seven towns. In that year, a steady stream of Jewish refugees arrived in the estates around Warsaw. By 1792 they formed nearly ten percent of the population, numbering 6,750 individuals.

PARTITIONED POLAND

Poland lost approximately one-third of its territory when it was partitioned in 1772 by Austria, Prussia, and Russia. Another partition was carried out in 1793. In the midst of this national calamity, Poles began to regard the Jews in a new light. Poland was in the process of being erased from the world map; its citizens could no longer view themselves as a geographic entity but as a martyred nation. Living side by side with this nation were a people who were different in their religion, language, education, customs, and even clothes. It had always been this way, but the partitions of Poland led to a reevaluation of the relationship between Poles and Jews. Poles often pointed to the Jews as the scourge of the nation, a foreign entity that was the reason for the country's tribulations.

But in this sea of scapegoating hysteria, there were some refreshing approaches to the "Jewish question." Some Polish intellectuals and politicians recognized that the Jews were a separate people largely because the Poles had issued so many edicts to oppress and to segregate them. In the Polish Diet of 1788–1792, certain members began to discuss in earnest what should be done with the Jews. The conservatives advocated no changes, but the liberals pushed for complete emancipation and Polonization. Their goals were quite similar to those of Josef II in Austria, Bohemia, Moravia, and Hungary: to eliminate all differences between the Jews and the outside world, including religious autonomy. The most liberal propositions included placing Jewish children in Polish schools, placing a cap on the total number of Jewish holidays, and forcing Jews to dress like Poles. All this was in the name of desegregation, but the Jews—who were still overwhelmingly Orthodox—understandably viewed such proposals askance. Eventually the Diet adopted only one privilege: The Jews could not be imprisoned without trial. In this regard and no other, the Jews were made equal to Christian Poles.

But the dangling fruit of emancipation did appeal to many. After the second partition in 1793, the Polish nation organized around Thaddeus Kosciuszko in a national insurrection in 1794. The Jews saw this as a grand opportunity to demonstrate their loyalty to Polish soil and to create a new Polish society based on religious equality. Jews volunteered as guards and fought in battle. The most famous among them was Berek Joselewicz (c. 1770–1809). Joselewicz, a Jewish revolutionary living in Praga, requested of Kosciuszko permission to create a special Jewish regiment in the Polish army. Kosciuszko eagerly granted the request, and Joselewicz organized five hundred Jewish soldiers, including volunteers, to fight in the uprising. Joselewicz spoke to Jews all over Poland, calling on them to fight "like lions and leopards." The insurrection was defeated, but Joselewicz had become a military hero who advanced the debate on Jewish emancipation. Later he was killed fighting the Austrians at Kock in 1809.

Jews were so loyal to the 1794 insurrection that when it was defeated, the Russian armies massacred the Jews. After the fall of Praga in 1794, the pogrom was especially fierce. According to Warsaw legend, Shmuel Zbitkower put two barrels in front of his house: one filled with gold, one with silver. He claimed that any soldier who brought him a live Jew would receive a ducat in gold; any soldier bringing a Jewish corpse would receive a ruble in silver. By the end of the day, both barrels were empty.

UNDER PRUSSIAN RULE

In 1795, Warsaw passed into the hands of Prussia. In general, life under the Prussians was good for the Jews. The Prussians wished to Germanize the Polish capital; one peg in their plan was to Germanize the Jews. Jews were permitted to organize an autonomous communal structure to manage Jewish affairs. Wealthy Jews and German-speaking Jews were given privileges. As was the case in the Hapsburg Empire, Jews were required to adopt German surnames. The Prussians permitted the Jews to establish a synagogue and a cemetery.

In 1797, though, Warsaw Jewry was strapped with several economic restrictions included in the "*General Juden Reglement.*" In 1799, new residential decrees were issued that favored wealthier Jews. Jews who had settled between 1796 and 1799 had to pay an annual toleration fee of thirty-five thousand thalers, and new Jewish settlers and merchants had to purchase daily one-zloty tickets for temporary residence. Wealthy, German-speaking Jews were given favorable status. The decrees resulted in an influx of wealthy Jews to Warsaw. Poorer Jews were forced to enter the city in circuitous, and often illegal, fashion.

In 1802, the Prussians officially abolished the edict of *non tolerandis Judaeis* in Warsaw and Jews were finally permitted to settle in the city. At this time, Jewish Warsaw embarked on a population growth that was to continue throughout the century. From 1797 to 1804, the Jewish population increased from 7,688 to 11,630. Jews now made up over seventeen percent of the total population. The first area of Jewish settlement in Warsaw was near the Great Theater, a bustling commercial center in the heart of town that was an ideal location for Jewish merchants. From there, settlement spread to Tlomackie Street and other areas that already had Jewish inhabitants from the days of the *jurydyka*. Although anti-Semitic legislation continued to exist, including a prohibition from governmental posts, Jews began to make strides in various avenues of Polish society.

The Jewish Community as an official institution originated at this time, and soon a Jewish hospital and orphanage were built. Early in the century, a wooden synagogue was built on Graniczna Street near the Saxon Gardens. In 1825, when Graniczna Street was no longer open to Jewish residents, the synagogue was destroyed. In addition, a so-called "German synagogue"—it was used mostly by German immigrants—was erected on Danilowiczowska Street in 1802. The synagogue later became one of the first in Warsaw to include Polish sermons in the liturgy. Resentful Orthodox Jews mocked the synagogue as the "*Daytshe-Shul.*" Later, when the synagogue became too small, the Tlomackie Street Synagogue was erected as a symbol of Warsaw Jewish prosperity.

But Jewish rights in Warsaw were by no means viewed with enthusiasm by the neighboring Poles. Economic competition, coupled with the suspicion that the Jews were an arm of the Prussian regime, fueled a rising backlash that exploded on the Christian holiday of Corpus Christi, 1805. A procession carrying the sacrament near the Great Theater was evidently hit by some shingles from a neighboring roof. Immediately a rumor swept the crowd that Jews had thrown rocks to desecrate the sacrament. The rumor turned to hysteria; some even whispered that priests had been injured in the "attack." The mob attacked the Jewish quarter and began to beat up Jews and to loot and destroy Jewish homes and businesses. Only after three days was the Prussian army able to quell the pogrom. One newspaper report mentioned 95 arrests of the looters as well as arrests of Jews who were blamed for agitation, but numbers of Jewish casualties were omitted. One personal account expressed the uncertainty over the number of Jewish deaths, putting the number at anywhere from 50 to 1,000. Perhaps as a response to Christian hostility, the Prussian government decided to expel the Jews from several streets in Warsaw. However, the Prussian administration was ousted before the decree could take effect.

THE DUCHY OF WARSAW

It was Napoleon's army that ousted the Prussians. In 1806, the army defeated a combined Prussian-Russian force and captured the partition of Poland controlled by Prussia. In 1807, Napoleon formed the Grand Duchy of Warsaw with a Polish-controlled administration tied to France. The resulting upsurge in Polish nationalism led to another wave of anti-Semitic agitation. The Jews, after all, were associated with the despised Prussian regime, which had tolerated them and had even given them German names. The president of Warsaw, Pawel Bielinski, attempted to abolish all Jewish rights adopted since the first partition. Suddenly, the recently formed Warsaw Jewish Community found that it would be all but ignored by Warsaw's leaders. Bielinski sought to replace the Jewish Community administration with a single representative whom he would appoint himself. This had been the method of government contact with the Jews before the partitions. After great protests among the Jews of Warsaw, the plan was abandoned and the Jewish Community's role reinstated.

The Jews had reason to rejoice when Napoleon issued his Duchy Constitution, which granted freedom of religion and equality to all citizens. However, Napoleon immediately dashed these hopes in 1808 when he issued his "infamous decree." The decree sharply curtailed Jewish freedoms and postponed Jewish citizenship rights for ten years.

Soon the issue of Jewish settlement rights in Warsaw returned to the government's agenda. The Warsaw municipal authorities joined the guilds in demanding an expulsion of Jews from Warsaw, and in 1809 the Jews were expelled from the Old Town and various other streets. The only exception to this law was a quota of two Jewish families per street. These families were required to be indistinguishable from Gentiles in language, dress, and education. In addition, only the wealthiest Jews were permitted the privilege of residence.

Jews were initially expelled from their burgeoning neighborhood in the district of the Great Theater. It was at this time that the dense Jewish neighborhood in the northern district of Warsaw began to develop. Among the most famous of these streets were Nalewki and Franciszkanska, which soon became a hubbub of Jewish entrepreneurial and social life. Over the course of the nineteenth century, the neighborhood was to become a legendary quarter for Polish Jews and the cradle of one of the most remarkable communities in the Diaspora.

At the same time, Hasidism made sweeping inroads among the Jews of Warsaw. Earlier, in 1781, a fierce debate had been held in the Praga district between Rabbi Avraham Katzenellenbogen of Brisk for the *mitnagdim*, or opponents of Hasidism, and Rabbi Levi Yitzchak of Berditchev, who stood for Hasidism. The *mitnagdim* considered theirs an overwhelming victory, but their celebrations were short lived: Within the coming generations, Hasidism was to earn massive public support among the poorer Jews of Warsaw.

ST. PETERSBURG ON THE VISTULA

In accordance with the Congress of Vienna convened after Napoleon's defeat, Congress Poland (also known as the "Kingdom of Poland" or, later, the "Vistula lands") was established in 1815. Congress Poland was to exist as a domain of the Russian empire, with varying degrees of autonomy, until the Polish state was reborn after the First World War.

From the beginning of life in Congress Poland, Warsaw's Jews continued to be barred from the center of town—and thus confined to restricted residential areas. In 1816, there were 15,600 Jews in Warsaw, or 19.2 percent of the total population. Aristocrats, wary of Jewish incursions in the financial sector, were opposed to the campaign for Jewish civil rights that was gaining strength elsewhere in Europe. Jews continued to be barred citizenship, and from 1825 Jews again had to purchase tickets to enter the center of town. In 1846, the government tried to force the Jews to dress only in "European" clothing. After a great deal of protest among traditional Jews, the authorities relented. Only in 1862 were anti-Semitic prohibitions abolished in Congress Poland.

In contrast with Galicia and other areas of partitioned Poland, Congress Poland experienced rapid industrialization and economic growth during the nineteenth century. Several Jews distinguished themselves at this time as industrialists and traders. In 1847, seventeen of the twenty bankers in Warsaw were Jewish, and in 1849, roughly half of the people involved in commerce in Warsaw were Jewish. Even earlier under the Russian reign, several Jewish financiers had flourished as suppliers of the Russian army. At the time, golden opportunities were ripe, with the military's annual budget peaking at 30 million zloty. Among the chief suppliers of the army were Warsaw Jews, who dealt in linen, clothes, shoes, braid, horse accessories, food, and other equipment. Warsaw Jews such as Jacob Epstein (1771–1843) and Berek Sonnenberg (1764–1822), buried near each other in the Warsaw Jewish Cemetery, both supplied the Russian Army from the earliest years of Congress Poland. Epstein was later appointed banker of Poland's treasury council.

JEWISH REBELS

The rise of this Jewish industrial class sparked a campaign for Polonization among many Jews in the second half of the nineteenth century. An increasingly popular term emerged that cleverly obfuscated one's identity: "Pole of the Mosaic Faith." It is interesting that assimilated Jews chose the Polish nation, rather than the dominant Russian empire, as the object of their assimilationist swoon. It turned out that many Jews identified with the Poles as partners in subjugation. The Poles, after all, were themselves a somewhat persecuted nationality under Russian rule. There were even some Poles who saw a future redemption through unity with the Jews. The nineteenth-century revolutionary Aleksander Wezyk boldly stated,

> Divided, we shall both perish . . . only mutual assistance and aims can be effective. In an independent Poland there shall in future be no differences between the Christian Pole and the Pole of the Mosaic faith. In a future Poland, if through work God permits us to have it, all will be free, all will enjoy equal rights, we will all be joined by a bond of brotherly love. (quoted in Stefan Kieniewicz's "The Jews of Warsaw, Polish Society and the Partitioning Powers 1795–1861")

It was the dream of full equality that compelled many Jews to join forces with Poles not only in cultural projects but in the Polish revolts against the Czarist regime. Jewish solidarity with the Poles surged in the Kosciuszko insurrection of 1794 (see above), as well as in later anti-Russian insurrections in 1830 and 1863.

In the November Uprising of 1830–31, wealthy assimilated Jews as well as Orthodox Jews served in the National Guard. In fact, the issue of the Orthodox in the National Guard became a celebrated—and hotly contested—issue of the day. It seemed that Polish merchants, fearful that Jewish participation in the armed struggle would help the Jews win accolade and emancipation, tried to erect barriers to the Jews. They demanded that all Jews in the National Guard erase their distinguishing marks—ie., their beards. Warsaw's first chief rabbi, *Solomon Zalman Lipschitz* (1765–1839), known as the "Chemdat Shlomo," argued that Jews should be permitted to express their patriotism without abandoning Jewish law. He argued that a compromise could be reached through a nicely groomed trim. Polish soldiers preferred a different compromise: a separate "Civil Guard," nearly equal in status to the National Guard, that would be reserved for Jews. In order to maintain their superiority, soldiers in the National Guard insisted that Civil Guard uniforms be decorated with brown, and not amaranth, lapels. The Civil Guard eventually included 1,000 Jews; an additional 300–400 Jews served in the National Guard with clean and well-shaven faces.

But it was the January Uprising of 1863 in which Jewish-Polish unity reached mythic proportions. After a series of anti-Semitic decisions by Czar Nicholas I and his successor, Russian rule had become more onerous in the eyes of Warsaw's Jews. Chief Rabbi Dov Berush Meisels (1798–1870), a beacon of Orthodox Jewish activism in the nineteenth century, went down in Jewish and Polish history as a charismatic patriot who rallied the Jews in the struggle against Russian rule. Two years before the official uprising, demonstrations in Warsaw set the stage for unprecedented unity between Poles and Jews. In February 1861, after the first casualties in street fighting, Rabbi Meisels was among the first prominent men in Warsaw to sign a proclamation to the Czar asking for Polish rights. He issued an appeal for solidarity with the Polish struggle whose fiery message was compared to a declaration of war on Russia. Churches and synagogues, starting in Warsaw and then spreading throughout the entire country, sang the national anthem as part of the service. Many churches even exchanged gifts with synagogues, as a symbol of their fraternal and patriotic bonds.

Another symbol of the age was the teenage martyr Michal Landy (1844–1861). Landy was shot and killed after he lifted the cross of a fallen priest during patriotic demonstrations in Warsaw in 1861. He instantly became a mythical figure among Christian Polish nationalists, who interpreted the Jew with the cross as a symbol of Jewish magnanimity and Jewish-Polish unity. The legend immediately entered some of the most seminal literature of the period. The anonymous revolutionary poem *Dwa Izraele* ("The Two Israels") addresses Landy directly:

> You sacrificed the heart of your nation
> Oh, you chosen among the chosen people
> To unite forever the two nations
> To seal by blood their eternal union.
>
> quoted in Magdalena Opalski and Israel Bartal, *Poles and Jews: A Failed Brotherhood*

Throughout the country, there was a feeling of euphoria among Poles and Jews united in their struggle against an oppressive regime. Although the insurrection was ultimately a failure, it represented the historic peak of Jewish-Polish solidarity that has never since been matched.

JEWISH LIFE IN THE NINETEENTH CENTURY

In the middle of the nineteenth century, a specifically Jewish form of national politics and activism had not yet fired the imagination of Warsaw's assimilated Jews. Such movements would only become widespread late in the century, with a massive influx of Jewish immigrants from the east. Even Reform Judaism did not have the same intoxicating hold on Warsaw's Jews, as it had elsewhere in Europe. The esteemed Tlomackie Street Synagogue, built in 1875–1878, was less a center of progressive Jewish thought than a triumphant symbol of rising Jewish affluence. Generally speaking, those Jews in Warsaw who had repudiated religious tradition found little interest in replacing it with either Zionism or with religious reform.

In spite of this resistance to Jewish national movements, many assimilated Jews worked to modernize the infrastructure of the Jewish Community. Perhaps the most prominent of these was **Ludwik Natanson** (1822–1896), a renowned physician who served as chairman of the Jewish Community starting in 1871. Supported by the growing elite of Jewish assimilationists, Natanson reorganized the Community's finances, modernized the Jewish Community structure, and created such indispensable facilities as a Jewish Community building on Grzybowska Street and a Jewish hospital. In addition, Jews began to make inroads into various cultural fields, notably in art, science, and publishing. Notable among Warsaw's publishers were **Henryk Natanson** (1820–1895)—a brother of Ludwik—and **Samuel Orgelbrand** (1810–1868), who produced the first general Polish encyclopedia.

But aside from these noteworthy exceptions, the overall picture of nineteenth-century Warsaw Jewry was a religious life dominated by traditional Orthodoxy, and an economic and social life defined by relative poverty. Most Jews worked as peddlers, shopkeepers, artisans, laborers, and porters.

By the second half of the nineteenth century, Jewish Warsaw was overwhelmingly hasidic. It is estimated that two-thirds of the Jews in Warsaw were hasidic. By far the most popular branch of Hasidism was Gerer, led by the charismatic Rabbi **Yitzchak Meir Alter** (1799–1866), author of the *Chiddushei HaRim*. The seat of Gerer was a tiny town located just outside Warsaw, called Gora Kalwaria but known in Yiddish as Ger. Rabbi Alter divided his time between Gora Kalwaria and the Jewish district of Warsaw, where he garnered a massive following in the 1860s. Rabbi Alter has been credited with singlehandedly changing Warsaw into a capital of Hasidism. Rabbi Alter's successor, Rabbi **Yehudah Aryeh Alter** (1847–1905), also known as the *Sfas Emes* after his most famous work, transformed Gerer Hasidism into one of the strongest hasidic movements in the world, attracting hundreds of thousands of followers up until the Holocaust.

LITVAK WARSAW

The Warsaw Jewish Community experienced an enormous surge in its numbers for much the same reason the Jewish population increased in America: Pogroms in Russia and the hope for economic betterment. In the second half of the nineteenth century, an easing of border restrictions led many Jews to life in Congress Poland, with its less anti-Semitic stance in Jewish affairs. Specifically, Jews were attracted by less stringent army requirements and easier rules of residency in Congress Poland. Warsaw, with its growing trade links to Western Europe, had long been considered a golden city among Russian Jews.

In the 1880s, state-sponsored anti-Semitism throughout Russia caused further emigration to Warsaw. Using the 1881 assassination of Czar Alexander II as a pretext, mobs throughout Russia launched pogroms against the Jewish population. The hatred even spilled over into Congress Poland, and on Christmas in 1881, a pogrom was launched in Warsaw from the steps of the Church of the Holy Cross. Nonetheless, the situation in Russia was far more somber. The so-called "May Laws" of 1882 prohibited Jews from further settlement in rural Russia, imposed severe restrictions on Jewish residence within the Pale of Settlement, and instituted a suffocating quota on Jews in academia and the workforce. As a result, tens of thousands of Jews began to move west. Jewish life in Russia continued to deteriorate with the Imperial ukase of Passover, 1891, that expelled all the 20,000 Jews of Moscow. Expulsions from St. Petersburg and Kharkov were soon to follow.

Immigration from these tumultuous regions in the east, in addition to ongoing immigration from the provinces, made Warsaw the largest Jewish Community in Europe. The Jewish population in Warsaw grew from 72,800 in 1864 to 130,000 in 1882. By 1897, the Jewish population had risen to 219,128. Jews accounted for over one-third the population of the city.

Most of the immigrants had come from Lithuania and Belorussia and were commonly referred to as "Litvaks" (Lithuanian Jews). Interestingly, native Warsaw Jews had mixed feelings about the newcomers. First, there was the unwanted economic competition from similarly skilled men. Their fluency in Russian even put the newcomers at a competitive advantage, for they could navigate Warsaw's Russian bureaucracy with relative ease. In addition, Warsaw's native Jews claimed, the newcomers worked for lower wages than the locals and isolated themselves from the Community. Among many Jews, "Litvak" came to be a term of derision and contempt. One of the greatest complaints was that the Litvaks, with their Russian speech and foreign ways, would make the Jews look like an arm of the ruling empire. The fear was that these Jewish "Russians" would thwart Jewish efforts at greater civil rights and unity with the Poles.

Although much of the resentment of the Litvaks was old-fashioned xenophobia, on the issue of Jewish-Polish relations, Warsaw's native Jews had reason to fear. Many Poles viewed the Russian-speaking Jews as outsiders and as collaborators with the Russians. Anti-Semites, goaded on by such hot buttons as Russian-language Jewish schools and the burgeoning Yiddish press, spoke of the ultimate incompatibility of Poles and Jews. Jews, they contended, were an alien element who used their Russian contacts to profit off the Poles.

Thus the Litvak presence in Warsaw became a lightning rod in the anti-Semitic campaign against the integration of Jews into Polish society.

But before too long, the Litvaks blended into the Community of Jews in Warsaw, appealing in particular to non-religious, cosmopolitan Jews. For the Litvaks imported much more than the Russian language to Warsaw. Far more importantly for the social evolution of Warsaw Jewry, the Litvaks brought with them radical concepts of Jewish socialism and Zionism that had been incubating for years in Russia. It was largely due to Litvak influence that, from the end of the nineteenth century right up until the Holocaust, Warsaw had become one of the world's most important centers of Jewish national culture.

THE JEWISH UTOPIAS

By the beginning of the twentieth century, Warsaw could boast one of the most diverse Jewish cultures in Europe. In the years between the two World Wars, that culture would blossom even further, as Zionist youth movements and a national Orthodox party entered the fray. In spite of the precarious political situation, one could argue that Jewish Warsaw experienced its ultimate Golden Age in the modern period. The number of avenues with which Warsaw's Jews expressed their Jewishness remains unmatched, in any part of the world, to this day.

Much of the cultural and political activities among non-religious Jews centered on grand, utopian solutions to the Jewish national question. Perhaps the most popular expression of this utopia was the various forms of socialism that captivated Jews throughout Eastern Europe. Jews were active in the Polish Socialist Party and the illegal Polish Communist Party, but the movement that attracted the most Jews in the period was the Bund. The Bund, or "General Jewish Workers' Union," envisioned a Yiddish-based, autonomous Jewish culture within a socialist state on the Eastern European soil where Jews had lived for centuries. Formed in Vilna in 1897, the Bund rejected both religious Orthodoxy and the Zionist idea that Jewish fulfillment could be achieved only in a separate state. The catchword among Bundists, "*Doykeyt*" ("Hereness"), expressed it all: Jewish life *here* in Eastern Europe, as part of a tolerant, multicultural socialist society, was the most perfect fulfillment of the Jewish experience in the Diaspora.

The Polish Bund was formed in Warsaw in 1914 as a body independent from the Russian Bund. Far more than a trade union, the Bund built schools, workers' kitchens, a youth club, a women's organization, and a sports club. The Bund made spectacular strides among Poland's Jews in the years before the Second World War. In 1936, Bund representatives resoundingly defeated the Orthodox party Agudath Israel in elections to the Jewish Community Council. In elections to the Warsaw City Council, the Bund won the majority of Jewish votes before the war.

Another utopian movement was, of course, Zionism. In many ways, Zionism was the most widely supported political movement among Polish Jews in the interwar period. Reasons for this ranged from a rising Polish nationalism to a rising Polish anti-Semitism. There was a fertile breeding ground for Zionism among a massive Jewish population that was neither religious nor overly assimilated into Polish society.

Zionism itself was a movement with more strands than it was easy to sort out. The movement seemed to add new meaning to the saying, "Two Jews, three opinions." Before the Second World War in Poland, there were six socialist or labor Zionist parties such as the Poale Zion, five General Zionist parties, and youth movements such as Ha-shomer ha-tsair and Gordonia. Most religious parties were anti-Zionist, but the Mizrachi was a movement of Orthodox Jews who were strongly Zionist. There were socialist Zionists and antisocialists; Yiddishists and Hebraists; Diaspora-oriented and Palestino-centric; centrist and Revisionist. The diversity of Zionist life was one factor that made it appealing to such a broad sector of Warsaw's Jews. Perhaps the most visionary and idealistic Zionists were the members of Hehalutz (Pioneer) youth movement. Hehalutz made no bones about it: Its purpose was to create a new Jewish nation to be shipped out to colonize Palestine. Arguing that the Diaspora had produced a weak Jewish type, Hehalutz worked for the evolution of the Jewish people into a classless proletarian society that would reach fruition in a Jewish state.

Internal disputes abounded, such as the question of priorities. Should they concentrate on emigration to Palestine or on the campaign for Jewish rights and Jewish cultural renewal here in Poland? In the 1920s, most Polish Zionist work was concentrated on Diaspora activities. In addition, in spite of the Hebraic emphasis of traditional Zionism, Poland's Zionists were unabashedly Yiddishist. After all, Yiddish, and not Hebrew, was the living language of East European Jews.

In the midst of this nationalist Jewish carnival, the Orthodox were not to be left out. Partly in response to the growing power of assimilated Jewry, traditionally observant Jews decided to channel their populist energy into a movement, complete with offices, a newspaper, and seats in government, that would defend the interests of Orthodox Jewry. The movement, originally formed in Germany in 1912, was named Agudath Israel ("League of Israel"). Agudath Israel was anti-Zionist, regarding the Zionist movement as a usurpation of God's Providence and plan for redemption. The movement had a firm base among hasidic Jewry, especially among Gerer Hasidism, which was by far the most widespread and influential hasidic group in pre-war Warsaw. It almost always dominated the leadership of the Warsaw Jewish Community, and established an impressive network of Jewish schools. During the years of the Pilsudski regime (*see page 164*), the Agudath Israel succeeded in forming a relatively strong alliance with the Polish government. The government, preferring Agudath Israel's conservatism to the revolutionary incitement of both the Bund and the Zionist parties, sanctioned the movement's yeshivah system and assisted the movement's supremacy within the Jewish Community. In return, Agudath Israel supported the government with the backing of a widespread base of Orthodox voters. In the 1930s, with the massive rise of anti-Semitism in Poland, Agudath Israel lost much of its popularity as Jews opted for more radical movements in the growing climate of terror.

JEWISH CULTURE IN WARSAW:
THE TRIUMPH OF DIASPORA JEWRY

In 1939, 380,567 Jews lived in Warsaw, giving the city the world's largest Jewish population outside of New York. Jews had been arriving to the Polish capital throughout the interwar period, attracted to the freedom and opportunities rampant in Europe's great Jewish metropolis. Warsaw was like New York City: Sure, there were other centers of Jewish life, but nothing could compare to the bustling exhilaration of the capital. By that time, streets like Nalewki and Franciszkanska in the northern district had become legendary as the vital arteries of Jewish life. The Jewish district had also stretched west and south to encompass several streets that were predominately Jewish. From the second half of the nineteenth century until the Second World War, the Jewish population in Warsaw hovered around one-third the total population. In the second decade of the twentieth century, the proportion came close to 40 percent.

Warsaw's Jews were mostly tradesmen and merchants. In 1918, 73 percent of private business in Warsaw was owned by Jews. Most of these businesses were small, family-run shops. With the increase in anti-Semitism in the interwar period, this proportion shrank to 54 percent by 1928 and continued to shrink in the coming years. Over the course of the same period, Jews turned to industry in ever-increasing numbers. Unlike the Jews of Warsaw in the nineteenth century, when the city was ruled by Russia, Warsaw's Jews in the interwar period had far fewer opportunities to become great businessmen. Nonetheless, certain individuals became successful. The Jewish Merchants Association, founded in 1906, claimed 6,000 members in Warsaw in 1928. In spite of rising obstacles to Jews in the professions, Jews continued to be active as doctors, lawyers, and teachers in the interwar years.

Although anti-religious movements such as the Bund and the Zionist parties were widely popular in Warsaw, Jewish spiritual life in the city was very much dominated by Orthodoxy. Side by side with cultural forays into the arts, science, and literature, Jewish Warsaw maintained a strong religious core that was entirely unmatched in Jewish metropolises in Western Europe. This was one aspect that made the community unique. Even assimilated Jews did not press for any more religious reform than Polish-language sermons and male choirs. In fact, Jewish religious life in Warsaw was best represented not by the stately Tlomackie Street Synagogue, but by the countless hasidic prayer halls dotted throughout the city. In the 1930s, there were 300 *shtiebels*, or Jewish prayer halls, in Warsaw. These prayer halls were not ostentatious; usually the synagogues were converted from apartment flats. Franciszkanska Street alone had 35 *shtiebels*. In addition, there were hundreds of *hadarim*, or Jewish elementary schools, throughout the city. Many hasidic rebbes settled in Warsaw during the interwar years.

From the end of the nineteenth century, Yiddish language, literature, and theater experienced a booming renaissance in Warsaw. By the end of the 1930s, there were 230 Yiddish newspapers in Poland. Most of the widely circulated newspapers, including the two mass circulation dailies, *Haynt* and *Moment*, were based in Warsaw. **Isaac Leib Peretz** (1852–1915), the first modernist Yiddish writer, transformed the language into a highly sophisticated literary medium. **Isaac Meir Weissenberg** (1881–1938) developed a graphic, naturalist style out of the literature. The world-famous **Isaac Bashevis Singer** (1904–1991) began his career in Warsaw and went on to immortalize the city's prewar life in much of his writing. Countless other Jews turned to Yiddish literature as a means of self-expression. The famous Writers' Club on Tlomackie Street became the center of activity among dozens of writers and journalists. The Yiddish language also thrived in the theater. Yiddish theater had thrived in the late nineteenth century in a regulated form: The Russian authorities, as well as Orthodox censors in the Community, limited the performances in their language and content. In 1905, though, the Literary Company was established in Warsaw, and modern Yiddish theater experienced a colorful heyday. **Esther Rachel Kaminska** (1870–1925), the "Mother of Yiddish Theater," was one of the most famous Jewish actresses of the age, giving performances throughout Europe and the United States.

POLAND AND THE JEWS BETWEEN THE WARS

In 1918, the Polish state was reborn after nearly a century and a half of partition. In the new map of Central Eastern Europe drawn after the First World War, one of the most pressing concerns was how the new states would safeguard the rights of their national minorities. Within the borders of the Polish state, around 40 percent of the citizens were not ethnic Poles. The biggest minority was Ukrainian. As long as one considered Judaism to be a nation, and not simply a religion, Jews constituted the second largest minority. Roughly three million Jews, or ten percent of the total population, found themselves within the borders of this new state. Over half of Poland's Jews lived in central Poland, in the area formerly known as Congress Poland. There was a high concentration of Jews in cities; in eastern provinces, Jews sometimes comprised over half the urban population. In Warsaw, the population of Jews approximated one-third the total population.

Over the course of the interwar years, the relationship between Poles and Jews—including, among other things, the degree to which Poles were ready to integrate the Jewish minority, and the degree to which the Jews themselves wished to integrate into Polish society—was to become a pressing national concern. It all began with the Minorities' Treaty, negotiated in Paris between the victorious Allies and various new states and signed in 1919. The Minorities Treaty ensured political and civil rights for minority groups, including a prohibition against discrimination in the workplace. It forbade the state from forcing Jews to violate *Shabbat*, and spoke of the establishment of state-subsidized Jewish schools. In 1922, **Yitzchak Grunbaum** (1879–1970), leader of the General Zionists in Poland, formed a minorities bloc that attempted to unite Jewish, Ukrainian, German, and other minority concerns into a single party. In 1922 elections to the Sejm, the minorities bloc won 22 percent of the vote. But although many secular Jewish groups considered the Minorities Treaty to be a "Magna Carta" for the Jews in Poland, Polish opinion was much more cynical. By and large, Poles viewed the campaign for Jewish cultural autonomy as evidence that Jews were not concerned with the welfare of the Polish state. Such views were enforced, for instance, when the state refused to subsidize Jewish schools, when graduates of Jewish schools were denied entry to universities, and when Jews were all but barred from jobs in the public sector. With the wide popularity of the right-wing, rabidly anti-Semitic National Democratic movement, civil rights for Jews—as well as for all other minorities in Poland—were often trampled upon.

In 1926, Marshal Jozef Pilsudski, a Polish military hero who had staved off the Bolsheviks in 1920, staged a coup d'etat and became leader of the Polish state. To this day, historians have had an awkward time with Pilsudski. He started as a socialist but drifted increasingly to the right throughout his reign, ultimately dissolving parliament in 1930. Still, Pilsudski was not quite a dictator and his government, especially when compared with other governments of the period, stopped short of Fascism. From the start, Poland's Jews were optimistic about Pilsudski's reign. Pilsudski was not anti-Semitic and did not tolerate anti-Semitism among his followers; indeed, he was an enemy of the right-wing National Democrats. His federalist bias led many Jews to believe he would set up a multinational state in Poland. Although a multinational state never emerged, Pilsudski quelled the waves of populist anti-Semitism while he was in office. The situation for Jews continued to deteriorate in the economic sector, but at least Pilsudski did not use anti-Semitism as an organized state policy during his reign. When seen in light of the crisis that followed his death in 1935, Pilsudski appears to have been a genuine beacon of stability at the time. To this day, many Jews consider him a hero.

After Pilsudski's death in 1935, anti-Semitism burst into an unprecedented, nationwide phenomenon as the government was increasingly moved by Catholic anti-Semitism and totalitarian principles. Political parties modelled themselves on the Nazi party, and from 1936 the government led an open economic campaign against the Jews. Polish gangs forced an economic suffocation of Jewish merchants. "Aryan" signs went up in Polish shops; lists of those who disobeyed the boycott were published in right-wing newspapers; Jewish shops and stalls were destroyed. The campaign spilled into pogrom: according to one conservative estimate, hundreds of Jews were murdered and over 1,000 Jews were wounded in over 150 Polish towns during pogroms of 1935–1936.

In the universities, the so-called "ghetto benches" were established as segregated seating for Jews. Some Jews, refusing to be humiliated in the classroom, preferred to stand defiantly in the back of the room rather than sit on these benches. Gangs of right-wing students roamed the halls looking to attack Jewish students. Several Jews were murdered in these pogroms of the Polish intelligentsia. In 1936, the Sejm tried to outlaw the kosher slaughter of meat. Meanwhile, the government used every means short of brute force to encourage the Jews to emigrate. The government tried to convince Britain to relax its restrictive quota of Jewish immigrants to Palestine, and even researched Madagascar as a possible place to unload the Jews. With the government united with the opposition in their abrogation of human rights, the Polish Socialist Party was the only large Polish organization that stood by the Jews and combatted anti-Semitism.

The increasingly uncompromising attitude of the Poles led to a rise in Jewish involvement in the Bund and the Communist Party, with their campaign against Polish Fascism, and in Revisionist Zionism and the Pioneer movement, with their emphasis on evacuation to Palestine. In 1936, Zev Jabotinsky (1880–1940), leader of the right-wing Zionist Revisionists, made a public appeal to evacuate 1.5 million Eastern European Jews—half of them from Poland—to Palestine. The Polish government loved the plan, but many Jewish leaders, especially in the Bund and Agudath Israel, rejected it in favor of continued work in the Diaspora. In the years 1919 to 1942, 139,756 Polish Jews emigrated to Palestine. This number represented less than five percent of the Polish Jewish population. Many more Jews left for the United States and other countries, during the years that those countries were willing to accept Jews.

There is one thing to keep in mind about pre-World War II Polish treatment of the Jews. As anti-Semitic as it was, Polish policy was not racially based, as it was at the time in Germany. Rather, it was based on the idea that the Polish nation would not tolerate minorities. In other words, the Poles viewed the Jews as an entirely separate nation that could not coexist with the Polish people. It was an idea wholeheartedly advanced by the Zionist movement as well. This should go some way toward explaining why devout anti-Semites in the Polish government actively assisted young Zionists in military training and other matters. The Bund and Agudath Israel, by contrast, viewed the Jews as a separate nation that could and must coexist with the Poles.

At the time, it was a fierce Jewish debate: Which policy was best for Poland's Jews? By 1939, the debate was swiftly silenced with the German invasion of Poland and the beginning of the Holocaust of Poland's Jews.

THE HOLOCAUST

In September 1939, with massive aerial bombardments and swift troop advances, the German army overwhelmed Poland's relatively unprepared resistance. On Warsaw alone, the Germans rained between ten and thirty thousand shells daily. By the end of the month, the Soviet Union had annexed Lithuania and other territories in accordance with its none-too-secret intention to dissect the spoils of a conquered Poland. Hitler was left with an area that included approximately two million Polish Jews, including the entire territory of Warsaw. A few thousand Jews managed to escape Poland, but during the summer of 1940 the doors to emigration were closed.

The effect on the roughly 360,000 Jews remaining in Warsaw was immediate. Even during the initial bombardments, which targeted the civilian centers and destroyed or damaged twenty-five percent of the city, Jewish districts in the northern parts of Warsaw were singled out for particular severity. In keeping with its perverted obsession with the Jewish calendar, Germany made unremitting air raids on the Jewish districts during Rosh Hashanah and Yom Kippur. One week later, Jewish school teacher Chaim Kaplan wrote in his diary, "Beautiful Warsaw, city of royal glory, queen of cities—has been destroyed like Sodom and Gomorrah. There are streets which have been all but wiped off the face of the earth. . . . In the midst of the ruins thousands of human beings lie buried" (Chaim Kaplan, *Scroll of Agony*).

After Warsaw fell to the Nazis, there were mixed rumors and colliding opinions regarding Hitler's intentions. Many elderly Jews, who recalled their experiences in the First World War, remembered the dignified behavior of German troops and were quick to downplay rumors of impending horrors. When the German soldiers entered and proceeded to loot and riot through the city, forcing themselves into Jewish apartments and making off with valuables, there were those who interpreted it as proof that the occupiers had no intention of staying long. But all hopes were dispelled when the Germans kidnapped Jews from the streets for forced labor, forced Jews violently out of soup lines, "Aryanized" all Jewish business and property, and cancelled all pension rights for Jewish retirees. Jews were to be removed from all areas of commerce. Early in 1940 the Jews were issued separate ration cards from the Poles, which denied them various foods. They could not walk on certain streets and gardens, and riding on trains was forbidden. Meanwhile, the propaganda machine was quickly set into motion. In his first public address on October 26, Hans Frank, the governor-general of German-occupied Poland, declared, ". . . there is no place for agitators, profiteers, or Jewish parasites in the area that has been placed under German sovereignty." By the end of 1939, all Jews in Warsaw, twelve years of age and up, were required to wear a Star of David imprinted on a white armband.

As early as November 11, 1939, Chaim Kaplan recorded his prophetic fear:

> This is not the eve of destruction, but destruction itself. Our personal degradation is calamitous, and material impoverishment is bound up in our degradation. The entire administrative machinery is geared toward this end. Everywhere—"no Jews allowed." Czarism used to do this, but without sadism. (Chaim Kaplan, *Scroll of Agony*)

The Nazis established the Judenrat, a body similar in structure and composition to the prewar *kehillah*, or Jewish Community council. The main difference, though, was that the Judenrat's primary responsibility was to implement German decrees concerning—i.e., against—the Jews. One of its first activities was mobilizing Jews for slave labor for the Germans. Soon enough, the Judenrat's main activity became the establishment and administration of the Warsaw ghetto.

The first pretext for the creation of a ghetto was German propaganda that the Jews were diseased and must be quarantined. This was an obvious lie; although many Jews had already succumbed to typhus, the epidemic had been contained and was on the verge of being eradicated when the Germans announced the quarantine. Nonetheless, in March 1940 the Jewish district was labelled "A Plague-Infected Area." Posters were pasted throughout Warsaw with a caricatured Jew and the words "Jew—Louse—Typhus." At the end of March, when the Judenrat was ordered to pay for and construct a wall surrounding the designated area, signs were posted on thirty-four streets leading into the Jewish district with the words "Danger: Epidemic Zone." To the Poles the Germans spoke of containing the epidemic, but to the Jews they spoke of protecting the population from Polish pogromniks.

Early on, the Germans had wanted to establish a ghetto away from the city center, where it wouldn't interrupt Warsaw's transportation and economy. Plans included locating a ghetto across the river, in the suburb of Praga, as well as erecting two ghettos on the outskirts of the city. But after considering the daunting task of resettlement, the Germans chose the crowded Jewish district as the site for the ghetto. Again showing their perverse predilection for Jewish holidays, the Germans chose October 12, 1940—Yom Kippur— to set up loudspeakers throughout Warsaw and blast the decree to establish a Jewish ghetto. The Jews and Poles had until November 15 to separate along racial lines.

Once it was sealed, it became apparent that the true purpose of the ghetto was not to quarantine the Jews but to exterminate them gradually through disease and starvation. As Hans Frank boasted about the situation in Poland in 1942, "We are sentencing 1.2 million

Jews to death" through lack of food. To gain a sense of the physical conditions of ghetto life, note the following statistics catalogued in Yisrael Gutman's *The Jews of Warsaw, 1939–1943*:

1. The fact that there were only 375 acres of living space when the ghetto was established meant that thirty percent of the population of Warsaw was forced into 2.4 percent of the city's area.
2. Of the eighteen hundred streets in Warsaw, only seventy-three were contained in the ghetto.
3. The population was over two hundred thousand people per square mile in the ghetto.
4. There was an average of 9.2 people living in each room of the ghetto.
5. In 1941, the daily caloric content of food distributed to the Germans was 2,613 calories; to the Poles, 699 calories; to the Jews, 184 calories. (As a point of comparison, the minimum daily caloric intake for an ordinary-sized adult is 2,000–2,400 calories.)

Basic living conditions in the ghetto were appalling. Forced to construct a separate city on the burned-out remains of the German bombardments, with neither a treasury nor an endemic economy by which to subsist, the Jews were being condemned to die in a collective, open-air prison. Often when we think of the Holocaust we imagine the most extreme images—the gas chambers and crematoria—but the ghettoes themselves were also factories of death; they differed from extermination camps only in the speed and efficiency of genocide. In this way, the situation in the ghetto was worse than that of a prison or POW camp. As Holocaust historian Lucy Dawidowicz once noted, "Death bestrode the Nazi ghetto and was its true master, exercising its dominion through hunger, forced labor, and disease" (Lucy Dawidowicz, *The War against the Jews 1933–1945*). Even the most common comparison—that of the Christian-decreed ghettoes, which defined six hundred years of European Jewish existence—is misleading. In those ghettoes, isolation was not absolute. And in those ghettoes, the intention was to separate and oppress the Jews, not to murder them outright.

At the beginning of 1941, there were about 380,000 people crammed into the ghetto. The population rose as the Germans deported Jews from other cities to Warsaw. By the spring of 1941, refugees in the ghetto numbered 130,000. One out of every three Jews was a refugee. At its peak in March 1941 the ghetto population reached 445,000. The one factor that kept the population from expanding indefinitely was the skyrocketing mortality rate of the ghetto. It has been estimated that one hundred thousand people died while interned in the ghetto. The main cause of death was starvation and disease.

Since the Germans controlled all the food entering the ghetto, they had free rein to institute a policy of starvation. It was hard enough to find and purchase food in "Aryan" Warsaw. For the Jews, obtaining food on the free market was forbidden, and any food sold on the streets had a price that reflected its scarcity. Rationing, which was instituted by the Germans in December 1939, discriminated severely against the Jews. Ration cards were dubbed *bona*, implying that it was like throwing a dog a bone. Stale bread and potatoes were the staple of almost every meal, accompanied by the worst quality cabbage, beets, carrots, turnips, radishes, and horseradish, and occasionally horsemeat or fish. When horsemeat was no longer available, some people would spread a mixture of coagulated horse blood, salt, and pepper on bread. One diarist, Yehuda Elberg, wrote, "A *dybbuk* has entered my belly. My belly talks, shouts, even has complaints, and drives me mad" (quoted in Lucy Dawidowicz, *The War against the Jews 1933–1945*). The ghetto's wealthier inmates would sell or barter furniture, clothing, and jewelry in order to buy the most meager portions of bread. In the summer of 1941, non-Jews marched through the street markets of the ghetto, buying up family heirlooms for a pittance. Every day, a total of almost one million zlotys were spent at these markets. Starving beggars filled the ghetto streets day and night. Emmanuel Ringelblum wrote in his diary in August 1941, "In the surrounding silence of night, the cries of the hungry beggar children are terribly insistent, and, however hard your heart, eventually you have to throw a piece of bread down to them—or else leave the house. . . . It's a common thing for beggar children like these to die on the sidewalk at night. I was told about one such horrible scene that took place in front of 24 Muranowska Street where a six-year-old beggar boy lay gasping all night, too weak to roll over to the piece of bread that had been thrown down to him from the balcony" (Jacob Sloan, ed., *Notes from the Warsaw Ghetto: The Journal of Emmanuel Ringelblum*). Horror stories abound of people reduced to eating feces, of relatives hiding the corpse of an infant so as to use the additional ration card, of people tripping over cadavers lying in the streets. The number of deaths due to starvation rose ominously as conditions in the ghetto continued to worsen. At the end of 1939, four Jews died of hunger. In 1940, the number increased to 91; in 1941, starvation took 11,000 lives.

One factor that kept starvation from killing the entire ghetto population was smuggling. The serpentine paths of smuggling were so intricate and varied that they became the primary means of survival for many in the ghetto. There were individuals—mostly children—who every day would sneak into "Aryan" Warsaw and bring back bare essentials. Then there were organized smuggling rings, which supplied most of the ghetto's food. Adam Czerniakow, chairman of the Judenrat, stated that eighty percent of food entering the ghetto was smuggled in. The professional rings became so efficient that it was not uncommon for one hundred sacks of wheat or sugar to be passed through an opening in a dozen minutes. Food, furniture, disassembled machinery, even entire cows passed into the ghetto in this manner. German and Polish policemen often permitted the smuggling in return for hefty bribes. At other times, though, a policeman might even shoot a child he caught sneaking through the gate. The "professional" class of smugglers mostly came from the prewar lower classes and even the underworld, accustomed as they were to danger. Ironically, it was due to these people—often the objects of disdain in prewar days—that the Jews of Warsaw could survive a little longer. A study of smuggling found in the Ringelblum Archive states emphatically that the smugglers were "in the front line of the ghetto's struggle against Hitlerism." Of course, some of them became relatively wealthy from the business, and were seen wining and dining in the ghetto's relatively fancy restaurants. Smuggling reached such life-saving proportions in the ghetto that a tongue-in-cheek jingle emerged:

> Hitler won't be able to cope
> With the English fleet
> And with the Russian sleet,
> With American dollars
> And Jewish smugglers.
>> (quoted in Lucy Dawidowicz,
>> *The War against the Jews 1933–1945*)

It should be mentioned that the assistance of individual Poles in the smuggling was not as magnanimous as is implied in postwar Polish reminiscences. Nothing was donated; the Poles profited from the black market prices they charged.

In spite of the best efforts of the smugglers, hunger continued to plague the ghetto inhabitants. This, combined with the overcrowding and awful sanitary conditions, led to a genuine outbreak of the typhus disease. Ironically, the Nazis had used typhus as their pretext for establishing the ghetto in the first place. In fact, the ghetto had the opposite effect. The Germans progressively curbed the water supply to the ghetto; the resulting hygienic conditions made the ghetto a breeding grounds for lice. Nurses would remove bandages from the poor to find hordes of lice underneath. One doctor reported seeing a boy covered with lice in the hair and inside the ears. He was "practically eaten alive by lice, and looked more like a corpse than a human being. I didn't even find out if he had typhus. He died before being moved to the ward" (quoted in Charles G. Roland, *Courage under Siege: Starvation, Disease, and Death in the Warsaw Ghetto*). But in general, it was the lice that carried typhus. A jingle from the period expresses the suffering:

> When we had nothing to eat,
> They gave us a turnip, they gave us a beet.
> Here have some grub, have some fleas,
> Have some typhus, die of disease.
>> (quoted in Lucy Dawidowicz,
>> *The War against the Jews 1933–1945*)

By spring of 1941, after the influx of huge numbers of Jewish refugees from outside Warsaw, reported cases of typhus began to increase. By July, it had reached epidemic proportions. Over eight hundred new cases were reported in June; the number was two thousand by September. In August alone, over fifty-five hundred Jews died of typhus. The actual numbers were far greater; the Judenrat tried to conceal the rising statistics from the Germans in order to avoid punitive action. At the same time, the Germans refused to allow sufficient treatment and ruled out any measures to prevent the disease. When a patient was reported, the Germans would seal off the entire house for two weeks, often causing more deaths by starvation. Terror of the disease quickly enveloped the ghetto. People would buy "typhus belts" lined with mercury, which were known to kill lice. All told, over one hundred thousand Jews suffered from typhus from the time the ghetto was established until the mass deportations began.

In addition to typhus, tuberculosis preyed on the starving and congested ghetto masses. According to one statistic, 33.7 percent of ghetto deaths in 1941 were due to tuberculosis, thus making it more of a scourge than typhus itself. But because tuberculosis was not dreaded like the typhus epidemic, and because it was frequently misdiagnosed, it is often omitted from recollections of the ghetto.

THE MASS DEPORTATIONS OF JULY 22–SEPTEMBER 21, 1942

For a long time, Warsaw's Jews believed that if they could somehow survive disease and hunger until the end of the war, they would make it out alive. Reports had been streaming into the ghetto about the systematic slaughter of Jews during the German invasion of the Soviet Union, but the majority of Jews in Warsaw were convinced that the Nazis would not dare liquidate the largest Jewish city on the continent. In fact, however, the Nazis considered the size of the Warsaw ghetto an ideal testing ground for genocide; if its liquidation was successful, Warsaw would be the "feather in the cap" of the Final Solution. With this in mind, Reichsfuhrer-SS Heinrich Himmler ordered on July 19, 1942, that the Final Solution in Poland must be finished by the end of the year.

Three days later, at noon on Wednesday, July 22, posters appeared throughout the ghetto bearing the following text:

"Upon order by the German authorities, all Jewish persons, regardless of age and sex, living in Warsaw, will be resettled in the East."

The Nazi Germans insisted on at least six thousand deportees per day. Their goal was to exterminate ninety percent of the Jews in Warsaw; the remainder would serve as laborers in a new, concentration-camp version of the ghetto. To increase the impression of "resettlement," the Nazis permitted the deportees to take up to seven pounds of belongings and valuables, as well as food for three days. These suitcases would form giant piles at the entrance to Treblinka as their owners were filed into the gas chambers.

There were four stages to the seven-week deportation to Treblinka, each one more vicious than the last. In the first phase, Jews were rounded up from the streets of the ghetto by the two-thousand-strong Jewish police force. In the next phase, SS men together with their Ukrainian, Latvian, and Lithuanian colleagues, rounded up the Jews themselves. The third phase disregarded almost all exemptions as the SS became increasingly frantic to meet its quotas. The fourth phase, called the "Cauldron," was the most brutal. All the remaining Jews were ordered to come to the streets surrounding the Umschlagplatz, the site of the deportations. Except for those who received a "life ticket" indicating they were essential employees in the ghetto, the assembled masses were sent to death in Treblinka.

The twisted meticulousness of the Germans is revealed in the opening and closing dates of the Aktion: It began on the eve of *Tishe Bi'av*, the Jewish day of mourning for the destruction of the First and Second Temples in Jerusalem, and ended on Yom Kippur, the Day of Atonement. Both these days are fast days on the Jewish calendar. All totalled, 265,040 Warsaw Jews, or seventy-five percent of the ghetto population, were deported and murdered at Treblinka by the end of the seven-week Aktion. Ten thousand more died during the Aktion, over ten thousand were deported to forced labor camps, and almost ten thousand escaped to "Aryan" Warsaw. By the end of September 1942, about fifty-five thousand Jews remained in the ghetto—over a third of whom were living in hiding, called "wildcats." According to Judenrat reports, 2,305 Jews died of gunshot wounds during August 1942 and in September, the number reached 3,158.

The second Aktion took place from January 18 to 22, 1943. Compared with the terrible summertime Aktion, this Aktion was relatively mild. Despite Himmler's demand that eight thousand Jews be rounded up, only five thousand were taken to the Umschlagplatz. Sobered from the summer of 1942, the Jews had gone into hiding and had begun to respond to the Germans with armed resistance.

THE WARSAW GHETTO UPRISING

The Warsaw Ghetto Uprising, the first urban uprising in all of German-occupied Europe, was waged from April 19 until the end of May 1943.

Some points should be made about the Uprising. First, it was not an uprising of the entire ghetto population. For various reasons—including the fierce secrecy of the Jewish Fighting Organization (ZOB) itself—there was a total of approximately 750 fighters from the ZOB and the other military group, the Jewish Fighting Union (ZZW), when the fighting broke out. Second, the Uprising was launched only after approximately ninety percent of the Jews in the ghetto had been murdered. Only forty thousand Jews remained in the ghetto by the time of the Uprising. In addition, the Jewish District was no longer a single ghetto but several reduced enclaves, some of which resembled concentration camps composed of factories where Jews worked. Finally, the fighters were not fighting with any hope of defeating the German army, saving their fellow Jews, or even saving their own lives. There were no illusions as to what would become of all the ghetto inmates. After the massive deportations of 1942, the population realized that they had all been sentenced to death. As they saw it, theirs was not a life or death choice but a choice between death with disgrace and death with honor. By fighting, they would seize their destiny from the Germans. As Mordecai Anielewicz, the commander of the ZOB, wrote in one of his last letters, the Uprising was like "a last desire in life."

It was the ubiquitous slaughter of the 1942 Aktion that actually gave the underground the freedom to plan a revolt. Before that, many young people had feared what would happen to their relatives if they were caught. While there was still hope for survival, they could not risk the lives of their families. After the Aktion in the summer of 1942, young Jews were paradoxically given the freedom to take up arms against the Germans.

During the Aktion itself, several Zionist youth movements founded the ZOB. With no weapons other than a single revolver, it set out to publicize the mass murders at Treblinka, to forge work permits so that people could remain in the ghetto, to assassinate members of the treacherous Jewish Police, and to sabotage German factories in the ghetto through arson attack. From the outset, the ZOB was faced with two options: either attack the Germans immediately during the Aktion itself, using whatever primitive weapons they could find, or wait, organize, and finally launch the most effective military attack possible. After some debate, the ZOB chose the latter route.

On August 21, 1942, the ZOB acquired its first arms, purchased through the Polish Workers' Party in "Aryan" Warsaw. The arms consisted of a mere five revolvers and eight hand grenades. These were discovered and confiscated by the Germans within two weeks.

In October, the ZOB expanded to include various Zionist pioneer groups and political parties. The commander was **Mordecai Anielewicz** (1919–1943). Most of the members of the ZOB were between nineteen and twenty-five years old. They immediately set out to create an infrastructure to collect money, purchase arms, train fighters, publicize rebellion, and plan the revolt.

During the Aktion of January 1943, the ZOB made its first attack. Several fighters, including Anielewicz himself, infiltrated a procession of Jews marching to Umschlagplatz. Each attacked a different German guard using pistols and hand grenades. There were casualties on both sides, and Anielewicz himself just escaped being killed. Meanwhile, other fighters attacked Germans who had charged into buildings to round up deportees. After the January resistance, the impressed Polish underground sent the ZOB forty-nine revolvers, fifty grenades, and nine pounds of explosives. It was one of the only acts of military aid given to the Jews by the well-armed Poles. By the time of the Uprising in April, the ZOB possessed only ten rifles and one submachine gun; the ZZW had several more rifles and submachine guns. The ZOB also possessed around two thousand hand grenades and two thousand Molotov cocktails. Before the Uprising began, each fighter was equipped with one revolver, ten to fifteen bullets, four or five hand grenades, and five Molotov cocktails. By contrast, the Germans used heavy weaponry normally found on the front lines: tanks, cannons, anti-aircraft weapons, and flamethrowers. They were equipped with eighty-two machine guns, 135 submachine guns, and 1358 rifles.

At dawn on April 19, the Uprising began. The Germans had surrounded the ghetto in preparation for its final liquidation. Heinrich Himmler even posted a new man, General Jurgen Stroop, to make sure the liquidation proceeded efficiently. Eight hundred fifty German soldiers entered the ghetto in two columns. One column marching up Nalewki Street was ambushed by a ZOB force on the top floors of a building. Meanwhile, at the corner of Zamenhofa and Mila, ZOB fighters attacked the makeshift German headquarters and barricades. The third point of attack was orchestrated by the ZZW on plac Muranowska (today around the corner of Andersa and Stawki), where the Germans were repelled with a single machine gun. As a result of these battles, the Germans were able to round up only 580 Jews. The next day was similar: only 505 civilians were caught.

After three days of battle, the Germans decided that the only way to reach the Jews and destroy the Uprising was to burn down the ghetto, block by block. But even this didn't force out the Jews, who had already prepared elaborate and interconnected bunkers beneath the ground. For the next three weeks, the Germans burned, bombed, and gassed all the buildings in the ghetto. Many Jews hiding in bunkers died from fire, suffocation, or collapsing buildings. During all of this, the ZOB continued its attacks in partisan manner, using the bunkers to launch assaults on the Germans. According to the historian Yisrael Gutman, the "battle of the bunkers" turned the Uprising from a three-day revolt into a nearly month-long rebellion.

Finally, on May 8, 1943, the central command bunker of the ZOB was located and attacked. The Germans threw cannisters of poison gas inside. Some of the holed-up fighters, including Anielewicz himself, committed suicide rather than be killed by the Germans. Marek Edelman, a leader in the uprising, later estimated that eighty people took their own lives in Mila 18.

Fighting in the ghetto continued until May 16, when Stroop declared victory. As a symbol of his triumph over the Jews of Warsaw, Stroop had the Tlomackie Street Synagogue blown up. After the ghetto was completely demolished, Stroop issued a scrapbook of documents and photographs entitled, "The Jewish Residential Quarter of Warsaw Is No More!"

Individual groups of armed fighters continued to fight the Germans in the bombed-out ghetto for weeks after the Uprising had been quelled. Some continued to hide in bunkers until as late as January 1944. But for all intents and purposes, Jewish Warsaw was finished.

THE GENERATIONS AFTER

After the war, Jews returned to Warsaw from concentration and death camps, from hiding in "Aryan" Poland, and from the Soviet Union. Many of these returnees were looking for relatives and recovering from the ravages of the Holocaust. It has been estimated that there were as many as 280,000 Jews in Poland after the war. The number was fleeting, though; most were to emigrate.

The postwar Jewish numbers game has become one of the great hobbies of the Polish people: How many are among us? It is a common Polish suspicion that Poland is filled with Jewish Marranos who deny their identity. Although such a numerical witch-hunt is tainted by anti-Semitism, it is true that many more Jews exist in Warsaw than are recorded. The official number of five thousand Jews at the end of 1945 is obviously unrepresentative of its Jewish population then. Prominent American Jewish organizations like to speak of untold tens of thousands of Jews in Warsaw and the rest of Poland after the war.

The number may be true, but we should remember that Jews who chose to stay in Poland after the war were not a representative sample of the Jewish people. Scarred beyond imagination in the Holocaust, they rejected emigration and placed their faith instead in assimilation and/or communism, both of which might finally erase the differences that had brought them so much grief. These Jews sought so fervently to hide their Jewishness that they indeed succeeded in wiping their identities out of Polish society. Many of them, in fact, had been so practiced at hiding their identities during the war that it was only natural to do so afterwards. Thus the numbers game among both anti-Semites and Jewish philanthropists. We should realize that the term Marrano is misleading here. The Marranos of fifteenth to sixteenth century Spain hid their Jewish identities but practiced the religion in secret. The secret Jews in Warsaw, by contrast, attempted to erase all signs of Jewishness, even to themselves.

The urge to hide became all the more compelling after 1946. Before that year, there had been at least some Jews in Poland who had returned from the camps with the hope of beginning Jewish life anew. But the well-publicized Polish rampages after the war tested the faith of both the "Jewish Jews" and Jews who wished to hide. The most notorious pogrom occurred in Kielce. Of the eighteen thousand Jews from Kielce before the war, approximately two hundred returned from the Holocaust to start a new life. On July 4, 1946, their Polish neighbors—inspired as much by a blood libel accusation as by a refusal to relinquish Jewish homes and businesses—charged into Jewish homes to kill the remnant. A total of forty-two Jews were murdered, with many more injured. Kielce was not an exception but a culmination of several postwar murders all over Poland that left hundreds of Holocaust survivors dead. The illusions of the Jews were put to the test: "Jewish Jews" had no place in Poland, and "Hidden Jews" had all the more reason to hide themselves further. After Kielce, almost all Jews who wished to remain Jewish fled the country. This unnatural selection left a sample of Polish Jewry so weak in its identification as Jews as to be almost invisible. In 1948 the official count of the Jewish Community of Warsaw was two thousand Jews. Their outlook was mostly non-religious in temperament and Yiddish in culture.

The velvet bunker of postwar Jewish identity was opened quite forcefully in 1956 and 1968. In 1956, a wave of populist anti-Semitism erupted against Jews who were, in the eyes of many Poles, the most prominent members of the Communist Party. It was true that many Jews were active in the Communist Party, for reasons that included ideology, a sense of gratefulness to the Soviet liberators of the camps, and an urge to assimilate into a society free of religion. But nationalists summoned the demon of a Jewish-Communist conspiracy to label all Jews as anti-Polish. The nationalist hysteria led to an emigration of fifty thousand people, including many Jews from Warsaw who had never identified publicly as Jews.

The situation was much worse in 1968. This time anti-Semitism was shrewdly exploited by Party hardliners to gain power. General Mieczyslaw Moczar orchestrated a sweeping purge of Jews from the Party. But the anti-Semitism did not stop there. Jews in all areas of Polish national and social life were branded as traitors. The newspapers spoke of Zionist conspirators working for the overthrow of Poland. Jews were fired from their jobs and expelled from universities. Jewish suffering in the Holocaust was minimized. Encyclopedia workers were fired after writing that ninety percent of the victims of Nazi concentration camps were Jewish. Jews were even considered German collaborators who brought the Polish state ruin during the war. Soon, the delicately orchestrated "anti-Semitism from above" spread among the general populace. Jews were shouted at, beaten up on the streets, and told to leave Poland. The official Jewish Community was no help; its leader had issued a hate-filled condemnation of Israel after the Six Day War. In this period, even the most assimilated Jews in Warsaw were startled back into their Jewish identities. The result was another mass emigration. Twenty thousand Jews left Poland by 1970. Again, those who stayed had to hide themselves even more meticulously than before. Hiding one's Jewish identity in postwar Poland had become almost a full-time occupation.

There was an unintended outcome of the purges of 1968. The first generation of Jews born after the Holocaust was coming of age and many Jews learned of their identity for the first time during the purges. Often, the immediate reaction was to internalize the slurs and to view themselves as different or even inferior to their former friends. But after some time, these Jews became interested in their newly discovered Jewishness. By the late 1970s, the "Jewish Flying University" had formed as an offshoot of the Flying University, an underground study group that concentrated on uncensored Polish history, literature, politics, and the like. The purpose of the Jewish Flying University was to learn about Jewish roots and religion. According to one of its creators, "It was a study group, it was a Jewish consciousness group, it was a mutual reliance group." It met fortnightly until the advent of martial law in 1981, when most of its members became active in the anticommunist underground. But the spark had been lit. Suddenly, it wasn't only elderly people who were affiliated with Jewish communal institutions on 6 Twarda Street. Dozens of younger people began to take interest in both the cultural and religious dimensions of Judaism.

What is the situation today? Officially, there are less than five thousand Jews in Warsaw. But here, more than anywhere else, one learns to discard official numbers. Certainly there are tens of thousands of Jews in the capital, but the question is: What do we mean by a Jew? In Poland this question is more complex than that of mixed-marriage offspring. If a person lives a full life without ever knowing that she is Jewish, should she be counted in the statistics? For demographic studies, certainly. But for studies of the strength of the Jewish Community, can she really be considered a vital component? All the talk about tens of thousands of Warsaw Jews is a moot point on the mornings that the Nozyk Synagogue cannot draw a *minyan*. It is a fact that the vast majority of Warsaw's twenty to fifty thousand inactive Jews hide their Jewishness even from themselves. In this sense, the city cannot be considered to have a vibrant Jewish life, and there are indeed only a handful of Jews in Warsaw.

Nonetheless, the number of people interested in their roots is increasing. The youngsters of the 1970s are today middle-aged; their roles as newcomers to the faith have been replaced by a new generation born in the late 1960s and 1970s. The Polish Union of Jewish Students claimed a couple hundred members in the 1990s. It should be mentioned that today's youth are not necessarily children of the generation of '68. Warsaw will never have a shortage of hidden Jews; some of their children can be expected to return to their heritage in every generation. As long as hidden Jews outweigh actively identified Jews, there will be a constant stream of newcomers to Jewish life and tradition.

The youth today are much different from the generation that preceded them. For one thing, in the 1970s Jews were forced to fend for themselves if they had a serious interest in their heritage. The infrastructure of the Warsaw Jewish Community was not prepared for growth or education. Today, by contrast, there has been a revitalization of Jewish communal bodies in Warsaw. Much of this turnaround is the result of the active involvement of the American Ronald S. Lauder Foundation, which has sent a frisky and energetic rabbi to the capital to lead religious events. The Lauder Foundation established a Jewish day school, the first of its kind in generations, which has grown to ninety children in grades one through six, and thirty-five children in the preschool, in the late 1990s. Friday evenings and holidays are celebrated family-style in the Lauder Center on 6 Twarda Street. Thus the youth today have an outlet for their renewal of identity that was denied the prior generation.

There is another difference in the two generations that came of age after the Holocaust. Active Warsaw Jews who grew up in the 1960s or 1970s insist on being called "Polish Jews," to defend Poland's attitudes toward Jews, and to work at a rapprochement between Jews and Gentiles in today's Poland. Younger Jews don't feel this need. "Don't call me Polish! I am a Jew!" is a common retort among twentysomething Warsaw Jews who actively identify as Jews. This is not simply a cynical sneer at assimilation. It reflects the blossoming of a full Jewish identity without the cautious apologetics used by the previous generation. The earlier generation had to fend with virulent anti-Semitism in the late 1960s; it was difficult not to absorb some of these anti-Semitic attitudes even as they themselves began to identify with the Jewish people. Also, to label oneself "Jew" in a totalitarian regime is a risky matter. It was a first step, but because of the hostile atmosphere, the term "Jew" had to be tempered by a constant insistence on their Polishness. The term "Pole of Jewish origin" was commonly used by members of that generation. Not today. Young Jews in today's Warsaw talk about Judaism on their own terms. If forced to choose, they will proudly state "Jews of Jewish origin!" or at least "Jews living in Poland." This divulges a fullness of Jewish feeling and a rejection of assimilation that calls to mind the attitudes of the Jewish renewal movements in Warsaw before the war. Although it is too early to tell which of these generational attitudes will fare better in today's Poland, the difference in the two generations is crucial. It is a natural evolution from the timid self-denial that followed the Holocaust to the rebirth of a full Jewish spirit among younger Jews in today's Poland.

Spotlight: Emmanuel Ringelblum (1900–1944)

It seems a cruel trick of history, but the man responsible for most of our knowledge about the Warsaw ghetto is a little-known figure in the Jewish world today. A high school teacher before the war, Emmanuel Ringelblum rose to prominence in the ghetto as founder and director of the Oneg Shabbat, the secret archive that by the end of the war had compiled tens of thousands of pages documenting the extent of Nazi barbarism in Warsaw and elsewhere in Poland.

It was not much of a stretch for him. Born in 1900 in the Galician town of Buczacz, Ringelblum studied Jewish history at the University of Warsaw; his Ph.D. thesis concerned the medieval history of Warsaw's Jewish Community. Ringelblum's dream was to detail the history of Warsaw's Jews up until the twentieth century. When the war broke out, he had reached the end of the eighteenth century and had published 126 articles and books.

Motivated by the concept of active historicism—i.e., not simply recording events, but striving to affect change in the world—Ringelblum became involved in the Polish branch of the American Jewish Joint Distribution Committee. When the Germans invaded Poland in 1939, he headed the social welfare department of what was later called the Jewish Organization for Social Care. In this capacity he was instrumental in the organization of soup kitchens for the starving and needy. His interaction with the most desperate denizens of the ghetto ultimately made Ringelblum decide to record the horrors of everyday life in Jewish Warsaw. As early as October 1939—before the ghetto had even been formed—Ringelblum began to take notes on what he witnessed. Soon he began to meet with various figures in the ghetto, including leaders of the underground, to gather information about what was happening to the Jews. Since the group met on Saturdays, they code-named themselves "Oneg Shabbat," or "Shabbat delight," after the relaxed study and song meetings that traditionally fall on Shabbat.

The domain of Oneg Shabbat was enormous. Funded by the JDC (Joint Distribution Committee), they collected documentary materials, testimonies, and information about the Jewish underground. Ringelblum directed dozens of researchers and hundreds of participants conducting extensive surveys and research into all aspects of ghetto life. Report titles ranged from "Jewish Women during the War and in the Ghetto" to "Humor and Folklore" in the ghetto. It was Ringelblum's intention both to document the history of Polish Jews during the war, and to create a testimonial record that would be proof for posterity of the horrors surrounding him.

The archives did not stop at passive documentation. As news of the Nazi extermination program trickled into the ghetto, the Oneg Shabbat evolved into an active participant in the struggle for Jewish survival. As Ringelblum wrote, "Every associate of Oneg Shabbat knew that his effort and suffering, the risking of his life twenty-four hours a day while carrying materials from one place to another, served a great idea. . . ." The Oneg Shabbat established a news agency and published an underground newsletter detailing the exterminations. Even more importantly, the members worked day and night collecting evidence and recording testimonies that were smuggled to London. It was from the Oneg Shabbat that, as early as March 1942, the Allies received the first testimony from a man who had escaped from the death camp of Chelmno. By the end of that year, Ringelblum's team had smuggled to London a meticulous account, entitled "Annihilation of Jewish Warsaw," of the Warsaw Aktion in which close to three hundred thousand Jews had been deported to death in Treblinka. As a result of Ringelblum's fearless activity, the British and American governments knew full well of the German extermination of the Jews almost from the moment it began.

Ringelblum managed to secure a hiding place in "Aryan" Warsaw in March 1943. He returned to the Ghetto a month later and was deported to the Trawniki labor camp. He escaped and returned to his family, but in March 1944 his hideout was discovered. Ringelblum, his wife and son, thirty other Jews, and the Poles who had hidden them were summarily murdered by the Germans.

Before Ringelblum went into hiding, the Oneg Shabbat hid its archives in three milk containers underneath the cellars of three different ghetto buildings. Two of the containers, containing around forty thousand pages, were exhumed in 1946 and 1950. Today they form the most precious materials of the Jewish Historical Institute and the most vital collection anywhere of documents pertaining to the Holocaust in Poland. The third container, hidden underneath the building at 34 Swietojerska Street, could not be found and is presumed to be lost. It is possible that somewhere below the streets of Warsaw this last archive, which specifically detailed the life of the Jewish Fighting Organization, remains to this day.

Although he died before he could systematize his history of the ghetto, Emmanuel Ringelblum brought his youthful dream of active historicism to fruition. Under constant threat of capture and death, he recorded the history of twentieth century Warsaw Jewry. Perhaps more than any other human being this century, Emmanuel Ringelblum fought, and ultimately died, for the sake of truth.

The Jewish Essentials

The Jewish Community of Warsaw
Twarda Street 6
Telephone (48–22) 620 4324

The Jewish Community handles the administrative, religious, and welfare needs of the Jews of Warsaw and serves as the central administrative authority for the rest of Polish Jewry. Services and maintenance of the Nozyk Synagogue are managed by the Jewish Community. Offices of the Jewish Community are partly located in the annex of the Nozyk Synagogue.

The Socio-Cultural Society of Jews in Poland
plac Grzybowski 12/16, in the Jewish Theater building.
Telephone (48–22) 620 0554

The Socio-Cultural Society promotes Yiddish culture in a Jewish monthly, organizes meetings, and plans Jewish retreats in a cottage outside Warsaw. The Society has come under fire in recent years for its solid alliance with the former communist regime in such matters as the condemnation of Israel, but it continues to function as a social center today.

The Ronald S. Lauder Foundation
Twarda Street 6
Telephone (48–22) 620 3496 or 652 2152
Fax (48–22) 654 3156

The Ronald S. Lauder Foundation is the most active and visible Jewish organization in Warsaw today. With world headquarters in New York City and Polish headquarters in Warsaw, the Lauder Foundation has invested time and resources in invigorating Jewish communal life in the capital. The Foundation's greatest success is its preschool and elementary school, headed by Helise Lieberman and Ania Szyc, which had a combined enrollment of one hundred twenty-five children in 1997. The Foundation also supports associations for the youth and the elderly and sponsors summer and winter camps that have become popular among young Jews. Feel free to join the Foundation's *Kabbalat Shabbat*, held every Friday evening in Twarda 6 after services in the Nozyk Synagogue.

Rabbi Michael Schudrich, the Foundation's full-time rabbi and director in Warsaw, is an energetic man who will go out of his way to assist you in any Jewish query.

The Jewish Historical Institute
Tlomackie Street 3/5
Telephone (48–22) 279 221
Fax (48–22) 278 372

The Jewish Historical Institute maintains a library and resource center. For more information about the Institute, *see page 238*.

If you're researching your Polish Jewish ancestry, it would be a good idea to speak with Yale Reisner, director of research and archives of the Ronald S. Lauder Foundation Genealogy Project, operated in conjunction with the Jewish Historical Institute. Mr. Reisner can be reached at telephone (48–22) 827 9221.

PRAYING IN WARSAW

The Nozyk Synagogue
Twarda Street 6
Shacharit: 8:30 A.M.
Kabbalat Shabbat: According to sunset
Shabbat Mornings: 9:30 A.M.
Daily *Minchah/Maariv:* Twenty minutes before sunset

The Nozyk Synagogue was the only house of prayer in Warsaw to survive the German occupation and is today the only site of Jewish worship in Warsaw. Services today attract a mixture of elderly Jews from Warsaw, personnel from the Ronald S. Lauder Foundation, several young Jews, and, depending on the season, tourists. Rabbi Michael Schudrich of the Lauder Foundation succeeds in investing the services with energy and verve. Chief Rabbi Pinchas M. Yoskowitz, an Israeli who spends much of the year in Warsaw, delivers Torah commentaries in Yiddish. With so few Yiddish speakers in Warsaw today, many people are confused as to why he does this. Rabbi Yoskowitz is not very active; the general rule is to pursue him energetically if you need his assistance.

Unfortunately, heated arguments sometimes erupt between elderly worshippers in the middle of services at the Nozyk Synagogue. Sometimes hostility is directed against younger worshippers and tourists. One of these men once insisted to a young congregant that there is not a single Jewish youth in Warsaw. Similar conduct is not uncommon in Prague, but in Prague it derives from a fear of foreigners and newcomers, as the local congregants are weary of constantly being examined for Jewish Life In Action. In Warsaw, it's somewhat more complex. One woman who works in the Community explained to me that the elderly congregants romanticize themselves as the last Jews of Warsaw. When they see signs of incoming life, they perceive it as a threat to their mission. Whether or not this is true, don't be surprised if elderly worshippers are less than friendly.

You can be certain of open hospitality from the happy people working for the Lauder Foundation. After services on Friday night and the holidays, the Lauder Foundation prepares an open Kiddush and meal of light salads followed by a selection of *zemirot* and *birkat hamazon*. These are held on the ground floor of the white building next door to the synagogue.

> **Tips to Torah kissers:** Unlike most synagogues, which carry the Torah around the sanctuary before reading it, the Nozyk congregation tends to make a beeline from the *aron hakodesh* to the *bimah*. So if you want to kiss the Torah, it's best to stand near the *bimah* as soon as it is taken from the ark.

MIKVEH

A *mikveh* can be used by appointment. Ask Rabbi Pinchas Yoskowitz at the Nozyk Synagogue, Twards Street 6, or call Rabbi Michael Schudrich of the Lauder Foundation at (48–22) 620 3496 or 652 2152.

Keeping Kosher in Warsaw

RESTAURANT

Menora
plac Grzybowski 2
Tel. (48-22) 620 3754
Open 10:00 A.M.–10:00 P.M.
Credit cards accepted

    The complete lack of competition for this restaurant has not exactly done wonders for the quality of food, service, and decor. It's not very good, but kosher travellers in Warsaw haven't the luxury of options.

BUYING FOOD

There is no place to purchase kosher food in Warsaw. In 1996, leaders of the Warsaw office of the Lauder Foundation began looking into methods of importing kosher goods from Prague. A plan hasn't materialized as of this writing. It is best to call the Lauder Foundation and ask about recent developments. In general, though, kosher-minded travellers are best advised to stock up in Budapest, western Europe, or America before coming to Warsaw.
    On Friday nights, the Lauder Foundation prepares *Kabbalat Shabbat* meals in the white building at Twarda Street 6. The meals are fairly light, consisting of various salads and challah.

Orientation and Suggested Itinerary

Of the cities discussed in this book, only Warsaw has a Jewish history that is best appreciated in its cemetery. The cemeteries in Prague and Cracow are sublime but not solitary; they are complemented by ancient synagogues that reveal the living dimension of Jewish history in the region. In Warsaw, though, the only sizeable Jewish communal institution that remains from before the war is the cemetery. Oh, but what a cemetery it is!

No trip to Warsaw would be complete without a visit to its Jewish Cemetery. Serious visitors should arrive in the morning; give yourself a few hours to comb its graves and absorb the breadth of Jewish life in this city before the Holocaust.

The other main site in Warsaw is the series of memorials marking the destruction of Warsaw Jewry in the Holocaust. The memorials seem like an anachronism, juxtaposed as they are against the postwar topography of Warsaw. In fact, because the entire city was levelled during the war, almost nowhere is it possible to appreciate the vitality of its prewar Jewish life. For this reason, I have included a special walking tour meant to exhume the past flavor of the city on streets built after the war. Other common points of interest in Jewish Warsaw—for instance, the Jewish Historical Institute or the Nozyk Synagogue—are incorporated into this stroll, and you can turn right to those pages if you wish to see only those sites.

The Holocaust memorials are all located outside, so you can visit them at any hour. The cemetery's opening hours are listed below and sites such as the Nozyk Synagogue in the walking tour are best approached in the morning or early afternoon.

Finally, a stroll through parts of Praga (see "Elsewhere in Warsaw") is a nice way to spend an afternoon. You can even combine a trip to Praga's formerly Jewish buildings with a visit to the Praga Zoo nearby. Make sure to visit during daylight hours, as Praga is not the safest area of Warsaw.

THE JEWISH CEMETERY IN WARSAW

Address: Okopowa Street 49–51

The Jewish Cemetery starts on the western side of Okopowa Street, just after the junction with Mordechaja Anielewicza Street.

The Jewish Cemetery in Warsaw

Full View Including All Plots

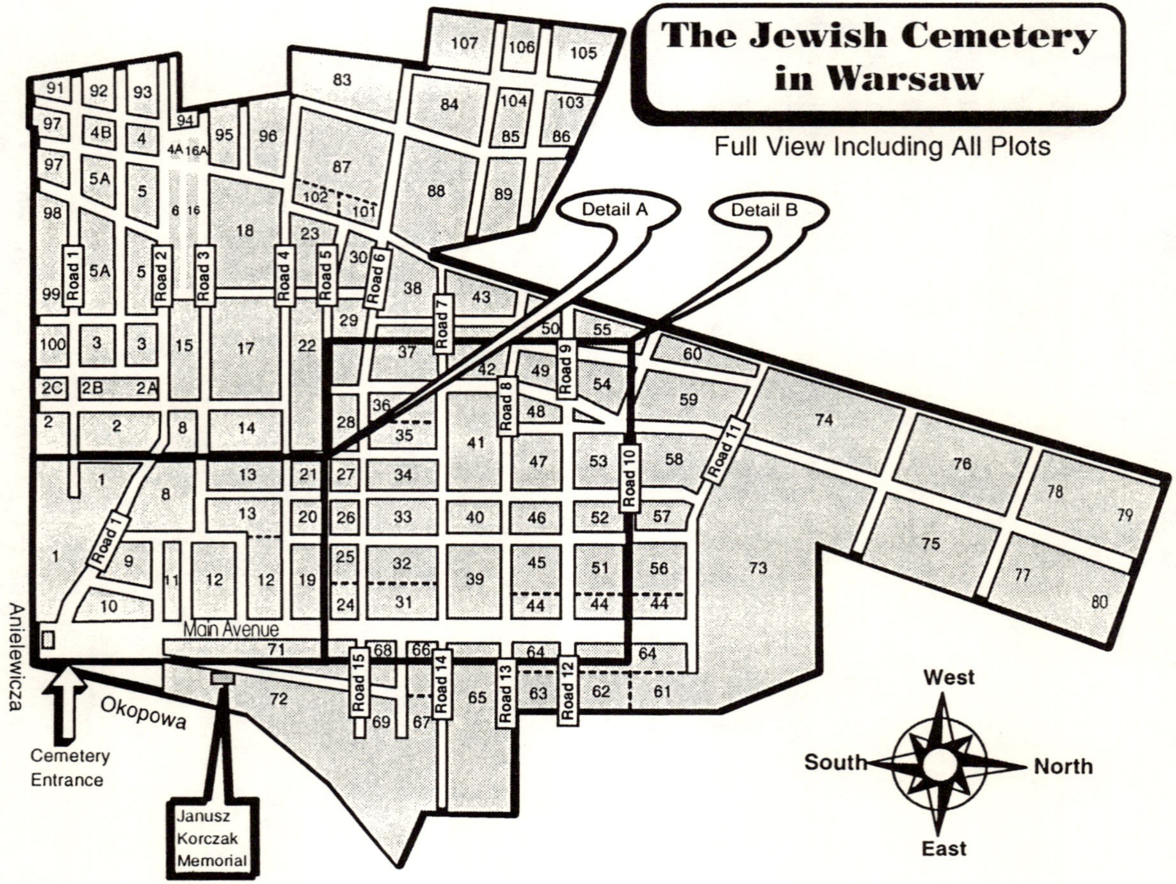

Cemetery hours:
Sunday–Thursday: 9:00 A.M.–3:00 P.M.
Friday: 9:00 A.M.–1:00 P.M.
Closed Saturday

Getting There

BY BUS: Take line 107, 111, 180, or 516 to the final stop, fittingly called "Esperanto." From the bus stop, walk to the end of the street and cross Okopowa; the entrance to the cemetery is on the corner.

BY TRAM: Take tram 1, 22, or 27 to the Cmentarz Zydowski stop. The cemetery entrance is across the street.

Just as the cemetery in Prague is the one place to glimpse the topography of Prague's former ghetto, the Warsaw cemetery is the only place to appreciate the rich fullness and diversity of Warsaw's prewar Jewish Community. It is easy to get lost amid the Polish tombstones of doctors, professors, bankers, publishers, actors, and philanthropists or the Hebrew tombstones of wonder-rabbis, teachers, students, hasidic miracle-workers, and their entire courts. It is a kaleidoscopic testament to the vibrancy of what was once the second-largest Jewish Community in the world.

The Jewish Cemetery in Warsaw was established in 1806 with two sections, one for men and one for women, just outside the city limits. The trenches of the city actually ran along today's Okopowa Street (*okopy* is Polish for trenches). Burials began in 1807, but after only five years, space ran out. At the time, the Jewish Community could afford only a small addition to the cemetery grounds. The enlargement began in earnest in 1824 and 1840, when additional fields were purchased from sources ranging from the nearby Franciscan monastery to a hospital. During the following decades, the cemetery was expanded several more times to accommodate the needs of the growing Community. Nevertheless, there was a constant lack of space in the cemetery. For this reason, the Jewish Cemetery in Warsaw adopted the practice most famously used by Prague's Jews: layered graves. From the beginning of the 1830s, bodies were placed on top of older graves, soil was added, and new tombstones were added next to the original tombstones, which were raised. In the densest areas, the Jewish Cemetery in Warsaw became more mountainous than even the Prague Jewish Cemetery. Warsaw saw fourteen layers compared to Prague's twelve.

The burial pace continued to increase. At the beginning of the twentieth century, there were fifteen hundred burials a year in the cemetery. The Jewish Community planned to establish a new cemetery next to Warsaw's Russian Orthodox Cemetery, but the plans were never realized. By 1939, there were approximately 130,000 graves in the cemetery.

Jews were also buried in an older Jewish cemetery, established across the Vistula River in Praga in 1780 (*see page 253*). The Praga cemetery eventually became impoverished, filled mostly with poor Jews who couldn't afford to be buried in the Warsaw cemetery. There were free burials in the Warsaw cemetery, but most fell into one of four price categories.

The current entrance to the cemetery was once the entrance only for hearses carrying bodies. In fact, the cemetery office is housed in a postwar building; before the war, it was the site of stables for the horse buggies and carts bringing in the bodies. It was by this entrance that the cemetery was popularly known, called *Gesia beis olam*, or Gesia cemetery, because the entrance was located on Gesia Street (today's Mordechaja Anielewicza Street). Across from the entrance, where blue benches surround a B'nai B'rith memorial, there used to be a one-story building for the *Chevrah Kaddishah*, or Jewish Burial Society. It was so small that it was used only for *taharah*, or the ritual cleansing of bodies. Originally, the Jewish Community couldn't even afford this *taharah* building; it wasn't erected until 1828. It was later rebuilt, but no longer remains. The nearby water tap, built in 1907, is the only remaining part of the prewar office complex.

On the other side of the water tap was a two-story administrative building, complete with offices and private flats for workers. Between the two buildings, around the area of the water tap, was the entrance to the cemetery for visitors and mourners. If you stand outside the cemetery you can view the original gate: Facing the current entrance, look down the road a dozen or so meters to the right and you'll see the cemetery wall jutting out. That was the original entrance; it was filled in with bricks after the current entrance became the only entrance.

During the war, the *Chevrah Kaddishah* and administrative buildings remained and carried out their functions, but on May 15, 1943, at the end of the Ghetto Uprising, the Nazis dynamited them. One day later, the Nazis blew up the Tlomackie Street Synagogue. The buildings were destroyed in a symbolic act of triumph over the Jews. All the cemetery archives had been stored in these buildings.

During the War

During the period of the Warsaw ghetto, the Jewish Cemetery continued to exist "beyond the trenches," as the area of the ghetto extended to, but did not include, Okopowa Street. There was a gate at the end of Gesia Street (today's Mordechaja Anielewicza Street) in front of the current entrance to the cemetery, where Germans controlled entrance into and out of the cemetery. Because of the constant traffic of bodies into the cemetery, the Judenrat proposed that an overhead pass be built over Okopowa Street, similar to one that existed over the "Aryan" Chlodna Street, which intersected the ghetto. But when they considered that bodies of the deceased would have to be carried up and down the stairs to the bridge, the idea was abandoned.

The cemetery gate was one of the chief areas of smuggling during the war. The sheer size of the cemetery and its borders with Christian cemeteries made it a preferred place to sneak unnoticed into Gentile Warsaw and return with desperately needed food. According to Adam Czerniakow, smuggling accounted for about eighty percent of the food entering the ghetto. Children would often pose as mourners and then enter the depths of the cemetery, where they would scale the wall. Sometimes they would sleep in the *ohelim* (room-size monuments) of famous *tzaddikim* and then leave the next morning. Other times, smuggled food would be loaded into emptied hearses to be carried back into the ghetto. Mourners would often leave the cemetery with loads of food bought by smugglers. Even whole cows were known to be pushed through holes in the walls of the adjacent Christian cemetery. Once in a hearse, they would be carried into the ghetto through the Gesia Street gate.

In addition to food, the Jewish Cemetery was an important site for the smuggling of people into hiding on the "Aryan" side. Cemetery workers even developed a system: in late 1942, it cost about seventy-five zloty to be assisted with a ladder over the wall. Often a family would stage a funeral and, once inside the cemetery, escape over the wall. In one recorded instance, a baby girl was injected with a drug that made her unconscious and apparently lifeless. The family formed a funeral procession to the cemetery, where an empty casket was buried. After bribing the appropriate people, the family escaped over the wall.

Eventually, though, funerals ceased. In 1941, burial in mass graves began. Approximately one hundred thousand Jews inside the Warsaw ghetto died of disease and hunger. Wealthier people, particularly early in the war, could afford to have individual graves, but the vast majority of those who died were buried naked in mass graves. Ritual cleansing (*taharah*) as well as the custom of wrapping the body in a linen shroud were both abandoned for lack of resources. Even paper could not be spared as substitute for linen.

Another war phenomenon was the gangs known as "dentists." These were volunteer cemetery workers who, instead of salaries, would pick out gold teeth from bodies. They became relatively wealthy from this, but eventually were disciplined by the Judenrat. However, in September 1941 members of the Jewish police itself were found to be exhuming bodies for their gold teeth and scarcely used shrouds. Noting this in his diary, Emmanuel Ringelblum wrote, "In a word—the deepest pit of degradation" (Jacob Sloan, ed., *Notes from the Warsaw Ghetto: The Journal of Emmanel Ringelblum*).

A grotesque feature of burials during the war was that German visitors and soldiers used the cemetery as leisure grounds. They could always be found following the mourners, taking pictures of both the relatives and the bodies buried. On Sundays they took their girlfriends to watch with them.

The Cemetery Today

Although the Germans actively controlled the cemetery during the war, they never spent the time to destroy it. Apparently, they didn't need the tombstones as paving material and they were too busy elsewhere to vandalize for its own sake. Nonetheless, some tombstones were destroyed. The retaining wall of Plot 10, at the beginning of the cemetery, contains fragments of destroyed tombstones. When broken fragments of tombstones were collected in the 1970s, it was impossible to tell from which graves they came. The mosaic was built from 1973 to 1978 by cemetery director Pinkus Szenicer, father of the current cemetery director. According to the latter, ninety-five percent of the fragments come from this cemetery. He explains that the stones were not destroyed during the Nazi occupation but by hooligans since the war; others claim that some of the fragments were destroyed during the war. The wall recalls the similar Wailing Wall in the Old Jewish Cemetery in Cracow, not to mention walls in scores of other Jewish cemeteries in the region.

Today the cemetery, with its roughly one hundred thousand tombstones over the graves of more than twice as many people, is the second largest in Poland after Lodz. It is in a serious state of deterioration. Funds are desperately needed for the upkeep of its sprawling thirty-three hectares, much of which is overgrown by weeds. The first trees in the cemetery were planted in 1851; today, it is almost a jungle, with roots and branches growing into and over tombstones. Vandalism continues to occur throughout the cemetery, which cannot afford an adequate security system. One man active in the preservation of Jewish monuments sadly quipped, "All that we can do is put up a big sign on the cemetery wall saying, 'Please do not vandalize the Jewish Cemetery.'" Much of the destruction is motivated by theft. Anything even semi-valuable is at risk of theft, from marble headstones to gold-plated letters on tombstones. There is also anti-Semitic vandalism, the most infamous being the fire set to the Berek Sonnenberg tombstone while it was being reconstructed in 1991.

The Jewish Cemetery in Warsaw is still active today. In fact, some claim that this is where the "hidden majority"—the thousands of Warsaw Jews who maintain no contact with the Jewish Community—show their faces. Before both Christian and Jewish holidays, people can be found throughout the cemetery, tending the graves of loved ones and leaving flowers and candles.

A walk through the Jewish Cemetery in Warsaw is not only a visit to the most eminent Jewish personalities of the city, but to the entire fabric of Jewish life in the nineteenth and twentieth centuries. Here are graves of bankers as well as beggars, world-famous rabbis as well as unknown *shamashim* of the *shtiebels*. You will see tombstones inscribed exclusively in Hebrew as well as tombstones inscribed exclusively in Polish, a vivid reminder of the split that occurred in all parts of Jewish life in the nineteenth century. You will find exquisite monuments erected during the most prosperous period of Jewish life in Warsaw, as well as mass graves from the Holocaust.

Because the cemetery is the single enclosed area in the city that has maintained its prewar appearance, what follows is a detailed walking tour of the grounds. Even this is only a sampling of the great rabbis, writers, scientists, and entrepreneurs the cemetery contains. Weeks can be spent in the cemetery and still there will be something new to surprise you. Because the cemetery is so expansive and potentially overwhelming, included are meticulous instructions, linked to the maps on *pages 189 and 190*, to keep you on track. Two detailed maps will help you locate the graves. "Detail A" covers the first half of the walk, and "Detail B" the second half. All map references during the walk refer to the graves indicated in Detail A and Detail B. Be aware that the entire walk, if followed to the letter, can easily take three hours.

Enter the cemetery at the first path on the left, or Road 1.

About five meters in on the left side, there is a large white cabin behind a smaller one. These are *ohelim*. Unlike the Jewish cemetery in Prague, where the term *ohel* designates a sarcophagus-style tombstone, the *ohelim* in Warsaw's Jewish cemetery resemble, quite literally, little houses. They are placed over the graves of *tzaddikim*, sometimes singly but often over an entire family of *hasidim*.

The Jewish Cemetery in Warsaw: Detail A

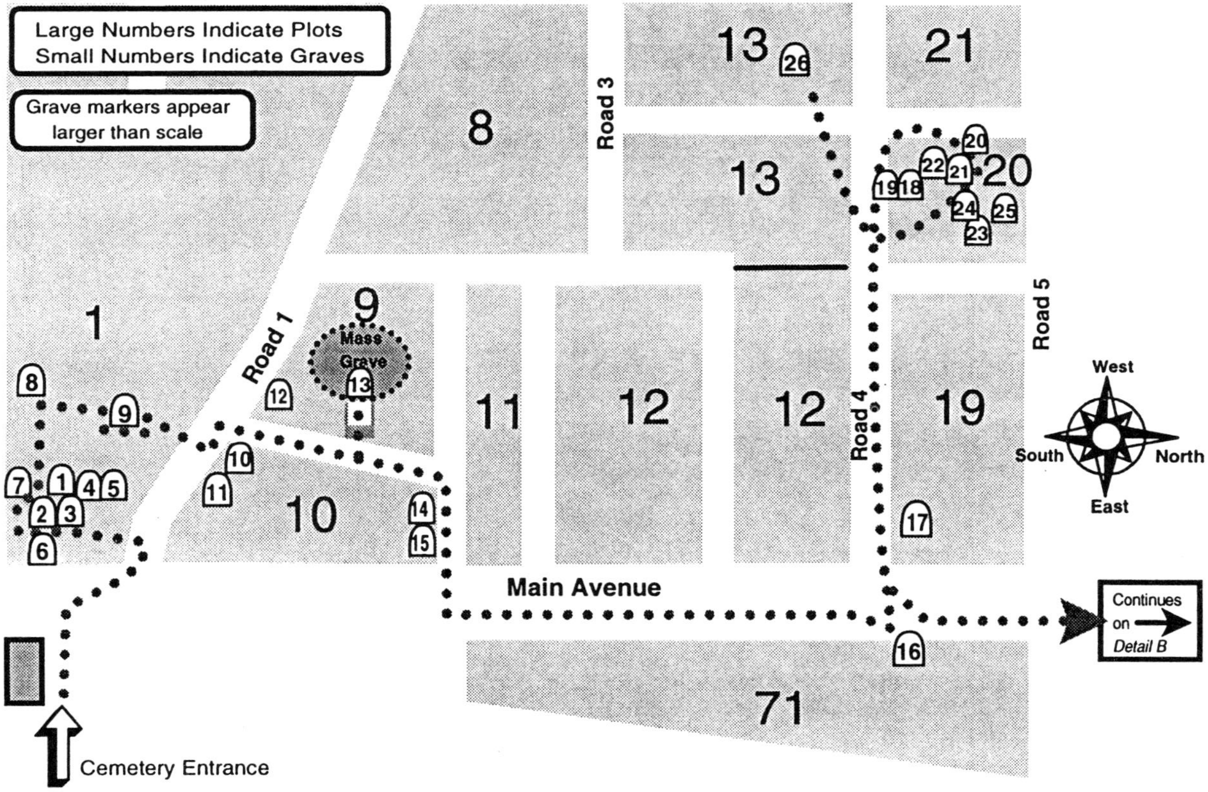

The Jewish Cemetery in Warsaw: *Detail B*

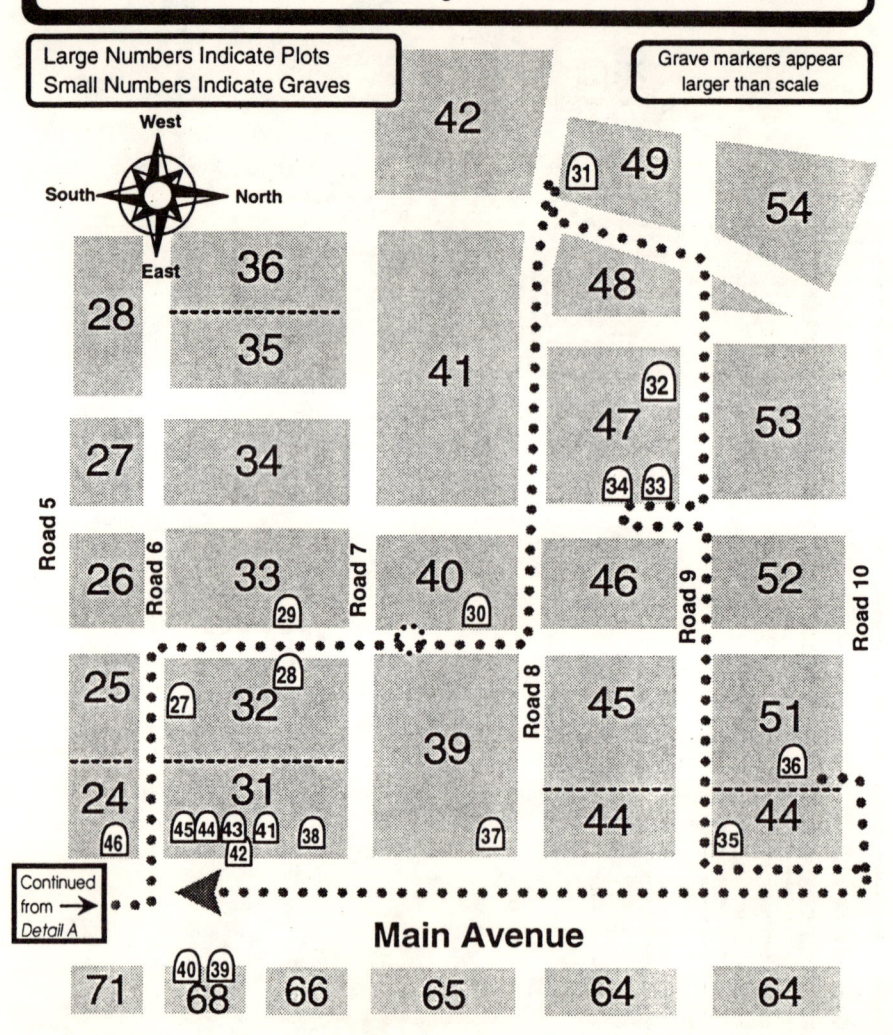

Large Numbers Indicate Plots
Small Numbers Indicate Graves

Grave markers appear larger than scale

Compass: West, South, North, East

- 42
- [31] 49
- 54
- 28
- 36
- 35
- 48
- 41
- [32] 47
- 53
- [34] [33]
- 27
- 34
- Road 5
- 26
- Road 6
- 33 [29]
- Road 7
- 40 [30]
- 46
- Road 9
- 52
- Road 10
- 25
- [27] 32 [28]
- Road 8
- 45
- 51 [36]
- 24 [46]
- 31 [45][44][43][41][38]
[42]
- 39
- [37]
- 44
- 44 [35]

Continued from → *Detail A*

Main Avenue

- 71
- [40][39] 68
- 66
- 65
- 64
- 64

LIST OF NAMES FOR MAPS A AND B

1. Solomon Zalman Lipschitz (the *Chemdat Shlomo*) (1765–1839)
2. Yeshayah Mushkat (1801–1866)
3. Avraham Tzvi Perlmutter (1844–1930)
4. Dov Berush Meisels (1798–1870)
5. Chaim Davidsohn (1760–1854)
6. Antoni Eisenbaum (1791–1852)
7. Jacob Epstein (1771–1843)
8. Berek Sonnenberg (1764–1822)
9. Avraham Mordechai Alter (d. 1855)
10. Majer Balaban (1877–1942)
11. Samuel Abraham Poznanski (1864–1921)
12. Henrietta Epstein
13. Mass Grave
14. Adam Czerniakow (1880–1942)
15. Ludwik Zamenhof (1859–1917)
16. Chaim Zelig Slonimski (1810–1904)
17. Jan Sierota
18. Zelig Natanson (1795–1879)
19. Ludwik Natanson (1821–1896)
20. Michal Landy (1844–1861)
21. Levi Lesser (1791–1870)
22. Aleksander Lesser (1814–1884)
23. Henryk Wawelberg (1813–1891)
24. Hipolit Wawelberg (1844–1901)
25. Samuel Orgelbrand (1810–1868)
26. Menachem Mendel of Worke (the *Worker Rebbe*) (1819–1869)
27. Yaakov Aryeh Guterman of Radzimin (1792–1874)
28. Yakov Yitzchak Shapiro of Balandov and Chaim Meir Yechiel of Mogelnice (d. 1882)
29. Wilhelm Landau (1833–1899)
30. Abraham Shalom Frydberg (1838–1902)
31. Naphtali Tzvi Yehudah Berlin (the *Netziv*) (1817–1893) and Chaim Soloveitchik (*Reb Chaim Brisker*) (1853–1918)
32. Yisrael of Modzhitz (1849–1921)
33. Moshe Mordechai of Pelcovizna
34. Shmuel of Slonim (the *Divrei Shmuel*) (1850–1916)
35. Isaac Leib Peretz (1852–1915) Jacob Dineson (1856–1919) S. An-ski (1863–1920)
36. Baruch Shulman (1886–1906)
37. Esther Rachel Kaminska (1870–1925)
38. Bund Monument for Henryk Ehrlich (1882–1941) and Victor Alter (1890–1941)
39. Henryk Wohl (1836–1907)
40. Majer Wolanowski (1844–1900)
41. Abraham Goldberg (1881–1933)
42. Leib Naidus (1890–1918)
43. Shlomo Biber (1875–1931)
44. Isaac Meir Weissenberg (1881–1938)
45. Hersh David Nomberg (1876–1927)
46. Felix Perl (1871–1927)

Walk over to the small *ohel*, so that you're facing the inscriptions on the adjacent tombstones. This is the area where Warsaw's chief rabbis were once buried, and as such is filled with well-known personalities from the nineteenth century.

Map: 1 The large *ohel* is the grave of Warsaw's first chief rabbi, **Solomon Zalman Lipschitz** (1765–1839), known as the *Chemdat Shlomo* after his most famous work. In 1819 Rabbi Lipschitz became rabbi in Praga, and in 1821 he moved over to Warsaw, where he established a renowned *yeshivah*.

Whether you were a *hasid* or a *mitnaged* (an observant Jew who opposed the *hasidim*), the Chemdat Shlomo was beloved throughout the city. Although he himself was a *mitnaged* who once even rejected a post because Hasidism was widespread in the city, the Chemdat Shlomo encouraged the development of Hasidism in Warsaw. Assimilationists, however, he wouldn't tolerate, and campaigned against their increasing influence in the early nineteenth century. In the November Uprising of 1830–31, the Chemdat Shlomo entered the public debate over Jewish beards. Many Polish soldiers had argued that Jews should be admitted to the national guards only if they shaved. The Chemdat Shlomo defended the rights of the Jewish soldiers to keep their beards, suggesting instead that they simply trim them a bit. When the Chemdat Shlomo died, Jewish women all over Warsaw did not wear their jewelry for four weeks.

Map: 2 The small *ohel* is the grave of Yeshayah Mushkat (1801–1866), the rabbi from the other side of the Vistula River, in Praga.

Map: 3 In front of the *ohel* of Chemdat Shlomo, and next to the *ohel* of Rabbi Mushkat, is the grave of Avraham Tzvi Perlmutter (1844–1930). It is decorated with books, a symbol of knowledge.

Perlmutter was a prime example of rabbinical activism in the early twentieth century. Before he came to Warsaw in 1909, Rabbi Perlmutter served in Radom, where he succeeded in establishing a kosher army kitchen for Jewish soldiers. He went on to serve in sundry Polish parliaments throughout his career. After Poland gained independence, he represented the Agudat Israel party in the first Polish Sejm, in which he campaigned for Jewish religious and cultural autonomy. During Agudat Israel's anti-Zionist era, Perlmutter delivered a speech in the Sejm in which he said that until the Messiah came, "We must live here where our forefathers have lived and are buried. . . . We shall remain in Poland as long as it takes, until Providence calls us forth to the Land of Israel" (quoted in Celia S. Heller, *On the Edge of Destruction: Jews of Poland between the Two World Wars*).

Map: 4 Behind Perlmutter's grave and two over from the right of the Chemdat Shlomo is the white marble grave of Dov Berush Meisels (1798–1870). Rabbi Meisels was one of the most respected Jews in all of Polish history. Before coming to Warsaw, Rabbi Meisels served as chief rabbi of Cracow for two and a half decades, from 1832 to 1856. He was actively involved in Jewish thought, Jewish communal life, and, most famously, Polish revolutionary activities. In 1848 he was elected to the Austrian Parliament, adamantly fighting for Polish rights. When the speaker of parliament asked him why he sat with the Leftists, Rabbi Meisels gave his famous reply, "Jews have no Right(s)!" In 1856 Rabbi Meisels became chief rabbi of Warsaw, where he continued his campaign for Polish sovereignty.

Rabbi Meisels became famous throughout Poland during the patriotic demonstrations of 1861. He sermonized for the Polish cause, attended the Christian funerals of those killed in the riots, and even closed the synagogues as an act of civil disobedience against the Russian authorities. In November of that year he was arrested. What followed was truly remarkable: Polish patriots throughout Warsaw fought for Rabbi Meisels's release, selling pictures of the rabbi throughout the city. Eventually two hundred thousand rubles were raised from Rabbi Meisels's picture. It was given to him upon his release from jail in 1862 as an honorarium for his patriotism. The Russians deported Rabbi Meisels repeatedly, but he returned each time to the capital. Thousands of mourners, both Jewish and Christian, attended his funeral in 1870. It was as much an act of defiance against the regime as a funeral. The funeral was enveloped in silence, as the Russians prohibited eulogies from being read, and, though no obituaries appeared in the newspapers, all of Warsaw knew that one of Poland's greatest national heroes had died.

Map: 5 To the right of Rabbi Meisels is the grave of Chaim Davidsohn (1760–1854), who proceded Rabbi Meisels as the chief rabbi of Warsaw. When the Chemdat Shlomo died, the Warsaw Jewish Community had wanted Rabbi Yitzchak Meir Alter, the famous Gerer Rebbe, to lead the rabbinate. Rabbi Alter politely declined, suggesting instead the seventy-nine-year-old Rabbi Chaim Davidsohn, a merchant and scholar who had fallen on hard times. Rabbi Davidsohn became the chief rabbi and was ensured of a decent salary. A perfectionist to the core, Rabbi Davidsohn burned all his writings before he died at the age of ninety-four.

Map: 6 Turning around to face the cemetery entrance, you'll see tombstones with Polish inscriptions. The first stone of this type, standing in front of a tree, is that of Antoni Eisenbaum (1791–1852). The tombstone depicts a pillar bearing Eisenbaum's name.

Eisenbaum, a fierce assimilationist who campaigned for Jewish emancipation in Poland, supervised and later directed the Warsaw Rabbinical Seminary beginning in 1826. With its secular cocurriculum, the seminary earned both the approval of the Russian government and the animosity of Warsaw's Orthodox Jews. The Orthodox considered the school a breeding ground for assimilation, and they were partly right: Many of the graduates of the Warsaw Rabbinical Seminary went on to convert to Christianity. One rabbi today claims that "Sixty-eight percent of its students converted!" but this might be an exaggeration.

Eisenbaum was controversial not only in life, but apparently after he died as well. His burial sparked one of the biggest internal feuds in Jewish Warsaw's history. Originally, all the tombstones in the cemetery were stone or marble slabs covered in Hebrew text accompanied by an occasional depiction. That wouldn't do for Eisenbaum's followers, who decided that his tombstone would reflect the new age for the Jews. Although a crucifix was deemed excessive, a tall obelisk was constructed and was immediately seen as the most radical monument in the cemetery. The rabbis didn't protest until they heard of the planned inscription: It was to be in Polish. Previously, only Hebrew characters had been used in tombstone inscriptions. When Yiddish was introduced in the 1840s, it was naturally printed in Hebrew characters. The Polish inscription on Eisenbaum's tombstone was considered too much, an abrogation of Jewish tradition in the sacred grounds of a cemetery, and the rabbis forbade it. Incensed, Eisenbaum's followers complained to the government, which passed a ruling that tombstone inscriptions must have a second language in addition to Hebrew—whether it be Polish, German, or Russian. This outraged the Orthodox Jews. They threatened to bury their dead without any tombstones at all, rather than include writing in the vernacular. Fearing a serious escalation of hostilities, the powerful statesman Rabbi Meisels (see above) met with the government to break the impasse. A decision was not reached until 1855, three years after Eisenbaum died. According to the compromise, Orthodox Jews could continue using only Hebrew in specially designated parts of the cemetery; in other designated areas, assimilated Jews could use the vernacular.

The compromise ushered in a unique form of segregation in the cemetery: traditionalist Jews from assimilationists. The area of Eisenbaum's grave is the first vernacular-designated area in the cemetery. Nearby, the second tombstone to use Polish is that of the publisher Jan Glucksberg (1784–1859), who printed the first ever guide to Warsaw. Glucksberg went even further than Eisenbaum by decorating his grave with a shrouded vase, a typical Greek symbol of mourning.

As you walk through the cemetery, you'll find blocks of Hebrew language graves and blocks of Polish language graves, sometimes separated by a mere path—all the result of a compromise reached in 1855 after a battle over a single provocative tombstone.

※

The Jewish Cemetery in Warsaw was a veritable battleground of Orthodox and assimilated Jews in the mid-nineteenth century. Practically everything about Jewish burial became a topic of dispute as religious and non-religious Jews struggled for supremacy in the Jewish Community.

Even the funeral processions came under attack. Traditionally, the body was carried into the cemetery on a stretcher. With a greater emphasis on mores of elegance in the nineteenth century, assimilated Jews wished to use a carriage to accompany the body from the house of mourning to the cemetery. Orthodox Jews rejected this idea, arguing that it was forbidden to turn one's back on a deceased body. The horseback riders would be doing just that. After some deliberation, a typically Jewish compromise was reached: The riders would walk alongside the procession, rather than sit on the horses.

A more contentious debate developed over the use of Polish text on tombstones. Jews had almost always used Hebrew text for inscriptions on tombstones. In the nineteenth century, with greater Polonization of the Jews in Warsaw, many wished to adorn their tombstones with Polish text. The Orthodox were adamantly opposed to the idea, considering it a first step in a repudiation of Jewish practice. After the death of Antoni Eisenbaum, the campaign for Polish inscription centered on his tombstone (*see page 193*). Rabbi Meisels, the great conciliator within the Jewish Community, issued a compromise: Orthodox Jews would continue using Hebrew-only tombstones, while special plots would be set aside for assimilated Jews to use Hebrew and Polish.

Then there was the gender issue. Poland and Galicia had developed the unique custom of burying men and women separately. This was not according to a particular Jewish law, but a custom unique to the region. Before the seventeenth century, families were customarily buried together. No less a halachic authority than Rabbi Moses Isserles, buried in Cracow in 1572, is buried next to his sister, grandmother, and wife. But in the seventeenth century, it became the custom to separate the sexes into all-male and all-female sections. This changed in the 1840s, when assimilated Jews began calling for family plots. They saw no reason why husbands should be separated from wives and mothers separated from sons. Assimilated Jews came to Rabbi Meisels to request gender integration, reminding him that the separation has nothing to do with Jewish law. The *mechitzah* might be traditional for a synagogue, but there is no Jewish law to bring it into a cemetery. This time, there was no extended debate; it was, after all, only a custom to separate the sexes. At the end of the 1840s, Rabbi Meisels agreed to set aside Plot 20 for family burials. Over the course of the next decades, the plot would become the final resting place of Warsaw's most illustrious, and assimilated, Jewish families. Elsewhere in the cemetery, the plots were divided into three categories: Orthodox Jewish men, Orthodox Jewish women, and assimilated families.

Today, the Warsaw Jewish Cemetery is like a museum of Jewish religious stratification in nineteenth-century Europe. Each plot will tell you a story about the religious affiliation of the people buried in its borders. All-female plots indicate that the women buried here were Orthodox. Bilingual plots and male-female plots indicate that the people buried here were assimilated. The cemetery reveals the intense segregation within European Jewish life in the nineteenth century. We all know that the Orthodox and the assimilated found it difficult to live together, but it seems they had trouble dying together as well.

Map: 7 Continue your walk by going around the Chemdat Shlomo's *ohel* on the left. To the left is the tall, rusting obelisk atop the grave of Jacob Epstein (1771–1843). Epstein, a banker and philanthropist, was one of the increasingly prominent Jews in nineteenth-century Warsaw who made successful inroads into secular Polish life. According to one source, he was the first Jew in Warsaw to commit the then-scandalous act of dressing like a European. This largely symbolic gesture gave Epstein access to the worldly society routinely denied his fellow Jews. He was honored to sit among Polish noblemen—another triumph for a Jew—on a council of charities. The Russian Emperor himself, Nicholas I, granted Epstein the title of "hereditary honorary citizen" after he visited the illustrious Jewish hospital Epstein had founded.

Epstein served with Poles as an officer during the November Insurrection of 1830–31, but in spite of this rebellious streak the Russians appointed him banker of Poland's treasury council in 1838.

Map: 8 Walk past the grave of Epstein, heading into the cemetery and parallel to the wall. (The easiest route might be right next to the wall.) About ten meters ahead is the magnificent tomb of Berek Sonnenberg (1764–1822).

The most detailed sculpture in the cemetery stands on the grave of one of its most esteemed Jews. Berek Sonnenberg was the son of the legendary Shmuel Zbitkower (1730s–1801), the entrepreneurial merchant who built up the Jewish Community in Praga. Among other things, Zbitkower built sawmills, bought estates and woodlands, operated a brewery, and hauled timber on the Vistula. His name was given to an entire Praga neighborhood, "Szmulewizna," by which it is still known to this day. Zbitkower established the Praga Jewish Cemetery, but this became an impoverished secondary cemetery after the Jewish Cemetery in Warsaw rose in prominence in the nineteenth century. It was a mark of the

Praga cemetery's lesser importance that Sonnenberg, the son of its founder, chose to be buried in the Warsaw cemetery.

Sonnenberg, who took his surname during Prussian rule, was the only son of Zbitkower not to convert to Christianity. He turned his father's impressive wealth into an even greater fortune through industrial and trade expansion. Czar Alexander I gave him the rights to unrestricted residence, to dress like a traditional Jew, and to keep his beard. In his will Sonnenberg sent most of his five million gulden to charity.

His wife, Temerel, is even more famous among Orthodox Jews as a great benefactor of the nineteenth century. She gave Torah scrolls to synagogues, financed *yeshivah* educations, and subsidized entire courts of *hasidim*. Among her beneficiaries were the first *rebbes* of the hasidic courts of Gerer and Worke. Some say it was really Temerel who managed her husband's widespread business activities. Nahum Sokolow wrote, "Berek would have been forgotten, were it not for his wife Temerel. The loveliness of a flower, the modesty of a dove, a soul with wings of gold, and fruitful as an olive tree" (Nahum Sokolow, "Henri Bergson's Old-Warsaw Lineage" in Lucy S. Dawidowicz, ed., *The Golden Tradition: Jewish Life and Thought in Eastern Europe*).

Their children and grandchildren became even more renowned, taking the name Bergson, literally "Berek-son" or "son of Berek." Mihal Bergson (1818–1898) became a famous pianist who spread Chopin's name all over Europe. His son was Henri Louis Bergson (1859–1941), the world-famous French philosopher who was awarded the Nobel Prize for Literature in 1928.

Berek Sonnenberg's tombstone is filled with imagery from his life and livelihood that suggests various interpretations. On the right side is a view of his father's stomping grounds in Praga, complete with the Praga Jewish Cemetery. It seems that Sonnenberg wished to pay homage to the Praga cemetery even though he himself is buried in Warsaw. One branch has broken and fallen to the earth from the tree in the foreground, a common image on Jewish tombstones. The Sonnenberg tombstone continues this imagery with a broken bridge crossing a river and empty boats, both signs of mourning and the end of one's life. They can also be seen as a symbol of the broken foreign trade with the death of Sonnenberg, the great merchant.

The left side of the tombstone repeats the image of boats, this time broken ships on the river. The Hebrew word "mourning," *oniyut*, is phonetically similar to the word "boats," *aniyot*. Above the scene is a Hebrew passage from the oft-quoted Psalms 137: "By the rivers of Babylon, there we sat, sat and wept, as we thought of Zion. There on the poplars we hung up our lyres." The entire scene on the tombstone may be said to depict this passage. Jerusalem stands on the left, Babylon on the right. You can even see lyres hanging from the trees.

This, the most ornate tombstone in the entire cemetery, has been the subject of several attacks by vandals. The most shocking occurred in 1991, when the tombstone was covered in wooden scaffolding during refurbishing. Some teenagers broke into the cemetery, added more wood to the scaffolding, and set it all ablaze. The tombstone became a pyre; by the time the fire went out, the monument was in worse condition than before. There are those who wish the tombstone to be replaced by a replica, but at this writing the original monument remains in the cemetery.

In front of Sonnenberg's tomb, there is a row of tombstones with exquisite imagery, including a Torah crown, a Levite's pitcher, books as a symbol of wisdom, a hand placing a coin in a box symbolizing charity, and a hunched-over eagle representing God supporting the universe. Look at the decorations on the bottoms of the stones as well. The litany of images is so pervasive that one is shocked this is still the Orthodox section of the cemetery. At the end of the row there's even the depiction of a man—but, so as not to go too far, his face is covered by a hat. A couple meters to the right of this grave you can see a tombstone with a chimerical creature. The head is that of a mammal and the body is that of a fish. This symbolizes the grave of a *tzaddik*, who would eat both beef and fish on Shabbat.

Return in the direction of Road 1. Five meters before the road lie the graves of the esteemed Alter family on the right-hand side. The inscriptions face the other way, so you'll have to walk around to see them.

Map: 9 The grave featuring a light outline of a hand holding a book is that of Rabbi Avraham Mordechai Alter (d. 1855). The drawing is rather faint; if you cannot read Hebrew, it might be easiest to locate by using a landmark: The grave topped by a depiction of books stands to Alter's right. Rabbi Alter was the son of the great Reb Yitzchak Meir Alter (1799–1866), called the *Chiddushei HaRim* after his most famous work. The Chiddushei HaRim founded a hasidic dynasty in Gora Kalwaria, a town near Warsaw, that by the 1930s had become arguably the most widespread and influential hasidic court in the world. It was known by the Yiddish name for the town, *Ger*; its followers are called *Gerer hasidim*. The Chiddushei HaRim himself is buried in Gora Kalwaria.

Rabbi Avraham Mordechai Alter did not live long enough to achieve the fame of his father. He was the only child of thirteen to live past childhood, but he was sickly throughout his life. Once, his father even admonished him at his sickbed to "Choose life!"

Nonetheless, in the loving words of Avraham Yitzchak Bromberg in his *Rebbes of Ger*, "This did not prevent [Rabbi Avraham Mordechai Alter's] kindheartedness and magnanimity from reaching the point of self-sacrifice, if need be, for the sake of any fellow Jew. Though outstanding in his scholarship, his sanctity, and his good name—for he was loved by all who knew him—he was humble and retiring. Simplicity marked his entire conduct...." His simplicity was expressed in his chosen occupation: Instead of teaching in *yeshivah*—a guaranteed career for the son of the Chiddushei HaRim—Rabbi Avraham operated a small grocery store and later a bookshop, making a very meager living. The bookshop stood on the famed Krochmalna Street (*see page 240*). The drawing on his tombstone refers to his scholarship but also, perhaps, to his chosen profession. The Chiddushei HaRim, who survived his son, inscribed the following on the top of the tombstone, "My eyes spring tears that my only son, the delight of my eyes, was taken from me on account of my sins."

It was Rabbi Avraham Mordechai Alter's own son, Rabbi Yehudah Aryeh Alter (1847–1905), who turned *Gerer Hasidut* into such a powerful force in the Jewish world. Known as the *Sfas Emes* after his most famous work, Rabbi Yehudah Aryeh Alter attracted hundreds of thousands of Jews to the movement. The town of Gora Kalwaria became filled with tens of thousands of hasidic pilgrims during each of the Jewish festivals. For Orthodox Jewry, the tiny Gora Kalwaria far outshone Warsaw as the true capital of Poland.

The vast majority of *Gerer hasidim* were murdered in the Holocaust. After the war, the survivors of the dynasty settled throughout the world. Today, *Gerer* Hasidism has rebounded considerably, particularly in Israel.

Two graves to the left of Avraham Mordechai Alter's, there is a tombstone depicting sheep drinking from a water basin underneath a broken tree. Judaism often compares the head of a family to a shepherd. When this man died, his children put up a tombstone representing themselves as sheep without their guide.

Map: 10 At the juncture alongside Road 1 is the grave of Majer Balaban (1877–1942). (His name is pronounced "Meir.") Balaban was one of the great historians of the twentieth century. In all of prewar Poland, whose three million Jews constituted ten percent of the total population, there was only a single university chair devoted to Jewish studies. This was filled by Balaban at the University of Warsaw. During his tenure there, Balaban wrote definitive histories of Jewish communities throughout Poland. Covering topics as diverse as Jewish communal organization, ancient synagogues, and the eighteenth-century Frankist movement, he is considered the father of Polish Jewish historiography. His works on the Jews of Cracow are still the preeminent works in the field today. This is partly because Balaban's erudition was immense, but also because many of the original archives he used were destroyed during the war.

Balaban refused to leave Warsaw when the Nazis entered in 1939. When he died in 1942, he was one of the fortunate ones buried in individual, identified graves in the cemetery.

Map: 11 As if great scholarly minds have their own gravitational force in the cemetery, the grave of another fierce intellect lies to the right of Majer Balaban. The tomb atop the steps is the grave of the rabbinical polyglot Samuel Abraham Poznanski (1864–1921). Poznanski was one of the revered rabbis who presided over the Tlomackie Street Synagogue. In the 1920s he translated the *siddur* into Polish. Educated at Berlin University and the esteemed College for the Science of Judaism in Berlin, he published hundreds of eclectic studies ranging from Hebrew grammar in the Middle Ages and Jewish-Arabic literature to Jewish communities in North Africa. Over the course of his life he became one of the world's chief authorities on the Karaites, the Persian Jewish sect that rejects the Talmud in favor of rigorous obedience to the letter of Torah law.

Return to Road 1 and make a right onto the path after the grave of Balaban. This path separates Plots 9 and 10.

Map: 12 On the left side is an unusual iron tomb, in Gothic style, atop the graves of Jacob and Henrietta Epstein. Actually, you've already seen Jacob Epstein's grave near that of the Chemdat Shlomo. This is the grave of his wife, Henrietta. The tombstone inscribes both names to remember them together. This is one area where Orthodox women are buried *(see pages 194–195* [special section]).

Map: 13 Fifteen meters farther down the path, on the left side, there is an opening that leads to the site of a mass grave of Jews from the Warsaw ghetto.

There are two mass graves inside the cemetery itself, with additional larger mass graves in Skra Stadium nearby. The area here is the site of one of the mass graves, but there is no consensus on where the second one is. It is most likely in the area at the end of the Main Avenue in Plot 73, but historians aren't certain. The total number of Jews in the mass graves is close to one hundred thousand.

People buried in the mass graves fell into two categories: those lined up and murdered in the cemetery by the Germans, and the much larger numbers of those who died in the ghetto of disease or hunger. Of the first category, sometimes it was prisoners who were executed for reasons such as trying to scale the ghetto wall or being found on the "Aryan" side of Warsaw. The elderly and sick who were murdered at the start of the mass deportations to Treblinka were buried in Skra Stadium (see *After The Cemetery*, page 213).

The memorial stones on the site were designed by the same individuals, architect Hanna Szmalenberg and sculptor Wladyslaw Klamerus, who designed the Memorial Route of Jewish Martyrdom and Struggle and the Umschlagplatz Memorial (*see page 214*). As with the Umschlagplatz Memorial, the memorial on the mass grave employs the motif of a *tallis*, or Jewish prayer shawl, through the use of thin black stripes on white stones.

Continue on the path between Plots 9 and 10. Among the graves of Orthodox women in Plot 9 on the left are more recent memorials to families killed in the ghetto. At the end of the path, make a right.

Map: 14 The second grave on the right side is that of Adam Czerniakow (1880–1942). During the siege of Warsaw in 1939, the mayor appointed Czerniakow, an industrial engineer, to be leader of the Warsaw Jewish Community; soon the Gestapo itself appointed him chairman of the Judenrat. As such, he was the object of much ill will on the part of the Jews, who considered the Judenrat an ineffectual Nazi organ. A common epithet in the ghetto was *Judenverrat*, or "Betrayal of the Jews."

Czerniakow, as the most visible Jew in the ghetto and the one in daily contact with the Nazis, was an easy scapegoat for the misery of ghetto life. In fact, he labored night and day to bring some relief to the largest Jewish Community of Europe. The way the ghetto was structured, his job was impossible; Czerniakow was supposed to lead and administer a Community that was literally being starved to death by the Germans. As his terse diary attests, Czerniakow maintained a superhuman equilibrium while trying to alleviate the horrors of ghetto life. "The ability to work in such conditions, to follow through on a plan, is to be commended," he wrote. "Still, we do our everyday tasks. Tears will not help us. Again, in the words of Dickens: 'You cannot wind the clock with tears'" (excerpted in Lucy S. Dawidowicz, ed., *A Holocaust Reader*).

The Nazis repeatedly harassed and humiliated him. On one occasion they placed a fully lit menorah on his desk and commenced a film on "Jewish degeneracy" in the ghetto; another time they threw him in prison and tortured him. According to his diaries, as early as January 1940 Czerniakow tried to abdicate: "Confronted with all this, I turned to the SS asking that I be relieved of my office, for in these abnormal circumstances I cannot lead the *Kehilla* [Community]. They said, in response, that they would not recommend such a step" (excerpted in Lucy S. Dawidowicz, ed., *A Holocaust Reader*).

Still, even a man of Czerniakow's composure had his limits. On July 20, 1942, when rumors of impending mass deportations had reached frantic proportions, Czerniakow went from office to office, practically begging the Germans for information. The Germans said nothing. Then, on July 22, Czerniakow was informed that deportations of six thousand Jews a day were to commence at once—and that should there be any problems, his wife would be the first person shot. On July 23 he desperately roamed the offices of the SS, asking for exemptions for various groups. In his diaries he had written that "the most tragic problem is that of the children in the orphanages" (excerpted in Lucy S. Dawidowicz, ed., *A Holocaust Reader*). He pleaded with the SS to save the orphans, but the Germans were intransigent. The horror was too great; Czerniakow took a cyanide tablet he had saved for such an occasion as this since 1939. In the suicide notes he left to his wife and to his colleagues, he wrote, "I am powerless. My heart trembles in sorrow and compassion. I can no longer bear all this. My act will prove to everyone what is the right thing to do" (quoted in Lucy S. Dawidowicz, *The War against the Jews 1933–1945*).

But what was the right thing to do? Czerniakow's suicide was seen by many as an act of moral courage. Many others, particularly in the underground, were enraged. They argued that he should have warned the ghetto and mobilized the populace to resist. Historians today are much more judicious, citing Czerniakow's impotence in the face of the Nazi murder machine, as well as the impotence of the entire ghetto Community in 1942, including the underground itself. With this in mind, Lawrence Langer writes in *Admitting the Holocaust* of "the poverty of traditional moral vocabulary when we address the subject of human conduct during the destruction of European Jewry."

On Czerniakow's tombstone is a Polish inscription that reads in part, "It will take much more than an instant for the world to absorb the tranquil rest of a person like you. . . . It is not important in which urn you rest, for one day they will reopen your grave and weigh your good deeds in a new way."

In the same grave lies Jan Czerniakow, Adam's son, who passed away in a sanatorium in Russia just days before his father took his own life. In addition, Adam Czerniakow's wife, Felicja, is buried here. She survived the Holocaust.

Map: 15 *Du tomboj, sube kaj dekstre estas la tombostono de doktoro Lazaro Ludoviko Zamenhof, kreinto de Esperanto.* That's Esperanto for "Two graves down on the right side is the tomb of Ludwik Zamenhof (1859–1917), creator of Esperanto."

At a time when Jewish utopian ideals, from Zionism to the Bund, captured the fancy of Jewish intellectuals, Ludwik Zamenhof fostered the most utopian vision of all: A single global tongue to unite all the people of the world.

Zamenhof, a doctor and philologist born in Bialystok, published a pamphlet of Esperanto ("Hope"), his new language, at the fresh age of 21. Zamenhof argued that Esperanto was not merely a language but a means of achieving peace and understanding in the world.

At first, there were only 900 roots and 16 grammatical rules to the language. Zamenhof was convinced that Esperanto could serve as an international language. To prove it, he translated classics of world literature into Esperanto. Like his direct contemporary, Theodor Herzl, Zamenhof did not live to see the fruition of his dream. But unlike Herzl's dream, Zamenhof's never reached fulfillment. There are Esperanto speakers throughout the world, hosting societies, seminars, and the like, but the language never became the linguistic panacea its creator had hoped for.

Janusz Korczak, the famed leader of orphans in the Warsaw Ghetto (*see page 211*), jotted down these impressions of Zamenhof:

> Naive, audacious: He wanted to rectify God's error or God's punishment. He wanted to fuse the misplaced languages into one again. (Janusz Korczak, *Ghetto Diary*)

Zamenhof, who had originally worked on a book of Yiddish grammar and who sympathized with the Zionist movement, was committed to Jewish concerns throughout his life. His vision of a unifying language, sort of the converse of the tale of the Tower of Babel, was perhaps most emblematic of the nineteenth-century Jewish dream of a world without boundaries.

The lush mosaic on his grave was constructed by Esperanto enthusiasts in the early 1960s. It contains the traditional five-pointed star, the symbol of Esperanto. Green is the symbol of Esperanto hope. The "E" stands for Esperanto.

To the left of Zamenhof's grave is the grave of his wife, Klara, and below it a memorial stone for his daughters, Zoeia and Lioia, who were murdered in Treblinka.

Map: 16 Return to the main avenue and turn left. About thirty meters ahead, on the right side, is the grave of Chaim Zelig Slonimski (1810–1904). Slonimski, a sort of Carl Sagan of the nineteenth century, wrote popular science books for the masses of the Jewish *Haskalah*, or Enlightenment. He even founded a Hebrew antecedent to *Discover* magazine, called *Ha-Zefirah*. This, the first science magazine published in Hebrew, was instrumental in the nineteenth-century rebirth of the language. Slonimski dabbled in invention as well, and in 1844 was awarded a twenty-five-hundred-ruble prize by the Russian Academy of Sciences for his calculating machine. In 1856 he pioneered a method of sending quadruple telegrams, thus paving the way for the technique of multiple telegraphy in 1858.

Among the subjects Slonimski explored were mathematics and astronomy—in particular Halley's Comet, which appeared in 1835. He drew acrimony from Orthodox Jews, ending only after thirty years, when he pointed out an error of four days in the Hebrew calendar. However, because Slonimski remained Orthodox throughout his life, his work was well received even by those observant readers who saw science as a threat to tradition. His tombstone reflects this, reading "He was great in Torah and wisdom." Some of his mathematical explanations actually wound up in certain editions of the Talmud.

His grandson Antoni Slonimski was one of the leading Polish poets of the twentieth century.

Map: 17 Roughly opposite Slonimski's grave is a path, Road 4, that divides Plots 12 and 19 and leads back into the heart of the cemetery. A few meters down this road and on the right side, you'll see the grave of Jan Sierota, which was designed by *Abraham Ostrzega*, a virtuoso twentieth-century sculptor whose work can be seen throughout the cemetery. This monument, an expressionistic masterpiece, is titled *Trapped in Stone* because it depicts a man attempting to emerge from the stone that threatens to bury him.

The son of a tombstone maker, Ostrzega himself designed cubist and expressionistic tombstones that almost unfailingly earned him the contempt of Orthodox circles. At issue was one of the fundamentals of Jewish tradition: the Torah expressly prohibits the depiction of graven images. Of course, for centuries observant Jews had decorated tombstones with such common images as a hand giving charity or pouring water. But Ostrzega took it a step further with his depiction of entire human forms. That he himself was assimilated didn't earn him any points either. It was not uncommon for Orthodox Jews to vandalize and destroy Ostrzega's monuments in the cemetery.

During the war, Ostrzega found work in the Warsaw ghetto not as a sculptor—there was no stone, let alone demand—but as a craftsman. He cut thin strips of sandstone to sell as knife sharpeners. He was killed in Treblinka in 1942.

Continue on Road 4 into the heart of the cemetery. After a short walk you'll see a number of impressive tombstones in Plot 20 on the right. The monument style differs from that of more traditional Jews because this was the original area chosen by Rabbi Meisels for the burial of women and men together. Remember that there were two main issues in the cemetery that divided observant and assimilated Jews: language on tombstones and segregation of graves by sex. Assimilated Jews argued that the segregation of sexes was not a question of religion but of custom. Meisels, the great conciliator of Warsaw Jews, established Plot 20 for assimilated Jews to bury in family gravesites. Ironically, a new form of segregation thus evolved: the Orthodox from the assimilated.

Taken as a whole, Plot 20 is a testament to the great strides Jews made into Polish society in the nineteenth century. Some of the most influential Jews in Polish history are buried here. Their spheres of influence included Polish commerce and culture, but also extended to the Jewish Community itself. Here are the creators of Jewish books, schools, synagogues, and hospitals. They were the leading figures in the Warsaw Jewish Community in the nineteenth century

But you will be hard-pressed to find evidence of grandchildren in this area. Most are buried in Christian cemeteries. The families buried here were so assimilated that the children often converted for reasons of greater social and economic mobility. Baptism was often the final barrier to acceptance in the Gentile world.

Map: 18 In the fenced-in area next to the road lies the illustrious Natanson family. Zelig Natanson (1795–1879), the patriarch, was one of the major soap magnates of nineteenth-century Warsaw. He also ran clothing stores, sugar factories, a banking house, and Warsaw's second progressive synagogue above his shop on Nalewki Street.

Map: 19 His son, Ludwik Natanson (1821–1896), was the key player in Warsaw's Jewish Community during its period of unprecedented growth and transition. In the secular world, Natanson was a prestigious doctor; he founded and edited one of the first journals of medicine written in Polish, served as president of the Polish Medical Society, and fought against the Warsaw cholera epidemic of 1848–52. In the Jewish Community, Natanson was no less active. A symbol of the rising power of assimilationists in Warsaw Jewish circles, Natanson became chairman of the Jewish Community of Warsaw in 1871. It was under his tenure that the Tlomackie Street Synagogue—the triumph of assimilated Jews—was built. He also built the Jewish Community office building on Grzybowska Street, which was later destroyed by the Nazis. In addition, he began work on an enormous Jewish hospital, later known as Czyste Hospital because it was located in the Czyste quarter, that would serve as a workplace for Jewish doctors and nurses who were denied work at Polish hospitals. In 1939 Czyste Hospital, with 1,490 beds and 147 doctors, was the largest hospital in all of Poland.

Natanson represented the upper echelon of Warsaw's Jewish bourgeois that was certain of Poland's ultimate hospitality toward the Jews. He was unflinchingly devoted to the theory that Jewish assimilation was the surest remedy to anti-Semitism. Even after he bravely led Warsaw's Jews through a pogrom in 1881, Natanson declared that Jews would truly be accepted into Polish society only when they eliminated the differences between themselves and their neighbors. Poorer Jews and traditionalists were, needless to say, unconvinced. It was one more example of the nineteenth-century fissure between tradition and modernity.

As a testament to the enduring power of the Natanson family name—and to the flourishing of nineteenth-century assimilated Warsaw Jewry—in the same gated area you'll find Ludwik's brothers Henryk (1820–1895), one of the major publishers in Warsaw, and Jakub (1832–1884), a distinguished industrialist and professor of chemistry.

Map: 20 A few meters along the western edge of Plot 20 on the path beyond the Natanson family gate is the simple grave of Michal Landy (1844–1861). (On the stone, his name is conjugated as "Michala Landego.")

Michal Landy is one of the few figures in European Jewish history whom Christians turned into a legend.

The story itself is beguilingly simple: During the unarmed patriotic demonstrations on Warsaw's Castle Square in 1861, a priest was shot down by a Russian soldier. Michal Landy, a seventeen-year-old student demonstrator, kneeled down to the priest and lifted his cross. Immediately Landy himself was shot down.

These ten seconds of Polish national history became a symbol of rapprochement between Poles and Jews. In Poland, the cross is not only a symbol of Christianity but of Poland's fate. By symbolically dying for the cross, the Jews displayed to their Christian neighbors that they were devoted to Polish national sovereignty. In Polish Christian circles, exalted opinions of the Jews became widespread; if Landy was a Jesus-type martyr, then the entire Jewish people were a noble race. There is, of course, the patronizing implication of Jewish baptism to the legend, but basically the myth shows sincere reverence toward the Jewish people. Immediately after his death, Landy was emblazoned in Poland's psyche and in its art and literature.

Map: 21 & 22 In the same plot, next to the gate of the Natanson family, is the white marble tombstone of Levi Lesser (1791–1870), a merchant who owned a department store on plac Bankowy, and a smaller monument to his son Aleksander (1814–1884). Aleksander Lesser was one of the great historical painters of nineteenth-century Poland. His portraits of kings and barons can be found in palaces throughout the country. One of his paintings, *The Funeral of the Five Victims*, incorporates the legend of Michal Landy and includes the famous Rabbi Dov Berush Meisels in the funeral procession. Fittingly, a simple palette and brushes is depicted on his tombstone.

Map: 23 Northeast of the Lesser graves there is a large stone coffin atop the tombstone of the banker Henryk Wawelberg (1813–1891). On top of the stone coffin are the Greek letters alpha and omega. He was not a fraternity boy. The first and last letters of the Greek alphabet symbolize that Henryk was first and last in all that he did. This sudden appearance in the cemetery of Greek letters certainly raised the eyebrows of observant Jews; in ancient Israel under Assyrian domination, Greek was a blatant symbol of assimilation. (Now you see why there is a special assimilated section of the cemetery. "It was enough they insisted on Polish—now this?" the rabbis must have lamented.)

Map: 24 In front is the grave of Henryk's son Hipolit Wawelberg (1844–1901), probably the only Polish Jew to have an Argentinian city named after himself. The philanthropist Hipolit was so taken by the idea of a Jewish homeland in Latin America that he counted the Argentinian settlement project among his favorite charities. After a particularly generous donation in 1899 to the Jewish Colonization Association, the latter changed the name of its settlement Santa Elena to Wawelberg.

Hipolit was active in secular Jewish causes throughout Poland and Russia. He published journals that, among other things, fought against Polish anti-Semitism. Perhaps motivated by his own call for a cultural rapprochement between Jews and Poles, he was one of the nineteenth century's greatest patrons of Polish literature. Within the Jewish Community itself, he helped finance the Warsaw Jewish Community's crafts school on Grzybowska Street, established a Jewish agricultural school in the southern Polish city of Czestochowa, and in 1895 helped found a Warsaw industrial school in which Jews would not be discriminated against. In spite of the efforts of his heirs, the ban on discrimination was revoked during the interwar period.

Map: 25 To the left of the Wawelbergs are the white-columned graves of Samuel Orgelbrand (1810–1868) and his wife, Anna (1811–1884).

When Jewish book publication was restricted inside Russia, Samuel Orgelbrand founded a publishing house that printed in Polish and Hebrew. It became such a success that Orgelbrand became the most powerful publisher in Warsaw in the mid-nineteenth century. Of the 520 volumes he published in his career, one hundred were in Hebrew. He published the *Tanach* with commentaries, *siddurim*, *machzorim*, and an edition of *Ze'enah u-Re'enah*—a Yiddish version of the Torah for women. In the 1860s he published the entire Babylonian Talmud in twenty volumes. The work sold twelve thousand copies. As if that wasn't enough, he spent a decade publishing the first Polish general encyclopedia in twenty-eight volumes, including a comprehensive survey of Judaism.

Before he entered the publishing world, Orgelbrand was a graduate of the Warsaw Rabbinical Seminary where he also taught for a short time. As such, his tombstone-column is inscribed on one side in Polish, but on the other side in a much more extensive Hebrew. Both of Orgelbrand's sons were somewhat assimilated; in the 1890s they converted to Christianity and when they died were buried in Christian cemeteries. In 1901 they disbanded the Hebrew department of the family publishing house.

Although her father converted and is not buried in this cemetery, Romana Orgelbrand (1880–1899) is buried next to her grandparents Samuel and Anna. Her tombstone is striking in its marble depiction of vines climbing over the text. She died at the age of nineteen. On the left, you can see lilies, a Christian image that has become a universal symbol of virginity.

Map: 26 Return to Road 4. Facing west (deeper into the cemetery), you'll see on the left side the *ohel* of Rabbi Menachem Mendel of Worke, the Worker Rebbe (1819–1868).

The son of the esteemed founder of the school of Worke, Rabbi Yitzchak of Worke, Reb Mendel was known as the "silent *tzaddik*." From the start, Reb Mendel spurned the life of the hasidic court, going off with friends for mystical forays in the forest instead. There is a story that on his wedding day, when the *badhan*, or Jester, sang, "Pray and learn and serve your God," Reb Mendel responded, "Don't pray and don't learn and don't anger your God."

When he was crowned successor to his father, Reb Mendel tried to refuse, but the *hasidim* of Worke were adamant. Over the course of Reb Mendel's tenure, Worke *Hasidut* became legendary for its humility, its humanism, and its silence. Reb Mendel explained that the fact that vanity can be found in wicked people proves that it is bad. He was known to sit through entire private meetings without uttering a word. He did not deliver sermons and did not make commentaries on the Torah. When asked once why he didn't give Torah commentary, Reb Mendel responded, "The Psalms speak of the Heavens: 'There is no utterance, there are no words, their sound is not heard. Their voice carries throughout the earth'" (Psalms 19:4–5). This very silence is what attracted scores of *hasidim* to his court. As Elie Wiesel wrote in *Somewhere a Master: Further Hasidic Portraits and Legends*, "He would spend sleepless nights sitting around his table with fervent disciples. The silence would be overwhelming, total. Soon there was nothing else in creation but this silence, and soon it reached farther still, higher still. A primary force, it would grow more and more intense and pure and true. Time stood still, for it had not been disrupted by words."

Once Reb Mendel was asked where he had learned the secret of silence. Reb Mendel refrained from answering.

The unkempt plot north of the *ohelim*, Plot 21, is one area where Orthodox Jewish women were buried. Walk back on Road 4 to the Main Avenue, turn left, and continue until you come to the second path on the left, or Road 6, which leads back into the cemetery. The road begins between Plots 24 and 31. As a point of reference, the gravestone at the corner of Plot 31 is for Bernard Grunbaum. At this point, turn to the "Detail B" map, which continues the walk.

After you enter Road 6, you can see another Ostrzega monument a few meters in on the left. It is no less beautiful—or controversial—than the rest of his work in the cemetery.

Map: 27 About twenty meters down Road 6 you'll find the *ohel* of the famous miracle worker Rabbi Yaakov Aryeh Guterman of Radzimin (1792–1874) on the right side. This *ohel* was one of the preferred locations of smugglers for spending the night after sneaking in food from "Aryan" Warsaw during the war. Nearby lie the graves of several leaders of *Gerer Hasidut*, some of whom were killed in the Holocaust.

Take the first right from Road 6 onto the path between Plots 32 and 33.

Map: 28 Halfway down the path, on the right side, you will find the *ohel* of Yakov Yitzchak Shapiro of Balandov and his father, Reb Chaim Meir Yechiel of Mogelnice (d. 1882).

Map: 29 Opposite this *ohel*, inside a gate, is the ornate marble sculpture of a cloth covering a coffin. This is the grave of the wealthy banker Wilhelm Landau (1833–1899). The Landaus, unsatisfied with the tombstone sculpture available in Poland, had Wilhelm's exquisite stone crafted in Frankfurt.

Continuing on this path, you will notice Hebrew tombstones on the right side and Polish on the left. That's because the right side was reserved for Orthodox Jewish men and the left for assimilated people. This also means you'll find women as well as men on the left.

After the next intersection there is a sewer opening right in the middle of the path (watch your step).

Map: 30 A few meters beyond the sewer, on the left, is the grave of the writer Abraham Shalom Frydberg (1838–1902). His monument is a greyish stone topped by a stack of white marble books. Frydberg, a member of the Hebrew literati of nineteenth-century Warsaw, translated various German and Russian works into Hebrew. He served on the editorial board of Slonimski's popular science journal *Ha-Zefirah*, and worked for a short time as Warsaw's official censor of Hebrew books.

Frydberg also went by the Hebrew version, *Har Shalom*, of his German name. This is a literal translation of "Frydberg," which means "peaceful hill" in German. His name is symbolically rendered on the tombstone, with two hands shaking ("peace") in front of a hill. In the open book is inscribed Psalms 137:5: "If I forget you, O Jerusalem, let my right hand wither." Quite a hefty promise, coming from a writer.

Continue on the path, making a left onto Road 8 at the first intersection. Now you'll have to walk a good distance, deep into the cemetery, to arrive at the graves of two hasidic sages.

Map: 31 You'll see two *ohelim* in Plot 49 on the right. The one deeper inside the plot is the most-visited *ohel* in this part of the cemetery. It holds the graves of two of the greatest rabbinical thinkers of the twentieth century, Rabbi Naphtali Tzvi Yehudah Berlin (1817–1893) and Rabbi Chaim Soloveitchik (1853–1918).

Rabbi Berlin, known as the *Netziv* after his initials, was the legendary leader of the *yeshivah* at Volozhin. The Volozhin *yeshivah* was one of the most important centers of Jewish learning in Russia, with four hundred students deeply immersed in talmudic study. In 1892, after the Netziv refused to comply with Russian regulations concerning enrollment and curriculum, the *yeshivah* was closed by the authorities. The Netziv was forced to leave Volozhin. He wished to emigrate to Palestine, but he died in Warsaw in 1893.

Rabbi Soloveitchik, also known as Reb Chaim Brisker because he served as rabbi of Brisk, studied at the Volozhin *yeshivah* and eventually became one of its most outstanding instructors. Rabbi Soloveitchik pioneered a method of talmudic study involving an analytical breakdown of the entire Talmud. At the time, it was considered a revolution in talmudic study. Today, the highest level of *yeshivah* is known as "Brisker," after Rabbi Soloveitchik.

Walk back on Road 8 and make a left, then take the first right, onto Road 9. On your right will be Plot 47, a veritable garden of *ohelim*. Many hasidic rebbes visited or moved to Warsaw after the First World War. There is no space here to explore each one in great detail, but what follows are some of the most famous:

Map: 32 The second *ohel* adjacent to the path is that of Rabbi Yisrael of Modzhitz (1849–1921). The rebbe of Modzhitz could easily have been called the rebbe of music. He was the author of countless melodies, many of which are still popular today. One of his most famous melodies is called "Ezkerah." He allegedly composed it while undergoing surgery without anaesthesia. In some Modzhitzer synagogues, music is such an important part of the liturgy that adult (male) choirs harmonize during the service. Rabbi Yisrael's most famous book was *Divrei Yisrael*. It is a compilation of hasidic commentaries on the weekly Torah portion.

Continue in the same direction down Road 9 and make a right at the corner, where you'll find three *ohelim* side by side.

Map: 33 The first one is the *ohel* of Rabbi Moshe Mordechai of Pelcovizna, who was the father of the famous theologian Abraham Joshua Heschel.

Map: 34 Two doors down is Rabbi Shmuel of Slonim (1850–1916). Reb Shmuel is also known by the title of his most famous book, *Divrei Shmuel*. Reb Shmuel made Slonimer Hasidism one of the most well-known hasidic courts in the Jewish world. He also published a series of advice letters, entitled *Avodat P'nim* (Inner Work), in which he counseled people in all manner of problems, from employment to childbirth.

Turn right on Road 9 to go back to the Main Avenue.

Map: 35 When you get there, you will notice on the left corner the famous Ostrzega monument to three giants of Yiddish literature: Isaac Leib Peretz (1852–1915), Jacob Dineson (1856–1919), and S. An-ski (1863–1920).

Peretz is by far the most famous of the three. He is regarded as both the intellectual figurehead of Yiddish literature as well as the first modernist writer in the Yiddish language. His first book appeared when he was twenty-seven. In his thirties, he moved from Zamosc to Warsaw, where he became involved in the Jewish Community.

Peretz insisted on using Yiddish neither as an imitation of nor as a springboard to European literature. Instead, Peretz developed this uniquely Jewish language until, by the end of the nineteenth century, its expressive power ranked with the most sophisticated languages and literature of Europe. Although he began his literary career in Polish and often wrote in Hebrew, Peretz ultimately insisted that Yiddish was the language of the Jewish people. He wrote about hasidic Jews but was not himself observant; he believed in Jewish national renewal but was not a Zionist. Stylistically, Peretz was influenced by the modes of neo-romanticism and modernism that were gaining strength in western Europe in the late nineteenth century. But today, he is as well known for his content as his style.

Born to observant Jewish parents, Peretz witnessed the withering of tradition in Jewish daily life. He himself harbored no yen for Orthodoxy, which he considered narrow-minded, but he had even more disrespect for the herds of assimilated Jews dandying about in Polish society. Peretz had left traditional Judaism, but he considered its myths and ideals a fertile breeding ground for a national Jewish culture—even a Renaissance—in the Diaspora. One of the chief harbingers of this Renaissance would be Yiddish literature. As he wrote in his essay "Escaping Jewishness," "Jewish life must burst into blossom again. With the Bible as germinating seed and with folk symbols and folk legends as dew and rain, the field will sprout again, the people will revive, the Jews will rise once more to suffer anew for their truth and will reaffirm their faith in ultimate victory" (Sol Liptzin, ed., *Peretz*).

Peretz's home in Warsaw was considered the central address of Yiddish literature. He opened his doors and hosted a salon for the most talented writers of the day. Eventually, after Peretz died, this salon was transferred to the Writers' Society on Tlomackie Street. At Peretz's funeral, it is said, all of Warsaw crowded into the cemetery. The Jews were mourning en masse for a national hero, the patron saint of the Yiddish language and of the Diaspora itself.

An-ski (real name: Solomon Zainwil Rapaport) is as distinguished for his Yiddish writing as for his Jewish ethnographic studies in Eastern European villages. His most famous work is the play *The Dybbuk*, which was first performed in Vilna in 1920 and has since appeared all over the world on stage, opera, and film. An-ski spent most of his life in Russia and came to Warsaw only after World War I, two years before he died.

Dineson was a devoted follower of Peretz who labored to spread Peretz's fame throughout the Jewish world. A Yiddish writer himself, his second novel sold over two hundred thousand copies. He was also known for his "Dineson schools," elementary schools that introduced secular subjects to the Jewish education system.

From the Peretz Monument, continue along the Main Avenue toward the end of the cemetery. After about ten meters you'll come to Road 10 on the left. On the far corner of the junction is the grave of Ester Pave. It is another sculpture designed by Ostrzega. This one looks innocent enough; certainly it would arouse no resentment among the Orthodox. But look again: On the back of the monument there is a fully realized human form hiding, as it were, behind the monument itself. In such a way the tombstone could get past the cemetery censors of the day.

Map: 36 Ten meters into Road 10 (on the left side, inside the plot a little) is a rectangular, black and white monument resembling a stone wall. If Peretz was buried with all the pomp and circumstance of a lavish prince, the funeral of this man was like that of a prayer. Under the cover of night, Baruch Shulman (1886–1906), a leading socialist in the early twentieth century, was buried here after he was killed for throwing a bomb on plac Grzybowski *(see page 244)*. The Russians would not permit the funeral, so it had to be performed at night. During preparations for the Warsaw Ghetto Uprising, some fighters viewed Shulman as a source of inspiration. There are even photographs of fighters posing proudly before his tomb.

Map: 37 Walk back to the Main Avenue and turn right. About fifteen meters beyond the Peretz monument is the grave of Esther Rachel Kaminska (1870–1925), near the edge of Plot 39 on the right. Kaminska was called the "Mother of Yiddish Theater," partly because with her husband she established the Yiddish Theater of Warsaw; partly because her acting propelled Yiddish theater to the world stage; and partly because her most famous roles were of mothers. She captivated audiences not only in Warsaw but in St. Petersburg, Paris, London, and in the United States. On plaques throughout the tombstone, she is referred to as "Mother," predominately in the main Yiddish inscription. The tombstone is notable for its depiction of four animals, referring to the passage from *Ethics of the Fathers*, which reads, "Be bold as a leopard, light as an eagle, swift as a deer, and strong as a lion, to carry out the will of your father in Heaven" (*Ethics of the Fathers* 5:20). The passage could easily pass for a credo in the dramatic arts.

Kaminska's daughter Ida Kaminska (1899–1978) directed the state Jewish theater in Warsaw, started in 1950, but she emigrated after the anti-Semitic purges in 1968. She is most famous for her role in *The Shop on Main Street* from 1967.

Two graves to the left of Kaminska's is a monument to three leaders of the socialist Zionist Po'alei Zion party who died in the Warsaw Ghetto Uprising. They were Pola Elster, Hirsch Berlinski, and Eliyahu Ehrlich. They were active in the formation of the Jewish Fighting Organization.

Map: 38 Farther along the Main Avenue, a set of stairs on the right leads to a modest Bund monument commemorating Henryk Ehrlich (1882–1941) and Victor Alter (1890–

1941), Polish Bund leaders in the first half of the twentieth century. The Bund was a uniquely Eastern European form of practical Jewish messianism. It stood against both rabbinical Judaism and Zionism, arguing that Jewish life would reach its fruition only in an autonomous, socialist, and Yiddish-based society within Eastern Europe.

Ehrlich and Alter became heroes in trade unions all over the world for their stance on workers' rights. They also became objects of government crackdowns: Ehrlich was repeatedly arrested and Alter was sent to Siberia before World War I, though he escaped.

Ehrlich and Alter were the only representatives of the Polish state who issued a formal protest after the Red Army invaded on September 17, 1939. This sounds surprising, given that Hitler had invaded from the other side, but Ehrlich and Alter were committed democratic socialists. They viewed the Russian invasion as a totalitarian crime no less invidious than Hitler's. Both men were arrested by the Soviets. Later, after they had been released, Stalin ordered their re-arrest; on December 4, 1941, they were executed on Stalin's orders in Kuibyshev. Numerous organizations throughout the world expressed their outrage. New York Mayor Fiorello LaGuardia condemned the executions at a memorial in March 1943.

The most moving memorial service was undoubtedly the one held in the Warsaw Jewish Cemetery in April 1987, when this symbolic tombstone was unveiled. It was organized by Marek Edelman, one of the last surviving fighters of the Warsaw Ghetto Uprising and a committed Bundist to this very day. Edelman, who as an undeterred Bundist refused to leave his home country even after the war, became one of the most vociferous leaders of the Solidarity movement against communist rule. The memorial ceremony for Ehrlich and Alter turned into a semi-spontaneous Solidarity demonstration. Thousands of people from all over Poland streamed into the cemetery in a procession that became an act of resistance. All types of Solidarity supporters came, from activists who had never even heard of the Bund to Polish nationalists strutting, somewhat bewildered, with the obligatory yarmulkes covering their skulls.

Those who were there remember it as one of the most inspiring shows of strength Solidarity had ever arranged. But why did Solidarity feel united with these two Jewish revolutionaries? Was it because they protested a Russian occupation? Was it a symbolic gesture of identification with two men executed by Stalin? Was it an attempt to uncover the concealed parts of Polish history? Ehrlich and Alter, who had not previously experienced posthumous fame in their own country, certainly became symbols of resistance against a totalitarian regime backed by Russia. Was there also possibly an identification with the Bund? Marek Edelman was probably the only Bundist in Solidarity, and most activists had no idea what the Bund once stood for. But there was a connection. One Polish Jewish intellectual, who was a leader in Solidarity, explained it to me like this: "There is a surprising spiritual continuity between the Bund and Solidarity. . . . The [ideal] is so similar, the idea of a movement becoming really the society you live in, that it's not only a fight for union rights or political rights but it educates, it promotes; it's your family, it's your life. It embodies the noblest ideas of humanity. I mean, if you read early Solidarity manifestos, they sound as if they were translated from the Yiddish."

The original bronze plaque was stolen in 1995. It was replaced by a stone plaque.

Map: 39 Immediately on the left as you continue along the Main Avenue is the grave of Henryk Wohl (1836–1907), another anti-Russian revolutionary whose grave became a magnet for demonstrations. Wohl was active in the 1863 insurrection against Russian rule and was later arrested by the Russians and sentenced to death. His sentence was commuted, and after twenty years in a labor camp he returned to Poland. Until his death—and even afterwards—Wohl lamented the occupation of his country. His unique tombstone, with its three boulders, symbolizes the three partitions of Poland between Austria, Prussia, and Russia in the eighteenth century. It is inscribed, quite simply, "The Good Son of the Homeland—His Countrymen." Like the later memorial plaque for Ehrlich and Alter, Wohl's tombstone attracted activists demanding an end to the Russian occupation.

Map: 40 Half a dozen graves past Wohl's is a fenced-in area containing black pillar-tombstones for Majer Wolanowski (1844–1900) and his wife. Wolanowski was one of several Polish Jewish tycoons of the nineteenth century. His business was nails, wire, and roofing material, later expanded to include railroad materials and even telegraph and telephone parts. Wolanowski's windfall came when the Russian government commissioned him to supply all of Russia's railroad and telegraph service. In 1894, he purchased 14 Prozna Street, one of the few buildings remaining today from the prewar Jewish quarter (*see page 248*).

Opposite the Wolanowskis, on the other side of the Main Avenue, is an area dense with the graves of Warsaw's Yiddish literati. Most of the inscriptions are in Hebrew characters, so if you cannot read Hebrew it is best to start with the most visually arresting tombstone.

Map: 41 The four stone pillars supporting a dome stand above the grave of Abraham Goldberg (1881–1933). Goldberg was a journalist in three languages: Hebrew, Yiddish, and Russian. He is most famous for his Yiddish work as editor-in-chief of the famous Yiddish newspaper *Haynt*. Goldberg transformed the *Haynt* into an impassioned voice for Jewish national rights in Poland. He was also a correspondent for the New York Yiddish daily *Der Tog*, or "The Day."

Map: 42 One row in front and a couple of graves to the left of Goldberg's is the marble and granite tombstone for the poet Leib Naidus (1890–1918). On its side you'll find his name in Polish. Born in Grodne, Naidus studied in a Bialystok trade school until he was thrown out at the age of fifteen for Bundist activities. By the time he was twenty-one years old, he had devoted himself completely to poetry. Naidus couldn't publish in Warsaw because the Germans, who occupied the city in World War I, restricted publishing. For this reason, Naidus couldn't receive criticism while he was alive. His first collection was published in Vilna in 1915.

Naidus was hailed as an innovative European voice that refined Yiddish poetry from the inside. The Yiddish poet Jacob Glatstein remarked, "He did not imitate world poetry, but rather conquered world poetry for the Yiddish language. He was only productive for eleven years, but in that time . . . he demonstrated that Yiddish could be used as a modern medium for poetry" (quoted in Shmuel Niger and Yakov Shatsky, eds., *Leksikon fun der Nayer Yidisher Literatur*).

Naidus died at the age of 28. His original tombstone, designed by Ostrzega, was destroyed in 1950, and this monument was erected in its place.

Map: 43 Above Naidus is Shlomo Biber (1875–1931). Biber is probably best known for his journalistic account of the Beilus blood libel trial in Russia, based on the stenographer's original records. In 1924 he wrote a book of memoirs entitled *Disappearing Characteristics of Jewish Warsaw*.

Map: 44 Next to Biber on the left is the grave, with the name inscribed in both Hebrew and Polish, of Isaac Meir Weissenberg (1881–1938). One of the best known of Peretz's disciples in Warsaw, Weissenberg was the leader of a new trend of realism and naturalism in Yiddish literature. His most famous work is *A Shtetl* from 1906. Instead of portraying a Jewish village as a romanticized fairyland, Weissenberg depicted it as factionalized, filled with internecine hatreds and all the "isms" he could muster: socialism, Bundism, Zionism, and the like. This was the first time the *shtetl* was portrayed in Yiddish literature in a harsh, even violent, light.

Map: 45 To the left of Weissenberg is the imposing tomb of Hersh David Nomberg (1876–1927). A dedicated disciple of Peretz, Nomberg originally wrote in Hebrew but was ultimately swayed to the Yiddish side. Later he entered politics and was a founder of the *Folkspartey*, or "People's Party," in 1916. His impact on Warsaw Jewish life could best be felt in the Writers' Society, which met on 13 Tlomackie Street (since destroyed) (*see pages 239–240*). Nomberg helped build the society and directed it for several years.

Map: 46 Five or ten meters farther back on the main avenue, in the raised area, is the peculiarly broken tombstone of Felix Perl (1871–1927). In 1892 Perl founded the Polish Socialist Party, and beginning in 1919 he served in the Polish Sejm.

His is one of the relatively few examples of a tombstone broken deliberately and not by vandals. The broken monument, like the broken trees depicted throughout the cemetery, represents the cutting off of life. It is particularly interesting in light of the custom of visitors placing pebbles on tombstones to break the balance of the tombstone and thus symbolize the disharmony the death has caused (*see pages 252–255*).

(The "Detail B" map ends here. The final sites are located in Plot 72 toward the cemetery entrance.) Continue back along the Main Avenue. Toward the entrance to the cemetery, there is a parallel road protruding on the left, where there are additional memorials.

The first one is in memory of the one million children killed in the Holocaust. Three succinct words on the memorial echo, like nowhere else, the forces behind the most thought-out crime in human history: "Nazi German barbarians."

The next memorial is to Janusz Korczak.

The Memorial to Janusz Korczak

Janusz Korczak (1878–1942) was the Polish pseudonym and ultimately the assumed name of Dr. Henryk Goldszmit. Before the war, Korczak was known throughout Europe as a writer, doctor, educator, and campaigner for children's rights. In 1911, he was founder and director of an orphanage that became renowned for its progressive approach to child care. The orphanage was located at Krochmalna Street 92. (It stood in the western end of Krochmalna Street, far from the district explored in the Warsaw Walking Tour on *page 240*. The building of Korczak's orphanage still stands and is still used as a children's home, on a part of Krochmalna preserved and renamed Jaktorowska. The current address is Jaktorowska 8.)

Korczak, a self-proclaimed "son of a madman," was consumed by a passion for the redeeming power of childhood. He had dreams of a pedocratic Children's Republic, with an international Children's Parliament with representatives from all nations, religions, and races. Convinced that the human race would one day evolve into a perfect society, Korczak invested the utmost trust in children as the redeemers of mankind. Childhood innocence, Korczak felt, contained the seeds of pure justice that were lacking in the corrupt world of adulthood. The path to his utopia would be paved by the International Children's Congress, held either in New York or Jerusalem.

Called the "Karl Marx of the Children," Korczak was respected throughout Europe for his views on childhood and education. Korczak's theories were more than just castles in the air. He instituted judicial and penal systems in which the wards in his orphanage were given an unprecedented degree of control over their own lives.

When anti-Semitic decrees were promulgated early in the war, Korczak would not comply. Not only did he refuse to wear a "Jude" armband; he continued to wear the uniform from his service in the army as a doctor. The Germans, enraged, threw Korczak in jail. It was only through the appeals of several prominent Poles that he was released.

As soon as the ghetto was erected, Korczak's vision of an international Children's Republic was crushed. His Jewish orphanage was immediately moved into the ghetto and his wards labelled a subspecies. As the ghetto was reduced in size, the orphanage was again forced to change buildings. Nonetheless, Korczak kept his vision alive in modified form, enacting a children's society in his orphanage even within the terrible confines of the ghetto. The orphanage had to contend with famine, typhus, tuberculosis, and dysentery as well as a shortage of supplies and an increasing pool of new wards. Nonetheless, it maintained a well-organized children's government and produced plays, a newspaper, and even children's courts. Several times during the existence of the ghetto, Korczak had the opportunity to escape. Gentile friends had given Korczak Aryan documents so that he might go into hiding. The Germans themselves repeatedly offered to spare Korczak's life, hoping to land a propaganda coup with the defection of an international celebrity from the plight of his people. Korczak replied with a resounding "No," refusing to abandon his children at any time.

An entry from Korczak's diary less than three weeks before his death reveals the conditions under which the orphanage was forced to operate:

> . . . An injection of caffeine for a hysterical new inmate following a collapse.
>
> His mother, wasting away of ulcerated intestines, was unwilling to die until the child had been placed in the Home. The boy was unwilling to go until the mother had died. He finally yielded. The mother died propitiously, now the child has pangs of conscience. In his illness, he mimics his mother: he moans (screams), complains of pain, then gasps, then feels hot, finally is dying of thirst.
>
> "Water!"
>
> I pace the dormitory to and fro. Will there be an outbreak of mass hysteria? Might be!
>
> But the children's confidence in the leadership prevailed. They believed that as long as the doctor was calm there was no danger.
>
> Janusz Korczak, *Ghetto Diary*

It was this belief that led to one of the most well-known events in the Warsaw ghetto. On the morning of August 5, 1942, German and Ukrainian police surrounded the orphanage and ordered everybody to march at once to the Umschlagplatz, where the trains departed to Treblinka. The children were already prepared, dressed in holiday clothes and carrying small bundles of bread and water. Assembling the children in orderly rows, Korczak led his wards through the streets of the ghetto until they arrived at the Umschlagplatz. At their head, the children waved a green flag emblazoned with a golden four-leaf clover: the flag of the orphanage. The image of 200 children, preternaturally tranquil amid the bedlam of the deportations, instantly became a tragic symbol of the European Jewish disaster. Many survivors were there to witness the procession through the ghetto streets.

Later accounts have it that Korczak told his wards they were going on a journey to open fields, where they would have a picnic. Other memoirs attest to the children singing in the streets on their way to the Umschlagplatz. Whether or not this was the case, there was no doubt that it was the presence of Korczak among his wards that gave the orphans their sense of security. At the Umschlagplatz itself, Korczak was entreated to escape. Once again, he refused. He arranged the orphans into rows of four and, holding the youngest children in his arms, the doctor led the way into the freight cars.

The statue in the cemetery was sculpted by Mieczyslaw Smorczewski in 1982. It depicts Korczak leading some of his 200 wards in the procession to the Umschlagplatz.

It should be mentioned that although Korczak was the most visible orphanage director to die with his wards, he was by no means the only one. Many doctors and leaders of children's homes shared the same fate. In Korczak's orphanage alone, several other staff members accompanied the children to Treblinka. The most famous was Stefania Wilczynska, Korczak's dedicated assistant who managed the orphanage since its establishment in 1911. These are the names of the other staff members of Korczak's orphanage who remained with the children: Henryk Asterblum, Felix Grzyb, Balbina Grzyb, Roza Lipiec-Jakubowska, Sabina Lejserowicz, Natalia Poz, Roza Sztokman, Dora Solnicka, and Henryk Azrylewicz.

After the Cemetery: The Former Skra Stadium

After exiting the cemetery, turn right and then right again at the corner, walking along the cemetery wall until you come to a gate. Fifty meters to the left is the site of the former Skra Stadium. Today there is a neglected memorial on the site erected by the Nissenbaum Foundation, a Polish Jewish philanthropy.

During the war, after the two mass graves inside the cemetery walls became filled, there was not enough space for the massive numbers of dead. For this reason, Skra Stadium was chosen as a site for auxiliary mass graves of the Warsaw ghetto. Mortuaries were built alongside the field, and additional grave diggers were employed.

During the years 1941 and 1942, bodies arrived in increasing numbers at the cemetery gate, usually without any identification. These were buried in the mass graves. In addition, prisoners from the Gesia Street Prison, which was run by the Jewish police and which included mostly smugglers and those who had left the ghetto illegally, were lined up by the mass graves and shot by the Nazis.

When the mass deportations to Treblinka began on July 22, 1942, children, elderly, and sick people were taken not to the Umschlagplatz but to Skra Stadium, where they were shot and buried in mass graves. Abraham Karmi, who secretly lived in the cemetery during the war, recorded these murders in a memoir:

> One day the Germans arrived with two carriages of the "horse-tram" filled with old and sick people. They were transferred to the "Skra" field, being supported by the grave diggers. One "polite" German even picked up a parcel that an old woman had dropped, or a scarf that fell from her hand. Everything was conducted quietly. There was no shouting. This thing continued for a number of days. Every day they used to bring one or two groups there in the evening hours, and shoot them all. The Germans claimed that it was impossible to transfer these people to the "East."
>
> (Abraham M. Karmi, "The Jewish Cemetery in Occupied Warsaw," *Yad Vashem Bulletin 16*)

In his Warsaw ghetto diary, Abraham Lewin wrote about these killings of the sick and the elderly. He added a harrowing detail: "On the fourth day of the expulsion, Saturday 26 July, a car drove to the Jewish cemetery and a middle-aged German woman with two young children got out. She took them inside the cemetery and led them to the place where our old people were being murdered. She wanted to show the children how the Jews were dying. A typical illustration of the character of this evil and brutal people. New Amlekites" (Abraham Lewin, *A Cup of Tears: A Diary of the Warsaw Ghetto*).

When news of these killings reached the ghetto, there was a paradoxical sense of relief among certain Jews who were terrified of the deportations. They reasoned that if the Germans were killing the elderly and sick, who were unable to work, perhaps the massive deportations really were a movement to labor camps and not to imminent death.

After the war, the bodies of 6,588 Jews were exhumed from the area and placed in a Warsaw cemetery for soldiers and civilians who died in the Polish Uprising. During a building project in 1988 many more bones were uncovered, at which point the Nissenbaum Foundation erected the current memorial.

THE MEMORIAL ROUTE OF JEWISH MARTYRDOM AND STRUGGLE

Take Bus 111, 119, or 516 to the Nalewki stop. The series of monuments begins at the corner of Anielewicza and Zamenhofa Streets.

All of the monuments are located outside and are open 24 hours a day.

The focus of most visits to the Jewish quarter of Warsaw is the Warsaw ghetto memorial district located just north of the city center. The memorials are prominent partly because they rise indomitably out of a monotonous postwar landscape. Incongruous in the surrounding housing blocks, they command the viewer never to forget what was perpetrated here. They are also prominent because they have no competition: There are so few living Jewish sites in Warsaw that the tragic monuments have taken a singular hold on the tourist imagination. Warsaw used to be known for its *shtiebels*, or Jewish prayer halls, on

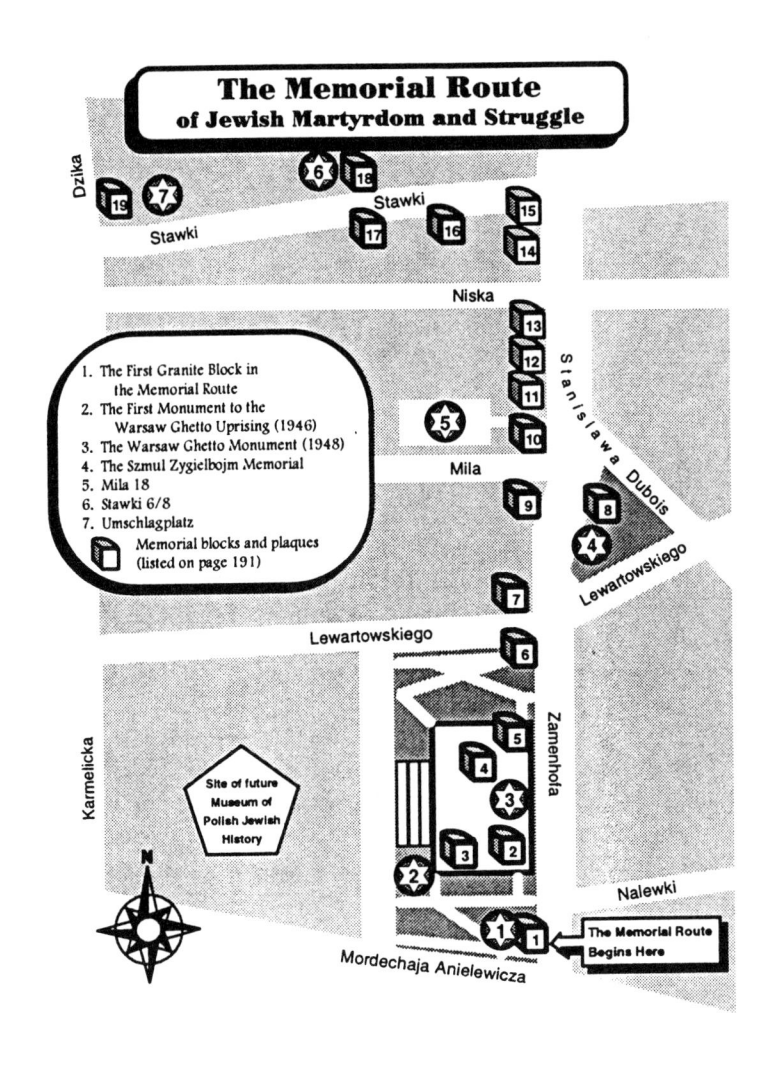

The Memorial Route
of Jewish Martyrdom and Struggle

1. The First Granite Block in the Memorial Route
2. The First Monument to the Warsaw Ghetto Uprising (1946)
3. The Warsaw Ghetto Monument (1948)
4. The Szmul Zygielbojm Memorial
5. Mila 18
6. Stawki 6/8
7. Umschlagplatz

   Memorial blocks and plaques (listed on page 191)

Site of future Museum of Polish Jewish History

The Memorial Route Begins Here

every corner. Now it is known for the plaques and monuments marking, in silent requiem, the mass murder of its Jewish population.

The proliferation of memorials became so widespread in the postwar period that it was easy to become lost amid the monuments. Partly with this in mind, in 1988 a system of memorial stones and plaques was installed to unify the landscape of memory. *The Memorial Route of Jewish Martyrdom and Struggle* was designed by architect Hanna Szmalenberg and sculptor Wladyslaw Klamerus and unveiled on April 19, 1988, marking the 45th anniversary of the Warsaw Ghetto Uprising.

The Memorial Route begins near the Warsaw Ghetto Monument and travels north, culminating in a new memorial installed at the deportation center at Umschlagplatz. Along the way, the Memorial Route encounters seventeen granite blocks, each of them three feet high, which jut out of the sidewalk to memorialize events, places, and individuals from the ghetto's history. An additional two plaques are embedded in the facades of buildings near the Umschlagplatz Memorial. The shape of the written surface is said to correspond to Jewish tombstones. When it was unveiled, the Memorial Route broke Warsaw's tradition of anonymous monuments and actually personalized the history of the ghetto. There are granite blocks for poets, rabbis, Zionists, historians, and Bundists.

The Memorial Route does more than give individual identities to various ghetto inhabitants: It also unifies several blocks of the former ghetto into a single, sprawling passage of memory. In the rather dull cityscape, the granite blocks stand upright and demand that one remember what happened here. Lining the streets, they serve as checkpoints marking a trail through the horrors of the ghetto. It is not chronological—the Uprising occurs earlier in the path than the deportations—but it is not meant to be a one-way route. The first and last granite blocks bear identical inscriptions concerning the formation of the ghetto. The repeated blocks make the route less a line than a cycle of grief, caving in on itself like the very ghetto it seeks to memorialize.

Finally, the route reminds the viewer that everything in the Warsaw ghetto was inextricably connected. This mirrors the cohesiveness of the Nazi strategy. All the diverse aspects of life in the ghetto—from incarceration to starvation to deportation—were part of a meticulous, centralized, and unified plan of genocide.

Guide to the Monuments

What follows is a walking tour that explains the main monuments (including the Warsaw Ghetto Monument and Umschlagplatz) within the context of the Memorial Route. The walk heads in a general south-to-north direction, until it turns west toward Umschlagplatz at the end.

The first granite block sits on the corner of Anielewicza Street and Zamenhofa Street.

Over the course of the walk from here to the Umschlagplatz Monument, you will encounter nineteen blocks and plaques devoted to various people and events. Because the inscriptions are in Polish and Hebrew, what follows is an English summary:

1. *The Creation of the Ghetto in 1940, the Murder of 450,000 Jews from 1940 to 1943.*
2. *The Warsaw Ghetto Uprising:* 19 April–15 May, 1943.
3. *The Tree of Remembrance.*
4. *The Warsaw Ghetto Uprising* (same as #2).
5. *Emmanuel Ringelblum* (1900–1944): Historian, leader of the Oneg Shabbat team documenting ghetto life.
6. *Jozef Lewartowski* (1895–1942): Polish Workers' Party.
7. *Michal Klepfisz* (1913–1943): Bundist, fighter in the Uprising.
8. *Szmul Zygielbojm* (1895–1943): Jewish leader in the Polish Government-in-Exile in London.
9. *Arie Wilner* ("Jurek") (1917–1943): Hashomer Hatza'ir, active in the Ghetto Uprising as liaison to the Polish underground.
10. *Mordechai Anielewicz* (1917–1943): Leader of the Ghetto Uprising.
11. *Meir Majerowicz* ("Marek"): Group commander in the Ghetto Uprising.
12. *Pawel Frenkiel* (1919–1943) and *Dawid Apfelbaum* (1914–1943): Commanders of the Jewish Military Union active in the Ghetto Uprising.
13. *Frumka Plotnitzka* (1914–1943): Organizer of armed struggles in ghettos throughout Poland.
14. *Itzchak Nyssenbaum* (1868–1942): Rabbi, leader of the Mizrachi party, and member of the ghetto underground.
15. *Janusz Korczak* (1878–1942): Writer and orphanage director who accompanied his wards to the gas chambers of Treblinka.
16. *Itzchak Katzenelson* (1886–1944): Poet.
17. *SS Command at 5/7 Stawki Street.*
18. *Jewish Hospital, Umschlagplatz Holding Center at 6/8 Stawki Street.*
19. *The Creation of the Ghetto in 1940, the Murder of 450,000 Jews from 1940 to 1943.*

The First Monument to the Warsaw Ghetto Uprising

From the first granite block, walk down Anielewicza and bear right with the path, until you come to the circular, red sandstone monument. It was constructed in 1946 on the third anniversary of the Ghetto Uprising. The memorial is the first monument commemorating the Warsaw ghetto. Indeed, it was the first World War II monument unveiled in all of Warsaw. The memorial is often overlooked, situated as it is in the shadow of the Nathan Rapoport monument *(see pages 218–221).*

The red disc commemorates the fighting that began early in the morning of April 19, 1943. It is pointed toward the gate (since destroyed) where German tanks tried to enter the ghetto.

In front is the Hebrew letter *bet*, which begins the Torah as the first letter of the word *bereshit*, "The Beginning." Unveiled in 1946, the monument pointed to the beginning of a new life for the survivors of the Holocaust. But it also contains a note of disharmony. *Bet* is the second letter of the Hebrew alphabet. The first letter, *alef*, is missing here, indicating the absence of nearly half a million Warsaw Jews and their descendants. Situated asymmetrically and at the end of the disc, the letter points to a gaping wound in postwar Warsaw.

To the right and behind this monument is the famous Warsaw Ghetto Monument, designed by Nathan Rapoport and constructed two years later, in 1948.

THE WARSAW GHETTO MONUMENT

The monument is located at the end of the large square bordered by Anielewicza, Zamenhofa, and Lewartowskiego streets.

The Warsaw Ghetto Monument, designed by Nathan Rapoport and unveiled on the fifth anniversary of the Warsaw Ghetto Uprising, is to many Jews around the world a symbol of Jewish existence in Warsaw. The image of seven fighters literally emerging from granite blocks in a pose of confrontation has become a modern Jewish archetype. In the art world, the monument is often dismissed as a prop of Soviet-style social realist representation. Perhaps this is true, but it is preferable to the original Polish design for the monument: two hasidic Jews hoeing potatoes! Monuments should be perceived in the context of their times. Social realist art though it is, this has not prevented the monument from being a focal point of both foreign visitors and Poles seeking to encounter and interpret their country's Jewish past. Official visits in the past by the pope, the West German chancellor, and even by the PLO chairman have sparked international discussion and debate. In 1983, for the fortieth anniversary of the Ghetto Uprising, the communist regime organized memorial ceremonies at the monument. These were boycotted by the Solidarity trade union, which staged its own demonstration at the site one day before the official ceremonies. It was broken up by police. The Warsaw Ghetto Monument had become a stirring symbol not only for the Jews but for the Polish struggle for freedom.

Nathan Rapoport, born in 1911 in Warsaw, had already distinguished himself as a promising young sculptor before the war. He won various competitions, including a "Sports in Art" contest sponsored by the Warsaw Academy of Art in 1936. His winning entry, *The Tennis Player*, was to be sent to an international exhibition sponsored by the Berlin Summer Olympics. But Rapoport, disgusted by the thought of exhibiting in Nazi Germany, forfeited his prize money and refused to submit his piece.

After Germany invaded Poland, Rapoport fled with many other Jews to Russian-controlled Bialystok, and later to Minsk. After spending time in a labor camp in Novosibirsk, Siberia, he was installed by the Russians in a studio in that city. There he resumed sculpting, but along the rather grotesque aesthetic lines dictated by the Russian Communist Party. All his work was commissioned by the state, and thus Rapoport sculpted busts of Russian war heroes and superlative laborers that one can still find throughout the former Soviet Union today. Rapoport absorbed the aesthetic sensibility of worker-heroism, and this became the guiding force in his construction of the Ghetto Monument.

When news poured in of the extermination of the Jews of Poland and Russia, Rapoport was determined to channel his grief into a memorial cut in stone. In the late spring of 1943, when he heard of the armed uprising of Warsaw's Jews, he was so moved by the heroism that he immediately began designing a monument. He submitted a model to the Stalinist authorities as early as mid 1943, but it was dismissed on the grounds that it focused too heavily on the Jewish dimension of suffering. This, too, should be kept in mind when viewing the decidedly neutral, non-Jewish figures on the front of the monument. Rapoport knew what the government would accept and refuse. Back in Warsaw after the war, a modified design was approved by the Warsaw Jewish Committee and, after some hesitation, by the Warsaw Arts Committee. One year later, the monument was unveiled. It was April 19, 1948: five years after the start of the uprising and 25 days before the establishment of the State of Israel.

The monument is replete with symbolism, not all of which is evident at first sight. First, the destroyed ruins of the ghetto provide the base of the monument. Unable to clear away the massive congestion of burned-out ruins and debris in time for the opening of the memorial, the designers poured tons of concrete onto the ruins and turned the site into the monument's base. Keeping the monument in a historical continuum, sand from Israel was added to the base. As for the large granite blocks supporting the sculpture, they were found in a Swedish quarry in 1947. The blocks had been requisitioned by Arno Breker, the German sculptor, for a Berlin monument to celebrate Hitler's victory. Thus the rocks themselves symbolize the turnabout in the war, and hence a victorious "uprising" against Hitler's plans to cleanse the world of Jews. As it stands, the granite wall represents both a giant tombstone for the martyrs of the Holocaust, and, in Rapoport's own words, "a support and symbol of the vanished ghetto."

Another aspect to the wall is its allusion to the Western Wall in Jerusalem. This latter image is perhaps the most pertinent, as the Western Wall is the last remaining piece of an earlier massacre of the Jewish people, perpetrated by the Romans in the year 70 C.E. Original designs for the monument show that the stones were intended to be rougher in appearance, recalling the stones of the Western Wall. By linking the destruction of the Warsaw ghetto with the destruction of the Second Jewish Temple, the monument places the modern Jewish catastrophe into a broader context of Jewish history and suffering. In fact, such a linkage transforms the monument, which at first glance seems to lack any specifically Jewish symbolism, into a modern religious icon. The addition of the menorahs flanking its base helps make the monument into a sort of secular Temple. According to James Young, author of *The Texture of Memory: Holocaust Memorials and Meaning*, the rabbi who dedicated the monument on April 19, 1948, insisted that the human forms be kept veiled when he recited the mourner's *kaddish* before the twelve thousand spectators. Evidently the rabbi was afraid the monument, sitting behind a temporary *aron hakodesh* brought for the ceremony, would become a massive idol for the assembled people. "In his sensitivity to the spectacle of so many Jews praying before such an icon," Young writes, "the rabbi appears to have been prescient: for over the years, it has been the monument and its square (not the synagogue) that serves as a gathering place for both religious Jewish visitors from abroad and the largely unaffiliated young Jews in Warsaw. Ironically, it is as if the monument had retained the sense of sacred space created by the temporary Holy Ark and altar."

The second reference to the destruction of the Temple in Jerusalem is also one of the only distinctly Jewish motifs on the monument. Behind the monument is the bas relief image of twelve Jews, representing the twelve tribes of Israel, being marched off to their deaths by the Nazis. Unlike the image of warriors on the front, the dorsal image attempts to describe the horror and despair of the Holocaust. In both style and content, the bas relief recalls the Arch of Titus in Rome, which celebrates the destruction of the Temple. This again places the Holocaust in historical context, particularly with regard to the initial exile from Israel that resulted in the Diaspora. Here, there are specifically Jewish themes: Unlike the bearded man on the front of the monument, who is lifting a rock in self-defense, this bearded man is carrying the Torah and beseeching God for deliverance. It is a tragic image that extends its reach throughout the history of the Jews in exile. The Germans were not the first people to try to annihilate the Jews. The message is that despite repeated tragedies that have befallen the Jews, they have survived and will survive. Such a view was even voiced in the Warsaw ghetto itself, where in March 1942, four months before the mass deportations began, an underground Jewish newspaper printed: "From generation to generation, we are troubled by the burden of passivity and lack of faith in our own strength; but our history also contains glorious and shining pages of heroism and struggle. We are obliged to join these eras of heroism . . ." (quoted in Yisrael Gutman, *The Jews of Warsaw 1939–1943*).

Rapoport's monument is unique in that it immortalizes resistance without ignoring the larger dimension of the all-consuming genocide. Thus the large stone wall gains perhaps its most moving interpretation: a place for the fusion of both heroes and victims into one complete whole.

There is also another view. Look more closely at the back of the monument. As a bas relief, it is cut into Hitler's victory stones themselves. Rapoport even continued the line axes of the stones over the bas relief itself, so that the condemned Jews are embedded into Hitler's stones as well as into the symbolic tombstone and the Western Wall. Indeed, the twelve figures are engulfed almost entirely by the wall, vanishing into the monument. This is in stark contrast to the heroes, who are cast in bronze and thus separate themselves from Hitler's victory stones. In this light, the stone wall does not join but actually distinguishes heroism and victimhood. Delegated as they are to the back of the monument, where few people actually walk, the condemned figures and their placement reveal the awkwardness—particularly in 1948, on the eve of another potentially catastrophic struggle for the Jewish people—of dealing with genocide so soon after it was perpetrated.

In this respect, the dichotomy between hero and victim—as if the victims weren't heroes, and vice versa—is the most disturbing aspect about the monument. The dangerous implication is that, unlike the Jews of the Uprising, those who went "passively" to their deaths were a source of shame and embarrassment to the people. It is this peculiar manipulation of fighter versus victim that firmly places the monument into the context of its times. Neither the communist authorities nor the founders of modern Israel wanted to memorialize, first and foremost, genocide. It is interesting that at the unveiling ceremony, two types of banners were waved in the crowd: the red banners of the communist youth, and the prenatal flags of the State of Israel. Nathan Rapoport himself was a member of Hashomer

Hatza'ir. In his memoir of the monument, Rapoport wrote, "We were for life. We hold the tree of life. My purpose was to give back, at least spiritually, what had been taken away by deadly destruction" (Nathan Rapoport, "Memoir of the Warsaw Ghetto Monument," in James E. Young, ed., *The Art of Memory: Holocaust Memorials in History*). Thus, when he sought live models for his monument, Rapoport chose Jewish settlers from Palestine, who were living in Paris at the time. It is these vibrant forms leaping out of the monument, and not the ghetto dwellers on the back, who point the way toward a Jewish future of self-determination.

Indeed, the Warsaw Ghetto Monument was unveiled quite literally on the threshold of a new era for the Jews. This makes it interesting to consider in the context of modern Israeli society. The day established by Israel to commemorate the Holocaust is entitled *Yom Hashoah Vehagvurah*, "Day of Remembrance of Holocaust and Heroism." This day was fixed as close as possible to the day of the Warsaw Ghetto Uprising, in spite of complaints from Orthodox circles that the day would distract from redemptive contemplation during the month of Nisan. Likewise, *Yad Vashem* is called "Martyrs' and Heroes' Remembrance Authority." This reflects the already-mentioned discomfort in early Israeli society regarding the slaughter of Europe's Jews. But in another sense, the name distinguishes heroism from victimhood as much as does the Warsaw Ghetto Monument. According to this logic, the martyrs and heroes were two distinct groups. Unfortunately, this can lead to a bifurcated emotional response to the Holocaust: Pride for the armed warriors, shame for the murdered victims.

Needless to say, such a view comes perilously close to insulting the six million martyrs of the Holocaust. However, the celebration of resistance—or, at least, armed resistance—has quickly been translated into modern myth. Thus the fighters are associated with Jewish vigilance in Israel, and the victims are associated with the hopelessness of Diaspora Jewry. In this vein, the bas relief victims are looking downward, seemingly to the past, whereas the bronze heroes are looking upward to the future. The Jews of the bas relief come straight out of the European ghettoes; they are resigned to their fates in Exile. The frontal figures, on the other hand, have decided to seize their own destiny. The front and back of the monument resemble nothing less than the distorted view of Israeli and Diaspora Jewry. The most overwhelming tragedy in all of Jewish history has sadly become a tool used to define the modern Jew.

ELSEWHERE ON THE MONUMENT SQUARE

In front and to the right of the Warsaw Ghetto Monument is the third granite block of the Memorial Route of Jewish Martyrdom and Struggle. It refers to the large oak tree planted there when the Memorial Route was unveiled on April 19, 1988. The oak commemorates both the Polish Jews murdered in the Holocaust and the Poles who died while trying to save Jewish lives.

In front of this is a small monument commemorating Zegota, the Council for Aid to the Jews operated by the Polish Government-in-Exile in London. The underground organization emerged in late 1942. It was composed of Polish democratic and socialist activists as well as Jewish functionaries. Zegota was responsible for providing Jews with food, shelter, false identity papers, and money once they had gone into hiding in "Aryan" parts of Poland. Priority was given to children, Jewish activists, and famous Jews. In Warsaw, Zegota provided some form of assistance to about four thousand Jews, or roughly twenty percent of those in hiding in "Aryan" parts of the city. Zegota publicized the plight of the Jews and urged Poles to assist Jews in hiding. It even established a secret medical service in "Aryan" Warsaw that assisted Jews who otherwise would have been killed had they made their illnesses public. Secret mailboxes were set up into which lists of ailing Jews were deposited; Zegota channelled these lists to the head doctor, who dispensed treatment accordingly. Zegota also established the infrastructure for Jews to transmit information and appeals, from the beginning of 1943, to Jewish leaders around the world.

Zegota was an anomaly in Nazi-occupied Europe. Poland was the only state among the occupied countries that established an organization whose specific purpose was to rescue Jews. This is a shining credit to the Polish state, and it should never be forgotten.

The Jewish Historical Institute has plans to build a museum and educational center on the square opposite the Nathan Rapoport monument. The museum would be an unprecedented addition to the itinerary of most visitors: It would concentrate on the centuries of Jewish life in Poland *before* the Holocaust. The proposed site of the museum was the location of one of the headquarters of the Judenrat during the war. It was destroyed and buried under rubble during the Warsaw Ghetto Uprising. The Jewish Historical Institute hopes it will find documents from the Judenrat's basement or bunker during excavations. For this reason, archaeologists are examining the site before the construction workers begin. The Institute hopes the museum will be built by the year 2000.

From the Warsaw Ghetto Monument, turn left up Zamenhofa Street. You will pass by more granite blocks of the Memorial Route along the way.

After the first intersection on the right, there is a square named after Szmul Zygielbojm (pronounced "Shmul Zygelboym"). A building has recently been added to the square, but it stands on stilts above the ground. At this writing, there were plans to install a memorial or plaque in the area of the building stilts, to be completed in the late 1990s.

The Szmul Zygielbojm Memorial

Perhaps because he was not living in Warsaw at the time, it is often forgotten that Szmul Zygielbojm (1895–1943) was another hero and martyr of the Warsaw Ghetto Uprising.

Zygielbojm was a prominent leader of the Bund in Warsaw before the war. When the Germans occupied Warsaw and ordered the establishment of the Judenrat, Zygielbojm became its most radical member.

An incident that illuminates Zygielbojm's passion for his people occurred during the early existence of the Judenrat. On November 4, 1939, the Gestapo made its first attempt to construct a Jewish ghetto in Warsaw by convening an emergency meeting of the Judenrat. As soon as the meeting began, the Gestapo seized the twenty-four alternate members as hostages and issued a decree that within three days, all the Jews in

Warsaw were to be assembled in a ghetto. If anything went wrong, they would kill the alternates one by one.

Panic swept the Judenrat. The German decree was not only barbaric, but physically impossible. How could they transfer so many people in just three days? Early the next morning the Judenrat met to decide a course of action. Zygielbojm stood up and passionately demanded that they fight the decree. He felt that it was the only moral response to the Germans. By refusing to obey the order, the Judenrat would maintain its ethical purity and gain the trust of all the Jews of Warsaw.

But most members of the Judenrat disagreed. Quelled by fear, they felt if they didn't obey the decree, the Germans would brutally enforce it themselves. Zygielbojm did not see compliance with the Germans as an option, and handed in his resignation. Eventually the Judenrat appealed directly to the military commander of Warsaw, and the establishment of the ghetto was put off for about a year.

The incident expressed both the untenable dilemmas that plagued the Judenrat and Zygielbojm's own uncompromising vigilance in the face of German barbarism. Zygielbojm sought a course of action entirely foreign to almost all the Judenrate in occupied Europe: total noncompliance with German decrees. This type of civil disobedience—neither passively acquiescent, nor militantly recalcitrant—was a novel approach to the unforeseen terror the Jews faced. Whether such methods would have worked against the Nazi murder machine is doubtful, but Zygielbojm's stance showed a brave defiance that earned him the respect of his peers.

It also earned him the wrath of the Nazis, who immediately began to hunt him down. In early 1940, Zygielbojm fled Poland. He travelled through various countries, including America, before settling in London in 1942. In London he became one of the two Jewish representatives in the Polish Government-in-Exile. He continued his impassioned appeal for the Jewish people, this time by campaigning for the Allied governments to end the Nazi genocide. He worked tirelessly to elicit a moral reaction from the world, shuttling from office to office with specific news of extermination camps he had obtained from underground reports. The Allied governments did not budge. Zygielbojm was forced into an impotent rage as his office filled with reports of German mass murder while the world refused to listen. Messages from the Warsaw Jewish underground were increasingly desperate and personal, singling Zygielbojm out as the man responsible for the fate of the Jews.

On February 7, 1943, the underground Bund leaders sent Zygielbojm a coded radio message detailing the German Aktion in January and the liquidation of ghettos throughout Poland. It said that in mid-February—about a week's time—the Germans were to decimate the remnant of the Warsaw ghetto. Appealing to Zygielbojm tc do anything and everything to stop the massacres—it even suggested he solicit the assistance of the pope—the message ended with a frantic, personal appeal: "We suffer terribly. The surviving two hundred thousand await annihilation. Only you can save us. The responsibility with regard to history will rest on you" (quoted in Lucy S. Davidowicz, *The War against the Jews 1933–1945*).

Neither the pope nor the western governments were moved enough to act. In April and May 1943, news reached Zygielbojm of the Warsaw Ghetto Uprising and the total liquidation of the ghetto. Ravaged by grief for the destruction of his people and his own inability to stop it,

Zygielbojm decided to commit a final act of protest. On May 12, 1943, at the age of forty-eight, Zygielbojm committed suicide. It was a final example of Zygielbojm's purity of heart carried into the realm of civil disobedience: He relinquished his comfortable diplomatic life in London in order to join the common grave of his Warsaw Jewish brethren. In a letter addressed to the Polish Government-in-Exile and forwarded to the British and American governments, Zygielbojm gave the reasons for his suicide:

> News recently received from Poland informs us that the Germans are exterminating with unheard-of savagery the remaining Jews in that country. Behind the walls of the ghetto is taking place today the last act of a tragedy which has no parallel in the history of the human race. The responsibility for this crime—the assassination of the Jewish population in Poland—rests above all on the murderers themselves, but falls indirectly upon the whole human race, on the Allies and their governments, who so far have taken no firm steps to put a stop to these crimes. By their indifference to the killing of millions of hapless men, to the massacre of women and children, these countries have become accomplices of the assassins.
>
> Furthermore, I must state that the Polish Government, although it has done a great deal to influence world public opinion, has not taken adequate measures to counter this atrocity which is taking place today in Poland.
>
> . . . I cannot remain silent. I cannot live while the rest of the Jewish people in Poland, whom I represent, continue to be liquidated.
>
> My companions of the Warsaw Ghetto fell in a last heroic battle with their weapons in their hands. I did not have the honor to die with them but I belong to them and to their common grave.
>
> Let my death be an energetic cry of protest against the indifference of the world which witnesses the extermination of the Jewish people without taking any steps to prevent it. In our day and age human life is of little value; having failed to achieve success in my life, I hope that my death may jolt the indifference of those who, perhaps even in this extreme moment, could save the Jews who are still alive in Poland . . . (excerpted in Jacob Glatstein, ed., *Anthology of Holocaust Literature*)

A passage from the letter will be incorporated into the memorial tablet: "I cannot remain silent. I cannot live while the rest of the Jewish people in Poland . . . continue to be liquidated."

Zygielbojm's death was a final act of protest, but it was also more than that. The Jewish experience was bound up in a single, intertwined collective in which individuality mattered less than the unity of the people. If this was true before the Holocaust, how much the more so, then, when the Jews were grouped into a single subspecies by German decree? When the Jewish collective was being murdered and destroyed, Zygielbojm had no option but to join his people. As he himself put it, "I did not have the honor to die with them but I belong to them and to their common grave."

Continue on Zamenhofa Street. After the next intersection you'll find the site of what was once Mila 18 on the left side.

Mila 18

In the first few months of 1943, before the Ghetto Uprising in April, Warsaw's Jews devoted much of their energies to the creation of elaborate, well-stocked bunkers. These were sophisticated, camouflaged burrows beneath the ground, containing everything from water pumps to electricity to alarm systems. When the Germans entered the ghetto for the intended final Aktion, tens of thousands of people were already holed up beneath the earth. As Yisrael Gutman writes, "It is no exaggeration to state that the network of cells and tunnels resembled a subterranean Jewish city" (Yisrael Gutman, *The Jews of Warsaw 1939–1943*). It was the existence of these bunkers that turned the Uprising from a three-day struggle into almost a month of rebellion. The Germans could not liquidate a ghetto that had moved beneath their feet.

The bunkers hid not only civilian Jews, but also the armed fighters. In order to get to these underground passages, the Germans began to set entire blocks of the ghetto on fire. They entered the ghetto with dogs, listening devices, and canisters of poison gas. Many ghetto inhabitants preferred to die in the bunkers rather than surrender to the Germans.

The bunker the Germans wanted the most was located at Mila Street 18. This was the location of the command headquarters of the Jewish Fighting Organization (*ZOB*). The bunker had not been built by the *ZOB* itself but by prominent smugglers securing their own survival. The *ZOB* used this sophisticated bunker to devise strategy, parlay information, stockpile equipment, and supply refuge.

On May 7, 1943, the Germans discovered the bunker at Mila 18. The next day, they surrounded the bunker and blocked up each of its five exits. Then they burst open the entrance and filled the interior with poison gas. At this point the command of the *ZOB*, including the leader Mordecai Anielewicz, decided to commit suicide rather than die at the hands of the Germans. Approximately one hundred fighters, including much of the *ZOB* and underground leadership, were entrenched in the bunker. Many died either through the poison gas or by suicide. Others, probably civilians, were apprehended by the Germans. Some managed to escape through a new exit, but each of the survivors was killed later in the war. The destruction of the bunker at Mila 18 marked the end of the central command of Jewish resistance.

The memorial is situated on a mound the same height as the rubble of the ghetto when it was destroyed.

Continue to the end of Zamenhofa and make a left on Stawki Street.

The first building on the left, at Stawki 5/7, was used by the German SS in 1942–43 as the command center from which it supervised the deportations to Treblinka from the nearby Umschlagplatz. A granite stone embedded in the building explains its wartime history. It is also part of the Memorial Route of Jewish Martyrdom and Struggle.

On the opposite side of the street is a long building at Stawki 6/8 that served as an archives building before the war and is used today as a primary school. Toward the right end of the building are two memorial plaques.

One plaque remembers August 1, 1944, when Polish resistance fighters freed fifty Jews from this site. The Nazis had shipped thousands of Jews here from Auschwitz in order to clear the rubble from the ghetto uprising. In another part of the former ghetto, 350 Jews were rescued.

The second plaque speaks about the use of this building during the war as a detention center for Jews awaiting transport to Treblinka. But before the mass deportations, the building was used as a Jewish hospital in the ghetto. What happened within its walls was so horrifying that it warrants some elaboration.

Stawki 6/8

In 1939 the Warsaw Jewish Hospital, known as Czyste Hospital, was the largest hospital in all Poland. Built in the nineteenth century to provide a workspace for Jewish doctors forbidden access to Polish hospitals, it formed a complex of buildings in the vicinity of Dobra Street, near the Vistula River.

Soon after the Nazis ordered the formation of a ghetto, Czyste Hospital was forced to enter the newly defined district as well. There is perhaps no other image so expressive of German inhumanity in Warsaw than hundreds of terminally ill and handicapped Jewish patients hobbling and wheeling toward the ghetto gates. No operating tables, beds, or machinery were permitted to be transferred. Beds were constructed inside the ghetto out of scrap metal pipes.

The ghetto, of course, had no room for a modern hospital compound. Instead, Czyste moved into various unrelated buildings randomly dotting the landscape. This building at Stawki 6/8 became the main nonsurgical division of the hospital. The departments of infectious disease and internal medicine were housed here. The basement was turned into the pathology lab, where doctors performed autopsies in a desperate attempt to curb epidemics. Eventually, Stawki 6/8 became filled to overflowing with people suffering from typhus, typhoid fever, acute tuberculosis, diphtheria, and other diseases. Although the Stawki branch had the best-equipped pharmacy in the ghetto, the strangulating lack of supplies caused many patients to starve to death. Commenting on this, the Judenrat's chief of medical affairs, Dr. Izrael Milejkowski, referred to the ghettoized hospitals as "places of execution" (quoted in Charles G. Roland, *Courage under Siege: Starvation, Disease, and Death in the Warsaw Ghetto*). Two or three patients were put in each bed. In terms of hygiene, there was little difference between the building and the rest of the ghetto. Lice, the messengers of typhus, were everywhere.

On July 22, at the start of the Aktion, the Nazis ordered the evacuation of the hospital at Stawki 6/8. The building was to become an overnight waiting point for Jews being deported to Treblinka. Adam Czerniakow, the chairman of the Judenrat, protested this inhumane decision—but, of course, evacuating the hospital was only one small step in the meticulous strategy of genocide. When he realized this a day later, Czerniakow took his own life. Meanwhile, the Germans had taken the hospital manager as a hostage until evacuation was complete. The hospital was forced to discharge as many as 750 patients; the rest were transferred to other Czyste branches in the ghetto.

Overnight, the building at Stawki 6/8 became a teeming house of bedlam. Every Jew who was condemned to death at Treblinka but had not found a spot on the day's trains was forced to wait the night in Stawki 6/8. Sometimes the number of detainees reached the thousands. Toilets and tap water were unusable. Rooms became sewers as the floor was the only available space to relieve oneself. Survivor Frank Stiffel recalled the transformation of the hospital into a deportation way-station:

> We were now approaching the Umschlagplatz. I was thinking how different the same place can be if it is seen on different occasions. It didn't even resemble the Stawki Hospital in which I had worked for three months and which I had known so well. Now it was a set of gloomy buildings surrounded by barbed wire and inhabited by a huge crowd of Jews who had been brought there before us. . . . People were everywhere: sitting people, standing people, lying people. The corridors, the wards, the stairways, all smelled of people and their excrements. People were sitting in their own feces, jealously clutching their bundles and their bread.
>
> (Frank Stiffel, *The Tale of the Ring: A Kaddish*)

Very rarely, one was able to bribe an official and escape; much more often, people were trapped the entire night in Stawki 6/8 before being loaded onto cattle cars in the morning.

Stories abound of the sadistic Jewish policemen and Ukrainian guards who tortured the detainees. Marek Edelman, one of the few people who survived the ghetto uprising, described a gym on the fourth floor of Stawki 6/8 into which several hundred people were crammed:

> There was a niche in this gym. And in this niche one day several Ukrainian guards—six, maybe eight—were raping a young girl. They waited in line and then raped her. After the line was finished, this girl left the niche and she walked across the whole gym, stumbling against the reclining people. She was very pale, naked, and bleeding, and she slouched down into a corner. The crowd saw everything, and nobody said a word. Nobody so much as moved, and the silence continued.
>
> (Hanna Krall, *Shielding the Flame: An Intimate Conversation with Dr. Marek Edelman, the Last Surviving Leader of the Warsaw Ghetto Uprising*)

In early September 1942, just as the most brutal phase of deportations was about to begin, the Nazis ordered all Czyste hospitals emptied within 24 hours. The patients were to assemble at Stawki 6/8, which had been designated a hospital again. Trucks pulled up with the sickest patients and dumped them in the mud outside the building. Even those with open wounds were forced to lie in the mud until the medical staff, who had been forbidden from accompanying their patients, arrived to assist them. Of course, after its use as a holding ground for thousands of detainees, the building was in no condition to serve as a hospital. But this, too, was a moot point. Soon enough, almost all the patients and medical staff were themselves deported to Treblinka. The Nazis ordered the doctors to decide which ten percent of their patients would be spared deportation.

On September 8th, the hospital was liquidated. Marek Edelman spoke of a doctor who performed an act of mercy by administering her precious supply of cyanide to sick children. The picture reflects the contorted moral universe of the ghetto:

> On the upper floor there were a few rooms with children. As the Germans were entering the ground floor, a woman doctor managed to poison the kids.
>
> . . . She saved these children from the gas chamber. People thought she was a hero.
>
> In this hospital, sick people were lying on the floor waiting to be loaded onto the train cars, and the nurses were searching out their parents in the crowd and injecting them with poison. They saved this poison for their closest relatives. And she, this doctor, had given *her own* cyanide to kids who were complete strangers!
>
> (Hanna Krall, *Shielding the Flame: An Intimate Conversation with Dr. Marek Edelman, the Last Surviving Leader of the Warsaw Ghetto Uprising*)

After September, the hospital ceased to function at this site.

Farther down Stawki Street is the final site in the Memorial Route of Jewish Martyrdom and Struggle. The Umschlagplatz Monument is located on the right side of the street.

UMSCHLAGPLATZ

On this site, between July 22 and September 12, 1942, 265,000 Warsaw Jews were herded onto freight cars and led to immediate death in the gas chambers of Treblinka. Referred to as a "Hell on Earth," the Umschlagplatz was a scene of terror and chaos as thousands of Jews awaited deportation among SS forces; sadistic Ukrainian, Lithuanian, and Latvian guards; and Jewish Police—called "Jews outfitted in boots and caps"—who were there to ensure a swift transit. Although initially the Jews had no idea where they were being sent or what awaited them—most considered it yet another Nazi resettlement program—the Umschlagplatz became a symbol of the end of life in the Warsaw ghetto.

The terror on the streets as Jews were forced to the Umschlagplatz is difficult to imagine on the streets of today's Warsaw. Emmanuel Ringelblum, the great historian of the Warsaw ghetto, recorded the increasing brutality and murder as the Aktion reached its final stage: "The tens of thousands who remained on Niska Street—the continual slaughtering—seventy people killed in one apartment on Wolynska Street—in two days, one thousand people killed, taken to the graveyard—hundreds killed in the street during the selections, all forced to kneel on the pavement [to be killed]" (Jacob Sloan, ed., *Notes from the Warsaw Ghetto: The Journal of Emmanuel Ringelblum*). In Charles G. Roland's *Courage under Siege*, a superb account of the medical and social conditions of the ghetto, there is a diary excerpt of a survivor who barely escaped an Aktion:

> How did it look, the catching of people on the street? I had an occasion to "satisfy" my curiosity about it walking one day on Leszno Street. . . . All of a sudden, a truck approached with Germans, Ukrainians, and SP [Jewish police]. They blocked the exits on Karmelicka, Solna, and Zelazna Streets in order to direct the traffic toward Karmelicka Street. They did it at a very fast pace. In front of each house there was a Ukrainian standing with a gun ready to shoot.
>
> (quoted in Charles G. Roland, *Courage under Siege: Starvation, Disease, and Death in the Warsaw Ghetto*)

In the second Aktion of January 1943, an additional five thousand Jews were loaded onto freight cars to Treblinka.

The Umschlagplatz Square

The point of departure was the Umschlagplatz. Prior to the mass deportations, the Umschlagplatz was a railroad freight zone on the northern border of the ghetto, used by the "Transfer Authority" to control food and materials entering the ghetto and factory products exiting it. Located on the train lines, it was used in a similar vein before the war for goods entering and exiting Warsaw. "Umschlagplatz" itself simply means "place for transfer." On July 22, 1942, it became exclusively the transfer site of human cargo exiting the ghetto.

There were two areas in the Umschlagplatz. The first was a square adjacent to the former hospital on Stawki 6/8. Deportees who spent the night in Stawki 6/8 were ushered, from a back door, to the first Umschlagplatz square. When the square was filled with Jews, the deportees were herded through a team of SS guards, who would pick out a few hundred young men for forced labor camps. The rest would enter the second square, where the train cars were stationed. Midway into the Aktion, the Germans abandoned the forced labor camp *selektion* and sent all the gathered throngs to Treblinka. It is disturbing to note that one of the supervisors at Umschlagplatz was a ruthless Jew named Schmerling—"the hangman with the whip," according to Emmanuel Ringelblum. He would rip the badges off Jewish policemen found smuggling people out of the Umschlagplatz.

One week into the Aktion, on July 29, huge lines of *volunteers* began crowding the corner of Stawki and Dzika, next to the Umschlagplatz. The Germans had instituted the policy of distributing three kilograms of bread and one kilogram of jam to each volunteer deportee. It seems incomprehensible that people would volunteer, but we should recall that at the time, the Jews were literally starving to death. Marek Edelman, a survivor of the Warsaw Ghetto Uprising, remembered the scene:

> Do you have any idea what bread meant at that time in the Ghetto? Because if you don't, you will never understand how thousands of people could voluntarily come for the bread and go on with this bread to the camp at Treblinka. Nobody has understood it thus far.
> (Hanna Krall, *Shielding the Flame: An Intimate Conversation with Dr. Marek Edelman, the Last Surviving Leader of the Warsaw Ghetto Uprising*)

In addition, many young people and especially children, incredulous about the reports of death camps, felt that by volunteering for deportation, they would be reunited with parents and relatives who had already been deported. Eventually, thousands of volunteers showed up at Umschlagplatz.

During the daily roundup of deportees, there was a frenzied activity on the Umschlagplatz itself to save the lives of children, leaders of the Community, rabbis, relatives, and others. The motives were not always pure; outlandish bribes were often paid to smuggle oneself out of the mob. German businesses actually appointed representatives to stand in the Umschlagplatz and handpick essential workers. In other instances, individuals feigned death to be loaded into an undertaker's cart; they put on smuggled hats and badges of the Jewish Police Force and escaped; they donned smuggled nurse's caps and exited with other nurses; they squeezed through a hole in the wall to "Aryan" Warsaw at night. People dyed their grey hair in order to appear younger for the increasingly arbitrary *selektionen*. Rabbis began to mass-produce false wedding contracts, so that women could be protected on men's "life tickets." In such a manner brothers would even marry their sisters to protect the sibling from death.

Special mention should be made of the selfless doctors and nurses who saved condemned Jews during the Aktion. They risked their own lives smuggling medical clothing onto the Umschlagplatz so that people could masquerade and escape. Emmanuel Ringelblum noted "the heroic nurses—the only ones who saved people from deportation without [asking for] money" (Jacob Sloan, ed., *Notes from the Warsaw Ghetto: The Journal of Emmanel Ringelblum*). Exceptional among these rescuers was Nachum Remba, who was not actually a doctor but the personnel secretary of the Judenrat. Dressed in a doctor's coat, Remba operated a special two-room first aid unit on the side of the Umschlagplatz, while several nurses—known as the "Rescue Brigade"—would comb the square for important people to save. At one point Remba and his wife seized an ambulance in order to steal children away from the Umschlagplatz. It was Remba who tried to save Janusz Korczak and his orphans from the waiting trains. He begged Korczak to make a personal appeal with him at the Judenrat offices, but Korczak refused to leave the children. In the end, Korczak led his children, in a quiet, stately fashion, into the trains.

The smuggling of human life became a highly intricate endeavor. Everything had to be managed under the noses of the SS and their vicious Ukrainian, Latvian, and Lithuanian guards, not to mention the ruthless Jewish commander Schmerling. When they weren't masquerading as medical personnel, rescued individuals had to feign illness. Sometimes the nurses would help the process along. Marek Edelman, who assisted the Rescue Brigade, spoke about the creation of injuries:

> In order to pull somebody out from the lines at the Umschlagplatz, it was necessary to prove to the Germans that the person was seriously ill. They would send those sick people home in ambulances: Till the last moment, the Germans tried to maintain the illusion in people that they were leaving in those trains to work, and only a healthy person could work, right? So these girls from the emergency rooms, those nurses, would break the legs of those people who had to be saved. They would wedge a leg up against a wooden block and then smash it with another block. All this in their shiny white robes of model students.
> (Hanna Krall, *Shielding the Flame: An Intimate Conversation with Dr. Marek Edelman, the Last Surviving Leader of the Warsaw Ghetto Uprising*)

The "injured" people would be taken to the first aid unit, from which they were often whisked away from the Umschlagplatz in a hospital ambulance. Hundreds of Jews were saved in this way—a paltry number compared with the hundreds of thousands who were loaded onto the trains and taken to the gas chambers, but it indicates at least a small spark of mercy amidst the evil of Umschlagplatz.

The Monument

The Umschlagplatz Monument was designed as part of the Memorial Route of Jewish Martyrdom and Struggle in 1988 by Hanna Szmalenberg and Wladyslaw Klamerus, the architect and sculptor who designed the overall Memorial Route. They also designed the memorial over the mass grave in the Jewish Cemetery (*see pages 198–199*), and repeated the image of a *tallis*, or Jewish prayer shawl, in both monuments. Here the black strip across the white outside walls recalls the traditional appearance of a *tallis*.

One enters the monument underneath a granite block with a depiction of a destroyed forest. Both in shape and content, the slab alludes to Jewish tombstones. In Jewish cemeteries, the symbol of a broken tree is a common image of mourning, and the symbol of a leafless tree often refers to a childless individual. Here, the image of an entire forest of fallen trees indicates genocide. The destroyed, broken trees are given a counterpoint on the inside of the monument: The narrow gap in the wall looks out onto a healthy, blooming tree. Also, if you stand inside the monument and look on the reverse side of the entrance slab, you will see a living reflection of the tree against the black granite. In the spring and summer, the back of the archway reflects a multitude of leaves from the tree. Thus the tombstone itself is given a nuance of life. The pain of mourning is soothed in the affirmation of rebirth after the Holocaust.

The walls of the monument are three meters high, alluding to the walls of the ghetto. Some say that the monument represents the train cars that left from this site. Because of this, some visitors assume that the trains were located where the monument is, or that Umschlagplatz consisted only of the monument's space. It is important to point out that the memorial is only a corner of the space into which the Jews were herded and then forced into freight cars. The trains, in fact, were located farther back. This area was the place where Jews were initially rounded up and forced to proceed to the waiting trains.

The four plaques on the interior describe the crimes at Umschlagplatz in Polish, Yiddish, Hebrew, and English. Around these are inscribed the four hundred first names of people who were sent from here to Treblinka. This is meant to personalize the tragedy, to summon individual names out of the otherwise anonymous mass of three hundred thousand human beings. On the right side of the monument is a passage from Job 16:18: "Earth, do not cover my blood; Let there be no resting place for my outcry!"

Future plans include a reconstruction nearby of the train rails, wagons, and railway platform used during the deportations.

Warsaw: The Walking Tour

In one of Isaac Bashevis Singer's many books about prewar Warsaw, he writes, "Yes, people died, but things lived on. The least cobblestone in the street was millions of years old." Part of the exuberance in walking the streets of a former Jewish Town is the knowledge that in previous centuries, one's ancestors tread an identical path. Thus in Cracow we walk the same streets the Community traversed when it flocked to the court of the Rema. Even in Prague, whose ghetto streets were levelled at the turn of the century, one finds so many synagogues clustered around the cemetery that it is not difficult to imagine masses of Jews rushing home to prepare for Shabbat on a Friday afternoon.

What makes Warsaw's tragedy especially compelling is that this is impossible today. In 1943, German General Jurgen Stroop printed a wartime memory book triumphantly entitled, "The Jewish Residential Quarter of Warsaw Is No More!" Indeed, the Nazis levelled the entire ghetto, not to mention eighty-four percent of Warsaw proper. Afterwards, the goal of postwar reconstruction was not the recreation of a destroyed Community but pragmatic urban renewal. Thus the narrow streets once teeming with *shtiebel*s, secondhand stores, sweatshops, literary cafes, socialist cells, Zionist clubs, Bundist offices, prostitutes, porters, petty thieves, and nouveau riche—often on a single block—have given way to wide boulevards dotted with grey, communist era high-rise housing blocks separated by lots and untamed plots of grass. Often the original streets were not even included in the new city plan; at other times the street names were moved to other locations. A tourist in Warsaw has nothing other than memorials to the Holocaust that recall anything about a Jewish presence in the city; the streets themselves are empty and altered.

It is this dilemma that the following section is intended to ease. A description of the former sites of today's urban terrain will bring back a sample of its erstwhile atmosphere. By recreating the urban landscape of prewar Jewish Warsaw—even in areas where a former street no longer exists—the reader will be able to imagine the former Community. The purpose of this is twofold: to relive and perceive the way Jewish Warsaw was, and to realize all the more tangibly its searing absence today.

It should be kept in mind that this is only a small sample of Warsaw's multi-hued Jewish district. The prewar Warsaw Jewish Community was so diverse, with writers, actors, rabbis, politicians, scientists, and industrialists, that it is impossible to pluck a single strand of life as it was. Therefore, this section is intended not to show the whole gamut of Jewish

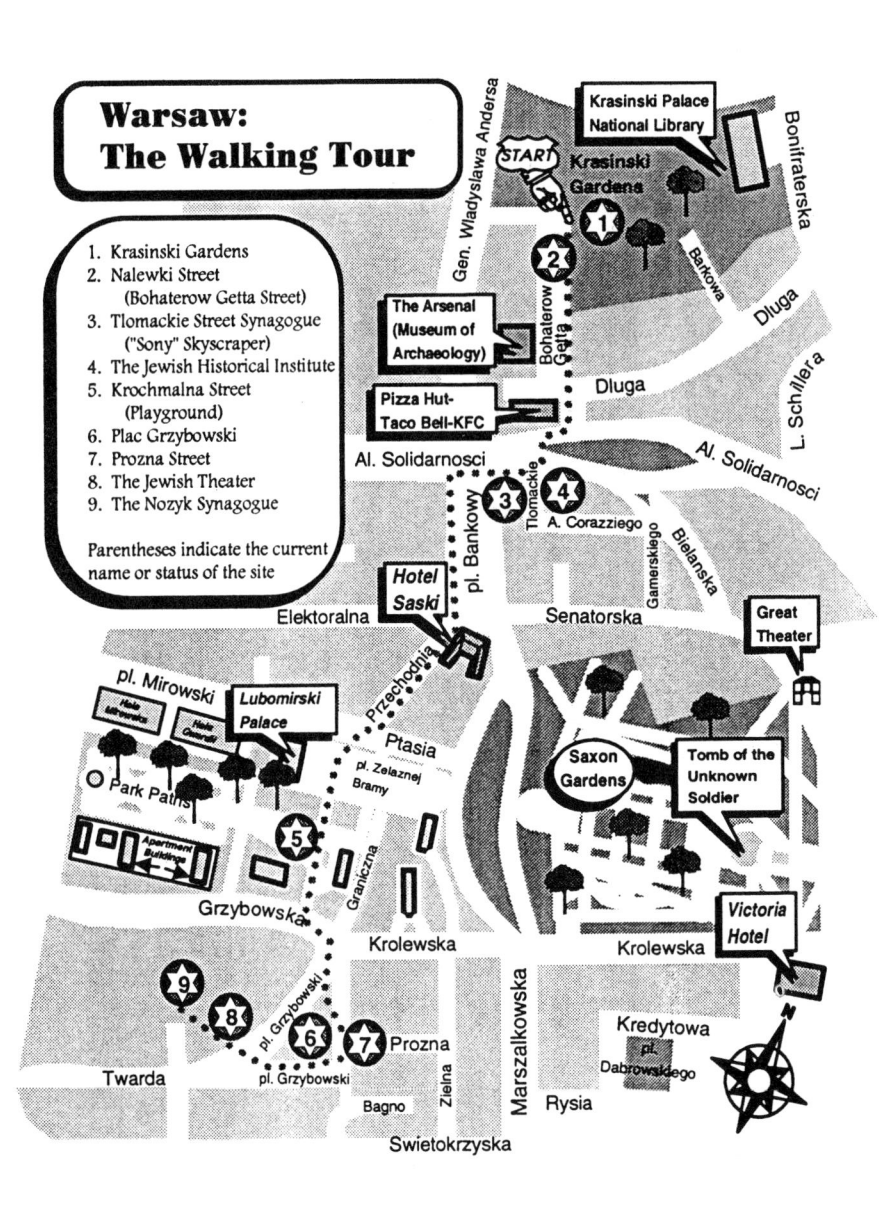

Warsaw: The Walking Tour

1. Krasinski Gardens
2. Nalewki Street (Bohaterow Getta Street)
3. Tlomackie Street Synagogue ("Sony" Skyscraper)
4. The Jewish Historical Institute
5. Krochmalna Street (Playground)
6. Plac Grzybowski
7. Prozna Street
8. The Jewish Theater
9. The Nozyk Synagogue

Parentheses indicate the current name or status of the site

life but to provide a glimpse of what once existed here. Hopefully this glimpse will help your own imagination fill in the enormity of Warsaw's Jewish civilization.

To facilitate orientation, the walk generally proceeds from north to south. It begins with Nalewki, a Jewish street that no longer exists, and culminates with the Nozyk Synagogue, a symbol of the continuity of Jewish life in Warsaw to this day.

※

The walk begins at the northern end of the short street called **Bohaterow Getta**. Bohaterow Getta Street extends north from Dluga Street into the Krasinski Gardens. The gate on the left, just north of the tip of Bohaterow Getta Street, is one of the original entrances to the Gardens. Because the Gardens were completely rebuilt after the war, they only wistfully approximate their original shape and appearance. The Krasinski Gardens used to be known as the "Jewish Gardens" before the war. Unlike the respectable Saxon Gardens (Ogrod Saski), where Jews could not enter without dressing in "European" clothes, in the Krasinski Gardens Jews could dress however they wished. This, and its bordering some of the most bustling streets of the Jewish District, made Krasinski Gardens one of the most popular leisure spots for Jews before the war. On any given day it was filled with young Jewish couples, elderly retirees, and *hasids* on their way home from *heder*.

Back on Bohaterow Getta Street, you will notice original cobblestones and tram tracks, which end rather abruptly.

BOHATEROW GETTA (NALEWKI STREET)

Bohaterow Getta, or "Heroes of the Ghetto," is the last remaining piece of what was once one of the most vibrant and beloved streets in the Jewish district, Nalewki Street. You might notice a Nalewki Street on current city maps; that Nalewki was built after the war and bears no relation to the original Nalewki. Its location is entirely different. The original Nalewki extended from today's Bohaterow Getta to plac Muranowska on the north, running roughly parallel to today's Andersa Street. At the end of the war, with most of Nalewki in ruins (the first battle of the Uprising occurred farther north on Nalewki Street), only this tiny snippet was preserved and renamed Bohaterow Getta. The rest was completely obliterated by the postwar city gridwork.

Nalewki Street! Any Jew who lived in Warsaw before the war will smile at the mention of this name. "Ah, Nalewki! Let me tell you a story . . ." Everybody has a Nalewki Story. Jews began to settle Nalewki in large numbers in 1780. In the early nineteenth century, the Warsaw municipal authorities passed laws restricting Jewish settlement to areas outside the center of town. As a result, streets in the northern district of Warsaw—streets like Nalewki, Franciszkanska, and Gesia—became populated by large numbers of Jews. Eventually Nalewki became one of the most densely built streets in Warsaw.

Starting in 1815, new three-story-high, neo-classical, stone buildings emerged on Nalewki to replace the older wooden structures. It became one of the richest Jewish streets in Warsaw. Nalewki was known all over town for its specialty shops and textile industry. Each building, built deliberately on an elongated plot, hid an entire village inside—packed with so many merchants and customers that they resembled frantic bazaars. There were flats, shops, synagogues, study halls, warehouses, and countless small factories. It is said that as you travelled deeper and deeper into these endless courtyards, the residents became poorer; the wealthiest residents had views of Nalewki itself, with its commotion of people making deals, trading cloth, wheeling out pushcarts, and bending over to carry enormous loads as porters. It was once called the "Street of Disorder." There were no trees on Nalewki, only tall, posh streetlights.

Alfred Doblin, a German Jewish writer, made a trip through Poland in the interwar years and recorded his impressions in a charming travelogue. It was in Poland that this assimilated German intellectual discovered his roots as a Jew. In the Jewish district of Warsaw, he immediately wrote about Nalewki, "filled and teeming with Jews":

> I enter a courtyard; it's rectangular and, like a marketplace, full of loud people, Jews, mostly in caftans. The back wings contain furniture shops, fur shops. And, after passing through a back wing, I stand in another swarming courtyard full of crates, teams of horses; Jewish porters loading and unloading. . . . Toward the city, in the southern part, along the Dluga, large, open, modern stores: cosmetics, stamps, textiles. I read strange names: Waiselfisch, Klopfherd, Blumenkranz, Brandwain, Farsztandig, Goldkopf, Gelbfisch, Gutbesztand.
>
> (Alfred Doblin, *Journey to Poland*)

Unlike many other streets in the Jewish district, where both Jew and Gentile lived, Nalewki was almost exclusively Jewish—with the exception of Gentile shoppers looking for the best clothing selection in Warsaw. During the interwar years it even became something of a tourist attraction. Everybody wanted to see that "Jewish world." Nalewki postcards were sent all over Europe with messages like "I visited Jewish life in Poland." People came to watch swanky Nalewki residents march around the street. There was a semihumorous label, *Elegant z Nalewek* (Nalewki Elegance) that referred to a so-called "Jewish face" dressed completely in the latest European fashions. The wealthiest industrialists eventually moved to non-Jewish quarters to the south, but they kept their workshops on Nalewki. Doblin made his own observations on the style of Nalewki's denizens:

> Jewish women pass through the crowd; they wear black wigs, small black veils on top, a kind of flower in front. Black shawls. A tall young man in modern clothes with his elegant sister looks strange; he walks proudly, with a skullcap on his head. Families converse in the street; two youngish men in clean caftans with their wives in modern garb and piquant Polish makeup. . . . Young girls stroll arm in arm, they don't look very Jewish, they laugh, speak Yiddish, their clothes are Polish down to the fine stockings. They amble erect. The shoulders of the men are slack, their backs crooked, they shuffle.
>
> (Alfred Doblin, *Journey to Poland*)

It was unthinkable for Nalewki to be empty during the workweek, but come Shabbat, Nalewki Street shut down completely. Even the horse-drawn trams knew better than to make their usual stops on Nalewki. They just drove on through. Policemen who normally wandered the street extorting money from unlicensed merchants would disappear on Friday evening: Nalewki, the teeming quarter of shopowner deals, was penniless on Shabbat.

There were unwritten cultural rules on and around Nalewki Street. Wealthy Jews who remained would send their kids to public or trade school outside the Jewish quarter, and if they were Orthodox their children developed a certain way of walking. On Nalewki and its immediate environs, they walked in two distinct groups, boys separated from girls. As soon as they crossed onto plac Bankowy, though, the two groups merged into a single, chattering mass. The same was true of language. Jews strolling down Nalewki Street would speak nothing but Yiddish. When they crossed into streets whose populace was both Jewish and Christian, their language would automatically shift into part Yiddish, part Polish. On strictly Polish Streets like Marszalkowska, their speech was strictly Polish. When they got back to Nalewki, Yiddish embraced their speech once again.

The flavor of Nalewki Street in the early twentieth century was captured in a nostalgic memoir by Bernard Singer entitled *Moje Nalewki* (My Nalewki). Here he describes Nalewki's typical character:

> All its beauty was dependent upon its unhealthy, incessant, and arrhythmic rush. During the day, all the people were rushing, not glancing to the left and right, and pushing one against the other. The entire street was running. The rush hour was exactly between 1:30 and 2:00. People ran from store to store for just the right amount of cash necessary to pay for their goods.... All the pushcarts were in motion. The customers who came from the provinces joined in the rush. People uttered prayers as they ran, muttering the last sentences as they ran from the synagogue to the shop. I don't know how many shops there were in Nalewki. In any event, during the first years of our century, the number increased tenfold. A big store was divided into parts, and in every part a different merchant set up his own shop. After a while there were five, six of them. A stand for soda water was turned into a store. Pubs were changed into warehouses. The long houses with the big courtyards had their own swarms of merchants without shops. They paid a guard and a policeman for the right to make their business there.

Farther north, Nalewki ran into Franciszkanska Street. From the early nineteenth century, Franciszkanska was an area where Jews were allowed to live on the condition that they build their own houses. As a result, Franciszkanska became one of the most beautiful streets in Warsaw, built by preeminent Jewish architects in around 1825–40. Franciszkanska houses were similar to the houses on Nalewki. Before the war, there were approximately 35 *shtiebels*, or Jewish prayer halls, on Franciszkanska Street alone.

Walk south along the tram lines. The street was once lined with stores and flats. The heart of Nalewki actually lay farther north, but all we have left are these stones and tram tracks at its southern tip. Bohaterow Getta is used today as a parking lot.

At the end of the street, on the right side, is a yellow building called the Arsenal. It used to be a prison, playing an evocative role in Isaac Bashevis Singer's novel *Scum*. Today it is a museum of archaeology.

Walk south from the corner of Bohaterow Getta and Dluga Streets toward a large blue skyscraper until you reach Al. Solidarnosci. Your back will then be to a Pizza Hut–Taco Bell–Kentucky Fried Chicken franchise.

You are now standing on what was once Tlomackie Square, and the skyscraper is built on the exact spot of the Tlomackie Street Synagogue.

"SONY" SKYSCRAPER (TLOMACKIE STREET SYNAGOGUE)

The Tlomackie Street Synagogue, also known as the "Great Synagogue," was a monument to the rising affluence of Warsaw Jewry in the late nineteenth century. It was an immense building flanked by two menorahs and topped by an enormous crown.

Although the Reform movement was extremely small in tradition-minded Warsaw, the Jewish Community was led by progressive Jews in the late nineteenth century. In particular, the wealthy Ludwik Natanson (1822–1896) assumed leadership of the Community in 1871. Natanson spearheaded a complete reorganization and modernization of the Jewish Community, establishing everything from vocational schools to a Jewish hospital. Orthodox Jews were wary of his assimilationist bent, but Natanson had the support of the wealthy Jewish bourgeois. With their help, he engineered the construction of the Tlomackie Street Synagogue as early as 1872.

After the early designs were rejected, the building commission gave the assignment to Leandro Marconi (1834–1919). The synagogue, which sat eleven hundred men and nearly as many women, was built in 1875–78. It was partly classicist in style, with its Corinthian columns and dome reminiscent of the Roman Pantheon, and was ringed by pavilions that were used during various ceremonies. In the interior, which measured twenty-eight by thirty-eight meters, there were seven bays. The *bimah* was located in the front, and above it stood the choir loft. The synagogue also had an organ, which was not used on Shabbat. Women sat in the galleries, but the partitions were not as strict as in other synagogues of the time; their faces could be seen down below.

The synagogue opened onto Tlomackie Square and was recognizable from afar by its distinctive crown-shaped dome adorned by a Star of David. It was the exact opposite of the hundreds of crouched and diminutive *shtiebels* in Warsaw. The Tlomackie Street Synagogue announced itself for all the world to see. The synagogue distanced itself from nineteenth century Reform synagogues in that its exterior did not mimic a church or use the Moorish style so widespread at the time. This fierce independence revealed the degree of comfort and self-assurance Warsaw's Jews felt at the time.

Although the liturgy at the Tlomackie Street Synagogue liturgy remained Orthodox, the yarmulkes of its ritzy worshippers were covered by top hats.

Alfred Doblin, the German Jewish journeyman in the interwar years, made the following comments about the closest thing to a German synagogue in Warsaw:

> The great synagogue on Tlomacki Street; a classical temple, narrow, lofty. Above it, the dome with the Star of David. A short beadle chats with a Polish policeman at the foot of the stairs. It's Saturday morning. They pour up the steps. Few of them wear caftans and skullcaps, this is the synagogue of the middle class, also the enlightened, the emancipated, and the assimilated. . . . Upstairs, women sit behind a high wide gate; I see fashionable modern hats. . . . Most of the men wear prayer shawls, white with blue and black stripes. Some wear them like scarves, some wrap them around their arms, tightening them. Many young men walk about, including almost a dozen soldiers, and more join them afterward. . . . On either side of the room, I count seven windows, small, unadorned. Lofty columns rise from

the gallery, partitioning off seven round arches. A small stairway leads to the altar. The red burning lamp, the central curtain.

(Alfred Doblin, *Journey to Poland*)

One of the most interesting aspects of the synagogue was that the *aron hakodesh* faced south, not the traditional direction east. This was revolutionary, and still is; European Jews have always built their prayer halls to face the east, the presumed location of Jerusalem. But Warsaw's upstart rabbinical scholars reasoned that Jerusalem was more south than east, and they were right. A bigger question is why it took so long for European Jews to realize they had been praying not toward Jerusalem but toward Moscow. Perhaps the east was viewed as a metaphorical concept and not as the literal location of Jerusalem.

The Tlomackie Street Synagogue was incorporated into the Warsaw ghetto in 1940. It was like an island, attached to the body of the ghetto by a narrow street. When the mass deportations to Treblinka began in July 1942, the synagogue was removed from the redrawn ghetto map. At 8:15 P.M. on May 16, 1943, as a symbol of its triumph over the Warsaw Ghetto Uprising, the German army dynamited the Tlomackie Street Synagogue.

In the 1960s, construction work began on the huge skyscraper that sits on the site today. For some reason, the building work met with several small disasters, including unexplained phenomena like walls collapsing and machinery malfunctioning. A modern legend spread through Warsaw that when the synagogue was destroyed, a rabbi placed a curse on the site. Finally, after thirty years of construction, the building was finished in 1993. It is known among foreigners as the "Sony Building" because of the logo on top, but in Warsaw it's called the "Blue Building" because its mirrored facade reflects the sky. The building's owners have agreed to set aside two hundred square meters of space for temporary exhibitions of the Jewish Historical Institute across the street, but at this writing the space had not yet been opened. Ask at the Jewish Historical Institute (*see below*) about temporary exhibitions.

THE JEWISH HISTORICAL INSTITUTE

Address: Tlomackie Street 3/5

Opening Hours (subject to change):
Museum: Monday to Friday 9:00 A.M.–3:00 P.M.
Library: Monday to Thursday 8:00 A.M.–3:00 P.M.
           Friday 9:00 A.M.–12:00 noon
Archives: Monday to Friday 9:00 A.M.–3:00 P.M.

This building, one of the rare sites to have survived the war, was originally built to be the library of the Tlomackie Street Synagogue across the street. The leaders of the synagogue wished to begin building early in the twentieth century, but the First World War forced them to abandon their plans. After the war, the synagogue lacked the funds to build the library. Construction began only in 1928 after a design by Edward Zacharia Eber. It took eight years before the building was finished in 1936. Three years later, it would be closed in the German occupation.

The building housed both the synagogue's library and the Institute for Judaic Studies, which held lectures, meetings, and cultural events. Esteemed professors such as Majer Balaban (*see page 198*) lectured here.

On October 25, 1939, Chaim Kaplan lamented in his diary the passing of the building into German hands:

> The day before yesterday, like true Vandals, the conquerors entered the Tlomackie Library, where rare spiritual treasures were stored. They removed all the valuable books and manuscripts, put them on trucks, and took them to some unknown place. This is a burning of the soul of Polish Jewry, for this library was our spiritual sanctuary where we found respite when troubles came to us. Now the fountain which slaked our thirst for Torah and knowledge is dried up.
>
> (Chaim A. Kaplan, *Scroll of Agony*)

From 1940 until the summer of 1942, when the mass deportations to Treblinka began, the building was part of the ghetto. It was here that Emmanuel Ringelblum (*see page 177*) headed the social welfare department of the Jewish Organization for Social Care, organizing soup kitchens to assist the most needy Jews in the ghetto. But Ringelblum's clandestine work is even more well known than his welfare activites. It was in this building that he secretly organized and led the Oneg Shabbat group that documented all aspects of life in the Warsaw ghetto. One of the large containers in which Oneg Shabbat documents were hidden during the war used to be displayed in the Jewish Historical Institute. It is possible that this display will be reinstalled in the future.

On May 16, 1943, when the Tlomackie Street Synagogue was blown up, the Germans also set the library on fire. In parts of the main lobby, you can still see burn marks from the fire.

In 1947, after the building was reconstructed, the Jewish Historical Institute began working here. Its first priorities were to gather information regarding German war criminals and to collect information on the wartime experience of Polish Jews. It gathered testimony from around seven thousand survivors in its earliest stages and broadened to cover the history of the Jews in Poland in the centuries before the Holocaust. Some of the top Jewish scholars in postwar Poland worked at the Institute but after the anti-Semitic purges of 1968, most emigrated. It began to regain its strength as a Jewish research and cultural association only in the 1990s.

Today the Institute includes a museum, library, archives, research department, and educational center. The Lauder Foundation has funded the archives and created a genealogical research center (come here to search for Jewish ancestors in Poland—*see page 180*). There is an exhibition in the building, supplemented by planned temporary exhibits in the skyscraper across the street. The Institute also plans to build a museum focusing on the millennium of prewar Polish Jewish history. It will be located on the square opposite the Warsaw Ghetto Monument.

Today Tlomackie Street is only a small strip; it used to be a large square in front of the synagogue that curved around the building on its eastern side. Elsewhere on Tlomackie Street was the Writers' Society, which evolved out of a salon in Y.L. Peretz's own home. Instigated by Peretz's disciple Hersh David Nomberg (1876–1927), the Writers' Society—

also known simply as "Tlomackie 13" after its address—was a haven for Jewish writers seeking a little food, a little chess, and a lot of intellectual banter. It is regarded as one of the legendary sites of the Jewish Renaissance before the Holocaust. Unfortunately, the building no longer exists today.

On the other side of the skyscraper from the Jewish Historical Institute is plac Bankowy. Cross this major thoroughfare, turn left, and continue until you reach the end at the Hotel Saski. Walk along the right side of the Hotel Saski to Przechodnia Street, a small street that extends in the same southern direction. At the end of Przechodnia cross Ptasia Street and keep heading south along the right side of Iron Gate Square (plac Zelaznej Bramy). To your right you'll see a large building, the Lubomirski Palace. The building was once situated on a forty-five degree angle from its current position; during urban reconstruction projects after the war, the Polish authorities actually pushed the entire building away from Ptasia Street to create the square you see today.

To your left, there once stood the Iron Gate entrance to the Saxon Gardens. (Today the Saxon Gardens—Ogrod Saski in Polish—begin on the other side of the main avenue.) Before the war, the Saxon Gardens were the most luxurious gardens in the center of Warsaw. In order to preserve the pleasant and "untainted" atmosphere, the authorities put up a sign by the Iron Gate that prohibited entrance to all individuals not clothed in "European dress." It was meant to bar from entrance all Jews who dressed in traditional Jewish clothing. No gabardines or *striemels* were permitted. The blockade, which also applied to the exquisite Lazienski Park to the south, was the single anti-Semitic law of Czarist times that was not abolished by independent Poland after 1918. The rule affected poor Jews more than the rich, since the rich had long abandoned the unique dress of Orthodox society. The ban was one reason the Krasinski Gardens, with their more tolerant rules, was the favored spot for Jews in the interwar years.

Continue heading south, into the grassy park area. About ten meters into the park on your right is a children's playground with sliding boards, swing sets, and, weather permitting, pony rides. At approximately the site of this playground, Krochmalna Street used to exist.

KROCHMALNA STREET

You can find Krochmalna Street on any city map today, but this is misleading. Krochmalna Street once stretched from Karolkowa Street all the way to the area near Iron Gate Square. Today Krochmalna Street is only a random segment of the original—and even there, most of the original buildings no longer exist. The heart of the original Krochmalna Street—and the area that was most decidedly Jewish—was the eastern end, where the playground now stands in the park.

This portion of Krochmalna Street was one of the handful of Warsaw streets whose tenants and workers were, with almost no exceptions, Jews. It was also one of the poorest streets in Jewish Warsaw, which goes some way toward explaining its demographics: By the end of the nineteenth century, wealthier individuals had moved from the Krochmalna district to upper-class Gentile neighborhoods to the south. This insured the ghetto-like containment of Jewish poverty on Krochmalna. The street was so poor that nobody ever bothered to photograph it, much to our chagrin today. There were no postcards of Krochmalna, and neither the Warsaw City Archives nor the Jewish Historical Institute of Poland possess a single photograph of Krochmalna in their vast collections.

But Krochmalna did not despair. It was a self-contained slum as much as New York's Lower East Side could have been considered a slum at the time. Krochmalna, for all its dilapidation and grime, was one of the most robust and dynamic streets in all Warsaw. It was less a street and more an organic byway, a meeting point where the sundry crosscurrents of European Jewish life intersected. Krochmalna was loud, earthy, sometimes vulgar. All the fiery spices of twentieth-century Warsaw converged on Krochmalna Street in a pungent stew. During the interwar period, one could find hasidic study houses next to communist propaganda offices next to boisterous taverns and brothels, with children playing in the street and women shouting from one balcony to the next. It was this fertility that served as incubator for Krochmalna Street's most celebrated son, Isaac Bashevis Singer.

If all writers can be identified with a single great city—James Joyce with Dublin, Franz Kafka with Prague—then Isaac Bashevis Singer is forever linked with this single, unpretentious street in Warsaw. Singer grew up at Krochmalna 10. As the narrator confides in the first paragraph of *Shosha*, "We lived in Warsaw on Krochmalna Street, which might well have been called a ghetto." Elsewhere, in his story "The Betrayer of Israel," the young narrator boasts, "What could be better than to stand on a balcony and be able to see all of Krochmalna Street (the part where the Jews lived) from Gnoyna to Ciepla and even farther, to Zelazna Street, where there were trolley cars! A day never passed, not even an hour, when something did not happen. One moment a thief was caught and then Itcha Meyer, the drunkard—the husband of Esther from the candy store—became wild and danced in the middle of the gutter. Someone got sick and an ambulance was called. A fire broke out in a house and the firemen, wearing brass hats and high rubber boots, came with their galloping horses . . ."

Singer's father was a modest rabbi who headed the street's only rabbinical court of law, called *Bet Din* in Hebrew. Singer devoted an entire book, *In My Father's Court*, to reminiscences of the nutty characters who flooded his home. His courtship of Krochmalna pervades so much of his work, in fact, that it is difficult to say whether Singer immortalized Krochmalna or vice versa. As Aaron Greidinger, the narrator of *Shosha*, relates, "When I thought of it, I had the strange feeling that my experience there constituted something removed from the world. . . . Krochmalna Street was like a deep stratum of an archaeological dig which I would never uncover." So much of Singer's fiction and memoir is precisely this: the patient exhuming of layer after layer of his childhood home on Krochmalna.

Shosha itself is a sublime example. In this seminal work, Greidinger takes virtually the same walk we have taken today, beginning with a street parallel to Nalewki and heading south to Krochmalna. His description of Krochmalna is one of Singer's most indelible recreations of Warsaw as it was:

> We reached Krochmalna Street and the stench I recalled from my childhood struck me first—a blend of burned oil, rotten fruit, and chimney smoke. Everything was the same—the cobble-

stone pavement, the steep gutter, the balconies hung with wash. . . . Every house here was bound up with memories. No. 5 contained a *yeshiva* in which I had studied for a term. There was a ritual bath in the courtyard, where matrons came in the evening to immerse themselves. I used to see them emerge clean and flushed. . . . The only change I could observe was that the houses had lost most of their plaster and grown black from smoke. Here and there, a wall was supported on logs. The gutters seemed even deeper, their stink even stronger. I stopped before each gate and peered in. All the garbage bins were heaped high with refuse. Dyers dyed clothing, tinsmiths patched broken pots, men with sacks on their shoulders cried, "Ole clo's, ole clo's, I buy rags, ole pants, ole shoes, ole hats; ole clo's, ole clo's." Here and there, a beggar sang a song—of the *Titanic*, which had gone down in 1911, of the striker Baruch Shulman, who had thrown a bomb in 1905 and been hanged. Magicians were performing the same stunts they had in my childhood—they swallowed fire, rolled barrels with their feet, lay down bareback on a bed of nails.

Singer's stories and novels about Warsaw paint a meticulous, house-by-house portrait of the once vibrant street that is today a grassy park and playground. Number 4 contained "Yanush's Court," a food bazaar where they sold "everything," as Singer writes in *Shosha*: ". . . fruit, vegetables, dairy, geese, fish. There were stores selling secondhand shoes and old clothes of all kinds." Number 5, as mentioned above, contained a *yeshivah*. Number 6, in the story "Elka and Meir," contained a brothel, referred to as "a windowless cellar, a living grave." In the novel *Scum*, Number 6 has become a tavern of the underworld. Number 8 housed Asher's milk shop. In *Shosha*, the narrator hears a tall tale about Number 8: "A ditch was dug and they found a dead Russian sapper, with a sword and a revolver." Number 17 contained another tavern, referred to in *Scum* as "much more orderly" than the one in Number 6.

And then there was the "Square." One of the most exciting—or notorious—spots on Krochmalna was the area adjacent to Number 13, known alternately as "The Place" or "Krochmalna Square." The Square epitomized the discordant hodgepodge of sacred and profane that had free reign on Krochmalna. Singer returns to the Square throughout his fiction and memoir. In *In My Father's Court*, Singer recalls the harmonious contradictions of the Square: ". . . No. 13 bordered on the ill-famed Krochmalna Square, where pickpockets and hoodlums loitered and dealers in stolen goods carried on their trade. The houses facing the Square also harbored a number of brothels. Even regular commerce was carried on in an underhand manner: if one wanted to buy a *tchaste*—a kind of chocolate-covered cracker—one pulled numbers from a hat or spun a wooden wheel. Yet in these same houses dwelt decent men, pious women, chaste girls. There were even a few hasidic study houses."

The unifying force on Krochmalna Street, whether for the pious or the profane, was the transforming power of Shabbat, the day of rest. Shabbat was a time when the seemingly abysmal contradictions of the street came to a close, and Krochmalna became a single vehicle of *Yiddishkeit*. From the balcony of Number 10, the hero of Singer's novel *Scum* surveys the street as it readies itself for Shabbat:

> In every nook and cranny of the street preparations were being made for the Sabbath. The bakers were not carrying rolls but challah, *shtritsl* (white bread loaves), and cakes. Men were coming

back from the ritual bath, as their red faces, damp beards and sidelocks revealed. Here and there the half doors of stores were being shut. Through open windows you could see men or women setting candles firmly in molten wax and girls carrying *cholent* to the bakeries.

Max looked at No. 15 and recognized Esther, the baker's wife; their encounter had ended so disastrously. She was sitting on a bench by the gate, weighing a huge twisted challah on a scale. All over the square, which usually swarmed with thieves and loose women, there hovered a Sabbath-eve peacefulness.

Today, that tranquil unity amid the apparent chaos of Krochmalna Street is entirely removed, perplexingly replaced by a playground that belies the site's former appearance. One can spend hours here and still not believe it is the same geographic area Singer rhapsodized about. In *The Certificate*, Singer's narrator again waxes nostalgic when he returns to his childhood home of Krochmalna: "Nothing had changed; time had congealed here. It occurred to me that here in my old street I might discover the secret of time." It seems that Singer, knowing what he knew had become of Krochmalna, is eulogizing, as well as reconstructing, his childhood home.

There should be a footnote to the nostalgic reverie. Krochmalna Street, the retina of Singer's prewar childhood vision, became one of the most squalid streets in the Warsaw ghetto. This is not at all surprising: A poor street in prewar Jewish Warsaw became infinitely more destitute during the occupation. It is particularly eerie that this should have happened to Singer's street, for it was Singer who, time and again, warned of the cruelty and violence that are fixed at the end of all man's endeavors.

Before long, Krochmalna was one of the most horrid places in Warsaw. Decomposed corpses of Jews who had starved to death littered the streets. At the refugee center in Krochmalna 21, all four hundred residents died of typhus or starvation.

Typhus hit Krochmalna particularly hard. During the first epidemic, which occurred at the beginning of 1940, the Germans used Krochmalna Street as a sort of guinea pig for their planned formation of a ghetto. When they began separating Jews from Christians in Warsaw, one of the focal points of separation was this street. In March 1940, Emmanuel Ringelblum wrote, "The health authority says that Krochmalna Street is the chief source of infection for the whole city. If they could, they would burn it down" (Jacob Sloan, ed., *Notes from the Warsaw Ghetto: The Journal of Emmanuel Ringelblum*). In May, Krochmalna Street was roped off and quarantined for twenty-three days. Approximately twenty thousand inhabitants of the street were forced into isolation. The majority of the inhabitants were, of course, Jewish. Thus the Krochmalna quarantine was in effect the first German experiment at creating a ghetto. Had it not been for the active efforts of smugglers, all the residents would have starved to death. After the ghetto was formed, in August 1941, Krochmalna Street faced another "Typhus Aktion." All the residents were marched far from Krochmalna Street to public baths. The two-day disinfection was accompanied by such a degree of pandemonium that, once again, the residents were starved as much as cleansed. So many people died during this "cleansing" procedure, and so much crime occurred in the emptied flats during the disinfection, that the Aktion was never repeated.

The Jews of Krochmalna became so starved for food that on at least one occasion a resident was driven to desperation. One of the three documented cases of cannibalism in the Warsaw ghetto occurred in Krochmalna 18. A starving thirty-five-year-old woman was found eating the severed buttocks of her deceased twelve-year-old son.

Thus Singer's childhood wonderland of inexplicable innocence and sin turned into one of the most horrifying streets in Warsaw during the Nazi terror.

Today, the parents and children clustered around the swing sets, sliding boards, and sandbox have no inkling of what this place used to be.

From the playground, continue south on the path until it ends at Grzybowska Street. The Warsaw Jewish Community had its administrative center on Grzybowska 26, but the building was destroyed during the war. Crossing Grzybowska Street, you'll see the triangular plac Grzybowski (Grzybowski Square) beginning at the intersection slightly to the left. As a point of reference, you'll see a church rising from the far end of plac Grzybowski.

PLAC GRZYBOWSKI

This area used to be a separate town that, during the centuries in which Jews were forbidden from Warsaw proper, opened its gates to the Jews. In the nineteenth century it became an area of increased Jewish settlement, with several shops as well as the palatial home of the Jewish entrepreneur Shaja Privus. It was the center of Warsaw's hardware trade, a role it still fills today—with one difference. If you look at the signs on the doors and above the shops, you'll see dates like 1945 and 1946. These are the dates the stores were "established," although for the most part they were pre-existing businesses taken over by Poles after their former owners had been murdered by the Germans.

Plac Grzybowski was known less as a Jewish center than as the site of constant worker unrest and demonstrations. Bundists demonstrated here, and so did the Polish Socialist Party. In 1905, the square was the site of clashes between Polish workers and the Russian army. Nineteen-year-old Baruch Shulman, a radical member of the Polish Socialist Party, headed a faction that wanted to assassinate the chief Russian policeman. He hid a bomb on the square, near Prozna Street, and then ran to hide on Zielna Street. But he didn't run quickly enough. The bomb exploded near him, killing a policeman and one or two bystanders and injuring Shulman himself. After he was found hiding in a courtyard, Shulman was executed.

If you are still facing south, Prozna Street begins on the left side of plac Grzybowski.

PROZNA STREET

Step into Prozna Street and, for a moment at least, you are standing on a piece of the past. Amid the endless rows of apartment blocks and patches of grass, Prozna is an oasis. Over half a dozen buildings on Prozna were destroyed during the war and its immediate aftermath, but four remain. It is thus the single street from prewar Jewish Warsaw that still has buildings on both sides. There are, elsewhere in the former Jewish district, rare examples of buildings, walls, or gates, but only Prozna remains as a genuine, tangible street. It was originally named Prozna, meaning "vacant," because it joined two vacant lots. Today the name has added significance, as Prozna is a vacant island of prewar Jewish Warsaw. It never distinguished itself as the heart of the Jewish Quarter. It was no Nalewki, no Franciszkanska or Gesia. But today, it's the only piece we have. In this vein, it can be considered the highlight of one's walk through Warsaw's bypassed streets.

Because of its unparalleled historical status today, Prozna is quickly becoming the focus of world attention. In 1996, the World Monuments Fund placed it on its first annual World Monuments Watch List of 100 Endangered Sites, side by side with such world heavyweights as Ancient Pompeii, the Yucatan Indian Chapels, Ayuttaqya temples in Thailand, and Ancient Tyre. The problem on Prozna is that the buildings are literally falling apart. Walk up the collapsing stairs in any of these structures (at your own risk) and you'll see just how deteriorated they are. Gone are the once-stately facades. Scaffolding was erected in the 1980s to shield pedestrians from falling bricks. In one case, a portion of the building seems to be held up by emaciated wooden beams. American Express donated $50,000 toward preliminary survey work and the Ronald S. Lauder Foundation gave $25,000. After surveying is finished, the charities are expected to declare what many people already fear: that reconstruction work here will cost millions of dollars. These buildings can't be just knocked down and rebuilt; because they're on the World Monuments Watch List, preservation work means a painstaking internal-external restoration, brick by precious brick.

Assuming Prozna finds a benefactor, expect scaffolding to cover the site in the near future. If this does occur, try your best to see as much as you can. It's the closest one can come to experiencing what was once the world's second-largest Jewish Community.

The Street

Prozna existed, in a slightly reduced form, as early as the eighteenth century. Toward the end of the nineteenth century, it was extended to reach plac Grzybowski. At that time, construction began on the buildings that remain today. When the buildings were finished, its flats soon became filled with middle class and wealthy individuals.

By then the street was almost entirely Jewish. Practically all the landlords, tenants, shopowners, and pedestrians were Jews; one building had a prayer hall; and there was even a kosher restaurant on the street. As an offshoot of plac Grzybowski, Prozna Street boasted its own gaggle of hardware and metal goods shops, also run by Jews. Because it was a market center, and because it was located toward the southeastern rim of the Jewish District, Prozna Street had a unique cosmopolitan flavor created by the intermingling of Jewish and Christian marketers. Craftsmen walked up and down the street, selling products they carried on their backs; shopowners leaned on their doorposts, shouting out the day's deals; organ grinders stood by the sidewalk, playing tunes for a coin or two. It was not always so leisured: As a thoroughfare for many of Warsaw's laborers and marketers, Prozna Street was also a hotbed of worker tension. Properly harnessed, this tension sometimes exploded into full-blown riots on the adjacent plac Grzybowski.

To give you an idea of city life on a Jewish street in Warsaw, take for example the riots at the end of May 1905. The eastern end of Prozna Street, beyond the area of the prewar buildings that remain today, was the scene of harsh fighting among Jews themselves when a citizens' task force decided to rid the area of the pimps, extortionists, criminals, and other nifty characters who had transformed the neighborhood into a hunting ground for crime. What is interesting is that both the sleazy underworld characters and the "Neighborhood Watch" group were Jews.

Jewish workers, fed up with the underworld, broke into a pimp cafe on the corner of Sienna and Zielna and chased the occupants up Zielna Street. When they reached Prozna, so-called "trials" and beatings began. Crowbars, knives, and clubs flashed through the air as the Jewish workers pummelled the neighborhood grime into submission. A number of casualties were sent, seriously wounded, to the hospital. That was only the beginning. For the next three days, the Jewish workers invaded brothels and underworld haunts in the entire area, sending the inhabitants fleeing. As Blind Mayer, the deposed "rabbi of the underworld," relates in Isaac Bashevis Singer's *Scum*:

> Here there was rioting and the old gang was knocked off. . . . During the riots the shoemakers and tailors ganged up on us. There was nobody to fight back. Everybody on the square was beaten up. They scattered like rabbits. The workers went into the whorehouses and beat up the girls. Twenty bastards attacked me, and with twenty against one, no one's a big shot. They took me away to the hospital in Czyste and I lay there six weeks.

Soon enough, all of downtown Warsaw joined the war against the underworld. What had begun as a Jewish self-cleansing program turned into a city-wide campaign.

Before the Second World War, Prozna Street had come into its own as a bustling commerce center catering, as it still does today, to the hardware industry. The tenants were relatively well-to-do; they included merchants, businessmen, musicians, artists, journalists, philanthropists, doctors, and lawyers.

When the Germans invaded Warsaw, they incorporated about two-thirds of Prozna—amazingly, the two-thirds that still exists—into the Jewish ghetto. The other third, beyond Zielna Street, was incorporated into "Aryan" Warsaw. A wall thus intersected Prozna Street. In 1941 the remainder of Prozna was removed from the ghetto territory. During the Polish uprising in 1944, Prozna Street was the scene of fierce battles as Polish partisans fought for the Polish Telephone building around the corner on Zielna Street. This same building on Zielna Street is today the home of the Nissenbaum Foundation, a Jewish philanthropy that restores cemeteries and erects Holocaust memorials throughout Poland. During the battle for the building, many Poles were killed on Prozna and the Germans riddled Prozna's buildings with bullets to pick off any remaining partisans. Some buildings were burnt out or partially destroyed, but a few remained. It is a miracle they survived.

Oddly enough, it was only after Prozna survived Nazism that it entered its most precarious era. The postwar Office for the Reconstruction of the Capital, dominated by architectural fanatics, insisted that any relics from the capitalist period were a scourge on the capital's beauty. Thus, in 1945 and 1946 four buildings on Prozna Street were demolished. Later, during Stalinist urban planning of the 1950s, another building came down. The remaining structures were left in unrestored squalor, waiting for eventual demolition. Only in the 1980s was a campaign mounted to save the four remaining buildings that you see today.

The Buildings

Of the dozen or so buildings that once stood on Prozna Street, only four buildings remain: numbers 9 and 7 on the southern side, and 14 and 12 on the north. The facades have completely disappeared and most of the furnishings have been looted or destroyed. Nonetheless, on many doorways to apartment flats, you can still find marks where *mezuzahs* once were. What follows is a re-creation of the history and nuances of each building. Feel free to stop by each one, read the appropriate text below, and try to imagine Jewish Warsaw as it once was.

Nine

Number Nine, on the corner of plac Grzybowski, was the home of Zalman Nozyk, the founder of Nozyk Synagogue. His is the only surviving synagogue in Warsaw today (*see* Nozyk Synagogue, *page 249*). Nozyk was part-owner of the building until he bought the remaining share for twenty-seven rubles. Built in 1880–82 by the prominent Warsaw architect Franciszek Brauman, the building featured an oak staircase and mosaic floors.

Nozyk ran his own iron goods shop on the ground floor. A competing store was opened on the same floor by Chaim Rosenfeld. The other stores at Number Nine continued the metal goods theme: Shaya Bucharski opened a shop for bronze goods he produced himself; David Lebensold had a bronze hardware shop. Creating his own niche was David Fallinower, who sold ceramic tiles. In 1919, the building's new owner, Boruch Cukierman, opened one of the most popular nut and bolt shops in all of Warsaw.

Seven

Number Seven was also built by the architect Brauman in 1880–82. The building's eventual owner opened a workshop and warehouse on the ground for his ostrich feather company. Where the ostriches lived is not recorded. Also on the ground floor was the trading house of J. Lipschitz and the iron sheeting shop of Lebensold & Berlewi.

In 1910, Number Seven was the place to go if you had a craving for *cholent* and *kugel*. The building retains the interior from the kosher restaurant that took up three rooms of the ground floor before the war. The restaurant, which included a bar as well, was opened by Itzek Blumenfeld. It became quite popular among both locals and visitors, particularly during the interwar period. Two wooden double doors entered into the restaurant, which boasted a wooden bar lit with gas lamps, mirrors on the walls, and tables supplied with bread for the customary blessing. It was strictly kosher; the proprietor was so devout that he even put up a *mezuzah* in the cloakroom.

Fourteen

The remarkable corner building of Number Fourteen has a second address, Number Six, on the side facing plac Grzybowski. It was most likely built by Brauman in approximately 1899–1900, and instantly transformed the skyline around Grzybowski Square into a relatively modern, urban area. Smaller buildings were built in the expansive courtyard. It was noted for its metal balconies on the fourth floor, as well as an exquisite marble staircase adorned with a hand-wrought bannister. The metal fixation is no surprise; the building was owned by the family of hardware magnate Majer Wolanowski, one of the main suppliers to Russia of railroad, telegraph, and telephone parts.

On the ground floor facing plac Grzybowski, one could find metalmen at all times of the day. There were hardware stores, an iron goods shop, a shop devoted exclusively to nails, a shop for water pipes and valves. On the Prozna side were, among other shops, the tin and iron warehouse of H. B. Lebensold and the framing and carpetlaying supply shop of P. Brykier. Later, a saddle shop was opened, as well as a jewelry store and a wire and nails shop. Of particular interest was an entire apartment in Number Fourteen made into a *shtiebel*, one of the three hundred *shtiebels* found in Warsaw apartments before the war.

During the First World War, the building housed a shelter for homeless Jewish children. After the Warsaw Ghetto Uprising, it housed a secret bunker of the Jewish Fighting Organization [ZOB], which was discovered by the Nazis after a betrayal in 1944. There was a short battle, at the end of which the hidden Jews were killed.

Twelve

Number Twelve was built later than the other buildings on Prozna Street, and it shows. Prozna Street's most wealthy residents lived in this sumptuous six-story structure with a white marble staircase and crystal mirror. Even if you couldn't afford to live in Number Twelve, you could get your hair done to look like you did. On the ground floor was M. Braun's hairdressing salon, as well as a grocery, a hardware store, an electronics bureau, and two trading houses.

One of Number Twelve's most renowned tenants was Abraham Gepner (1872–1943), chairman of the Jewish Merchants' Association and a Warsaw city councilman. During the war, Gepner served as the head of the Supply Authority, which controlled the supply of food in the ghetto. Gepner was one of the few members of the Judenrat who was respected and admired by his fellow Jews. In spite of his advanced years, he maintained positive contacts with the underground. During the Warsaw Ghetto Uprising he was murdered at the corner of Gesia and Zamenhofa.

Number Ten, which no longer exists, was once one of the most well-known buildings in Warsaw. It was on the rooftop of Number Ten that the Bell Telephone Company set up Warsaw's first telephone transmission station, where it remained until 1904.

On the other side of plac Grzybowski are the communal institutions of the Warsaw Jewish Community today. The Jewish Theater, along with several administrative offices of the Community, are housed in the building with the "Deutsche Bank" sign. The entrance to the Jewish Theater is on the left side.

THE JEWISH THEATER

plac Grzybowski 12/16

The Jewish Theater contains offices of the Socio-Cultural Society of Jews in Poland. Naturally, it also hosts theatrical performances. However, it is a far cry from the heyday of Yiddish theater before the war. It's also a far cry from the State Jewish Theater led by Ida Kaminska after the war. Today, many of the actors are not Jewish; most do not speak Yiddish. The productions are nonsensical. Unfortunately, the theater is one of the few Jewish cultural forums in the capital.

Behind the Jewish Theater and beyond the parking lot is a white building at Twarda Street 6. Before the war, the building housed a Jewish medical clinic. There are remains of paint labelling an x-ray room on one of its interior walls. Today the building houses offices of the Ronald S. Lauder Foundation, the Association of Hidden Children of the Holocaust, a youth club, as well as Jewish tour guide services for sites throughout Poland. Next door and to the right is the Nozyk Synagogue.

THE NOZYK SYNAGOGUE

Address: Twarda Street 6

The synagogue is open during regular office hours, roughly 9:00 A.M.–4:00 P.M., and during services. Access to the synagogue is not through the main entrance on the far side, but through the attached office building of the Jewish Religious Union in Poland.

All cities in Europe have their Jewish mysteries, unexplained phenomenon that beg a suspension of disbelief. Is the Golem really sleeping in the attic of the Altneuschul in Prague? Did Cracow's King Casimir the Great really have a Jewish mistress named Esterka?

In postwar Warsaw, most of the mysteries revolve around what is hidden beneath the ground, where wartime rubble buried human life and human memoir. But the Nozyk Synagogue has its own mystery, if relatively mundane. Even though it was built as recently as the turn of the twentieth century, we do not know the identity of its architect. Scholars have their ideas, but to this day who designed the building remains a perplexing mystery.

We do know who had it built. Zalman and Ryvka Nozyk, who lived nearby at 9 Prozna Street (*see page 247*), were a wealthy couple who had no children throughout their marriage. Perhaps eager to leave something for future generations, and perhaps yearning to be remembered after their deaths, they had the Nozyk Synagogue built in 1898–1902. In his will, Nozyk made it clear that the congregation was to say the *El male rachamim* prayer for him and his wife during all *yizkor* services.

The synagogue's dimensions are over nineteen by fifteen meters. It holds three hundred men and three hundred women. Unfortunately, there are no unique details on the interior to mention. The Nozyk Synagogue is famous today not for its design but because it is the only synagogue to have survived the German occupation and the only synagogue in use in Warsaw today. There is some symbolism: The *aron hakodesh* contains twelve columns, symbolizing the twelve tribes of Israel. In 1923, the choir space was added behind the *aron hakodesh*. In front of the *aron hakodesh* are two *parochet* curtains. The Joint Distribution Committee supplies the yearly *parochet* and a special white *parochet* has been supplied by the Ronald S. Lauder foundation for the High Holidays. Both *parochets* point to the murders during the Holocaust and new life afterwards.

For some time during the war, the Nozyk Synagogue continued to remain in use for the ghetto's Jews. Baptized Jews who were trapped in the ghetto attended the nearby All Saints Church, off plac Grzybowski. When services coincided in both buildings, there were often scuffles outside between the two groups. In many cases, Jews felt betrayed by their baptized peers, and baptized Jews felt hatred for a nation they had tried so hard to escape.

After the ghetto was destroyed in 1943, the Germans used the synagogue as a stable for horses. It was renovated from 1977 to 1983, and is now the single place of prayer for the Warsaw Jewish Community. It is no accident that this walk ends at the primary symbol of Polish Jewish continuity today. In the coming years, the Nozyk Synagogue will hopefully serve as the cradle of a growing Jewish Community in the capital.

The preceding walk was about a mile long, or the equivalent of a dozen or so city blocks of what were once predominantly Jewish streets of Warsaw. Had you taken this route during the interwar period, you would have passed literally thousands of Jews walking from work, picking up food for dinner, preparing for a special rendezvous, or just standing around on the streets that once comprised Jewish Warsaw.

Elsewhere in Warsaw: Praga

Praga, the threshold of Warsaw—the aroma of the country, with its broad fields, so many times desolated by wars and fires and rebuilt, remnants of trenches, a battlefield and a cattle market, too large to be a suburb and too small to be a separate organism, a gateway to Warsaw. But for us, Jews, an older Community, squeezed together—where the old synagogue was secluded and the old cemetery hidden, with large stores and the tiniest shops, and where Jews had the right of residence when they did not yet have it in Warsaw proper . . .

Nahum Sokolow, "Henri Bergson's Old-Warsaw Lineage," in Lucy S. Dawidowicz, ed., *The Golden Tradition: Jewish Life and Thought in Eastern Europe*

Nathan Sokolow wasn't exaggerating when he spoke of the magnetic aura of Praga. Located on the other side of the Vistula River, Praga hosted a thriving Jewish Community starting in the eighteenth century. It is a highly recommended addition to any visit to Warsaw.

A BRIEF HISTORY OF PRAGA

While the Jews were strictly excluded from residence in Warsaw, an adjacent Jewish Community sprouted in the then-separate city of Praga. Although it technically shared the "privilege" *de non tolerandis Judaeis*—to exclude Jews—Praga was much more lax in enforcing the law than its sister city Warsaw. Whenever there was an outbreak of anti-Semitism in Warsaw—and there were many—Jews would come streaming across the river to the hospitable shores of Praga. Toward the middle of the eighteenth century, a cemetery was established. It was closed in 1760 but reopened in 1780. By 1787, Jews counted for twenty percent of the population of Praga.

Praga was the home of the legendary Shmuel Zbitkower (1730s–1801), a merchant who singlehandedly built the Jewish quarter. To this day, that quarter is unofficially known as "Szmulewizna," named after Zbitkower. From the moment he moved from Zbitkow to Praga in 1756, Zbitkower jump started the appearance and economy of the city. His entrepreneurial successes ranged from real estate deals to lumber shipping, from sawmill construction to brewery management, from operation of salt mines to management of a kosher slaughterhouse. He was beloved by King Stanislaw Augustus. He was apparently beloved even by the Russian Cossacks, who thanked him for his military supplies during the Russian occupation. Under the Prussian occupation, King Frederick gave him permission to live in Warsaw, but Zbitkower was a dedicated Praga man and he remained in Praga until his death.

Almost all aspects of Praga Jewish history, from its cemetery to the Russian slaughters of 1794, touched in some way upon Zbitkower. He served as tax collector, or "Elder of the Jews," from 1773. In 1788 he was made *parnas* of the Community. King Stanislaw Augustus bought the area containing the Jewish cemetery and rented it to Zbitkower from 1780. Zbitkower also had the Praga Synagogue built (it has been since destroyed). His descendants continued to serve as leaders of the Praga Jewish Community until the twentieth century.

Polish nationalism among the Jews of Praga spread quickly after the first and second partitions of Poland. In the failed insurrection of 1794, Jews played an active role as city guards and soldiers. Berek Joselewicz (c. 1770–1809), a Praga Jew, became a hero of the insurrection, leading a regiment of five hundred Jews. After the insurrection was defeated, the Russian armies vented themselves on Jewish communities throughout the occupied land, particularly on Praga. The Jewish streets of Praga were subjected to wholesale slaughter, and most of the Jews living in Praga were murdered. But even this defeat has a legend: Shmuel Zbitkower allegedly placed two giant barrels in front of his home: one filled with gold ducats, the other with silver rubles. He paid the Russian soldiers in gold for every live Jew they brought back, and in silver for every Jewish corpse. In this way, he saved a remnant of Praga's Jews. By the end of the day, both barrels were empty.

Jews returned to Praga soon after the carnage, and rebuilt a thriving Community that remained vital during the ascendance of Warsaw as the center of Jewish life in the nineteenth century. Praga was incorporated into Warsaw in the 1830s, but it wasn't until 1870 that the two Jewish Communities merged under the banner of the Warsaw Jewish Community. Eventually, Praga lost much of its prominence and became an area where poorer Jews lived; nonetheless, it retained both its vibrancy and its legendary mystique right up to the Second World War.

Originally, Praga had been the Germans' chosen location for the Warsaw ghetto. They felt that its separate location across the Vistula made it perfectly suitable for isolating the Jews. Later an idea was floated to contain the Jews in two suburban ghettos. Ultimately, though, both plans were abandoned. Instead, they decided to use the Jewish district in Warsaw, where the Jewish population was densest. Moving the remaining Jews there would be the quickest and most expedient method of incarceration. The Jews were given until October 31, 1940, to move into the ghetto, but the Jews of Praga kept thinking that a separate Praga ghetto would be created. By the last week of October, it became clear that these rumors were unfounded, and the Jews of Praga hurried in a large stream over the Vistula into the Jewish district of Warsaw. Along with the rest of the Jews of Warsaw, almost all of the Jews of Praga were murdered by the Nazis in the Warsaw ghetto and in Treblinka.

VISITING PRAGA

An excursion across the river into Praga is highly recommended for two reasons. First, this district was settled by Jews while the doors of Warsaw were still sealed tight. Second, only in Praga are there entire neighborhoods whose buildings completely survived the war.

This second reason is probably the most compelling, given the aesthetic nightmare that is downtown Warsaw today. Unlike Warsaw itself, where eighty-four percent of the city was destroyed in 1944, Praga survived the war virtually intact. In fact, while the Germans were carpet bombing Warsaw, the Red Army was stationed right across the river in Praga, casually smoking cigarettes and observing the spectacle. Some say it was in the Russian interest to have a prostrate Poland ripe for a postwar communist takeover, and so they let the Germans do their dirty work. In any event, today's Praga is filled with buildings from the nineteenth and twentieth centuries.

Here in Praga, one can at least imagine what the streets were like over in Warsaw. Of course, you should keep in mind that as Warsaw rose in importance in the nineteenth century, and as barriers to Jews were successfully broken down, Praga became a more impoverished section of town, for both Jews and Gentiles.

Visitors to Praga should also be aware that parts of Praga are not the safest areas of town. Although crime in the district is relatively mild compared to any American city, you should be alert: no flashy cameras, and don't go wandering alone at night. In 1996, a scholar of Jewish history was videotaping tombstones in the cemetery. He was held up in broad daylight and his camcorder was stolen.

Don't let these precautions dissuade you from strolling through Praga's streets and summoning an image of Warsaw before the war.

SELECTED HIGHLIGHTS

What follows are some of the more interesting streets and addresses in Praga's former Jewish district. It is a sample: a former *mikveh* here, the site of a synagogue there. The district of Szmulewizna is situated northeast of Targowa Street. However, in the nineteenth and twentieth centuries the Jewish district moved west, closer to the river.

The Praga Jewish Cemetery

The cemetery stands at the junction of Odrowaza and Wincentego streets. The entrance is at the end of Biruty Street.

The earliest Jewish settlers in Praga buried their dead in this area from the 1740s. When Christians protested against Jews maintaining a cemetery, it was closed in 1760. Four years later, before he was coronated, King Stanislaw Augustus himself purchased the land. The king was a friend of Shmuel Zbitkower, and he rented the land to him for forty years starting in 1780. Zbitkower paid rent for the land and gave an annual supply of one hundred kilograms of wax to a local church. Burials began in earnest in 1780. Toward the end of the nineteenth century, the Praga Jewish Cemetery became the burial place mostly for poor Jews. Wealthier Jews could afford to be buried across the river in the Jewish Cemetery in Warsaw.

During the war, the Nazis destroyed most of the cemetery. The most famous tombstones stood over the graves of Zbitkower and Abraham Stern (1762–1842), inventor of the calculating machine. Both tombstones were destroyed during the war. Although parts of the cemetery have been restored, it is still in a badly deteriorated condition. The Germans used many of the tombstones in road building; others were later shifted to make room for a park. The area where tombstones are today is the oldest part of the cemetery. However, some of the tombstones were moved here from other parts of the cemetery after the war. The two columns at the entrance of the cemetery memorialize the beginning and end of Jewish life in Warsaw: One remembers Shmuel Zbitkower, the other remembers the Jews of Praga mass murdered in the Holocaust.

The streets northwest of Szwedzka and Al. Solidarnosci are a well-preserved representation of what used to be a Jewish district in Praga. Typical brick houses had two or three floors, balconies, stripped facades—like parts of the Lower East Side of New York at the turn of the century. For instance, you'll find a classic prewar building at 14 Brodnowska Street, and there are dozens of similar buildings in the area. Brodnowska is fairly close to the cemetery.

Strzelecka Street 11/13

This building, at the corner of Strzelecka and Srodkowa, contained a *shtiebel*, or Jewish prayer hall, before the war. It was mostly used by poorer Jews in Praga. Today, the building no longer has any Hebrew or other identifying marks on the facade or inside. This building is one of only two remaining former *shtiebel* buildings in Praga. In all of Warsaw, there were approximately three hundred *shtiebels* before the war.

Parallel to Strzelecka Street is Stalowa Street, where you'll find the area of a former *mikveh*:

Stalowa Street 42

In the courtyard of this building, on the left side (when you're facing the back), there used to stand a *mikveh* before the war. A wooden part of the enclosure still exists, but the rest of the extension was destroyed in a fire in the 1990s.

Mala Street

This little street is a perfect place to experience the look and feel of a prewar Jewish neighborhood in Praga or Warsaw. Of course, none of those places was purely Jewish, but in many instances, the streets were populated mostly by Jews. Mala Street can give you some idea of what Krochmalna Street (*see page 240*) looked like before it was destroyed. When film crews want to shoot a scene of "Old Warsaw" before the war, they use Praga's Mala Street as the natural backdrop.

In the courtyards of these buildings you can often find broken water pumps that predate private apartment plumbing.

The area of Praga around Jagiellonska Street contains several buildings that once served the Warsaw Jewish Community.

Klopotowskiego Street 31

This private high school used to house another *mikveh* before the war. Further down, to the left of the building, you'll see a fenced-in garden park that was the site of the *beit midrash* built by Berek Sonnenberg, Shmuel Zbitkower's son *(see page 195)*, in the early nineteenth century. In 1840, a round-shaped synagogue was built next door. It was destroyed in the 1950s.

On the left side of the *mikveh* building at 31 Klopotowskiego Street (on the side facing the park), there used to be a kosher butcher.

This area was the center of Jewish life in Praga before the war.

Jagiellonska Street 8

This building was built in 1915 by the Jewish architect Henryk Stifelman. It served until the war as an Orthodox Jewish school, with as many as eight hundred students at any time. In the same building was a foster home for orphaned Jewish children. The construction of the school was spearheaded by Michal Bergson, a nephew of the famous pianist of the same name, who headed the Jewish Community before the war. Bergson was also a descendant of the famed Shmuel Zbitkower. The building is used today as a fairy tale theater for children.

III

Cracow:
City of Legends

Introduction

Of the half-dozen or so streets named after Jews in the Kazimierz quarter of Cracow, perhaps the most enchanting is Esther (*Estery*) Street. A physical landmark named for a pseudo-mythical figure, the street bears witness to the playful union of fact and fantasy in the city.

According to legend, Esterka, a Jewish woman from the town of Opoczno, was the mistress of the famed King Casimir the Great (1300–1370). In one version of the legend, Casimir the Great rescued the infant Esterka from a pogrom; years later, Casimir met the fully grown Esterka by chance during a hunting expedition. Captivated by her beauty, Casimir became infatuated with the Jewess and eventually brought her to the Polish capital, Cracow. Some versions of the legend, borrowing heavily from the story of Purim, have Esterka wedding the king and becoming queen of Poland. It is said that Esterka bore the king two sons, who were raised as Christians, and one daughter, raised as a Jew. Alternate endings to the story include Esterka distraught over the death of her lover, either living a life of seclusion or committing suicide.

But was it only legend? No less an authority than the first Polish historian, Jan Dlugosz, recorded the coupling in his fifteenth-century chronicle of Polish history. A century later, the affair was recorded again by David Gans, the famous Jewish chronicler who lived in Cracow and later settled in Prague. Gans went so far as to imply that Esterka was married to the king. Whether mistress or wife, the figure of Esterka pops up throughout the country, in her alleged home in Opoczno, or in castles said to have been built for her by King Casimir in Bochotnica and Nieolomice. Her grave was said to lie near Cracow in the town of Lobzow.

Cracow itself, the seat of royal power in Wawel Castle, became linked to Esterka as the site of her romance with the king. Tradition has it that Esterka left the home of her father, a humble tailor, to live in Cracow near the king. She resided below the castle Kazimierz; her house was said to stand at 46 Krakowska Street. In one version of the tale, King Casimir had a secret tunnel built from Wawel Castle to Esterka's basement. The lovebirds surreptitiously continued their affair away from public scrutiny.

The history-legend has become part and parcel of Cracow lore. Even today, there are dozens of businesses, from pharmacies to discotheques, which proudly bear the name "Esterka." Although the name might also refer to the business owner, one cannot escape a *double entendre* whenever the name Esterka crops up in Cracow.

Thousands of Jewish legends have emerged from Galician cities and hamlets, but few are as well-known as the story of King Casimir and Esterka. For this reason, Esterka has become a sort of vanguard for the fertile imagination of Polish Jews. That Esterka became a symbol for Cracow is also no coincidence. Perhaps more than any other city in Poland, Cracow was a breeding ground for over five hundred years of Jewish legend and anecdote, whispered rumor, and murmured fancy. In Cracow, rabbis flew on magic carpets; priceless treasures were hidden in simple homes; righteous men were tested by the Devil himself. A walk through the Old Jewish Cemetery of Cracow is a trip through tales of inexplicably missing graves and transplanted mystics.

Although Cracow has since shorn its mantle of "Mother of Israel," the streets of Kazimierz, its formerly Jewish district, have maintained much of their erstwhile charm and allure. Indeed, it is here in Cracow that one comes closest to apprehending that which was once commonly accepted in Judaism: That one's actions in the material world are inseparable from goings-on in the transcendent realm. The manifold legends connected to the Jewish district hark back to a day when all aspects of Jewish life were touched by mystical explication.

The Cracow section of this book attempts to recreate as much of this atmosphere as possible by bringing these legends back to life. In the stories of the Jewish district of Cracow, you will encounter an era where sheer wonder was once the defining feature of Jewish life. It was an age in which the harmony of God and man was so fine that there was no distinguishing between the earthly and heavenly spheres: The mundane and the sublime had been joined as one.

A History of the Jews in Cracow

LIFE BEFORE KAZIMIERZ

Long before the Jews were concentrated in Kazimierz, a Jewish Community flourished in Cracow itself. At the time, Cracow stretched no further than the Old Town and Wawel Hill. (The Cracow city walls were destroyed in the beginning of the nineteenth century; in their place Planty encircles the Old Town today.) A permanent Jewish Community existed in Cracow from as early as the thirteenth century.

Ibrahim ibn Jakub, the same travelling scribe who observed Jews in Prague in 965, rode his horse and carriage for three weeks until he arrived in Cracow after leaving Prague. There he also observed Jewish merchants, but implied that the Jews were migrants and didn't have a permanent footing in the city. What is interesting is that Ibrahim ibn Jakub recorded a trade route between the Jews of Cracow and Prague. Even in the tenth century, the two cities had a Jewish connection.

Most of the Jews entered Cracow from the west: from Germany and Bohemia, especially from Prague. In Silesia, the first records of Jewish communal buildings are from the twelfth and thirteenth centuries. From there, Jews moved northeast during the thirteenth century to greater Poland. Finally, in the last decade of the thirteenth century, the Jews migrated to southern Poland, where they settled for the most part in Cracow. The oldest document that notes a permanent Jewish presence in Cracow is from 1304, in which a certain "Jewish Street" is mentioned.

The "Jewish Street" mentioned in 1304 is St. Anne's Street today. It runs off the main square in the Old Town, and was once the home of most of Cracow's Jews. The street extended all the way to the city walls, where there stood a so-called Jewish Gate. Beyond the gate, past water and gardens, was the Jewish cemetery. There are two theories about this cemetery. Some scholars think it was located just outside the city walls, while others believe it was much farther from the Old Town, where Kaviory Street is located today. The name Kaviory, in fact, probably has roots in the Hebrew word *kever*, or "grave." The cemetery was destroyed when the Jews were expelled from Cracow in 1494, and no traces remain.

There were two synagogues on Jewish Street. The first record of one is from 1356. It was located where the Jagiellonian Library later stood. Records exist of a *mikveh* on the street in 1358. Today, no traces of either the two synagogues or the *mikveh* remain.

There were difficult times for the Jews during the Black Plague of 1348–1349. The Christian population was enraged that Jews died in fewer numbers during the epidemic, unaware that ritual purity associated with *halachah* made the Jews much less susceptible to the Plague. The Christians insisted that the Jews were poisoning the city water supply, and massacred many Jews in riots on Jewish Street.

As was usually the case, though, life was worse in Germany. The resulting waves of immigration deposited increasing numbers of Jews in places like Poznan, Kalisz, and Cracow, where they became active in trade, craft, and moneylending. In the second half of the fourteenth century, there were around four hundred or five hundred Jews living in Cracow. During the fourteenth century, Poland was probably the safest place for the Jews in all of Central and Eastern Europe.

KING CASIMIR THE GREAT

Every city has its benevolent Gentile leader who merges into myth as a benefactor of the Jews. In Prague it was the deranged Rudolf II; in Cracow, this hero was King Casimir the Great. As usual, the legend machine went into overdrive. One story says that the greatest number of Jewish immigrants to Poland came during King Casimir's reign. One of Cracow's most inexplicable legends—the Esterka story (*see page 259*)—attempts to explain King Casimir's kindness toward the Jews.

Under King Casimir, the Jews received the royal protection necessary for survival, not to mention prosperity. In 1334 the king reissued the Royal Charter, originally granted in 1264, of legal residency for the Jews in Poland, free movement from place to place, the safety of Jewish life, religious freedom, and free trade in both currency and goods. One important aspect of this charter was that the Jews would be judged either by the waywode—the regional administrator—or, in special cases, by the king himself. City councils, which were known to issue draconian restrictions on Jewish life and trade, were severely weakened in their authority over the Jews. Another important point involved free trade privileges. The Jews were allowed to lend money on the security of property and land. The Royal Charter was reissued in 1364 and 1367.

During the reign of King Casimir the Great, many Jews found office in the Royal Court. The most successful among them was a Jewish banker named Lewko ben Jordan. Lewko (who lived till around 1395) was the wealthiest man in the Cracow Jewish Community in the middle of the fourteenth century. The king's treasurer, Lewko lent money to both the king and the court, traded real estate, ran a beer brewery, and leased the king's most profitable industry: the salt mines in Wieliczka and Bochnia.

Jewish involvement in trade and tax collecting led to a rising jealousy among the Gentile population. It didn't help that certain Jews such as Lewko were highly visible as counselors to the king. Legends arose—with their usual anti-Semitic twinge—that Lewko had a magic ring that he used to wield power over King Casimir. With economic tensions mounting between Jew and Gentile, the fifteenth century ushered in an immediate change in Jewish fortune.

THE DARK AGE OF THE FIFTEENTH CENTURY

Those who point to Polish anti-Semitism as a peasant phenomenon would be interested to note that in Cracow, attacks were largely perpetrated by students at the university. What this says about the Polish intelligentsia has not yet been fully determined.

The crucial date is 1400. In the summer of that year, King Wladyslaw Jagiello re-established the Cracow Academy right in the middle of Jewish Street, in two houses purchased from Jews. We do not know why the king chose this street, but it was to be a source of acrimony for years to come. It wasn't only the overcrowding that resulted on the street, but student hostility in economic matters. In order to placate the Jews over the loss of their houses, the king created the position of Jewish banker who would loan money to the students. As a "privileged servant" of the university, the banker would defend his fellow Jews against abuse by the students. Naturally, the students resisted having to pay interest to a Jew. In addition, the Jews had to pay a sort of blackmail: The students would "protect" the Jews from attacks by their own, as long as the Jews paid for all of the students' books and supplies.

On the third day of Easter in 1407, an infamous pogrom was launched in Cracow, using as its pretext the perennial slander of blood libel. A Catholic priest named Budek delivered a speech claiming that Jews had murdered a Christian baby. Immediately there was a rush to Jewish Street to massacre the Jews. Even the city bells were rung, as the entire city was enveloped in a thirst for blood. The sewers became filled with stolen bounty, which the Christians hid until the storm blew over. On Jewish Street, an orgy of looting and violence, many Jews hid in St. Anne's Church. The Cracowians surrounded the building and actually burned their own church to the ground in order to exterminate the Jews inside. The fire killed the Jews and destroyed several Jewish homes as well. In the midst of the carnage, many Jews accepted baptism in order to save their lives. After the pogrom, King Wladyslaw Jagiello accused the City Council of inciting the riots and the council was forced to try the perpetrators in court. After much haggling, thirty-five rioters were turned over. It was obvious, however, that practically all of Cracow took part in the riots. The trial dragged on for two years; the outcome is unknown.

The change from tolerance in the fourteenth century to fanatical hatred in the fifteenth resulted from several factors. First of all, King Wladyslaw Jagiello had no inclination to protect the Jews as did King Casimir. Increasing Jewish competition in trade, as well as the success of individual Jews in the Royal Court, was a source of hostility among jealous Cracowians. Rising Christian intolerance toward everything non-Christian was also a crucial factor, as was the constant struggle between students and Jews on Jewish Street.

In 1423 and 1454, the Jews of Cracow were subjected to further pogroms for reasons largely economic: the Gentiles detested the Jews as moneylenders and as unwanted trade competition. Had it not been for Christian dogma, however, it is possible that the Cracowian crowds would not have been aroused to murder. Christian speeches, designed as they were to dehumanize the Jews and thus to justify slaughter, were sparks thrown into a powder keg looking for an excuse to erupt. The pogrom in 1454 was connected with the visit of Jan Capistrano, the notorious Franciscan counselor to the Pope who inspired killing in the name of Roman Catholicism throughout Europe. That year, a fire next door to the Church of St. Peter burned down a hundred homes and four churches. Jews were accused of starting the fire, and the resulting pogrom took many Jewish lives.

By the 1460s it became apparent that the growing Cracow Academy would not be satisfied until it had taken over all of Jewish Street. In 1469 the Jewish Community was forced into a "transaction" with the university, represented by the famous and not entirely philo-Semitic historian Jan Dlugosz. The Jews were forced to relinquish to the academy both synagogues, the cemetery, *mikvehs*, hospitals, and all other buildings on Jewish Street. In return, they received Szczepanska (St. Steven's) Square, next to a pre-existing fifteenth-century synagogue (since destroyed).

In 1485 the Jews had to accept an even more crippling City Council decision. The Jews were allowed to remain in Cracow only on the condition that they resign all commercial rights in the city. Jews were permitted to sell only materials that they had obtained as security for moneylending, and nothing else. Even this they could do only on Tuesdays, Fridays, and market days. The only handcrafts the Jews were permitted to make and sell were bonnets and collars sewn by Jewish women. The law effectively disenfranchised the Jews of Cracow, erasing most of the economic rights they had been granted in the previous two centuries. The Jews had no choice but to accept the ruling if they wanted to remain in the city. According to Majer Balaban, the great historian of Cracow's Jews, "For life, they gave up life. In order to remain in Cracow, they resigned their commercial rights" (Majer Balaban, *Historja zydow w Krakowie i na Kazimierzu, 1304–1868*).

The turning point came one night in June 1494. A huge fire erupted on Szewska Street, near the heart of Jewish Cracow. Three gates—St. Nicholas, Florianska, and Slawkowska—were burnt down. The crowd, as was its custom by now, used the conflagration as an excuse to loot Jewish Street and massacre Jews. This time, the Jews took up arms to defend themselves. Many were killed in the ensuing street battles. When it was over, both the Jewish Community and the City Council went to King Jan Olbracht with complaints. The king sided with the City Council and imprisoned leaders of the Jewish Community, including Rabbi Jakob Polak, who started the first *yeshivah* in Cracow. Thanks to the intercession of the famous humanist Filippo Buonaccorsil, who served as the teacher of the king's children, the leaders were freed. In fact, King Jan Olbracht changed his attitude toward the Jews as a result of Buonaccorsil's intervention. As usual, though, the City Council was protected and encouraged in its anti-Semitism by the Church. The king's brother, Cardinal Frederik, coerced his brother into settling the Jewish question once and for all. Swayed by his brother, Jan Olbracht expelled the Jews from Cracow. In 1495, the Jews left Cracow for Kazimierz. All their homes and synagogues that had not been destroyed were appropriated by the Cracow Academy.

THE JEWS IN KAZIMIERZ

One of the most common misunderstandings about Cracow Jewish history is that the city forced the Jews into the ghetto-like enclave in Kazimierz, so chosen because it was isolated like an island, surrounded at the time by water on three sides.

In fact, the king did not send the Jews to Kazimierz. He decreed only that they could not remain overnight in Cracow. The Jews themselves *chose* Kazimierz for many reasons: It was close to Cracow; there was already a Jewish Community established there; and the Kazimierz City Council was willing to sell additional grounds to the Jews. Even after they had moved to Kazimierz, the Jews referred to themselves as the Jewish Community of Cracow. Some even hoped that when the fury passed they would be readmitted into Cracow itself.

Cracow and Kazimierz were twin cities at the time, separated by water. Dietla Street was once an arm of the Vistula River, as were parts of Grzegorzecka Street and Daszynskiego Street. Kazimierz was connected to Cracow by bridges; the waterways were filled in with land only at the end of the nineteenth century. Jews were still permitted to come to Cracow during the daily markets, and some Jews opened shops on Tomasza Street in the city. At night, though, they had to return to Kazimierz.

Kazimierz was founded by King Casimir the Great in 1335. Even before the Jews were expelled from Cracow in 1495, a smaller, sister Community had existed in Kazimierz. Two Jews are mentioned in the archives as early as 1386. According to some accounts, this is the period when the wondrous Altschul (*see page 294*) was built. A century later, in 1485, is the first mention of a *mikveh* in Kazimierz. In 1488 there was a Jewish marketplace. From these facts we know that on the eve of the expulsion of Jews from Cracow, there already existed in Kazimierz a Jewish Community, a synagogue, a cemetery, and a *mikveh*. It is no wonder, then, that Cracow's Jews chose Kazimierz as their new home.

THE JEWISH QUARTER OF KAZIMIERZ

The Jewish Quarter of Kazimierz was established in the northeast corner of the city. In the beginning of the sixteenth century, the Jews were concentrated almost exclusively on Szeroka Street, known at the time as Hoykhegas (High Street). Their borders were easily demarcated by the synagogue and by the Kazimierz city walls: the Altschul stood at the southern end, and the city walls along Miodowa Street and Dajwor Street formed the borders to the north and east. The cemetery was probably located in the northern part of Szeroka Street, where there is a fenced-in yard today (*see The Cemetery Square, page 337*). Everywhere else was off limits; the blatantly anti-Semitic City Council of Kazimierz refused to allot any further land to the Jews. As a result, the Jewish Community was in open confrontation with the City Council for the next 350 years. These disputes concerned both the expansion of the Jewish Quarter and the granting of equal commercial rights to the Jews.

Needless to say, the Jewish Quarter soon became overcrowded. Throughout the first half of the sixteenth century, Jews continued to pour into Cracow from nearby Bohemia, which was experiencing a resurgence of anti-Semitism. In 1542, after the expulsion of Jews from Bohemia, Polish King Sigismund I allowed the refugees to build homes and shops in Kazimierz. In addition, Jews came to Cracow from places as diverse as Germany, Italy, Spain, and Portugal. By the middle of the century, the Jewish Quarter was bursting at the seams. Jews began to pay outlandish sums for illegal space outside the ghetto; some even built illegal shops there. This infuriated the City Council, which repeatedly entreated the king to pass further decrees against the Jews. In 1543, only one year after sanctioning the influx of Bohemian Jews, King Sigismund I relented to pressure and closed the borders. Still, wealthier Jews managed to trickle in. The king also forbade Jews from buying any homes outside the Jewish ghetto. Meanwhile the City Council prohibited Jews from dealing in wine and honey, two of the more lucrative industries in Cracow. As if all this weren't enough, the cemetery on Szeroka Street was full, and the Jews were desperate for new burial space. The Jewish Community had bought nearby land for an additional cemetery in 1533 (today's Old Jewish Cemetery), but the City Council was dragging its feet on issuing a cemetery permit. If an agreement wasn't reached soon, the ghetto would explode.

Finally, in 1553, a deal was struck. It was the first of three deals that were to expand the perimeter of the ghetto to more breathable dimensions. The Jews were permitted to buy some land south of the Altschul and west of Szeroka Street. It was agreed that a wall be built around the Jewish Quarter. A total of three gates would connect the Jewish Quarter with the Christian areas of Kazimierz. The Jews would pay for the land as well as an annual tax for the right to live there. In addition, the Jews were finally permitted to turn their new cemetery land into a cemetery.

As if a dam had at last been lifted, the Jews erected a wave of synagogues in the new territory. The Rema Synagogue was built in 1553. Almost immediately afterwards, the High Synagogue was built a block away. But after only a decade, the additional land again proved insufficient. Enough Sephardic Jews arrived in the 1560s that they established their own subCommunity in Kazimierz, complete with Sephardic prayer houses. Immigration mixed with increased births in the enclosed ghetto quickly led to overcrowding. Although the Jews were required to return to the ghetto by nightfall, many began to live—again illegally—beyond the ghetto walls. King Sigismund August tried to help in 1564 by forbidding Christians from living in the Jewish Quarter. This helped matters a little, but soon enough the City Council began arguing that Jewish trade as well as residence should be restricted to the ghetto.

The next deal between the City Council and the Jewish Community was brokered in 1583. The Jewish Quarter was somewhat extended, and the three gates were reduced to one. This single gate stood at the corner of Jozefa and Jakuba Streets, near the High Synagogue. In 1608–09, the final land expansion agreement was signed between the City Council and the Jewish Community. The Jewish Quarter was now defined by the city walls of Kazimierz on two sides (Miodowa Street and Dajwor Street), by Wawrzynca Street to the south and Bozego Ciala Street to the west. Of course, problems arose in reference to the Church of Corpus Christi, whose land and gardens encroached on twenty percent of the new Jewish Quarter. Eventually the Jews were forced to surround the church area with a wall, to exempt it from Jewish jurisdiction, and, in an interesting twist of logic, to pay the church 250 zlotys per year. Waska and Jozefa Streets became the new southern borders of the ghetto. This agreement was ratified in 1627. Over the course of the next decade, affluent Jews built homes in the new part of the ghetto.

In the 1570s, the Jewish population of Kazimierz topped two thousand. By the middle of the next century, the population reached forty-five hundred. In comparison, around five thousand Christians lived in Kazimierz, in an area that was five times the size of the Jewish ghetto. Although the Jewish Quarter had expanded, it was still the most overcrowded and congested district in Kazimierz.

THE KAZIMIERZ GHETTO?

There is some debate regarding use of the term "ghetto" for the Jewish Quarter of Kazimierz. This is largely due to the disparate meanings of the term "ghetto" in Polish and English. In the Polish language, "getto" conjures up memories of the Second World War, when Jews were consolidated in enclosed areas prior to their systematic murder. The word "getto" is linked to this extermination, and some Polish Jews argue that use of the term in prewar contexts distorts the uniqueness of the Holocaust. However, in the English language, "ghetto" means any restricted urban enclosure—even, as the term is used in modern American English, when the restrictions evolve not out of legal precepts but out of economic circumstance.

In Kazimierz, the Jews were surrounded by walls and gates, and were permitted outside the district only during certain daytime hours. In the English language, that was a ghetto. But be prepared for some misunderstanding if you use the term "ghetto" when speaking to Jewish or Gentile Poles.

THE GOLDEN AGE

When the Kazimierz ghetto began to expand in the second half of the sixteenth century, the Jews of Cracow entered roughly four decades of unprecedented prosperity. But it wasn't only the new living space that changed Jewish fortune: Golden Ages for Europe's Jews were often linked to royal indulgence, and Cracow was no exception. The Golden Age for the Jews in Cracow occurred from 1548 to 1586, during the reigns of King Sigismund August and King Stefan Batory.

Sigismund August was known for his religious tolerance. His mother, Queen Bona, was an Italian who essentially brought the Italian Renaissance to Cracow. Mingling with the Jews in his mother's royal court, Sigismund August acquired an appreciation for religious pluralism that was centuries ahead of his time. When he became king, the Jewish question became a chief concern. He was dedicated to alleviating the overcrowding in the Kazimierz ghetto. In the 1550s, the king assisted the Jews in enlarging their living space.

It was during the reign of King Sigismund August that the Jews built two synagogues in addition to the Altschul: the Rema Synagogue and the High Synagogue. The Rema Synagogue was built by Israel Lazars, a merchant with much influence in the royal court. The synagogue was named after his son, Rabbi Moses Isserles, known by the acronym "Rema" and one of the greatest halachists in Jewish history. The Rema, who codified Jewish law for all of Ashkenazic Jewry, was a cornerstone of Jewish learning and wisdom throughout

Poland. It was under his tenure that Cracow cemented its reputation as the most dynamic Jewish center in the Diaspora.

A mark of Jewish achievement was the number of Jewish doctors who served the king during these years. Samuel Bar Meshulam was imported from Italy by the king's mother. When he died, King Sigismund August brought in another Italian Jewish doctor named Solomon Ashkenazi. After he left, the king chose yet another Jewish doctor, the Spanish-descended Solomon Calahora.

Majer Balaban, the great historian of Cracow Jewry, wrote about July 7, 1572, the day King Sigismund August died: "When news of Sigismund August's death came to the Jewish city, Jews burst out in tears with the same grief as on the day Jerusalem was destroyed" (Majer Balaban, *Historja zydow w Krakowie i na Kazimierzu*). Aftershocks of the death spread all over Europe. In Prague, the famous Renaissance Jew David Gans (*see page 12*) scribed an inimitable, Rabelaisian entry concerning the king's death in his history book *Tzemach David*.

In 1576, after a short interim with an anti-Semitic monarch, Stefan Batory was coronated. He continued the spirit of tolerance pioneered by King Sigismund August. At his coronation, King Stefan Batory reaffirmed the rights of the Jews and went on to protect them from intolerance and attacks. King Stefan Batory was well aware of the contribution of the Jews to the kingdom's economy, and he helped them gain trade rights as well as further expansion of the ghetto in Kazimierz. He added two Jews to his court—Felix, who traded precious stones, and Jakub Ezra, who served as the royal jeweler.

The death of King Stefan Batory in 1586 is commonly considered the end of the Golden Age for the Jews of Kazimierz. His successor, Sigismund III, surrounded himself with Jesuits who campaigned fiercely against the Jews. Soon the Jews found themselves thrown out of the royal court. Cracow itself fell into a political and economic decline starting with King Sigismund III, who moved the capital of Poland from Cracow to Warsaw.

Thus ended a Golden Age catalyzed by the friendly disposition of sixteenth-century monarchs. No longer buoyed by royal protection, the Jewish Community entered a more precarious phase in the seventeenth century in its relationship to Gentile Cracow. Christian fanatics used the opportunity to burn several Jews at the stake during this time. Nonetheless, in terms of Jewish religion and culture, the Golden Age can be said to have extended well into the seventeenth century. Both the illustrious Isaac Synagogue and the Popper Synagogue were built by wealthy *machurs* in this period, while the Jewish Community itself built the Kupa Synagogue. Equally important were the great rabbis who officiated and taught in Cracow at this time. Nathan Nata Spira, the so-called *Megalleh Amukkot* ("Revealer of the Depths"), soared through the heights of kabbalistic wisdom in the early seventeenth century. The preeminent talmudic scholar Joel Sirkes, known as the "Bach," also served as rabbi and head of the *yeshivah*. Rabbi Joshua ben Joseph, called the *Meginnei Shlomo*, gave dazzling explanations of the eleventh-century commentaries of Rashi. Finally, there was Yomtov Lippman Heller, the talmudic genius who came to Cracow to find peace from nasty politics in Prague.

Some of the greatest Jewish legends of all time originated right here in Cracow, amidst the hubbub of wonder-rabbis in the first half of the seventeenth century.

THE COMMERCIAL LIFE OF THE JEWS

Side by side with their struggle for more living space, the Jews continuously fought the City Council of Kazimierz for equal commercial rights. It was not an easy battle. The City Council was committed to protecting Christians in Kazimierz from any sort of economic competition from the Jews. As mentioned above, the council even sought to limit Jewish trade to the ghetto itself.

In 1609, Jews received the right to free trade in Kazimierz and Stradom, with certain exceptions. They could deal in leather, but were prohibited from dealing in leather crafts. Jews were permitted to buy vodka and beer only from Christians in Kazimierz, and could sell it only to fellow Jews. They were not permitted to employ Christian workers. Only eight kosher slaughterhouses were permitted in the ghetto, and only two *mikvehs* (ritual baths).

In spite of the procession of prohibitions, Jewish trade continued in the seventeenth century both in Kazimierz and in Cracow itself. During market days in Cracow, Jews were permitted to deal in wholesale merchandise. Since their shops had to be closed at all other times, Jews paid exorbitant fees to rent warehouse space in Kazimierz, where they stored their goods until the next Cracow market day. If they didn't bring their goods out of Cracow, they were required to sell all their wares at once, normally at rock bottom prices, and only to Cracow buyers.

Among the Jewish merchants in seventeenth-century Kazimierz, a few stand out. The Horowitz family was the largest Jewish family in Cracow. A branch of the Czech Horowitz family that built the Pinchas Synagogue in Prague, the Horowitzes of Cracow were successful merchants who had a magnificent home in the Kazimierz ghetto. Chief among the Cracow Horowitzes was a man named Pinchas; in fact, this Pinchas was most likely the namesake of Prague's Pinchas Synagogue. A senior on the board of the Jewish Community, Pinchas Horowitz helped broker the 1609 deal for trade rights. It was said that nothing happened in Jewish Kazimierz without Pinchas's consent. Another wealthy merchant family was the Jekeles. Jacob Jekeles, known as "Jacob the Rich," loaned five thousand zlotys to King Sigismund August in 1573. His son, the legendary Reb Isaac Reb Jekeles, was the chief benefactor of the Jews. He built the Isaac Synagogue in 1638. Other merchant families included the Poppers, who built the Popper Synagogue, and the family of Saul Wahl, the Jew who served, according to legend, as the king of Poland for a single night.

TERRIBLE TIMES

Disaster struck when the Swedish army occupied Cracow and Kazimierz in September 1655. What followed was the classic Jewish experience of being attacked by both sides in a war. First the Swedes spent three days murdering and looting throughout Kazimierz. Then Polish soldiers entered the Jewish Quarter and stole everything that wasn't rooted to the ground. A total of seven hundred thousand zlotys were stolen and the Jews lost around one million zlotys from the combined Swedish and Polish rampage. Many Jews fled the devastated city. By the end of the two-year Swedish occupation (1655–57), there were only eighteen hundred Jews in the ghetto, where before there had been roughly forty-five hundred. During the occupation, the Swedes destroyed sixty Jewish houses and stationed soldiers inside synagogues and homes, forcing into servility the Jews that remained. The Poles interpreted this as collaboration. After the Swedes were driven out, the Poles accused the Jews of welcoming the Swedes into Kazimierz and of assisting the Swedes in looting church vestments. Obviously none of this was true, but that didn't stop the Poles from handing possession of the entire ghetto to two noblemen, who forced the Jews to buy back their living space. The Jews paid sixty thousand zlotys "punishment" money to the king, and ten thousand zlotys to the church for objects the Swedes had pilfered. The atmosphere following the Swedish occupation was charged with anti-Semitism, leading to pogroms and show trials. In 1663, a well-known Jewish apothecary named Mattathias Calahora was framed for blasphemy, tortured, and burned at the stake.

The harrowing situation was exacerbated by the plague of 1677, which, according to one account, took one thousand Jewish lives and caused most of the remaining Jews to flee Kazimierz. The Jewish Community was so far in debt that in 1679 the king granted it a respite from taxes, but the indigence continued for the Jewish Community authority as well as for most of the Jews of Kazimierz. The Jewish Community took loans wherever it could find them. In the early eighteenth century, it owed money not only to the king, noblemen, and merchants, but even to churches and monasteries. In 1719, this debt totaled six hundred thousand zlotys. Meanwhile, the Jewish Community had to deal with a continuous population drain to the increasingly pivotal capital of Warsaw. As if things couldn't get worse, economic desperation drove Cracow merchants to take their most stringent measures against competition from the Jews. In 1766, Jews were forbidden from all crafts and trade in Cracow.

In 1772, after the first partition of Poland by Prussia, Austria, and Russia, the northern branch of the Vistula became a border between Poland and Austria. Kazimierz thus became Austrian for four years. During this time, Christian merchants argued that the Jews were no longer Polish citizens, and should therefore have absolutely no trade rights in Cracow. All of the daytime Jewish stalls in the Cracow marketplace were liquidated. Most of these Jews opened shops in the Christian district of Kazimierz. Soon there were 350 Jewish merchants in Christian Kazimierz, including forty-five financiers, fifty-two textile merchants, and eighteen innkeepers. In 1796, there were 4,138 Jews living in Kazimierz.

INTO MODERNITY

At the end of the eighteenth century, the most sweeping social change that transformed the Kazimierz Ghetto was the hasidic movement. Hasidism was brought to Cracow almost singlehandedly by Rabbi Kalonymus Kalman Epstein (c. 1763–1823), a mystic who served as a disciple of the hasidic pioneer in Poland, Elimelech of Lizensk. When Rabbi Epstein introduced Hasidism to Cracow, he was met almost instantly with reprobation. In 1785 and 1797, the chief rabbi of Cracow issued a *cherem*, or religious ban, against all hasidic prayer houses and the people who prayed in them. It was no use; by the middle of the nineteenth century, the hasidic movement had become so widespread that it chose its own rabbi and ignored the chief rabbi of the Community. Soon the majority of Cracow's traditional

Jews were hasidic. As a movement it was the most decisive force in the social life of Cracow's Jews until the early twentieth century.

With the creation of the Cracow Republic in 1815, the government began to break down the physical and social barriers that had isolated the Jews in the ghetto. Jews were permitted to settle in parts of Christian Kazimierz, provided that they shed certain defining characteristics of Jewish life. In 1822, the wall of the Jewish ghetto was broken down. Jews were also permitted to live outside Kazimierz if they had a secular education, dressed like Christian Poles, and owned at least five thousand zlotys. It was not an easy qualification to meet: In 1848, only 196 of the thirteen thousand Cracow Jews could meet the requirements. Meanwhile, the state campaign to assimilate the Jews was crude and often destructive. The autonomous Jewish Community was abolished; in its place a Committee for Jewish Affairs was established, headed by a Christian and a rabbi with secular education. In 1830, a Jewish elementary school was opened in which Jews were instructed in secular subjects. Jewish marriages were strictly controlled by the state. Marriages beyond the permitted quota were allowed only for Jews who were relatively well-off, at least 30 years old, dressed like Christian Poles, and had a secular education.

Cracow became part of Austria again in 1846. Decades of emancipatory gestures toward the Jews culminated in 1867, the year Austria and Hungary formed the dual monarchy. In that year, Jews throughout Austro-Hungary were given citizenship rights.

It was with these citizenship rights that Jews were finally permitted to return to Cracow proper without having to meet stringent requirements. The district of Stradom soon rivalled Kazimierz as the best-known Jewish neighborhood in Cracow.

In the second half of the nineteenth century, the divisions between Orthodox Jews and progressive assimilationists reached a critical point. Cracow had been one of Europe's main centers of traditional Jewish life for centuries, and active Orthodox rabbis were determined that this would not change. Cracow's chief rabbi Simeon Sofer (1820–1883), son of the famed Chatam Sofer of Bratislava, founded the *Machzike Hadas* ("Strengthening of the Faith"), a Galician Orthodox organization whose primary aim was to stop the flood of assimilation. Nonetheless, several prominent Jewish intellectuals and activists called for complete Polonization as the surest deterrent to anti-Semitism in Polish society.

By the end of the nineteenth century, Jews in Cracow made strides in all areas of Polish culture and society, from science and education to art and literature. Unlike Prague, which experienced massive erosion of Jewish tradition in the nineteenth century, Cracow maintained a firm bedrock of Yiddishkeit that was expressed even among secular Jews. While Jews in Prague produced a culture that had no relation to Judaism, contemporary Jewish culture in Cracow took a distinctly Jewish turn. **Maurycy Gottlieb** (1856–1879), hailed today as the "Jewish Rembrandt," was an internationally acclaimed Cracow painter who produced indelible depictions of Jewish social and religious life. One of his most famous paintings, "Jews Praying on the Day of Atonement," in which the artist included a self-portrait, is one of the most famous depictions of East European Jewish life to this day. **Sarah Schnirer** (1883–1935) was a pioneering Jewish feminist within the Orthodox world. Dissatisfied by the lack of a Jewish educational system for young girls, Schnirer started the *Beis Yaakov* (House of Jacob) school for Jewish girls in Cracow in 1918. By the 1930s, there were over two hundred *Beis Yaakov* schools with over 25,000 students throughout Central Eastern Europe. Another Jew who pioneered a distinctively Jewish form of modern culture was **Mordecai Gebirtig** (1877–1942). Gebirtig, a carpenter by trade, wrote Yiddish folk songs that became popular throughout the Jewish world. His lullabies, socialist hymns, love songs, and lamentations are still known today. Gebirtig was murdered on the streets of the Cracow Ghetto in 1942. A memorial plaque on his home on Joselewicza Street was installed in 1992.

The Jewish population of Cracow jumped from around 26,000 in 1900 to 45,200 in 1921. In 1938, there were 64,348 Jews living in Cracow. Throughout this time, the Jews constituted about one-fourth the population of the city.

THE HOLOCAUST

The Germans invaded Cracow on September 6, 1939. Two days later, they ordered all Jewish businesses and restaurants to display a Star of David.

At the time, Cracow's Jewish population numbered over 68,000 people, due to the influx of several thousand refugees from other areas under Nazi control. The Jewish Community of Cracow was soon placed under the authority of the Judenrat. Judenrat were set up throughout Nazi-occupied Europe as Jewish Community organizations whose duties were to carry out and enforce all German decisions regarding the Jews. Later that month, the Jews were commanded to fill in all the trenches in and around Cracow that had been dug to protect the city from German troops. The date chosen for this work reflected the meticulousness the Nazis unerringly showed for Jewish festivals. It was September 22 and 23, or the eve and day of Yom Kippur. All furnishings, from typewriters to curtains, were removed from Jewish businesses. The Germans removed all ritual objects from Cracow's synagogues.

In October the Nazis decided to make Cracow, not Warsaw, the capital of the so-called "Generalgouvernement" of Poland. Hans Frank was appointed head of the Generalgouvernement. One of his first decrees was a ban on all kosher slaughtering of meat. One month later, the Jews of Cracow were forced to wear a blue Star of David on a white band. Punishment for non-compliance increased from a fine of around 10 *zloty* (roughly $20 today) to death by hanging. Over the next several weeks, Jews were thrust out of all aspects of Cracow economic and social life. The Germans regulated Jewish populations by forbidding Jews from owning motorized vehicles, forbidding Jews from using public transportation and trains, and by forbidding Jews from changing residence. In order to meet the Germans' increasing demands for Jewish forced labor, the Judenrat drew up lists of all Jews, male and female, between the ages of 18 and 55. In December, the Germans closed off the Jewish district of Cracow for two days, giving soldiers complete reign to loot money and valuables from the trapped Jews. On December 11, all Jewish schools were closed down.

Eventually, though, Frank was disgusted to have Jews in his capital city. On May 18, 1940, he gave the Jews three months to leave the city with their belongings. When the time had elapsed and some Jews still remained, most were forcibly removed; the remaining Jews were sent to a ghetto. Many Jews expected the ghetto to be established in Kazimierz, but apparently this was deemed too close to the seat of Nazi power in Wawel Castle. Instead, the suburb of Podgorze was chosen largely because it was separated from Cracow proper by the Vistula River. Fifteen thousand Jews were crowded into the ghetto, three thousand of whom lived there without permits. In the midst of terrible living conditions, in which each person had an average living space of two square meters, Jewish cultural and welfare organizations operated inside the ghetto.

In June and October, 1942, the Germans launched massive Aktions in the ghetto, in which thousands of Jews were rounded up and sent to death camps. In the course of these Aktions, German officers stormed through buildings, searching for any Jews hiding from the deportations. A total of five thousand Jews were sent to the Belzec death camp during these deportations. June 4 became known as "Bloody Thursday" after German officers randomly shot women and children on streets throughout the ghetto, massacring entire crowds of captured Jews. It was on Bloody Thursday that the renowned Cracow folk singer **Mordecai Gebirtig** (1877–1942) was shot and killed on the corner of Janowa Wola and Dabrowki streets. Gebirtig. His ballad, "Our Town Is Burning," written in anguish over a pogrom perpetrated in 1938, became an anthem in the ghettoes of occupied Europe. All three of Gebirtig's young daughters were later murdered.

The next massive deportations were perpetrated on October 28, 1942. German soldiers combed hospitals, orphanages, and elderly centers for Jews, whom they shot on site. Six thousand Jews were murdered during this Aktion.

After the massive deportations, the Cracow branch of the Jewish Fighting Organization (ZOB) came into existence. Its most dramatic—and final—act was the bombing of the Cyganeria Cafe on Szpitalna Street. The cafe, located far from the ghetto in the Old Town of Cracow itself, was a popular social spot among German officers. Soon after the attack, all members of the Cracow ZOB were caught and arrested.

Meanwhile, the Nazis began to convert two Jewish cemeteries near Plaszow, southeast of the Cracow ghetto in Podgorze, into a labor and concentration camp. The command post of this camp was eventually assumed by Amon Leopold Goeth, who was notorious even by Nazi German standards for his acts of arbitrary sadism. It was he who commanded the liquidation of the Cracow ghetto in March of 1943. Throughout the winter of 1942–43, Jews were taken from the Cracow ghetto to work on the construction of the Plaszow camp. In the midst of their work, they were faced with the constant threat of murder at the hands of Goeth. Countless reminiscences exist of Goeth, irritated by a factor as irrelevant as the weather, firing into a crowd of Jews.

The final destruction of the Cracow ghetto was executed on March 13 and 14, 1943. By that time, the ghetto had been divided by barbed wire into "Ghetto A," filled with employed Jews, and "Ghetto B," filled with the unemployed as well as with children, the sick, and the elderly. On March 13, the Germans emptied Ghetto A by marching its six thousand inhabitants to Plaszow. On March 14, the Germans entered Ghetto B with the intention of exterminating all of its inhabitants. Hospital patients were murdered in their beds; children were shot *en masse*; elderly women were lined up and killed. All the welfare institutions of the ghetto were emptied. By the end of the day, the streets of Podgorze were filled with corpses and blood. Over one thousand Jews were murdered in this way; two thousand others were deported to death in Auschwitz-Birkenau; four thousand others were sent to Plaszow.

After March, 1943, most of the survivors of the Cracow ghetto were interned in nearby Plaszow. The Plaszow camp, divided into a Polish partition and a larger Jewish partition, was a camp in which people were literally worked to death. Over time, the camp changed from a labor camp into a forced labor camp and, finally, into a concentration camp. In 1943, Plaszow became a part of the Majdanek concentration camp. The next year, Plaszow became autonomous, thus increasing in size and authority. The prisoners had to contend with exhaustion, hunger, disease, beatings, and daily executions of unfit laborers. The pace of the camp was set by its murderous commander, **Amon Goeth**. The cruelty ascribed to Goeth in the 1993 Steven Spielberg film "Schindler's List" was not an exaggeration. Goeth constantly used his Jewish prisoners as targets for random shootings. An additional threat facing the prisoners of Plaszow was frequent deportations to Auschwitz. Due to the influx of prisoners throughout 1943, the number of prisoners interned at Plaszow reached 25,000. Most of these were Jews. Thousands of Jews were murdered in Plaszow. Only a couple thousand Cracow Jews survived the war.

POSTWAR TO TODAY

Early in the 1990s, an idea was floated in the back rooms of one of America's largest Jewish philanthropic institutions: What if we hire American Jewish families to pick up and move to Cracow? If we get ten families, they figured, we will have a Community.

The idea was discarded as being too outlandish and desperate, but it points to the tragedy of Cracow's Jewish Community today. Sadly, of the four cities discussed in this book, Cracow's current situation is the most difficult.

After the war, approximately six thousand Jews from throughout the region settled in Cracow. Cracow was one of the main destinations of Galician refugees, and so its postwar Jewish communal institutions were invested with some life. However, Jews left Cracow in large numbers in 1948, with the establishment of the State of Israel, and in 1957 and 1968–70, in response to state-sponsored anti-Semitism. There were six hundred Jews registered in the Cracow Jewish Community in 1978, but most were elderly. In 1988 the number was 180. Today, there are barely over one hundred Jews registered in the Jewish Community, the vast majority of them elderly.

Jewish culture has become popular in Cracow, with cafes and artist studios opening shop in Kazimierz, but for Jews themselves, Cracow is painfully lacking. The Ronald S. Lauder Foundation has recently sent a young, Yugoslav-born rabbi to Cracow to work with Poles who have Jewish roots. This is a commendable plan, but it seems almost quixotic. With so few Jews left in the city, it is difficult to expect results commensurate with Lauder success stories elsewhere in Poland.

The legendary city of Cracow is now practically a closed book on Jewish life.

Spotlight: Rabbi Moses Isserles
1525 or 1530–1572

By far the most famous and widely respected Jew ever to reside in Cracow was Rabbi Moses Isserles, known by the Hebrew acronym "Rema" (or "Remuh," depending on your accent). To Ashkenazic Jews his word is, quite literally, the law. On every page of the *Shulchan Aruch*, the guidebook to Jewish law, the Rema's commentaries are inked in side by side with the main text by Rabbi Josef Karo. Rabbi Karo's compilation of the law concerns the customs of the Sephardic Jewish Community. For every point on which Ashkenazic custom differs from Sephardic, you'll find the Rema's glosses, called *haggahot*, next to the text.

The Rema was born in either 1525 or 1530 to one of the most prominent leaders of the Cracow Jewish Community, a successful businessman and talmudic scholar named Israel Lazars. Israel was widely known as "Isserl," and the Rema's name Isserles derives from that name. From his early youth, it is said, little Moses was destined for greatness. In one story, it is told how the Community once asked the small child to sing the hymn, "*Adon Olam*," or "Master of the Universe," after evening services. Young Moses sang the hymn in a beautiful melody, and when he was finished he announced, "I'd like to thank the Cracow Jewish Community for honoring me with the *Adon Olam*. And I can only hope that one day, the *Adon Olam* will honor me with the Cracow Jewish Community." He was confident that one day he would become the chief rabbi of Cracow. Meanwhile, he went through teachers so quickly that soon there was not a scholar left in Cracow who could impart something new. On his *bar mitzvah*, his instructor Rabbi Moses Halevi Landau, the chief rabbi of Cracow, gave him *semichah*. Young Moses was then sent to Lublin to study at the famous *yeshivah* of Rabbi Shalom Shachna, one of the two chief rabbis of Lesser Poland. He studied seven years at Rabbi Shachna's *yeshivah* and was such an exemplary student that Rabbi Shachna delightedly married off his daughter Golda to him.

After he finished his studies in Lublin, the Rema returned home in 1550 and was soon appointed chief rabbi of Cracow. He was perhaps the youngest man ever appointed chief rabbi in Cracow's history. In one legend, when the Rema was scheduled to meet with the Catholic archbishop of Cracow—who was permitted to approve or reject all nominees for chief rabbi—the Rema's beard suddenly turned white, so that he would appear older and more mature in the eyes of the Catholic. In another legend, the archbishop, angry that the Jews should choose such a young man to preside over them, demanded a debate with the Rema. When the Rema arrived, the archbishop spoke only in Latin. To his surprise, the Rema not only answered him in Latin, but displayed a tremendous knowledge of all forms of philosophy and science. From that day on, the archbishop had nothing but respect for the Rema's genius.

As chief rabbi of Cracow, the Rema was admired as much for his talmudic acumen as for his humility and generosity. In one of his 132 Talmud-probing letters included in the book *She'elot u'Teshuvot Rema*, the Rema characteristically begins, "These are the words of the insignificant person who wishes to roll in the dust of wise students and to drink thirstily their words. I speak only in order that I may learn, to become accustomed with their qualities, to be like one of their lowest servants" (quoted in Yaakov Dovid Shulman, *The Rema: The Story of Rabbi Moshe Isserles*). In the introduction to another book he writes, "Do not suspect me of thinking that I am competent to compose books or speak before kings without embarrassment. I know that my well is a dry source, empty of flowing waters . . ." As for his generosity, the Rema headed a *yeshivah* in which, due to his independent wealth, he was able to finance the education, room, and board of his students.

Tragedy struck the Isserles family in the form of the plague of 1551. In the span of a year, three of Rabbi Isserles's closest relatives died of the plague: his mother, Malkah Dinah; his wife, Golda; and his grandmother, Gittel. They were among the first people buried in the Old Jewish Cemetery, which was opened early because the plague necessitated new burial space. In memory of his departed wife, Israel Lazars built the New Synagogue, later called the Rema Synagogue (*see page 307*).

The Rema's writings include decisions on the *halachah* (Jewish law), for which he is most famous today, as well as forays into philosophy and *Kabbalah*. Claiming that "The *minhag* (custom) is the Law," Rabbi Isserles stressed the resiliency of tradition—as opposed to the Law itself—in determining one's behavior. In the realm of philosophy, the Rema wrote *Mechir Yayin* ("The Price of Wine"), a commentary on the Book of Esther. *Mechir Yayin* takes the story of Esther to an entirely new level by treating it as an allegory for an individual's life, with the three parts of the story representing one's youth, middle age, and old age. The Rema's analysis employs four methods of interpretation: the literal, allegorical, homiletical, and mystical, known collectively as the "Pardes" technique. A more mystical work is his *Torat ha'Olah*, which he considered a sequel to *Mechir Yayin*. It took the Rema eight years to complete. Inspired by a similar work by Moses Maimonides, *Torat ha'Olah* interprets the structure and ceremony of the Old Temple in Jerusalem in mystical and philosophical terms. For instance, the Rema interprets the women's courtyard of the Old Temple as active intelligence; its four chambers signify the four kingdoms produced by active intelligence: mineral, vegetable, animal, and rational.

The Rema's most enduring literary legacy did not emerge without a twinge of frustration. *Darkei Moshe* ("The Ways of Moshe"), his magnum opus several years in the making, was written as a commentary on the fourteenth-century *Tur* by Rabbi Jacob ben Asher. The *Darkei Moshe* is both a guidebook of Jewish law as well as an index of opinions that were used to form that law. But on the very same nights the Rema was toiling in his study, a similar work was taking shape thousands of miles away, in Tsfat, Israel. Josef Karo, the great Sephardic rabbi originally from Spain, was busy compiling his own compendium of Jewish law, the *Beit Josef* ("House of Joseph"). Indeed, it is said that a Heavenly Being, the personification of the *Mishnah*, would often drop down for a visit. On one occasion, the

Heavenly Being prodded Rabbi Karo to speed up his writing so that he would publish before the Rema. Thus it was that *Beit Josef* hit the presses just as the Rema was putting the finishing touches on his beloved *Darkei Moshe*. When the Rema saw the first printed edition of *Beit Josef*, he was crushed. It was almost identical to his own *Darkei Moshe*. As he later wrote, "I was seized with trembling and clothed in shock. The light of Israel, the head of the exile, the lion, had arisen . . . and composed the *Beit Josef*. I was stunned. My work had been in vain and my toil a useless waste; in vain had I robbed myself of sleep" (quoted in *Yaakov Dovid Shulman, The Rema: The Story of Rabbi Moshe Isserles*). After he had read the *Beit Josef* in greater detail, he saw that there were discrepancies between his work and that of Rabbi Karo. First of all, Rabbi Karo had consulted the decisions of sages only up to the thirteenth century. The Rema's work considered opinions of later authorities as well. Moreover, Rabbi Karo had focused on the customs of Sephardic Jewry, omitting large areas of Ashkenazic tradition. The Rema, whose book addressed the Ashkenazic Jews of Poland, found that his research—if not the book itself—could serve as an Ashkenazic companion to the *Beit Josef*. Thus the Rema rewrote and published his *Darkei Moshe*, and his literary nightmare had a happy end. The Rema's commentaries are included in every edition of the *Beit Josef*.

In 1567, when Rabbi Karo published his classic halachic compendium the *Shulchan Aruch*, the Rema again noted the omissions concerning Ashkenazic Jewry. He wrote the *Mappah* ("Tablecloth"), which was intended to be placed alongside the *Shulchan Aruch* ("Prepared Table"). The *Mappah* was first included in the Cracow edition of the *Shulchan Aruch* in 1571 and today, all editions of the *Shulchan Aruch* contain the Rema's notations. It is considered the Rema's great and enduring contribution to Jewish civilization.

Legends of Cracow

The following are selected tales from the reservoir of Jewish creative thought that emerged from Cracow.

THE BIRTH OF THE REMA

The Rema's father, Rabbi Israel Lazars—also known as Reb Isserl—was a very pious man. In his day, he was one of the wealthiest Jews in Cracow. He ran a fabrics store that supplied textile to buyers throughout Poland. But, as an honest and God-fearing Jew, it was his custom to close the shop every Friday at twelve o'clock sharp, in order to give himself the entire afternoon to prepare for Shabbat.

Satan, as was his wont, decided this was a perfect opportunity to test Reb Isserl. "I'll give him such temptation that he'll never be able to say no!" squeaked the Evil One, and hatched a devilish plot.

One Friday at around 11:30, a nobleman, oozing with wealth, drove his carriage up to Reb Isserl's shop. (You know and I know that the nobleman is Satan in disguise.) The nobleman marched into the store wearing a crimson cape, ebony stockings, and the finest satin gloves. He was so wealthy that as he walked, little gold coins fell from his pockets onto the ground, and he had a special servant whose duty it was to brush the littered money into a special purse. Slapping one of his gloves on the counter, he demanded, "Who's in charge here?" He spoke in a deep, well-modulated nobleman's voice.

Reb Isserl stood up and offered his hand. "How can I help you?"

"I need some satin, and I need it quick!" the nobleman thundered. He snapped his fingers to the rhythm of his own voice.

"Of course. What color do you wish, and how many meters would you like?" asked Reb Isserl deferentially.

"Meters? I want whole bolts!" responded the nobleman, snapping his fingers. "Give me thirty bolts of purple satin, forty-five bolts of crimson, give me your finest turquoise, I want the most expensive turquoise you have in stock—make it fifty bolts even. And pink, I love pink—give me sixty bolts of pink."

Reb Isserl, making notes as the nobleman spoke, interjected, "Fine, fine, we have all the bolts in the back. I just want you to know that I close at noon, so if you like the material, you'll have to purchase it before then."

The nobleman smirked. Snapping his fingers, he bellowed, "Don't worry about it! First I've got to see the goods though. Let's see a sample of your pink."

Reb Isserl went to the back room and brought out a sample bolt of pink satin. It was 11:44 A.M.

The nobleman ran his gloved hand over the satin. Then he removed one glove and felt the material with his bare hand. "Have to test it with body oils," he muttered. He stretched the satin between his fingers and held it up to the light. He rubbed it over his forehead. Murmuring softly, he put it up to his nostrils and sniffed it. It was 11:51 A.M.

"Excuse me. Sir? Sir?" said Reb Isserl politely. The nobleman was lost in a reverie with the pink satin against his cheek. "Sir, if you like it, I'll have to ask you to be so kind as to purchase it now," said Reb Isserl, in a slightly louder voice.

The nobleman, startled out of his reverie, began snapping his fingers again. "But wait!" he declared. "I've only begun to sample! I love the pink—it's just my type—but I still need to try the turquoise. Make sure it's your finest! If I like it, I'll buy it, whatever your price."

"My dear sir," said Reb Isserl, "If you like, you can continue sampling the material on Sunday. But now, I see the time, and I really have to close the shop. It's almost noon."

"What are you talking about?" cried the nobleman, sternly squinting his eyes. "This is big money we're talking about here. With this one sale, you can go on vacation for the rest of the year! Name your price; let's do business."

"I'm sorry, sir, but with all due respect, this has been my policy ever since I started my shop. I told you up front. And it is not in my power to change the policy."

The nobleman responded with a tirade of vulgar, unprintable expletives. "What kind of store closes at midday? Are you crazy? If you kick me out now, I won't come back Sunday, I won't come back ever! How do you like that? You'll lose the best business deal of your life!" The nobleman began foaming at the mouth. His fangs glinted in the gaslight of the store.

But, true to his word, at exactly twelve o'clock Reb Isserl escorted the raging nobleman out from his shop. He shut the windows, turned out the lights, locked the door, and went home to get ready for Shabbat.

When he told his wife the news, she wasn't angry that they had lost more money than they would have been able to spend in a lifetime. On the contrary. She was pleased and gratified that the holiness of Shabbat was more important to her husband than his business.

High in the sky, the Heavenly Court watched the proceedings with undivided attention. When the Court saw such purity of heart, it decided that Reb Isserl was worthy to have a son who would become one of the greatest lights of Israel. The same night that the nobleman rode huffing in a tantrum out of Kazimierz, Reb Isserl's wife conceived the baby Moses Isserles.

YAKOV AND THE HEAVENLY COURT

Once, during the time of the Rema, there was a Jew in Cracow by the name of Yakov. The people in town used to call him any of three names: Yakov Tregger, Yakov Shikkur, or Yakov Shabbat.

They called him Yakov Tregger because that was his job. A *tregger* is a person who carries in water from a well. They called him Yakov Shikkur because that was his hobby. A *shikkur* is a drunk. The name Yakov Shabbat came about because every Friday at exactly twelve o'clock, he put down his buckets of water and went straight to the local tavern, where he bought a bottle of vodka, a bottle of rum, and a bottle of whiskey. It was Yakov Shabbat's goal to down all three bottles before the sun set. In the wintertime he had to rush. Every Friday afternoon he would stand on the street corner and, between shots of alcohol, shout, "Shabbat, Shabbat," in a singsong slur to passersby. This was his custom every Friday.

One Friday at noon, on his way to the tavern, Yakov heard a woman's voice calling from a window. He turned his head up. "Oh look," scolded the lady, "There he goes again to buy his three bottles. We have no money to buy Shabbos candles or challah, and yet he can go traipsing about town with three bottles of liquor."

Vodka isn't liquor, thought Yakov. But all the same, he felt a pang of guilt. Why should he be getting drunk when a family couldn't even afford bread? He thought about his weekly ritual—he always liked to drink the rum first and save the whiskey for last—and then wondered if, for just one Friday afternoon, he could live without the fix. It was a tough decision. "A shot of rum would certainly taste good right now," he thought. The woman in the window started to cry. "Alright, alright, I'll go," Yakov decided. "So I won't get drunk today. I'll read the newspaper instead." And, hardly believing what he was doing, Yakov turned away from the tavern and climbed the steps of the woman's apartment. He gave her every last coin of his tavern money, thus breaking his custom of 25 years.

The next evening, after Shabbat had ended, the Rema was sitting in his home, going over the next week's Torah portion. Suddenly Yakov entered the room. Yakov was shivering. He still had on his Friday clothes. Every couple seconds he would dart his eyes about, as if he suspected he was being followed. "Rabbi, we have to talk," he said in a hurried, gasping voice. "I know it's late, but—can I sit down?"

Without waiting for a response, Yakov sank into a chair opposite Rabbi Isserles. There was a smell about him that was hard to identify.

"Well, what seems to be the problem?" asked the Rema, charmed by Yakov's audacity.

"Well, for one thing, I'm dead." Yakov cracked his knuckles, as if that proved his death. "Do you have anything to drink?"

The Rema, broad in his learning, knew that he shouldn't serve alcohol to a drinker. He brought Yakov a glass of apple juice and sat back down opposite him. Soothingly, he said, "Perhaps you should explain."

Yakov told the Rema everything that happened the day before. "I gave the lady all my drinking money. Only it wasn't any normal lady. It was Queen Esther! And when I gave her the money, it was the purest *mitzvah*, so now I'm a Heavenly Messenger, that's what I am!"

The Rema brought Yakov a couple aspirin.

After a few minutes, Yakov had calmed down some. "You see, yesterday, not long after I helped that lady, I died. As soon as I went up to Heaven, I heard that the lady was a *gilgul* (reincarnation) of Queen Esther.

"Apparently, when Queen Esther died, there was an argument up in Heaven. One of the angels claimed that Esther had everything she could ever want. She was married to a king, she ruled with him over a kingdom, she had a lot of money. So she had freedom to do whatever she wanted. That's nothing. It's not so hard to be good when you have it easy. But what if she had lived a poor life, without money? Maybe she wouldn't be so good? Maybe she would, you know, be bad? So the Heavenly Court decided to try her again, this time with poverty. Queen Esther was sent back to this world as that poor woman I helped."

Yakov drank some more apple juice, grimacing as if it were stronger than whiskey. "When I gave her my drinking money," he said with a hand on his chest, "I had no idea it was Queen Esther I was dealing with. Who could tell these things? She didn't have a crown. Up in Heaven I learned that I had helped her a lot with that money, and I'm proud—Purim's one of my favorite holidays, as you can probably guess why. But I also helped myself, without even knowing it. The *mitzvah* was so pure that when I went up to Heaven, they found no sins on me. They said, 'Sure, he was a *shikkur*, but he never sinned.' And so, because of my purity, they wanted to make me a judge on the Heavenly Court. Just think, Rabbi—me, a Heavenly Judge!" Yakov struck a pose he deemed Judge-like, scratching his eyebrows and then pulling his beard.

The Rema, meanwhile, listened with all the patience that had made him famous in the Jewish world. In truth, though, he thought poor Yakov Shikkur had finally drunk himself into a delusion. Trying a gentle approach, the Rabbi said, "But Yakov, are you sure you know enough Jewish law to serve the Heavenly Court?"

Sheepishly, Yakov stopped pulling his beard and looked to the floor. "Yes, well that's the problem," he said. "What do I know about laws and rules? I just know that if you drink hard liquor after beer, you'll feel sick, and rum from the north can give you a nasty headache the next morning, and you should never mix vodka with plain milk, and—well, that's it. So they made me a sort of apprentice. A messenger."

At that, Yakov dropped his head again. It was the first moment in the entire evening that he fell silent.

"Well, you should be proud. It's a great honor to be a messenger of the Heavenly Court." the Rema offered. Noticing Yakov's distraction, he added, "Is something wrong?"

Yakov kept his eyes pinned to the floor. "It's my first mission," he whispered. "I've been sent by the Heavenly Court to inform you . . . that you, righteous Rema, will pass away from this world."

Rabbi Isserles was amused by Yakov Shikkur's creativity. He made a mental note to check into the alcohol Yakov favored—surely it wasn't a tad dangerous? Continuing to humor his guest, he said, "Is that all?"

"Well, no," replied Yakov. "The Heavenly Court asked me if you help the poor. They asked if you help not only with your own money, but if you go around collecting money for the poor. So I told them, 'Yes, I've seen Rabbi Isserles go to the rich people and request alms for the poor.' And the Heavenly Court looked at me and said, 'Only the rich? That's nothing. He should try to collect charity from everybody.' It was a bad scene. They said that just like Queen Esther, the Rema himself would be reincarnated as a poor man. Because you are rich in this life, you will be tested with poverty in the next."

By this point, Yakov's gibberish had become a bit too personal. As much as the Rema resented the use of nicknames, he could finally see why they called this man Yakov Shikkur. "Yakov," the Rema shouted, trying to sober up his guest. "Are you still drunk from Friday? Shabbat is over, you have to work tomorrow."

Yakov looked in a vacant direction away from the Rema. Absently, as if responding to a silent call, he muttered, "I must go now." He left as quickly as he came.

"The things a rabbi must listen to," thought the Rema, returning to the next week's portion. Then he stiffened. "How did Yakov get into my house?" he asked aloud. "My door is locked." It was true. The Rema always used a double-barrelled lock on his iron door. "And how did he leave?" mused the Rema. "It's like he just vanished!"

Rabbi Isserles put on his coat and left the house. He went up to his synagogue, where one could always find people studying. "Has anybody seen Reb Yakov Tregger here?" The Rema made sure not to use the mocking nickname "Shikkur" in public.

A young man looked up from his Rashi text and said, "Rabbi, I just heard that Reb Yakov Shikkur—I mean Tregger—passed away Friday evening."

The Rema rushed back to his apartment, where he found Yakov waiting for him. Immediately, the rabbi told his ghostly guest, "Go back to the Heavenly Court and tell them that from now on, I'll collect charity from everybody. Neither the rich, nor the middle class, nor the poor, will be exempt from my exhortations to give *tzedakkah*."

From that evening forward, Rabbi Isserles fulfilled this obligation. He could always be found, in the synagogue and on the street, asking all members of his Community to give money to charity. And because of this change in his behavior, the Heavenly Court granted Rabbi Moses Isserles a longer life.

THE TEST

On the tomb of Nathan Nata Spira (1585–1633), also known as the *Megalleh Amukkot*, is written: "It is said of him that Elijah conversed with him face to face." Many legends surround the friendship between Rabbi Spira and the Prophet Elijah. The following tale is one of the most awe-inspiring legends ever to emerge from Kazimierz, not only because it attests to the purity of a great Cracow rabbi, but because it attempts to explain one of the most cataclysmic events in all of Jewish history.

Once upon a time, in the middle of the seventeenth century, there was a heaving commotion up in Heaven. It appeared that the birthpangs of the Messiah were about to begin. A hidden, uninvited guest at this Heavenly hullabaloo was Satan, flicking his tail and rubbing his hands together in mischievous glee.

Satan was an opportunist. Ever vigilant in his crusade to thwart Redemption, he saw the present commotion as a perfect time to put Israel to the test. "Let's see if the Jews accept just anybody as their Messiah," he snickered, and, in a burst of bluish smoke, flew down to the Earthly realm.

"Form of—a humble man!" Satan screeched, and before you could cry "hoax!" he was seen ambling down Szeroka Street in Kazimierz, dressed as a pious Jew with a grey beard.

Turning to the *beit midrash* of the Megalleh Amukkot, Satan kissed the *mezuzah* on the door and walked inside.

Rabbi Spira, the Megalleh Amukkot, was in a corner, tutoring a young man on the finer nuances of the *Gemarah*. Satan approached the Rabbi, took off his hat (he made sure to wear a *kippah* underneath), and said it was of the utmost importance that they speak. The young man dismissed himself at once. Gingerly taking a seat opposite Rabbi Spira, Satan summoned all the integrity he could muster and said, "Rabbi Nathan Nata Ben Shlomo Spira, author of the Megalleh Amukkot, I have been sent from The Holy One, Blessed be He, to inform you with the greatest humility that you, honored servant of the Lord, have been chosen to be the Messiah!"

Satan fixed the Megalleh Amukkot's gaze with a mixture of reverent intensity and sublime joy. If nothing else, Satan was an accomplished performer. "The time has come for Redemption," he chanted, "And you are the man chosen for the task!" He gripped the Megalleh Amukkot's arms. He made his hands shiver and quake. He was going to burst forth in tears, but he thought that would be melodramatic.

As for the Megalleh Amukkot, he was at once skeptical. An unassuming disposition led him instantly away from such delusions of grandeur. Besides, he met with Elijah every night; wasn't it odd that the prophet himself had never made mention of it?

The Megalleh Amukkot was about to say, "Sure, sure, don't call me, I'll call you," but decided that would be rude. Instead he told his guest to return at the same time the next day.

That night, when Elijah arrived for their study session, the Megalleh Amukkot told the prophet what had happened. "I don't want to be an egotist," said the rabbi, "But is it true?"

Elijah, prophet that he was, knew just what Satan was up to—but there was only so much he was permitted to reveal. "It's a test," Elijah cryptically responded. "I am not privileged to reveal the answer, for that would ruin the test. However, I can give you a small hint. The sign of Truth is the complete alphabet adorning the man's essence. The sign of Falsehood is the first, middle, and last letters missing."

The next day, when they had their meeting (Satan was five minutes late), the Megalleh Amukkot saw the Hebrew alphabet dancing around his guest. But three letters indeed were missing: the first (*alef*), the middle (*mem*), and the last (*taf*). Together these letters spell *Emmet*, Hebrew for "Truth." This is how Rabbi Spira could see that his guest was missing Truth, that he was enveloped in Falsehood.

The Megalleh Amukkot jumped from his chair. "Be gone from Cracow!" he shouted, pointing to the door. "Leave, Satan, and don't ever step foot in my presence again!"

Satan was astonished. He considered himself a fine actor. Grinding his fangs in exasperation, he headed for the door.

After a few years, Satan came back with renewed ardor, plus an acting degree. He approached a young man residing in Salonica, decidedly less righteous than the Megalleh Amukkot, and informed him that he was the Messiah. The young man instantly failed the test and accepted Satan's message.

The man's name was Shabbetai Tzvi, and he went on to become one of the most dangerous false Messiahs in all of Jewish history.

THE *CHEREM*

The following is a legend concerning two of the rabbinical kingpins of Cracow, Nathan Nata Spira, known as the Megalleh Amukkot, and Joel Sirkes, known as the Bach. As the two were contemporaries, they shared the spotlight in many Cracow stories.

When the Bach first arrived in Cracow, the Jewish town was abuzz with excitement. Everybody felt honored that such a great talmudic master was to grace the humble quarter of Kazimierz. People in the street cried, "*Shalom aleichem!*" as soon as they saw the new rabbi. When he stepped inside the *beit midrash*, the students and teachers rose and said, "*Shalom aleichem!*" Soon enough, all the rabbis in Cracow came out to greet the Bach in a single group. When they met him they, too, shouted, "*Shalom aleichem!*" with joy in their hearts. But there was one man in the whole town of Cracow who didn't say, "*Shalom aleichem*," who didn't even offer a cordial "Hello." This was the Megalleh Amukkot. When he saw the new rabbi walking down Szeroka Street, he quickly turned away and ducked down a side street.

This caused an instant uproar. The Bach had reason to feel insulted, but the rabbis of Cracow were no less offended. "The nerve of Rabbi Spira! The arrogance!" one fumed. Another rabbi exclaimed, "Is he so threatened by a new rabbi that he can't even show his face? Is he so insecure that he must resort to childish games? If this be so, then perhaps he is no longer suited to be our rabbi!"

The very next day, the rabbis of Cracow convened an emergency meeting in the Altschul to decide what to do. They discussed the behavior of the Megalleh Amukkot at length. The Bach was called in, to ask what he thought. The Bach had felt offended, but he insisted that it wasn't his duty to interfere so soon in Cracow Jewish politics. Finally the rabbis decided to put a *cherem* on Rabbi Spira. A *cherem* is a rabbinical ban on a person or group of people who have shown themselves to be heretics. Because of the disrespect Rabbi Spira had shown the Bach, he had earned a *cherem* on himself.

What the rabbis didn't know was that listening in on their meeting was the prophet Elijah, who—as we all know—was a special friend and study partner of the Megalleh Amukkot. Elijah rushed to Rabbi Spira and warned him of the *cherem*.

"What should I do?" asked Rabbi Spira, gravely worried about the meeting.

"Go and explain the truth. You had every reason to behave as you did," responded the prophet, and snuggled up in an easy chair with a copy of *Sanhedrin* in his lap.

So Rabbi Spira left his home and walked the length of Szeroka Street to the Altschul, repeating Elijah's pep talk in his head. Once inside, he went up to the offices and knocked on the door of the proverbial smoke-filled room. "Open the door. It's Rabbi Spira," he called through the door frame.

The rabbis inside were startled. The meeting was shrouded in the utmost secrecy. How could Rabbi Spira possibly have known they were there? Exchanging nervous glances, each of the rabbis was too afraid to open the door. Finally one of them rose and let Rabbi Spira inside.

As soon as he entered, Rabbi Spira greeted the assembled leaders of Kazimierz. He held out his hand and said, "*Shalom aleichem*" to each of the rabbis seated before him, including a rather perplexed Bach.

This made the rabbis even more confused. Why did he avoid the Bach the previous day, only to greet him warmly today? Was he cynically trying to change their minds about the *cherem*?

Before the rabbis could even begin to launch an offensive, the Megalleh Amukkot explained, "I was not able to greet the Bach until today, because he himself was in a *cherem* for 40 days. That *cherem* ended today, and so now I can greet him. A warm '*Shalom aleichem*' to you, Rabbi Sirkes!" He walked over to the Bach and, with a kind smile, patted the latter on the back.

There was a perplexed murmur all through the room. "The Bach in *cherem*?" they whispered. "Is this possible?" All eyes focused on Rabbi Sirkes, who was no less dumbfounded than the rest.

"Is it true? Were you in *cherem*?" the incredulous rabbis asked.

"I beg your pardon?" answered the Bach.

The Megalleh Amukkot continued, "It wasn't an Earthly *cherem*, but a Heavenly one. When the Bach left his town to come to Cracow, a widow came running after him, begging him for a moment of his time to speak. The Bach was in a terrible rush and couldn't stop even for a moment. As his horse and carriage left, the widow began to cry bitter tears. Her tears went straight to Heaven; it was there that the Bach was placed in *cherem* for 40 days."

The rabbis turned to the Bach and asked, "Was there indeed such a widow?"

The Bach, furrowing his eyebrows and tugging at his beard, searched his memory. After a moment his eyes lighted in recognition. "Yes, yes, I remember now. She ran after me as I was hurrying to the horse and carriage. I thought the carriage was about to leave, so I had no time. I hoped the woman would speak with the town's new rabbi." The Bach looked at the Megalleh Amukkot. "How could you possibly have known this?" he said.

The Megalleh Amukkot just smiled. "I keep company with prophets."

It was decided at once to not issue a *cherem* on Rabbi Spira, and instead to thank him for following a Heavenly decree at the expense of public favor.

And this is the story of how two *cheremim* converged in the Jewish town of Cracow.

THE CUSTOM OF THE WALL

Some stories arose not for the purpose of revealing a miracle or lauding the special powers of wonder rabbis, but to illustrate a certain rabbi's views concerning Jewish life and practice. Rabbi Joel Sirkes, known as the Bach, held profound views concerning the codification of Jewish law. The Bach felt that when Jewish law was observed in a rote manner from a manual, it lost its living presence among the Jewish people. The following story shows the potentially absurd end result of mindless codification of the law:

> Before the Bach was rabbi in Cracow, he spent time as a rabbi in many other Polish towns. When he first came to the city of Brisk as their rabbi, it was *Shabbat Mivurchan Hachodesh*, the Shabbat when the Jewish Community blesses the new month. The Bach came to synagogue to pray with the Community for the first time. When it came time to say the prayer for the new month, the *shamash* of the Community said, "Everybody face west." All the people in the congregation rose and faced the back of the synagogue.
>
> The Bach found this odd. It was the usual custom to face east, not west. He had never heard of such a unique custom in a synagogue. He had travelled to many towns, serving as rabbi in quite a few places; he had learned all the holy books and the books of customs and law; and nowhere had anybody mentioned such a custom. Perhaps, thought the Bach, it's a special custom associated with this Community. The congregants remained facing west through-

out the entire prayer for the new month. When it was over, they turned around to the front again.

After services, the Bach went to the *shamash*. He asked the *shamash* what was the reason for facing west during the prayer for the new month. The *shamash* responded, "I really don't know, but I'm certain it's an old custom here."

So the Bach approached the elderly people in the Community. "Why do people face the back of the synagogue?" he asked. But even the elderly didn't know. One of them said, "Ever since I was a small boy, this has been the custom. But I don't know the reason for it."

The Bach continued searching for people who might have the answer. Finally, after scores of interviews, he arrived at the house of the oldest man in Jewish Brisk. The man was already in his late nineties. He was poor and sick in bed, and never stepped foot outside his home. When the Bach arrived, the man was overjoyed. Nobody ever called on him, but the esteemed new rabbi was paying a personal visit. Propping himself up on two pillows, he asked, "To what do I owe this pleasure, rabbi?"

The Bach responded, "I've been searching day and night for the answer to a riddle that has confounded me since I arrived in Brisk. Perhaps you can help me. Do you have any clue as to why the congregation turns to face the back wall during the prayer for the new month?"

The elderly man laughed, revealing a toothless mouth. "Yes," he said, "I know why they do this. In my time, when I was a child, there weren't many *siddurim* (prayer books) in the synagogue. Most of the people were ignorant. They could read, but they didn't know all the prayers by heart. The only prayers they could memorize were the basic ones. The prayer for the new month, that was a tough one, because it wasn't said very often."

The man shifted onto his side. "Now there was a rich Jew in Brisk who wanted to do a *mitzvah*. So he went and had the entire prayer printed onto a poster, to put up in the *shul*. There was no room on any of the other walls, only the back wall. So they put it up there. To remind the people that they should say the prayer, the *shamash* just announced, '"Everybody look up to the western wall, where the poster is.'"

The old man sighed in his memories and took a sip from his bedside glass of water. The Bach, meanwhile, was just as perplexed as when he'd arrived. "But there's no poster in the synagogue," he insisted.

"Ah, yes, well that's true," admitted the man. "It was taken down when we finally had enough money to buy *siddurim*. But the custom—that remained."

The Bach was frustrated. "But there's no point to it. It's not Jewish law. It's not even Jewish custom. There's no spiritual or practical reason for it."

The old man shrugged his shoulders. "It's a custom," he repeated, and went to sleep.

But to the Bach, such a "custom" distorted the meaning behind Jewish ritual. And so, in his first ruling as rabbi of Brisk, the Bach abolished the practice of facing the back of the synagogue during the prayer for the new month.

The Jewish Essentials

The Jewish Community of Cracow
Skawinska Street 2
Telephone (48–12) 656 2349

This office, which is responsible for the religious affairs of the Cracow Jewish Community, manages most aspects of the Jewish Community today. Large groups wishing to gain access to the Rema Synagogue and Old Jewish Cemetery on Sundays (when these sites are normally closed) are advised to contact the office prior to arrival. Questions concerning use of the *mikveh* can also be directed to this office.

The Ronald S. Lauder Foundation
The Cracow branch of the Foundation may be contacted through its Warsaw office (*see page 179–180*).

The Lauder Foundation has recently assigned a director of religious education for Poland, Rabbi Sacha Pecaric, who is stationed in Cracow. Rabbi Pecaric, a Yugoslav-born graduate of Yeshivah University, teaches classes, assists in the Rema Synagogue, and leads a weekly *Kabbalat Shabbat* in the Isaac Synagogue. Rabbi Pecaric will be able to assist you with religious matters during your visit. He can be reached by mobile telephone at (48) 602 35 0671.

The Center for Jewish Culture
Meiselsa Street 17
Telephone (48–12) 633 7058
Fax (48–12) 634 4593

The Center for Jewish Culture opened in 1993 in the building of a former *beit midrash* from the nineteenth century (*see page 363*). Staffed entirely by non-Jews, the Center sponsors cultural and educational projects regarding Jewish life, both past and present. Long-term plans include a kosher restaurant and, eventually, a hotel to serve international tourists.

In its eagerness to arrange lectures, conferences, and exhibits, to promote Jewish culture in Cracow, and to educate Poles about a people that once lived among them, the

Center is a vital and necessary institution in Cracow. But in terms of its actual knowledge about Jewish culture and tradition, both inside and outside Cracow, the center is ill-equipped to answer questions. Visitors with specific questions about Jewish history and life would do better speaking with an experienced Jewish guide.

The Ariel Cafe
Szeroka Street 17
New branch at Szeroka Street 6

The Ariel is *not* a kosher cafe or restaurant. However, it is the closest thing to a Jewish "hangout," both for locals and visitors, that exists in Cracow. Unlike several other cafes in Kazimierz, The Ariel Cafe tries to be tasteful in its recreation of prewar Yiddish atmosphere.

PRAYING IN CRACOW

The Rema Synagogue
Szeroka Street 40

> *Kabbalat Shabbat:*   Approximately 45 minutes prior to sunset.
>   The Rema congregation meets a little earlier than is usual on Friday evenings.
>
> *Shabbat* and Holiday Mornings: 9:00 A.M.
> There are no weekday services and no services at the conclusion of Shabbat.

Shlomo Carlebach composed one of his most famous melodies, "*Cracow Niggun*," during services in the Rema Synagogue. The melody, which begins slowly and then turns joyous and exciting, could well be the anthem of the Rema Synagogue during the year. In the winter months, it is slow and sad: The wait for a *minyan*, the predominately elderly congregation, the lack of participation in prayers. But in the summer months, the rhythm changes completely: A full congregation, lively participation, devotion, and excitement in prayer. The symphonic change is entirely dependent upon the tourist season. In the summertime, droves of excited Jewish visitors from throughout the world crowd into the small hall of prayer, eager to pray in the synagogue of the great Rabbi Moses Isserles. A visitor's experience in the Rema Synagogue often hinges on what season he or she arrives.

Things are picking up in the winter months, however. In the past, the congregation relied on tourists to read from the Torah on *Shabbat*. In the winter, with so few tourists, the Torah often could not be read. This changed in 1997, when the Ronald S. Lauder Foundation sent a young rabbi, Sacha Pecaric, to Cracow. With the assistance of Rabbi Pecaric, the Torah is read throughout the year in the Rema Synagogue.

The Lauder Foundation also operates a traditional *Kabbalat Shabbat* after the main service on the first floor of the Isaac Synagogue, Kupa Street 18.

The Rema Synagogue is the only synagogue used on a regular basis in Cracow. However, when large groups of visitors wish to pray, the Tempel is occasionally opened for services as well.

For a full description of the Rema Synagogue, *see page 307*.

MIKVEH

The Cracow *mikveh*, located behind the Temple, is currently not functioning. However, there are plans to renovate it. Assuming the *mikveh* becomes active in the near future, visitors can make appointments to use it. Ask at the religious administration at Skawinska Street 2, telephone (48–12) 656 2349, or call Rabbi Sacha Pecaric.

Keeping Kosher in Cracow

As is the case in Prague and Warsaw, there is only one kosher restaurant in Cracow.

The Nissenbaum Kosher Restaurant
Szeroka Street 39, adjacent to the Rema Synagogue

The Nissenbaum Foundation opened this kosher restaurant in 1995 amid controversy that the building intrudes on the serenity of the Rema Synagogue and other buildings on Szeroka Street. One point of complaint was that the gate of the restaurant was designed to dwarf the ancient gate of the Rema Synagogue next door.

The restaurant, which relies on tourists, is expensive by local standards. It is also unreliable: The restaurant has been known to shut down completely when there are no tourists, as is sometimes the case in the winter months. The most recent controversy involved the resignation of the *mashgiach* in the autumn of 1997. At this writing, the certificate of *heksher* for the restaurant claims that the restaurant is kosher when the *mashgiach* is there. It is unclear whether there will be a permanent *mashgiach* in the restaurant. Strictly kosher tourists are strongly advised to be certain there is a *mashgiach* on the premises before eating there. If you wish, call Rabbi Sacha Pecaric at (48) 602 350 671 for updated information.

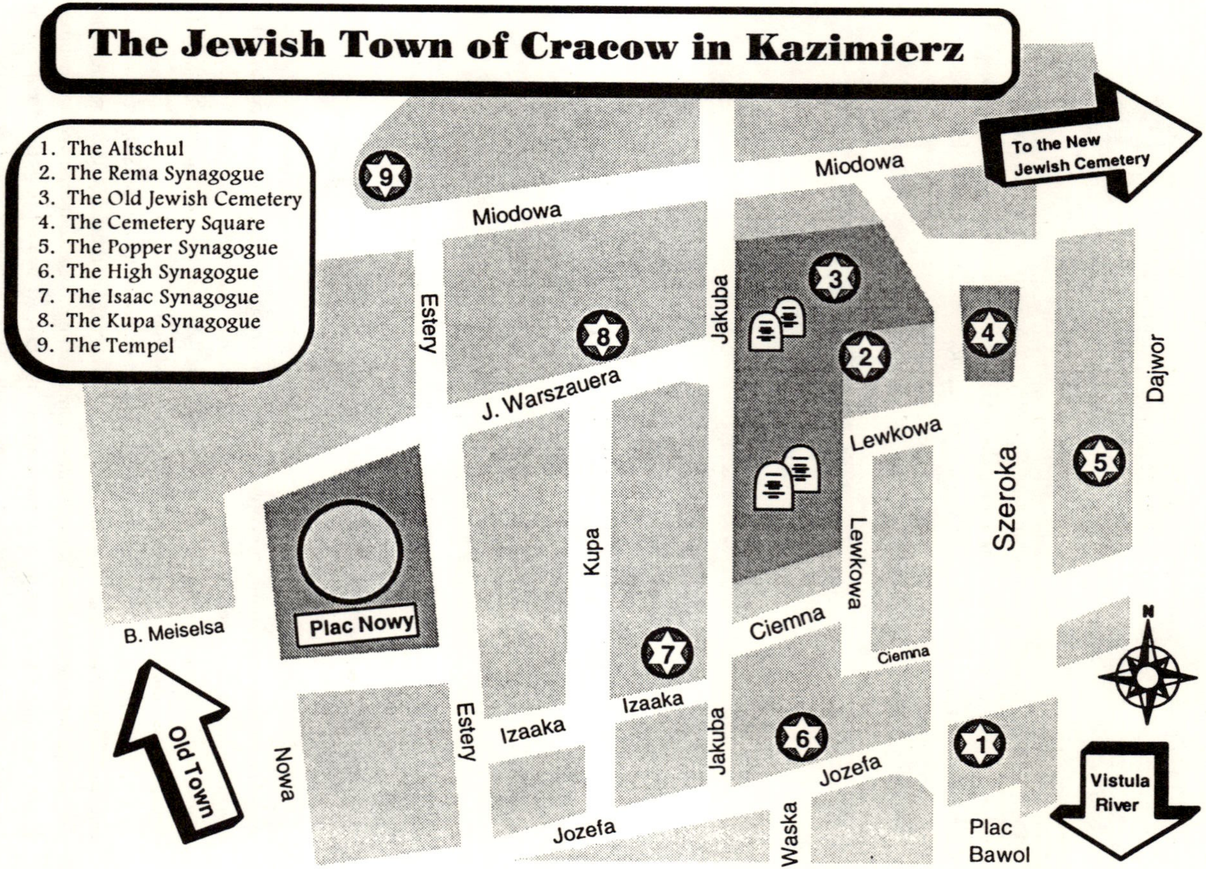

The Jewish Town of Cracow in Kazimierz

1. The Altschul
2. The Rema Synagogue
3. The Old Jewish Cemetery
4. The Cemetery Square
5. The Popper Synagogue
6. The High Synagogue
7. The Isaac Synagogue
8. The Kupa Synagogue
9. The Tempel

Orientation and Suggested Itinerary

Ever since the Jews were expelled from Cracow in 1495, a small district in Kazimierz has been the heart of the Jewish Community. Kazimierz is a fifteen-minute walk southeast from Old Town. It used to be a distinct city, separated from Cracow proper by arms of the Vistula River, which were filled in at the end of the nineteenth century. Although Kazimierz is today integrated into the city of Cracow, you'll notice as soon as you arrive that there is something distinctly unique about the Kazimierz district. The streets themselves point to the Jewish culture that once prevailed here, with names like Estery, Maiselsa, Kupa, Izaaka, Lewkowa, Joselewicza, Jakuba, and Warszauer.

A trip through the six centuries of Jewish life in Kazimierz appropriately begins on Szeroka Street—"Broad Street"—which has always been the Jewish center of Kazimierz.

For a historical perspective, the first stop is suitably the Altschul, the oldest synagogue in Poland, situated at the southern end of Szeroka Street. As the public hours of the Altschul are rather quirky, however, it must occasionally be pushed to the second or third day of one's visit to Cracow. I suggest you check the schedule (*see page 292*) before you arrive.

After visiting the Altschul, head up Szeroka Street to the famous Rema Synagogue, near the end of the street on the left side. After visiting the synagogue, enter the Old Jewish Cemetery from the synagogue's courtyard. You should also see the enclosed park just outside the Rema Synagogue gate, in the middle of Szeroka Street. It has its own history and legend, which are described on *page 337*.

Halfway back down Szeroka Street you'll find the Popper Synagogue. Then walk back to the Altschul and make a right on Jozefa Street and you'll come almost immediately to the High Synagogue on the right side. From Jozefa Street, make a right on Jakuba, a left on Izaaka, and a right on Kupa to get to the Isaac Synagogue. The Kupa Synagogue is at the intersection of Kupa Street and Warszauera Street. The Kupa Synagogue is usually closed, but sometimes one of the entrances on the other side, from Miodowa Street, is unlocked. From there it's a short walk to the Tempel, which braces the corner of Podbrzezie and Miodowa.

Not all of these synagogues will be open to visitors, but the tour can easily take the greater part of a day, depending on how much time you spend in places like the Altschul and the Old Jewish Cemetery. Time permitting, I recommend you visit the New Jewish Cemetery and the sites in the "Elsewhere" section.

A local Jewish guide popular with American tourists is Henryk Halkowski. He's active in the Jewish Community, and can be reached at Al. Slowackiego 11A, Apt. 6, 31159 Cracow, telephone (48 12) 633 15 64 or tel/fax (48 12) 421 38 70.

THE ALTSCHUL

Address: Szeroka Street 24
The synagogue lies at the southern end of Szeroka Street.

> Hours:
> *Pay careful attention and read to the end; the Altschul's opening hours are labyrinthine.*
> Monday and Tuesday: Closed
> Wednesday and Thursday: 9:00 A.M.–3:30 P.M.
> Friday: 11:00 A.M.–6:00 P.M.
> Saturday and Sunday: 9:00 A.M.–3:00 P.M.
> The Altschul is closed the first Saturday and Sunday of the month.
> The Altschul is open from 9:00 A.M.–3:30 P.M. on the first Monday and Tuesday of the month.

True to its name, the Altschul is the oldest remaining synagogue not only in Cracow, but in all of Poland. In fact, it is the only two-naved, two-pillared synagogue remaining in the country. As such, it has become a symbol both of Jewish antiquity in Poland and of the vitality of Jewish civilization in the Polish state.

Legends descend on the Altschul in even greater numbers than the famous rabbis who once officiated here. One tale recounts how King Casimir the Great gave the Jews permission to build the synagogue. It is said that the king endowed a royal gift to the Jews of several swords to be recast as candleholders. The swords bore depictions of angels, which is prohibited in Jewish tradition as a desecration of the Second Commandment. Nevertheless, the Jews used the swords as candleholders so as not to offend His Majesty. Another legend holds that King Casimir founded the Kazimierz building himself in order to house the Cracow Academy of Science. When the Jews were expelled from Cracow, the building was given to them as reparation for the synagogues they had to abandon in the Old Town. Of course, by all historical accounts the synagogue was built after the reign of King Casimir. Still, there are those who insist there was once a book in the Altschul that contained a special prayer for King Casimir.

Like all ancient synagogues, the Altschul incorporated historical milestones into both its customs and appearance. For instance, there is a charity box memorializing the 1407 pogrom launched on St. Anne's Street in Cracow and its Simchat Torah celebrations are drastically altered in order to remember another pogrom that occurred on that very holiday. This is the synagogue where the famous Thaddeus Kosciuszko addressed the Jews in his revolutionary call to arms in the 1794 Insurrection. He wasn't the only one to speak here. Rabbis throughout Poland considered it an honor to give *d'var Torah* from the pulpit in the Altschul, the hallowed centerpiece of Polish Jewish life.

When you face the synagogue from the outside and look to the left, you can see partially reconstructed remnants of the Kazimierz city walls. The Altschul, built at the border of the Jewish quarter, ran right into the walls of the city. Before the war, there was another, smaller synagogue in the same area, connected to the city walls next to the Altschul. It was called the Oyfn Berg Shul, meaning "Synagogue on the Hill," and was built in the seventeenth century by the illustrious Jekeles family. Nearby stood another building owned by the Jekeles family, later rebuilt as the red-and-white building at Szeroka 22. Moses Jekeles, the brother of Reb Isaac Reb Jekeles (the namesake of the Isaac Synagogue), built the Oyfn Berg Shul for his son-in-law, the great Nathan Nata Spira, or Megalleh Amukkot. Above the synagogue the Megalleh Amukkot kept his personal kabbalistic study chamber. According to legend, a candle could be seen burning in this chamber every night, as the Megalleh Amukkot delved into the depths of mysticism. Everywhere was darkness in Kazimierz, and the candle above the *shul* was the single light that could be seen throughout the town. When the great rabbi died, the candle finally went out. The building was destroyed during the war.

There is some belief that the first Jewish cemetery in Kazimierz was once located beyond these city walls.

Old and Old New, Cracow and Prague

If you've been to Prague, you'll notice that the interior of the Altschul bears a striking similarity to Prague's Altneuschul (the exteriors, by contrast, look completely different). Both synagogues feature a Gothic twin-nave design, both consist of six vault bays, and both descend underground. Even their size is similar. The interior of the Cracow synagogue is much larger than its counterpart in Prague, but outside the Altschul aces out the Altneuschul by less than half a meter in height!

There are those who explain the similarity by insisting that the Altschul was built by Bohemian Jews. Since the fourteenth century, there lived a colony of Bohemian Jews in Cracow. It is said that after the notorious Prague Easter Pogrom of 1389, which occurred inside the Altneuschul itself, many Bohemian Jews fled here, where they built the Altschul in the same style as the Prague synagogue. A similar view has it that Bohemian Jews built the Altschul in the fifteenth century. Why later? Because the synagogue in Cracow bears a much later appearance than the Altneuschul. The thinner columns and walls of the Altschul reveal more sophisticated developments in construction than those used in the Altneuschul. Bohemian Jews continued to flow into Cracow during the fifteenth century, when Jewish life in Bohemia was particularly precarious. They established their own colony in Kazimierz, and became so well to do that they could easily have built a paean to their hometown synagogue. The Bohemian colony was so independent, in fact, that eventually it seceded from the Cracow Jewish Community.

In the early sixteenth century, there were intense conflicts between Polish-born Jews and the Bohemian Jews living in Kazimierz. It reached the point where each Community elected its own rabbi and ignored the decisions of the other. There was Rabbi Asher for the Polish Jews, and Rabbi Peretz for the Czechs. Soon enough, both the Polish-born and Bohemian Jews marched to the Altschul and insisted on exclusive rights to the building. During the holidays, such synagogue squabbling shot to its peak. Eventually, in 1519, the conflict over the Altschul was brought to King Sigismund. After listening to both sides, the not-quite impartial king decided that the Altschul had been built by Polish Jews, who were given full rights over the synagogue.

Whether or not the Altschul was actually constructed by Bohemian Jews, there is no denying some degree of influence. How could there not have been, with a Prague Jewish colony living in Kazimierz?

The line of influence extends even beyond Prague. The Altschul is not only remarkably similar to the Altneuschul but to earlier synagogues, since destroyed, in Worms and in Regensberg, as well as the buried Great Synagogue of Budapest (*see page 417*). What is most fascinating about the similarities is that we can use synagogue architecture to trace the movement of Jews on the continent. As the Jews moved from Germany to Prague and then to Cracow, they built synagogues using the same basic design, refining and adjusting it along the way. Today, the synagogues form a map of Jewish migration on the continent. Thus the Altschul, built at the end of that migration path, is the last of the medieval twin-naved synagogues that remain in Europe. It is no coincidence that it is also the highest and largest of them all.

How Old Is Old?

The original date of the Altschul is unknown. As a European Jewish mystery, it ranks up there with the unknown architect of Warsaw's Nozyk Synagogue. Dates from the late fourteenth to the late fifteenth century have been proposed, but as yet there is no agreement and there may never be.

No less an authority than Majer Balaban, this century's greatest scholar of the Jews of Kazimierz, put the date of construction at the 1380s. This would mean the synagogue predated the large influx of Bohemian Jews to Cracow. Others point to the famous *tzedakkah* box in the synagogue inscribed with the year 1407 (*see page 298*). The year probably memorializes a pogrom, but it might also mark the beginning or the end of construction of the Altschul. These two periods, the late fourteenth century and the early fifteenth, are close enough to not cause problems. Buildings took a long time to build in the Middle Ages.

However, just when we think we know the date, along comes another historian to throw an entire century into the mix. Some experts believe the synagogue was built during the second half of the fifteenth century, while others contend that it was only after the Jews were expelled from Cracow in 1494 that construction of the Altschul began in Kazimierz. These experts argue that if such an expansive synagogue were built in the fourteenth century, it would have been built in the Old Town of Cracow itself. Only after 1494, when Jews were expelled from Cracow, would Kazimierz have been the spot for a central synagogue.

Unfortunately, those visitors who wish to hear a single, tangible date for the construction of the synagogue are inevitably disappointed.

The name "Altschul," meaning "Old Shul," came about in the sixteenth century in order to distinguish the synagogue from a new house of prayer called, fittingly, the "Neuschul" or "New Shul." This Neuschul, built by Israel Lazars in 1553 and then rebuilt after the fire of 1557, soon came to be known as the Rema Synagogue. In later centuries, the name "Altschul" took on added resonance, as it became clear that the Altschul was the oldest remaining synagogue in Poland.

The earliest picture we have of the Altschul is from a drawing of Kazimierz from the 1530s. In the illustration, the Altschul is topped by a Gothic roof tower that no longer exists today. According to Balaban, this tower housed the Jewish prison. Rather than hand over lawbreakers to the often sadistic Christian authorities, the Jews kept their own prison right in the synagogue. Only in cases of severe crimes, which were extremely rare in the Jewish quarter, would the guilty party be handed over to city authorities. Balaban describes the holding cell in the tower as relatively comfortable, while an additional jail in the cellar was more rugged. By the seventeenth century, the Altschul prison had been moved next to the *mikveh* on Szeroka Street.

The first Altschul date about which we can be absolutely certain is 1570. In that year a thorough reconstruction was finished, following a fire that had damaged the synagogue in 1557. Hoping to redesign the building with the signature flair of the Renaissance, the Jews brought in the Italian architect Matteo Gucci. This is why the Altschul is not strictly Gothic in structure but a blend of Gothic and Renaissance (thus the ever-selfless Altschul avoids smearing Prague's claim to have the world's only *purely* Gothic twin-naved synagogue). Gucci heightened the main wall of the synagogue, rounded the tops of the formerly pointed windows, and added an arcaded attic, which was typically added to Renaissance buildings in Poland in order to protect the roof from fire. Before this flat roof was introduced by Gucci, the Altschul's roof was most likely gabled. The *bimah* and *aron hakodesh* were also restyled during the Renaissance, but it is not clear if Gucci himself supervised the reconstruction.

European synagogues served not only as houses of prayer, but also as the social, administrative, and legal centers of the Jewish Community. This was nowhere more obvious than in the Altschul, where a special building was erected at the time of the Gucci renovations. The building served the administrative needs of the Community. It was physically connected to the Altschul on the ground floor and first floor of the western side—a visible symbol of the dominance of tradition and prayer in the everyday lives of the Jews. The building was destroyed in the 1880s, and at the beginning of the twentieth century the Jewish Community office moved into a new building at Skawinska Street number 2, where it continues to operate today.

The Twentieth Century and Beyond

In the early part of this century, the synagogue underwent an extended renovation in the neo-Renaissance style. Work was carried out in 1904, 1913, and 1923 by the famous Cracow architect Zygmunt Hendel. Working also on the surrounding land, Hendel decided to lower the area surrounding the synagogue to the level it had in the sixteenth century. This is why you climb down steps to reach the Altschul's doors today. Hendel also added the elegant fence that surrounds the synagogue. The other noticeable change in the exterior is the stairs added along the western side of the synagogue, where the Jewish Community building stood until it was pulled down at the end of the nineteenth century. At that time, the western facade of the synagogue was renovated and a set of stairs was added, but the stairs were redesigned during Hendel's renovations. The canopied stairs look so distinguished as to be the main entrance to the synagogue, but actually they lead directly to the upstairs women's gallery. Women visitors will be happy to note that their entrance was considerably more splendid than the men's.

When the Germans entered Cracow in 1939, they ordered an end to prayers and turned the building into a storehouse. All of the Altschul's precious relics and furnishings were either looted or destroyed by the SS. When the storehouse was closed later in the war, Germans came in and, in an orgy of looting and destruction, stripped the entire building of its metal, wood, gothic vaulting, and columns. They stripped away so much that the entire ceiling and roof collapsed. It rained and snowed so much in the Altschul that weeds overtook the dilapidated walls and floor. By the end of the war, the Altschul was popularly used as a public toilet. In October 1943, the Nazis brought 30 Polish (Gentile) patriots to the square in front of the synagogue and executed them. The site of execution is marked by a granite monument outside the synagogue.

The Altschul stood in ruins for an entire decade after the war ended. Finally, the state Social Fund for the Protection of Monuments reconstructed the Altschul in 1956–58. The material used in that renovation (the bricks, for instance) is generally the same material that supported the Altschul before the war. The renovators were careful to respect the Gothic and Renaissance styles that had defined the building since the Gucci renovation of 1570.

Technically, the Altschul is owned by the Jewish Community of Cracow, but the ownership is only symbolic. On January 13, 1958, an intriguing "restitution" was effected between the state and the Jewish Community of Cracow. The Altschul was returned to the Jewish Community on the condition that it would be rented to the state, at a cost of one zloty per year, for ninety-nine years. The Altschul thus became the Jewish History branch of the state-run Cracow Historical Museum. After the fall of communism in 1989, the Polish state gave the Altschul to the city of Cracow, which continues to use the site as the Jewish component of the city museum. The collection in the Altschul belongs to the city museum as well.

Although it is commendable that the city runs a Jewish Museum, one might think that the Altschul, as the primary symbol of Jewish longevity in Polish history, should be maintained and controlled by the Jews themselves. Certainly the ticket revenues would well serve the dwindling Jewish Community of Cracow, most of whose active members are survivors of the Holocaust. But therein lies the problem: There are so many visitors to the Altschul that the city museum is reluctant to give it up. More tourists come to the Altschul than to the several other branches of the Cracow Historical Museum combined. Ironically, the city museum supports the Altschul less than the Altschul supports the city museum. Thus the financial anchor of the Cracow Historical Museum will remain in the city's hands, according to the ninety-nine-year contract, until the year 2057—and every year the Jewish Community of Cracow will receive its annual check of one zloty. The Jewish Community, decimated in numbers, has not tried to seize control and insist that the contract of 1957 amounts to theft.

Because the Altschul itself is far more precious than any of the exhibits contained within it, what follows is a detailed description of the building, complete with all its nuances and special secrets. Afterwards, you'll find a brief description of some of the more interesting items on display in the museum.

The Vestibule

The first room, where today tickets are sold, used to serve as the meeting place of the *beit din*, or rabbinical court. All the internal Jewish disputes in Cracow were settled by a religious court of three *dayanim*, or judges, in this room. It used to be filled with benches and candles, and the litigants would sit on one side with the *dayanim* on the other. One book recounts that during heated disputations, shouting would reach such a feverish pitch that the candles would be blown out and the litigants would be left sitting in the darkness. The *dayanim* would always maintain their composure, issuing a verdict based on talmudic precedent.

In the corner left of the entrance are three steps leading to a reconstructed stone well. It is a custom to keep a lavabo of "living water" in a synagogue for the purpose of cleansing the hands, particularly before the traditional third meal on Shabbat. The Altschul interpreted this custom in the purest way possible by digging an actual well into the synagogue itself. Before the war, the well was deemed impractical and replaced by a barrel and a modern faucet. When the synagogue was restored after the war, a replica of the original well was made and remains today.

The antechamber also contains a plaque commemorating the famous speech delivered in the Altschul by Thaddeus Kosciuszko in 1794.

Kosciuszko, a Polish revolutionary inspired by the ideals of the Enlightenment, moved to America in 1775 and became the leading engineer of the American War of Independence and a personal friend of Thomas Jefferson. He built fortifications for the battles at Saratoga, West Point, and elsewhere. It is interesting to note that when the newborn American government awarded him property after the war, he did the unthinkable and freed all the slaves bound to the land.

Kosciuszko returned to Poland in 1784 and ten years later led his country in its own war of independence, called the 1794 Insurrection, against Russia and Prussia. Recalling his memories of Jewish fighters at the Battle of Saratoga, he came to the Altschul to muster Jewish support and participation in the Insurrection. From the *bimah* of this synagogue, Kosciuszko declared that Polish independence would benefit the Jews as well. The text of his speech was excerpted in the Cracow newspaper *Gazeta Rzadowa*. Implicit in Kosciuszko's speech was the belief that Poland was a country belonging to both Gentile and Jew, who must defend it together. The actual fighting, though, was done separately.

The plaque honoring Kosciuszko was unveiled in 1966, on the occasion of the one thousandth anniversary of the Polish state, by the Jewish Youth of the Polish People's Republic. It contains a famous quote uttered by Kosciuszko himself: "The Jews proved to the world that whenever humanity can gain, they would not hesitate to spare their lives." An English translation was put up by a United Jewish Appeal youth mission in 1990.

Surrounding the plaque are pictures highlighting other patriotic activities of the Jews. You'll find Berek Joselewicz, who is also memorialized in the name of a Kazimierz street. During the 1794 Insurrection, Joselewicz organized and led a segregated Jewish unit in the Polish army. Calling on the Jews to fight "like lions and leopards," he had asked Kosciuszko if he could create a separate Jewish regiment. The regiment consisted of five hundred Jews.

Also pictured is the great Polish rabbi Dov Berush Meisels, also immortalized today by a Kazimierz street (*see pages 192–193*). There is also a photo of Rabbi Kornitzer and President Landau awaiting the visit of Polish President Ignacy Moscicki in 1927. It is such a heady occasion that the entourage has brought out the *chupah*, or wedding canopy, which would also be used on such special occasions as the ordination of a new rabbi.

Entering the Main Sanctuary

Above the gateway to the main sanctuary is the traditional synagogue inscription, in Hebrew, "This is the gateway to God, righteous people enter here."

The steps leading down into the main sanctuary most likely do so for the same reason as those found in the Altneuschul in Prague. As it was forbidden to the Jews to build a synagogue higher than any church in the city, they had to build underground in order to achieve the high Gothic ceilings.

In the gateway itself, you can see the remains of what used to be a box for *tzedakkah*, or charity, on the left side. Still remaining is the Hebrew word *Li'yerushalayim*, meaning "For Jerusalem." Thus the box contained donations earmarked to help the Jews of the Holy Land, who maintained a continual presence in Jerusalem throughout the centuries of Exile.

The Main Tzedakkah Box

Around the corner in the main sanctuary itself is a stone-and-iron *tzedakkah* box whose history far exceeds that of the *tzeddakah* box in the archway. It is one of the most remarkable relics remaining in the Altschul today.

The box was crafted in Baroque style in the seventeenth century, but an earlier one preceded it in the same spot. There has been much discussion about the inscription underneath the metal lock. It reads, "Because through *tzedakkah* you make stronger the divine throne." The *gematriah*, or numerical sum, of the letters topped by circles reveals the year 1407, or over two centuries before the *tzedakkah* box was built. There are several theories regarding the meaning of the year 1407 on the box. Some scholars believe the date is related to the founding of the synagogue. As mentioned earlier, the age of the synagogue is shrouded in mystery. It is possible that the synagogue was originally built in the early fifteenth century and the *tzedakkah* box commemorates its construction.

A more widespread opinion is that the date refers to the notorious pogrom perpetrated on March 27—the third day of Easter—1407. A Catholic priest named Budek spread the age-old slander of the blood libel, in which Jews were accused of killing Christians in order to use their blood in Passover matzoh. At the time, Jews lived on St. Anne's Street in Cracow and several Jews sought refuge during the pogrom in St. Anne's Church. The

Christians were so blinded by their rage that they actually set fire to their own church in order to kill the Jews inside. The entire church, as well as surrounding houses, burned to the ground in the resulting conflagration. (Today's St. Anne's Church was built in Baroque style on the site in 1689–1705.) The pogrom, which was described in detail by the first Polish historian, Jan Dlugosz, became embedded in the psyche of Cracow's Jews. Even centuries after the pogrom was perpetrated, it would have been a custom to give charity in memory of the martyred souls. Thus the year memorialized on the *tzedakkah* box almost certainly refers to the tragedy of 1407.

Perhaps both theories about the year are accurate. After the pogrom, several surviving Jews fled to Kazimierz, before it was officially the Jewish Quarter. It is possible that the Altschul, or an earlier synagogue, was built at that time.

Above the metal lock, you can see a much more traditional (and easier to interpret!) inscription. *Mavi*, a Hebrew word meaning "the bringer," refers to the bringer of charity. But on another level, the word is an abbreviation of *Matan biseter yichapeh af*—"A gift in secret subdues anger" (Proverbs 21:14). This inscription adorns *tzedakkah* boxes throughout the Jewish world; you'll see the same inscription on a box in the Altneuschul in Prague. The anger that is subdued in the proverb is God's. Judaism teaches that one of the highest forms of charity is that which is done anonymously. Then the donor performs the good deed through the purest motives of altruism, and not in order to reap public acclaim or control. At the same time, the receiver does not feel humiliated or unnecessarily obliged to his benefactor.

Note to charity-givers: As mentioned above, until the year 2057 all revenues of this museum go to the city museum. If you wish to leave charity to the Jewish Community itself, it is better to do so in the *tzedakkah* box of the Rema Synagogue.

Above the *tzedakkah* box there is a tiny fragment of former wall decorations from the seventeenth, eighteenth, or nineteenth century (it's too small to determine exactly). Another fragment can be found above the other door on the same wall. These fragments seem to be teasing us, offering only a tiny hint of the luxurious frescoes that once paraded through the interior of the Altschul. More fragments can be found in the southern women's section *(see page 300)*.

The interior is where you'll notice the Altschul's most striking similarities to the Altneuschul in Prague. It has two columns, two naves, and six vaults. The benches placed behind the *bimah* are misleading; the Altschul originally contained moveable lecterns similar to those found in the Altneuschul. You can see these lecterns in the painting by Jan Kanty Hruzik, "Jews Praying in the Old Synagogue in Cracow," displayed on the southern wall. From the interior, the Altschul is more spacious than the Altneuschul. This, as well as its thinner columns and walls, serve as evidence that it was built later than its mirror image in Prague.

You'll also notice that, unlike the Altneuschul, the Altschul incorporates many Renaissance details, added during Matteo Gucci's 1570 renovations. The windows, originally pointed, are rounded on top, and the *bimah* and *aron hakodesh* bear Renaissance designs.

The two main columns, like much else in the synagogue, were reconstructed in the late 1950s. Some original parts were used, but the lower parts are obvious reproductions.

The Women's Sections

Women might be pleased to know that at various times they could choose from four *ezratei nashim*, or women's sections, in the Altschul.

The first women's section was built on the west side, where today the museum shop is located. It was most likely built of wood. Later, at the end of the sixteenth century, a small women's section was added to the southern side of the main sanctuary. (As a point of reference, the *aron hakodesh* is always on the eastern wall.) This section was once on the same level as the main sanctuary; only in the past century were the stairs added. The door leading into the southern section is even newer. It used to be a second window looking onto the main sanctuary, and was transformed into a door only during the 1950s restoration of the synagogue. The real door was in the back of the room.

There are two things to notice in this southern room. First, you'll see the original stones from the buttresses of the synagogue, before there was a women's section. When the women's section was built, these were incorporated into the wall. The other unique find in the southern annex are remains of antique text and floral decorations that once covered the walls. On the wall above the window-cum-door, there are fragments of two different frescoes, presumably painted at different times. Unfortunately, they are too withered away to actually read today. There are other fresco remains in the annex; seek and you shall find. Since we can also see fragments of frescoes above the *tzedakkah* box by the entrance (*see page 299*), we know that decorations were not limited to the women's section but covered all the walls of the synagogue.

In the second quarter of the seventeenth century, the women's section on the north side of the sanctuary was built. From the outside of the Altschul, this northern women's gallery is the white, jagged-roofed extension to the main building. Women had a separate synagogue entrance that led straight into the northern women's section. The jagged roof was built after the war, because the architects believed that the women's section had such a roof in the seventeenth century. A similar reconstruction was made on the main roof of the synagogue, but it is hidden behind Gucci's Renaissance attic. The roof design was common to Polish synagogues.

The most recent women's section is a gallery added on the west side in the nineteenth century. It was to this gallery that the exquisite set of canopied stairs was added to the western side of the synagogue in the early twentieth century, as a very posh entrance for women congregants.

This upstairs women's gallery was home to a phenomenon not uncommon in European synagogues. There was a special window reserved for the *zogerke*, a specially designated woman who understood the prayers as well as the cantor himself and served as a sort of women's cantor. She sat at the window and listened to the cantor in the main sanctuary. As he prayed, she would repeat the prayers for the women in her section who could not read. This was in keeping with the idea of the passage from *Berachot*, "Greater is he who answers amen than he who makes the blessing." Just as the cantor is considered the "messenger of the Community," because he repeats the blessings for those who cannot read Hebrew, the *zogerke* serves as the special "messenger" of the women. The women would respond "amen" to the chants of the *zogerke*, and thus count as if they had recited the prayers themselves. Often the *zogerke* was the rabbi's wife.

The special window for the *zogerke* is high on the left side of the western wall. It is the yellow window, and its bottom part swings open for the *zogerke* to be able to listen discreetly. You can see the window better—and pretend to be the *zogerke* herself—by going upstairs to the former women's gallery, which serves as part of the museum today.

The Bimah

In the center of the main sanctuary is a postwar reconstruction of the Renaissance-era *bimah*, made of wrought iron. According to tradition, this *bimah* was originally constructed from 150 pieces of iron to symbolize the 150 chapters in the Book of Psalms. It is said that Jewish iron craftsmen of the sixteenth century sang the 150 chapters while they built the *bimah*.

The spectacularly high *bimah*, tapering off at the top, enclosed the most famous personalities who ever visited Kazimierz as they delivered speeches and sermons in the synagogue. This is where Thaddeus Kosciuszko rallied the Jews to fight for love of Poland in 1794, where the Orthodox leader Maurycy Krzepicki made a similar call in 1846, and where Rabbi Dov Berush Meisels gave a stirring patriotic sermon in 1848. Indeed, before he moved to Warsaw, Rabbi Meisels orated from this *bimah* for 24 years.

There was once a time when a speech delivered from this *bimah* was considered the pinnacle of one's career. All the great Cracow rabbis, including the Bach (*page 326*), the Tosefot Yomtov (*page 334*), the Meginnei Shlomo (*page 329*), and Rabbi Simeon Sofer (*page 361*), ascended these steps and addressed the Jews of Cracow from inside the iron grill. Even the Rema (*page 315*) and the Megalleh Amukkot (*page 321*), who prayed in their own synagogues, would deliver their most consequential sermons in the Altschul. According to tradition, the first chief rabbi of Warsaw, the Chemdat Shlomo (*page 192*), delivered his first speech from this *bimah* in 1799 before heading to Warsaw. The experience was one he never forgot. Even while he led the Warsaw Rabbinate, he would sign all documents with the title, "Head of the Cracow Rabbinical Court, Residing in Warsaw"!

This is the site where all the king's decrees were announced and where the Jewish Community promulgated its own decrees as well. For instance, in the fall of 1785 when the leaders of the Cracow Jewish Community worried that the rising influence of Hasidism would lead to hereticism along the lines of the false messiah Shabbetai Tzvi a century before, Chief Rabbi Isaac Halevi ascended the *bimah* of the Altschul and read off a *cherem*, or ban, against Hasidism. Although the *cherem* was signed by himself and sixteen other leaders, it did little to contain the intoxicating allure of the populist mystical movement. A second *cherem* issued here in 1797 was equally ineffective.

The primary function of the Altschul, of course, was prayer. The *bimah*, representing the altar of the Jerusalem Temple sacrifices, is the place where the Torah is read during the service. Every Shabbat, the Torah portion is read in seven installments. Seven members of the Community are called up to recite a blessing before and after each of these installments in what is called an *aliyah* (literally, "ascent"). As is the case in most synagogues, the *bimah* is raised to represent this ascent as well as to symbolize the throne of God.

In the Altschul there developed a tradition of reserving the third *aliyah* for the chief rabbi and the fourth *aliyah* for the head of the *yeshivah*. There was also a coveted position referred to as the "Assistant." This was the man who would stand on the *bimah* next to the *gabbai* and point out the congregants who were to be called up for *aliyot*. The position was so powerful that the title Assistant was rented out to members of the Community.

On more than one occasion, the Assistant became embroiled in scandal. To have an *aliyah* is considered a high honor; when there are only seven *aliyot* awarded to a congregation that may exceed one hundred, then *aliyot* become status symbols. It is often the custom that the man who receives an *aliyah* to the Torah donates charity to the synagogue after Shabbat is over. So the Assistant had more power than many people realize. It often happened that the Altschul Assistant would call off names that hadn't been decided upon by the rabbi and *shamash* or that he'd pad the *aliyah* roster by calling off eight, nine, or ten *aliyot*. It was usually the case that the Assistant, on his own initiative or at the behest of others in the synagogue, was moonlighting by selling *aliyot* on the side. This, of course, drew down the charity the synagogue would receive. In 1632 the leaders of the Jewish Community issued a special ordinance that prohibited *aliyah*-padding in all the synagogues of Kazimierz. "Concerning recent events involving certain individuals who behave like bosses, pressuring the Assistant to add more than seven to be called to the Torah—this is not from any ancient custom, and it is not from the rules of the synagogue, and it causes a great damage to *tzedakkah*." The decree, posted in each of Cracow's synagogues, stressed the Assistant's ultimate culpability: "If anybody should disobey, no matter who he is, the Assistant will be punished with two coins toward *tzedakkah*, without exception" (quoted in Aryeh Bauminger et al., *Sefer Krako: ir ve-em be-Yisrael*).

The Aron Hakodesh

The stone portal of the *aron hakodesh* was built in the late Renaissance, possibly during the Gucci renovations. The stairs and lectern are reconstructions but the ark itself, with certain refurbishments, is original. The stone columns flanking the ark, for instance, are original, but their capitals are semi-reconstructed. If you look behind the *parochet* (the curtain in front of the *aron*) you will see stonework from the sixteenth century. It used to be painted with vibrant colors in Renaissance Arabesque style. In the nineteenth century, a sumptuous red fresco was painted all around the *aron hakodesh* to give the vital furnishing an even larger appearance. The fresco was lost during the postwar restoration.

Above the *aron hakodesh* you'll see a *keter Torah*, or crown of the Torah, carved in stone. As Jewish mystics sought the loftiest symbols with which to compare the grandeur of God and Torah, the magnificence of royalty was always a favorite metaphor. The other side of this metaphor is that Jews obey the Torah as if it was their king.

Specially made silver crowns are placed on the Torah when it is carried around the synagogue. As a sign of humility and aversion to idolatry, such crowns are never worn by people.

There is an added meaning to this Torah crown, indicated by the passage printed beneath it: "Through me kings reign" (Proverbs 8:15). It is only God who has the supreme power of endowing one with royalty.

As was the custom in Cracow, the *ner tamid*, or everlasting light, is placed on the eastern wall, in a container beside the *aron hakodesh*. The *ner tamid* on the left side was remade after the war. In an active synagogue, the light is a symbol of both the burnt offerings to God in the Old Jerusalem Temple as well as the flame of the Temple menorah.

As in many other synagogues, the space in front of the lectern is marked by a depression. This physically represents Psalms 130:1, "From out of the depths I call to you God." When the cantor stands here to recite the prayers of the liturgy, his lowered position represents both humility and the depths of his soul.

The chandeliers hanging in the Altschul were not necessarily hanging there before the war. Most of them were placed in the Altschul during its reconstruction, culled from among the few remaining chandeliers left in Cracow synagogues. We know that one of them— the second one from the left side of the *aron hakodesh*—spent time in Cracow's Wawel Castle. In the nineteenth century, Wawel was used by the Austrian Army as part of its barracks. Before the First World War, the Poles bought it back and made it into a museum and special residence. During the refurnishing of the castle, a rich Jew had the chandelier made and donated it to Wawel's museum exhibit. It's quite possible that other chandeliers in the Altschul found their way into Wawel during Hans Frank's looting binge when he became the Nazi leader of the Generalgouvernement in Poland. After Frank set up his official residence and office in Wawel, he took the chandeliers from the High Synagogue and brought them to the castle. The Chanukkah menorah to the left of the *aron hakodesh* used to be situated next to the *aron hakodesh* of the High Synagogue. Hans Frank destroyed the eagle that once adorned the candelabra and brought the lamp to the castle. During the 1950s, it too made its way to the Altschul.

None of the chandeliers hanging here are older than the eighteenth century. Countless other chandeliers that once hung in Cracow synagogues are now hanging in private homes throughout Germany.

The Museum Exhibit

At this writing, the museum exhibit is a somewhat random display of generalized Judaica, history of the Altschul, items and pictures from Jewish history in Cracow, and a Holocaust exhibit upstairs. Among the more interesting items on display in the museum are two paintings by Marcin Gottlieb, the brother of the famous painter Maurycy Gottlieb (*see pages 271, 361–362*). One of these is a copy of one of Maurycy Gottlieb's most famous works, *Shylock and Jessica*, which disappeared during the war. The original painting won Maurycy his first major prize, in 1876 in Munich. The other painting is an original by Marcin, *Portrait of a Rabbi*. Elsewhere, in front of the *bimah*, you'll find the famous Polish edition of the Bible, translated by Rabbi Isaac Cylkow in Warsaw and printed by the renowned Fischer printing house in Cracow in 1895. In the women's section you'll find amulets used to protect against Lilith during childbirth. Also shown, both in the women's section and upstairs, are photographs from the Cracow studio of Ignac Krieger from 1870. The photographs are somewhat humorous today because they are posed. Normally it was assimilated Jews who took pictures of themselves, but here even the Orthodox were dazzled by inventions in photography. The Jews are real, but the environment—sometimes involving a bucolic stage set—are artifice. Elsewhere in the women's section there is a touching memorial illustration of a woman, Scheindl Bina Fuchs, that gives the exact dates for the *yahrzeit*, or death anniversary, for forty years after her death in 1912. Since the Hebrew and Roman calendars are different, this allowed her family to know exactly when to say memorial prayers each year. Upstairs, in the exhibit on the Holocaust, there is an iron art composition around the original Shield of David that adorned the gate of the Czestochowa ghetto.

Customs of the Altschul

Walking through the Altschul today, it is difficult to imagine the synagogue as it once was. One constantly has to remind oneself that this edifice was the core of Jewish life in Cracow and a symbol of Jewish longevity in all of Poland. Today, the synagogue holds no services; instead, a rather sterile exhibit of Judaica is all that remains to remind the visitor of the building's former greatness. In this regard, the exhibit could just as easily have been staged in a modern museum. It is our goal, however, to remember the Altschul in its function as a house of prayer.

What follows is a selection of ancient customs and traditions unique to the Altschul. All synagogues have characteristic habits during daily services and the holidays—all the more so a synagogue that absorbed five centuries of Jewish prayer.

Simchat Torah

Perhaps the most well known customs regarding the Altschul surround the holiday of Simchat Torah, or "Rejoicing over the Torah."

On the eve of Simchat Torah, candles would be placed in the windows of homes throughout the Jewish Quarter, but particularly in homes that lined the streets between the home of the chief rabbi and the Altschul. A large group would carry a *chupah*, or wedding canopy, to the home of the chief rabbi and escort him underneath it, amid song and dance, to the steps of the Altschul. The parade was a festive mix of torches, flags, and decorations as the entire Jewish Quarter burst into song.

As soon as they entered the synagogue, the party was abruptly halted. All songs ended in mid-note; the chupah was dismantled; the torches were silently extinguished in a deliberate show of mourning for a pogrom that had once befallen the Jews on Simchat Torah.

Historians point to various attacks that could have been the basis of the Simchat Torah memorial in the Altschul. The most likely is a pogrom that occurred after the Polish-Swedish war in 1655. After the war, the Jews were accused of supporting the invading Swedes. A rumor was spread that the Jews had assisted the Swedes by opening up the gates to Kazimierz. Prompted by such slander, physical attacks against Jews increased and, according to the Altschul tradition, a pogrom occurred on the holiday of Simchat Torah. During the Simchat Torah celebrations, several Cracow university students came to Kazimierz to launch their riot against the Jews. The Jewish Community was praying in the Altschul when they heard horses galloping in the streets. This was the beginning of the pogrom, in which the students killed Jews, looted homes, and set fire to buildings. Quickly sensing the danger, the

Jews in the synagogue halted the service to hide the Torahs, which the students would surely burn. They were in the middle of the *hakafot*, seven circuits around the synagogue in which all the Torahs are taken from the *aron hakodesh* and carried amid singing and dancing. It was during the fourth *hakafah* that the tragedy struck, and it was during the fourth *hakafah* that the Torahs were hidden from the invaders.

Thus arose the most bizarre aspect of the Altschul's Simchat Torah tradition: Every year on Simchat Torah, the synagogue would interrupt the fourth *hakafah* and turn all the benches onto their sides, as is the custom on Tishe B'av, the day that commemorates the destruction of the First and Second Temples in Jerusalem. The congregants would then sit on the overturned benches or on the floor and hold small candles in their hands. Together they would sing a *selichah*, or penitential prayer-poem, composed to remember the tragedy that befell Cracow's Jews. It is said that the congregants sang the same dirges and lamentations sung on Tishe B'Av. Afterwards, the benches would be returned to normal, the remaining *hakafot* would be finished, and the festive atmosphere would resume.

What makes this custom especially compelling is that Simchat Torah is one of the most joyous holidays of the Jewish calendar. Tishe B'Av, on the contrary, is one of the saddest. Such a synthesis of joy and despair is not uncommon in Jewish tradition. The breaking of a glass at a wedding to symbolize the destruction of the Jerusalem Temples is the most obvious example, but there are many others. More than anything else, the custom in the Altschul reveals the extent to which a tragic event could chisel itself into the consciousness of the Jews.

Rosh Hashanah

On the eve of the New Year, the Altschul *shamash* would march down the streets of the Jewish Quarter and call out to the inhabitants that it was time to begin *selichot*. "Come out, Jews, for *selichot*! Come out, Jews, for *selichot*!" Then he would add, in a much deeper voice, "Our fathers—Abraham, Isaac, Jacob, Moses, Aaron, David, and Solomon—arise for holy *selichot*! Rise, rise, for the Jews remain in Exile!"

Yom Kippur

Before the Day of Atonement, the *shamash* of the Altschul would enter the Old Jewish Cemetery and approach the graves of the holy *tzaddikim*. He would shout out for the Rema, the Bach, the Megalleh Amukkot, the Tosefot Yomtov, and he would entreat them to "Rise up to pray for the nation of Israel!"

What was so astonishing was that he didn't call them by their titles or monikers but more directly, by their personal names. "Moses, son of Israel Lazars!" he would shout. "Rise up, your children await you!"

Havdallah

The Havdallah ceremony occurs every Saturday evening throughout the Jewish world, officially ending Shabbat and ushering in the new week. The symbols of the ceremony are a cup of wine, a spice box, and a candle with two or more wicks. Havdallah is customarily performed in the home, but it is often held communally in the synagogue.

What was unique about the Altschul Havdallah was that when the ceremony ended, the *shamash* would use the Havdallah candle to light a series of extra candles. These candles were handed out to each of the congregants, and were said to supply luck and protection. This was no superstition; the ancient custom originated before the time when streetlights had been installed in Kazimierz. As Shabbat ended at nightfall, the candles were used to guide the congregants through the twisting alleyways as they made their way home.

Mornings in Kazimierz

The *shamash* of the Altschul awoke before dawn each morning so that he could visit all the houses in the Jewish Quarter, knocking on doors with a hammer in order to wake people for the *vatikin* prayer in the Altschul. He shouted, "Rise up, Jews, to serve the Creator!"

This custom was not unique to the Altschul. Throughout Galicia the *shul Klaper* would go from house to house with his hammer, knocking on each door to wake the inhabitants for morning prayer. In Cracow, though, the Altschul *shamash* had a special code. If he knocked three times on the door, it was a signal that all was normal and well. When he knocked twice—his sign of mourning—the inhabitants knew that someone in town had passed away during the night.

The Midnight Prayer

There is a Jewish tradition in Cracow that all the souls of the departed gathered in the Altschul every night at midnight to recite the *tikkun chatzot*, or midnight prayer. The souls were so devout that they extended the prayer until morning struck. At dawn, the *shamash* would use a hammer to knock three times on the door of the Altschul, in order to alert the dead that they must leave to make room for the living. Then the gate would be opened, and Cracow's living Jews would enter the synagogue for *shacharit*, the morning service.

Weddings

Since the time it was built, the Altschul hosted all Jewish weddings in Cracow. The custom was that the wedding party gathered at the home of the bride's parents and paraded the couple through the streets of Kazimierz to the Altschul. Just like on Simchat Torah, torches and lanterns were held high and all the homes en route to the synagogue were adorned with burning candles in their windows.

Eventually, an ordinance was passed that weddings would be held in the synagogue of the bride's father. At that point, the Altschul ceased to be the sole sanctuary of Jewish weddings in Kazimierz, but to be married in the Altschul was always considered a singular honor.

New Chief Rabbis in the Altschul

When a new chief rabbi was elected, a procession similar to the wedding parade was staged, this time involving scores of *shofar*s, or rams' horns. All the Jews of Kazimierz would line the streets and the new chief rabbi would be marched through underneath a *chupah*. (Such a *chupah* can be seen in the vestibule, to the left of the plaque honoring Thaddeus Kosciuszko, in the photo of the Jews awaiting the arrival of President Moscicki in 1927.) Three of the tallest *shamashim* in Cracow would be chosen to accompany the chief rabbi with torches held high. As he was marched down the street, spectators would blow from *shofar*s in a public show of exultation. By the time he reached the Altschul, the air resonated with the siren call of dozens of *shofar*s. Once inside, he would mount the *bimah* and deliver his first official sermon as the chief rabbi of Cracow.

THE REMA SYNAGOGUE

Address: 40 Szeroka Street

Opening Hours: Monday through Friday 9:00 A.M.–4:00 P.M.
In the winter, the synagogue is closed to tourists on Fridays before sunset.

Once upon a time, there lived in Kazimierz a Jew, Israel ben Joseph Lazars—widely known as "Reb Isserl"—whose enormous fortune was matched only by his inner virtue. Aside from being one of the richest Jews in the city, he was pious and learned in all the holy books. He served on the board of elders of the Jewish Community of Cracow, negotiating with the City Council for better living conditions for the Jews. His businesses spread throughout the country and even to distant lands, and he even had influence with the king. His son Moses Isserles (the "Rema") was fast becoming the most respected rabbi in all of Poland. His wife, Malkah Dinah, was known far and wide for her devotion to the Torah and her acts of charity. Reb Isserl had great reason to rejoice and to give thanks.

But in 1551, Reb Isserl's good fortune was swiftly turned on its head. A plague consumed the entire Jewish quarter, taking as many as 220 lives in the course of two years. The plague was prodigiously contagious, spreading through the streets of the ghetto with little hope of containment. In 1552, the plague killed Reb Isserl's daughter-in-law, Golda bat Shalom Shachna. Once the tragedy began, it would not cease. Only two weeks after Golda's death, Reb Isserl's mother, Gittel bat Moshe Auerbach, passed away. Reb Isserl then pleaded with his wife, Malkah Dinah, to apply restraint in her charitable activities, so that she too would not come into contact with the plague. But Malkah Dinah would not relent, and every day she left her home to feed and comfort the dozens of sick Jews in the Ghetto. After eight months, she too succumbed to the plague.

Reb Isserl was distraught. In the span of nine months, the time it takes to bring life into the world, the three most important women in his life had been taken from him. The most cataclysmic loss was that of his wife, his lifelong partner who was such a trusted confidante that she even managed much of his business. Reb Isserl finally decided that the only way to split the web of grief would be to build a lasting monument in his wife's memory that would serve as spiritual shelter to all the Jews in Cracow.

The synagogue, an exquisite building crafted out of wood, was built in Malkah Dinah's memory as the plague subsided in 1553. It was built out of one of Reb Isserl's houses in the recently expanded area of the Jewish Quarter that had been intended for a cemetery. Rabbi Isserl's urge to be near his wife was so great that he broke the custom of separating prayer halls from cemeteries. Indeed, the synagogue was built just next to the graves of the Isserl family's loved ones, as if protecting them with the merit of the synagogue's constant prayer. The capacious windows in the back of the synagogue looked out onto the family plot, thus uniting Reb Isserl with his wife all the days of his life.

But the synagogue, which later became known as the Rema Synagogue, was more than a memorial to Reb Isserl's loved ones. In building the synagogue, Reb Isserl wished to quell a fierce dispute that had polarized the Jews of Kazimierz.

In the sixteenth century, there was a conflict in Kazimierz between Polish Jews and a sizeable Community of Czech Jews who had immigrated during repeated persecutions in Bohemia in the fourteenth, fifteenth, and early sixteenth centuries. There was an obvious culture gap: Even then, Czech Jews were known for their westernized ways and their relative prosperity. Polish Jews, by contrast, were less worldly and more focused on Jewish mysticism than the Czech Community. Conflicts between the two communities came to the surface in the early sixteenth century, when the Polish Jews in Kazimierz elected an intense kabbalist as the chief rabbi. The Czech Jews, who didn't want a kabbalist at the helm, elected their own rabbi (*see page 292*). The dispute eventually reached King Sigismund I, who sanctioned the existence of two separate Jewish Communities in Kazimierz in 1519.

Two communities, but only one synagogue, the Altschul. Sure enough, Czech Jews began to fight Polish Jews over rights to the Altschul. The conflict even reached the king, who allowed the Polish Jews to preside over the Altschul while urging them to find a separate prayer space for the Czech Jews. For various reasons, the Polish Jews refused to do so. Reb Isserl, hoping to end the internecine feud once and for all, decided to build his synagogue to give Czech Jews their own place of prayer in Kazimierz. It was yet another example of Reb Isserl's boundless generosity of matter and spirit. In 1556, King Sigismund August gave the synagogue his official sanction.

Originally, the synagogue was called the Neuschul ("New Synagogue"), to distinguish it from the Altschul ("Old Synagogue"). It was the second synagogue the Jewish Community built in Kazimierz. At the end of the sixteenth century, when newer synagogues were planned for Kazimierz, the name had to be updated. By this time, the fame of the Rema (Reb Isserl's son, Rabbi Moses Isserles), had already spread throughout the Jewish world. Since this was the synagogue where the Rema prayed each day, its name was changed to "The Rema Synagogue." The Hebrew inscription above the gate on Szeroka Street combines both names: "The New Synagogue of the Rema, blessed be his memory."

"New" acquired added meaning four years after the synagogue was built. On April 1, 1557, a fire swept through the Jewish quarter, devastating much in its path. Reb Isserl's synagogue was one of dozens of buildings burnt to the ground. Undaunted, Reb Isserl went to King Sigismund August in October of the same year and obtained permission to build a new synagogue. This time, Reb Isserl used brick and stone in the construction.

One of the wealthiest Jews in Kazimierz, Reb Isserl certainly had the means to rebuild. In his codification of Jewish law, the Rema often pointed out exceptions to the rules noted by his contemporary, Rabbi Joseph Karo, in cases involving the risk of great monetary loss. To this day, yeshivah students jest that the Rema knew what he was talking about: he came from such a wealthy family and understood just what it meant to risk such a loss!

In 1829, the synagogue was renovated from floor to ceiling. The ceiling, in fact, was replaced in that year by wooden vaulting. In addition, the large, semi-circular windows were installed at this time. Earlier windows resembled those on the south side. The main addition, though, involved the women's section built on the western side. Before this, there might have been a women's gallery on the northern side of the synagogue, where you can see window shapes today. In a guide to Jewish sites in Cracow published in 1935, the great historian Majer Balaban noted that the Rema Synagogue's roof "is reminiscent of a Chinese temple" (Majer Balaban, *Przewodnik po zydowskich zabytkach Krakowa*). He also described an ornate, sixteenth-century copper lavabo at the entrance—"One of the most beautiful monuments of Renaissance art"—which is no longer to be found in the synagogue. The lavabo was impressive for its human depictions along its sides, including Moses and the Ten Commandments, Isaac carrying wood for the supposed sacrifice, and Jacob and his angelic dream.

During the German occupation of Poland, the Nazis looted the synagogue and turned it into a warehouse for body bags and fire equipment. The synagogue was restored in the 1950s. It is today the only synagogue in continuous use in Cracow.

Inside the synagogue, a beautiful stone *tzedakkah* box for charity is situated at the entrance to the main sanctuary. The inscription on the top implores worshippers to give, like in the days of the Bible, "gold, silver and copper" (Exodus 35:5). Another inscription, destroyed but later repainted in slightly altered form, exhorts people to give "Charity for the peace of the soul of the Rema of blessed memory."

It is interesting that the Rema himself, following the opinion of Maimonides, maintained that a synagogue's *bimah* is best situated in the center of the sanctuary. During the war, the Rema Synagogue's *bimah* was carted away and melted down by the Nazis. The *bimah* you see here is a post-war reconstruction, using some materials from other surviving synagogues. On its doors, dating from the early eighteenth century, are depictions of various furnishings of the Old Temple in Jerusalem, including the altar of incense, the menorah, the crown of the Torah, the twelve-piece bread of display, and Levite pitchers.

The *aron hakodesh* on the eastern wall is composed of four pillars from the late Renaissance, supplemented by other decorations from later eras. On top of the *aron* is an inscription identical to that of the Altschul's aron: "Through me kings reign" (Proverbs 8:15). Beneath this is a *keter Torah*, or crown of the Torah, surrounded by the verse, "Look down from Your holy abode, from heaven, and bless Your people Israel" (Deuteronomy 26:15). Embedded in the pillars on the left side is the *ner tamid*, or everlasting light. The inscription states that the light burns for the soul of the Rema.

In front of the *aron* on the right side is a lowered space, symbolizing Psalms 130:1, "From out of the depths I call to you God." This is where the cantor leads the service. On the podium is a simple Sh'viti Tablet (*see page 64—Altneuschul*), adorned with the verses, "I place God in front of me always" (Psalms 16:8) and "Know before Whom you stand" (Babylonian Talmud, *Berakhot* 28b).

Inside the *aron hakodesh* there once sat a unique Torah scroll, scribed by the Rema himself, that gained fame for its fourteen points of difference from other Torah scrolls.

To the right of the *aron hakodesh* is a plaque above the place used by the Rema himself during services and study sessions. The seat is left vacant during services to this day. The plaque reads, "It is a tradition among us that at this place stood the Rema, blessed be his memory, to pray and to pour out his thoughts before the Holy One, Blessed be He." It is interesting that the plaque indicates not that the Rema sat here but that he stood here. Evidently the Rema used the space in front of the seat to deliver prayers that are read while standing.

The plaque on the southern wall of the synagogue was installed after Reb Isserl's death in 1568. It refers to the construction of the original synagogue in 1553. It reads:

> The man Reb Israel son of Josef, blessed be his memory, with the assistance and for the honor of the Holy one, blessed be He, and for the memory of his wife, Malkah daughter of Reb Eleazar, may their souls be bound in the bundle of the living, built a house of God from the wealth that she left in the year and in the week "Return, O Lord, unto the ten thousands of the families of Israel."

The final verse incorporates the Hebrew date the synagogue was built, written in the form of a verse from the Torah (Numbers 10:36).

In the course of his tenure as chief rabbi of Cracow, the Rema promulgated several rules for the synagogue. These rules were designed to preserve the sanctity of the house of God. Included are prohibitions against eating, drinking, smoking, idle chattering, sleeping, joke telling, chuckling, and loitering. It was forbidden to use the synagogue simply as a shelter against heat or rain. It was forbidden to use the candles of the synagogue to light private candles. Perhaps most importantly, it was forbidden to disrespect any person in the synagogue because such an act, the Rema maintained, was akin to disrespecting the honor of God.

On the western wall of the synagogue are three murals painted in the early twentieth century. From left to right, the images are the grave of Rachel, Noah's ark, and the Western Wall in Jerusalem.

Outside the synagogue, just next to the gate to Szeroka Street, stands a building that used to house the *shamash*, or synagogue sexton.

THE OLD JEWISH CEMETERY OF CRACOW

Address: The cemetery is accessed through the entrance to the Rema Synagogue at Szeroka Street.
Opening Hours: Monday–Friday 10:00 A.M.–4:00 P.M.
In the winter, the cemetery closes Fridays before sunset.

The Old Jewish Cemetery of Cracow

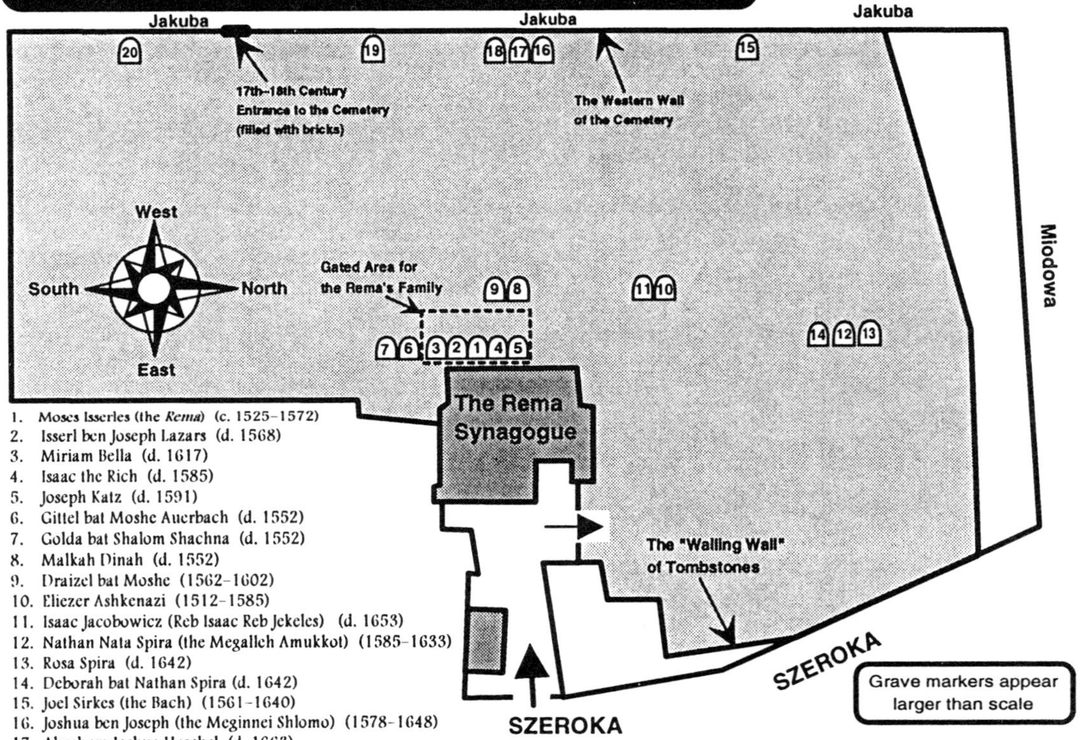

Miodowa

Jakuba

Jakuba

The Western Wall of the Cemetery

17th-18th Century Entrance to the Cemetery (filled with bricks)

Gated Area for the Rema's Family

The Rema Synagogue

The "Wailing Wall" of Tombstones

SZEROKA

SZEROKA

Grave markers appear larger than scale

North / South / East / West

1. Moses Isserles (the *Rema*) (c. 1525–1572)
2. Isserl ben Joseph Lazars (d. 1568)
3. Miriam Bella (d. 1617)
4. Isaac the Rich (d. 1585)
5. Joseph Katz (d. 1591)
6. Gittel bat Moshe Auerbach (d. 1552)
7. Golda bat Shalom Shachna (d. 1552)
8. Malkah Dinah (d. 1552)
9. Draizel bat Moshe (1562–1602)
10. Eliezer Ashkenazi (1512–1585)
11. Isaac Jacobowicz (Reb Isaac Reb Jekeles) (d. 1653)
12. Nathan Nata Spira (the Megalleh Amukkot) (1585–1633)
13. Rosa Spira (d. 1642)
14. Deborah bat Nathan Spira (d. 1642)
15. Joel Sirkes (the Bach) (1561–1640)
16. Joshua ben Joseph (the Meginnei Shlomo) (1578–1648)
17. Abraham Joshua Heschel (d. 1663)
18. Michael Calahora (late 17th cent.)
19. Isaac ben Mordechai Halevi (d. 1799)
20. Yomtov Lippman Heller (the Tosefot Yomtov) (1579–1654)

There are a couple of things to keep in mind as you enter the Old Jewish Cemetery of Cracow. The first is that some of the greatest minds of the Diaspora are buried here. This small plot of land is the final resting place of such famed rabbis as the Rema, the Tosefot Yomtov, the Bach, and the Megalleh Amukkot. Its graves are the third oldest in all Poland, next to Wroclaw and Lublin.

The second thing to keep in mind is that it is very difficult to call this a cemetery today. Under the Nazi occupation, the cemetery was utterly destroyed. The tombstones were demolished and the land was turned into a dumping ground. After the war, it was difficult to imagine that the area had once been anything other than a junkyard.

During archaeological research carried out in the years 1958–61, many of the original tombstones were exhumed from the ground and arranged in the cemetery. Though the renovators tried to approximate the original locations of the tombstones, the stones only roughly correspond to the graves they represent. Chances are that an individual is not buried directly beneath his or her tombstone. What's more, before the war the cemetery had a more helter-skelter and hilly appearance. In the renovations, it was decided to arrange the rediscovered tombstones in an even gridwork of rows and columns.

These factors have led the director of the Cracow Jewish Museum to refer to the site not as a cemetery but as a "stone museum." This is tragic for those who wish to visit the graves of ancient relatives or *tzaddikim*. It is frustrating for anybody to stand before a monument but to not know where the person is buried.

Thus arises the paradox of Cracow's Old Jewish Cemetery: It contains some of the most remarkable people in Jewish history, and yet we cannot be sure exactly where their graves are. The all-star cemetery of European Jewish history is in effect no longer a cemetery at all.

History

The Old Jewish Cemetery is actually not the oldest Jewish cemetery in Cracow. That honor belongs to the cemetery established outside the Cracow city walls as far back as the beginning of the fourteenth century. That cemetery might have existed in the same area as today's Kaviory Street, in which case the street's name probably comes from the Hebrew word *kever*, or "grave." After 1494, when the Jews were expelled from Cracow and moved to Kazimierz, the tombstones from the cemetery were either destroyed or taken by the City Council to use as building foundations. No traces of the cemetery remain.

Even in Kazimierz, though, the Old Jewish Cemetery isn't the oldest. There was an older cemetery, from at least the fifteenth century, that was located either in the park on Szeroka Street in front of the Rema Synagogue (*see page 337*), or nearby the Altschul. After Cracow's Jews were expelled and settled here in 1494, that cemetery filled up quickly. By the early sixteenth century, it was already far too overcrowded. But the congestion of the Jewish quarter wasn't limited to the cemetery: All the streets were overpacked, and the Jews desperately needed new land to grow into. Thus in 1533 the Jewish Community bought the plot of land now called the Old Jewish Cemetery. At the time, there was no Rema Synagogue on the site. It was just an empty plot of land adjacent to the then-boundaries of the Jewish Quarter.

Even after the Jews bought the land, the City Council dragged its heels over granting a cemetery permit for the new area. Ironically, it was land for the dead that initiated the tug-of-war over whether the Jews should be granted more space for the living. Nearly two decades later, the city still hadn't decided whether to permit another Jewish cemetery in Kazimierz. Then in 1551 an epidemic broke out in Kazimierz. During the next two years, the epidemic took 220 Jewish lives. The Jews had no choice but to begin burying in the new space. The first person buried in the cemetery was a woman by the name of Hendela bat Gershon. Because the status of the land was still unresolved, the first funerals in 1551 and 1552 were technically illegal and had to be performed semi-surreptitiously.

Finally in 1553, in one of the most important acts in Jewish history in Kazimierz, the Jewish Community won permission from the city to expand the Jewish Quarter. Included in the deal was the permission, at last officialized, to use the new plot of land as a cemetery. One of the representatives of the Jewish Community was Israel Lazars, the father of the Rema, who built the Rema Synagogue next to the cemetery plot.

When the cemetery was first opened, the entrance was from the east, in the same general area as today's entrance. This was the only place a gate could be placed, as the cemetery's other walls bordered either the Kazimierz city walls or the walls of the Jewish Quarter. In 1608, when the boundaries of the Jewish Quarter expanded west, it was considered a symbol of prosperity to move the cemetery entrance to the west as well. Thus a new gate was established on the newly secure Jakuba Street. You can still see this gate, filled in with bricks, from inside the cemetery (in the middle of the western wall) and from outside, on Jakuba Street. At the turn of the nineteenth century, when the cemetery was no longer in active use, the main entrance was again moved, this time to the gateway next to the Rema Synagogue. This gateway serves as the main entrance to this day. You can see the plaque describing the establishment of the cemetery, originally placed on the Jakuba Street gate, above the modern entrance.

From the middle of the sixteenth century until the year 1800, the cemetery was used for a seemingly endless number of illustrious rabbis, scholars, doctors, printers, and merchants, as well as simple artisans, poor beggars, and unknown wedding jesters. In 1799 the ruling Austrians insisted that the cemetery was overcrowded and too close to nearby apartment buildings. They demanded that for hygienic reasons the Jews close the cemetery and buy a new area for burial outside the congested Jewish Quarter. Thus the cemetery stopped being used in 1800, when the New Jewish Cemetery was established east of the Jewish Quarter. An important rabbi or communal leader occasionally would be buried in the Old Cemetery until the middle of the nineteenth century, but for all intents and purposes the cemetery was closed for burials. Unlike the Old Jewish Cemetery in Prague, this cemetery survived the pipe dreams of nineteenty-century city planners. In 1845, during the same urban renewal that created the plac Novy ("New Square," commonly referred to—even today—as "Jewish Square"), the city wanted to pave a street right through the cemetery. The great Rabbi Dov Berush Meisels (*see pages 192–193—Warsaw Cemetery*) tirelessly lobbied the city senate until it abandoned its designs.

As unbelievable as it seems for a holy site of such stature, the Jewish Community rarely tended the cemetery after it was closed to burials. Throughout the nineteenth century the cemetery fell into deeper and deeper neglect. By the eve of World War II, its condition had reached a critical state. According to one account, practically all the tombstones were already buried beneath the earth at this time. It is said that at the beginning of the eighteenth century, when the Swedes invaded Cracow a second time, the Jews hid the tombstones under layers of earth in order to protect the cemetery from destruction. Later they exhumed the tombstones of the most eminent personalities, but never got around to renovating the entire cemetery. As a result, there were only about seventy standing tombstones in the Old Jewish Cemetery before the war.

The German devastation finished in an instant what an entire century had only begun to wreak. Soldiers using mallets, hammers, and axes hacked away and toppled all but a dozen or so of the remaining tombstones. The entire area soon became a favorite dumping ground for the occupying army.

Soon after the war ended, the Jewish Community of Cracow started to rebuild. The tombstones of the most famous individuals were presumed lost forever, so the Community created replicas of the originals and placed them in the cemetery. Then at the end of the 1950s, the National Fund for the Restoration of Cracow's Historical Monuments conducted archaeological research in the cemetery. Over seven hundred tombstones from the sixteenth to nineteenth centuries, as well as countless broken fragments, were found buried in the ground. The fragments were embedded into the cemetery wall on the Szeroka Street side. The mosaic is titled "The Wailing Wall" because, like the Western Wall in Jerusalem, it represents the last piece of a destroyed Jewish society. When you enter the cemetery, you will find this wall on the right-hand side.

As for the rediscovered tombstones, they were placed in the even rows and columns mentioned above. In places where a replica tombstone had already been made—as is the case for practically all the well-known personalities—the original tombstone was placed either back-to-back or nearby the replica. As a result, you will often find two tombstones for a single person. Often the replicas have easier to read inscriptions than the faded and semidestroyed originals. However, the inscriptions on the replicas are almost always altered or abridged versions of the originals. Many of the tombstones are supported by cement bases made during the postwar cemetery renovation. They should not be confused with decorative *ohelim*. The aluminum "hats" atop the tombstones are not a quaint Cracow custom, but a deterrent to acid rain.

Unlike the Old Jewish Cemetery in Prague, there is no tourist-friendly path that encircles this cemetery and stops at the most famous graves. In general, though, the noteworthy graves in the Old Jewish Cemetery of Cracow can be found in three areas: near the Rema Synagogue, in the center area of the cemetery, and in the last row next to the western wall. What follows are some of the most prominent individuals, with explanations as to their location. Most, but not all, of the famous personalities have noticeable tombstones. With the help of the map, you should be able to locate these important stones.

The grave of Rabbi Moses Isserles [see page 275] is located directly behind the Rema Synagogue. In the fenced-in section are prominent members of the Isserles family. Rabbi Isserles's grave is the middle one among the five tombstones.

Moses Isserles (1525 or 1530–1572): The **Rema**

The grave of Rabbi Isserles, known commonly by the acronym "Rema," is without a doubt the most-frequented grave in the cemetery. The position of the grave is no coincidence. In fact, it is said that his father constructed the Rema Synagogue so that it would look out on his family. Today, the windows from the women's section offer a clear view of Rabbi Isserles's tombstone. As people pray in his synagogue, they are said to be spiritually guided and protected by the merits of the Rema himself.

For a rabbinical heavyweight such as the Rema, you can expect a wealth of legends and traditions concerning his life (*see page 278—Legends*). The first is the most all-inclusive: it is said that his entire life was framed by the number "33." He was chosen as chief rabbi of Cracow when he was 33 years old, on the holiday of *Lag Ba'Omer* (the 33rd day of the Omer); he wrote 33 books; he died on *Lag Ba'Omer* in the 333rd year of the fifth millennium; finally, at his funeral, the eulogizers listed 33 merits. For centuries after the Rema died, thousands of Jews from all over Poland would sanctify the holiday of *Lag Ba'Omer* by making a trip to Cracow to pray at the grave of the Rema. The Rema shared this holiday with Yochanan ben Zachai, who also died on *Lag Ba'Omer*, and whose grave in Meron, Israel, still attracts thousands of Jews on that holiday. Here in Cracow, however, there are too few Jews to make the *Lag Ba'Omer* celebrations anything like those before the war.

The Rema's tomb was one of the only ones to survive the Holocaust unscathed. Even the nearby graves of his family were demolished, but the Rema's was untouched. Photographs taken after the war show a veritable wasteland with a solitary monument—that of the Rema—emerging from the rubble. This has led to several legends. The main legend is that during the destruction of the cemetery, an SS commander ordered one of his underlings to destroy the Rema's tombstone. The worker went in, but stopped as soon as he reached the grave. Something kept him from moving forward. He came back to the SS commander, spent and terrified. The commander sent in another man, who returned even more panic-stricken, trembling and struck with a sickly pallor. After two more men came back with similar non-results, the commander was infuriated. He marched into the cemetery, grabbed a sledgehammer from the ground, and swung it with all his might at the tombstone of Rabbi Isserles. The sledgehammer bounced off the stone and returned with equal force to the commander's head, striking him dead.

Of course, such Holocaust legends ultimately leave a bitter taste in one's mouth. When we spin tales that a man was saved through his holiness, what are we implying about those who were murdered?

On his tombstone is the celebrated inscription, "From Moses to Moses, there was none like Moses." The aphorism originated in the Middle Ages to compare Moses Maimonides to his biblical forebear, the Moses of the Torah. On the Rema's tombstone it takes the Moses progression one step further, and likens the Rema to Maimonides himself. Such a linkage is not accidental. Of all the philosophers in Jewish history, Moses Maimonides is the one who most influenced the Rema's thought and work.

In fact, the Rema was known as the "Maimonides of Polish Jewry" partly because he felt Jewish study might be supplemented by the study of secular thought. When one rabbi criticized the Rema for having used an Aristotelian approach in his decisions, the Rema defended himself by saying that all his knowledge of Greek philosophy he had learned through the writings of his spiritual and intellectual mentor, Maimonides.

You'll find an inscription on the back of the Rema's tombstone as well. That's actually the original inscription. In the eighteenth century, the Jewish Community decided to make the Rema's tombstone more aesthetically ornate. Instead of using a new tombstone, the Community flipped the original around and wrote on its back side. Today, the "front" of the tombstone is really its back.

To the left of the Rema is the grave of his father, Israel ben Joseph Lazars (d. 1568), the prestigious merchant who built the Rema Synagogue. Israel ben Joseph was widely known as Reb Isserl. The text on his tombstone indicates that "His great merit should assist those who come to pray at his gravesite . . . He will solicit compassion on our behalf before the One Who neither slumbers nor sleeps." The final verse is a reference to Psalms 121:4.

To the left of Isserl ben Joseph Lazars is the Rema's sister, Miriam Bella (d. 1617). On her tombstone she is described as "The sister of Moses and Aaron." This relates her to the original Miriam of the Bible, who also had brothers named Moses and Aaron.

The grave to the right of the Rema is that of Isaac "the Rich" (d. 1585). Isaac the Rich, one of the Rema's brothers, was a wealthy banker in Cracow who held a high position in the Cracow Jewish Community.

To the right of Isaac the Rich is **Joseph Katz** (1511–1591). Although he was not himself an Isserles, Rabbi Katz was a relative: The Rema chose Rabbi Katz's sister as his second wife. Rabbi Katz also worked closely with the Rema, serving with him on the Cracow *beit din* and co-signing a number of his important rulings. The decisions of Joseph Katz, the Rema, and the third member of the Cracow Beit Din, **Moses Landau** (d. 1562), were hailed throughout the Diaspora as definitive explanations of Jewish law.

After marrying into a wealthy family, Rabbi Katz was free to pursue scholarly studies and Jewish Community work his entire life. He directed the main yeshivah in Cracow from 1576 until his death. His most famous work was *She'erit Yosef*.

In 1551, a plague struck Kazimierz, which lasted two years. As many as 220 Jews died in this plague. To put this in some perspective, the average annual death count among the Jews in sixteenth-century Kazimierz was roughly twenty to fifty when there was no epidemic. The plague was so catastrophic that it necessitated the immediate opening of this cemetery. Because the land was not yet licensed as a cemetery, the burials were technically illegal. Among those who succumbed to the epidemic—which, according to one source, was cholera—were three women in the Rema's family. First the Rema's wife, Golda, died (the Hebrew date was 11 Sivan 5312). Two weeks later, the Rema's grandmother, Gittel, passed away (27 Sivan 5312). After seven months, the Rema's mother, Malkah Dinah, succumbed as well (20 Tevet 5313). It was the most tragic period in the life of the illustrious Isserl Lazars and his son, the Rema. The mourning was no doubt compounded by the fact that the funerals had to be covert, as the City Council had still not authorized the land to be used as a cemetery (authorization came only in 1553). After the mourning period, the original Rema Synagogue was built as a way of memorializing Isserl Lazars wife, Malkah Dinah, as well as the other matriarchs of the Rema dynasty.

Golda and Gittel are buried immediately to the left of the fenced-in graves, and Malkah Dinah is buried behind the fenced-in area.

Thus, just outside the fence, to the left of Miriam, is the grave of Gittel bat Moshe Auerbach (d. 1552), the Rema's grandmother. Her inscription reads:

> Here is hidden a distinguished woman, all of whose deeds were performed in faith, Mrs. Gittel, daughter of Reb Moshe Auerbach, of blessed memory. Every eye will tear. She was generous to the poor all the days of her life. All her life she rose early to come to *shul*, and she passed away in her old age. She went to her world on Sunday, the 27th of Sivan, in the year 5312 (1552), with the rest of the righteous people of the world, in the Garden of Eden.

To Gittel's left is Golda bat Shalom Shachna (d. 1552), the first wife of the Rema. Golda was the daughter of one of the most famous rabbis of the sixteenth century, Rabbi Shalom Shachna of Lublin. The Rema himself studied under Rabbi Shachna, who was so impressed with the Rema's genius that he suggested the Rema marry Golda. Golda died only two weeks prior to Gittel's death. These two graves were among the first burials in the cemetery. Golda's tombstone is badly damaged, but some of the original text reads:

Woe on the breaking of the daughter of my nation, praise her.
How can this golden amulet be dulled?
The Rebbetzin Mrs. Golda, may her memory be a blessing,
Daughter of our teacher Rabbi Shachna, leader of the congregation, head of the Exile
In all her deeds and traits she was exemplary
A daughter of twenty, she was as a daughter of one hundred
Not a fault to be found in her.
In her good memory, this tombstone shall remain standing everlastingly,
Until those that are resting in the dust shall rise with joy.
The year 5312, the 11th day of Sivan
This catastrophe took place.
May she be bound up in the bundle of life with the other righteous people in the world, in the Garden of Eden Amen Selah.

Behind the fenced-in area, on the right corner, is the grave of the Rema's mother, Malkah Dinah (d. 1552), the third close relative of the Rema to die from the plague. Distraught, he composed her tombstone inscription himself, using the text of the well-known "Woman of Valor" chant (Proverbs 31: 10–31) as inspiration. The "Woman of Valor" is normally sung by husbands before beginning the Friday evening meal on Shabbat. Unfortunately, the tombstone is all but unreadable today. Here is the original text:

> This is the tombstone of my precious mother, Malkah Dinah
> On the twentieth of Tevet our hearts' happiness ceased
> She made tapestries, her clothing was fine linen and purple
> She did not fear for her household because of snow,

For her entire household is dressed in crimson
She extended her hands to the destitute,
She was like a merchant fleet, bringing her food from afar, in her youth,
In wisdom, in humility was my mother
Her spirit and soul flew away
In the year "Return to Him."

The year of Malkah Dinah's death (*shin-yud-gimel*) was rewritten (*shin-yud-bet-alef*) in order to begin the sentence "Return to Him," ie., "Return to your Creator."

It was after the death of Malkah Dinah that the Rema's father, the illustrious Isserl Lazars, embarked on the construction of the Rema Synagogue.

To the left of Malkah Dinah is the grave of Draizel bat Moshe (1562–1602), the Rema's first daughter. She was married to Rabbi Simchah Bunim Meisels of Lublin.

To the left of the graves of the Isserles family is a hilly and unkempt area of the cemetery that was once covered in tombstones as well. The archaeological renovations in the 1950s were confined to the central area of the cemetery, and so there are without a doubt hundreds of tombstones still buried beneath the ground here. Before the war, the entire cemetery resembled this area. The hills in the main part of the cemetery were levelled when the tombstones were exhumed and reset at the end of the 1950s.

The stone of Eliezer Ashkenazi is located northwest of the Rema Synagogue, three rows in. Its most distinguishing characteristic is the snake that adorns the top of the stone.

Eliezer Ashkenazi (1512–1585)

To call Eliezer Ashkenazi a rabbi of Cracow would not do justice to the breadth of the rabbi's reign. Indeed, the rabbi arrived in Poland only at the age of sixty-three. A wealthy Renaissance globetrotter of epic proportions, Rabbi Ashkenazi experienced the colorful panorama of Diaspora Jewry in all its international vitality. Through his activities in communities as far afield as Egypt, Italy, and Poland, he embodied both the divergent traditions and underlying unity of the Jewish world at the time.

After studying in Salonica under the venerable Joseph Taitzak, Ashkenazi became a rabbi in Egypt at the ripe age of twenty-six. He spent twenty-two years in Egypt, after which he officiated in Cyprus, Venice, Prague, Poznan, Gniezno, and finally Cracow. His predilection for town hopping was due partly to his internal drive to see the world, partly to disagreements with other rabbis, and partly to politics, both within the Jewish communities and in relation to the Gentile world.

Or it might have had to do with his magic carpet. There is a beautiful legend about Rabbi Ashkenazi that marvels at both his enormous frequent flyer miles and the exoticism of his experience. Rabbi Ashkenazi, who was endowed with great wealth, owned an exquisite set of gold and silver dishes, which he used only on Passover. One Passover, as he set his table with the resplendent plates and platters, his Egyptian neighbors caught a glimpse of his lavish wealth. Overcome with jealousy, they ran off to the governor of Cairo and accused Rabbi Ashkenazi of stealing from the Egyptians.

That evening, the Ashkenazi family gathered for the Passover seder. After eating the traditional *afikomen* desert, they opened their door to Elijah the Prophet, as is the custom. In the blink of an eye, two Heavenly messengers rushed into the Ashkenazi household. One of them spoke: "We are here to inform you that there is a *gezerah* (decree) from Heaven that you should leave the country at once." Rabbi Ashkenazi assembled his wife and daughter on the living room carpet and said, "Let's all hold hands together." The carpet rose high into the sky and began to fly, far across the Mediterranean Sea and all the way to Venice. The entire journey took only minutes; when the Ashkenazis disembarked from their carpet, they finished the seder in Venice. Rabbi Ashkenazi went to the rabbi of Venice and quoted from the *selichot*, or penitential prayers: "*Mimitzrayim v'ad heynu, v'sham ne'emar* . . ." This means, "[And God brought us] From Egypt until here, as it is said . . ."

Rabbi Ashkenazi is known both for his works and his activities in diverse Jewish communities. While in Egypt, he maintained contacts with the kabbalists of Tsfat and became friends with Josef Karo, the author of the *Shulchan Aruch*. In Poland, the Rema considered him an equal. While in Prague in 1564, Rabbi Ashkenazi created the Prague *Chevrah Kaddishah*, or Jewish Burial Society. He worked closely in this project with Rabbi Judah Loew (*see page 118*), who was an active participant in the society and who codified the society's rules. It was the first *Chevrah Kaddishah* to serve an entire Jewish Community. Future burial societies throughout the Jewish world were to look to the Prague society as their model. (For an inside look at Prague's legendary *Chevrah Kaddishah* created by Rabbi Ashkenazi, *see pages 117–120*.) While in Prague, Rabbi Ashkenazi also wrote eight *selichot* that were used in prayers throughout Bohemia.

Rabbi Ashkenazi was fiercely independent in his thought. He got in trouble in Venice, for instance, for eschewing tradition and ruling that, if a wife desired it, the Community could force her immoral husband to divorce her. In Cracow he caused a minor commotion when he dismissed as oppressive a ruling that forbade *yeshivah* students from forming new academies anywhere near their former *yeshivahs*. As a result, his contemporary and fellow Renaissance man Joseph Delmedigo cheekily quoted the Psalms (80:9–14) in describing Rabbi Ashkenazi: "You plucked up a vine from Egypt; You expelled nations and planted it . . . Why did you breach its wall so that every passerby plucks its fruit, wild boars gnaw at it, and creatures of the field feed on it?" He meant that Rabbi Ashkenazi, a sophisticated and worldly man from Egypt, was forced to live among the uncultured Polish Jews.

His most famous work is the Torah commentary *Ma'asei Ha'Shem*, published in 1583. It was noted for its rationalistic bent. Four centuries before the universities were to tout "new" methods of reading, Rabbi Ashkenazi insisted that the Torah was a constantly regenerating text, from which each generation—indeed, each individual reader—could find his own personal interpretation. Calling on all Jews to search for the meaning of the Torah, Rabbi Ashkenazi wrote, "Let us not permit the opinion of someone else—even if of an earlier generation—to hinder us from research. . . . Research and choose: For that you have been created and reason has been given you from heaven." Rabbi Ashkenazi held the radical view that the less rational aspects of Jewish tradition were the result of everything from misspellings to religious sabotage.

A Renaissance Jew of the sixteenth century, Rabbi Ashkenazi spoke twelve languages and was well versed in philosophy, physics, and medicine. He himself was a physician (the snake adorning Rabbi Ashkenazi's stone is the symbol of medicine). When he wrote, in a commentary on the Book of Esther, that the miracles described therein probably didn't really take place, he earned himself the future censure of several hasidic groups.

Rabbi Ashkenazi said that whoever came to his grave with a request would be assisted. Heaven would come to the seeker's aid and supply the solution. Today, however, it is unclear whether the placement of his tombstone corresponds exactly with the grave itself. It can't hurt to make a wish, though.

Eerily enough, there is a legend regarding Rabbi Ashkenazi's tombstone that predates the chaos wreaked on the cemetery during the Holocaust. It is said that as soon as Rabbi Ashkenazi was buried, the Jews of Cracow underwent a kind of collective amnesia regarding his gravesite. They had the text of the tombstone recorded in the annals of the Cracow Burial Society, but nobody seemed to know where was the site of the grave itself. Centuries later, in 1861, Simeon Sofer, the son of Bratislava's venerable Chatam Sofer, became rabbi in Cracow. When a quandary hit the Jewish Community, Rabbi Sofer went straight to the cemetery to pray at the graves of *tzaddikim*, or righteous people. It was felt that the merits of the *tzaddikim* would help the Jews resolve the problem. As he left the cemetery, Rabbi Sofer told his entourage, "Everything should turn out all right. We have the merits of such bright lights of Jewish tradition—the Rema, the Bach, the Megalleh Amukkot, Tosefot Yomtov, Eliezer Ashkenazi—"

The rabbis of Cracow, wide-eyed and gasping, interrupted him. "Did you say Eliezer Ashkenazi?"

"Sure," said Rabbi Sofer. "He might not have been the Rema, but we can still use his merit."

The astonished rabbis declared, "But the gravesite of Rabbi Ashkenazi has been missing for generations!"

"What do you mean?" responded Rabbi Sofer. "I was just there. It's right near Reb Isaac Reb Jeckeles's tombstone. There's a snake on top." Rabbi Sofer then proceeded to recite the text off the tombstone.

The rabbis couldn't believe it. Murmuring in bewildered tones, they asked themselves how a grave could simply vanish for centuries, only to reappear again. And how come Rabbi Sofer, a newcomer to Cracow, was the first person to find it? "There's only one way to find out," declared an older rabbi, and the entourage made a beeline back into the cemetery. When they arrived at the place Rabbi Sofer had indicated, the site was once again empty. "That's funny," said Rabbi Sofer. "It was here a minute ago!"

Years later, in 1925, there was an effort to clean up the cemetery, which had become overgrown and untidy after years of neglect. In one area, right near the grave of Reb Isaac Reb Jeckeles, there was a large pile of stones. Clearing away the rocks and debris, they found the grave and tombstone of Rabbi Eliezer Ashkenazi. It was in the exact spot that Rabbi Sofer had indicated over half a century earlier.

The legend has added meaning today, after the post-Holocaust reconstruction of the cemetery. At first replicas were made, and then later the originals were found. Thus there are often two tombstones representing a single individual. Searching for graves today is like searching for Rabbi Ashkenazi's grave after he died. It is further interesting because, since the tombstones were replaced in locations that only roughly approximated their former positions, it is difficult to say today whether this is the exact spot of Rabbi Ashkenazi's grave. We need another Simeon Sofer to tell us.

As an illustration of this confusion, to the left of Rabbi Ashkenazi's tombstone you'll find the stone of Isaac Jacobowicz, also known as Reb Isaac Reb Jekeles (d. 1653) [see Isaac Synagogue, page 346]. However, it's one of the replicas made after the war. The original, ohel-style tombstone is located two rows in front of the replica, one grave over to the left. The inscription has faded drastically and it's almost impossible to read today.

The tombstone of Rabbi Nathan Nata Spira, the Megalleh Amukkot, is located in the northern section of the cemetery. From the northwest corner of the synagogue, walk on the path to the right, up the hill, to the three ohel-style tombstones separated from the other tombstones in the area. The largest of these ohelim—and, in fact, the largest grave on the hill—is that of Rabbi Nathan Nata Spira.

Nathan Nata Spira (1585–1633): The Megalleh Amukkot

Long before the Nobel Prize recognized mathematical genius, centuries before Jews were even allowed into universities, there was a humble rabbi by the name of Nathan Nata Spira who was such a maven with puzzles and numbers that Einstein and Kasparov would surely have found in him a worthy match.

Born in Cracow in 1585, Rabbi Spira married the niece of the wealthy Reb Isaac Reb Jeckeles, the namesake of the Isaac Synagogue. When he was thirty-two years old, Nathan Spira's father-in-law passed away, and Nathan himself was appointed to the Cracow rabbinate and made director of his father-in-law's *yeshivah*. Rabbi Spira was exceptional in that, most likely due to his family wealth, he consistently refused a salary from the Jewish Community. By the end of his life, he headed Cracow's *beit din*, or rabbinic court.

Rabbi Spira is most famous for his forays into the *Kabbalah*. Inspired by the sixteenth-century innovations in *Kabbalah* that came pouring out of the Galilee city of Tsfat, he disseminated these teachings in his popular *yeshivah* as well as through his writings, and became one of Polish Jewry's pioneers of the new form of *Kabbalah*.

The type of mystical revelation that most appealed to Rabbi Spira was that of the *gematriah*. According to the *gematriah*, every Hebrew letter has a numerical equivalent; through additions, subtractions, and combinations of letters, one can find new meanings for passages in the holy texts.

Possessed of an intricate mathematical mind, a superlative memory, and a feisty inventiveness, Rabbi Spira was perfectly suited to the arcane universe of the *gematriah*. A man who was said to be intoxicated with numbers, Rabbi Spira literally thought in acrostics and equations. He was known to seize verses from distant reaches of the *Tanach* and stitch them together with such surgical precision that their association became at once self-evident to the reader.

Rabbi Spira's most famous work illustrates his uncanny numerical acumen. Published posthumously in 1637, his magnum opus *Megalleh Amukkot* (literally, "The Revealing of the Depths") became an instant classic in the world of Jewish mysticism. Indeed, "Megalleh Amukkot" has become the moniker by which hasidic scholars refer to Rabbi Spira to this day. The entire book focuses on a single verse in Deuteronomy 3:26. Moses, eager to enter the land of Israel, is told by God, "*Rav lach*,"—"Enough to you." God is saying that Moses has experienced enough already, and therefore should stop begging God. The numerical sum of the Hebrew phrase *rav lach* is 252. Taking this as his cue, Rabbi Spira etched out 252 commentaries on the single passage. Each of the 252 explanations revealed not only the geometric symmetry of the Torah, but also the brilliant digital mind of Rabbi Spira.

In another book, *Elef Ulfanim* ("A Thousand Ways"), Rabbi Spira scrutinizes the first word of the book of Leviticus. He notices that in the Torah, the first word, *vayikra*, features a tiny *alef*. Of course, the numerical equivalent of *alef*—one—does not leave much room for mathematical gymnastics. But Rabbi Spira, hardly one to get discouraged, points out that when *alef* is spelled out, it has the same letters as *elef*, which is the Hebrew word for one thousand. Additionally, in the *Kabbalah* it is said that when you come to the number one thousand, it is like you have come around in a circle back to the number one. So instead of underachieving with the number one, Rabbi Spira seizes the thousand and goes on to find *one thousand* reasons for the diminutive *alef*, each of them more ingenious than the last.

You'll notice that there are actually two tombstones, back-to-back, over Rabbi Spira's grave. The one in the front is the seventeenth-century original, which was considered lost after the cemetery was demolished during the Holocaust. During reconstruction of the cemetery, a new tombstone was constructed along roughly the same lines as the original and placed over Rabbi Spira's grave. Then in the late 1950s, the original tombstone was found. It was returned to its original location, with the more recent replica tombstone placed at its backside.

On the Megalleh Amukkot's tombstone there is a famous and oft-repeated inscription: "It is said of him that Elijah conversed with him face to face." The inscription reveals the immense hold Rabbi Spira had on the Cracow Community even during his own lifetime.

According to hasidic lore, the great prophet would descend every night from Heavenly bliss down to Kazimierz for a cup of cocoa and kabbalistic conversation right in the Megalleh Amukkot's home. Elijah would give the Megalleh Amukkot holy insights and divine double entendres, which the latter used in both his kabbalistic writings and his rabbinical decisions. Many legends evolved out of the Megalleh Amukkot's friendliness with Elijah; you can find a gem of a legend on *page 282*.

The Revealing of the Depths

In his most famous book, *Megalleh Amukkot*, Rabbi Nathan Spira gave a whole new meaning to the term exegesis when he offered 252 explanations for the passage in Deuteronomy 3:26 in which God says to Moses, "*Rav lach*,"—"Enough to you." To give you a peek into the synapses firing in Rabbi Spira's mind, here is a select example of one of the 252 commentaries:

There is a *midrash* written one thousand years ago that explains the passage in Deuteronomy in terms of a poor man speaking to a rich man. The poor man speaks in an obsequious tone, while the rich man responds with strength and chutzpah. The word used in the Hebrew is *azut*, meaning "impudence." Thus, the *midrash* relates that Moses was like a poor person asking a favor from God that he would be able to enter the land of Israel. God, in turn, is the rich man, who answers Moses with *azut*.

But Rabbi Spira found this inconceivable. How could God, the Supreme Being, speak with *azut*? How can the *midrash* refer to the Holy One with a word that means "impudence"?

The Rabbi, in response to the dilemma, takes us on a journey of speculation. Had Moses been allowed to enter the land of Israel, Rabbi Spira explains, he most certainly would have been the Messiah. But as a result, successive generations of Jewish history would have been terminated. Thus, Moses was not permitted to enter the land of Israel so that history would be permitted to continue. This history gives us the story of Ruth, who married Boaz. After many more generations, Ruth's descendant is King David. Many, many generations later, from the same lineage as King David, the true Messiah will ultimately rise. In this respect, God is saying to Moses, "You have such a burning desire to go to the land of Israel, but look what you'll cause—we will lose the entire story of Ruth and Boaz, with its lineage that leads to the Messiah."

According to Rabbi Spira, the passage in the Torah melds with the *midrash* to summon this explanation. The word *rav* from *rav lach* is composed of two letters, *resh* and *bet*. These letters are the abbreviation for Ruth and Boaz. But this is only an abbreviation; the remaining letters are waiting to be heard. If you take the remaining letters from the name Ruth, you get *vav* and *taf*. The remaining letters from Boaz are *ayin* and *zayin*. Taken together, *Ayin-zayin-vav-taf* spells out *azut*, the problematic word from the *midrash*. Thus, the *azut* in the *midrash* is connected to the *rav* in the Torah passage in a way nobody before had imagined. In this instance, Rabbi Spira bypasses the numerical pyrotechnics of the *gematriah* in favor of wordplay wizardry. He demonstrates that it was never in God's demeanor to behave with *azut*, and that the word was used purely because God wished to inform Moses that future Redemption hinged on the existence of Ruth and Boaz. And because it was so important that Ruth and Boaz eventually be born, God says, "I beg you, *rav lach*, enough, don't ask me anymore."

For one thousand years, nobody understood why the *midrash* ascribed to God a disagreeable quality such as *azut*. Rabbi Spira saw through to the deeper meaning of the *midrash*, and used it to give an entirely new twist to the original passage from Deuteronomy.

There are 251 other explanations of *rav lach* in *Megalleh Amukkot*.

To the right of the tombstone of the Megalleh Amukkot is his wife, Rosa, who died on the holiday of *Shemini Atzeret* in 1642. It is very difficult to read her tombstone, which is partially destroyed. The postwar replica on the reverse side contains only the essential information. It was once easy to read on her tombstone a beautiful wordplay involving the year Rosa Spira passed away. The Hebrew calendar year was *taf bet*. On her tombstone the letters *taf bet* were reversed, in order to spell out the word *bat*. As *bat* is Hebrew for "daughter," this supplied an enchanting double entendre: Rosa Spira died in "*bat*" years from the creation of the world, and Rosa Spira is the "daughter" of creation as well.

To the left of the Megalleh Amukkot is the grave of his daughter, Deborah, who also died in 1642. As in the case of Rabbi Spira and his wife, his daughter also has a double tombstone configuration. The stones you see are the originals found in the late 1950s, whereas the stones on the opposite side are the replicas constructed after the Holocaust.

Rabbi Spira had two other daughters, Chavelesh and Gitelech, and three sons, Shlomo, Moshe and Yitzchak. His oldest son, Shlomo, delivered a commentary on the Torah when he was seven years old, inside the synagogue in Kosov. His father was so proud that he included this commentary—called a *drasha*—in his masterpiece, the *Megalleh Amukkot*.

***

There is a mysterious story about this gravesite that was recorded in the memorial book of the Burial Society of Cracow. Sometime after the death of the Megalleh Amukkot, an itinerant foreigner arrived in the Jewish quarter of Kazimierz. Nobody knew who he was or where he was from. He slept in the *hekdesh*, which was a special lodge for out-of-town travellers as well as a hospice for the poor.

One night, the vagabond Jew knocked on the door of the *gabbai* of the Burial Society. "I'd like to buy a small plot in the cemetery," he said in a muted voice. Then he added, "Close to the Megalleh Amukkot."

The *gabbai* looked at the young beggar, whom he had never seen before, and laughed to himself. Nobody, not even the richest *machurs* in the Community, would be so bold as to seek a space next to the holy Megalleh Amukkot. After the Megalleh Amukkot died, his grave was deliberately surrounded by empty plots to symbolize the rabbi's untouchable greatness. And now, some waif thinks he can seize one of these plots? Who does this *schnorrer* think he is?

But the man was insistent. He said he'd pay whatever the *gabbai* wanted, if only he could be buried next to the Megalleh Amukkot.

The *gabbai*, tired and bleary-eyed, thought the man might be a little crazy, or that it was a joke. Why was he so adamant? Perhaps if he named an outlandishly high price, the man would go away. "A thousand rubles," he said. "And not a kopeck less."

Swiftly, the man withdrew from his pocket five two-hundred-ruble notes. "May I have a receipt?" he asked.

The *gabbai* was shocked. Such money in the purse of a drifter? Exchanging glances between the money and the man, the *gabbai* thought, "Suppose I just take the money. This guy can't be a day over thirty-five. By the time he passes away, he'll be far from Cracow and nobody will be the wiser." He wrote out the receipt.

In the morning, the *gabbai* heard that somebody had died in his sleep at the *hekdesh*. When he arrived, he was astonished to see that the deceased man was the same wanderer that approached him the night before. What's more, the *gabbai* learned that the man had no relatives and that nobody even knew him. Certain that his deal with the dead man was a secret to the world, the *gabbai* allowed him to be buried by the end of the cemetery, where the poor people lay.

That night, the *gabbai* dreamt that he was standing in the synagogue. Suddenly the beggar appeared on the *bimah* and announced, "The *gabbai* must come to the Torah!" Being called to the Torah is a euphemism for passing away from this world. The *gabbai* awoke in a sweat, but then laughed it off. A silly dream.

The next night, though, the dream recurred. "I call you to the Torah," said the beggar. "I call you to the Heavenly Court for not keeping your obligation!" Lest his meaning be unclear, the beggar then added, "If you don't take this seriously, you will pass away at once."

In the morning, the *gabbai* ran to Rabbi Joel Sirkes, known as the Bach. After hearing the story, the Bach was infuriated that the *gabbai* had stolen the beggar's money. "Let this serve as a lesson to you," he admonished the *gabbai*.

"Fine, this is a fine lesson," gasped the frantic *gabbai*, "But what do I do now? I can't very well move his grave—the Community would throw me out for having sold a plot near the Megalleh Amukkot! But if I don't, the beggar will kill me!"

After thinking a moment, the Bach said, "We will have to convene a *beit din*, a rabbinical court. When he comes in your dreams tonight, ask him for the favor of appearing tomorrow morning in my office. We will decide the case there."

The *gabbai* did as he was told, and the next morning arrived at the Bach's *beit din*. There was a chair for the *gabbai* across from an empty chair, on which the Bach had laid a *tallit*, which designated the chair for the soul of the beggar. Also present in the room were two other rabbis, who together with the Bach composed the *beit din*.

The Bach asked to hear the beggar's case.

"I bought the plot next to the Megalleh Amukkot," said a voice from the direction of the chair. "Now the *gabbai* has reneged on his word. I demand justice."

Then the Bach asked to hear from the *gabbai*.

"I thought it was a joke. I can't go burying somebody in the Megalleh Amukkot's area. If I did, I'd incur an even greater wrath than the beggar's."

The Bach consulted in privacy with the two other rabbis. He rubbed his eyes and pulled his beard. Finally, when they had reached a decision, he returned to the *gabbai* and the soul of the itinerant Jew. "Both of you have viable complaints," he began. "The beggar has bought the plot next to the Megalleh Amukkot, but the *gabbai* risks losing his livelihood if he fulfills this obligation." Then, looking directly at the empty chair, the Bach said, "The *gabbai* is truly repentant. I therefore ask of you a favor of compassion. To save the *gabbai*'s job, please move to the new plot yourself, without his assistance. If you are truly worthy to be buried next to the Megalleh Amukkot, and if Heaven recognizes you as such a holy man, then surely you are powerful enough to do so on your own."

The *beit din* was adjourned.

The next morning, Cracow's Jews came out to the cemetery and were amazed to find that the day-old grave of the wandering Jew was empty. At the same time, a fresh mound had appeared next to the grave of the Megalleh Amukkot. The Community wanted to place a tombstone over the new grave, but nobody knew the wanderer's name. Therefore they inscribed the words: "In this place was found a grave. We do not know who is buried here, but the greatest sign for us that he is a great man is that he is buried near the Megalleh Amukkot."

The new tombstone lay near the grave of the Megalleh Amukkot until the Second World War, during which time it was either lost or destroyed.

The "Back" of the Cemetery: The Western Wall

Many of the most important personalities of the seventeenth century were buried next to the western wall of the cemetery, which at the time was the front of the cemetery [see page 335]. If you come to this wall and face the first row of tombstones, the eighth grave from the left side is that of Rabbi Joel Sirkes.

Joel Sirkes (1561–1640): The Bach

Rabbi Joel Sirkes has two tombstones in the cemetery. This one is the replica made in the 1950s. The other tombstone, located four graves to the left, is a late-eighteenth-century stone prepared when the seventeenth-century original had fallen into disrepair. The recent replica is much easier to read than the partially destroyed eighteenth-century tombstone.

Rabbi Joel Sirkes was commonly known as the Bach after the initials of his most famous work, *Bayit Chadash* ("New House"). The Bach was one of the most formidable talmudic scholars in Polish Jewish history. It is said of him that when a person was sick, he could approach the Bach while the latter was studying. The Bach would tell him, "I hereby give you the merit of this learning," and the person would recover from his illness.

Born in Lublin, Rabbi Sirkes was constantly on the move for the simple reason that he was expelled of one Community after another. He served as rabbi in Pruszany, Lubkow, Lublin, Miedzyboz, Szydlowka, Brisk and Belz. Shlomo Carlebach once said, "The Bach—you know it's very, very strange, you know, sometimes, if you're mediocre, you always find your place, very easily. If you're special, you know, you may not find it, ever" (Shlomo Carlebach, "The *Taz* and the *Bach*," in *Agada* 3:1). Luckily for us, he finally found his place in Cracow. It seems that only there was the Bach at peace both intellectually and financially. In Belz, he received a pittance from the Community and there were many who made trouble for him.

In one story from Rabbi Sirkes's days in Belz, a pregnant woman went into labor in the middle of the night, in a house that had no fire. At the time, it was the custom for the town rabbi to remain awake the entire night, studying and learning. The woman's family sent a messenger to Rabbi Sirkes's home, certain that he would have a lit candle they would be able to use. But when the messenger arrived at the Bach's home, all was pitch black.

The next day, the entire town was up in arms. Why wasn't the rabbi studying all night? He can't be the rabbi in our town!

But indeed, Rabbi Sirkes *was* studying all night. The problem was, his salary was so minuscule that he couldn't afford candles. So he studied the entire night without opening a book, using only his thoughts. (This story was probably not told with pride at gatherings of the Jewish Community of Belz.)

Eventually, the Bach left Belz. In another story, Rabbi Sirkes was preparing for Shabbat one Friday when some birds flew his way and spoke in his ear. He ran to his wife and confided, "You know what the birds told me? That I'm becoming a Rav in Cracow! So please prepare *Shabbos* for three more guests, who should arrive this evening." Sure enough, three messengers from the Cracow Jewish Community arrived that evening, with an invitation for Rabbi Sirkes to become rabbi in Cracow.

In 1619 Rabbi Sirkes became head of the Cracow rabbinical court (*beit din*) and director of the *yeshivah*. The work that gained him the highest esteem in Jewish circles was his *Bayit Chadash*, which was published between 1631 and 1639.

Indeed, yet another story involves the Bach and the Megalleh Amukkot, who was Rabbi Sirkes' contemporary and Cracow's other prominent rabbi at the time (*see page 321*). In this story, Rabbi Sirkes approached the Megalleh Amukkot for a *haskamah*, or recommendation, for *Bayit Chadash*, which was just being published. But every day, the Megalleh Amukkot pushed off Rabbi Sirkes, cancelling their meetings and avoiding him in the streets. Eventually the Megalleh Amukkot went so far as to ask the printer not to publish the work. When Rabbi Sirkes heard this, he was naturally upset. He cornered the Megalleh Amukkot and said, "Why are you doing this? Is my book somehow inadequate? Do you disagree with my ideas?"

"On the contrary," the Megalleh Amukkot allegedly responded. "I know that when this book comes out, you will have fulfilled your life's purpose and accomplished your mission in this world. It is the culmination of your life's work; when it comes out, you will leave this world."

In spite of the warning, Rabbi Sirkes went ahead with the publication. Sure enough, soon after the final volume of *Bayit Chadash* was issued in 1639, Rabbi Sirkes passed away.

Bayit Chadash provides an exhaustive etymology of Jewish laws from their origins in the Talmud through their fine tuning throughout generations of clarification. A commentary on Jacob ben Asher's *Arba'ah Turim*, *Bayit Chadash* focuses on the reasons behind the laws as expressed in the *Mishnah* and *Gemarah*. Even today, volumes of the *Turim* feature a column of Bach's commentary gracing every page. Rabbi Sirkes was dismayed at what he considered the petrification of the oral law when it was written down. He felt that one must never forget the ethical background out of which Jewish law sprang. As such, he was also an opponent of *pilpul*, the popular method of Talmud study that often ignored the ethical firmament of the laws.

Rabbi Sirkes was a proponent of the *Kabbalah*, but he never lost sight of the binding nature of *halachah*. Nonetheless, the Bach felt the law should remain in synch with the humanity it was created to serve. Thus he adjusted laws in order to make Jewish holidays more enjoyable, and disagreed with the rule that prohibits men from hearing the sound of a woman in song.

A lot has been said about the Bach, but perhaps a few words are in order about the Bach's eminent daughter. She was such a wise and learned woman that she made a match with one of the greatest halachic commentators of the age, Rabbi David Ha'levi (1586–1667), who earned himself the hip nickname "the Taz," abbreviated from the title of his masterpiece, *Turei Zahav* ("Rows of Gold"). The Taz was chief rabbi of Lemberg (Lvov), but he also lived for a while in Cracow. Thus it was that two of the most penetrating minds of the Diaspora, the Bach and the Taz, lived together under a single roof.

Back to the Bach's daughter: Not only was she knowledgeable and wise, but she also had a savvy sense of humor. In those days, it was a custom that a girl would not go to synagogue until she was married. The Bach's daughter always yearned to pray in the synagogue, so when she got married she was overjoyed. She found a verse from Psalms in which King

David proclaims, "I was very happy when they told me, 'Let's go to the House of God.'" (King David was speaking about the Temple in Jerusalem.) During the wedding of the Bach's daughter, the Taz recited the customary words of the groom: "You are bound to me." The Bach's daughter, realizing that this meant she would be able to pray in a synagogue at last, later made a play on the psalm and exclaimed, "I was so happy when he told me this, because now I can go to the House of God!"

The love story of the Bach's daughter and the Taz is one of the great romances in Jewish history. It is said that when his daughter was very young, the Bach gave her a blessing that she would one day marry a scholar who was at least as great as he was. But as his daughter grew up, she couldn't seem to find the right partner. There would always be a problem, and all potential matches ultimately turned sour. Eventually, the Bach realized that his words were less a blessing and more a curse! Where in the world were they to find a man as ingenious as the Bach himself? His wife, at her wit's end, urged him to revoke his blessing so that their daughter wouldn't die a maiden. The Bach, equally desperate, made a vow: "The first unmarried man I see in the synagogue can marry my daughter."

It just so happened that that was the day the eighteen-year-old Taz arrived in Cracow. The Taz, still a young man, had not yet achieved fame in the Diaspora. In fact, he was in the middle of a personal odyssey, wandering around the world dressed in rags, longing to capture the lifeblood of Jewish existence. He had just arrived at the *beit midrash*, carrying all his belongings on his back, when the Bach rushed in.

"Are you married?" asked the Bach. When the Taz replied no, the Bach said, "Well, do you want to marry my daughter? I'm the chief rabbi of Cracow."

The Taz, without much enthusiasm, agreed.

On his way home, the Bach had his doubts. "Who is this *schlep*?" he thought. "Here I am, the chief rabbi of Cracow, and he isn't even excited to marry my daughter?"

When the Bach got home, he told his wife what had happened. "Maybe there's something wrong with him," he wondered. Then his doubts started to grow. "You know what?" he said. "I know I already broke my first blessing, but I think I'm going to have to break my vow, too. Who knows who this man is? I'm going to the *beit din* to annul the vow."

At that moment his daughter walked in the room. She had a frantic look about her. "Father, don't do it," she pleaded. "It might have been rash and it might have been foolish, but it must also have been ordained from Heaven. That man you met in the synagogue must be my soul mate."

Before the wedding, the Taz spoke with the Bach's daughter. Looking her in the eyes, he said, "I am your soul mate. And I want you to know that your father did not break his promise. As penetrating a halachic mind as he has, I am indeed his equal. But please, do not reveal this until the time is ripe."

After the wedding, the Taz lived with his wife in the home of the Bach. A Torah giant himself, he nonetheless craved the fruits of the Bach's wisdom. But he didn't want to shatter his humble image of ignorance. Every night, the Bach would study in the kitchen, as that was the single room in his home that was heated. It was his custom to think out loud while studying. So the Taz, dragging in his blanket at nightfall, would say, "It's too cold to sleep in my room. Is it okay if I sleep on the stove?" Supine on the stove, he would lie awake and gather the gems of Torah knowledge that fell from the Bach's tongue. After filling his storehouse of knowledge, he would get up and return to his soul mate in the bedroom.

Eventually, the Taz instructed his wife to inform the Bach that he was no *schlep*. She did so, and the Bach realized that his son-in-law was indeed a genius equal to himself. At that point, the Taz's great knowledge was finally revealed to the world.

Why is a romance story being told in the cemetery? Because this is where it reaches its tragic conclusion. The Bach's daughter suffered a protracted illness while still very young and when she died, the entire family came to this cemetery for the funeral. The Bach delivered a eulogy for his daughter and then the Taz stepped forward and delivered his own eulogy. Those who had gathered for the funeral were spellbound. The Taz's eulogy was the most intricate sermon they had ever heard. It had a precise poetic harmony and it was filled with ingenious references to every aspect of the Torah. Over the course of the eulogy, the Taz connected all the mysteries of the universe to his beloved wife. By some accounts, the eulogy lasted three days.

When the mourning period was over, the Taz thought perhaps it would be proper to marry one of the Bach's other daughters. When he approached the Bach with the idea, he was instantly rebuffed.

"Never!" shouted the Bach. "Be gone from my presence!"

The Taz was bewildered. His mouth dropped. "What is it? What have I done?" he pleaded.

"That eulogy, that eulogy," the Bach repeated darkly. "There is no way you could have written that in a single day. You wrote it while my daughter was still among the living. For this, I shall never forgive you."

An even greater tragedy is that the tombstone of the Bach's daughter has been lost in the undergrowth of buried and demolished tombstones.

Twelve tombstones to the right of the Bach replica is the tombstone of Rabbi Joshua ben Joseph, better known by the title of his most famous work, the Meginnei Shlomo.

Joshua ben Joseph (1578–1648): **The Meginnei Shlomo**

Born in Vilna, the Meginnei Shlomo served as Rabbi in communities throughout the region, from Grodno to Przemysl to Lvov. In 1640 he was made head of the *yeshivah* in Cracow, where he became the final arbiter on questions pertaining to Jewish law and observance. His popularity enabled the *yeshivah* to expand considerably during his tenure.

Rabbi Joshua's wealth was legendary. Like the Megalleh Amukkot before him, he refused to accept a salary from the Jewish Community, though at one point he practically held two jobs at once. In the last years of the Bach's life, when he became too ill to perform the rigorous duties of chief rabbi, it is said that Rabbi Joshua—who already served as head of the *yeshivah* in Cracow—took on the additional burden of acting chief rabbi of Cracow. Finally, when the Bach passed away, Rabbi Joshua became chief rabbi in title as well as deed.

Then along came Yomtov Lippman Heller. Fresh from the betrayal of the Prague Jewish Community, the expulsion by the Austrian Monarch, and the internecine warfare of the Polish countryside (*see below*), a rather haggard Rabbi Heller arrived in Cracow in 1643 to fill the vacant post of *yeshivah* director. This disturbed Rabbi Joshua. Why should the financially strapped Rabbi Heller receive a smaller salary than Rabbi Joshua, who had no need for monetary recompense? So Rabbi Joshua made the selfless decision to effectively trade places with Rabbi Heller. He left the chief rabbinate and returned to the leadership of the *yeshivah* so that Rabbi Heller would have a greater source of income as chief rabbi of Cracow. This singular act of generosity must have revitalized some of Rabbi Heller's battle-worn faith in his fellow man. Of course, Rabbi Joshua insured a crucial condition: whenever a Council of Rabbis was called, Rabbi Joshua would serve as its president.

The title of Rabbi Joshua's most famous work, *Meginnei Shlomo* ("Shield of Solomon) bears no relation to his name. It refers to Rabbi Joshua's ancestor, Rabbi Shlomo ben Isaac (1040–1105), known by the acronym Rashi. The purpose of the *Meginnei Shlomo* was, quite literally, to shield Rashi from the mist and fog of later commentaries. In the *Gemarah*, the main text is surrounded on one side by Rashi's commentaries and on the other by the *tosefot*. The *tosefot* were written to explicate Rashi's analysis. Sometimes, though, the *tosefot* disagree with Rashi's point. This is where Rabbi Joshua ben Joseph entered the picture. He concentrated on every aspect of Rashi that the *tosefot* had failed to understand, and explained it so that Rashi's intentions were clear. *Meginnei Shlomo* wasn't published until 1715, sixty-seven years after Rabbi Joshua died. It was an immediate success; the first edition sold out almost at once, and several editions were printed throughout Europe in later generations.

It is said that one half hour before he died, the Meginnei Shlomo was in perfect health. He was in his study, learning the holy books, when suddenly an apparition appeared. The visitor was none other than Rashi himself.

The Meginnei Shlomo was flabbergasted. His revered ancestor, whom he had spent his entire life defending, was paying a personal call! He jumped up and asked, "Oh eminent ancestor, to what do I owe the honor of your presence?"

Rashi smiled broadly. "I've got some terrific news for you."

"What, dear ancestor?" asked the Meginnei Shlomo, clutching his chest in anticipation.

"In roughly half an hour, you're going to die!" exclaimed Rashi, his arms opened wide.

Rabbi Joshua's face dropped. "*Nu*, you call this good news?"

"But I've come to inform you, dear protector, that your place in the World to Come is enormous. You have rescued me from the *tosefot*! Those tenacious lions of commentary would have muddled my meaning were it not for your wisdom. For this, your life has been rich, but your hereafter shall be even richer. I hereby invite you into the World to Come with me and with all my students. You have half an hour to prepare." And Rashi set his stopwatch and disappeared.

Rabbi Joshua gathered all the leaders of the Jewish Community of Cracow, along with his students (who were many) and his family. When his room overflowed with his dear ones, Rabbi Joshua instructed those present to make room for one more person. "Our teacher Rashi is among us," he declared, "He has come to deliver me to the Next World."

His disciples were shocked. Rabbi Joshua showed no signs of ill health.

But the Meginnei Shlomo continued, "Just as I stood by the side of our master Rashi throughout this lifetime, he has come to stand by my side in the next."

At that very moment, to the surprise and consternation of the entire Jewish Community of Cracow, the Meginnei Shlomo breathed his last breath.

The original tombstone was destroyed and rebuilt by Rabbi Joshua's great-grandchildren. Two hundred fifty years later, the Nazis destroyed the replica. Today's tombstone is a new replica, constructed after the war.

To the left of the Meginnei Shlomo's tombstone is a replica tombstone for Rabbi Isaac Ha'levi [see below], constructed at the end of the nineteenth century. To the right of the Meginnei Shlomo is a 1950s replica tombstone for Rabbi Abraham Joshua Heschel.

Abraham Joshua Heschel (d. 1663)

Not to be confused with the famous twentieth-century theologian, this Abraham Joshua Heschel was one of the last great talmudists in Cracow in the seventeenth century. Precocious from the start, he began as a teacher in Brisk, then followed his rabbi-father to Lublin in 1630 and after several years succeeded him as the head of the renowned Lublin *yeshivah* and chief rabbi. When Rabbi Yomtov Lippman Heller (*see below*) died in 1654, Rabbi Heschel became Cracow's chief rabbi and head of the Cracow *yeshivah*.

He didn't stay long. In 1655 the Polish-Swedish war compelled many Jews to flee Cracow; Rabbi Heschel ended up in Mikulov, the heart of Jewish Moravia, and later Vienna. All this time, he continued to act as chief-rabbi-in-absentia for Cracow's transplanted Jewry. During his travels he solicited massive assistance for victims of the notorious Chmielnicki pogroms, which ravaged Jewish communities throughout Galicia. It was even said that Rabbi Heschel had an audience with the Austrian monarch. As for his rabbinical decisions, Rabbi Heschel became known for his leniency as well as his matter-of-fact terseness.

Rabbi Heschel returned to a burnt-out Cracow in 1660. The Jewish Community was in terrible disrepair and Rabbi Heschel himself had lost his sight. During the Calahora show-trial (*see below*), Rabbi Heschel, already quite frail, was brought to Piotrikow as a witness for the defense. The emotional strain of the show trial, as well as the torture he likely endured during his statements, was too much for the blind rabbi to bear. Just before the trial ended, in December 1663, Rabbi Heschel passed away.

A beautiful verse from the Torah was connected to Rabbi Heschel: "I will be standing there before you on the rock . . ." (Exodus 17:6). The passage describes how Moses struck water from a rock during the wanderings in the wilderness and is linked to Rabbi Heschel because he supplied the Jews with support, both spiritually and materially. The *gematriah*, or numerical sum, works even better. The *gematriah* of the first four words in Hebrew is equivalent to Rabbi Heschel's name. The *gematriah* of the last two words is equivalent to "Cracow." So it was a biblical verse tailor-made for Rabbi Heschel.

Rabbi Heschel's second marriage was to Dinah, one of the granddaughters of Saul Wahl. Saul Wahl was the Jewish merchant who, according to legend, served as the king of Poland for just one night.

To the right of Rabbi Heschel is the tombstone of Michael Calahora, one member of a great dynasty of doctors and pharmacists that once made their home in Cracow.

Michael Calahora (Late Seventeenth Century)

The Calahoras, a Sephardic family with roots in Calahora, Spain, came to Cracow in the sixteenth century. The first Calahora to settle in Cracow was Solomon (d. 1596). A Renaissance man who felt equally at home among talmudic scholars, fabulous physicians, and wonder-merchants, Solomon was the court physician to Kings Sigismund August and Stephen Batory. His grandson, David (d. 1656), was a pharmacist in Kazimierz who supplied socialized medicine to poor Jews, both in their own homes and in the *hekdesh*, or poorhouse. David's son, Mattathias, took over his father's apothecary. It was this Mattathias Calahora, the father of the man buried here, who was subjected to a sadistic Christian show trial that, although not unique in European history, deserves to be mentioned here.

On August 8, 1663, the Dominican friar Servatius Hebelli found a note on his church altar, written in Gothic German script, that blasphemed against Jesus and Mary. A Jewish convert to Christianity, Yironim Rubinkowski, had had a property dispute with Mattathias Calahora and decided to frame the Jew. The astonished Calahora, who had been popular among both Jewish and Christian customers, was accused of blasphemy and instantly imprisoned. In the face of torture, Calahora maintained his innocence and insisted that he couldn't even write German, let alone Gothic script. But after Hebelli and Rubinkowski testified, the court ordered Calahora to be tortured and burned alive.

The case was appealed to the royal tribunal in Piotrikow. When Calahora was transferred there, riots broke out against the Jews of Kazimierz and several Jews were murdered in the streets. These pogroms continued even after the appeal had ended. Meanwhile, no less an authority than Rabbi Joshua Heschel (*see page 331*) testified on Calahora's behalf, but to no avail. The tribunal not only upheld the ruling of the lower court, but ordered that Calahora be tortured and killed in the marketplace of Piotrikow itself. On December 14, 1663, Calahora was led to a giant stage before masses of spectators. The executioner used a knife to cut off Calahora's lips from his face. Afterwards, he placed the incriminating note in Calahora's right hand, doused it in oil, and set the hand on fire. Then Calahora's tongue was cut out and thrown into the fire. During all this, the crowd roared with approval. Calahora was then taken outside the city and burnt, while alive and conscious, on a pyre. His ashes were shot from a cannon in the joyous celebrations that followed.

The Jewish Community of Cracow purchased whatever ashes remained and buried them in the cemetery. It was a time of never ending pogroms, so Calahora had to be buried secretly, without any fanfare, lest the Christians find yet another excuse to rage through the Jewish Quarter. The situation was so bad, in fact, that after 140 Jewish homes were robbed in a single night, the Jews were forced to pay four thousand florins and agree that the rector of the university—where most of the pogromniks attended school—not punish the culprits.

The grave you see here is of Mattathias's son, Michael, who continued his father's apothecary trade in spite of the horrors that had befallen his family. Presumably Michael was buried near the unmarked ashes of his father.

It is a mark of the Calahora family's resilience that one of Michael's sons, Aaron, was the first Jew to qualify at the University of Cracow, in 1724, in the family field of medicine.

⋘◎⋙

Six tombstones to the right of Calahora's is the original black marble tombstone for Isaac Halevi.

Isaac ben Mordechai Halevi (d. 1799)

Rabbi Isaac Halevi was the chief rabbi in Cracow and director of its yeshivah from 1776 to 1799, as it stood on the brink of the modern age. He is most famous today as the author of an invective-filled *cherem*, or writ of excommunication, against the burgeoning hasidic movement in Cracow. Cracow had been introduced to Hasidism by Rabbi Kalonymus Kalman Epstein, an iconoclastic rabbi known for his innovations in prayer. Rabbi Epstein formed hasidic prayer groups in 1785. The Cracow Jewish Community viewed the popular mystical movement with alarm; Rabbi Isaac Halevi was at the forefront of the campaign to stop Hasidism in its dancing tracks. In 1785, Rabbi Halevi mounted the stairs of the Altschul *bimah* and excommunicated all Jews who prayed in hasidic groups. The proclamation was remarkable for its derisive imagery when referring to the early *hasidim*:

> Some of them shake their heads, others clap their hands, others shuckle back and forth, muttering that the focus of our religion is not the Talmud but the *Kabbalah*, the Zohar. . . . And they splash in the water like bluebirds, and make the prayers last until the sun reaches midday. . . . They destroy the basis of science and the times of prayers which were established by our fathers. And around them there are gathered empty and foolhardy people. Now only God knows how far it will take them, because so many people follow them, those empty people who call themselves hasidic, which means "devout!" . . . And during those prayers they make grotesque gestures with their lips and their hands, and twirl around like drunkards, and alter the text and order of the prayers which were handed down from our forefathers. . . . If anybody dares to organize separate prayer groups, he will be excommunicated from both worlds—this world and the future world. He will be excluded from the holiness of Israel and he will be buried like a dog when he dies.
>
> (quoted in Majer Balaban, *Historja zydow w Krakowie i na Kazimierzu, 1304–1868*)

The hateful proclamation did little to stem the growth of Hasidism in Cracow. Jews who were interested in alternative prayer continued to meet outside the Cracow jurisdiction of Rabbi Halevi. Rabbi Halevi issued another *cherem* in 1797, but it was equally powerless. Cracow could not contain the new movement, and in 1815 the first hasidic prayer house was opened in Kazimierz. Within a short period, Cracow was largely hasidic, a trend that continued right up to the Second World War.

On your way there, you'll pass a couple of interesting sites along the western wall of the cemetery. First, over halfway down, you'll find the seventeenth- and eighteenth-century entrance to the cemetery, filled in with bricks. This was once the main entrance to the cemetery, leading in from Jakuba Street *(for details, see "The Birth of a Legend," page 335)*. Just past that, you'll see a stone basin set in the cemetery wall. This was formerly used for washing hands as people left the cemetery by the nearby entrance. Rabbi Heller's grave is three or four tombstones farther down from the stone basin. His grave is decorated by a large Levi's pitcher.

Yomtov Lippman Heller (1579–1654): The Tosefot Yomtov

In the back of the Altneuschul in Prague, the name of Rabbi Yomtov Lippman Heller is memorialized on the *yahrzeit* board as one of the great rabbis of the city. What isn't mentioned is that the famed Rabbi Heller was literally run out of Prague, a victim of the mercilessness leaders of the Prague Jewish Community in the seventeenth century.

It all started in 1627, in the middle of the Thirty Years' War. In order to continue gorging its military appetite, the government imposed an annual tax of 40,000 thalers on the Jews of Prague. Rabbi Heller, a brilliant talmudic commentator who had served in Vienna and Mikulov, was called in to allot the distribution of the tax burden. Although he tried to avoid being drawn into the bureaucratic tangles of the Jewish Community, Rabbi Heller had no choice. He ultimately decided on a graduated income tax divided according to one's earnings. A cabal of wealthy men, outraged by the share they were asked to pay, rushed off a letter of complaint to King Ferdinand II. Unappeased, they then accused the rabbi of having blasphemed against the Christian religion in his published writings. In 1629, Rabbi Heller was jailed and taken to Vienna, where he stood trial.

In the course of the trial, Rabbi Heller was assailed for his defense of the Talmud after it had been burned by order of the Vatican. He was sentenced to death, but King Ferdinand II commuted the punishment to a fine of 12,000 thalers (later reduced to 10,000). Rabbi Heller's incitive writings were censored, and he was forbidden from any rabbinical post in and around Prague. Rabbi Heller had no access to such a large sum of money, and only through the intercession of prominent Jews was he able to avoid being publicly flogged in the squares of Vienna and Prague. The rabbi had been imprisoned for 40 days.

After the debacle in Prague, Rabbi Heller decided to leave Bohemia altogether. He served as rabbi in small Polish towns, but once again, Rabbi Heller's strong ethical beliefs ran him afoul of the powers that be. Rabbi Heller criticized wealthy Jews for buying their way onto the administrative Council of Four Lands. As a result, he moved from one office to the next; only when he arrived in Cracow, in 1643, could Rabbi Heller be at peace. He served as chief rabbi of Cracow from 1643, and from 1648 as the director of the yeshivah as well. But he did not forget his former trials. He penned *Megillat Eiva* ("Scroll of Hatred"), a memoir of his struggle, and obliged all his descendants to read it. Likewise, he established a fast day on the fifth of Tammuz, the day he was arrested, and a joyous day on the first of Adar, the day he was chosen as rabbi of Cracow. His descendants were obliged to observe these days in addition to the regular Jewish holidays.

Rabbi Heller's fierce ethical buttress was part and parcel of all his decisions. In 1648–49, when tens of thousands of Polish Jews were murdered in the Chmielnicki pogroms, Rabbi Heller advocated a progressive approach to the issue of *agunot*. According to Jewish law, *agunot* are married women whose husbands have either disappeared or have refused to issue a *get*, or writ of divorce. In cases of a missing husband, an *agunah* is not permitted to remarry unless there is evidence of her husband's death. Because Jews were subjected to capricious slaughter so often in European history, the tragedy of *agunot* was often a very real dilemma facing Jewish communities. In the midst of the Chmielnicki pogroms, in which Jews were at constant risk of attack, Rabbi Heller interpreted the law in such a way so as to allow Jewish wives greater freedom to remarry.

Today, Rabbi Heller is most famous for his incredible halachic acumen, having served in Prague as a *dayan*, or judge, from the age of 18. His magnum opus was the *Tosefot Yomtov*, a commentary on the *Mishnah* by which he is known by name and which accompanies the main text in standard editions of the *Mishnah* with commentaries.

Many Jews have encountered Rabbi Heller's work without even realizing it. It was Rabbi Heller who wrote the "*Mi she-berach*" prayer recited for the recovery and well-being of individuals on Shabbat mornings in synagogue.

It has been said that Rabbi Heller was so pure of heart that he never accepted recompense from dishonest sources. Thus, when he died, he did not have enough money to pay for burial shrouds.

His tombstone has been restored several times. The front tombstone dates from the beginning of the twentieth century, whereas the back tombstone dates back earlier, probably from the eighteenth century. On the top of the front tombstone, there is the depiction of a pitcher, indicating that Rabbi Heller was descended from the Levite tribe. It is meant to recall the pitchers used to cleanse the hands of the *Cohanim* in the Old Temple in Jerusalem.

Unfortunately, repeated inscriptions have led to inadvertent spelling mistakes in the Hebrew text. In 1996, the word "Prague" was particularly deteriorated, as if recoiling from the memories of Rabbi Heller's experience in that city.

The Birth of a Legend

Many people find it peculiar that so many eminent personalities, such as the Bach, Rabbi Joshua Heschel, the Meginnei Shlomo, and the Tosefot Yomtov, are buried at the back of the cemetery. Traditionally, less distinguished members of the Community, as well as poor people, were buried on the outer rim of the cemetery. So why should such great rabbis be placed there as well?

In fact, the area in question was not always the back of the cemetery. Jakuba Street, which runs along the western wall of the cemetery—where people like the Tosefot Yomtov are buried—was once the border of the Jewish district. When the cemetery was established in the sixteenth century, Jakuba Street was indeed its back end. But in 1608, the Jewish district was expanded past Jakuba Street. At this time, the main entrance of the cemetery was changed from its original eastern location, around the area of Szeroka Street, to a gate on Jakuba Street. This gate, which served as the seventeenth- and eighteenth-century entrance to the cemetery, can still be seen today. It was used from 1608 until the turn of the nineteenth century, when no further burials were made here. At that time, it was considered impractical to service a cemetery gate that was no longer in use. The Jakuba Street gateway was filled in with bricks and a new entrance was made by the Rema Synagogue. This is how the Jakuba Street wall, which for two centuries had been the front of the cemetery, became the back. When the eminent rabbis of the seventeenth century passed away, they were buried in a place that was, at the time, the most respected area of the cemetery. The entrances changed, and that which was sacred became mundane.

Needless to say, the explanation of the gates did not appease the fantasy of Cracow's Jewish storytellers. In the nineteenth century, legends began to flourish to explain the placement of Cracow's greats at the supposed back of the cemetery. One legend in particular offers an ingenious explanation as to why Rabbi Yomtov Lippman Heller is placed there.

There was once a Jew in Cracow whose enormous wealth was equalled only by his stinginess. When the *shamash* rattled his charity box, seeking donations for the weekly *kiddush*, the miser would fake a sneezing fit and beat a hasty departure. When the sundry benevolent societies wound their way through the Jewish streets and arrived at his house, he'd pretend he wasn't home, or he'd promise to give the next week, or he'd say he ran out of money that very day, or he'd declare that the political position of their board of trustees was reprehensible.

This happened for weeks, months, and finally years, until the benevolent societies gave up all hope of receiving a *groschen* from him. Looser lips in the Community labelled him "Mr. Next World," because it seemed that the man was saving all his wealth for the hereafter.

Throughout his prosperous life, Mr. Next World was admonished by the Cracow rabbinate to reform his ways. "The High Court judges us based on our charitable acts," the rabbis pleaded. It was to no avail; Mr. Next World would always respond, "They'll judge me for who I am. You can't buy your way into Heaven." Shrugging their shoulders, the rabbis would leave in despair.

When Mr. Next World became old and sick, the beggars of Kazimierz formed a line outside his magnificent home. Rumor had it that now that the miser's end was near, he would make a last ditch effort to buy his way into Heaven. Tall paupers, fat paupers, paupers in rags, and paupers in borrowed coats mobbed the yard outside his house. But each time a pauper approached his bedside, Mr. Next World shielded his eyes so that he wouldn't have to see the supplicant. Looking out the window, he uttered a simple, sneering "No." He must have said "No" a thousand times that day. The rabbis of Cracow sent an emergency delegation to urge Mr. Next World to change while there was still time. "The gate to repentance is always open," they purred. But they too were rebuffed.

That night, Mr. Next World passed away. The Community, disgusted by his incorrigible bitterness, refused to bury him in the front of the cemetery, where wealthy patrons and learned rabbis were buried. As a sign of their scorn for his ways, they buried him at the far reaches of the cemetery, where the poorest and most miserable Jews in Cracow found their final rest.

The day he was buried, though, strange things began to happen in Kazimierz. It started when a beggar woman came to the rabbi and asked if something was wrong with the mail.

"Every morning for the past twenty-five years I've received food money in the mail," she said. "Today I received nothing." Other complaints were lodged. One man claimed that every morning at sunrise there would be three bottles of milk on his doorstep for his five children. Now the bottles stopped coming. The orphanage wondered why its shipments of toys had been terminated. New clothes stopped arriving at the doors of the poorhouse. Even the rabbis, although they would never say it, used to receive weekly gifts of *kiddush* wine produced in the Holy Land. It was anybody's guess why the wine stopped flowing.

Peopled whispered that the benevolent societies were to blame for mismanagement. But the mystery deepened when the various societies denied ever being involved in such charities.

When Shabbat came, the confusion turned to pandemonium. Hundreds of paupers had received a Friday allowance on their doorsteps to pay for Shabbat candles, challah, fish, eggs, and a little *cholent*. Now the allowance was gone. Mobs of the needy swarmed the offices of the benevolent societies, pleading for some assistance for Shabbat. It was similar to the scene outside the home of Mr. Next World before he died.

Finally the pieces of the puzzle came together. The Community realized that it was Mr. Next World himself who had been Kazimierz's great benefactor. He refused to give charity to the benevolent societies because then he would have been given recognition and honor; he wanted nobody to know about his goodly deeds. According to Maimonides, one of the highest forms of charity is that in which the donor does not know the supplicant, and the supplicant does not know the donor. In this manner, charity is given out of the purity of one's heart, not out of the desire for credit and reward. By avoiding all honor for his charity, indeed by incurring the undeserved wrath of his peers, the so-called miser was indeed a righteous man who most certainly entered the next world, as his name implied.

The Tosefot Yomtov declared that this man was a true *tzaddik*. He requested that he be buried next to such a holy man. And that is why the grave of the venerable Rabbi Yomtov Lippman Heller is found at the back of the cemetery.

THE CEMETERY SQUARE

In front of the Rema Synagogue on Szeroka Street is a fenced-in plot of grass studded with trees. This is the site of one of the most enduring legends ever to emerge from Kazimierz.

Before beginning the history of the site and the legend, a word is in order about the stone memorial facing the southern edge of the grass. The rock was erected by the Polish Jewish Nissenbaum Family Foundation, which erects Holocaust memorials throughout Poland. However, no act of genocide took place on this plot of grass. A more appropriate place for the memorial would be on the other side of the river in Podgorze, where the ghetto was, or in the nearby Plaszow forced labor camp. But as Szeroka Street is the destination of most of the tourists to Jewish Cracow, the memorial was placed here. It might seem tasteless to tell ancient legends in front of Holocaust memorials, but keep in mind that this plot of grass had nothing to do with the Holocaust—and everything to do with the ancient history of the Jews of Kazimierz—until the rock was put here in 1994.

The History

At one point there existed a cemetery on the site of the fenced-in park. Majer Balaban, the great twentieth-century historian of Cracow's Jews, claimed that the oldest Jewish cemetery in Kazimierz was located on this site. It continued to be used as a cemetery when Cracow's Jews were expelled in 1494 and settled in Kazimierz. By the year 1533, the cemetery had become vastly overcrowded, and the Jewish Community bought another piece of land—today's Old Jewish Cemetery—where they started burying people during the epidemic of 1551–52.

A more recent view is that the oldest Jewish cemetery in Kazimierz was located outside the Kazimierz city walls, nearby the Altschul around today's Dajwor Street. There used to be ponds in the area, and it has been suggested that the oldest cemetery was situated between the ponds. According to this view, the plot here on Szeroka Street was established as a cemetery during a plague epidemic.

There is no argument, though, that there was once a cemetery in this place. It used to be larger, but during nineteenth-century city planning, it was shortened to provide more space for the expansive Szeroka Street. At that time, the remaining area, which had by now lost its tombstones, was surrounded by a wall.

Today, the wall is gone, replaced by a fence and a confusing memorial rock. But in the old days, legends surrounded the unused cemetery, the space in front of the venerable Rema Synagogue, a mysterious plot of land shielded from the public by an impenetrable wall.

The Legend

One Friday afternoon during the time of Rabbi Moses Isserles (the Rema), Szeroka Street was host to a spectacular wedding. Scores of guests gathered for the ceremony of two of the most beautiful and well-to-do Jews of Kazimierz. Musicians performed on flutes and banjos, jugglers tossed torches of fire in the daylight, comedians told bawdy tales, and magicians pulled white doves out of the air. There was more food than anybody knew what to do with. It was one of the most festive events Szeroka Street had ever seen.

After the reading of the *ketubbah*, or marriage contract, which took place under a scrumptious, hand-embroidered *chupah*, or wedding canopy, the merrymaking really began. At dizzying speeds, the men danced in their own circle, the women danced in a separate circle, and the children danced among themselves. Both the bride and the groom were hoisted on separate chairs, between which they held a thin red ribbon that connected the dancing groups.

The wedding guests were so caught up in the frivolity, in fact, that they didn't notice when the sun began to set. They kept dancing and singing and drinking and eating in an even greater frenzy.

Finally, the grey web of twilight approached. In a short while, Shabbat would begin. Still there was no relaxation of the merriment. The Rema, observing the jubilee from his synagogue, sent a messenger to alert the partygoers that Shabbat was approaching. According to Jewish law, music is forbidden on Shabbat. Therefore weddings, which almost always employ music in some form, are not permitted either.

The messenger tried speaking with the partygoers, but they didn't listen. They were dancing and drinking too quickly even to hear the message, let alone to cease their merriment.

The sun set. Fearing the desecration of the Shabbat, the Rema himself hurried out of his synagogue and declared in a loud, authoritative voice, "You must stop the music at once! Shabbat is upon us!"

The wedding guests stopped dancing long enough to laugh at the Rema, whom they derided as an "old man." They saw no reason to abandon their fun. As if to prove their point, they sang and danced with even greater abandon.

The Rema took a couple steps closer to the fray and called out, "If you don't stop now, you will regret it!" Still no response. After the third warning, Rabbi Isserles remonstrated the guests with the most severe punishment. "It says in the Torah," he uttered darkly, "that if a person disrespects the Shabbat, he earns a death sentence upon himself."

The guests laughed with open mouths. Who could think of death during a wedding?

Just then, the earth on Szeroka Street split in two. Before anybody knew what was happening, all the wedding guests—the bride, groom, relatives, musicians, magicians, and caterers—were instantly swallowed up into the area of today's fenced-in yard. As quickly as it began, the earth moved back and sealed itself shut. Not a trace of the wedding remained.

Everybody who saw the miracle on Szeroka Street knew that there is a God in Heaven. The swallowed site of the wedding was instantly considered sacred ground. This was the site where God showed Himself in all His wrath. But also, because the grounds now contained buried bodies, they had to be separated from the rest of the street. If not, an unsuspecting *Cohen*, who is not permitted to step foot in a cemetery, might accidentally trespass the yard. Even the government heard of the spectacle on Szeroka Street, and ordered a wall erected around the yard, to keep it consecrated. Although the wall has since been removed, the yard is still fenced off as a reminder of God's vengeance here on Szeroka Street.

The Original Story

The legend has its roots in a similar, true story. There actually was one such wedding in Cracow on a Friday, but this one was officiated by the Rema himself.

According to this account, there was once an orphan in Cracow named Esther. Esther's life was filled with abandonment over the loss of both her parents. Just when she had resigned herself to a life of solitude, a match was arranged for her with a sensitive and kindhearted *yeshivah* boy named Mordechai. Finally, there was hope for Esther. The dowry was arranged between her brother and Mordechai's family, and the wedding was set for a Friday.

On the day of the wedding, there was a fierce scuffle among the guests. Apparently, Esther's brother couldn't agree on a proper amount for a dowry. Both parties shouted, and Mordechai's family threatened to call off the wedding. Both Esther and Mordechai were terrified that their dreams together would be ruined.

Enter the Rema. He summoned Esther's brother and Mordechai's father into his office to discuss the dowry. Both sides refused to compromise. They squabbled over market values, percentages, and taxes on the dowry, all but ignoring the holy sanctimony of the occasion. As in the legend, the sun began to set—but the Rema, realizing that there was an orphan involved, knew that the wedding must take place. If the wedding was postponed until Sunday, it was possible that Mordechai's family would change its mind during the Shabbat. This would spoil a partnership that both the bride and the groom longed for. Additionally, since Esther was an orphan, responsibility for her welfare rested ultimately with the Community. If the match failed to proceed, then the entire Jewish Community would be at fault.

Using this as his rationale, the Rema continued negotiating with the families well into Shabbat. Finally, after night had fallen, they emerged from his office with an agreement. The Rema jubilantly announced, "Prepare the *chupah*, it's time for a wedding!"

One of the bystanders gasped. "A wedding on Shabbat?"

"It's better than no wedding at all," replied the Rema.

And so, Esther and Mordechai were joined together. There was no catastrophe on Szeroka Street, no earthquake to devour the party—but there was controversy. Many rabbis wrote that the Rema had erred in his decision to allow a wedding on Shabbat. In response, the Rema wrote a lengthy explanation, emphasizing that compassion toward the orphan was a more crucial factor than any other. According to Yaakov Dovid Shulman's charming biography of the Rema, the rabbi wrote,

> "This was an emergency situation. If the wedding were to be postponed until after *Shabbos*, the bride would be shamed. . . . There could be no greater emergency than the bride being shamed. . . . So great is the honor of people that it pushes off the negative commandment of 'Do not turn aside from all the things that [the Sages] teach you,' regarding a matter like this, which is only a rabbinic prohibition. . . . Besides, regarding the prohibition against playing music on *Shabbos*, people generally allow clapping and dancing on *Shabbos* everywhere, and they even command Gentiles to play musical instruments. . . . This is especially so when the wedding may be otherwise broken off. . . ."
>
> (quoted in Yaakov Dovid Shulman, *The Rema: The Story of Rabbi Moses Isserles*)

The wedding decision served as a sublime example of the Rema's concern for human welfare. So dramatic was his decision that it inspired the altered, cataclysmic legend related above. It's interesting to note that the legend is filled with austere judgment, whereas the true story is overflowing with compassion.

In response to the Rema's Friday wedding controversy, the Jews of Cracow passed a special ordinance. Never would there be a wedding scheduled for any part of Friday. This ordinance was designed to avert a Shabbat wedding in the future. If a couple wanted to have a wedding on a Friday, they would load up their carriages and do so across the river, in the suburbs. Even before the war, when the district had already been incorporated into Cracow proper, the Jews of Cracow would convene Friday weddings only in that part of town. Cracow was unique in the entire Jewish world for such a custom.

Naturally, such an idiosyncratic practice gave ammunition to fathers who told their wide-eyed children, on rainy nights, about the terrible earthquake that struck Szeroka Street during the time of the Rema.

Near the Cemetery Square

Szeroka Street 6, at the northeast corner of the street, is a building that once served as a *mikveh* for the Jewish Community. It was built right next to the eastern walls of Kazimierz. It is not known exactly when the *mikveh* was built; the first mention of it was in 1567. The historian Majer Balaban noted a tragic event that occurred in 1567: The floor of the *mikveh* collapsed and ten women drowned. In the nineteenth century the *mikveh* was rebuilt.

During the war, the *mikveh* was appropriated by the German authorities. After the war, the Polish state claimed the building under the pretext that it was either German or abandoned property. In the 1970s, the same "preservation" society that altered the High Synagogue set to work on the *mikveh* building. The exterior of the building was changed and the interior was remodelled into simple rooms for workshops and offices.

In 1989, ownership of the *mikveh* was handed to the city of Cracow. The Jewish Community made a claim to the building in 1995, but the city was reluctant to return it, fearing that it would set a precedent of property restitution to the Jews. To avoid such a scenario, the city sold the building back to the Jewish Community for a symbolic price.

At the end of 1995, the Jewish Community rented the building to the friendly owners of the Ariel cafe. Ariel set up an additional space in Szeroka 6 to complement its other cafe at Szeroka 17. (Although Ariel is not a kosher cafe, it has maintained very good relations with the Jewish Community and with Jewish visitors from abroad.)

The *mikveh* is located in the cellar. You can see the stairs leading down from the outside. Because of unsturdy floors, the *mikveh* is no longer in use and is closed to the public.

From at least the seventeenth century, there was a Jewish prison located next to the *mikveh*.

THE POPPER SYNAGOGUE

Address: Szeroka Street 16

> This building is now used as a cultural center, so it is relatively easy to enter on weekdays. Some nights and weekends it is open as well. The exterior is also viewed well from the other side, on Dajwor Street 1.

The Popper Synagogue was built by Wolf Popper (also known as Bozian) in 1620. Popper, a merchant and money trader, was one of the richest Jews in Cracow at the time. According to one account, Popper owned seven stores in Cracow and possessed a fortune worth three hundred thousand Polish zlotys. Of course, this account was by Sebastian Miczynski, one of the most virulent anti-Semites of the seventeenth century, who in 1618 authored a hate-filled brochure against the Jews entitled "The Mirror of the Polish Kingdom." In that brochure, he even summoned the age-old accusation of the blood libel to accuse Popper of killing Christians for their blood! Further investigation reveals that Cracow experienced an economic slump in the early seventeenth century. As usual, a visible Jew received the brunt of the blame. But in spite of Miczynski's lies, there is no doubt about

Popper's enormous wealth. In his will, he spoke of a chest containing gold and silver, as well as four bags filled with Silesian coins, deposited in the city of Wroclaw.

Originally from Checiny (near Kielce), Popper became a trader of goods from Wroclaw and cloth from Cologne. His main business, though, was currency trading, particularly in regional fairs. He was also known as "the Stork," according to one legend, because he would stand on one foot while immersed in thought. A devout Jew, he built the Popper Synagogue as a private prayer hall for his family. Eventually it became one of the many synagogues used by the Jews of Cracow. Adjacent to the synagogue he built a *beit midrash*.

One year after he built his synagogue, Popper's wife, Cyrl, died. Cyrl had herself been a prominent denizen of the Jewish Quarter, as her father was the illustrious Judah Lewek Landau, one of the leaders of the Jewish Community. Four years after his wife's death, Popper returned from a business trip and suddenly fell ill. The next day, December 2, 1625, he died. The death was especially tragic because only one of his six children—Lewek—was married. The rest—Jelen, Lazar, Marik, Solomon, and Rose—were either teenagers or small children. The Community immediately came to their aid and the children were raised by two of the other wealthiest Jews in Cracow, Isaac Jakobowicz, builder of the Isaac Synagogue, and Wolf Doktorowicz. In his will, Popper left all his property to his children on the condition that they would never sell it. If they did sell it, however, he wrote that the money earned must be used "in a Jewish way."

When it was founded in the seventeenth century, the Popper synagogue was one of the more affluent prayer halls in Kazimierz. Later years, however, took their toll. The Popper family lost some of its prosperity, and by the nineteenth century the Jewish Community of Cracow had taken over control of the synagogue. The Community did not tend the building much at all, and eventually parts were whisked away. The silver Torah ornamentation, for example, had to be sold in order to raise money for the synagogue. The wood furnishings became wilted from neglect.

Nonetheless, the synagogue was continuously used by Orthodox Jews in Cracow until September 1939. Then it was closed and its remaining precious objects, from floor to ceiling, were looted by the Nazis. Many of its valuables were methodically sent to the Museum of an Extinct Race the Nazis established in Prague.

Today the Popper Synagogue is unique among Cracow's other prewar synagogues in that it has absolutely no traces of its former function as a house of worship. Only the walls remain. The building was abandoned until 1965 and is now used as a cultural center. Rented from the Cracow Jewish Community, the center schedules drawing classes for children, cultural events, and art exhibits. Occasionally, the exhibits have a Jewish theme. Nonetheless, nobody seems to find it odd that every year before Christmas, a large, decorated tree is placed in a corner of what was once the main sanctuary.

On the northern side of the synagogue is the women's gallery (you can still see the former gallery's windows), but the wooden stairs were added in recent years. Originally, women had their own separate entrance to the synagogue. During the interwar period, the walls of the synagogue were covered with figurative murals painted by Leon Schenker. Before the war, the seventeenth-century *bimah* was noted for its beauty, but the real treasure in the synagogue was the *aron hakodesh*, with its sumptuous doors carved out of oak.

Featured on the doors were a lion, an eagle, a deer, and a panther, mixed with images of trees and homes. This refers to *Ethics of the Fathers* 5:20, which reads, "Be bold as a leopard, light as an eagle, swift as a deer, and strong as a lion, to carry out the will of your father in Heaven." The idea is that one must adopt the positive qualities of all God's creations during prayer.

After the war there was a rush to save—or pilfer, depending on your view—the remaining synagogal relics not seized by the Nazis. Among many Jews, the prevailing view was that although the Jewish communities of Eastern Europe were decimated, the surviving Jews would continue their tradition in places far removed from the source, such as America and Israel. But in doing so, they wanted to preserve a piece of the source in their new homes. Since Polish law forbade removing historical objects from the country, an entrepreneurial few resorted to law bending. Thus the doors of the Popper Synagogue *aron hakodesh* were smuggled out of Poland hidden inside futons. *Aron hakodesh* doors from the High Synagogue were "rescued" in the same way. They went up for sale in the United States and were bought by various institutions in Israel. The doors from the Popper Synagogue *aron hakodesh* can today be found in the Wolfsohn Museum in Helchal Shlomo, the building of the Chief Rabbinate of Israel in Jerusalem.

At this writing, plans were under way to reproduce a photograph of the original *aron hakodesh* on the eastern wall of the synagogue.

THE HIGH SYNAGOGUE

Address: Jozefa Street 38

> The entrance to the High Synagogue is from the adjacent building at Jozefa 40. As the synagogue is used as a private workshop, it is closed to visitors and nearly impossible to get inside. The best advice—seriously—is to knock on the doors and beg.

Just as the Altschul bears an uncanny resemblance to the Altneuschul in Prague, the High Synagogue of Cracow looks remarkably similar to a Prague synagogue of the same name. Both synagogues are called "High" because their prayer rooms are located upstairs, on the second floor. Both were built in the middle of the sixteenth century, although unlike the Altschul the High Synagogue in Cracow was built slightly earlier than its sister *shul* in Prague. There is a special passageway in both synagogues that leads to an adjacent home. These striking similarities are yet another example of the cultural cross-fertilization that enriched the Jewish communities of Cracow and Prague.

Looking at the two synagogues today, we can see the starkly disparate situations of two communities in transition. Prague's High Synagogue was completely renovated and opened as a prayer hall that would hopefully complement the Altneuschul in 1996. A *beit midrash* with a library of books was opened in the women's gallery, and in the upstairs loft, also used as a *sukkah*, a Hebrew School for children was formed. In Cracow, on the other hand, the High Synagogue was taken over by the Historical Monuments Restoration Workshop in 1966, and continues to be owned and operated by the newly privatized enterprise.

The High Synagogue is the only synagogue that the Cracow Jewish Community—far weaker than Prague's both numerically and financially—does not officially own. Although the Workshop initiated basic repairs to the building, no renovation work has been undertaken. Essentially, the Workshop needed a free place to work and they found it. The once-majestic vaulted Renaissance ceiling, which had been utterly destroyed by the Germans, was taken down. In its place was put a flat modern ceiling, lower than the original, that obliterates almost all traces of what had been there before. Above the lowered ceiling the Workshop built a new floor and installed an additional workplace. In order to create even more workspace, the roof was made higher than the former one, which used to be lopsided toward Jozefa Street. The entire triangular attic structure you can see from the outside was added by the Workshop in order to bring more light to the loft. All this, so that the workshop would be able to restore the artifacts of Cracow's *other* historic landmarks! In 1997, the Workshop went bankrupt. It is not known what will become of the workspace or the synagogue itself.

The third oldest synagogue in Kazimierz today, the High Synagogue was built between 1556 and 1563. As mentioned, its name derives from the placement of the prayer room on the second floor, where the large windows are situated. The ground floor was filled with private shops and storage rooms that existed long before the building became a synagogue. The shops remained when the High Synagogue was established, thus making it probably the only synagogue in the world where one could buy laundry detergent on the way out of services. It is unknown today whether the High Synagogue was built with Jewish Community funds or by a private benefactor. Formerly, the building was used as a house.

The Nazis closed the synagogue and completely plundered it of all its valuables. Hans Frank, the Governor-General of Nazi-occupied Poland, personally pilfered the chandeliers from the High Synagogue and had them brought to his personal residence in Wawel Castle during the war. He also took the large Chanukkah menorah that stood in front of the *aron hakodesh* to Wawel. Disgusted with the Jewish and Polish symbolism on the Chanukkah lamp, he tore off the holder for the *shamash* (the ninth candle, used to light the others) and removed the Polish eagle that had once decorated the top. Today, the *shamash*-less, eagle-less Chanukkah lamp is on display in the Altschul Museum, to the left of the *aron hakodesh*.

During the "restructuring" of the building in the 1960s, the entrance to the synagogue was moved next door to number 40. A seventeenth-century *tzedakkah* (charity) box, which once stood on the western wall of the synagogue, was inexplicably placed near the stairwell of the next-door building. If you are lucky enough to gain access to the synagogue, you'll see the *tzedakkah* box on your way upstairs. This area was formerly the vestibule of the High Synagogue. In addition, a late-Renaissance archway from the western wall of the synagogue was restored and later placed in the new entrance from Jozefa Street 40. The current entrance into the main sanctuary was placed right next to the *aron hakodesh*, the holiest place in the synagogue. It is a lucky thing that Jews do not worship sites themselves, and that synagogues are only considered holy when they are used as houses of prayer; otherwise, the new entrance would be downright sacrilegious.

Very little of the original interior of the synagogue remains. The ceilings were once vaulted, with stucco decoration and a central chandelier, as is the case in the High Synagogue of Prague. Nineteenth-century wooden seats, each with its own pillow, as well as lecterns, once filled the synagogue. Each of the seats was decorated with a white heart, on which was printed a number in Hebrew. These corresponded to reserved seats for the regular congregants, particularly for those who would come every day for the morning *minyan*.

Much of the *aron hakodesh* can still be seen on the eastern wall, complete with its late-Renaissance fragments. The steps and the doors no longer exist, but the presently untidy hole was once where the Torahs were placed. You can still see two majestic, griffin-like creatures on either side of the words *keter Torah* (Crown of the Torah). The griffins themselves are clutching between their talons a Torah crown. Above, you can see flowers depicted in a vase. There used to be two Hebrew words surrounding the vase: *kodesh La'Shem*, or "Holy to God."

One of the great frustrations in visiting the High Synagogue today is that the marvelous paintings that once blanketed its walls are gone. All that is left are the teasing nineteenth-century remnants on the southern wall, so jumbled and deteriorated that they are almost impossible to decipher. Between the windows, there was a painted inscription of Jacob's trembling declaration in Genesis 28:17, when he awakes from his dream of the ladder: "How awesome is this place! This is none other than the abode of God, and that is the gateway to Heaven." This no doubt referred to the concept that every synagogue is considered a *Mikdash mi'at*, or a small version of the Temple in Jerusalem. Thus while people prayed in the High Synagogue, they were symbolically transported to the place where their forefathers prayed. Certain letters in the inscription were also highlighted. When the *gematriah*, or numerical equivalent, of these letters is computed, it indicates the year 1863, when the High Synagogue underwent a thorough renovation marking the three hundredth anniversary of its completion. In that year, the inscription was added as well.

What was most remarkable about the wall paintings was that they included human depictions, a practice usually shunned in traditional Jewish life. The painted scenes from the Bible included Noah and the ark, the binding of Isaac, Moses receiving the Ten Commandments, the Jews by the waters of Babylon (complete with harp-infested trees), the menorah, and the Bread of Display.

To paraphrase Jacob himself: How awesome was this place!

Nearby the High Synagogue

Two doors to the right of the High Synagogue, at Jozefa Street 42, there used to be a *beit midrash*, or study and prayer hall, from the beginning of the nineteenth century. The Hebrew words on the facade refer to the society that sponsored the *beit midrash*—*Koveah Etim La'Torah* ("Set Aside Time for Torah"). The Hebrew dates refer to the founding of the *beit midrash* in 1810 and its renovation in 1912.

On the other side of the High Synagogue, at the corner of Jozefa and Jakuba streets, once stood the gate to the Jewish Quarter. Beginning in 1583, this was the single passageway connecting the Jewish and Christian districts of Kazimierz.

The guards at the gate typically gave a hard time to visiting Jewish merchants and wedding parties entering the quarter, often exacting outlandish fees for the right to pass through. Finally, in response to the rampant corruption, the Jewish Community in 1595 established fixed rates that the bridegrooms would pay the guards when they entered Jewish Kazimierz for a wedding.

The gate was used until the Jewish Quarter was allowed to expand west, past Jakuba Street and all the way to Corpus Christi Street (*Bozego Ciala*), in 1608.

THE ISAAC SYNAGOGUE

Address: Kupa Street 18
Opening hours: Sunday–Friday 9:00 A.M.–7:00 P.M.
Closes Fridays according to sunset. Closed on Jewish holidays.
Cost: Six zlotys

> The synagogue can also be viewed Friday evenings. The Lauder Foundation hosts an Oneg Shabbat every Friday around the time services end in the Rema Synagogue. The Oneg Shabbat meets in the building next to the Isaac Synagogue, connected to it on the left. Just say, "Shabbat! Shabbat!" to the caretakers and they'll understand. The Lauder crew should let you in to see the breathtaking synagogue from its women's gallery. It will probably be unlit, though.

The Isaac Synagogue was once the jewel of Cracow's Jewish Community. It was built in 1638 by Isaac Jacobowicz (d. 1653), more commonly known as Reb Isaac Reb Jekeles because his father was named Jacob. A banker to King Wladyslaw IV, Reb Isaac was one of the wealthiest Jews in Cracow.

His father, known as "Jacob the Rich," made headlines in 1573 for his loan of five thousand zlotys to King Sigismund August. Following in his father's footsteps, Reb Isaac Reb Jekeles worked as a banker and merchant, amassing a small empire that included plots of land in Kazimierz and shops in Cracow. He spent much of his life serving as the main *parnas* of the Jewish Community. He chose one of his best plots of land to build the Isaac Synagogue, which became a symbol of Jewish prosperity in Cracow during the first half of the seventeenth century. Like Mordechai Maisel in Prague, Reb Isaac and his wealth were once a favorite theme of European Jewish storytellers. Although he obviously inherited a fortune from his father, he became the subject of an unforgettable rags-to-riches tale. The legend is one of Cracow's most enduring stories, with variations spread throughout Europe, Israel, and America.

The Legend of Reb Isaac Reb Jekeles

There was once a poor man in Cracow by the name of Reb Isaac Reb Jekeles. One night he had a dream. He dreamt that if he travelled all the way to Prague, he would find a secret treasure buried underneath Charles Bridge. When Reb Isaac awoke, he laughed. "A treasure for me," he mused. "Only in my dreams am I rich!"

The next night, he had the same dream. "I wonder: Should I test the dream, and travel to Prague? Nah—the trip would cost money; I would only lose more." The night after that, he had the same dream again. After a week of similar dreams, each of them more intense than the last, Reb Jekeles made up his mind. He would set out for Prague. "How can I argue with prophecy?" he thought.

It was a long and perilous journey, but finally he arrived in Prague. He went straight to the Charles Bridge and descended to the exact spot indicated in his dream. But once he was there, he didn't know what to do next. The place was crawling with soldiers. How could a Jew from Cracow just start digging up earth underneath Prague's Charles Bridge? Should he start digging in the middle of the night? As he was wondering what to do, one of the soldiers approached him. "Are you looking for something?"

"What have I got to lose," thought Reb Isaac. He told his dream to the soldier.

"You silly Jew!" laughed the soldier. "Do you chase after every dream you have? I have dreams, but you don't see me running after them like an idiot! Why, just last night I dreamt that if I go to Cracow and find the home of a Reb Isaac Reb Jekeles, I'll find a treasure buried beneath his fireplace. But do you think I'm going to run off to Cracow? A dream's a dream."

Reb Isaac was astonished. He had never met this man, and yet the man knew Reb Isaac's name. And such a dream! He realized then and there that this was what his dream meant: He should come to the Charles Bridge in Prague to find out that he has a treasure in his own home.

Reb Isaac left Prague as soon as he could. When he arrived home, he dug up the bricks underneath his fireplace and, sure enough, discovered a hidden treasure. Reb Isaac became one of the richest men in Cracow and built the Isaac Synagogue with the money from his treasure.

The Synagogue and Its Controversy

Although Reb Isaac received direct permission to build his synagogue from King Wladyslaw IV, the building was beset by problems from the beginning. During construction, the priest at the nearby Corpus Christi Monastery protested to the bishop of Cracow, complaining that the synagogue was too high, too close in proximity to a church, and far too close to a street—today's Jozefa Street—that had Christian residents. It should be noted that the Isaac Synagogue did not border any Christian street, but was built on a street *perpendicular* to a Christian street. This alone was considered scandalous. The priest told of his fear that during the processions around his church during the Corpus Christi holiday the mere presence of the synagogue would be an affront to the Christians, an insult, and a blight on the landscape. Specifically, the priest voiced his outrage that Christians would be forced to walk past a synagogue while carrying the Eucharist.

When the bishop received the complaint, the authorities sealed the site of the nearly finished synagogue with a lock, and revoked the permission to open it. That the bishop of Cracow could simply overturn the decision of the king, who had given express permission to build the synagogue, shows just how much authority the Church wielded in Cracow. The scheduled opening of the synagogue was postponed six years, until finally it was allowed to open in 1644.

Christian antagonism toward the Isaac Synagogue, and the extended verbal battles this engendered, gave rise to a semi-apocryphal tale when the synagogue finally opened.

When work was finished on the synagogue, the edifice was so magnificent that it attracted the attention not only of Polish Jews, but also of local Gentiles. Even members of the government came to marvel at the awe-inspiring beauty of the building and its interior furnishings. During the excitement that surrounded the opening of the synagogue, many anti-Semites in Cracow resented the attention the Jews garnered. They were filled with hatred for the sheer majesty of the building itself, which they considered to be an undesired symbol of Jewish success in Cracow.

On the day of the opening of the synagogue—its dedication, known as *chanukat habayit* in Hebrew—Reb Isaac Reb Jeckeles made his dedication speech in front of the entire Jewish Community of Cracow. In the middle of Reb Isaac's speech, a little Gentile boy entered the synagogue and squeezed his way through the massive crowd of Jews. He walked to the *aron hakodesh*, where Reb Isaac was standing, whispered something in Reb Isaac's ear, and left.

Reb Isaac turned white. He stopped his speech in midsentence.

"What is it? What's wrong?" cried voices in the crowd.

"The Gentiles are plotting in the church this very minute," he proclaimed in horror. "They plan to launch a pogrom to kill us all!"

There was instant panic in the crowd. All the members of the Community, from the wealthy leaders down to the poor *schnorrers*, ran to their homes amid cries of impending doom.

Reb Isaac Reb Jeckeles went to Yomtov Lippman Heller, called the Tosefot Yomtov, who had just become chief rabbi of Cracow. Reb Isaac told the rabbi everything the little boy had told him: that the Gentiles intended to attack after Shabbat, on Saturday night. "Be calm," the Tosefot Yomtov advised him. "Do not despair, God will protect us."

But the Tosefot Yomtov wasn't one for platitudes. He also had a plan. After meditating for a moment, he said, "Instruct every Jewish family to remain at home, with the exception of night watchmen, who will patrol the streets. Now I want you to find the twenty-six strongest men in Kazimierz. Tell them to prepare their *kittels*." *Kittels* are white gowns worn on Passover or Yom Kippur. They are also used as burial shrouds. "They should bring large sticks and attach burning candles to the ends. And in the middle of the night after Shabbat, at exactly twelve o'clock midnight, they should be assembled in the cemetery."

Not quite sure what the Tosefot Yomtov had in mind, Reb Isaac followed his advice. He found the twenty-six strongest men in the Jewish Community, and briefed them on the plan.

On Saturday night at midnight, the Gentiles secretly gathered outside the Kazimierz city walls to launch the massive pogrom. At the time, the northern wall of the cemetery bordered the city wall. In order to enter the walled-in Jewish Quarter, the Christians intended to hop the cemetery wall, and from there to enter the streets of Jewish Cracow.

Their first stop would be the hated Isaac Synagogue, which they intended to destroy completely.

Using each other as stepladders, the Gentiles hoisted themselves over the wall, and landed in the darkened cemetery. When they were all inside, they instantly began to scream.

"The Jewish dead have risen from their graves!" one of them cried, pointing to the men wandering about in *kittels*. "They're coming to kill us!" All at once, the terrified Gentiles stampeded back to the cemetery wall. From that night forward, they never attempted another pogrom on Cracow's Jews.

◆◆◆

That wasn't the end of the Isaac Synagogue's protracted trial at the hands of the Cracow Christian Community. In 1655, during the Swedish invasion, the Swedes destroyed the Church of St. Hedvik. The Isaac Synagogue, as the grandest, most opulent synagogue in Cracow, was instantly seen as an ideal substitute church. Architecturally, it was not too different from a church—not as different as was, say, the lilliputian Rema Synagogue. (The Tempel, which would have been an ideal choice for a church, would not be built for two hundred years.) The priest wrote to King Jan Kazimierz, asking the king to grant him the Isaac Synagogue as a sort of compensation for the destroyed church. The king agreed.

The Jewish Community was horrified. The Isaac Synagogue was their pride and joy; why should they be forced to just give it up? In a lobbying frenzy, the Jews wrote the king a series of letters imploring him to relent in his decision. Finally, the king effected a "compromise": the Isaac Synagogue would continue to be a synagogue as long as the Jews paid for the rebuilding of the church. The Jews, joyous that their religious site would not be confiscated, paid the fine—which was, of course, only one of many protection rackets they were forced to pay the Church.

◆◆◆

As soon as they entered Cracow, the Nazis pilfered practically all the interior furnishings of the Isaac Synagogue. Ironically, considering the synagogue's turbulent history at the hands of the Church, the Isaac Synagogue was itself slated to be a church after the war. The idea was eventually abandoned. In the 1980s, the exterior of the building was renovated.

In 1997, an enterprising young man in the Cracow Jewish Community rented space in the Isaac Synagogue for a video and photographic exhibit in the main sanctuary. The video consists of two pieces of archival footage: Cracow in 1936 and Jews moving to the wartime ghetto in Podgorze. Approximate running time is ten minutes.

Also exhibited are life-size reproductions of the famous Ignac Krieger photographs of Jews in the second half of the nineteenth century. This part of the exhibit has elicited a mixed response. Some visitors find it in poor taste to present life-size reproductions of "Jewish types" in a city where Jews were mass murdered in the Holocaust.

At this writing it is not known whether the exhibit will extend beyond an initial two-year period. If there is a change of exhibit, the opening hours may be altered as well. The synagogue is still awaiting interior renovation.

THE KUPA SYNAGOGUE

Address: 8 Warszauera Street

> During the renovation of this synagogue, it is often easier to gain entry from the other side, through the synagogue courtyard on Miodowa Street (opposite Number 26). Sometimes, however, it is locked tight. Try all the doors, including the doors to the women's galleries.

The Kupa Synagogue, built in the first half of the seventeenth century, is located in an area that was once the poorest district of Jewish Kazimierz. In fact, the street itself was once known as "The Poor Street." The synagogue, in turn, was labelled the "Poor Man's Synagogue" because it stood close to various Jewish Community welfare institutions such as an orphanage, a hospital, and a home for the elderly. You'll notice how relatively humble and unprepossessing the synagogue appears from the outside, compared with the grandeur of the Isaac Synagogue only a block away. The current street name, Warszauera, is no less appropriate than "The Poor Street," as it honors Jonatan Warschauer (1820–1880), one of the great Jewish social aid workers of the nineteenth century.

The synagogue itself was built by the Jewish Community, which began to collect funds for it as early as 1595. The name "Kupa" derives from the Hebrew word meaning "fund." The synagogue was built *mikuppat hakehillah*, "from the Community fund."

The Jewish Community's *kupa* eventually had its limits. In 1643 it became strapped for funds, and people feared that work on the synagogue would be halted. That's when the jewelers came to the rescue. The Jewish Goldsmiths Guild donated two hundred zlotys (at the time a sizeable sum) to help finish construction. In return, they were honored with two permanent seats in the synagogue, in front of the *bimah*.

The Kupa Synagogue is the oldest synagogue built in the relatively new part of the Jewish Quarter, which was expanded in 1608. Next to the synagogue there used to stand a small wooden building covered with hay. When it was destroyed at the beginning of the twentieth century, archaeologists made a great find: Original remnants of the city walls of Kazimierz. You can still see the fragment from the synagogue courtyard off Miodowa Street. The Kupa Synagogue, like the Altschul and the Popper Synagogue, was built right up against the city walls, perhaps to insure extra defense in case of pogrom. In the nineteenth century, when the Kazimierz city walls were taken down, the synagogue used the liberated space to build new windows, a courtyard, and a new entrance from the Miodowa Street side. From the courtyard, you can see the separate entrances to the men's hall and the women's galleries. From the other side of the synagogue, on Warszauera Street, you'll see two earlier doors that also led separately to the men's and women's sections. Both of these doors, visitors might be happy to note, are equal in size and shape.

The Nazis plundered the synagogue of all its valuables and destroyed as much as they could. After the Holocaust, the Kupa Synagogue was the first synagogue in Cracow opened for services. In 1947, the Jewish Community installed a factory for matzohs in a part of the synagogue, and in the 1950s a *shochet*, or ritual slaughterer, worked in one of the side rooms. Later, the synagogue was used by the state as a co-operative work station for invalids. The building was restituted to the Cracow Jewish Community, and today it is undergoing restoration: In 1995, mild renovations were carried out; in 1996 nothing happened; and in 1997 there were plans for a new roof. The repair costs are coming from a state fund for the restoration of historical monuments. There are plans to begin thorough restoration of the synagogue in 1998, to be completed in 2000.

At present, the interior of the synagogue gives few hints of its original appearance. There are no traces of either the *bimah* or the *aron hakodesh*, the two indispensable components of any synagogue. The *bimah*, which was traditionally located in the center of the sanctuary, was once decorated by a stately blue canopy. Although the *aron hakodesh* is gone, there still remains a window added in 1647 to bathe it in additional light. In the eastern wall, near the window, you can see a stone plaque, shaped like a gravestone and decorated with the hands of the *Cohen*, or priest, and the water pitcher of the Levite. It refers to a society of Cohens and Levites in Cracow that in 1647 donated the window to the synagogue. The text reads, "This window was donated to the synagogue by the Holy Society of Cohens and Levites for the glory of God and the glory of the synagogue, for its enlightenment." Then the text quotes from Numbers 6:25–26, using a double entendre comparing God's light with the light entering the windows: "May the Lord make His face shine upon you and be gracious to you! May the Lord lift up His countenance unto you and grant you peace!" In the biblical quotation, the highlighted letters indicate the Hebrew year 5407 (1647), when the window and plaque were built. The plaque is the oldest preserved object in the synagogue.

The other notable items in the synagogue are the remains of the deliciously colorful paintings that once covered the ceiling and the pillars in the women's gallery, including the heavily deteriorated images, in twelve medallions, of the signs of the zodiac. The ceiling's images are much more discernible. They were painted in 1912, most likely based on popular postcards from Palestine in the early part of the century, and reflect a renewed religious-Zionist intrigue with the sites of the Holy Land. There are twelve segments, each corner depicting the musical instruments used in the Jerusalem Temple. The remaining images, arranged two per side, are of the cities and landmarks in Israel that were always a source of inspiration to Jews in Exile. The Jewish national rebirth in the nineteenth and twentieth centuries made these images all the more compelling to Diaspora Jews, both Orthodox and those who were assimilated and in search of their roots. The paintings are of Hebron, Tiberias, Jaffa Gate, the Western Wall, Haifa, the terebinths of Mamre (where Abraham lived in Hebron), the Flood, and the Temple Mount. If the synagogue is ever restored, the ceiling promises to be its dazzling highlight, belying any suggestion that this was once the poor man's *shul*.

Near the Kupa Synagogue

On Warszauera Street:

To the left of the Kupa Synagogue, at the corner of Estery Street, there is a renovated building that since 1813 had served as a Talmud Torah religious school. True to the nature of the street, the Talmud Torah was attended mostly by poor children. A yeshivah continued to function here after the war, until 1948. In the 1990s, the Cracow Jewish Community made a claim for ownership of the building. The case went all the way to the supreme administrative court in Warsaw, which decided the Jewish Community had no legal rights to the building. In 1996 the building was renovated and now it is used as a children's health center. Of all the possible uses for the building today, perhaps that is the best one.

Its street address is Estery 6.

On Miodowa Street:

Across the street from the Kupa Synagogue courtyard at Miodowa Street 26 is the former primary and high school of the Mizrachi movement. The Mizrachi was an Orthodox movement that distinguished itself by wholeheartedly embracing Zionism.

After the war, the building was occupied by Jews who had survived the Holocaust or returned from hiding in Russia. In August 1945, a rumor sifted across the nearby plac Novy that the Jews had captured a child. Even after they had suffered the Holocaust, the Jews were still demonized with the infamous blood libel. A crowd gathered outside Miodowa 26 and shouted obscenities against the Jews. After their recent experience, however, the Jews were prepared: They carried arms to defend themselves and kept the rabble from storming the building. The Jews telephoned the police, who refused to come; eventually the state security came and dispersed the crowd. Afterwards, the crowd threw rocks at the Kupa Synagogue across the street, and in the ensuing confusion a Jewish woman was killed.

THE TEMPEL

Address: Miodowa Street 24, at the corner of Podbrzezie Street.

> **During the reconstruction of the Tempel, it's often easier to get inside through the back, often from the gate on Miodowa Street. The workers are normally kind and don't seem to mind visitors.**

> Not once did our fathers mention a person changing a word or even half a word in the prayers, and now, because of our great sins, new people have arisen who don't understand the Talmud, young people, spiritually deficient, who have decided to create their own altar, to change the old texts, and to create separate groups for prayers. . . . Such things must not be tolerated among the children of Israel!
>
> (quoted in Majer Balaban, *Historja zydow w Krakowie in na Kazimier zu, 1304–1868*)

The Tempel Synagogue, perhaps the most illustrious building erected in nineteenth-century Kazimierz, was also a symbol of one of the most heated Jewish polemics of the day. After a nearly twenty-year dispute in which Cracow's Orthodox Community opposed any Progressive synagogue in their midst, the Tempel was built in 1860–62 by an independent Jewish organization that called itself the Association of Progressive Jews in Cracow. It was to be the only non-Orthodox synagogue that would ever stand in Kazimierz. The acrimony was so great that the synagogue was never owned by Cracow's official Jewish Community. When it was finally built, *hasidim* were known to spit thrice as they passed it, or even to walk all the way around the quarter to avoid passing the building. On their way into Cracow, certain observant Jews even preferred passing the Corpus Christi Church to the Tempel. The message was clear: The church was a separate religion, but the Tempel was an insult within their own.

It should be mentioned that Progressive or Reform Judaism in Europe was nothing like today's Reform movement in America. Women sat in separate sections and music was almost never played once Shabbat had started. In Cracow of the nineteenth century, Progressive Judaism developed in response to the birth pangs of assimilation, when wealthier Jews who did not want to sever all ties with Judaism decided to pray in more grandiose and less stringently observant prayer halls. In fact, by today's American standards, the Tempel's congregants would be considered Modern Orthodox or "Conservadox," a perplexing label that has come to denote more observant Jews in the American Conservative movement. There were compromises, such as the service-stopping sermon or the use of languages other than Hebrew in prayer, but by and large, the ritual was quite similar to that of the Orthodox. Nevertheless, it swiftly met with the fury of strictly observant Jews, perhaps because it was considered the first step away from the tradition.

Ironically, some of the most avid opponents of Progressive Judaism—*hasidim*—were themselves embroiled in an identical controversy only half a century before. When Hasidism began to make inroads in Cracow in the late eighteenth century, the rabbinic authority panicked. It was feared that the new movement would lead to a breakdown in traditional Judaism, just as the seventeenth-century Sabbatian movement had threatened to destroy the very foundations of Jewish life. Nobody would argue today that Hasidism, which strictly maintains Jewish law, is anything like Reform or Progressive Judaism, but both movements emerged from the same wellspring of discontent. Hasidism, like Progressive Judaism, was initially a reaction in part to a perceived lack of spirituality in Jewish life. As a result, when Hasidism began, the movement was seen as an outright revolution. Thus the rabbis issued proclamations that literally excommunicated the *hasid*s from the Jewish Community, and outlawed any hasidic prayer hall in Cracow. Indeed, the vituperative excerpt above was not taken from the Tempel debate but from a proclamation against Hasidism read from the *bimah* of Cracow's Altschul in 1785! It seems uncanny, but the language and tone of that excerpt is virtually interchangeable with that used against Progressive Jews in the nineteenth century.

Why should two clearly disparate movements have provoked identical reactions in the Jewish leadership? Because, looking at their major trends, the two movements posed the same threat: Both *hasid*s and Progressive Jews were responding to what they perceived as the ritualized petrification of the normative tradition. Both movements appealed to broad segments of the population that had become disenchanted with the status quo. Finally, both movements, in their willingness to establish alternative synagogues and prayer halls, threatened the very unity and structure of Jewish communal life in their respective centuries. What is so incredible is that in only half a century the Jewish Community leadership should face not one but two fundamental challenges to its very existence. If nothing else, the disputes reveal the fissures that had spread through the European Jewish Community as it stood at the brink of the modern age.

Nowhere is the extended acrimony that surrounded Cracow's Progressive synagogue better epitomized than on the dedication plaque above the entrance portal. At first glance it seems innocuous enough: "In the year 5620 [1860] the foundations of the House of God were laid, in the month of Ziv. In the year 5622 [1862], in the month of Bul—that is the eighth month—the House was completed according to all its details and all its specifications." The year 5620 comes out to spell the word *keter*, or crown, and there is a charming little crown drawn above the word itself. All in all, it looks like any workaday plaque showing the dates a synagogue was built.

But in Cracow, nothing is workaday. The inscription on the plaque is actually a direct quotation from I Kings 6:37–38, describing the building of Solomon's Temple in Jerusalem. By rewriting the Book of Kings on their synagogue, the Association of Progressive Jews was likening its place of worship to the most holy site in all of Jewish tradition, a place that would be rebuilt only once the Messiah comes!

The Progressive Jews drew much inspiration from the practices of ancient Israel; as such, Solomon's Temple was an enchanting concept. The Hebrew line above the portal, "Enter His gates with praise, His courts with acclamation" (Psalms 100:4), describes not only the metaphorical elevation of prayer but quite literal pilgrimages the Jews took to Solomon's Temple in Jerusalem. Even the name "Tempel," used in common parlance today ("Temple") to designate Reform synagogues, was deliberately chosen to harken back to days of yore. But to observant Jews, it was considered a profanity even to imply that a synagogue, which is meant as a temporary prayer house to serve the exigency of Exile, could actually be an incarnation of the Jerusalem Temple. It is tantamount to saying the Messiah has arrived, and we all know what *tsuris* such proclamations have brought the Jews in the past.

Of course, nobody would claim that the new movement wished to speed up the clock toward Redemption. If anything, they sought to separate themselves from what they considered to be the dogma of religious life. At the same time, the orchestrators of Jewish Reform in the nineteenth century saw themselves as nothing less than revolutionaries of Jewish life, prayer, and ritual—and any new movement needs its Temple. The reformers were careful to weave ancient Jewish symbols into their prayers and prayer halls, both to insist that they were not leaving Judaism and to indicate that they were a logical progression from what had come before. You can see this in the stately Two Tablets of the Law emblazoned on the facade, a symbol on a par with the menorah, deliberately preserved in the Hebrew original (unlike, for example, the similar Reform synagogue of Prague, which inscribes the commandments in left-to-right, Roman numeral fashion). You can see this as well in the architecture of the Tempel, which borrows from Moorish styles in order to situate it in the continuum of Middle East art and architecture. The Association of Progressive Jews deliberately claimed the symbols of ancient Judaism as its own. In their own eyes, these Jews were simultaneously returning to the past and paving the way to the future.

It was this very manipulation of symbols that unleashed much of the fury of traditionally observant Jews. In their view, to leave the religion was one thing, but to try to change the religion from the inside amounted to heresy. This, too, the Progressive Jews shared with earlier hasidic innovators. After all, the upstarts were tampering with the most sacred symbols of Judaism.

Although the Tempel was originally built in 1860–62, it did not attain its current shape and appearance until the 1920s. The original Tempel building was smaller; in 1893, the building was substantially enlarged. The eastern wall was pushed back and a new *aron hakodesh* was placed in the new spot. In the early 1920s the synagogue was enlarged again, when the side naves were added for women. Before that, women sat in the built-in gallery. During the interwar period, women became part of the synagogue's choir. In the back of the gallery is the accompanying organ, which was never used on Shabbat or holidays.

Aside from the intricately painted Romanesque and Moorish decoration, the prized possession of the synagogue is its collection of stained glass windows, one of the best in Poland. Some of the windows date to the end of the nineteenth century; the last were added in 1924. Most were given as gifts from wealthy families in Cracow. The donors and the dates of donation are typically written on the windows themselves.

The centrally located *bimah* is actually a postwar construction. As in other Progressive synagogues, the *bimah* in the Tempel had been situated in the space in front of the *aron hakodesh*, in order to mimic the design of a church. It should be recalled that it was only in the nineteenth century that Ashkenazic Jews moved the *bimah* from its traditional central location to the front of the synagogue. American Jewish communities, influenced by the changes in nineteenth-century European Jewish life, built the majority of their synagogues with the same *bimah*-pulpit design. Many visitors are surprised when they hear that such a design has nothing to do with Jewish tradition and was actually borrowed from Christian ritual. Thus in the Tempel, the Torah was read in a place from where a priest would preach.

The benches, too, were added after the war. Originally the Tempel was filled with elegant chairs, reflecting the prosperity of its relatively wealthy congregants.

Depending on whether the Tempel is turned into an official museum, you may find a light switch in the area behind the *aron hakodesh*. This illuminates the *aron* itself, and creates a nice effect for photographs. Above the *aron hakodesh* is the traditional inscription from Psalms 16:8 that states, "I place God in front of me always." (For a further discussion of the uses of this verse in synagogues, *see pages 72–93*.) It is an inspirational message that transcends the Orthodox-Progressive polemic, and is customarily placed on the eastern wall—which the congregants face—in synagogues of all types. However, as if to further test the patience of Cracow's Orthodox Jews, you'll also find God's name written on glass inside the *aron hakodesh*. This would never be tolerated in the Orthodox world, because a well-aimed rock could shatter God's Holy Name into oblivion.

Before the Holocaust, the Tempel boasted two of the most outstanding Jewish figures in Cracow as its cantor and rabbi. Its cantor, or *chazzan*, was Joseph Fischer. In the 1870s, before he began to accompany the Tempel's lofty organ melodies, Fischer established the most important Hebrew printing house in Europe. Capitalizing on the strict censorship prevalent in Russia, Fischer printed the works of some of the greatest Russian Jewish writers of the time, including Chaim Nachman Bialik, Achad Ha'am, Mendele Mocher Sforim, Sholem Ash, and Shalom Aleichem. Fischer's publishing house, located on Grodzka Street 62, quickly shot to world fame; the greatest Jewish writers in Eastern Europe and Russia spent extended periods in Cracow to oversee publication of their works. Russian publishers would print their works at Fischer's house in Cracow and then import the books back into Russia. The same thing happened with periodicals and newspapers, since the Russian authorities made it a Herculean task to found a Jewish paper. Fischer published the oldest Hebrew weekly, *Ha'Maggid*, which relocated to Cracow in 1892. Other important periodicals carried names that signified the dawn of a new age: *Ha'Zman, Ha'Cheker, Ha'Dor, Ha'Eshkol,* and *Mi'Mizrach Umima'arav*. He also published the Bible in Polish, translated by the Warsaw rabbi Isaac Cylkow (1841-1908). It was the first Hebrew-to-Polish translation of the Bible.

Just as prominent was the Tempel's rabbi, Dr. Osias Thon, who officiated in the synagogue from 1898 until he passed away in 1936 *(see page 358—in New Cemetery)*. Rabbi Thon's brilliant orations used to pack the Tempel on Shabbat. Outside his synagogue activities, Rabbi Thon was an active Zionist, helping Herzl prepare the First Zionist Congress. He also worked as a writer, educator, and eventually as a public servant representing Jewish interests. In 1919 he began to shuttle to Warsaw after being elected to the first Polish Parliament, or Sejm, where he served until 1931. Rabbi Thon was a symbol of the fierce commitment to Jewish life that was possible even among those Jews who had assimilated into Polish society.

During the Second World War, the Nazis used the Tempel as a stable for horses. Evidently enamored of the design of the building, which they considered German in style, they considered turning the building into a concert hall after the war.

In the years following the war, the synagogue was renovated and used regularly until the 1980s. It is currently being restored under the supervision of the World Monuments Fund. The Jewish Community hopes to open it to visitors in 1999.

Today, the ironies and dizzying controversies of the Tempel have come full circle. When large groups of hasidic Jews come visiting from America and Israel, the diminutive Rema Synagogue cannot hold everybody. On such occasions, the Cracow Jewish Community gives them the keys to the Tempel, and the groups hold prayers in the formerly sacrilegious building. The centrally located *bimah*, built by an Orthodox remnant of Galician Jews after the war, makes the synagogue an ideal place for large Orthodox groups to pray, regardless of its history. There is perhaps no better example of how practical the Jewish tradition is when it comes to prayer: A synagogue is constructed only to serve the temporary needs of Exile, and as such it is simply the vehicle used for prayer—not the idolized goal itself.

Nevertheless, it's hard not to see the poetry here. The spiritual ancestors of *hasidim* would once walk all the way around Kazimierz to avoid passing this monument to assimilation. Today, *hasidim* fill the place up to pray. It's as if, given the intersecting origins of both Hasidism and Progressive Judaism, the services are an unspoken symbol of historical unity. Both groups, which today are frightfully intolerant of one another, have come to an imaginary meeting point here in Cracow. Since both rebellious movements were ostracized and made into pariahs when they began, Progressive Judaism (represented by the building) and Hasidism (represented by the congregants) are momentarily joined as one.

Back to reality: The last *bar mitzvah* in Cracow showed just how quixotic are such dreams of symbolic unity. It happened in September 1985. A thirteen-year-old American boy arrived with his parents and his Polish-born grandfather to stage the first *bar mitzvah* ceremony in Cracow since the 1950s. His rabbi, who happened to be a woman and who organized the trip, came as well, along with several journalists from NBC and *People* magazine hoping to film and photograph Jewish life (or at least American Jewish life) in Poland. When a New York *hasid* heard about the woman rabbi, he hopped a plane to Poland and made sure the ceremony wouldn't take place in the Rema Synagogue, a site of supreme importance to Orthodox Jews.

Thus the Tempel Synagogue became the site of yet another struggle—this time, a contemporary American struggle—over symbols and reform in Judaism. Here on the postwar *bimah* of the synagogue, the ceremony reached its embarrassing nadir when the woman rabbi and the *hasid* got into a shouting match over her right to lead the service. There was no union, no sublime harmony—on the contrary, there was almost a physical fight.

So it's not all poetry, and the cycles of Jewish history aren't always pretty. The grim and gritty reality is that the Tempel Synagogue has always been a battlefield on which the Orthodox and Reform wage their unseemly war for Jewish legitimacy.

THE NEW JEWISH CEMETERY

Address: Miodowa Street 55

> From the Jewish Quarter, take Miodowa Street east until you pass underneath the railway bridge (only a couple blocks away from Szeroka Street). The cemetery is just across the street. The main gate to the cemetery is closed; enter through the building on Miodowa 55. Walk through the front door and then out the back door, as if you were entering a courtyard.

Hours: 9 A.M.–2 P.M.
Closed *Shabbat* and Holidays
These hours are not strictly enforced; often the cemetery is open well past 2 P.M. Keep an eye on the exit, though, so you don't get locked in.

In 1799 the Austrian authorities ordered the Jews to close the Old Jewish Cemetery next to the Rema Synagogue. They claimed that the cemetery had become vastly overcrowded over the course of three centuries, and that the nearby apartment buildings were exposed to dangerous hygienic conditions. The Austrians made it clear that any new cemetery must be established outside the limits of the Jewish Town.

In 1800 the Jewish Community purchased a stretch of farmland, located outside the eastern edge of Kazimierz, from the local Augustinian Monastery. The first funerals took place in 1804. The cemetery was expanded at various times throughout its existence, beginning in 1836. With the exception of a few rabbis and family members, who continued to be buried in plots of the Old Jewish Cemetery, the new cemetery was the sole burying place of Cracow's Jews throughout the nineteenth century and well into the twentieth. As such, the tombstones are both a testament to the achievements of the Jews in Polish history and an image of the hopes and struggles of a Community in transition. As with the much larger Jewish Cemetery of Warsaw, which was established at roughly the same time, you can find graves of important rabbis, Zionists, socialists, artists, writers, and philanthropists. Likewise, you'll find special areas of the cemetery reserved for Orthodox Jews, reflecting the widening fissure of nineteenth-century Jewish life, when large numbers of Jews began to assimilate into mainstream civic society.

By the 1920s, the New Jewish Cemetery had become full and was closed to burials, with exceptions made for family plots or distinguished personalities. The Jewish Community established another cemetery on the other side of the river, near Plaszow, which was used until the Second World War.

During the Holocaust, the Germans destroyed part of the New Jewish Cemetery and used a section of the land for troop drills. The cemetery near Plaszow was completely destroyed when the Plaszow labor camp was established. (The sidewalk of tombstones seen famously in *Schindler's List* was made during the war from tombstones at the former cemetery near Plaszow.)

After the war, with no cemetery left in Plaszow, the Jewish Community had no choice but to literally overstuff the closed New Jewish Cemetery on Miodowa Street. Paths and roads in the cemetery were turned into cemetery plots. You will notice that most of the postwar graves—with the exception of the most eminent personalities—are placed single file on these previously used paths. Controversy arose when burials stretched into the area of the *Cohanim*. Many cemeteries reserve a special area, usually near the cemetery gate, for *Cohanim*. Because a *Cohen*, or priest, is not permitted to enter a cemetery, this practice enabled *Cohanim* to visit their relatives at the outskirts of the cemetery, without stepping foot inside. The *Cohen* area is customarily reserved exclusively for the priests, but the Cracow Jewish Community was so desperate for additional cemetery space that it had to encroach upon tradition and use the *Cohen* area for new burials.

The cemetery is still functioning for the Cracow Jewish Community today.

A Stroll through the New Jewish Cemetery

To give you a sense of the cross section of Jewish life represented here, what follows is a brief walk that will lead you to several selected graves.

From the back door of Miodowa 55, you'll see the *Chevrah Kaddishah* (Burial Society) building standing next door on the right. The building was erected in the second half of the nineteenth century and is the place where funerals are held to this day. The main path of the cemetery, where some of the most important communal leaders are buried, stretches into the cemetery from the entrance to the *Chevrah Kaddishah* building. Forty meters down this path, opposite a path starting on the right, is the grave of Osias Thon (1870–1936) on the left side. (In Polish his name is spelled Ozjasz; the Hebrew is Yehoshua.)

Born in Lvov and made rabbi in Cracow in 1897, Thon encapsulated practically all the major drifts that affected Jewish life in the late nineteenth century. He was a prominent Reform rabbi, whose sermons in the Tempel drew audiences from throughout Galicia. He was an ardent Zionist, leading the West Galician Zionist Federation and taking active part alongside Theodor Herzl in the Zionist Congresses. In fact, Rabbi Thon penned the first philosophical treatise on Zionism in 1897. Finally, he was a committed public servant, fighting for Jewish equality as an elected member of the first Polish parliament, or Sejm. He was such a gifted speaker that during his parliamentary addresses, the several anti-Semitic deputies in the Sejm refrained from their habit of howling and jeering during Jewish members' speeches. A settlement in Israel, Bet Yehoshua, is named after Rabbi Thon.

With such a prominent personality, the tombstone need not be prolix. Regarding Rabbi Thon, it says quite simply, *Posel na Sejm* ("Member of Parliament"). On the bottom there is a memorial inscription regarding Rabbi Thon's relatives who were murdered in the Holocaust. His wife, Maria, was shot in Radom in 1942; his son-in-law was tortured and murdered in Radom in 1942; and his only grandson, born in 1928, was murdered in the extermination camp of Belzec. The tombstone ends with *Czesc ich pamieci!* ("Honor to their memory!").

Return to the *Chevrah Kaddishah* building and walk to the side of the building away from the Miodowa 55 entrance, where you'll see the cemetery entrance used during funerals. Near this entrance is a Holocaust Memorial adorned by plaques memorializing individuals and families. One of those remembered is Dr. Rafael Landau, the last leader of the Cracow Jewish Community before the German occupation.

Beyond the Memorial in the cemetery wall are fragments of tombstones placed there during the postwar cemetery reconstruction, as was the case with the Old Jewish Cemetery's Wailing Wall.

Thirty meters into the cemetery alongside the wall is a path on the left that leads to the grave of Kalonymus Kalman Epstein (c. 1763–1823), who introduced Cracow to Hasidism *(see page 270)*. His tombstone is the black one on the right side of the path. The first letters of each line of the inscription spell out the name Kalonymus. Rabbi Epstein is known among *hasidim* as "Reb Kalmush" or by the title of his best-known work, *Ma'or va'Shemesh*, "The Luminary and the Sun." His tombstone reads:

> Lament over a man of multiple deeds,
> A luminary for the sages and a beacon for the intellectuals.
> His words are pure, refined seven-fold;
> We will glorify and praise him in the congregation of *hasidim*.
> . . . Lips shall kiss his holy words.
> He paved his study in the Hidden and the Revealed.
> He did not budge from the tent of Torah day and night.
> The pious, outstanding rabbi, a glory among the righteous,
> Rabbi Kalman, son of Rabbi Aharon Halevi, of blessed memory,
> Passed away in holiness and purity,
> May his soul be bound in the bundle of life . . .

To the left of Reb Kalmush is his son Reb Aharon (d. 1882). The *hasidim* made a play on his name and called him "Reb Aron," referring to the *aron hakodesh*. Such a prayer hall moniker had additional substance for Reb Aharon, who in 1815 opened the first ever hasidic prayer house, known as a *klaus*, in Cracow. The synagogue, located near the Altschul at Jozefa Street 33, was popularly known as "the Reb Aron Klaus." Reb Aharon succeeded his father in becoming the most important hasidic leader in western Galicia. He prayed in his *klaus* until he died in 1882, but the second floor of Jozefa Street 33 continued to be used as a hasidic *klaus* right up to the Second World War.

To the right of Reb Kalmush's grave is a tomb decorated with two lions touching a tree. Underneath the image is the famous Hebrew phrase, "The righteous bloom like a date palm," from Psalms 92. The psalm, read every Shabbat, continues, ". . . they thrive like a cedar in Lebanon; planted in the house of the Lord, they flourish in the courts of our God." This is the grave of Shlomo Zalman Yosef (d. 1858).

Reb Shlomo Zalman was the hasidic Rebbe of Vieliopoli. As one might expect, there are several hasidic legends about how the Vieliopoli Rebbe found his eternal rest in the city of Cracow.

The Vieliopoler, it is told, used to spend his days murmuring a phrase from the first page of the first book of the Talmud, called the *Berakhot*. The *mishnah* begins with a question asked by the rabbinical *Tannaim*: "Between what times at night can the Shema prayer be read?" The *Gemarah*, wondering why the *Tana* (rabbi) began the Talmud out of the blue like that, begins its commentary with a question: "Where is this *Tana* coming from? First he should tell us that there is a *mitzvah* to pray the Shema, and then he can launch into the permissible hours. And why does he start off with the nighttime Shema, and not the daytime one?" Then, as is its wont, the *Gemarah* answers its own question: "The *Tana* is basing this on the verse that you must read the Shema 'When you lie down and when you rise.'" It was this part of the *Gemarah* that struck the Vieliopoler Rebbe as catchy. In Aramaic, the phrase "The *Tana* is basing it . . ." reads, "*Tana Akra koee* . . ." The Vieliopoler Rebbe, for some reason fond of the phrase, would always mutter, "*Tana akra koee, akra koee, akra koee.*" Nobody understood why, but they let the Rebbe have his simple amusement.

Years later, the Rebbe fell ill and was taken from Vieliopoli to the skilled doctors in Cracow. The doctors, though, were unable to stop the spread of his sickness. Just before he passed away, the Rebbe said, "Reb Kalonymus Kalman once arrived at my father's home when I was only five years old. We didn't have many beds, so my father put Reb Kalmush in my bed, and said I should sleep on the floor. But Reb Kalmush looked at me and said, 'Such a child should not sleep on a floor.' He insisted that we sleep in the same bed." At that moment, the Vieliopoler breathed his last breath.

The people of Cracow knew what his anecdote meant: He wanted to be buried close to Reb Kalmush. But they knew that all the plots surrounding Reb Kalmush had been taken by relatives and students years before. Dejectedly, they came to the cemetery, and lo and behold, to everybody's surprise there was an empty plot to the right of Reb Kalmush's grave. So they buried the Vieliopoler there.

And at last they understood why he always said "*Tana akra koee, akra koee* . . ." "*Akra koee*," when rolled quickly off the tongue, comes out as "Cracow." The Vieliopoler Rebbe was psychically pointing to the place of his eternal rest.

Continue on the main path near the cemetery wall another thirty meters (you'll pass a large path on the left) to the graves of Shmul Shmulke Kornitzer and Yosef Nechemiah Kornitzer on the right side of the path. (As a point of reference for those who cannot read Hebrew, the Kornitzers are buried next to a path on the right in which is buried, in a large black tomb, Chaim Shalom Strassberg.) On the back of Yosef Kornitzer's *ohel* is a second tombstone with its own inscription. Yosef Nechemiah Kornitzer, the son of Akiva Kornitzer (*see below*), was chief rabbi of Cracow in 1925–1933. His son, Shmul Shmulke Kornitzer, was murdered in Auschwitz in 1940.

About ten meters farther along the path, make your first right. A couple meters in on the right is the grave of Simeon Sofer (1820–1883). The son of the famed Chatam Sofer of Bratislava, Simeon Sofer became rabbi of Mattersdorf in 1848 and rabbi of Cracow in 1861. When Rabbi Sofer arrived in Cracow, the Jewish Quarter was being torn asunder from the quarrels between the *hasidim* and the *mitnagdim* (observant Jews who opposed Hasidism). Rabbi Sofer was clever enough not to get mixed up in the controversy, and eventually he made peace between the two groups. Unfortunately, the same cannot be said for his relations with the *maskilim*, "Enlightened" Jews who had abandoned religious Orthodoxy. He founded the Galician Orthodox association Machzike Hadas, whose primary purpose was to battle the tides of Enlightenment and assimilation. However, his skeptical views on Jewish assimilation did not keep him from public service. From 1878, he served as a member of the Austrian Parliament in Vienna.

Rabbi Simeon's tombstone is a replica made in later years.

To the right of Rabbi Simeon's grave is that of his son-in-law, Akiva Kornitzer (1838–1892), who was the father of Yosef Nechemiah Kornitzer (*see above*). There is a legend that when Simeon Sofer died, the logical choice for his successor was Rabbi Akiva Kornitzer, but the *maskilim* in Cracow were vociferously against it. They had had enough secularism bashing during Simeon Sofer's day, and they suspected that Akiva would continue Simeon's campaign against assimilation. It was time, they argued, for a rabbi who represented their interests. The chairman of the Jewish Community agreed with them, and he blocked the appointment of Akiva Kornitzer as chief rabbi. As a result, there was no chief rabbi in Cracow for many years. Later, the chairman died a tragic death. His son, Rafael Landau, was appointed chairman in his father's place. As soon as Rafael assumed his position, he called a meeting of the Jewish Community of Cracow and declared, "My father died because of his decision, years ago, to stop Rabbi Akiva Kornitzer from being our chief rabbi. It is time at last to right the error done to Rabbi Akiva!" By that time, Rabbi Akiva had already died as well. So Chairman Landau, in an effort to repent for his father, appointed Rabbi Akiva's son, Rabbi Yosef Nechemiah Kornitzer, to be the new chief rabbi.

Continue along the path of Rabbi Sofer's grave until you near the end. You'll notice that all the gravestones are inscribed in Hebrew. Since Orthodox Jews were vociferously opposed to the use of Polish or German on their tombstones, they buried themselves in distinct areas separated from the assimilated. You might think this area exclusively Orthodox, but wait: close to the end of the path, on the left-hand side, you begin to see ornate columns and obelisks jutting from the ground. In the span of just a few graves, you cross from the most intensely Orthodox section to an area of assimilated and, as the tombstones indicate, highly successful Jews.

In this area of obelisks, about four rows in on the left, is the grave of Maurycy Gottlieb (1856–1879). The stone is decorated with a palette.

Maurycy Gottlieb was a great Polish-Jewish painter whose works were acclaimed throughout the continent. You can find copies of his work in the Altschul *(see page 303)*. In one of his paintings, Gottlieb painted the interior of a synagogue. On the Torah was written his own *yahrzeit*, or anniversary of death. Gottlieb's father urged him to remove the morbid inscription, but it can still be seen on the painting today.

The brief Polish inscription on the tombstone reads as follows:

> He wrote soaring songs with colors
> For brothers whom he loved.
> Death tore him from this world too early
> The world keeps his memory.

After another ten meters or so, you'll find the grave of Jonatan Warschauer (1820–1888) on the left. Warschauer, whose name is immortalized in a Kazimierz street today, was a doctor who was famous for opening his door to Cracow's impoverished denizens. He also established a Jewish hospital in Cracow in 1849.

ELSEWHERE IN KAZIMIERZ

Before the Second World War, Kazimierz was inhabited almost exclusively by Jews. As such, it boasted a gaggle of Jewish schools, communal centers, and its own marketplace, as well as countless kosher shops and scores of *shtiebel*s, or small hasidic prayer halls.

You might wish to visit some of these sights, none of which currently performs its former function, as you wander through the streets of Kazimierz. Because most of the sites have different functions today, they can be viewed satisfactorily from the outside. I have listed the sites in their order of placement, in a generally north-to-south direction. You can stroll past all of them in less than an hour.

The Jewish Crafts School

Podbrzezie Street 3 (around the corner from the Tempel)

This capacious building was erected by the Jewish Folk and Secondary Schools' Society in 1937–38 as a polytechnical school for craft making. Today the building is used by the Biology Institute.

Hebrew Grammar School

Podbrzezie Street 8/10 (across the street from the Crafts School)

This building housed a Jewish primary and secondary school, called a *Gymnasium*, that was built in the interwar period.

In Rafael F. Scharf's nostalgic essay "Cracow—blessed its memory," the author writes,

That school had a state approved secular curriculum, which entitled those who passed the matriculation exam to enter the University. But over and above that there was a comprehensive syllabus taught in Hebrew—Bible, Jewish history, and literature. Pupils came from far and wide, from Debniki, Pradnik, Krowodrza, even from Wieliczka. Fees were modest, most pupils had them reduced, nobody was barred from admission for lack of funds. The school was held in great affection by the pupils. It was kind of [an] oasis, where one felt free and on home ground, had the illusion that the world was and would remain benevolent. One could also—if one was so inclined—acquire a little learning.

(Rafael F. Scharf, Poland, *What Have I to Do with Thee: Essays without Prejudice*)

Plac Novy

The square on the eastern end of Meiselsa Street.

Before the war, plac Novy was the main market square of Jewish Kazimierz. "Plac Novy" means "New Square," but even today it's referred to as "Jewish Square" or, in slang, as "Jew" ("We'll meet at 7:00 at Jew!").

The round building in the middle of the square, called Okraglak, was built in 1900. At first it was a market hall, but in 1927 it was turned into a kosher slaughterhouse of poultry and was the poultry center of Jewish Cracow until the war.

Before the war, there used to be a hospital and shelters for the poor on plac Novy.

Today, plac Novy is once again used as a marketplace, but conspicuously lacking is the crowded, urban-Yiddish grit that once defined its essence. Nonetheless, fruits and vegetables are sold, as well as decidedly non-kosher meat. Every Sunday there's a flea market where you can find cheap clothes.

Beit Midrash B'nei Emunah

Meiselsa Street 17, just off plac Novy

This *beit midrash* was built in 1886 by the prayer society B'nei Emunah ("Sons of Belief") as both a study hall and *shul*. It was built by the famous Cracow architect Jacek Matusinski, who incorporated various Oriental elements into the building's appearance. Inside, there was an iron column in the hallway separating the men's section from the women's.

The *beit midrash* was used as a prayer house until the Second World War. After the war, workshops were housed in the building, leading to its eventual devastation. In 1990, the entire building was reconstructed and extended to house the Center for Jewish Culture, which officially opened in 1993. The Center works closely with the Research Center on Jewish History and Culture in Poland, established in 1986 at Jagiellonian University.

The Center for Jewish Culture is without a doubt the most modern building in the former Jewish Quarter. There are practically no interior traces of its former function as a *beit midrash*. If nothing else, the slick new facilities reflect the booming public fascination with Judaism in the years since 1989. For information about the Center, *see* page 287.

Vishniac's Gate

Next to the Center for Jewish Culture (see above) on Meiselsa Street is a courtyard made famous in one of Roman Vishniac's indelible photographs of Kazimierz. The title of Vishniac's 1937 photograph is "The entrance to Kazimierz, the old ghetto of Cracow." I'm not one to demystify legends, and no one wants to contradict the great chronicler of prewar Jewish life in Eastern Europe, but this courtyard gate was at no time the entrance or exit of the Jewish Quarter. In fact, the courtyard only became a Jewish neighborhood in the nineteenth century. This, of course, in no way detracts from the immense emotional appeal of his photograph, with its impressionistic grey rain, its arcs of light, its fences, cages, and stairways. Perhaps the most unforgettable part of the photograph—and the image that truly evokes the ghetto—is the solitary, caged pigeon on the left-hand side, perhaps the whitest object in the picture. So what if it wasn't the ghetto gate—it still makes a great photograph. If you've already seen the Vishniac photo, you can snap your own and then compare it with the master's.

Although the building was outside the Jewish Quarter, certain Jews received permission to run a kosher vodka factory in this courtyard in the eighteenth century.

Beit Midrash Chevrah Tehillim

Meiselsa Street 18, on the corner of Corpus Christi Street (Bozego Ciala).

Built in 1896, this building served as the study hall and prayer house of the Psalms Society, consisting of one hundred Jews. Membership was no piece of cake; every day, each of the members would read the entire Book of Psalms, from cover to cover. They also paid a *magid*, or preacher, who would lecture them in this building every day after the evening prayer.

Today (in keeping with the melody of Psalms), the building is used by a song and dance ensemble.

Corpus Christi Church

Kosciol Bozego Ciala **in Polish; it's the big church just off Corpus Christi Street (Bozego Ciala).**

Yes, this is a Jewish guide book, and we're not here to say Mass. But inside the Church of the Corpus Christi is an intriguing painting recommended for all those who crave the minute details of Jewish life and history in Cracow.

The painting is hanging on the wall of small paintings near the entrance. It depicts a fire that began in the Jewish Quarter in 1623. According to Christian legend, heavy winds were about to fan the fire over to the Christian side when Stanislaw Kazimiercek, the "patron saint" of Christian Kazimierz, convinced God to change the wind direction so that the Christian neighborhood would be spared the flames. As a result, the terrible fire burned the Jewish Quarter alone.

On the left side of the painting are Jewish homes in flames. The painting is celebrating this fact. For those who wish to view an image, however small and distorted by the flames, of Jewish Kazimierz in the seventeenth century, the painting is a good bet. You'll see how congested the Jewish Quarter was, which is exactly why fires raged there from generation to generation.

The painting, replete with what appears to be the outline of a burning Jew, is a horrifying depiction of Church insensitivity toward the Jews. Still, one wonders: If the situation had been reversed, wouldn't the Jews have developed a similar story, attributing their own salvation to Divine Providence?

In the seventeenth century it was this church that fought for, and almost won, the closure of the Isaac Synagogue, on the grounds that priests carrying the Host would have to walk by the synagogue—presumed to be a place of evil—on their way to the church.

Kazimierz Town Hall

On Wolnica Square (plac Wolnica), at the southern end of Corpus Christi Street (Bozego Ciala).

In 1875–76, when Kazimierz was already a part of Cracow, the sixteenth-century Town Hall was given a southern extension and turned into a school. As most of the neighborhood was Jewish, almost all of the school's students were Jewish. For some years, the school was even managed by the Cracow Jewish Community itself.

There is a plaque on the building commemorating the invitation of the Jews to Poland by the Angel of Poland. The original plaque was put up by the Jewish Community in 1910. It featured Casimir the Great instead of the Angel. During the war, the Nazis destroyed it. The plaque you see here is actually an earlier model, from 1907, that was kept in the storehouse of the Warsaw Museum after the war. It was put up on the Town Hall in 1996, in a ceremony featuring Ehud Olmert, the mayor of Jerusalem.

The artist of the plaque, Henryk Hochman (1879–1943), was an internationally renowned sculptor who lived and worked in Cracow. He was murdered in the Holocaust.

It is unclear whether it is the erosion of time that has given one of the pictured men the appearance that he is vomiting, or whether it was intended as a comment on Polish-Jewish relations.

Bochenska Street

Before the war, there were two Jewish institutions on Bochenska Street. At number 4 was a *beit midrash*, or study and prayer hall. After the war, number 4 was used as the cultural center of the city transport authority. Later it was given to the Medical Academy, which turned the space into offices. All that remains is the shell of the prewar building.

At number 7 was a Yiddish theater from 1927–1939. After the war, it became the site of a "Railwaymen's Theater." The prewar interior has been completely destroyed.

The Former Jewish Hospital

Skawinska Street 8

This hospital, built in 1822 and renovated in the 1860s, provided some of the highest quality medical care in Cracow until it was closed in 1938. After the war it became a public hospital. The Cracow Jewish Community has not tried to regain ownership of the building. In the early 1990s, however, there was a call to put a plaque on the building indicating its history. The Medical Academy did not wish to mention the Jewish origins of the hospital. It finally relented, but at this writing a plaque had not yet been erected.

THE CRACOW GHETTO IN PODGORZE

The Cracow Ghetto was located in what is today the suburb of Podgorze, in the streets around Plac Bohaterow Getta. From Kazimierz, walk down Starowislna Street until you come to the river (the bridge is called Most Powstanicow Slaskich). Plac Bohaterow Getta is located on the other side of the river, two blocks south.

The legendary innocence of Jewish Kazimierz finds a stark counterpoint on the other side of the Vistula River. Podgorze was the district chosen by the Germans as the site to contain the Cracow Ghetto. Over the course of 1941 and 1942, Cracow's remaining Jews were subjected to repeated deportations that resulted in the mass murder of most of the Jews confined to the area.

Millions of people around the world have already seen images of the Cracow Ghetto in Steven Spielberg's 1993 film "Schindler's List." Actually, those scenes were shot in Kazimierz in and around Szeroka Street, because several postwar buildings had altered the appearance of Podgorze since the war. The setting, though, is the Cracow Ghetto in Podgorze.

History of the Cracow Ghetto

On March 3, 1941, the Nazis put out a notice that parts of the Podgorze suburb would be transformed into a "residential district" for the Jews who remained in Cracow. The Jews had until March 21 to relocate to the district. There were 320 buildings in the ghetto, with anywhere from four to twenty people sharing a single apartment. Living space was so condensed that the average space for a single person was two square meters. Around 15,000 Jews lived in the ghetto, 3,000 of whom lived there "illegally" (i.e., without identity papers). The number would have been far higher (in 1940, over 68,000 Jews lived in Cracow), had the Nazis not actively displaced tens of thousands of Jews to the villages throughout 1940. In 1941, the Germans exacerbated the situation when they sent Jews from 29 surrounding towns into the Ghetto in Podgorze.

A three-meter high wall, topped by circular ornamentation to recall Jewish tombstones, surrounded the ghetto. It was accessed by four gates, the most prominent of which was situated at the northern end of Plac Zgody (today's Plac Bohaterow Getta), blocking access to the river.

In the first week of June, 1942, the first massive Aktion, or deportation of Jews to death camps, was carried out from the Cracow Ghetto. Jews employed in exploitable trades had been given stamps that exempted them from the deportations. The rest were pulled out of their homes and marched to Plac Zgody, where the transports departed for the Plaszow train station. Those who did not comply were shot and murdered on the streets of the ghetto. On June 4, the Nazis massacred a crowd of people on Plac Zgody. The day became known as "Bloody Thursday." The Nazis, dissatisfied with what they considered an inadequate number of deportees, had the president of the Judenrat, along with his family, sent on the transports as well. Even then the Nazis were dissatisfied. A second Aktion was organized on June 8. In all, 5,000 Jews were sent to the Belzec death camp.

On October 28, 1942, a new Aktion was perpetrated in a much more haphazard fashion, with little or no regard for the individuals' labor capacities. According to Malvina Graf, who survived the Cracow Ghetto, "The Nazis did not, for the most part, follow any usual pattern in this selection; among the ones that had been rejected were people of all ages—old, middle-aged, and young; there were both men and women; individuals both tall and short, good-looking and not." After the selection had departed, S.S. officers stormed through the ghetto, murdering Jews wherever they could be found. Graf writes,

> . . . . They began to shoot whomever they saw. They searched the buildings and apartments at random, looking for hidden Jews. Many sick and crippled people were thus killed. S.D. [*Sonderdienst* Special Police] and S.S. patrols also went into hospitals, where they killed many patients, dragging others outside to be finished off by a cleanup crew. They dragged a woman in the process of giving birth outside to join a group of other persons. Even some of the doctors were killed by the S.S.
>
> . . . . Whoever [the Germans] found, whether an old person, a sick person, or a child, was shot immediately. Many mothers, carrying their infants and small children in their arms, were shot on the spot.
>
> (Malvina Graf, *The Krakow Ghetto and the Plaszow Camp Remembered*)

Approximately 6,000 Jews were sent to death camps during the October deportations. After the deportations in June and October, the ghetto was reduced in physical size.

Soon after the October Aktion, the Nazis began to convert two Jewish cemeteries near Plaszow, not far from Podgorze, into a labor camp and concentration camp. Meanwhile, the Cracow Ghetto was divided into two sections, "Ghetto A" and "Ghetto B." Ghetto A was a labor camp; Ghetto B was for the unemployed as well as those who were too young, old, or infirm to work.

On March 13, 1943, the 6,000 inhabitants of Ghetto A were marched to the Plaszow concentration and labor camp. Several Jews escaped the deportation through the sewers, but after the Germans learned of this route they pumped poison gas into the sewer outlet.

On March 14, the Germans liquidated Ghetto B. Children were murdered on the streets of the ghetto; the infirm were shot in their hospital beds. The Germans forced Jews to race each other; those who were not quick enough to be sent to Plaszow were shot where they stood. Over 1,000 people were murdered on the streets of the ghetto, and 2,000 more were taken to be murdered in Auschwitz-Birkenau. Four thousand Jews were considered fit enough to work in the Plaszow camp.

With the exception of Jewish cleanup and German scavenger crews, the Cracow Ghetto was empty. Later, the few remaining Jews would be sent to the Plaszow concentration camp. The walls and barbed wire were taken down, and Poles moved into the newly opened area.

Selected Sites in the Former Ghetto

Plac Zgody

Today the square is called Plac Bohaterow Getta ("Heroes of the Ghetto Square").

As the largest open-air space in the Cracow Ghetto, Plac Zgody was chosen by the Germans as the site from which they arranged deportations. The square became the most feared spot in the ghetto during an Aktion. It was here on June 4, 1942, that Germans lined up Jews and shot them en masse when they were dissatisfied with the progress of the selection. The day became known as "Bloody Thursday." The Nazis separated the Jews on Plac Zgody; those Jews who were considered unfit were either deported to death camps or shot on the spot.

During the liquidation of the ghetto on March 13 and 14, 1943, Plac Zgody was the scene of even greater terror, as the Germans deported and mass murdered practically the entire remaining population of the ghetto. The square became a symbol of Nazi inhumanity, as infants, the infirm, and the elderly from "Ghetto B" were shot one by one on the square and in its side streets. On March 14, over 1,000 Jews were murdered on the streets; 2,000 Jews were sent to their deaths in Auschwitz-Birkenau.

Malvina Graf described the horrors of March 14:

> In the morning, exactly as in the previous Aktions, people gathered on the Plac Zgody. Their faces were unwashed, the men were unshaven, and in their eyes could be seen only fear or resignation. The Plac Zgody was filling up—there were men carrying their ritual religious attire and phylacteries, women holding small infants, and small children holding one another by the hand, some of the smaller ones clutching a favorite doll or stuffed toy. They—the very small ones—laughed and played happily with their toys, too young to understand the gravity of the situation and filled with curiosity about what they perceived as an adventure . . .
>
> Battalions of S.S. and *Sonderdienst* marched into the ghetto, heading straight for the Plac Zgody. They wore helmets and were fully attired in battle dress, and they all carried rifles. Following the neat rows of goose-stepping soldiers, Nazi dignitaries in large official cars drove into the ghetto. Anxious to put on a show to impress the dignitaries, the soldiers began shooting . . .
>
> On the Plac Zgody, the action was in full swing. The Germans were shooting at random the tired, ruined, and guiltless people of the ghetto, all the while wearing wide grins on their faces.
>
> . . . . Young children were taken into an alleyway and lined up in such a way that the Nazis could conserve their bullets, one bullet being used to murder two or even more children. . . .

Plac Zgody was soon empty. It looked like a battlefield, full of blood, corpses, and the blood-soaked packages of those who had gone on the transport.

(Malvina Graf, *The Krakow Ghetto and the Plaszow Camp Remembered*)

Parts of the square were changed and rebuilt after the war. For this reason, when Steven Spielberg filmed "Schindler's List," he chose to film scenes of the ghetto in the much more untrammelled landscape of Kazimierz.

"Under The Eagle" Pharmacy (*Apteka pod Orlem*)

18 Plac Bohaterow Getta
The Museum of National Commemoration is situated here.
Opening hours: Monday to Friday 10 A.M.–4 P.M.
Saturday 10 A.M.–2 P.M.
Closed Sundays and state holidays.

The pharmacy called "Under the Eagle" was the site of unique individual courage during the Holocaust. Under the Eagle was operated by a Polish man, Tadeusz Pankiewicz, before the war. When his pharmacy fell into the Cracow Ghetto in 1941, Pankiewicz chose to continue working in the ghetto and to help the Jews as much as possible. Along with his three Polish assistants, Pankiewicz used the pharmacy as a conduit of information between the Jewish and Polish underground. The pharmacy served all manner of purpose, from secret post office to covert hiding place during deportations.

In 1983, Pankiewicz was honored by the Yad Vashem Holocaust Memorial in Jerusalem. During shooting of "Schindler's List" in 1992, Steven Spielberg showed gratitude to Pankiewicz by giving him a small cameo in the film. Pankiewicz died in 1993.

A small museum was opened in the former pharmacy in 1983. The exhibit covers the Nazi occupation of Poland, focusing on the Ghetto of Podgorze and the inspiring figure of Pankiewicz himself. Included in the exhibit is a Torah held by Pankiewicz during the war. The rather crude images on the stained glass windows were commissioned by a local artist in the 1980s.

Headquarters of the Jewish Fighting Organization

6 Plac Bohaterow Getta

This building was used as the seat of the Cracow branch of the Jewish Fighting Organization (ZOB) during the war. Although the Cracow ZOB was not as large and renowned as its Warsaw counterpart, it was the first branch of the ZOB to launch an armed attack. This was the hand grenade attack on December 24, 1942, at the Cyganeria Cafe, located on Szpitalna Street in the Old Town. The cafe had been a social spot for German soldiers during the war. There were twenty German casualties in all. Days later, all members of the Cracow ZOB were arrested, and its activities were ended.

A plaque on the building commemorates the martyrs of the ghetto and the ZOB.

The Jewish Hospital
14 Jozefinska (today the building serves the Cracow Town Council)

During the years of the ghetto, this building served as one branch of the Jewish hospital. Lacking sufficient staff and supplies, the hospital was nevertheless known for its high level of care.

The Nazis regularly forced doctors to make decisions that defied human morality and reason. Malvina Graf offered this remembrance of Dr. Alexandrowicz, the director of the hospital:

> Gutter [the head of the Judenrat] had sent a policeman to the hospital, with orders for Dr. Alexandrowicz to conduct a selection among the hospital's patients. Dr. Alexandrowicz adamantly refused. . . . Only when he was informed that the hospital would be liquidated (and all its patients shot) if he did not comply with the Nazis did he reluctantly acquiesce; with the help of two OD [Jewish police] men, all of the patients were brought out into the street; after he had made the selection, most of his elderly patients were moved back into the hospital.

Dr. Alexandrowicz, along with his wife and son, later escaped the liquidation of the ghetto through the sewers.

During the liquidation of the ghetto, Germans came into the hospital and methodically shot, one by one, each of the infirm patients.

The Optima Building
7 Krakusa

Before the war, this building, which stretches from Krakusa to Wegierska streets, was a chocolate factory. After Plac Zgody, the Optima courtyard (since built over) was used as the site of deportations from the ghetto. During the deportations of June, 1942, the deportees were locked in the courtyard without food or water for two days. When they were released, on June 8, they were forced to march to the Prokocim railway station amid German shouts and blows. The trains took them to the Belzec death camp.

The Optima building was also the site of a German crafts factory during the war. Many Jews were employed here as tailors, knitters, shoemakers, furmakers, and leather and suede artisans. Employment for a German concern was arguably the best way to avoid deportation from the Ghetto.

Fragments of the Ghetto Walls

There are two remaining fragments of the stone wall, shaped like Jewish tombstones, which surrounded the Cracow Ghetto.

1 Lwowska street 25–29

  The wall is located on the west side of Lwowska street, between Jozefinska and Sw. Kingi.

  Here, you are looking at the wall from outside the ghetto.

  A plaque installed in 1983 reads, "Here they lived, suffered and died at the hands of the Hitlerite murderers. From here they began their final path to the extermination camps. Fragment of the walls of the Jewish Ghetto 1941–1943."

  During the liquidation of the ghetto, the Jews were marched down Lwowska to the Plaszow concentration camp.

2 By the primary school, or City Folk School (Miejska Szkola Ludowa) at 62 Limanowskiego Street

  To the left and behind the school, another fragment of the wall exists. Again, the view is from outside the ghetto. The wall fragment made the southeastern edge of the ghetto enclosure.

  The hill here formed a natural border of the ghetto. During the war years, the hill was bare. In "Schindler's List," it was from this hill that Oskar Schindler witnessed the liquidation of the ghetto.

Oskar Schindler's Factory
4 Lipowa Street
Today the building is a factory for Telpod Electronics

Oskar Schindler's factory was by no means the only enterprise to save Jews during the Holocaust. But after Steven Spielberg's 1993 film, it is certainly the most famous. Although Schindler started his factory with the intention of profiteering off the war, he was ultimately roused to rescue as many Jews as he could from the Plaszow concentration camp.

Behind the factory there once stood dozens of barracks in which Schindler housed most of his workers after the liquidation of the Cracow Ghetto.

IV

*Budapest:
City of Synagogues*

Introduction

There are those who maintain that the vitality of a Jewish Community can be measured best by its synagogues. No matter how many Jewish clubs and organizations a city might boast, it is the synagogue that is both cradle of Jewish Community and bedrock of Jewish faith.

According to this view, Warsaw's is an ailing Community, with only one synagogue and relatively few worshippers. Cracow, by contrast, is the site of several synagogues, but almost all of them are in various states of disrepair—a symbol of the decimation of that Jewish Community. In the former Jewish Town of Prague, almost all the synagogues have been converted into a highly lucrative museum, symbolizing the enormous wealth and spiritual aridity of that Community.

And then there is Budapest the triparitite city of Buda, Obuda, and Pest. With twenty synagogues open to divergent types of services, Budapest demonstrates a strength unseen anywhere else in Central and Eastern Europe. Of course, this is due entirely to the statistics of Jewish Budapest, unequalled in the region: Roughly eighty thousand Jews live in the city. Although most of these Jews are highly assimilated, there are enough who are active in Jewish life to allow so many congregations to continue operating today. The strength is epitomized by the synagogues, but it is seen elsewhere as well, most notably in the one thousand students attending Jewish schools in the city. Budapest has emerged from a half century of communism with one of the strongest Jewish communities in Europe.

For the visitor, synagogues are by far the most fascinating aspect of Jewish life in Budapest. Of the cities discussed in this book, only Budapest possesses a Jewish history that is not best seen in its cemetery. The synagogue diversity in this city is astounding. There is a Gothic synagogue buried underground, a breathtaking neoclassical synagogue by the riverside, a synagogue that is Europe's largest, a synagogue built from a former casino. There is a synagogue modelled after Babylonia and there are synagogues modelled after Vienna. There are synagogues built during the balkanization of Hungarian Jewish life, and synagogues built as sanctuaries of unity. Several synagogues are built inside courtyards; others can be seen from several blocks away.

One of the most intriguing aspects of one's trip to Budapest is often a visit to one of the lesser-known active synagogues in the city. I recommend you read the final section, "The Living Synagogue," before you arrive. Visits to synagogues off the beaten track are often the most rewarding. Choose a synagogue that interests you most, and stop in for a service. In this city of dozens of synagogues, active involvement in Jewish worship can be one of the most memorable parts of one's trip to Europe.

A History of the Jews in Budapest

In the first half of the nineteenth century, an auction was held in Pest at which various artistic relics were offered. One of the most intriguing objects on the block was a large stone decorated with the bas relief of a woman, man, and small boy. It was scooped up by a wealthy bidder who thought the apparently Christian artifact would look divine in his family's chateaux. There it sat for decades, embedded in the wall of the chateaux chapel as if shielding the illustrious family from danger. The man was depicted in a Roman robe. The woman stood by his side, holding the boy in her arms. Between the two adult heads, faintly inscribed, was a seven-branched candelabra.

It was only at the end of the nineteenth century that the Jewish origins of the stone became known. It turns out that the object sitting idly in the wall of the chateaux was actually a Jewish gravestone. Not only did it feature three inscribed menorahs, but also Jewish names and a repetition of the declaration, "God is One." It was placed over the grave of a young Jewish boy in the fourth century in Pannonia, a province on the eastern fringe of the Roman Empire. The site was Aquincum, a Roman fortress located on the right bank of the Danube River in what is today modern Budapest.

Unlike Prague and Cracow, and certainly unlike Warsaw, Jewish life in what is now Budapest began eighteen hundred years ago. This makes the Jewish presence a full millennium older than that of the other cities featured in this book. Not only did the Jews live amongst the Magyars who built a kingdom and later a state; they actually predated the Hungarian tribes by as many as seven hundred years. Dozens of relics, such as the famous tombstone mentioned above, attest to Jewish life in Pannonia.

In the late second century, two thousand Syrian troops were sent to reinforce the vulnerable Roman garrisons on the Danube. Over the course of several decades, many more troops arrived from Syria. Among these soldiers were many Jews. Indeed, two-thirds of the Jewish inscriptions recovered from Roman Pannonia refer to soldiers. Many of these invited their relatives to join them in the relatively favorable conditions in Pannonia. Jews were free to practice their religion and had their own synagogues. However, most were extremely assimilated into both Roman and Syrian cultures. They often adopted Roman names, were influenced by Roman paganism, dressed like Syrians, and even went so far as to violate the Second Commandment on their tombstones. Meanwhile, there was an Orthodox contingent that, infuriated by the assimilation of their peers, took axes to many of the monuments that showed the influence of paganism. Even in the third century, the banks of the Danube hosted the age-old battle over what constitutes "True Judaism."

THE MAGYARS ARRIVE!

That Jews were present under Roman rule is a certainty. That they were present when the Hungarians arrived is also known. The only question is what happened in the four-hundred-year interim. It is not known for sure whether there was a Jewish presence in the area of present-day Budapest between the times that Roman rule fell in the early fifth century and the Magyar (Hungarian) tribes arrived in the year 895. Jews were definitely living in what is today Budapest, working as merchants and traders, when the Magyar tribes settled the area.

The seven Magyar tribes came in a massive immigration of as many as two hundred thousand people. Before they arrived in present-day Hungary, the Magyars had lived in Central Asia relatively near the famous Khazars, who had converted to Judaism in the eighth century. When the Magyars left the area, many Khazar Jews joined them on their trek westward. In southern Hungary, archaeologists discovered a Khazar ring engraved with Hebrew letters. These Khazars joined the pre-existing Jews of Hungary and formed communities in the main cities, including Buda.

Until the end of the eleventh century, Jewish life under the Magyars was relatively unrestricted. King Istvan I converted the Magyars to Christianity in the symbolic year 1000, but Jewish and Muslim merchants were not forced to convert. Jews could own landed property and were allowed freedom of movement and trade consistent with the other non-nobles in the Hungarian kingdom. But the year 1092 marked the beginning of Christian antagonism toward the Jews of Hungary. In that year, the Christian Council of Szabolcs convened and prohibited Jews from marrying Christian women or from keeping Christian slaves. In addition, Jews were forbidden from working Sundays, as the Council declared, "so that Christendom should not be offended by it."

In 1096, King Kalman fought and almost defeated the invading Crusaders. The Christians had succeeded in butchering entire Jewish communities in almost every other land they entered and rumors soon spread among decimated Jewish communities that in Hungary, Jews could live in peace. As a result, many Bohemian Jews migrated to the supposed promised land of equality. This had by no means been King Kalman's intention in fighting the Crusaders, and the king, so as to let the Jews know where they stood in his land, issued his Jewish Law around 1101. The law enforced the economic barriers of the Council of Szabolcs and pushed the Jews more and more into the single field open to them, that of moneylending.

In Buda as well as elsewhere in Europe, Jews mostly were involved in buying and selling goods and in financial transactions. Since they couldn't own or even hire slaves, agriculture simply wasn't an option. Among the several Buda Jews working in finance in the early thirteenth century, by far the most prominent was "Treasury Count Teha." Teha, an estate-owning Jew who was so wealthy he was able to guarantee extravagant loans to King Endre, was put in charge of the royal treasury. The mint itself was located in the Castle District near what was once the first Jewish Quarter of Buda. Coins minted by Count Teha were marked with his Hebrew initial, *tet*. Jews also became salt officials and tax collectors. Jealous nobles eventually persuaded King Endre II to strip the Jews of these privileges; in his Golden Bull of 1222, the king did just that. Not only Jews, but also Muslims living in the country were forbidden from such public offices. However, most of the royal edicts were ignored, for the simple reason that the king wanted the Jews (referred to, in typical royal parlance, as "his" Jews) as tax collectors and administrators. Even in the late thirteenth century, coins produced at the royal mint bore the Hebrew initials of the treasury count.

Meanwhile, in Rome, Pope Honorius III was not convinced that the Hungarians were doing everything in their power to deprive the Jews—and the Muslims—of their rights. It was so bad that the Pope actually excommunicated the king until he promised to live up to the venomous tenets of the Church. It was only in 1233 that the king finally escaped papal censure. He made a holy vow and promised to forbid the Jews from holding public office and to allow the bishops full autonomy over all Jews, Muslims, and pagans under their jurisdiction. Included in the vow were several other prohibitions against non-Christians, but perhaps the most glaring was the introduction of the colored badge to be worn by all Jews and Muslims "in order to be recognizable." Thus Hungary joined the rest of Europe in creating physical barriers between the so-called redeemed and the so-called infidels. The pope was pleased and King Endre II was permitted to rejoin the Church.

THE JEWISH ILLITERATE

Unfortunately, few halachic writings have come down to us from early medieval Hungary. What makes this bizarre is that rabbis and scholars in neighboring countries achieved fame in the Middle Ages for their commentaries on Jewish law. However, there were so few rabbis and teachers in Hungary that many communities couldn't even hold prayers; there simply wasn't anybody who knew the liturgy well enough to lead them. Raphael Patai refers to the Community at the time as "Jewishly ignorant . . . Jewishly illiterate" (Raphael Patai, *The Jews of Hungary: History, Culture, Psychology*). The Jews were desperate for men of knowledge, and on the occasions that they found a literate man, they instantly made him a combination rabbi, teacher, and cantor for the Community. The situation was so dire that in the early thirteenth century, the Jews of Buda did not know if it was permissible for women to use the local hot springs as *mikvehs*, or ritual baths. Luckily, in 1217, Rabbi Isaac ben Moses (c. 1180–1250) *(see page 6 [in Prague History])* happened to be passing through Buda. The Jews scrambled to the visitor and presented him with their halachic quandaries, and Rabbi Isaac reassured them that the hot springs were indeed kosher. Apparently, there was no local Jew of Buda who was qualified to answer the question.

The main reason for this is the general ignorance that prevailed in Hungary until the fifteenth century. It was only then, for instance, that the Bible was translated into Hungarian. The Jews, who were more integrated into Gentile society than Jews in neighboring countries, shared this general ignorance and thus produced almost no rabbis of note until the end of the Middle Ages.

THE KING'S FAVOR, THE CHURCH'S RANCOR

Jewish rights were finally promulgated by King Bela IV in 1251. This doesn't mean the king was a big contributor to the United Jewish Appeal. The entire kingdom had recently been devastated by invading Mongol hordes, who had slaughtered approximately half the population. The king was desperate to reconstruct his country and the surest way to do so was to attract immigrants from abroad. King Bela's Jewish laws were orchestrated to do just that: "A Jew, wherever he goes in our country, should not be hindered, molested, or pestered by anybody . . ." As a result of the king's open position, Jews once again poured into the country, establishing the original Jewish District around the castle of Buda. Indeed, King Bela's Jewish laws became the primary source of Jewish rights for almost three hundred years. At almost every coronation, the new king would confirm the rights of Bela's laws. Whenever Jewish rights were abrogated, the Jews invoked the laws; in the fifteenth century, in the face of increasingly anti-Semitic City Councils, Jewish communities throughout Hungary scrambled to obtain authenticated copies.

The laws protected not only the life, religion, and property of the Jews, but also their rights as tradesmen and moneylenders. As was the case elsewhere in Europe, the monarchy compelled the Jews to act as financial lenders and tax collectors—intermediaries between the royalty and the peasantry. King Bela's laws firmly established Jewish rights as royal servants—or, to put it more bluntly, as royal chattel. The Jews were not an independent class but an instrument of the castle. Of course, such a relationship offered the Jews a degree of protection from the Church that they otherwise wouldn't have received. As was the case in Prague, such relationships between emperors and Jews came into effect partly as a response to the anti-Semitic laws passed by the Catholic Church in 1215. The Royal Charter in Bohemia, in fact, was issued only three years after King Bela's laws in Hungary.

But as was the case when King Endre II gave privileges to the Jews, the pope in Rome became infuriated. How can God-murderers, reasoned the Church, be employed by the King of Hungary? Losing his patience, Pope Urban IV reprimanded King Bela in 1262 for "giving opportunities to Jews, whom their own sin has condemned to eternal servitude, to exercise official authority over Christians" (quoted in Raphael Patai, *The Jews of Hungary*). In 1279, the Church held a Council in Buda that forbade Jews from collecting taxes and repeated the Jewish badge laws of 1233. This time, the badge would be a red circle sewn onto the left breast of the outer garment. The king, incensed that the Church should exercise authority over his Jews, forced the visiting priests out of Buda. Once again, we see the pendulum swinging between royal protection offered by the king and Christian enmity directed from within the walls of the Vatican.

EXPULSION

In the early fourteenth century, Hungary was perhaps the safest place in Europe for Jews, who were subjected elsewhere to unremitting attacks and expulsions. Then came King Lajos I, known as Lajos the Great for the prosperity he brought the country. In 1359 he tried to convince the Jews and pagans in his kingdom to convert to Christianity. Using the carrot approach Martin Luther would later adopt in Germany, King Lajos cooed that if only they would convert, the Jews would receive full emancipation and exemption from taxes. When the stiff-necked Jews refused, the enraged king grabbed his stick: He expelled all the Jews from Hungary in 1360. The Jews left for nearby countries, particularly to Austria and Moravia.

Of course, without his moneylenders and traders, King Lajos's economy plummeted sufficiently for him to allow their return in 1364, regardless of their adherence to the Jewish faith. To entice them to return, King Lajos established the position of national Jew Judge, stationed in Buda, who would both administer tax collection from the Jews and protect them from attacks by the Church and by City Councils throughout Hungary. This position, similar to that of diplomat or ambassador, was assigned by the king to a Christian nobleman of top standing position. The national Jew Judge appointed local Jew Judges—again, Christians—who served in cities throughout Hungary, mostly to mediate disputes between Christians and Jews. The office of national Jew Judge continued until the middle of the fifteenth century.

THE LAW BOOK OF BUDA

Much of Hungarian anti-Semitism in the Middle Ages was not a homegrown phenomenon, but rather imported from the outside. Not surprisingly, the most influential country on Hungary's attacks on the Jews was Germany, a haven for Jew-hatred during medieval times. A nineteenth-century historian pointed out that each and every pogrom in Hungary during the Middle Ages occurred in cities whose majority population was German. It was the German import of guilds into the cities that not only excluded the Jews but also gave rise to laws against them that coincided with anti-Semitic legislation in Germany and Austria. The practice of "letter killing," in which the king, in a single decree, absolved an entire city of all the debts it owed to Jewish moneylenders, became prevalent throughout the fifteenth century in Hungary; the country that had favored "letter killing" the most was Germany. Finally, in 1421, the *Law Book of Buda* was completed. One of the most anti-Semitic pieces of legislation to emerge from medieval Hungary, the *Law Book of Buda* derived its inspiration from anti-Semitic laws already in effect in cities throughout Germany.

The book, parts of which are interchangeable with Nazi propaganda of five hundred years later, refers to the Jews as "evil and villainous"; one section begins, "The Jews, the despicable, hard-necked, stinking betrayers of God. . . ." In one respect, the book admitted that Jews were humans by prescribing capital punishment for the murder of a Jew—the same punishment as for the murder of a Christian. But in almost all other ways, the *Law Book of Buda* continued the centuries-old European insistence that Jews, both individually and collectively, were equivalent to insidious vermin. With such proclamations rampant in European society, it isn't difficult to see how the populace could so easily be incited to spill the blood of Jews.

The book was filled with taxes, fines, and restrictions geared against Buda's Jews. For example, the Jews were required to pay a special tax on kosher wine, which by its very nature was divorced from Christian society. Jews could trade only on Jewish Street, and were forced to dress in cone-shaped hats usually reserved for witches. In addition, Jews had to wear red capes and, on their chests, a large yellow patch identical to the one worn by Buda's prostitutes. Thus by his costume alone the Buda Jew was firmly established as both a sorcerer and a whore.

THE FIRST BLOOD LIBEL OF HUNGARY

In the first half of the fifteenth century, the Jews of Hungary fared better than Jews in neighboring countries, which caused an influx of refugees from Germany and Austria. There was even French spoken on the Jewish Street of Buda. After the expulsion from France in 1394, many Jews found Hungary to be a relative safe haven in the smoldering pot of Europe.

It is interesting that although King Sigismund behaved heartlessly toward the Jews in the other countries under his reign, he reaffirmed and extended Jewish rights in Hungary. Later in the century, King Matthias Corvinus—considered the greatest king of Hungary—continued the policy of favoring the Jews of Hungary above those in his other realms. However, he did impose harsh economic laws against Hungarian Jews and cancelled more debts owed to Jews than any prior Hungarian king. In his own words, it was "the legal duty of every good Christian to avoid contact with Jews as far as possible." On a good note, it was King Matthias who established the venerated position of Jewish prefect (*see below*), in which the affairs of Hungary's Jews were administered by a Jew.

At that time, the most famous rabbi in Buda was Rabbi Akiva ben Menahem HaKohen. Known as "head of the entire Diaspora," Rabbi Akiva was celebrated not only for his talmudic acumen, but for his great riches and influence in the royal court. Ultimately, though, jealous Hungarian magnates conspired against Rabbi Akiva and forced him to leave for Prague, where he established a *yeshivah*. Rabbi Akiva was also known for his progeny: He sired twelve sons and thirteen daughters. On his tombstone in the Old Jewish Cemetery in Prague, Rabbi Akiva is referred to as "the *Nasi* [duke] of Buda."

King Matthias's death brought trouble for the Jews, who, designated as royal chattel in royal documents, were always in a precarious position during the interim period between two kings. Jewish property was confiscated by the mob and outstanding debts were ignored. It was at this time that the first blood libel accusation erupted on Hungarian soil. In 1494, after a Christian child went missing in the Hungarian city of Nagyszombat, rumor spread that the child had been murdered in the local synagogue by Jews, who drank the child's blood as he lay dying. Under torture, the Jews "confessed," among other things: that Christian blood remedied the circumcision wound, that it worked as an aphrodisiac, and that it remedied the menstruation that both men and women in the Jewish faith suffered. The Jews were offered clemency if they converted, but all refused. A total of twelve men and two women were consequently burned at the stake in the marketplace.

THE JEWISH PREFECT OF BUDA: KING OF THE JEWS

> In 1477, King Matthias Corvinus created a royal position unprecedented in European history. This was the office of "Jewish prefect," an imperial intermediary between the king and all the Jews of Hungary. What was so remarkable about this position was not that Jewish affairs would be administered by the royal court—such a situation had already been the norm for centuries—but that the position would be filled by a Jew. This royal Jew had unlimited access to the king and the royal court

in Buda. He was exempt from wearing the humiliating badge and hat forced upon the Jews (except when he travelled to Bratislava, a city that actually snubbed the royal decrees and forced the prefect to dress in the fool's costume). In most cases, all laws of segregation and discrimination were suspended in the case of this single Jew, who was included in royal ceremonies and even had his own battalion of armed horsemen to accompany him on his journeys. Indeed, in the early sixteenth century the prefect brought in mercenaries to protect the Jewish quarter of Buda from mob attacks.

In all respects, the Jewish prefect was truly the "king of the Jews." All royal decrees that concerned the Jewish people were personally addressed to him. When conflicts arose, it was he who mediated between the Jews and the city authorities. Jewish criminals were brought to the prefect's own jailhouse, which was situated in Buda. Perhaps the most telling evidence of the prefect's omnipotence in Jewish affairs was his control over even the most sacred aspects of Jewish life: He was empowered to choose chief rabbis for any and all of the communities of Hungary.

By far the most important task of the Jewish prefect was tax collection. After the king decided how much tax money the Jews should pay the treasury, it was the Jewish prefect who divided the burden among all the Jewish communities of the kingdom. If, as was often the case, a Jewish Community refused to pay its allotted portion, the prefect would send his troops to the city, have the Jewish leaders arrested, and bring them back to the Jewish jailhouse he administered in Buda. This, of course, did not endear the prefect to his fellow Jews. By parading in the royal court while jailing his coreligionists, the prefect risked turning into the worst sort of Jewish Uncle Tom. Luckily, the prefect was also empowered to help the Jews. He made sure the king honored the Jewish laws passed centuries earlier by King Bela IV, persuaded the king to repeal excessively onerous decrees on the Jews, interceded on behalf of the Jews whenever they faced danger, and filled the coffers of dukes and palatines (read: bribed) in thanks for their continued protection of Jewish life and property. Whenever there was a grave problem facing any of Hungary's Jewish communities, the prefect was propelled into action. One example of many occurred in 1502, when the citizens of Bratislava repeatedly attacked the Jews. Buda's Jewish prefect had a word with the king, who immediately issued an order compelling the recalcitrant Bratislava authorities to prevent such pogroms. In other cases of persecution, threats, or outright exploitation and economic abuse, it was the Jewish prefect who cajoled the king into action.

The most famous of the Jewish prefects were the Mendels, whose homes still stand in the Castle District today [see page 412]. Sometime after the Mohacs Disaster of 1526, the office of Jewish prefect petered out.

AMONG THE TURKS: GLORY DAYS

One of the most tragic dates in all of Hungarian history is August 29, 1526, commonly known as the Mohacs Disaster. On that day, the Hungarian army was routed by the Turks in the city of Mohacs, paving the way for Turkish occupation of all of Central Hungary. The next month, Buda fell to the Turks. Practically all the Christians in Buda were slaughtered during the capture of the city. Many Jews fled, without any possessions, along with the royal court and some noblemen. The remaining Jews, well aware of their inability to fight the invading Turks, covered themselves in mourning shrouds and pressed their faces to the ground, begging the Turks for mercy. In one account, they even handed over the keys to the abandoned castle in a gesture of submission. The Turks therefore spared the lives of Buda's Jews, and, in order to control the population, eventually sent about two thousand of them to various cities in Turkey. Sundry battles rocked the Castle Hill until 1541, when the Turks consolidated their control over the city and made it their Hungarian capital.

In the 1530s, Jews returned to Buda from other parts of Turkish Hungary and in the 1540s, the Turks themselves brought in Jews from the Balkans to replace those who had been sent to Turkey. By the end of the century, Jews had arrived in Buda from Hapsburg-controlled Royal Hungary to the west and north as well as from various parts of the Ottoman Empire, including Istanbul and Tsfat. In the 1580s, there were eighty Jewish families—a total of five hundred Jewish inhabitants—living in Buda. The Jews established themselves at twenty percent of the civilian population of Buda—a percentage that, according to Raphael Patai, remained unaltered in Budapest until the Holocaust.

The Jews fared considerably better under the Muslims than under the Christians. As long as the flow of taxes was unchecked, the Turks granted religious freedom to all the peoples of their empire. In the letters of Turkish leaders it was not uncommon to find such statements as "We have one God, we are one man, even if we differ in faith." Jews as well as Christians enjoyed religious autonomy under the administrative system of the Turkish *millet*.

Under the Turkish occupation, Buda's Jewish outlook turned eastward. The Jews established closer contacts with their Sephardic brethren, many of whom settled in Buda from other parts of the Ottoman empire. It was at this time that the so-called Small Synagogue was established by Sephardic Jews on the Jewish Street *(see page 414)*. Closer contacts with Palestine enabled many Buda Jews to seek and find burial in the holy Galilean city of Tsfat. Buda's most famous rabbi of the era, Rabbi Ephraim ben Jacob Ha'Cohen, was even asked to lead the Ashkenazic Jews of Jerusalem, but he died before being able to take up the position. The *yeshivah* he established in Buda, however, was known throughout the Jewish world.

The diversity of Buda's Jewish life led to many Jews becoming active in trade between Christian Europe to the west and the Muslim empire to the east. Likewise, in the local economy native Jews became partners with Turkish Jewish immigrants. In 1542, a Hungarian Jew joined with an Istanbul Jew to rent the candle works and the money exchange, in both Buda and Pest, from the Turks. Other Jews rented Buda's bridge toll. In 1556, a Turkish Jew managed the revenue office of the city. It was a Jew who served as comptroller for the wine tax, and Jews managed all the royal taverns and exchange offices in Buda and Pest. Thus developed a wealthy class of Jewish merchants living in the Jewish district of Buda. Of course, Jews also worked in the established trade of tax collection, while others worked as artisans. A profitable trade among Jewish women of Buda was cloth weaving. By the early 1680s, the Jewish Community of Buda had grown to one thousand.

In contrast to the flourishing Jewish life in Buda, Jews outside Turkish control—in the northern and western parts of the country—were subjected to the usual trials and persecution. They were expelled from Sopron and Bratislava, the two most important cities in western Hungary. A wave of blood libel accusations led to thirty Jews being burned at the stake in Bazin and the expulsion of the entire Jewish Community of Nagyszombat. Throughout the sixteenth and seventeenth centuries, Hungarian kings passed edicts that narrowed the scope of Jewish life and livelihood. There was no doubt that life under the Turkish Muslims was much safer than under the Hungarian or Austrian Christians.

It was no wonder, then, that the Jews of Buda longed to extend Turkish rule, and even assisted the Turks in the defense of the city during the repeated Austrian sieges (*see pages 415–416*). But eventually, in 1686, the Buda fortress was overrun. In the ensuing bloodbath, seventy-two Jews were murdered in the Great Synagogue (*see pages 417*), and many more were killed in their homes. A total of around five hundred Jews, or half the Jewish population of Buda, were killed by the rampaging soldiers. Hundreds of Jews were ransomed and freed, and hundreds of others had escaped before the siege to such cities as Constantinople and Belgrade. But in Buda itself, none remained after 1686. The Austrian capture of Buda marked the end of centuries of Jewish life in the city.

THE OBUDA CENTURY

The Hapsburg conquest of Hungary put a swift end to the century and a half of Jewish prosperity under the Turks. Jews returned to Buda only with great hesitation in the early eighteenth century and were never again to amass the same communal strength they had possessed in the seventeenth century. Throughout Hungary cities, propelled by economic pressure from the burghers and anti-Semitic propaganda from the Counter-Reformation, closed themselves off as much as possible to Jewish settlement. On the other hand, the royal authorities needed Jewish assistance to refill the coffers depleted by the war. It was between these two forces—the hostility shown by the cities and the cynical toleration shown by the central government—that Hungarian Jews found themselves at the turn of the eighteenth century.

But there was also a third competing interest that tipped the balance: that of the great magnates. These masters of huge estates found it expedient to open their gates to the Jews, who provided tax revenue, rents, and services. This was especially true in the early eighteenth century, when Hungary was reeling from a population drought following two costly wars. Allowing Jewish settlement was a quick and dependable way of generating income in this transitional period. The magnates coveted Jewish settlement so much that they were often at loggerheads with the imperial treasury over who would receive Jewish tax revenue. The most influential of these great magnates was the Count Zichy family, who were the lords of the domain of Obuda.

From the second decade of the eighteenth century, the benevolence of the Zichys toward the Jews—in return for a "protection tax"—led to a rapid increase in the Jewish Community in Obuda. In 1727, twenty-two Jewish families lived in Obuda; by 1785, the number had risen to 285 families. By this time, the Obuda Jewish Community had become the largest in the country. In order to increase Jewish settlement, the Zichy family permitted the Jews a degree of communal autonomy unmatched in Hungary. Not only were they given freedom of religion, but they could also buy and sell property and even plan out streets. In addition, the Jewish Community was given authority to judge in disputes not only among Jews, but also between Jews and Christians. The "protection tax" ranged from 1,350 to 1,800 florins annually, plus a two hundred-florin birthday and holiday gift given to the count.

It was a lucky coincidence for the Jews that at the moment Buda fell into oblivion as a Jewish city, the neighboring estate of Obuda sprouted into a stronghold of Jewish life. This clockwise turn of Jewish settlement would continue in the nineteenth century as Pest would take the title of the most thriving Jewish Community in the country. In fact, one reason the Jewish Community of Obuda grew to such prosperous proportions in the eighteenth century was that Jews were not permitted into Pest, except as temporary residents, until the end of the century. Many Jews waited in Obuda while their applications for temporary residence in Pest were processed. Indeed, as Pest began to grow into the economic center of the country, Obuda's Jews gazed longingly at the Promised Land across the Danube; once they were permitted into Pest, the Obuda Jewish Community fell into a slow but steady decline.

Aside from these shifts of Buda-Obuda-Pest Jewish fortune, Hungary experienced a Jewish population explosion throughout the eighteenth century. One reason for this was the Familiants Laws issued by Emperor Charles VI in 1726 and 1727. These laws capped the numbers of Jews permitted to reside in Bohemia and Moravia, forbidding all but the eldest sons in Jewish households to marry. As a direct result of these laws, over thirty thousand Moravian Jews emigrated to Hungary in the eighteenth century. Although most of these Jews settled in and around today's Slovakia (then a part of Hungary), some undoubtedly heard of favorable conditions in Obuda and settled there. According to a 1735 census, sixty-five percent of the Jews of Hungary were newly settled immigrants. In the second half of the eighteenth century, many Polish Jews immigrated to Hungary as well. All told, Hungary's Jewish population had grown eightfold by the end of the century. In 1787, there were eighty-three thousand Jews in Hungary.

Meanwhile, Austrian Empress and Hungarian Queen Maria Theresa, the Hapsburg monarch whose hatred of Jews exceeded the normal limits of royal scorn, established a toleration tax for the Jews of Hungary in 1746, only one year after she had ordered the expulsion of the Jews from Prague and Bohemia. The Hungarian Jewish Community was collectively responsible for paying two florins annually for every Jewish man, woman, and child living in the country. The Jews saw the bribe for what it was, and wryly dubbed it *malke gelt*, or "queen money." Nonetheless, Maria Theresa behaved more favorably toward the Jews in Hungary than to those elsewhere, which goes some way toward explaining the population explosion of Hungarian Jewry in the eighteenth century. In 1762, for instance, the empress—herself a devout Catholic—prohibited the Catholic clergy from forcing Jewish children to be baptized.

JOSEF II

A twinkling of Jewish emancipation began to show at the end of the eighteenth century. When Josef II ascended to the Hapsburg throne in 1780, he was determined to thrust his empire into the modern world. To Josef II, "modernity" meant a fully centralized state authority, an industrial economy, and an end to irrationality in human, economic, and political discourse. There was no way to modernize the empire without drastically changing the position of the Jews. First of all, Jewish communal autonomy was antithetical to a centralized state authority. Secondly, the severe restrictions against Jews in commerce seriously afflicted the economy of the state. Finally, the ubiquitous superstition and base hatred of the Jews was a vestige of medieval irrationality that Josef II wished to sever. This, in a nutshell, was what motivated the emperor to issue his Edicts of Tolerance to the Jews of Austria, Bohemia, and Moravia in 1781 and 1782 (*see page 116*). Of course, there was latent anti-Semitism in the bargain. Writing to the Hungarian Royal Chancellory, Josef II bared his personal bias when he claimed that Jews should be allowed into the economy "so that, at long last, by increased and broadened sources of income, they should be diverted from the usury and cheating commerce characteristic of them" (quoted in Raphael Patai, *The Jews of Hungary*).

In 1783, a year after Moravian Jewry received their Edict of Tolerance, Josef II issued his Systematic Regulation of the Jewish Nation to the Jews of Hungary. Like the Edict of Tolerance, the Regulation did not grant the Jews citizenship. Its priority, instead, was the secular education and integration of the Jews. In order to break the linguistic, cultural, and educational barriers that separated Jews from Christians, Hebrew and Yiddish were no longer permitted in legal documents and contracts. Jewish communities were to establish elementary and high schools or to send their children to Christian schools. There they would be taught German, Hungarian, or Slavic, as well as the normal range of secular subjects. The use of private Jewish tutors, which had been a popular method of teaching the young, was abolished. It was decreed that after several years, any Jew who could not provide evidence of matriculation from such a school would be prohibited from working in crafts, keeping taverns, or working in a profit-making commerce. After 1786, marriage certificates were withheld if the bride and groom had not completed secular elementary schools.

The first such school in Hungary was opened in 1784 in Obuda. It was enmeshed in controversy from the start: the rabbis of Obuda, fearing the school would lead the Jews away from the religion, tried to stop the construction. When the school was opened, an announcement was read in Obuda's synagogues that anybody who interfered with the school while it was in session would be punished with flogging. In spite of this controversy, the school eventually became so large that Emperor Josef II himself expanded it into the adjoining house.

In the economic realm, Jews were permitted to rent land but not to employ Christians to work the land. They were permitted to engage in crafts, but only if the nobility or guilds did not protest. The Regulation both liberated and narrowed the social life of the Jews. They were freed from distinguishing marks, but they were also required to shave their beards (after a great uproar among Hungary's Jews, Josef II repealed this decree). In 1787, a further decree was passed forcing Jews to adopt German surnames.

In the area today known as Budapest, by far the most consequential aspect of the Regulation was the ruling that all free royal cities should be open to the Jews. Buda reopened itself to Jews in 1783. By this time, though, the focus had already shifted across the river to Pest, which was rapidly becoming the country's main center of trade and commerce. After 1783, the City Council of Pest could no longer exclude Jews from settlement, leading directly to a population drain of Jews from Obuda to Pest at the end of the eighteenth century. Within a century, Pest would be the largest and most prosperous Jewish Community in the country.

As was discussed in the Prague history section, the reforms carried out by Josef II were not an unqualified embrace of the Jews. In fact, the Regulation arose as much from the idea that the Jewish religion was a diseased handicap that had to be shorn if the Jews were to be made useful members of society as from a spirit of general emancipation. This is one reason for the ongoing debate concerning Josef II's Regulation. On the one hand, the status quo of inequality and persecution had to be altered. Nobody would argue that the Jews didn't welcome greater economic rights. On the other hand, the education and language requirements were one of the prime factors in dissolving the communal structure of Jewish life in Hungary. Once they were legally required to assimilate, many Jews began to view their religion through the lens of the state: traditional Judaism was a harness that retarded their entrance into mainstream society. The solution, for many, was either to revise the religion or to repudiate it entirely.

THE NEOLOG MOVEMENT

Emancipation did not end with Josef II. If anything, the emperor's reforms ushered in an age of fierce public debate on the "Jewish question" throughout the first half of the nineteenth century. Josef II himself repealed most of his decrees soon before his death in 1790. At the end of 1790, it took a resolution from the Diet and from Emperor Leopold II to ensure that Jewish rights were not trampled upon. In the 1820s Pest merchants, disgruntled at the new level of economic competition, ushered in a campaign to disenfranchise the Jews. Luckily, it never gained enough strength to be a strong political force.

Meanwhile, the Hungarian Diet heard from various corners arguments for and against the further emancipation of the Jews. The delegation from the County Pest took a courageous stand, considering the obduracy of the Pest merchant bloc, and argued that "the Jews are not a separate nation, and therefore should be awarded the rights due to the Hungarian citizens" (quoted in Raphael Patai, *The Jews of Hungary*). Finally, in 1840, a compromise bill was passed extending Jewish rights without granting complete emancipation. Among other things, Jewish rights in the cities were confirmed and Jews could purchase property and establish factories.

The concept that "the Jews are not a separate nation" was put to the test toward the middle of the nineteenth century. Many members of the Diet responded to Jewish calls for emancipation by demanding reform in the Jewish religion. If the Jews wish to be like us, the parliamentarians reasoned, let them prove it. In its most basic form, the idea reasoned that the Hungarian government should not waste its time emancipating the Jews if the Jewish religion itself continued to segregate Jew from Gentile. If Jews eat separately, drink separately, marry separately, and raise their children separately, how can they demand to be considered Hungarians? Of course, these views presumed that in Hungarian society, equality and pluralism were mutually incompatible concepts. It was the perennial European Jewish problem, which peaked throughout the continent in the nineteenth century: If the Jews wished to be French, Germans, or Hungarians, they would have to cease being Jews.

The most extreme reform, of course, meant conversion. In response to the arguments of the Diet in the 1840s, there emerged, in the historian Raphael Patai's words, "a veritable epidemic of apostasy." At the same time, though, religious reform began to sprout in Hungary. The first pioneer of Reform in Hungary was also the first Orthodox rabbi anywhere to become inspired by Reform innovation. He was Rabbi Aaron Chorin (1766–1844) of Arad. One of Rabbi Chorin's most famous innovations was the substitution of a psalm for the *Kol Nidre* ("All Vows") prayer on Yom Kippur. Although he wasn't the most radical reformer of the time, Rabbi Chorin allowed vernacular prayer and sermons, permitted travel on Shabbat, and permitted the use of organs on Shabbat. As early as 1803, Rabbi Chorin was thrust into open confrontation with his more traditional friend and colleague, Rabbi Moses Muenz (c. 1750–1831) of Obuda. Nonetheless, as Jews in the area of today's Budapest became increasingly prosperous, the Reform movement gained respectability.

The most radical Reformnik in Budapest was a man by the name of Ignaz Einhorn (1825–1875). Einhorn operated first in Buda, and then in Pest, in 1848 forming the Israelite Reform Society of Pest, which seceded from the mainstream Israelite Congregation of Pest. In a prayer hall in Pest, Einhorn spearheaded some of the most zealous Reform innovations of the day, including the movement of Shabbat to Sunday and the abolishment of circumcision. Many wealthy Jews joined this novel congregation, and during its four years of activity the Reform Society registered over seventy births. The Israelite Congregation of Pest was alarmed by Einhorn's growing popularity, and gave voice to its concern in announcements, leaflets, and even open condemnation at a state-sponsored Jewish conference in Buda in 1851. Interestingly, the Israelite Congregation of Pest warned that the Reform movement was a subversive sect not unlike Hasidism (*see page 353—Cracow Tempel*). As a result, the government outlawed the Reform Society in 1852, only four years after it had entered the Budapest Jewish scene. The Reform Society's second rabbi, David Einhorn (1809–1879; no relation), left for America and became one of the leading architects of American Jewish Reform.

In contrast to the recalcitrance of the Reform Society, a moderate Reform congregation arose and was accepted by the official Israelite Congregation of Pest in 1830. This was the Cultus Tempel, modeled after a similar congregation in Vienna. Although it differed from Orthodox tradition, the Cultus Tempel took pains not to provoke its coreligionists. It was the Cultus Tempel that provided the core congregants of the Dohany Street Synagogue.

After the Hungarian Jewish Congress of 1868–69 (*see page 434*), Jewish Reform in Hungary became increasingly known as the Neolog movement. The word "neolog" comes from the Greek *neos logos*, or "new faith," and refers to any sort of innovation. Originally, the Hungarian term referred to progressive movements of any stripe. During the nineteenth-century era of nationalism, Hungary was filled with neologists. For instance, nineteenth-century philologists who modernized the Hungarian language by removing German and Latin terms were called neologists. In a sense, the Jewish Neolog movement was the same: it involved innovation in a specific discipline, motivated largely by the cause of Hungarian patriotism.

EMANCIPATION

In the Hungarian Revolution of 1848–49, the Hungarian statesman Lajos Kossuth claimed that twenty thousand Jews fought in the revolutionary army. It was partly in appreciation for Jewish valor that the Hungarian Diet issued a law that at long last made the Jews equal citizens to Hungarians. But after the Revolution collapsed, the bill was a moot point; Austria ruled with an iron fist for two decades, destroying the Diet and imposing particularly large taxes on the Jews.

Only in 1867, after the creation of the Dual Monarchy of Austria-Hungary, was the Diet able to issue a new law of emancipation. The Jews were proclaimed equal to the Christian citizens of Hungary and all laws that ran contrary to this proclamation were declared invalid. With nearly all anti-Semitic laws revoked from the books, the Jews of Budapest were able to continue their meteoric rise in the economic, cultural, and scientific life of the capital.

Unfortunately, the wellspring of emancipation also unleashed another current, the backlash of anti-Semitism—both religious and nationalistic—which attempted to thrust the Jews back into a disenfranchised position. In 1875, a parliamentarian in the Diet made the first "officially" anti-Semitic speech in any parliament of Europe. In 1882, a blood libel erupted in the northeastern Hungarian village of Tisza Eszlar. With the disappearance of a fourteen-year-old girl close to the holiday of Passover, the villagers accused the Jews of killing her for ritualistic purposes. The ensuing show trial, which had much in common with similar medieval affairs, grabbed the nation's attention. Although the accused were ultimately acquitted, pogroms were launched throughout the country.

After a thaw in anti-Semitic agitation in the early 1890s, the Law of Reception was passed in 1895. This law finally recognized Judaism as a sanctioned religion in Hungary. From 1895–1920, there was no law that discriminated against the Jewish people or religion.

After emancipation in 1867, Jews had become active in Hungarian culture, economy, and society. This trend increased prodigiously after the Law of Reception. Jews were highly successful in industry, and the most successful Jewish industrialists were made noblemen. In 1920, about forty percent of the factories in Hungary were owned by Jews. Jews also became highly prominent in literature, the arts, and the professions. In 1900, close to half the physicians in Hungary were Jewish, and in 1920 half the state's lawyers were Jewish. As if in thanks for the opportunities afforded them, Hungarian Jews became increasingly assimilated. By the beginning of the twentieth century, the proportion of native Hungarian speakers among Jews was over seventy percent, whereas among Catholics it was only around fifty-five percent.

From 1900–1910, the Jewish population of Pest grew from 168,985 to 203,687. After a peak population of 215,512 in 1915, the number of Jews in Pest began to decline, partly as a result of conversions and mixed marriages.

WORLD WAR I AND THE WHITE TERROR

The next great opportunity for Jews to demonstrate their loyalty to the Hungarian state came with the outbreak of World War I. All told, some ten thousand Jews died fighting for Hungary by the time the war ended.

The postwar Trianon Treaty devastated Hungary. The country lost seventy-one percent of its territory and sixty percent of its population in the newly redrawn map of Europe. This had a seismic effect on Hungary's Jewish population. Of the 911,000 Hungarian Jews before the war, 438,000 were truncated from the historic lands and fell under foreign rule. As a result of the redrawn borders, Budapest skyrocketed as the Jewish center of Hungary. A full 215,000 Jews now lived in Budapest. In 1920, they constituted 23.2 percent of the total population of Budapest.

In 1919, Hungary fell to a communist "Council Republic." Jews, it happened, were among the leading communists as well as the leading "enemies" of the communist system. Bela Kun, the commissar for foreign affairs and the figurehead of the Communists, was a converted Jew, as were several other members of the government. Meanwhile, prominent Jewish capitalists suffered the brunt of the Communist measures. It seemed that the converted Jews in the government sought to prove their distance from Judaism by persecuting the Jews themselves.

The overwhelming Jewish presence, albeit as converts, in the revolutionary government led to a backlash called the "White Terror" that followed the fall of the Communists. Thousands of people were executed, jailed, or forced into exile because of some connection with the Communist regime; many of these victims were Jewish.

The backlash against Jews culminated in the infamous Numerus Clausus law of 1920, the first anti-Semitic law issued in Hungary since the eighteenth century. According to that law, Jews would be able to constitute only five percent of the student body at all Hungarian universities. It is because of laws such as this that American Jews tend to be wary of university quotas in America today. The law not only limited Jewish enrollment in universities, but also led to riots against those Jewish students who did get in. The Numerus Clausus remained in effect, in one form or another, until the war, causing thousands of Hungarian Jews to emigrate. Before the war, there were around two hundred thousand Jews in the capital.

THE HOLOCAUST

Increasing anti-Semitism in Hungary, coupled with a clamor to keep up with Germany's anti-Semitic laws and a fear of a massive influx of Jewish refugees from areas under German occupation, led to the passage of the First and Second Jewish Laws in 1938–39. The First Jewish Law limited Jewish employment in the arts, professions, and commerce to twenty percent. Unlike the Numerus Clausus of 1920, the First Jewish Law mentioned the Jews by name. In 1939, the Second Jewish Law defined the Jews in racial terms and effectively disenfranchised them from all aspects of Hungarian society. Jews were barred or severely limited from most professions and subjected to a series of politically emasculating regulations.

After Hungary entered the war in September 1941, Jews from all over the country were sent to labor battalions on the front. The enforced labor was designed to kill them: They were forced to dig trenches in inhumane conditions and to act as human mine sweeps, being thrust across entire expanses of land on the Russian front. A total of 15,350 Budapest Jews died in these labor battalions or through other deportations.

But it was after the Germans invaded Hungary on March 19, 1944, that the killing of Hungary's Jews turned into systematized genocide. Adolf Eichmann himself coordinated the liquidation of entire regions. Budapest was saved for the end, after the provinces had been completely liquidated, and it is for this reason that half of Budapest's Jews survived the war.

With the arrival of refugees, Budapest's Jewish population climbed to 250,000–280,000 by the summer of 1944. On April 3, 1944, a decree was passed forcing the Jews to wear a yellow Star of David. The first movement of Jews into specified areas occurred in May 1944, when the government designated certain buildings as "yellow star houses," to be marked by a large Star of David above the doorway. By June, there were nineteen hundred such houses spread throughout the capital; by August, 170,000 Jews filled the houses up. In addition, 110,000 Jews lived in hiding in "Aryan" buildings. Thousands of Jews were saved with protection papers disbursed by such daring statesmen as Raoul Wallenberg of Sweden, Charles Lutz of Switzerland, and the Italian businessman Giorgio Perlasca.

In late August, Eichmann had to leave Hungary because of an anti-fascist insurrection in Slovakia. This gave the Jews a brief window of hope, but it was quelled six weeks later. The Arrow Cross Party of Hungarian fascists seized power on October 15 and immediately unleashed a wave of pogroms in the city. On October 15–16, hundreds of Jews were murdered; many were shot right into the Danube river. When Eichmann returned on October 17, the "yellow star houses" were locked tight for ten full days, trapping their inhabitants inside. The Dohany Street Synagogue and the Rumbach Synagogue were turned into prisons for six thousand Jews awaiting deportation. In late October, seventy-five thousand Jewish men and ten thousand Jewish women were taken to build trenches. As the Soviet army made advances west, most of these Jews were forced on a death-march toward the Hegyeshalom borderpoint with Austria. Those who could not withstand the terrible conditions of the march were shot or left to die. Raoul Wallenberg succeeded in saving five hundred of these Jews.

The ghetto of Budapest was formed in late November in the area east of and including the Dohany Street Synagogue. It soon reached a population of seventy thousand. Disease became widespread, food was in short supply, and members of the Arrow Cross made frequent raids, killing and pillaging the Jews. Even while Russian troops besieged the city, the Arrow Cross conspired with the Germans to liquidate the ghetto. Ten to fifteen thousand Jews were shot in the ghetto; some were brought to the Danube, where they were shot. Raoul Wallenberg managed to save thirty-three thousand Jews in an "international ghetto" protected by neutral countries. By the end of the war, there were 119,000 Jews alive in Budapest.

POSTWAR TO TODAY

After the war, Hungary's Jews were far less inclined to emigrate than were Jews from neighboring countries. Of the nearly 200,000 Hungarian Jews who survived the war, only five to six thousand left the entire country between 1945–46. By 1957, a total of 56,000 Jews, or roughly one-quarter of the Jewish population, had emigrated. This percentage was far lower than Jewish emigration rates in Czechoslovakia, Poland, Romania, and Bulgaria. It is important to keep in mind that even before the war, Zionism and other Jewish national movements were not as popular in Hungary as they were elsewhere in the region. When the war ended, emigration to Palestine or elsewhere was not as much a foregone conclusion in Hungary as it was elsewhere.

The majority that decided to remain embarked on a vastly accelerated process of assimilation. This trend was exacerbated by the new Jewish demographics after the war. During the war, the Jewish population in the countryside was almost completely exterminated, whereas the Jews of Budapest were spared total extinction because the Nazis began deportations there at a late stage in the war. Jews in the countryside tended to be mostly Orthodox, while Jews in Budapest were mostly assimilated. Because the Nazi genocide was concentrated outside Budapest, the Holocaust in Hungary practically eliminated Jewish Orthodoxy, leaving a Jewish remnant that was proportionately far more assimilated than the prewar Community. This was a major reason why there would be so little involvement in Jewish communal affairs in the decades after the war. Especially after living through the horrors of the Holocaust, the Jews of Budapest—where most of Hungary's Jewish Community was concentrated—were eager to shed all vestiges of Jewish identification.

One outlet of the assimilationist urge was the Communist Party, which promised an end to all forms of discrimination in an idealized socialist society. There were several reasons why the Jews turned to communism in disproportionate numbers after the war. Unlike the Gentile population, which viewed the Russian victory as the latest in a series of humiliating defeats at the hands of the Russians, the Jews rightfully saw the Russians as their liberators from total extermination. This was nowhere more profoundly felt than in Budapest, where half the Jewish population of the city was still alive when the Russians entered in January and February, 1945. Many Jews became lost in daydreams of communism, which vowed to erase the political, economic, and social stratification of Hungary. To many, the idea of a classless society seemed like the most feasible alternative to historical anti-Semitism in Hungary, the most recent expression of which was Hungarian apathy or complicity in the genocide of the Jews.

Most Jews did not become communists, but some of the most visible leaders of the Communist Party were indeed Jews. Of these, the most notorious was the Stalinist Matyas Rakosi (1892–1971), a Jew who became prime minister after the communists consolidated their power in 1947–48. Rakosi had long been active in the Communist Party, having served in the 1919 "Council Republic" and later sent to prison for clandestine communist agitation. Rakosi led a team of Jews and Jewish converts to Christianity in a brutal campaign against the Hungarian bourgeoisie that lasted until 1953. The Jewish roots of the ruling elite did little to protect Hungary's Jews; if anything, the leaders sought to prove their loyalty to Hungary and communism by lashing out at the Jews whenever possible. It is a sad fact of Jewish history that postwar anti-Semitism in Hungary was, to some degree, orchestrated and perpetuated by government ministers who were Jews themselves. Among the thousands of Hungarian citizens jailed and tortured during those years were many Jews who were branded as Western spies, Zionists, capitalists, and conspirators against the Hungarian state. The Jewish Community itself was crippled when Jewish schools became part of the state education system. From 1948–1958, practically no books were issued in

Hungary concerning Jewish history and the Holocaust. Israel was isolated from the Hungarian state, as it was from most communist countries, and little contact existed between Hungarian Jews and Jews in Western Europe and America.

The Soviets curtailed Rakosi's power in 1953 and again in 1956 as part of the political liberalization that followed Stalin's death in 1953. Populist dissatisfaction with the government culminated in the Hungarian Uprising of 1956, which was crushed by Russian tanks in a national catastrophe that took as many as 3,000 Hungarian lives. During and after the Uprising, 200,000 Hungarians fled the country. Among these were 20,000 Jews, or approximately one-fifth the Jewish population in Hungary. There were several reasons to leave. On the one hand, a repressive, Soviet-inspired dictatorship in Hungary could only spell trouble for the Jews. On the other hand, right-wing elements in the Uprising were ominously reminiscent of the right-wingers who launched the "White Terror" after the collapse of the communist "Council Republic" of 1919.

Although Hungary experienced a gradual political and economic thaw in the 1960s and 70s, Jews were undeterred in their campaign of assimilation. When considering postwar Jewish communities throughout Central Eastern Europe, one should keep in mind that after the Holocaust, survivors who remained in their nations of birth were generally much different than those who left. Jews who chose to rebuild their lives in countries that had, only months earlier, singled the Jews out for mass extermination were often convinced on some level that Judaism was a curse or a dangerous mark that must be kept hidden. The best way to hide this mark was to assimilate: To intermarry, to change one's name, to obliterate all differences between oneself and one's Gentile neighbors. Thus, in each of the cities discussed in this book, survivors of the Holocaust did not share many of the general traits noted among survivors in, for instance, Israel and America. In cities like Prague and Budapest, where Jews were already vastly assimilated before the war, the postwar Jewish population was more anxious than ever to expunge its roots and to meld into Gentile society.

There were various degrees of "melding." Although the western media tends to exaggerate the numbers of Eastern European Jews who learned of their Jewish identity only in their twenties and thirties, such cases did indeed exist. It was not uncommon for children to learn they were Jewish in the schoolyard, when classmates shouted anti-Semitic slurs at them. Sometimes parents actively hid their Jewishness from their children in order to spare them from suffering. Others downplayed Judaism not out of a fear for their children's security but simply out of apathy; Judaism was not considered a vital part of one's identity. Milder forms of melding were more common, and incorporated varying distinctions between one's public and private personas. For example, a family might be open about its Jewishness at home, but among neighbors, friends, and strangers, the fact would be concealed. Even among Jews who knew of their identity since earliest childhood and who made no attempt to hide the fact, there was rarely any interest in expressing a Jewish identity or affiliating openly with the Jewish institutions that continued to exist. Such behavior was passed from parents to children during the two postwar generations even when there was little anti-Semitism to contend with in the outside world.

After the political changes of 1989, Budapest's Jews found themselves in a vibrant position unequalled anywhere in the region. This position centered entirely on its population statistics. Although estimates vary, it has been said that there were roughly 100,000 Jews living in Hungary in the 1990s, with over 80 percent living in Budapest. This number is misleading, though. Jewish communal organizations boast only around 8,000 members, most of whom are elderly. The vast majority of Jews are highly assimilated. However, even if little over 500 Jews in Budapest regularly attend synagogue, this figure is exponentially larger that of Prague, Warsaw, and Cracow, whose synagogues attract no more than two dozen Jews in each city. Budapest has a higher Jewish population than any other city in Central Eastern Europe.

The contemporary situation in Budapest has indeed changed for the Jews. It is interesting that much of this change is not an independent Jewish response to the climate of freedom but rather a reaction to the anti-Semitism that emerged in the wake of the transition to a capitalist democracy. As Gabor Szanto, editor of the Jewish magazine *Szombat* (Sabbath), told me in 1997, "Anti-Semites do more for the resurgence of Jewish identity than do the leaders of the Jewish Community." What he meant was that Jews have become more aware of their identity less through a proactive initiative on the part of Jewish institutions themselves, and more through an increase in Hungarian anti-Semitism, which has made it almost impossible for Jews to forget their roots. Populist anti-Semitism returned to the Hungarian political and social scene after the fall of communism in 1989, with a rise in skinhead activity, the publication of anti-Semitic books and periodicals, and right-wing involvement in the majority party in the government. The level of anti-Semitism in Hungarian society was by no means great, but what made it unique was that it was visible and open after the fall of communism. And although the government officially condemned anti-Semitism and upheld equal rights for Jews in Hungary, it did little to combat the increase in specific anti-Semitic acts. Anti-Semitism became less pronounced by the mid 1990s—skinhead rallies, for instance, failed to draw the same crowds they had drawn immediately after the fall of communism.

But the renewed openness in Hungarian political discourse concerning a "Jewish question," combined with a rather obsessive fixation on the topic in the Hungarian media, have made the Jews of Budapest much less secure in the mantra of assimilation. Whereas before the political changes, Jews could tactfully avoid the issue of their identity, the new environment has poked many Jews into asking themselves who they are. The process of melding into the outside world is no longer painless. As Gabor Szanto told me, "Before 1989, most Jews here considered themselves Hungarian, internationalist, left wing, and the like; they weren't particularly interested in their Jewish roots. But after 1989, when anti-Semites said, 'You are Jewish, you cannot say you are Hungarians,' they were forced to look at themselves in the mirror." Many Jews were caught in limbo: they suddenly learned that they were not one hundred percent Hungarians. But after generations of assimilation, they hardly felt Jewish either. What were they?

In a move to answer this question, many Jews began to develop a heightened awareness of their ethnic identity. In the 1990s, Jews have expressed this rediscovered identity in various ways. This can be seen most noticeably in the enrollment in Budapest's three Jewish high schools. The relatively small Anne Frank High School, which operated throughout the communist era, was complemented in 1990 by two larger schools supported by western organizations. The Lauder Javne Jewish Community School and Kindergarten, started and funded by the Ronald S. Lauder Foundation in New York, has garnered respect as a superb private school that prepares its students for university while introducing them to general Jewish studies. In 1997 the Lauder Foundation opened a luxurious, modern campus for the Javne School, complete with state of the art facilities that rival top western institutions. A more religiously oriented school is the American Foundation School, also founded in 1990. The American Foundation School, supported by the Canadian Jewish Reichmann Foundation, includes an elementary school, high school, and business school. All told, over 1,000 students were enrolled in the three Jewish schools in the late 1990s. This number is truly remarkable, and represents the greatest hope for a revival of a deep sense of Judaism among the Jews of Budapest. In the future, the growth or decline of the Jewish Community of Budapest will depend largely on these 1,000 young Jews.

Other signs of a renewed interest in Jewish ethnicity are the several books and periodicals that have recently appeared on Jewish themes, the opening of a cultural center, the Balint Jewish Community Center, in 1995, and the continued popularity of the children's summer camp located in Szarvas, Hungary. True, there are serious problems. The intermarriage rate, for instance, is said to hover around fifty percent. There is a critical dearth of qualified Jewish teachers in the city. But still, other statistics are a source of pride: over twenty synagogues are currently in use in Budapest.

But even outside the schools and the synagogues, Budapest is an anomaly in Central Eastern Europe. When Jewish travellers visit the region, one of the first things they notice upon entering Budapest is the plethora of Jews in the city. In Prague, Warsaw, and Cracow, a happenstance encounter with a Jew can be jolting, like the sighting of an endangered species. Only in Budapest are encounters with Jews—on trams, in cafes, in movie theaters—both expected and natural. Melding, it would seem, did not work as effectively as many Jews had hoped. During the communist era and today as well, Budapest's Jews have disproportionately chosen professions that are Jewish favorites throughout the world. Jews are highly prominent in contemporary Hungarian literature, theater, film, journalism, and academia. Even Jews who do not identify with their religion or culture often discover that their good friends and acquaintances are also Jews themselves. A nouveau riche class of Jews is moving out to the rolling hills of Buda. Budapest is a cosmopolitan center that, for the Jews, looks more like London or New York than Prague or Warsaw.

None of this would be possible were it not for the large numbers of Jews in the city. In this way, Jewish history in Budapest is an unbroken chain to which new links are constantly being connected. Whereas for each of the other cities in this book, the unique urban culture of the Jews was terminated in the Holocaust, in Budapest that culture is both alive and evolving to this very day.

SPOTLIGHT:
Theodor Herzl (1860–1904)

Some would argue that to call Theodor Herzl a man of Budapest is as ludicrous as calling Josef Conrad a man of Poland. At the age of 18, the founder of modern political Zionism left Budapest for Vienna one week after the death of his sister from typhus. Herzl was thoroughly the product of late nineteenth-century Viennese culture. As a result, the influence of his native city has often been overlooked.

How did Budapest affect the development of Theodor Herzl? Without a doubt, the main influence was his birthplace itself, or rather, his next-door neighbor. Historians have duly noted that Herzl was born and raised in the building right next door to the world famous Dohany Street Synagogue. The building was since destroyed; today the Jewish Museum stands on the site. What hasn't been mentioned is that Jeanette and Jakob Herzl chose to conceive baby Theodor on almost precisely (give or take a month) the day the synagogue was ceremoniously unveiled. Given Herzl's later views, it seems that the matter was no accident. When it was built, the Dohany Street Synagogue was seen as the triumph of Hungarian Jewish assimilation—the same assimilation Herzl would reject as a failure in his adult years. At the same time, the facade of the Dohany Street Synagogue, with its bold Moorish design, celebrated the Eastern origins of the Jewish nation. Herzl himself was to insist that the Jews formed a unique nation that could thrive only in a separate state, preferably in the Middle East. In his grandest fancy, Herzl envisioned a rebuilt, albeit secular, Temple in Jerusalem that would resemble in many ways the familiar synagogue of his youth.

He was most likely given seeds of such thoughts during his *bar mitzvah* ceremony, which was held in the Dohany Street Synagogue itself. Simon Loeb Herzl, Theodor's paternal grandfather, traveled from Semlin to Budapest to attend the ceremony. Simon was a devoted follower of Rabbi Yehudah Alkalai (1798–1878), the Semlin rabbi who is largely regarded as the modern precursor of the Zionist movement and whose activities—from his courting of Jewish philanthropists to his appeals to the Turks—uncannily reflect those of Theodor Herzl decades later. Although Herzl only mentioned his grandfather Simon once in his writings, it is undoubted that this proto-Zionist relative influenced Herzl's thought.

In most other respects, Herzl's youth reflected the highly assimilated milieu of most of Budapest Jewry at the time. He did attend the popular Pest Jewish High Elementary School, housed in Sip Street 12 in the building that currently serves as the central headquarters of the Jewish Community of Hungary. The school had been built on the end of the expansive plot that later held the Dohany Street Synagogue; it owed its existence to the same pool of money that was used to create the Rabbinical Seminary of Budapest. Herzl later wrote of his years there:

> "My earliest memory of this school was the caning I received for not remembering the particulars of the Exodus of the Jews from Egypt. Nowadays many a schoolmaster would like to cane me for remembering that Exodus rather too well" (quoted in Ernst Pawel's *The Labyrinth of Exile*). From the age of five to nine, Herzl learned secular subjects as well as Hebrew and Jewish studies at this school.

From his earliest childhood, Herzl was coddled and indulged by his adulating mother; many credit this as the source of a rather superlative sense of self-destiny that found its ultimate expression as Redeemer of the Jews. According to his later recollections, the teen-aged Herzl once dreamt that the Messiah embraced him and flew him to a cloud where Moses stood. The Messiah then confided to Moses, "For this child I have prayed."

Such humility would be a lifelong trait. It was first expressed in Herzl's literary ambition, which he began at the onset of adolescence. In Vienna, Herzl earned a law degree but quickly returned to writing as a journalist and novice playwright. At the time, he was noticeably taciturn on the Jewish question, believing that assimilation and integration of the Jews would resolve any lingering "Jewish question" in society. It was only after 1891, when Herzl became the Parisian correspondent for the prestigious Viennese newspaper, the *Neue Freie Presse*, that he began to think deeply about Jewish national destiny. The eventual product of such musings was *The New Ghetto*, a play Herzl penned in 1894 that tried to expose the futility of assimilation.

Almost immediately after *The New Ghetto* was finished, France plunged into one of its most embarrassing episodes of the modern era with the Dreyfus Affair. Alfred Dreyfus was a Jewish captain in the French army who was framed for spying for Germany. Herzl wrote about Dreyfus's public humiliation, and the concomitant shouts of "Death to the Jews," for the *Neue Freie Presse*. One year later, when evidence was produced that proved Dreyfus had been framed because he was a Jew, a wave of anti-Semitic hysteria swept the country. Captain Dreyfus, an assimilated Jew to the core, represented for Herzl the ultimate failure of European integration. If even a man of Dreyfus's stature could not be considered a Frenchman, then the dream of assimilation was a bust; the only solution was to form a separate state for the Jews. He wrote that "the Dreyfus trial . . . which I witnessed in Paris in 1894, made me a Zionist" (quoted in Ernst Pawel, *The Labyrinth of Exile*).

Thus began a course of action, both frenetic and quixotic, on behalf of what Herzl himself termed "a gigantic dream." After vainly soliciting the assistance of Jewish philanthropists, Herzl outlined his plan in *The Jewish State* in 1896. Herzl chaired the First Zionist Congress in Basel in 1896, and was the leader of the World Zionist Organization from its inception until his death. Throughout the remaining years of his life, Herzl shuttled from country to country, meeting with Jewish leaders and secular rulers. His greatest public relations successes were his separate meetings with the German kaiser, the Turkish grand vizier, the pope, the king of Italy, and prominent members of the British government. All these meetings, however, were ultimately fruitless.

Herzl wasn't the first Jew to argue for a Jewish state. Ever since the dawn of Exile, a return to Zion formed a basic tenet of Jewish religious thought. But modern Zionism broke the mold of Jewish mystical longing. Previously, the hopeful return to Zion had been a cosmological drama acted out between the Jews and God. In the modern Zionist movement, the stage had changed: what was once Divine had become political. The new quest for Jewish fulfillment unfolded in the earthly realm between the Jews and their host nations of the Diaspora. The genius of Herzl—a secular Jew for whom the cosmological significance of messianism had only symbolic significance—was in his tireless skill as a leader in the political arena. Herzl attempted to persuade the world—both Jew and Gentile—that the only solution to the Jewish-Gentile dilemma lay in a homeland for the Jewish people.

Such a strategy was nothing short of revolutionary. Earlier Zionist theoreticians, who had emerged in the wake of the Russian pogroms of 1881, felt that the world was intrinsically and incorrigibly villainous against the Jews. For them, the only solution for the Jews was to remove themselves from that world. But Herzl, in many ways a typically Western European Jew, saw the world not only as a passive participant in the Jewish drama, but as midwife to the delivery of the Jewish state. He argued that anti-Semitism was painful both to the victim and to the perpetrator; the Jews did not belong in Europe, and only when the "Jewish Question" was resolved would the countries of the world be at peace. And the only solution to the Jewish Question was the creation of a Jewish state. "Zionism," Herzl declared at the First Zionist Congress in 1897, "is simply a peacemaker." Zionism, then, would heal Jewish wounds as well as Christian. In *The Jewish State*, Herzl's Zionist manifesto, he concludes with the universality of his plan: "The world will be liberated by our freedom, enriched by our wealth, magnified by our greatness. And whatever we attempt there for our own benefit will redound mightily and beneficially to the good of all mankind." Herzl's belief was so strong that he actually claimed he could feel the pain of the anti-Semite; both felt that there was no place for the Jew in European society.

Although Herzl spoke of Jewish national renewal almost strictly in political, as opposed to cultural or religious, terms, he was not unaware of the magnitude of his plan. At the First Zionist Congress in 1897, Herzl announced, "We returned home, as it were. For Zionism is a return to the Jewish fold even before it becomes a return to the Jewish land." At various moments, Herzl strived for Jewish states in Sinai, Cyprus, Argentina, and Uganda. But his main goal was a state in the Jewish homeland of Palestine.

Herzl died before seeing the fruition of his dream. Nonetheless, he succeeded in setting up the mechanism and the determination that, less than half a century after his death, would lead to the creation of the modern State of Israel.

The Jewish Essentials

The Jewish Community of Budapest
Sip Street 12
Telephone (36–1) 342 1335
Fax (36–1) 342 1790

The Jewish Community of Budapest serves all the administrative needs of the Jews of Budapest and Hungary. It is also the center of the religious administration of the Neolog congregations in Hungary. Most Hungarian and international Jewish organizations have offices in this building. Orthodox congregations have a separate religious and administrative office (*see below*).

The Autonomous Orthodox Jewish Community
Dob Street 35
Telephone (36–1) 351 0525, 351 0526, 351 0534
Fax (36–1) 322 7200

This is the communal office of Hungarian Orthodox Jewry. Information about the Orthodox Community and assistance in religious matters can be obtained here. Laszlo Herczog, the chief secretary of the Orthodox Jewish Community, offers helpful assistance to visitors in English.

Chabad House
Wesselenyi Street 4 I/1
Telephone (36–1) 268 0183

Chabad Lubavitch, led by Rabbi Boruch and Batsheva Oberlander, is very active in Budapest. The Oberlanders are extremely helpful in all matters of concern to Jewish visitors. If you require assistance in purchasing kosher foods or in using the *mikveh*, do not hesitate to call.

The Balint Jewish Community Center
Revay Street 16
Telephone (36–1) 111 9214, 131 5332

This cultural, social, and educational center was opened in 1995 in a renovated building with a modern interior. The Balint Center organizes a wide range of services and events, ranging from a Hebrew-speakers club to chess and Yoga classes. Cultural events such as lectures by psychologists attract the largest crowds. A complete program of the current month's lectures and activities can be obtained at the Center.

PRAYING IN BUDAPEST

Please *see* "The Living Synagogue" *on page 475.*

MIKVEH

Kazinczy Street 16
Telephone (36–1) 118 9224
Open mornings   5:30 A.M.–7:00 A.M. daily
                7:30 A.M.–9:00 A.M. Shabbat

These are approximate times; the *mikveh* does not follow stringent opening and closing hours. It is best to call in advance.

Before the war, there were several operating *mikvehs* in Budapest. The one on Kazinczy Street is the only *mikveh* currently in use. When it was built in 1927, it was divided into first, second, and third classes. First class was relatively exquisite: Four separate rooms, each with its own private *mikveh*, shower, and bed. Second class was a larger *mikveh* that held about five people, and third class was like a small swimming pool.

Today, since there are so few visitors to the *mikveh*, only the first class *mikvehs* are in use. Of the four *mikvehs*, one is reserved for women, one for men, and two serve as extras. There is never a wait.

Women are advised to call in advance for an appointment. The Orthodox Community can assist you, but it is easier to call Batsheva Oberlander of Chabad Lubavitch at (36–1) 268 0183, who speaks perfect English and who can accompany you to the *mikveh*. It is best to call her at least one day in advance.

Keeping Kosher in Budapest

For Central Eastern Europe, Budapest is a kosher-minded traveller's dream.

RESTAURANTS

Of the several restaurants in Budapest boasting Jewish "style" food, only two have Orthodox *hekshers*.

Hanna Restaurant
Dob Street 35
Tel. (36-1) 142 1464
Opening Hours:
Daily 8:00 A.M.–4:00 P.M.

Hanna Restaurant serves basic kosher food in a no-nonsense atmosphere inside the courtyard of the Kazinczy Street Synagogue. Orthodox members of the Jewish Community eat here often. On Shabbat, there is a family atmosphere around a long table, with rabbis and young people singing *zemirot*, or songs, after the meal. Tickets for Shabbat must be purchased in advance.

Meal ticket prices at Hanna Restaurant are one of the most mystifying aspects of life in Budapest. Anything will work for a discount (student ID's, etc.) just as anything will work to jack the price up (dressing like a tourist, speaking English).

King's Hotel Restaurant
Nagy Diofa Street 25/27
Tel/fax (36-1) 267 9323, 267 9324, 267 9325, 267 9326

This recently built restaurant inside the King's Hotel is fancier in quality and price than Hanna. Shabbat meals here must also be paid for in advance.

BUTCHERS

There are two strictly kosher butcher stores in Budapest, but because they only slaughter animals once a week, it is best to place orders in advance. If you need help ordering meat, you can call the very helpful Lubavitcher Rabbi Boruch Oberlander and his wife, Batsheva, at (36-1) 268 0183. The butchers' hours are fairly unstable, so it's best to call in advance. If you do come without calling first, be aware that Friday is a bad time to come, as they sell out early.

The butchers are located at:

Visegrad Street 16 Tel. (36-1) 132 0180
and
Dob Street 35 Tel. (36-1) 122 6620

The butcher here is located at the entrance to the kosher kitchen for Hanna Restaurant. Next door to the Dob Street entrance to the Orthodox Jewish Community center is the butcher. When he is out of meat, the door will be shut and locked.

SALAMI STORE

Kazinczy Street 41, in the courtyard, on the left.
Tel. (36 1) 142 1639
Open: Monday–Thursday 9:00 A.M.–5:00 P.M.
           Half day on Friday

The salami here, made on the spot, has been given top ratings by American tourists. Sometimes you can find other meats here as well.

MILK STORE

Dob Street 35, in the courtyard
Open: Mondays and Thursdays 7:30 A.M. until 10:00 A.M. or 12:00 P.M.

The milk is available boiled or unboiled. It's best to get there early, as the closing times vary.

GROCERY STORE

Each outlet in the Rothschild chain of grocery stores sells some kosher products (biscuits, etc.), but only one has a special section that is strictly kosher:

Rothschild Kosher Foodstore
Rakoczi Street 32
Tel. (36 1) 322 9276
Open: Monday–Thursday 10:00 A.M.–6:00 P.M.
Friday 10:00 A.M.–2:00 P.M.

PATISSERIE

(If you aren't so strict.)

Frohlich Patisserie
Dob Street 31

Frohlich's is a great little patisserie that keeps kosher, although it is not under rabbinical supervision. Depending on whom you ask, there are different versions as to why. But it is kosher. Try the flodni and you'll be floored.

HOTEL

King's Hotel
Nagy Diofa Street 25/27
Tel/fax—(see *King's Hotel Restaurant, page 401*)

Budapest's first "Kosher Hotel" in generations is open to anybody, but it's a favorite among travelling groups of *hasidim*. Everything is designed for the Orthodox traveller, from the restaurant to the Yiddish-speaking *mammele* manager to the Shomer Shabbos electricity policies to the two built-in *sukkot*. Costs are $60–$80 per room (2 single beds or 1 double bed) and $120 for a family room (2 double beds, 1 single bed). The hotel has 80–85 rooms.

Orientation and Suggested Itinerary

Most visitors, eager for a taste of "Jewish Budapest," head en masse for the looming Dohany Street Synagogue, the second largest synagogue in the world. Other synagogues in the area, as well as the distinct history of the former Holocaust ghetto, often make the left bank of the Danube the only stop for Jewish-minded tourists. As an unintended result, some of Budapest's most valuable finds are completely overlooked. For that reason this book tries to include some lesser-known parts of Budapest, particularly from the magnificent span of Jewish history in the Castle District.

Today's Budapest has really only existed since 1873, when the three distinct cities of Buda, Obuda, and Pest were united into a single municipal authority. Any foray into past centuries of the city should keep this in mind. This is all the more true regarding Jewish history in this jigsaw city. Jewish areas of settlement moved in a neat, clockwise fashion starting with the medieval Community in Buda, moving in the eighteenth century to Obuda, and finally landing in Pest from the end of the eighteenth century until the twentieth century. In this way, the otherwise unruly conglomeration of three cities becomes a more user-friendly landscape for the visitor. It gets even simpler: In each of the three districts, the trends of Jewish settlement fell along radically different lines. In Buda, for instance, Jews lived under the rule of the king and, later, the Turkish sultan. In Obuda, Jews lived under the protection of a noble family. Finally, the Pest Jewish Community developed as the town authorities slowly broke down discriminatory barriers against Jewish residence and trade.

Budapest's Jewish history is too diverse to describe in a single breath, but in its tripartite distinctions of Jewish settlement, the city is an invaluable microcosm of European Jewish life. For throughout European history, Jews were at the mercy and whim—always in varying degrees—of either kings, counts, or City Councils. In a single city, Budapest today tells the story of all three aspects of European Jewish history. For this reason, as well as for geographic simplicity, the sites of Budapest are here separated into their original divisions of Buda, Obuda, and Pest.

I recommend you begin your exploration of Budapest's Jewish past in the Castle District of Buda. The ancient Jewish Quarter here will place the large modern synagogues in their proper perspective by the time you cross the river into Pest. Even if you're in Budapest for one day, try to squeeze in at least an hour for the Castle.

Like Warsaw, much of the Castle District is a "virtual reality tour," since the earliest Jewish settlement was torn down in later centuries and the venerable Great Synagogue is today buried underground. Nonetheless, the Castle District includes a priceless sector in which Jews lived from the fourteenth through the seventeenth centuries. This is Jewish Street, today's Tancsics Mihaly Street in the northern part of the Castle grounds. The Small Medieval Synagogue is open weekdays from May through October, except Mondays.

When you've quenched your thirst for medieval Jewish life, cross over to the Pest side of the river to see what the Jews built when they were released from property and settlement restrictions. Although synagogues and communal centers can be found throughout Pest, the heart of the Jewish Community lies in the Seventh District (called Erzsebetvaros). This is also the area where Jews were confined in a ghetto at the end of 1944. In the span of several blocks, the triumph and tragedy of Budapest's modern Jewish history can be witnessed. First, of course, there is the inimitable Dohany Street Synagogue. Next door is the Hungarian Jewish Museum. Behind the Dohany Street Synagogue on Wesselenyi Street, you'll find the Holocaust Memorial of Budapest. Next door is the Heroes' Temple. From the Heroes' Temple, walk up Rumbach Street. On your right, next to Dob Street 12, there is a Memorial to Carl Lutz. Continuing up the street, you'll come to the Rumbach Synagogue on 11/13 Rumbach Street. From there, backtrack to Dob Street and make a left, following Dob Street up to Kazinczy Street. Make a right on Kazinczy and you'll find yourself at the Kazinczy Street Synagogue, a complex synagogue-cum-village managed by the Orthodox Community of Budapest. You should reserve the better part of one day for the Jewish sites on the Pest side of Budapest.

The Obuda section of Budapest hosted a thriving Jewish Community in the eighteenth century, between the times the Jews were expelled from Buda and settled in Pest. However, practically the only site to see today is the Obuda Synagogue, which is currently used as a studio for Hungarian Television. I highly recommend you visit this site, one of the world's rare examples of a neoclassical synagogue. However, since visitors are not permitted in the interior, you'll only be able to see it from the outside. This means the site is not limited by opening and closing times. Come to Obuda only after the other synagogues and museums in Budapest are closed. Located on the riverside, the Obuda Synagogue makes a stately impression at sunset.

Time permitting, I recommend you pay a visit to the Kozma Street Cemetery, with its astounding *ohelim*, memorials to the martyrs of World War I and the Holocaust, and tombstones for all aspects of the Neolog Community of Budapest from the end of the nineteenth century until today. As the cemetery is located far from the center of Budapest, a proper visit will take at least two hours with travel time.

Hardcore travellers eager for a rare glimpse into Budapest are encouraged to peruse the section titled "The Living Synagogue" (*page 475*). Budapest is unique in the region for its diversity of synagogues open for prayer. Most of these synagogues do not share the fame and glamour of Budapest's landmark synagogues, but if you're curious about the lifeblood of today's Jewish Community, you're more likely to find it in a small synagogue than on Dohany Street. If you will be here for Shabbat, I highly recommend visiting one of these synagogues off the beaten track. A couple have morning services during the week. In the active synagogues, you might even meet people about whom the future life of Budapest's Jewry will be written.

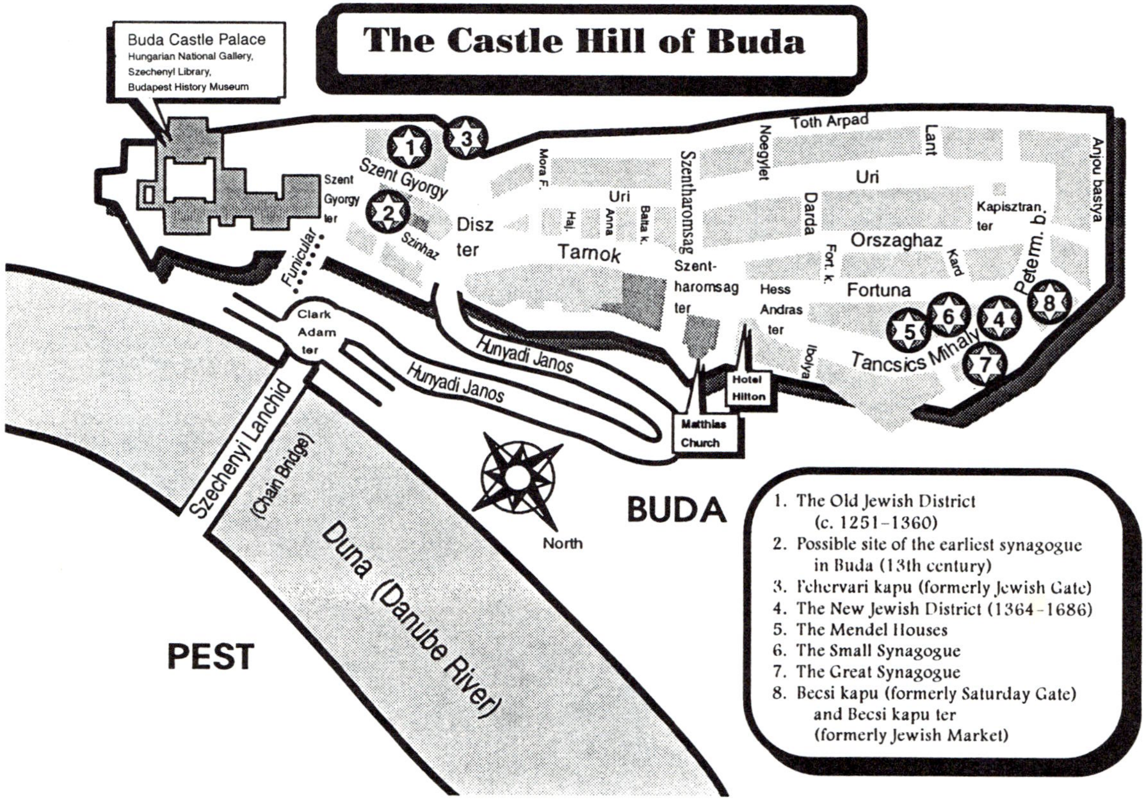

The Castle Hill of Buda

1. The Old Jewish District (c. 1251–1360)
2. Possible site of the earliest synagogue in Buda (13th century)
3. Tchervari kapu (formerly Jewish Gate)
4. The New Jewish District (1364–1686)
5. The Mendel Houses
6. The Small Synagogue
7. The Great Synagogue
8. Becsi kapu (formerly Saturday Gate) and Becsi kapu ter (formerly Jewish Market)

Buda Castle Palace
Hungarian National Gallery,
Szechenyi Library,
Budapest History Museum

Buda:
Jewish Life from the Middle Ages through the Turks

From the thirteenth century to the seventeenth century, Jews were almost entirely concentrated in and around the castle hill of Buda. If you want to explore Jewish Budapest in a chronological fashion, Buda is the place to begin.

When the Magyars entered Hungary in 895 and established settlements along the Danube, they undoubtedly encountered Jewish merchants who dealt in trade between Croatia and Russia. But it wasn't until the year 1000, when King Istvan I adopted Christianity and the Hungarian state was founded, that the Magyars began to settle in major cities, including Buda. Unlike his counterparts in other European countries, King Istvan did not weave anti-Semitism into his Christian belief. Jews migrated to major cities such as Esztergom and Buda, and were permitted to own property.

The earliest record of Jews in medieval Hungary is from the year 1050. The record speaks of two Jews from Germany who transgressed the Shabbat on a visit to Esztergom, which lies only thirty miles north of Budapest. The Jewish Community of Esztergom was so sophisticated that it certainly had a sister Community in Buda. At the end of the eleventh century, anti-Semitic laws were enacted that effectively threw the Jews out of agricultural fields and forced them by default to enter the mercantile professions. As a result, Jews began to flock to cities like Buda and Esztergom in great numbers.

THE OLD JEWISH DISTRICT OF BUDA
SZENT GYORGY STREET

Jews began to concentrate on a single street in the Castle District in the 1250s, under the reign of King Bela IV. Their position on "Jewish Street" was solidified by two factors. First, in the first half of the thirteenth century King Bela made Buda his royal residence and the capital city of Hungary. It was at this time that the Buda fortress was revamped into a genuine castle. Of course, the boon this gave the local economy made the city a natural destination for Jewish merchants and moneylenders. In addition, since the fate of the Jews in the Middle Ages often depended on the king's favor, the capital of a kingdom was often the safest place for Jews to live.

The second factor leading to the formation of a "Jewish Street" was King Bela's Jewish Law of 1251. The king was eager to reconstruct his country after the Mongol invasion; bringing in Jewish immigrants was one peg in his plan. The law granted the Jews of Hungary religious freedom as well as freedom of life, property, and trade. As expected, the privileges contained in this law resulted in an influx of Jewish immigrants to all parts of Hungary, including Buda.

Even more significantly, Bela's law made the Jews "servants of the royal chamber." As was the case elsewhere in Europe, the king had an interest in establishing the Jews as his chattel so that he could receive tax revenues directly as well as use the Jews as the moneylending engine for the economy (Christians could not fill this task because their religion forbade usury). In practice this meant that Jewish life, freedom, and fortune were bound up in the castle administration. Welded as they were to the royal treasury, it was natural that the Jews should populate an area near the royal residence itself. Thus, like medieval Jewish neighborhoods elsewhere in Europe, the "Jewish Street" developed near the castle both for economic expediency and for the protection of the king. By the end of the thirteenth century, with the Church taking an active interest in separating Christians from Jews, Jewish Street evolved into a semisegregated enclave. Christians who were seen fraternizing with Jews were regularly banned from churches.

Jewish Street was located where Szent Gyorgy Street is situated today. No houses or synagogues remain from the time of Jewish settlement. After the Jews were expelled from Buda in 1360, the houses were taken by Christians; eventually, during castle reconstructions, they were razed. Today, all that exists is a stretch of land where Jewish Street once existed. In 1996, the Budapest Historical Museum began excavating the area as part of its planned excavation of the entire Castle District. It remains to be seen whether the archaeologists find a fourteenth-century *mikveh* or the remains of a cemetery. Perhaps in five or ten years there will be an exhibit on Szent Gyorgy Street featuring the original foundations of thirteenth-century Jewish homes (this is an optimistic prediction; don't book your calendar just yet). Because the buildings have been demolished and records are meager, our information about this street is troublingly scant. The oldest known synagogue of Buda, from the thirteenth century, might have stood at the corner of Szent Gyorgy ter ("square") and Szinhaz Street. Because of the excavations and the previous demolition of the buildings, Szinhaz Street is today (in the late 1990s) like a path through a park. The exact whereabouts of the synagogue are unknown, but we do know that it was built as a direct consequence of the Jewish Law of 1251. It was probably a twin-naved synagogue similar to the Altneuschul in Prague, which was built after a similar edict in 1254. The synagogue was used from the 1250s until the Jews were expelled from Buda in 1360.

Because the street no longer exists, it is difficult to visualize Jewish life in the early Middle Ages in Buda. The place where you might best be able to imagine the Jewish district is by today's Fehervari kapu, which once was a sort of anchor of the Jewish neighborhood. The tower that stood by the gate was called Jewish Tower; the gate itself was called Jewish Gate. It was one of the main gates of the Castle District. The gate was also called Saturday Gate, because it was locked shut every Friday at sundown in order to prevent the desecration of Shabbat on Jewish Street. (In Israel today, observant neighborhoods block off their streets with barricades during Shabbat. As seen in Buda, such a custom is by no means new among the Jews.) The other reason the gate was shut was that it was part of the *eruv*. An *eruv* is a boundary around a Jewish neighborhood, within which Jews are permitted to carry certain objects (e.g., prayer books, keys) on Shabbat. Below the gate, in the district of Krisztinavaros, was the Jewish cemetery. It was discovered during a building project in 1894. The oldest identifiable tombstone was from 1278; it is the oldest extant thirteenth-century tombstone, for Jew or Gentile, in all of Budapest.

Nearby Jewish Street stood the royal mint, responsible for producing coins for all of Hungary. It was no accident that the mint bordered the Jewish district. As servants of the royal chamber, many Jews worked as moneylenders and tax collectors. Among them were several who rose to become leaders of the mint. Copper and silver coins produced throughout the thirteenth century often bore the Hebrew initials *alef*, *kaf*, *mem*, or *peh*, presumably the initials of the mint's various leaders. The most famous was the estate-owning "Treasury Count" Teha, who lived in Buda in the first half of the thirteenth century. The coins minted by Teha bore his Hebrew initial, *tet*. Teha was a prominent moneylender in both Buda and Vienna, where he lived for some time after Jews were barred from Hungarian public office in 1233. He backed up loans and lent money to noblemen and even to the king himself. Another famous treasury count was a German Jew named Henuk, who immigrated to Buda after King Bela IV passed his Jewish Law. In recognition of Henuk's services, the king granted him twenty-one villages and the castle of Komarom. Henuk's coins were marked with a *chet*. It is remarkable that in a Christian country Jews were actually permitted to sign the coins, but such license didn't last; toward the end of the century, King Laszlo IV prohibited the use of Hebrew on currency.

Long after the Jews had been moved to another part of the Castle District in the fourteenth century, exceptional Jews continued to live in the area of Szent Gyorgy Street. By far the most uproarious was an illustrious financier named Shneur Zalman (c. 1460–1526). When the authorities learned that Zalman had a Christian mistress, he had two choices: conversion to Christianity or painful death. Zalman chose the former option, became baptized, and was given the name Emericus Fortunatus. After he converted, Fortunatus found that the barriers that hindered his Jewish colleagues disappeared one by one. Eventually he became one of the most important men in the royal treasury. He lived in a palace on Szent Gyorgy ter right next to the castle wall. When the Turks began making inroads into the southern parts of Hungary, a wave of hysteria erupted that turned, as they often did, to the most visible Jew in the country—even though that Jew had been baptized. The nobility insisted Fortunatus be burned at the stake, the typical punishment meted out to unmasked Marranos. He was arrested and imprisoned for two weeks. When Fortunatus was released, he organized in his palace such a boisterous feast that the furious noblemen roused the castle mobs into a pogrom. Fortunatus escaped by climbing out the back window and sliding down ropes into the castle moat. The rabble ransacked his palace, taking out vats of wine, velvets, jewels, horses, and sixty thousand gold florins. The next day they attacked the Jewish Street, which by this time was situated on today's Tancsics Mihaly Street, and ransacked the entire quarter. As for Fortunatus, he rebounded almost immediately, becoming head of the treasury, head of the copper mines, tax collector for Buda, and personal financier of the king himself.

Aside from these extraordinary latter-day adventures, Jewish Street was the heart of Jewish life in Buda only for 100–150 years, until the middle of the fourteenth century. At that time, King Lajos I attempted to convert all the Jews of Hungary to Christianity. He forced them to attend proselytizing sermons and promised full emancipation if the Jews were to convert. In 1360, after all attempts had failed, King Lajos ordered the expulsion of the Jews from Hungary. The king permitted the Jews to keep their moveable property, but everything else, including their homes and synagogues, was given to Christians and court magnates. The expulsion of the Jews was effectively the end of the Old Jewish District of Buda.

THE NEW JEWISH DISTRICT OF BUDA
TANCSICS MIHALY STREET

Four years later, in 1364, King Lajos readmitted the Jews to Hungary. Evidently the king couldn't do without the Jewish class of financiers and moneylenders. In any event, when the Jews returned to Buda and found that their homes on the old Jewish Street had been taken by Christians, they settled in a new area in the northern part of the Castle District, on today's Tancsics Mihaly Street. Luckily for us, there is still much to see on this street.

At the time, it was called Jewish Street. It became a bustling quarter where the Jews again found themselves in the role of "servants of the royal chamber." In 1371, King Lajos encouraged Jews to return to Hungary by creating the position of a national "Jew Judge" to handle the affairs of Jews throughout the country. The Jew Judge, a Christian nobleman appointed by the king, collected Jewish taxes, protected Jewish rights, and mediated in all conflicts between Christians and Jews. Since these noblemen lived and worked in the royal court, the Jews of Buda had the security to grow and prosper on Jewish Street. Some of the most successful and affluent Jews in Hungary lived on this street. Buda's Jews had their homes here, but were free to trade in markets throughout the Castle District.

In 1421, the status of Jewish Street fell into decline with the issuance of the anti-Semitic *Law Book of Buda*. Although there was never an official Buda "ghetto" in which the Jews were confined, the *Law Book of Buda* limited Jewish trade and business to Jewish Street, and even there restricted selling to only one day a week. Any Jewish salesman found outside this single street had all his merchandise confiscated. In addition, Buda's Jews were forbidden from doing business with anybody from outside the city.

Perhaps the cruelest blow in the book was its prescription for Jewish dress. The thirteenth-century Jewish badge was enlarged into an entire costume: Jews were forced to wear red capes and cone-shaped hats normally forced upon witches and warlocks during public humiliation ceremonies. On their chests, they had to wear a large yellow patch identical to the one worn by Buda's prostitutes. This costume was legally binding on the Jews until it was abolished sometime before 1520.

As a result of the anti-Semitic hysteria, Jewish Street was subjected to several painful episodes. In one account, possibly anecdotal, Christians set up wax torches on Becsi kapu ter (Viennese Gate Square) at the northern end of Jewish Street. They announced that any Jew who did not convert by the time the fire burnt out would himself be burnt at the stake. The Jews refused, but it is unclear what happened next.

The situation on Jewish Street took a turn for the better after 1477, when King Matthias Corvinus established the position of "Jewish prefect." The Jewish prefect, or royally appointed intermediary between the king and the Jews of Hungary, was by far the most powerful Jewish position in all the kingdom of Hungary (*see page 381*). The prefect, who had free access to the king and the court, had no equal anywhere in Europe in the fifteenth century. He collected taxes from Jewish communities throughout the kingdom and secured royal protection for Jewish communities. It was partly the prefect's eminence that raised the stature of Jewish Street and its five hundred-odd inhabitants to relative prosperity toward the end of the fifteenth century. By far the most famous prefects were the members of the Mendel dynasty, whose houses we can still see today on Tancsics Mihaly Street 23, 26, and 28.

THE MENDEL HOUSES
TANCSICS MIHALY STREET 23, 26, 28

Prague had its Mordechai Maisel, Cracow its Reb Isaac Reb Jekeles; in Buda, the role of legendary affluent Jew was not confined to a single personality but stretched through an entire family of *machurs*. These were the Mendels, the most powerful Jewish family in all of Hungary in the late fifteenth and early sixteenth centuries. The Mendel houses at 23, 26, and 28 Tancsics Mihaly Street were a testament to the family wealth. It is said that they were the most lavish buildings on Jewish Street.

The founder of the dynasty was Judah Mendel (d. 1482). Judah served as leader of the Jewish Community of Buda and as such had intermittent contacts with King Matthias himself. When the king celebrated his wedding to Queen Beatrice in 1476, Judah Mendel topped the list of Jewish invitees. A fifteenth-century chronicle records Judah, a long silver dagger at his side, riding at the head of the Jewish notables entering the inner castle. Judah stopped at the castle fountain and delivered a speech before all the gathered dignitaries. He was accompanied by thirty-one lavish horses and twenty-eight Jews clothed in violet raiment with silver thread.

Judah Mendel went on to become the Jewish prefect, a position that remained in his family for seven generations. It was in these houses on the former Jewish Street that generation after generation of Mendels administered the affairs of dozens of Jewish communities. Whenever a Jew got in trouble with the law (or with a Mendel decree), Mendel's personal troops galloped away to seize the offender and bring him to Mendel's own jailhouse at Tancsics Mihaly Street 23. The Mendels were exempt from the special clothing Jews were forced to wear. They were invited to the king's celebrations and invariably were seen at the head of horseback processions. The Mendels could even appoint chief rabbis for communities throughout Hungary. In the early sixteenth century, Jacob Mendel II hired mercenaries to protect Jewish Street from assault or pogrom. He also employed special "Jewish jurors" who were sent all over Hungary to collect Jewish taxes. At the time, Hungary was the only country in Europe that allowed such privileges to a Jew.

From 1526 to 1541, the Turkish army made several attacks on Buda until the city finally fell under Turkish control. According to one account, when the Turks attacked Jewish Street in 1526, the Jews fought so valiantly that twenty-five hundred Turks fell before the street was taken. In the ensuing carnage, practically all of the thirty-five hundred Jews in the district were killed. This account, though, is certainly an exaggeration. In fact, many Jews escaped Buda, while the rest covered themselves in mourning shrouds and beseeched the Turks for mercy. The Turks spared the Jews and, in order to control their castle seat, sent off as many as two thousand of Buda's Jews to places in Turkey. At this time, the Mendel dynasty left Buda and continued its work in parts of Hungary outside of Turkish rule. Eventually, the office of Jewish prefect petered out.

By the 1530s, Jews had already returned to Jewish Street, and beginning in 1541 they basked in an era of unprecedented Jewish prosperity under the Turks. The Muslims governed with a degree of tolerance unseen in Christian Europe, allowing the Jews freedom of life and livelihood. As a result, Buda became the largest Jewish Community in all of Hungary. By the 1580s there were eighty-eight Jewish families, or five hundred individuals, living on Jewish Street. They worked in sundry professions, from purse making to royal tavern renting, from tax collecting to trade between the Ottoman Empire and western Europe. We know of two kosher butchers on Jewish Street, as well as two physicians. On Becsi kapu ter (Viennese Gate Square), at the northern end of Tancsics Mihaly Street, there was the Jewish Market. Becsi kapu (Viennese Gate) was known as Saturday Gate, much like its predecessor in the Old Jewish District (see above). The Jewish cemetery was again situated below the castle hill, this time in the district of Vizivaros. By the 1670s, there were one thousand Jews in Buda.

Greater contact with the Ottoman Empire turned Jewish Street into a veritable melting pot of Jews from the Ashkenazic and Sephardic worlds. It wasn't uncommon to hear several languages spoken at once on Jewish Street. As early as 1542, just one year after the Turks consolidated their control in Hungary, a Hungarian Jew teamed up with a Jew from Istanbul to rent from the Turkish authorities the candle factories and the money exchange of Buda and Pest. The cosmopolitan Jewish Community actually had three main branches: one each for the German, Spanish, and Syrian Jews living in Buda. Each of these groups had its own rabbi who led separate prayer services according to the rites of their countries of origin.

As a result, there were no less than three synagogues in Buda in the sixteenth century. One stood in the second Jewish settlement of Vizivaros, below the castle hill along the river (its exact whereabouts are unknown). The other two were situated across from each other on Jewish Street. In 1964, both of these synagogues were discovered. One of them, the Small Synagogue, is open for visitors today while the other, the Great Synagogue, is buried beneath a mound of earth, pending future excavation.

The Jewish Community of Buda thrived until the city was conquered by the Austrians in 1686. At that time, the Community was completely destroyed (*see page 421*). It was a long time before Jews resettled in Buda; their later Community never achieved the prosperity enjoyed under the Turks. However, in recent years several young, nouveau riche Jews have moved out of the city center to bucolic homes in the hills of Buda. Although it's no longer in the Castle District, there is once again a sizeable Jewish presence—if not quite a Community—in the Buda section of Budapest.

THE SMALL SYNAGOGUE

Address: 26 Tancsics Mihaly Street
The Small Synagogue is open only during the warm season, from May 1 through October 31. Opening hours: 10 A.M.–5P.M. weekdays; closed Mondays

Under the reign of the Turks (1526–1686) Buda became a multicultural metropolis bustling with both eastern and western peoples. Jewish Street was no different. Indeed, it was Jewish Street that hosted one of the most colorful communities of the Diaspora. Ottoman Jews, hearing rumors of prosperity in Buda, arrived in the capital city from such diverse locations as Istanbul, Salonika, and Tsfat. The Turkish rulers even thought it wise to bring in Jews from the Balkans. As a result, a thriving Sephardic Community of as many as thirty families established itself in Buda.

Although the Ashkenazic and Sephardic Jews enriched each other both professionally and socially, in religious matters the Sephardim did not want to abandon the unique customs they brought from the east. There were two Sephardic rabbis, one each for the separate Spanish and Syrian Jewish communities.

Sometime late in the sixteenth century, either the Spanish or the Syrian Community established a small Sephardic synagogue in this home, which had been formerly owned by the Mendel family. The entire building dates from the late fourteenth or early fifteenth century; later, when the Turks conquered Buda, the Mendels by and large left the city. When the Sephardim set up their prayer hall, they adjusted the room to suit their needs. Thus on weekdays and Shabbat, when the large Ashkenazic Jewish Community prayed in the Great Synagogue the *sephardim* conducted their own services just across the street.

The synagogue was identified during building reconstruction in 1964 when the red painted designs were discovered on the walls. None of its furnishings remain; instead, the small hall hosts an exhibition of Jewish objects. On the western wall, you can still see the windows that once connected to the *ezrat nashim*, or women's section.

Near the ceiling of the Small Synagogue, there are crude, red drawings of two distinct images specked with Hebrew text. Originating in the sixteenth or seventeenth century, these drawings are the most fascinating part of the synagogue today. The inscriptions are not written in classic Hebrew letters but in a cursive that has been identified as Eastern. This is one reason scholars decided the synagogue served the Sephardic rite. What is interesting here is not only the choice of images, but also the texts themselves were an interesting choice of inspiration for the Jews of Buda.

The Star of David

The first thing to mention about this Star of David is its very existence in a synagogue as early as the sixteenth century. Back then, the hexagram had not yet gained supremacy as a Jewish symbol. Its use here in the Small Synagogue forms a crucial part of the symbol's history, making the site one of Budapest's most secret treasures today. Gershom Scholem, the great Jewish historian of the twentieth century, wrote a history of the Star of David that was published in 1948 and revised in 1963—one year before the red Star of David was found in Buda. Although it probably wouldn't have changed his conclusions, Scholem would certainly have enjoyed the inscription around the emblem in Buda. In English it means, "The Lord bless you and protect you. The Lord deal kindly and graciously with you. The Lord bestow His favor upon you and grant you peace" (Numbers 6:24–26). This is the *birkat haCohanim*, or blessing of the Cohens, performed in front of the Old Temple in Jerusalem and repeated during synagogue ceremonies to this day. It is also the traditional blessing given by a father to his children on Shabbat.

The inscription appears to be a general benediction, recalling both divine favor and the glory of Old Temple rituals. But when viewed together with the adjacent image and inscription, the Star of David inscription takes on an ominous tone.

The Arrow

To the left of the Star of David there is a large shape that resembles a bell. It is one of the strangest symbols ever found in a synagogue: The image depicts an upwards-pointing arrow.

The image has caused consternation among scholars. Why an arrow in a synagogue? Jewish law prohibits graven images, but geometric and floral designs were commonly used to make a synagogue attractive. An arrow is hardly a pretty image to gaze at during prayer, however. The meaning of the arrow becomes more clear when we read its inscription. In English it means, "The bows of the mighty are broken, and the faltering are girded with strength" (I Samuel 2:4). It is from Hannah's prayer of thanksgiving when she dedicates her son Samuel to God. Although it is possible that this military image and inscription bears a kabbalistic explanation, the prevalent view is that the Jews praying in the Small Synagogue were aware of a very real danger to their lives. Especially in the context of the inscription on the Star of David, both images relate a fear in the Jewish District that was so great it could be felt on the synagogue walls.

What was this fear?

Though the citizens of Buda flourished under the Turks, the threat of annihilation was never far from home. The Austrian armies organized repeated attacks on the capital city, and even laid siege to it on more than one occasion. The Jews were always aware of the terror that would be unleashed should the Austrians ever gain control over Buda.

When the Austrians laid siege to Buda in 1598, the Jews fought valiantly alongside the Turkish forces encamped in the Castle District. According to one chronicler, the Jews declared, "Let us fight with courage for our children, our wives, our possessions, and let God do what seems good in His eyes" (quoted in Raphael Patai, *The Jews of Hungary*). It was partly due to Jewish assistance that the Austrian armies retreated. For Jews living in Austria, this raised the age-old specter of dual loyalty. There was a clamor in Vienna to expel the Jews from the country. But, according to legend, Emperor Rudolf II refused and declared, "Is it not a good thing that they fought for their ruler? Wouldn't our Jews do the same if they were required to? No, the Jews should never be punished for serving their country with honor."

During the next siege in 1602, Buda's Jews were not so fortunate. Faced with a famine and abject poverty, the Jewish Community of Buda had no way of supporting its most destitute members. In order to avert massive starvation, the Community had to send the poorest Jews to seek shelter elsewhere. Others, fearing a bloodbath, fled the city before the Austrians could enter. Those who remained were subjected to Austrian terror. Many were killed on the streets and in their homes, and twenty-two wealthy Jews were seized as hostages for ransom.

In yet another siege, the Austrians broke through the Vienna Gate, which lay right next to the Jewish District. The Jews parcelled out pieces of rat poison among themselves and prepared to swallow it should they fail to escape. "Escape or die!" they cried. One Jew ran to a large cannon standing in a defensive position inside Vienna Gate and lit the fuse. The attacking troops were so densely packed that the cannonball killed thousands (at least according to one chronicler's fancy). As a reward for defending the city, the Turks exempted the Jews from provincial taxes. Nonetheless, the fear and panic was so great that for years after the siege, there was a coded saying on Jewish Street: "Shall we lick?" meaning, "Shall we swallow the poison?"

Even when the city wasn't under siege, the Jews had good reason to fear Austrian incursions or stray Hungarian forces. In the seventeenth century, the Turkish traveler Evliya Chelebi wrote about Jewish Street: "If a Jew from this neighborhood falls into the hands of Hungarians, Germans, or Czechs, they roast him on a spit" (quoted in Raphael Patai, *The Jews of Hungary*). Unless, of course, they could extract a ransom for him. It happened repeatedly during Turkish rule that Hungarians captured a Jew and released him only for a lavish sum. In 1567 one of the wealthiest Jews in Buda, Moyses by name, was kidnapped by soldiers at the behest of a baron. Moyses was tortured and even put in chains in a dungeon until he paid nine thousand florins as ransom. Such a case was not unique in Buda.

In the context of these repeated battles and attacks, it is no wonder that the arrow was painted on the wall. It served as a decorative amulet symbolizing the constant vigilance of the Jews. The inscription by the Star of David offered the counterpoint: a blessing and prayer for peace. Thus the fear of war and the hope for peace were enshrined side by side on the synagogue's walls. After all, when Jews congregated in the synagogue, they offered each other support and prayed for deliverance. What is odd, though, is that the arrow is apparently an Austrian arrow, since the inscription speaks of the hopeful destruction of such weapons. It seems incongruous to place a symbol of the enemy's strength on the wall. Evidently the terror on Jewish Street was so endemic that this arrow was in everybody's waking thoughts, so much so that it even entered synagogue decorations. The threat of annihilation was always with them. Interestingly, the painted arrow is not broken, as the inscription describes. Nonetheless, the meaning is clear: The Austrians will lose with their weapons; we Jews will persevere.

The final siege of Buda in 1686 put these hopes to the test, with dismal results. The massacre that ensued (*see page 421*) showed just how real was the Jewish fear of Austrian rule. The arrow on the wall was much more than decoration.

Nearby the Small Synagogue

Just inside the entrance to 26 Tancsics Mihaly Street you'll find a group of tombstones behind a gate. This was not a cemetery. Jewish cemeteries in medieval Buda were situated below the castle hill, in the districts of Krisztinavaros and Vizivaros. After the Austrians reconquered Buda, the cemeteries were destroyed; many tombstones were carted off and used in building materials. Toward the end of the nineteenth century, several tombstones were discovered during building projects in the area of the castle hill. The oldest was discovered in Krisztinavaros in 1894; it dates from 1278. Oddly enough, more tombstones were discovered after bombing in the Second World War. Sometimes the tombstones were discovered as parts of later buildings, indicating that they had been used as building materials.

Today, for lack of a medieval Jewish cemetery, many of the tombstones are placed in the court of the Small Synagogue. The displayed stones date from the thirteenth to seventeenth centuries, encompassing the full range of the erstwhile Jewish Community of Buda. The bodies themselves were never exhumed or even located. For this reason, the tombstones here are simply an exhibit—albeit a priceless exhibit—but not a graveyard.

Tancsics Mihaly 26 also contains some remnants of the pillars of the Great Synagogue (*see below, The Great Synagogue*), brought here during excavations in the 1960s.

THE GREAT SYNAGOGUE

Address: 23 Tancsics Mihaly Street

> The synagogue is buried underground, completely inaccessible today. At the back of the courtyard of 23 Tancsics Mihaly utca, there are stairs running up a mound, underneath which the Great Synagogue lies in hibernating slumber. The courtyard is also accessible from the entrance at #21. If both doorways are locked, walk around the building to the other side. The gate offers a view of the mound.

Prague has its Altneuschul; Cracow has its Altschul. At Tancsics Mihaly 23, Budapest is one excavation away from joining these giants of medieval Jewish history with its priceless Great Synagogue.

Unfortunately, the synagogue is hidden from the naked eye. For over three hundred years, it has been buried four meters underground. Today we know it's there, but until enough money and interest come to the fore, the building will remain submerged beneath our feet. Nevertheless, a trip to Jewish Budapest would be incomplete without a discussion of this building. For one thing, it was the main house of prayer for the Jews from the mid-fifteenth century until the end of the seventeenth century. What's more, the synagogue placed Buda's medieval Jewish Community in the geographic continuum of European Jewish life: some of the most important Jewish communities on the continent built similar synagogues as expressions of their prosperity. Finally, the synagogue witnessed the destruction of Buda's Jewish Community when Turkish rule was overthrown in 1686. As such, the Great Synagogue is an invaluable piece in the mosaic of Budapest Jewish life.

The synagogue is yet another example of that uniquely Jewish spin on Gothic architecture, the twin-naved synagogue. Such synagogues were built in Worms, Regensberg, Prague, and Cracow; Prague's Altneuschul is today the oldest functioning synagogue of this type (*see page 64*). There were two reasons for building synagogues with only two naves as opposed to the traditional three so common in churches. The most oft-quoted reason is that the Jews wanted to avoid the number three, which symbolizes the Christian trinity. But there is a more subtle reason. In a traditional Jewish service, the entire congregation partakes in the liturgy. Because there is no competition for anybody's attention, there is no need to "wow" the congregants. A synagogue, in its pure form, is less theater and more communal prayer. (This is in sharp contrast, of course, to the Dohany Street Synagogue on the other side of the Danube, whose triple-naved interior is perhaps more churchlike than any synagogue in the world.) In its twin-naved design, the Great Synagogue epitomized all that was once token in Judaism: The humility of prayer and the emphasis on Community in all aspects of Jewish life.

In addition, the synagogue reflected the Community's presumably close contacts with its sister communities elsewhere in Europe. There are theories that the twin-naved Altschul in Cracow was built at the behest of Bohemian Jews who had migrated to the city. Likewise, the construction of Buda's Great Synagogue could very well have been instigated by the descendants of Bohemian and other Jews who arrived from the west in the eleventh, thirteenth, and early fifteenth centuries.

The Great Synagogue, referred to in contemporary documents as *the* synagogue of Buda, is proof of the prosperity of the Buda Jewish Community in the Middle Ages. It was also called the "New Synagogue" because it replaced an earlier synagogue that stood on Szent Gyorgy ter before the Jews were expelled from Buda in 1360 (*see page 409*). It rose close to eight meters high, and its interior was a spacious ten meters by twenty-six—which means it was almost twice as long as the Altneuschul of Prague. It was undoubtedly the largest and most active synagogue Buda had yet seen.

Unlike its counterparts in Prague and Cracow, the Great Synagogue of Buda probably had three large pillars instead of two in the main sanctuary. As in the Altneuschul, however, each pillar was octagonally shaped. The pillars supported the Gothic ribwork in each of either six or eight bays. During the 1960s excavations of the synagogue Hebrew inscriptions were found on one of the central pillars. The two letters of the first inscription, *shin* and *alef*, were said to represent numerals corresponding to the Hebrew year 5301. In the secular calendar, that date refers to 1541, or the year the Turks consolidated their control over Buda. It is possible that the Jews, who streamed back into the capital in the years following the Turkish invasion of 1526, were commemorating the year that brought peace to their capital. In the second inscription the date becomes more clear, though the inscription is equally terse: it consists of the word *bat* ("daughter") and the letter *peh*, whose numerical equivalent is eighty. Faced with such laconic inscriptions, historians matched wits to decipher the pillar's secret message. Finally they decided that in the year 1541, the Great Synagogue was "a daughter of 80," i.e., it had been built eighty years earlier, in the year 1461.

Buda, 1461: The city was three years into the reign of Matthias Corvinus, who was to go down in history as the greatest king of Hungary. In the Jewish District as well, a dynasty was being born that would prove more influential than any other family in Hungary. It was around 1460 that Judah Mendel rose to prominence and became leader of the Jewish Community of Buda. Judah had good relations with King Matthius and even greeted him with a Torah scroll at his coronation. It was most likely when he became leader of the Jewish Community that Judah initiated the building of the Great Synagogue in the courtyard of his own home. It lay near the Viennese Gate and adjacent to the Buda city walls, as if seeking to hide within its protection. Fifteen years later, Judah Mendel would lead the Jews to greet King Matthias at his wedding celebration and would soon afterwards manage the affairs of all the Jews of Hungary as the first royally appointed Jewish prefect. Seven generations of Mendels would serve in this vaunted position (see page 412). That the Great Synagogue was built on the Mendel lot most likely at Judah Mendel's own behest shows that it was not only the most venerable synagogue in Buda, but in all of Hungary as well. Nonetheless, the synagogue was built below the level of the ground. As vital a synagogue as it was, it still had to be kept hidden from the street and, according to church regulations, made lower than all the churches of Buda.

It was in the Great Synagogue that the Mendel family kept its prison, in which they held any Jew in Hungary who committed a crime or did not pay taxes. Similar prison cells have been noted in Prague's Altneuschul and in Cracow's Altschul. In the Altneuschul, the prison doubled as a safe deposit box for taxes, valuables, and pledges held against loans. Such was the case here in the Great Synagogue as well. It was logical to place valuables in the well-guarded fortress of the synagogue, but perhaps somebody wasn't thinking when they put them in the same room as the prisoners. In 1521, a Jewish criminal named Pelcz escaped from Mendel's jail—making off with the gold and silver objects that had been stored for safekeeping in the prison cell! Pelcz fled to Bratislava and then Vienna, until King Lajos II himself issued subpoenas for his arrest. It is not known how the matter ended.

The Great Synagogue served as the prayer hall of the Ashkenazic Jews of Buda and was where the chief rabbi of Buda worshipped. As was the case throughout the Diaspora, the rabbi followed certain customs unique to his particular city. For instance, there was a furnishing in the Great Synagogue that could not be found in similar twin-naved synagogues. It was a small podium, raised on two or three steps, that stood against the western wall of the synagogue. Every week, the rabbi ascended the podium to deliver his *d'var Torah*, or commentary on the weekly Torah portion. The entire congregation, which usually faced the *aron hakodesh* on the eastern wall, would turn to the back of the synagogue to face him. Thus the Great Synagogue took one more step in the direction of humility embodied in the twin naves: since the Torah was kept in the *aron hakodesh* on the eastern wall, the rabbi did not want to steal its glory for himself. It was also considered disrespectful to stand with one's back to the *aron hakodesh*. Both ideas express the traditional Jewish concern that people not supplant God's majesty, that spectacle not supplant substance. To impress upon the congregation the vitality of such concepts, the rabbi would march each week to the back of the synagogue, ascend the small podium there, and deliver his *d'var Torah* with as little artifice as possible.

The women's section of the Great Synagogue resembled that of the Altneuschul in Prague. It was connected to the south wall of the main sanctuary and opened up to it through windows. As was the custom in Ashkenazi synagogues, the prayer hall was filled with moveable seats owned by various members of the Community. According to the responsa of Rabbi Chayim ben Shabbetai, chief rabbi of Salonika, women as well as men owned seats in the Great Synagogue of Buda. Regarding this, he recounts an intriguing lawsuit that divided two Jewish women of Buda just after the Austrian siege in 1602. "Rachel" (the names were probably changed to protect their identities) owned a seat in the Great Synagogue, but because of the tribulation of the siege spent all her time trying to make ends meet in her home. As a result, her seat was left empty. "Leah" jumped at the chance to sit in Rachel's choice spot. When other members of the congregation protested, she explained that she intended to buy the seat from Rachel. Meanwhile, the famine in the city became so critical that the Jewish Community was forced to ask its most destitute members to find shelter elsewhere until the famine passed. Rachel was among those who left. When Leah died, she left the seat as an inheritance to her daughter "Dinah." Three years later, long after peace had returned to the city, Rachel returned to Buda. Entering the Great Synagogue, she was mortified to find Dinah sitting in her seat.

A lawsuit was promptly filed.

Although Dinah insisted her mother had bought the seat from Rachel, the rabbi of Buda sided with Rachel and returned the seat to her. In the appeal, Rabbi Chayim confirmed the decision and agreed that the seat was legally Rachel's.

We can see from the decision that a seat in the Great Synagogue was considered a vital symbol of both piety and status in Buda. It should be remembered that this was the most prominent synagogue in all of Hungary and as such its seats were prized possessions. Just as in the Dohany Street Synagogue centuries later, in which the sale of seats paid for the building's construction, one's seat in the synagogue reflected his or her position in society. Even more importantly, the case demonstrates that in this buried building, every pillar, stone, and seat has its own living story.

Another interesting gleaning on the Great Synagogue: It entered halachic lore in a curious case involving a *Cohen*, an archway, and a dead man. In the seventeenth century, a Renaissance archway ran from one side of Jewish Street to the other. Specifically, it connected two of the Mendel houses: one side stood on stone pillars next to what is today Tancsics Mihaly Street 23—connected to the Great Synagogue—and the other side stood on pillars next to Tancsics Mihaly 28. On number 23, the archway began on the left side of the facade, where a plaque is fastened today. (Although the plaque depicts a similar structure, it has nothing to do with the archway. It's a tribute from the City Council given when the building was renovated in 1987.) It is thought that the archway served as the gateway or entrance to the Jewish District. On the top of the archway, a roofed enclosure was built to allow Jews easy access from the houses on one side of the street to the Great Synagogue on the opposite side.

Ephraim Ha'Cohen, the great rabbi of Buda under Turkish rule, was presented with a quandary: If a person dies in the house across the street, is a *Cohen* permitted to attend services? The roots of this apparent non sequitur lay in the archway. A *Cohen* is not permitted to enter a cemetery because, as a member of the priestly tribe, he is on a special spiritual plane that must remain pure until the days of the Messiah, when the *Cohanim* will return to their priestly functions in the rebuilt Jerusalem Temple. Likewise, a *Cohen* must not be present in the same room as a corpse, because such a room has similar *teumah* (literally, impurity) to that of a cemetery. The problem was that the roofed archway connected the synagogue to an ordinary house. If any member of the household should die, then the *teumah* would rise up and enter the archway, cross Jewish Street, and make its way into the Great Synagogue, thus making the house of prayer impure. Instead of joining both sides of Jewish Street into a single union, the archway would serve to exclude a vital segment of the Community from prayer.

Rabbi Ephraim, who was himself a *Cohen*, was undoubtedly disturbed by the possibility that *Cohanim* would be forbidden from communal prayer. Concurring with an earlier opinion, he decided that if the roof of the archway was removed, the passageway would no longer resemble a house; consequently it would not be able to contain and transmit *teumah*. The roof was removed, *Cohanim* once again attended services, and peace was restored to Jewish Street. The only drawback was that during rainstorms congregants crossing the bridge to the synagogue might get a little wet.

The Churban of 1686

The end of the Great Synagogue spelled the end of the Jewish Community of Buda as well. Just as Prague's Altneuschul witnessed the Easter pogrom and Cracow's Altschul witnessed the Simchat Torah pogrom, the Great Synagogue of Buda was the scene of yet another carnage wreaked against the Jews. Indeed, it is hard to find a twin-naved synagogue that does not have its own account of horror.

Earlier assaults had damaged the synagogue—sieges in 1530 and 1541 had partly destroyed its Gothic arches, which were afterwards covered by a wooden ceiling—but the greatest damage occurred when the Austrians reconquered Buda. On September 2, 1686, the Austrian army, which had laid siege to Buda for ten weeks, broke through the castle defenses. What happened next we cannot call a "pogrom," because the Jews had allied their destiny with the Turks, and had even fought alongside them on more than one occasion (*see pages 415–416—Small Synagogue*). As a result, the Austrian forces did not distinguish between Turks and Jews during battle. Nonetheless, the zealotry with which they ravaged the Jewish District went beyond the norms of battle. As the soldiers neared Jewish Street, around one hundred Jewish men, women, and children fled to the Great Synagogue for protection. The synagogue, with its thick walls and lowered foundation, was considered the safest spot on the street. The strategy worked at first, but then the soldiers brought in a cannon and demolished much of the building. The roof and parts of the walls—six tons of stone—collapsed and buried people underneath. Then the soldiers charged in: Hungarian Hussars with their bent swords and Brandenburgian soldiers equipped with guns slaughtered a total of seventy-two people hiding in the synagogue. Meanwhile, the soldiers tore into the *genizah*. A *genizah* is a special chamber in which aged holy books that are no longer readable are stored until they are buried in the cemetery. Many of these books were destroyed as well, but the most precious among them were carted off as booty by leading soldiers. Some of these can still be found in libraries throughout Europe.

What happened next was truly bizarre. Either the soldiers or the surviving Jews loaded up the now empty *genizah* with the dead bodies of the Jewish martyrs. They probably planned to bury them the next day, but after nightfall the soldiers went on a drunken binge of looting and vandalizing. A huge fire consumed much of the city, including the Great Synagogue and the bodies stored inside.

The scene was not without its perverse poetry: the books from a *genizah* are often buried in the same grave as a rabbi or scholar. This emphasizes the holiness of Jewish thought as well as honors the individual who merits burial in this way. In the *genizah* of the Great Synagogue, the reverse happened. Jews were buried in the place for books and manuscripts. Although Judaism forbids cremation, it is hard not to imagine that in the conflagration that followed, the Jews and their books were united again.

Meanwhile, word of the siege of Buda had spread to Jewish communities throughout the Austrian empire. Because the rescuing of Jewish hostages is considered a holy act of utmost importance, a massive effort was launched to ransom the Jews of Buda. With this as his mission, a young Jew from Prague, Sender Tausk, arrived the next morning determined to save whatever he could of Buda's Jewish Community. He had secured the assistance of Samuel Oppenheimer, the great Jewish leader and banker in Austria, and was prepared to ransom the Jews. Accompanied by soldiers and a drummer, Tausk declared at every city gate that no Jews should be killed. Then he found the burning remains of the Great Synagogue. Hoisting the Austrian flag over the ruins, he announced that all those able to recite the *Shema* prayer should gather at once. Many Jews who had escaped the previous day's carnage emerged; by nightfall there were 274 Jews assembled, along with thirty-five Torah scrolls that had been hidden from the marauders. The Austrians later agreed on a ransom of twenty-one thousand florins for these Jews. After spending thirty-nine weeks in debtors' prison, Tausk visited Cracow, Metz, Frankfurt, Amsterdam, Cleve, and other cities until he raised the required amount. Meanwhile the rescued Jews settled in various parts of the world, but largely in Mikulov (Nikolsberg), the center of Moravian Jewry.

This marked the end, for the moment at least, of the Jewish Community of Buda. It had been one of the most fruitful periods in Budapest's Jewish history and the only period in Jewish history in which Ashkenazi Jews lived under Muslim rule.

⁂

As for the Great Synagogue itself, it remained burnt out and destroyed; the ruins were never cleared away. Soil and debris were piled over the site when the road lining the castle wall was raised, and the Great Synagogue wound up four full meters underground. A flat was built over it and the twin-naved structure with its broken pillars, charred floor, and blood-stained walls was completely forgotten.

It was only in excavations of 1964–65 that the synagogue was rediscovered. It was found exactly as it had appeared after being ravaged in the battle of 1686. In the ruins of the synagogue, littered with cannonballs and shrapnel, archaeologists found the charred bones of the martyrs who had been placed in the *genizah*. Among these was the skeleton of a man holding a *tallis*. The bones were placed next to the Holocaust Memorial in the Kozma Street Cemetery in 1968 (*see page 471*).

Regrettably, funding for the excavation ran out in 1966, just as archaeologists were nearing the end of their work. One problem was that the women's section of the synagogue was underneath an existing building and it was nearly impossible to fully excavate it without tearing the new building down. What is difficult to explain is why, after the excavations had halted in 1968, the city authorities permitted an additional home to be built over part of the site.

Aside from the teasing mound of earth, visitors can also view some salvaged remnants of pillars that were moved to the Small Synagogue across the street. Meanwhile, the Great Synagogue continues to live below ground. It will cost a huge sum of money to excavate it and it is difficult to imagine where such a donation could come from. The Budapest Jewish Community has too many concerns among its living members to justify such a spree and there are enough above-ground synagogues, in various states of neglect, that are literally dying for cash. If any money comes, it will have to be from abroad—unless, of course, the government steps in. As a Gothic relic from one of the most vital communities to live in the old Castle District, the site begs preservation by the state. In the 1990s, archaeological researchers embarked on castle-wide excavations, but it is unclear if their work will stretch all the way to the Great Synagogue. Again, the costs will be enormous. The Great Synagogue, an important piece of Hungarian Jewish history, will likely remain underground for the indefinite future.

Megillat Buda

Much of our knowledge about the destruction of the Great Synagogue of Buda comes from eyewitness Isaac Schulhof (1650–1733), a son-in-law of the Great Synagogue's eminent rabbi, Ephraim Ha'Cohen. Schulhof witnessed his own wife killed in the slaughter; his son was later killed in prison. Schulhof penned the rivetting *Megillat Buda*, a Hebrew memoir of the 1686 siege of Buda and the carnage in the Jewish District. He also wrote two books of poetry lamenting the siege. In this respect, Isaac Schulhof was similar to Avigdor Kara of Prague, who wrote a moving elegy after the Easter Pogrom of 1389 (*see page 78*). Both bloodbaths took place in the main synagogues of their cities; both men witnessed their loved ones murdered; both men went on to record the terrible events for posterity.

In fact, the connection doesn't end there. Schulhof himself was born and died in Prague; his gravestone is in the Old Jewish Cemetery of that city. He moved to Buda in 1666, when at the age of sixteen he married Esther, the daughter of Rabbi Ephraim Ha'Cohen. He became a Talmud teacher, instructing thirty men in *yeshivah*, as well as a leader of the Buda Jewish Community. After the carnage of 1686, Schulhof was taken hostage until he was finally rescued by a mysterious, unnamed "Lady." One of the most resilient personalities of the seventeenth century, Schulhof eventually made his way back to Prague, remarried, and raised a new family. However, another tragedy was lurking: the "flood of fire" that swept through Prague in 1689 (*see page 13*) destroyed his new home and belongings. Nevertheless, Schulhof pushed on, living to the ripe age of eighty-three.

Megillat Buda is an account not only of the siege of Buda and the murders in the Great Synagogue, but of Schulhof's own tribulations as a hostage immediately after Buda was conquered. Schulhof escaped death countless times during his travails, partly due to his shrewdness and partly, as he explains it, due to Divine intervention. His glimpse into the end of the Great Synagogue of Buda offers the visitor an unparalleled view of a site whose interior can only be imagined today. In addition, *Megillat Buda* is a memorial to the gravest tragedy that befell the Jews of Budapest until the Holocaust.

From *Megillat Buda*:

> I spent the entire day in the synagogue, from morning till nightfall, with my dear son Shimshon. I stood and prayed and served the Almighty. I was not aware of anything until many people fled into the synagogue to escape the guns. Everyone screamed, "Woe upon us! Our enemies have entered the town and ravaged the streets and squares! They broke into our houses! We are lost, we are all lost!" I didn't believe them, and I said, "But I never heard the horns sounded, as they always do when there is a siege." But I had hardly finished speaking when the entire crowd fled in from every corner of the Community. Men, women, and children, pushing and breathless, trying to flee from the guns. Everyone screamed and cried desperately. The cry of "Help" reached the Heavens. No one had heard such pain that we experienced. I stood up, I held my *tallis* and my prayer book, *The Gates of Zion*, and called my beloved wife and my only son, let his memory be blessed. . . . I took my wife and my son to the pulpit. As I gathered them in this great confusion, many musketeers broke in, holding their guns and their swords, and also Hungarian Hussars holding their bent swords, and slaughtered people in the house of God. They shed the innocent blood of the sons of Israel. As they say, Woe to our ears and woe to our eyes: one person kills, the next one pillages, the next one crushes the innocent. The cries that were sounded in the house of the Almighty were the sounds of a bitter day. One cannot even speak of such cries. I heard the sounds of suffering, weakness, and violence. O, let it never happen again. In the midst of this, the soldiers noticed me on the pulpit. Three musketeers rushed over and started to hit my back with their guns. I collapsed before them and begged them in tears, "Please, sirs, do not hurt me, since I am from a region of the Emperor . . ." . . . I continued to try to convince them, and ask for their forgiveness, when one of them faced me and shouted at me, "Give me your money and shut up!". . . He took hold of my clothes and started to leave the synagogue with us, to the court of the prayer house, where there were several other Jews who had everything taken from them. I was standing alone when Hussars attacked me and tried to kill me. I cried to my saviors, and they came to rescue me. When they were done with all the looting, they stepped to me and said, "Show me your house and all your possessions!" To this I answered, "Come with me!" From the court, we went out to the street. It was filled with people who had been slain, both the circumcised and the uncircumcised. As we proceeded, there was a great clash in front, where the Turks and the soldiers of the Emperor, may his glory rise, attacked one another. In this great confusion, the musketeers disappeared from my side. I managed to escape with my son, Shimshon, who clasped onto my coat. But my poor wife disappeared, she was carried by the waves of the crowd. And from that

hour, I did not know what had happened to her, but it is probable that she was killed. Shimshon and I, may his memory be blessed, ran home. But a soldier of the Emperor stood there with his sword unsheathed, took hold of my son and said, "This lad is mine!" I reached out for my son and dragged him back to me and pleaded with the soldier to let him go and I would give him a large ransom in exchange. But he swished his sword across and I had to jump backwards and fell through the open doors of a house, straight into the cellar. I was not aware of myself, whether I was alive or dead . . .

(Izsak Schulhof, *Budai Kronika*)

Obuda:
Count Zichy's Jews in the Eighteenth Century

The second area of Jewish settlement in today's Budapest became open to Jews a few decades after they were trounced out of Buda in 1686. With the end of Turkish rule in Hungary, the free royal cities did everything possible to forbid Jewish settlement. Not only was the Church experiencing a Renaissance of anti-Semitism with the rein of the Jesuits, but the city burghers and guilds refused to tolerate Jewish competition in commerce. Excluded from most cities, Hungarian Jews found themselves increasingly dependent upon the grace of the great magnates, who welcomed Jews to their estates for the commercial and tax revenues the Jews were sure to bring.

Such was the case with the baronial family of Zichy de Vasonykeo. Starting in the second decade of the eighteenth century, the Count Zichy family welcomed Jews to its domain of Obuda. In return, the Jewish Community paid annual taxes that started at 160 florins and eventually reached 1,800 florins, supplemented by annual gifts during the holidays. In 1727 there were twenty-two Jewish families in Obuda. The number rose in 1735 to forty-three families; by 1785 there were 285 families in the Count Zichy domain.

Life couldn't be better in Obuda. Fully aware of the prosperity the Jews brought, the Count Zichy family rolled out the red carpet of entitlement and privilege. First and foremost, the Jews were given freedom to practice their religion. Jewish judges were given sovereignty over Jewish disputes. Even in cases involving a Jew and a Christian, the Jewish court decided. Jews were given the unheard-of right to buy and sell grounds in Obuda, as long as they received prior permission in each case. They could make and sell beer, brandy, and kosher wine. In addition, they were permitted to bring their cattle to pasture on public lands. These rights, which were updated every six or ten years, provided the most favorable environment for Jewish settlement in all of Hungary. As a result, Obuda was the fastest growing Jewish Community in Hungary in the eighteenth century. The other major factor contributing to Obuda's rise was the prohibition of Jewish settlement in Pest. The only chance a Jew had to enter Pest was as a temporary resident; as a result, Obuda filled up with Jews waiting for their Pest temporary residency applications to be processed. Situated as it was on the river, the Jewish district of Obuda was teeming with Jews gazing longingly across the Danube at the tempting, forbidden city of Pest. By the end of the century, Obuda's Jewish Community had become the most populous in the country.

Owing to the tolerance of the Zichys, the Jewish Community of Obuda quickly became a fully autonomous body. It established its first synagogue and its cemetery in 1737.

The Zichy family sanctioned the erection of special posts and gates for the *eruv*, or the specially defined area within which Jews might carry items on Shabbat. The Jews were even given partial authority in such mundane municipal matters as planning out the streets of Obuda. Inside this riverside district, several Jewish institutions sprouted up. The Obuda *Chevrah Kaddishah*, or Jewish burial society, was founded no later than 1770. Over the course of the years, several private synagogues sprang up in Obuda. There was even a private commercial school. In 1780, twenty-four-year-old Joseph Manes Osterreicher, the first Jewish doctor to earn his M.D. in Hungary, was a pivotal figure in establishing a Jewish hospital in Obuda. The Obuda Jewish Community founded its own orphanage as well as a society for visiting the sick and a society that distributed bread to the poor and supported widows and children. In 1784, one year after Josef II's Systematic Regulation of the Jewish Nation called for the establishment of Jewish secular schools, Obuda opened the first such school in all of Hungary. This was quite a progressive move, and it was met by the expected outrage of religious Jews who feared secular studies would destroy Jewish observance. The opening of the school was surrounded by such acrimony that an order was declared in all the synagogues that nobody was permitted near the doors or windows of the school while classes were in session. Violators would be flogged. Eventually, though, the school became so large that Josef II himself granted the Jews an expansion in the adjoining house.

The autonomy of the Jewish Community of Obuda was best illustrated by its twenty-four-member council headed by a judge. Interesting facts surviving from this council include its ban on smoking during its twice-weekly meetings, the withholding of council members' salaries for lateness, and arrest for unexcused absence from three sessions. The judge, by far the most powerful man in the Jewish Community, walked through the streets of Obuda carrying a staff with a giant silver handle.

The most famous rabbi to serve in Obuda was Moses ben Isaac Halevi Muenz (c. 1750–1831), who served four decades in the district, from 1790 until his death. Called "a miracle of our times" by the venerable Rabbi Ezekial Landau of Prague, Rabbi Muenz was the most widely respected rabbi of the entire region, becoming chief rabbi and Jewish judge for the area of Pest in 1793. Although he was a fierce defender of traditional Judaism during the birth pangs of the Reform movement, Rabbi Muenz wrote a favorable introduction in 1803 to a book penned by Hungary's leading proponent of Reform, Rabbi Aaron Chorin of Arad. The book caused such a scandal in the Orthodox world that two years later, Rabbi Muenz was obliged to summon Rabbi Chorin to a *beit din*, or religious court, in Obuda. Rabbi Chorin arrived, but Rabbi Muenz was so embarrassed about his role that he didn't show up to the second day of hearings and refused to condemn his colleague. Meanwhile the remainder of the court ordered Rabbi Chorin to rescind his opinions or be punished by having his beard cut. The decision was cancelled by the government in 1806. This episode entered the annals of Jewish history as a landmark case in the battle over Judaism in the nineteenth century. In spite of his awkward involvement in the case, Rabbi Muenz was known as a talmudic authority to reckon with in Jewish communities throughout the Hapsburg monarchy. At Rabbi Muenz's behest Obuda's grandly neoclassical synagogue was built on the site of an earlier synagogue in 1821.

In the second half of the eighteenth century, Obuda had become a dam of wealthy Jewish entrepreneurs eager to sail into the bustling markets across the Danube. The dam burst in 1783, when Josef II issued his Regulation that decreed, among other things, that cities such as Pest could no longer forbid the settlement of Jews. All at once, Obuda's wealthiest Jews left for Pest and the prominence of Obuda fell into a slow but steady decline. Nonetheless, the Obuda Jewish Community charted an energetic course straight through the first half of the nineteenth century. Swelling with revolutionary fervor in 1848, the Community donated its silver Torah vestments to the national cause. The victorious Austrian army then exacted a fine that almost broke the Community. Only in 1889 did Franz Joseph forgive the Jews the balance of the payment.

THE OBUDA SYNAGOGUE

Address: 163 Lajos Street

The Obuda Synagogue is located at the northern end of Lajos Street. The clearest landmark is the Hotel Aquincum, which stands right next to the Obuda Synagogue on the riverfront. An easy way to get there is to take the HEV railway, which runs along the Buda riverfront, to the Arpad Hid station.

The Obuda Synagogue is today used as a television studio. As such, its interior is off-limits to visitors. The exterior, however, has no opening and closing hours. Feel free to visit even at night.

Obuda's famed Chief Rabbi Moses Muenz was instrumental in the construction of a new synagogue for the Community in 1821–22. This majestic neoclassical building, practically the only edifice that remains from the hyperkinetic Jewish communal authority in Obuda, is worth the trip down the Danube. Besides, there are so many Christian- and Islamic-influenced synagogues in Pest that it seems only fair to include a synagogue styled after a Greek Temple. It should be mentioned that since 1980 the building has been used by Hungarian Television as one of its studios. The television station restored the exterior of the synagogue, but the interior was totally reworked into a studio and offices. For this reason, there is very little to see on the interior today and the television station does not permit unauthorized visitors inside.

The synagogue is situated in what was once the heart of Jewish Obuda. Much of the site of the synagogue was originally a square, called "Jewish Square," from the early eighteenth century. The Jewish Community built a synagogue here in 1733. In 1737, Countess Susannah Zichy, one of the great benefactors of Obuda's Jews, permitted the Jewish Community to purchase the land itself. In selling the Jews this property as well as new land for a cemetery, the countess promised "to defend the Jewish congregation in the possession of this land against every one, native or foreign." Such a declaration was an oasis of relief in the eighteenth century, and Jews quickly filed into Obuda to put her words to the test. In 1760, the synagogue possessed over thirteen Torah scrolls. A new synagogue was built in 1769 on the plans of the famous Hungarian architect Matyas Nepauer. Unfortunately, its close proximity to the river led to the building's slow but irretrievable descent into the earth.

These were by no means the first synagogues in Obuda; private prayer halls had existed in the domain for decades. The synagogue on Jewish Square was commonly recognized as the Community synagogue, however.

After parts of the building were demolished in 1817, the Community decided to build a new synagogue that would preserve segments of the original. The Community almost chose the design of the renowned architect Mihaly Pollack (who built the Hungarian National Museum), but ultimately favored Andras Landherr's more cost-efficient and stable plans. The grand, neoclassical synagogue was erected from 1820–1821 and cost roughly 130,000 florins. When it was opened, there were 364 numbered seats in the main sanctuary and 298 numbered seats in the women's sections. The Hebrew inscription adorning the facade reads, ". . . any prayer or supplication offered by any person . . . when he spreads his palms toward this House . . ." (I Kings 8:38). The passage seems out of context, but gains stature when placed in its original milieu: "In any plague and in any disease, in any prayer or supplication offered by any person among all Your people Israel—each of whom knows his own affliction—when he spreads his palms toward this House, oh, hear in Your heavenly abode, and pardon and take action! Render to each man according to his ways as You know his heart to be . . ." (Kings 8:37–39). These were the exact words King Solomon used when he inaugurated the First Temple in Jerusalem. Such lofty imagery was not lost on Rabbi Muenz when he opened the synagogue on July 20, 1821, showing that Reform Jews were by no means unique when they fashioned their imagery of worship after the Old Temple (*see page 451*).

The classicism of the synagogue, best seen in its portico with six Corinthian columns, is offset by its decided lack of symmetry: the northern side has a staircase annex (the northern and western sides once contained a women's section) and the side windows are not uniform. Renovations in 1900 replaced the original tympanum, which consisted of two large leaves flanking a clock, with a new clock in a Secessionist design (the clock has since disappeared). It was at this time, too, that the Two Tablets were balanced on top of the synagogue. The Ten Commandments are faint but, with a little exertion, legible; reading numbers Five and Ten requires you to take a few steps back. Originally, fourteen extravagant menorahs stood near the entrance to the synagogue. An intriguing aspect of the exterior is that this stately, exalted building has a surprisingly lean number of steps. For an American accustomed to the endless stairway of the Lincoln Memorial, the Obuda Synagogue seems to be planted, like a ready-made model, right into the ground.

When the interior was still identifiable as a house of worship, its most awe-inspiring feature was its centrally located *bimah*. Four towering obelisks flanked the *bimah*, shooting up like giant nails toward the ceiling. Designed in the Empire style, each obelisk was decorated with musical instruments (a reference, perhaps, to the Levite orchestra in the Old Temple) and topped by perched eagles. By the middle of the nineteenth century, the Reform movement had penetrated the synagogue in the form of sermons delivered from the *bimah* in German one week and Hungarian the next. From the turn of the twentieth century, the walls were painted with Secessionist designs.

The area around the synagogue was always the core of the Jewish quarter. The Jews planned their own streets in Obuda, and saved the choicest piece of riverfront for the Jewish Square. It was here that the main offices of the Jewish Community were located. The

Jewish prison (since destroyed) was located in the yard of the synagogue. As was the case since medieval times, the Jews kept their prison either near or inside the synagogue, as this was considered the most secure part of the quarter. It was a mark of Jewish communal autonomy in Obuda that the Count Zichy family granted the Jews judicial authority in their own disputes.

The synagogue in Obuda experienced a tragicomic dose of slapstick during the era of intense Jewish patriotism in the nineteenth and twentieth centuries. In the Revolution of 1848, Obuda's Jews were so determined to show their loyalty to the cause that they marched out with most of the synagogue's silver Torah vestments, donating them to the Hungarian government to be pressed into silver currency. Similar donations were given from Jewish congregations throughout Hungary. After the revolution failed, Obuda's Jews were forced to pay the Austrians a fine of twenty thousand florins, plus fifty horses and thousands of uniforms for the army. Their magnanimity with synagogue vestments thus almost bankrupted them. The situation eerily repeated itself during the First World War, when emissaries from the state arrived in Obuda, climbed to the top of the synagogue, and removed all the copper from the roof to use in the war effort.

Pest:
The Jew in the Modern World

From the beginning of the nineteenth century until today, Pest has been the site of one of the most flourishing Jewish communities in Central European history. In everything from commerce to music, from medicine to literature, Pest exemplified the incredible achievements of which the Jews were capable once they were freed from anti-Semitic restrictions. Pest so outshone its twin neighbors of Buda and Obuda that modern Jewish history in Budapest is often told only on the left bank of the Danube.

Of course, it wasn't so simple. Jewish life in Pest did not begin in the nineteenth century. In the sixteenth century, Jews were active in the candle industry, money exchange, market rental, and Turkish revenue offices of Pest. Likewise, Jewish life in Buda and Obuda continued long after their respective golden ages had dwindled. Some of the most radical Reform innovations in the Jewish service occurred not in Pest but in a small *minyan* that met weekly in Buda. In general terms, though, Jewish life in Pest was relatively sporadic until the end of the eighteenth century, after which Pest became the defining Jewish section in the mosaic of Budapest.

In 1686 the comparatively small Jewish presence in Pest was forced to become negligible. In that year, the Austrians gained control of most of Hungary and forbade Jewish settlement in any of the free royal cities of Hungary (there were a total of eight). The guilds in the city, nervous about Jewish trade competition, lobbied to keep Jews out. Eventually, Jews were permitted to partake in the national market days held four times a year. The city levied huge taxes on these Jews, who stayed in the outskirts of the city and even opened makeshift kosher kitchens for the duration of the market days. Even then, they were not permitted into the city itself, and had to sell beyond the city walls. As soon as the market was over, the Jews had to return to their homes in nearby Obuda or Aszod.

Until 1783, the only opportunity for Jews to settle in Pest beyond the duration of the markets was as temporary residents. Such a resident was permitted to live in Pest only for a limited amount of time, buying tickets for each day, week, or month he spent in the city. Extended stays were thus infeasible except for the most wealthy applicants. Even the first rabbi of Pest, Israel Wahrmann, was officially registered as a migrant. Temporary residents were forbidden from owning land or property in the city. Even with these restrictions, the temporary residency waiting list was immense. Everybody, it seemed, wanted a piece of the booming economy of Pest. The City Council accepted few applicants in order to keep the Jewish presence—and thus Jewish trade competition—to a minimum. In 1773,

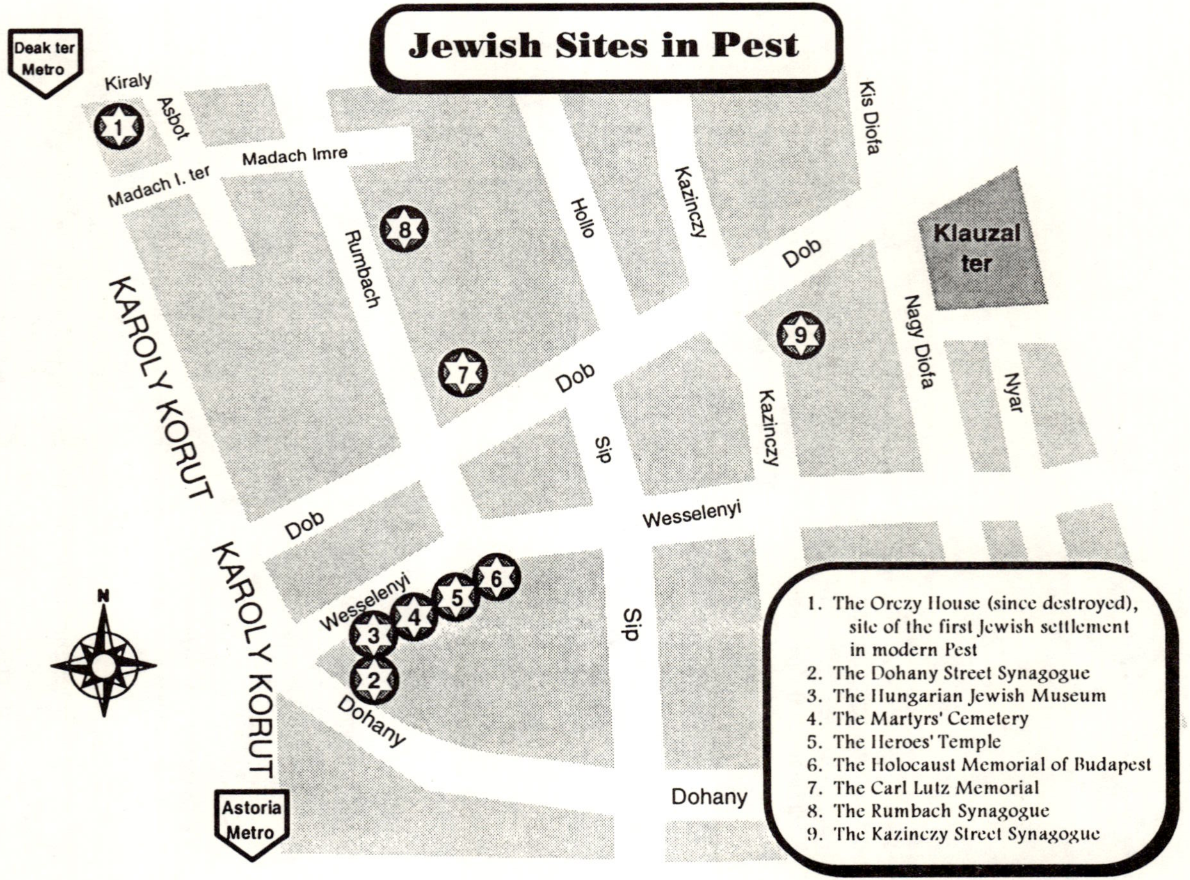

Jewish Sites in Pest

1. The Orczy House (since destroyed), site of the first Jewish settlement in modern Pest
2. The Dohany Street Synagogue
3. The Hungarian Jewish Museum
4. The Martyrs' Cemetery
5. The Heroes' Temple
6. The Holocaust Memorial of Budapest
7. The Carl Lutz Memorial
8. The Rumbach Synagogue
9. The Kazinczy Street Synagogue

the council officially stated that there were no Jews in Pest. In fact, fourteen Jewish families were registered in the city as temporary residents. The difficulty of entering Pest partly explains the flourishing Jewish Community of Obuda in the eighteenth century. Many Jews resided in Obuda while waiting for their Pest applications to be accepted. Once the contract was issued, they'd move to Pest.

Then came Josef II and his drive to modernize the empire. In his *Systematica Gentis Judaicae Regulatio* ("Systematic Regulation of the Jewish Nation"), the 1783 patent giving the Jews limited rights, it was prohibited that the free royal cities continue forbidding entrance to the Jewish people. The City Council of Pest was forced to open its city gate to "tolerated" Jews. Already in 1783, a kosher restaurant was opened in Pest. Undaunted, the council continued to erect barriers to Jewish immigration. Jews still had to apply for permission to settle and whenever it could find a reason the City Council declared Jews to be unfit for settlement. It established financial prerequisites by which only the wealthiest individuals could gain entry; the rest were summarily denied. The City Council even sought to put the Jews in a separate, ghetto-like district. That plan faltered, and in 1786 the council acquiesced to permit Jews both to settle and to rent property in the city. In 1788, the first Pest *Chevrah Kaddishah*, or Jewish Burial Society, was founded. A cemetery was established and used for a couple of decades; it stood in the area of what is now Nyugati Station, by Ferdinand Bridge.

Despite the obdurate xenophobia of the City Council, by the end of the eighteenth century there were some one thousand Jews living in Pest. They came largely from the overflowing pool of Obuda Jews eager to cross the Danube, but also from other cities in Hungary. There were even Bohemian and Moravian Jews who came to Pest after hearing of the burgeoning economy. The settlers opened two *shuls* in the 1770s and 1780s in the Terezvaros district of Pest, but the City Council shut both of them down, reasoning that fewer synagogues in Pest meant fewer Jews would come to settle.

The majority of immigrants settled in a single, sprawling building complex (it had three huge courtyards) on the corner of Kiraly Street and today's Karoly Korout, owned by the noble Orczy family. Just like the Zichy family did with its Obuda estate, the Orczy family allowed Jews to rent rooms, shops, storehouses, restaurants, a cafe, a bath, and even synagogues and a matzoh factory inside its capacious building. Referred to alternately as the "port" and the "cradle" of Jewish Pest, the Orczy House, which extended from the corner up to what is today Madach Square, soon became the unrivaled nucleus of Jewish life in the newly open city. It was even referred to as *Judenhof*, or "Jewish Yard." By the 1830s, 284 Jews lived in close to fifty flats in the Orczy House. Snobs whispered that the Orczys had tainted their noble blood with the teeming presence of Jews. In a single building, there was all the hustle and bustle one associates with the Lower East Side of New York at the turn of the century. It was part immigrant absorption center, part financial center, part religious center, and part social gathering place. In other words, it was a classic Jewish urban utopia. In 1796, with the grudging approval of the City Council, the first synagogue was built in the Orczy House, and in 1814 the first Jewish public school in Pest opened inside the building.

Near the Orczy House was the Jewish market (today a parking lot), which bordered the city market on today's Deak Ferenc Square. Soon enough, the district of Terezvaros became the main population center of Pest's Jews, with its vivid lifeline of Kiraly Street. At the beginning of the nineteenth century, Terezvaros was home to eighty-four percent of the Jews of Pest. In those days, Terezvaros was a suburb of downtown Pest. There were several reasons why Jews settled in Terezvaros as opposed to the city center. First, the City Council, while grudgingly permitting the Jews to settle, was reluctant to issue permits in the heart of the city. By contrast, the nobles who owned tracts of land in Terezvaros were more than willing to rent property to Jews. The second reason is that Jewish industrialists active in the leather, wool, and silk trades couldn't set up shop in the narrow streets of the city center, so they chose the larger land tracts in Terezvaros for their factories and workshops. Finally, Pest was filled with enclaved neighborhoods of Evangelicals, Calvinists, Lutherans, Greeks, and others. The Jews, too, wished to settle together. With the Jewish market and Orczy House situated right at the border of Terezvaros and the downtown area, the suburban territory was the obvious spot for the Jewish Community to blossom. The most famous Jewish factory in those times was the silk factory, established by Istvan and Tamas Valero at the end of the eighteenth century close to Kiraly Street. In the middle of the nineteenth century, the building housed the notoriously radical congregation of Ignaz Einhorn, where Shabbat, the *shofar*, and circumcision were abolished.

In 1830, there were 6,031 Jews living in Pest; by 1857, that number had risen to 23,101. The rise in the Jewish population of Pest coincided directly with the struggle for emancipation of the Jews in Hungary. The struggle brought two remarkable, intertwined traits to the Jewish Community in Pest: Jewish prosperity and Jewish Reform.

In 1840, the final official barriers to Jewish settlement in Pest were knocked down. A law was passed that guaranteed Jews the freedom to live practically anywhere in the country, as well as the right to own property. With a solidification of its urban rights, the Jewish Community of Pest could grow in earnest. It was this law that permitted the Jewish Community to buy the plot of land that became the site of the Dohany Street Synagogue.

THE HUNGARIAN JEWISH CONGRESS AND THE THREE SYNAGOGUES OF PEST

Some visitors find it odd that in the span of only a few blocks, three spacious synagogues were built in the nineteenth and twentieth centuries: the Dohany Street Synagogue, the Rumbach Synagogue, and the Kazinczy Street Synagogue. What's more, each of the synagogues hosted its own distinct group of worshippers who, in the worst of times, had little to do with one another. The segregation of Jewish prayer into three branches was not unique to Budapest. In fact, these synagogues reflect the larger crisis that tore asunder the Hungarian Jewish Community in the nineteenth century.

Three months after the Jews of Hungary were given full emancipation at the end of 1867, the Hungarian minister of education decided to prepare a unique Jewish Congress. The congress would establish a national organization to oversee the affairs of all the Jews of Hungary. He had no idea what he was in for. Hungarian Jewish life had undergone seismic shifts in the first half of the nineteenth century, with a vocal minority of Jews clamoring for increasing religious and social reform. This was seen most clearly in the building of the Neolog Dohany Street Synagogue, opened in 1859. Although the term "Neolog" had not yet been coined, it applied to that uniquely Hungarian brand of progressive Judaism. The Neolog, Magyarizing Jews of Pest had been the impetus for the congress.

From the start, Orthodox Jews throughout Hungary viewed the congressional fervor askance. In their view, the congress would impose centralized Neolog ideology on even the most Orthodox congregations of Hungary. They had good reason to fear: Most of the Jewish advisors preparing the congress were Neologs. However, unlike its weaker counterpart in western Europe, Orthodox Jewry in Hungary gained enormous strength throughout the nineteenth century, with Galician immigrants and famous rabbis buttressing traditional Jewish life. With this strength, Orthodox rabbis fought the calls for congress, forming a conservative political party and even suggesting a separate congress for Orthodox Jews. The minister of education declined, insisting that "the law knows only one Israelite religion."

When the Jewish Congress finally convened, from December 1868 to February 1869, it was composed of 126 Neolog deputies and 94 Orthodox deputies chosen in nationwide Jewish elections. They were at loggerheads from the start. The Neologs insisted that a Jewish Community was that which serves the religious needs of Jews; the Orthodox countered that a Jewish Community must be that which strictly follows the *halachah* and that governs by halachic criteria. The Orthodox were so disenchanted with the statutes of the congress that they proceeded to King Franz Josef in 1869, entreating him not to legalize the congressional resolutions. When the king refused, the Orthodox party went to the House of Representatives and adamantly claimed that there were two Judaisms and that they wanted no part of the Judaism of the congress. The House agreed to suspend the resolutions of the congress, and the Orthodox took the opportunity to establish their own, independent Community. In 1869, the Autonomous Orthodox Jewish Community of Hungary became an official body.

The divorce was unprecedented. At no other time in Jewish history had the entire Orthodox establishment declared itself separate from its fellow Jews. There had been excommunications, for instance against Sabbatians and *hasidim*, but never had there been such a withdrawal of an Orthodox Jewish Community into a separately defined group. The strife between Neolog and Orthodox was so great in nineteenth century Hungary that the entire context of Jewish communal life was thrown to the wind.

Neolog Jews organized along lines that followed the congressional statutes, while Orthodox Jews managed their own Communities. As if matters weren't confusing enough, a third group formed seeking to be a voice of reason in the midst of the acrimony. It was called the Status Quo movement, so named because its members repudiated both the Neolog statutes from the congress as well as the Orthodox separatism afterwards, opting instead to continue as things had been before the split.

> Although the Status Quo Jews followed strict *halachah*, the Orthodox felt betrayed and broke off ties to such a degree that even marriage between the two groups was forbidden.
>
> What do these prickly splinters have to do with Pest? The old joke that a Jew needs two synagogues, one where he worships and one into which he never steps foot, is nowhere better represented than in this city. The three large synagogues in the former Jewish District reflect the crisis in Hungarian Jewish life in microcosm. The Dohany Street Synagogue served the religious needs of Neolog Jews while the Kazinczy Street Synagogue was built as part of the separate communal authority of Hungarian Orthodoxy. The Orthodox even placed a *cherem*, or writ of excommunication, on the Dohany Synagogue itself. Orthodox Jews would cross the street in order to avoid passing the building. Meanwhile, although Status Quo never had an official outlet in Budapest itself, the Rumbach Synagogue became Budapest's Status Quo synagogue, both in its prayers and in its outlook. (The Rumbach is no longer an active synagogue.) The three synagogues in Budapest present the most graphic image of the fissure that has torn at Jewish life from the nineteenth century to this very day.

THE DOHANY STREET SYNAGOGUE

Address: Dohany Street 2
You can't miss this one. It looms at the corner of Dohany Street and Wesselenyi Street.
Opening Hours: Sunday–Friday 10:00 A.M.–3:00 P.M.

The synagogue on Dohany Street (literally, "Tobacco Street") is hailed throughout the world as the crowning achievement of Hungarian Jewry. Jews and Gentiles alike flock to this temple to witness the wondrous strides European Jews made in the nineteenth century. The largest synagogue in Europe and once the largest in the world, the Dohany Street Synagogue is today the looming castle of Jewish Budapest. From September 5, 1854, the day the foundation stone was laid, to September 6, 1859, the day the synagogue was ceremoniously opened, the Jews of Pest underwent a transformation into one of the most dynamic Jewish communities of the Diaspora. Until the Second World War, the Dohany Street Synagogue filled its three-thousand-seat capacity every Shabbat and festival. It was in this synagogue that Theodor Herzl, the father of Zionism, celebrated his *bar mitzvah*. Even today, the synagogue packs a full house during the High Holidays.

Highlights of the Building

The Dohany Street Synagogue is known more for its immensity than for the myriad details and nuances that typify more ancient houses of prayer. Nonetheless, the synagogue has several unique aspects that should be pointed out. Afterwards, we will examine in greater detail the history of the synagogue and its particular style.

Built in the Moorish style, the synagogue's most clearly identifiable signs are its two octagonal, forty-meter towers, immortalized by Ludwig Hatvany-Deutsch in his *Bondy Jr.*: "Then the synagogue loomed before them in the mist like a double-headed dragon, with its red brick and its two towers." In keeping with its Moorish style, the towers can be taken as references to the Muslim minaret. Some scholars point to the prominent clocks and claim that more than anything else the towers were fashioned after a church's bell tower. In this regard, the view holds, the Jews were eager to slice away the differences between themselves and their Christian neighbors. In fact, many Orthodox Jews consider the tower an emblem of a Neolog or Reform synagogue. However, a synagogue tower is really nothing new. In the Middle Ages, many synagogues were equipped with towers to serve as safes for valuables or as prison cells. In any event, the two towers on the Dohany Street Synagogue can be assured of a Jewish spin: They are said to represent the towers built by Hiram for the Temple of King Solomon: "He set up the columns at the portico of the Great Hall; he set up one column on the right and named it Jachin, and he set up the other column on the left and named it Boaz" (I Kings 7:21).

The colored brick facade was also given an Old Temple spin. In his original design proposal, Ludwig von Forster, the architect of the synagogue, thought of ancient Israel when he suggested a facade of molded bricks covering a red stone base: "The construction of walls using different stones and their embellishment with glazed bricks was a common practice in antiquity . . ." (Ludwig Forster, "Promemoria"). In antiquity it might have been commonplace, but in the nineteenth century it was quite unconventional to cover a building's exterior with brickface. The Dohany Street Synagogue, in fact, was the first monumental building in Budapest to use the technique. The bricks were not only avant garde but also economical, substantially lowering the total cost of the building.

The inscription above the doorway reiterates the Old Temple imagery: "And let them make Me a sanctuary that I may dwell among them" (Exodus 25:8). If you look closely, you'll see that twelve of the letters are marked by stars. The numerical sum of these letters indicates the Hebrew year for 1859, when the synagogue was opened.

The other striking aspect of the exterior is the extending wings on the right and left sides. (The arcaded building connected to the left wing was built in the twentieth century.) The wings hold conference rooms and administrative offices of the Jewish Community. Originally, the left wing had three archways, as opposed to the single one it has today. It was originally much longer than the wing on the right side, giving the exterior of the synagogue a deliberately lopsided appearance. This was to compensate for the oblique nature of the lot. You'll see that the right wing still has an oblique edge, parallel to the edge of Dohany Street. When the Jewish Museum building was built next door in the 1920s, the new architects shortened the wing on the left side considerably.

There are two main explanations for the yard formed between the two wings—one legalistic, the other romantic. The first reason is that when the Dohany Synagogue was built, the Hapsburg Empire did not permit synagogue buildings to be built right at the street. The most logical solution was to recess the building, in this case with wings.

The second reason harks back to the Middle Ages, when synagogues were often designed with inner courtyards that served as meeting places for the congregation. By following this tradition, the Dohany Synagogue made the much-needed claim that it was a site of unity for all the Jews of Pest. Regarding this point, the yard might also have been used for weddings. In the nineteenth century, one of the main wedges dividing traditional and progressive Jews was the site of the *chupah*: Orthodox law insists that the wedding canopy be held under the open sky, but progressive Jews wanted the entire ceremony performed inside the synagogue. With a yard as the site for weddings, perhaps the traditional Jews of Pest were mollified for the time being. Still, within a century the *chupah* was moved indoors.

Visitors to the Dohany Street Synagogue are often so taken aback by the immensity and "churchiness" of its interior that they miss one of its most controversial aspects: the construction material. Moorish synagogues reinvented prayer hall design in the 1850s, incorporating such innovations as gas lighting and steam heating. The most fundamental change involved the use of cast-iron foundations, pillars, and balustrades. The Dohany Street Synagogue was the first important building in Hungary to use such innovations. At the time, cast iron in a house of prayer was nothing short of revolutionary. It saved money, modernized the building, and created an atmosphere that at the time was linked to the avant garde aspects of Moorish architecture. As could be expected, such a novel technique caused a stir when it was introduced. Jakab Hirsch Kassowitz, a leading member of the synagogue's building committee, issued a letter as early as 1854—during the review of the architect's initial proposal—expressing his growing alarm over cast iron. Kassowitz was terrified that the designers valued innovation and economy over the safety of the worshippers. "Why has this newfangled building method not been applied at one single important building work in our country, if it is indeed so much cheaper and better?" he demanded. "And furthermore, even if such buildings have been recently erected, is it truly proven that they will indeed remain solid and stable in a hundred years' time?" (J. H. Kassowitz, "Memorandum").

Over a hundred years later the revolutionary cast iron continued to hold out—albeit in an increasingly dilapidated environment—and was still one of the most attractive features of the Dohany Street Synagogue. (Complete renovations in the 1990s reinforced the iron foundations.) You can see the cast iron most clearly in the oak-lined pillars stretching up to the galleries and ceiling. It is difficult to convey the shock these piers elicited in 1859 among people accustomed to thick, stone columns in churches and synagogues. The architect, Ludwig von Forster, claimed that stone pillars would severely hamper the view for the women in the galleries, and that a much larger sanctuary would be necessary as a result. In this view, cast iron can be seen as a material for women's rights! There is no doubt that women in the galleries of the Dohany Street Synagogue are afforded a more unobstructed view of the service. Forster, monomaniacal in his Moorish mission, also pointed out the Eastern exoticism of cast iron: "Nothing harmonizes better with Oriental architecture than cast iron whose very nature permits lightsome and freely flowing forms; and if this iron is decorated with glittering and light gold it will harmonize even better with the entire building" (Ludwig Forster, "Promemeria"). That's an interesting thought, but to the building committee the most appealing aspect of cast iron was its cheap cost. Without such intelligence of economy, the synagogue could never have been built. Other money-savers included the use of bricks, the marble-painted facade, and paper mache decorations.

The Pulpits of Dohany

In ancient synagogues, every brick has a story to tell after witnessing centuries of Jewish worship. Not so the Dohany Street Synagogue, which, in spite of its acknowledged size, is still a tiny infant in the lifespan of Jewish history. But even infants have their stories. Take the case of the two pulpits of Dohany. These pulpits are perhaps the most extreme example of Neolog Judaism appropriating Christian custom and practice. When the rabbi delivered his sermon, he would ascend the pulpit much like a priest ascends the pulpit in a church. But why are there two pulpits? Originally there was only one—on the right-hand side as you face the *aron hakodesh*. The left-hand pulpit is the direct result of a war over wounded egos in the early twentieth century. On one side was Dr. Simon Hevesi (1868–1943) and on the other Dr. Gyula Fischer (1861–1944). Both men were elected joint chief rabbi of the Dohany Street Synagogue in 1905.

This is what happened: In 1926, the Hungarian National Assembly decided to allow both an Orthodox and a Neolog rabbi to be represented in the denominations section of the Upper House of Parliament. The Orthodox position was quickly filled by Rabbi Koppel Reich of Pest's Kazinczy Street Synagogue. But the Neolog seat became a contested issue, divided between Rabbi Hevesi, chief rabbi of the Israelite Congregation of Pest, and Dr. Immanuel Low, chief rabbi of Szeged. Eventually, Rabbi Low was awarded the seat.

When Rabbi Hevesi lost the battle for the Upper House, the Israelite Congregation of Pest gave him the consolation title "leading chief rabbi." Rabbi Fischer was dumbstruck. He had served on the same level as Rabbi Hevesi for two decades—he was even seven years older than Rabbi Hevesi—and now he was being snubbed because of a political issue that had nothing to do with him. The wound grew until eventually the two rabbis were at complete loggerheads. Ultimately, the two rabbis were no longer seen together in synagogue. Rabbi Fischer would officiate one week and Rabbi Hevesi the next. But how could these two men possibly speak from the same podium? It was then that the second pulpit was built on the left-hand side. Even though they came to services on alternate weeks, Rabbi Fischer and Rabbi Hevesi would never touch each other's pulpit. This is how the unique placement of two pulpits arose in the Dohany Street Synagogue.

The Aron Hakodesh

The *aron hakodesh* in the Dohany Street Synagogue is so ornate as to be considered a separate synagogue in itself—which is not far from the truth. Its designer, Frigyes Feszl, had submitted one of the three competing designs for the synagogue, but his plans were rejected in favor of Ludwig von Forster's. Nonetheless, Feszl was commissioned to decorate much of the interior, including the frescos and ceiling, especially after Forster left the project when the exterior was finished. Feszl pounced on the opportunity to execute an *aron hakodesh* that would at least be an image of his original design, which had been partly Byzantine in style. Thus the *aron hakodesh* is like Feszl's temple plan in miniature, down to an identical crown-like dome.

The sheer depth of the *aron hakodesh*, accentuated by the round window to its rear, makes the ark of the Torahs the undisputed master of the synagogue, the focus of attention everywhere from the ground floor to the women's galleries. It vies with Forster's exterior design and demands its due. The tympanum stands on two pillars that, like the towers on the exterior, allude to the great portico of the Old Temple in Jerusalem. In fact, the entire *aron hakodesh* seems less like a receptacle than an entrance. One almost expects the rabbi to open the doors of the *aron* and vanish into another world.

In the tympanum, the four-letter *shem hamefurash*, or Holy Name of God, is written inside a golden sun. This would not have endeared the synagogue to Orthodox Jews in Pest, but there was not much risk of Orthodox Jews ever stepping foot inside the building. Orthodox rabbis had, in fact, placed a *cherem*, or writ of excommunication, on the building itself.

On the carpet lining the stairs to the *aron hakodesh*, there is a Hebrew variation of Psalms 95:6 that is found in the morning *Mah Tovu* prayer: "I shall bow down and kneel, bend the knee before the Lord my maker."

High up on the eastern wall is the Hebrew inscription, "From the rising of the sun until it sets the name of the Lord is praised" (Psalms 113:3). The psalm refers to place as well as time, from the eastern to the western corners of the world. The first word of the inscription, *mimizrach*, means "from the east." A *mizrach* tablet is traditionally placed on the eastern wall of homes, as a constant reminder of Jerusalem and a practical prompt for the direction of daily prayers. In the Dohany Street Synagogue, the entire inscription imitates a *mizrach* tablet, pointing to the eastern wall that is the focus of prayer. This is especially true in a Neolog synagogue, where the *bimah* is situated on the eastern side of the synagogue. The term *mizrach* has even more meaning in the arch of this particular hall. It was, after all, an eastern style of design that inspired the ornamentation and exterior facade of the Dohany Street Synagogue.

The Dohany Organ

The majesty of the *aron hakodesh* is reinforced by the tiara-like organ that rises behind it. The organ in the Dohany Street Synagogue is emblematic of the moderate Reform disposition of the synagogue. Although organs in the nineteenth century were viewed as overwhelmingly Christian additions in synagogues, the Dohany congregation respected Jewish law and forbade Jews from playing the organ on Shabbat. The organist, therefore, was always a Christian.

Originally, the organ was located on the ground floor. It was designed by Professor Wohler Gotthard, a music critic for the *Pester Lloyd* newspaper who later served for almost twenty years as the Dohany's chief organist. Constructed in Thurungia, Germany, the original organ had thirty-eight variations divided between two manuals and the pedals. One manual had fifteen variations and the other eleven, with twelve variations for the pedals. The number of variations was so high that it drew a good deal of attention when the organ was unwrapped in 1859. The immensity of the organ caused problems from the start. When it was played for the first time, the pipes created gusts of wind in the main sanctuary. For years, worshippers had to contend with organal drafts by holding down the pages in their prayer books. Finally, at the end of the 1880s, the pipe bellows were replaced with new ones. Still, the location of the organ continued to cause problems. It was topped by a glass roof that exacerbated its low position by hampering the projection of the sound.

As a result, the organ was completely rebuilt in 1902 at a cost of ten thousand Hungarian crowns. This time it was manufactured in the Hungarian city of Pecs. The glass roof was removed, a third manual with six variations was added, and the pipe system and keyboard were replaced. To help project the sound the organ was raised one story. In 1932, the organ was reconstructed once again, this time in a Pest organ factory. The new organ boasted seventy register pipes, four manuals, 5,030 pipes, and forty-nine bells. It was the largest organ in all of Hungary, incorporating all the latest advances in electro-pneumatic technology. With this organ, the Dohany Street Synagogue was the site of several sublime concerts throughout the 1930s.

During 1990s renovations, the organ was rebuilt in Dresden and equipped with sixty-three registers. Today the organ has been lifted even higher, where it serves as a stunning backdrop to the *aron hakodesh* and enhances the impression of depth on the eastern wall of the synagogue.

THE DOHANY STREET SYNAGOGUE: A LEGEND!

Legendmeisters visiting the Dohany Street Synagogue are due for a head-on collision with despair. There are no angels tiptoeing on the doors as at Prague's Altneuschul, no hidden treasure such as led to the building of Cracow's Isaac Synagogue. Some would say that Budapest's pride and joy is too young for legends to have sewn themselves into its fabric. That is a valid point, but consider also when and by whom it was built. The nineteenth century saw a marked rise in rationalism in mainstream Jewish life. This was all the more true among the Reformniks, many of whom wished to prove to their Christian neighbors that Judaism wasn't the bizarre and sinister occultism European society had branded it for centuries.

But this author was not content. The Dohany Street Synagogue is one of Europe's most emblematic houses of prayer, and as such, he told his friends, there *must* be a legend here somewhere, somehow. Undeterred by naysayers, the author conducted interviews with countless Dohany worshippers past and present, all the while perusing obscure texts in libraries across the world. Finally, after years of squandered leads, wasted bribes, and a frightening case of "the shakes," the author happened upon a faded manuscript tucked behind crumbling newspapers in the Library of Metz. "Eureka!" he cried. The legend had been discovered. Mythmeisters the world over can now breathe a sigh of relief.

It's about the organ. The story goes like this:

Franz Liszt (1811–1886), the world-famous Hungarian pianist, apparently had a soft spot in his heart for the organ in the Dohany Street Synagogue. In September 1865,

> Liszt obtained permission to drum the keys in the synagogue, playing a few religious compositions penned by the Dohany's chief organist. Ever since that day, he was hooked. When the French composer and pianist Camille Saint-Saens (1835–1921) rode into Budapest for a visit, Franz escorted him immediately to Dohany Street. "There is not a better organ in the entire capital!" confided an effervescent Liszt. When Saint-Saens saw the organ, he too was mesmerized. Almost at once, he wanted to play it. But alas, the leaders of the Dohany Street Synagogue had placed a ban on using the organ for anything other than service ritual; matinees were strictly forbidden. Saint-Saens was not to be deterred. He pulled all his sundry music strings, both in Hungary and abroad, until finally, in 1879, the executive committee acquiesced. Saint-Saens could play the organ.
>
> And so it happened. One fine morning in March 1879, Saint-Saens swaggered triumphantly down the main aisle of the synagogue and took his seat behind the organ. The sanctuary was filled with Budapest's finest: Franz Liszt was there, as well as the high statesman Count Albert Apponyi, the famous Jewish journalist Adolf Agai, and scores of dukes, benefactors, musicians, and writers—the cream of the crop in nineteenth century Budapest. All was silent in the sanctuary as Saint-Saens regally began the first notes of Bach's Fuge and Prelude in A Minor . . . and all continued to be silent. Saint-Saens kept pounding the keys, but not a single note, not even a whimper, emerged from the giant pipes. The audience began to whisper; eventually, they left the synagogue, scandalized. Saint-Saens was bewildered. How could this exquisite organ, which had operated so melodically the previous Shabbat, stop working all at once?
>
> The mystery of the organ in 1879 has never been solved, but there are those who insist that a curse was cast upon the organ when it was being prepared for a profane purpose. Could it be that the organ itself refused to utter a sound outside the service of God?
>
> You decide.

Origins of the Dohany Street Synagogue

The history of the Dohany Street Synagogue is not limited to the single year 1859, when the massive building was opened. To understand the historical importance of the synagogue, we must navigate back to the rise of Jewish settlement in Pest and the birth pangs of religious Reform.

The Orczy House

The seeds of the synagogue sprouted, appropriately, in what could be called the fertile crescent of Jewish settlement in Pest, the Orczy House (*see page 433*). In the first half of the nineteenth century, it was in the Orczy House that Jewish life, commerce, and culture flourished. In religious life as well, the Orczy House was where it all began.

In 1796, the City Council of Pest altered decades of intolerance by permitting the Jews to build a prayer room in their main place of residence, the Orczy House. In 1820, the Community had grown sufficiently to build a new synagogue, fittingly called the Large Synagogue, inside the same building. Although many private prayer rooms were to be established along Kiraly Street, this was the main synagogue for the Jews of Pest. It was also the core from which all offshoot congregations, including the Dohany Street Synagogue, would spring.

Chessed Neurim

Ironically, the impasse that brought progressive Judaism to Pest had nothing to do with women's rights, as is often the case in American Reform Judaism, but rather with the rights of *men*—bachelors no less. It was a custom in the Large Synagogue that *aliyot* to the Torah were given only to married men. A group of upstart young gents complained that they, too, wished to be called to the Torah, but their grievances were ignored. Unfazed, they decided to form an independent prayer house. It was in 1825 that they opened their congregation in the "White Goose" house on Kiraly Street. Thus emerged a new player on the Pest Jewish scene: the *Chessed Neurim* society, named for its determined young founders. *Chessed Neurim* was the kernel from which the Dohany Street Synagogue would emerge a quarter century later. It was through *Chessed Neurim* that Reform, which had previously been confined to the central Hungarian city of Arad, made headway into Pest. Its members not only permitted unmarried men to be called to the Torah, but took the further liberty of abridging the service.

Infatuation in Vienna

In 1826, when the *Chessed Neurim*ers heard about the new Reform temple in Vienna, they were enraptured. That same year marked the death of Israel Wahrmann (1755–1826), the rabbi of the Large Synagogue who had been opposed to change in religious ritual. The Chessed Neurimers possibly saw this as an opportunity for further innovation. Almost at once, they sent their new preacher, Joszef Bach, and cantor, Karl Denhof, for a crash course in Viennese Jewish Reform at the court of Rabbi Isaac Noah Mannheimer and the church-infatuated cantor Solomon Sulzer. When he returned, Bach preached in a finely nuanced, literary German. Denhof, for his part, dropped his eastern Ashkenazic delivery for a "polished" Sephardic intonation that was all the rage in western Europe. Services were supplemented by a couple of young boys who served as backup singers.

The Cultus-Temple

The Vienna baptism, so to speak, enabled members of the *Chessed Neurim* to form, in 1827, the so-called Chorus-Temple ("Choir-Temple"), later called the Cultus-Temple. The name was an homage to Vienna, whose Reform congregation used the same name. In Pest, the Cultus-Temple introduced a German-language sermon to the service. In 1832, they began to conduct weddings not under the open sky, as was the Orthodox tradition, but inside the synagogue itself. In addition, they introduced a choir to the service. Although the term "Neolog" was not yet in use, the Cultus-Temple founders would later form the heart of the Neolog Community. Traditional Jews were nonplussed; it seemed more like a church than a synagogue. As the worshippers sat silently in their pews, the choir sang the prayers. Soon the term "silent synagogue" was bandied about. Among the Reformers, it was used as a compliment: they had eliminated what they considered the uncivilized chaos of the Orthodox service. Among the strictly Orthodox, though, it was more like an epithet: the Reformers, in leaving the prayers to the choir, were absconding from their responsibilities as Jews.

It was a mark of the Cultus-Temple's rising popularity that the official Jewish Community of Pest recognized it in 1830 and permitted it to build a second "Community synagogue" in a courtyard of the Orczy House. This was remarkable. Practically side by side in the Orczy House, there now stood two divergent synagogues with two separate prayer rites, both officially serving the Jewish Community of Pest. Even the sizes were not too dissimilar: the Large Synagogue held 585 seats, while the Cultus-Temple held 491. It is even more remarkable that at that point, in 1830, there was no open animosity between the two groups. In a matter of decades, the two congregations, who were to be known as the "Synagogue Party" and the "Temple Party," would be at loggerheads, but in the first half of the nineteenth century, the Jewish Community of Pest was marked by an admirable sense of unity. From 1836, in fact, Chief Rabbi Low Schwab went scuttling from the Cultus-Temple to the Large Synagogue in the course of a single service. In the former he would deliver a modern sermon in German, and in the latter he would give a *derashah* in Yiddish.

It should be mentioned that as soon as it had established its synagogue in the Orczy House, the Cultus-Temple began a truly progressive tradition. At 11:00 A.M. every Shabbat, the Cultus-Temple held a special service exclusively for women, the first congregation in Pest officially to do so. The women's service was not quite what one would find in American Reform synagogues, however. Women were not called to the Torah. In fact, since there was no *minyan* of ten men, the Torah wasn't even read. Needless to say, observant Jews would see nothing wrong with such a service, which had been a custom in traditional communities throughout Jewish history.

In Pest in the first half of the nineteenth century, religious Reform occurred side by side with enormous economic and cultural advances among the Jews. The 1790 law "De Judaeis" permitted Jews to attend universities; the most popular course of study was medicine. In 1840 Jews were permitted to own both land and factories, and as a result a wave of Jewish industrialists emerged in the rapidly developing city of Pest. Enough Jews were active in financial transactions that another law was passed in 1840 that allowed the Shabbat and holidays to be rest days for Jewish businessmen. On the cultural front, the fields of literature, journalism, and art began to open as a new generation of Pest Jews came of age toward the middle of the century. Increased settlement meant that in a period of only five years, from 1852 to 1857, the Jewish population of Pest jumped from twelve thousand to twenty-three thousand.

Success in Hungarian society was much easier when the Jews broke down barriers between themselves and the outside world. In the 1840s, when the Jewish question became an urgent matter in the Hungarian Diet, the government itself linked Jewish emancipation to Jewish Reform. Lajos Kossuth, the great Hungarian statesman and revolutionary, argued as much in 1844: "As long as the Jews cannot eat together with their fellow citizens of other religions a little salt, a piece of bread, cannot drink one wine with them, cannot sit at one table . . . the Jews will not be emancipated *socially*, even if they should be emancipated politically a hundred times" (quoted in Raphael Patai, *The Jews of Hungary*). In the 1843–44 Diet, a delegate from one county emphatically declared, "The Jews should not be emancipated until they chisel off the trappings from the formalities of their religion."

This gave an added impetus to the Reform movement in the Cultus-Temple, as well as in other, more radical Reform movements in Pest. In a deeper sense, many of these Jews reflexively associated ancient Jewish ritual with the suffocating, impoverished ghetto life from which they were trying to escape. They sought a ceremony that could be considered clean and civilized, that would express their stature and success. Of course, their success was made in Christian society; was it not asking too much to attend synagogue in the same way as their Christian neighbors attend church?

The Cultus-Temple increasingly responded to this assimilationist need. As the need grew, the synagogue in the cluttered Orczy House was not sufficient. Luckily, the rise of a Jewish bourgeois also added to the coffers of the Cultus-Temple and made it ready and willing to turn its gaze outward, beyond the crowded tenement of the Orczy House.

Less than a decade after the Cultus-Temple established itself in the Orczy House, when the Jewish Community began to look for another, larger house of worship, it was the Cultus-Temple that planned it. The new house of worship would be the Dohany Street Synagogue and it was the members of the Cultus-Temple who would form the core of its worshippers.

The Beginnings of the Synagogue

By the middle of the nineteenth century, life was getting claustrophobic in the Orczy House synagogues. The worshippers were still on pleasant terms, but the Community was growing too quickly to be content with its twin halls of worship.

The real problem, though, concerned land. The Jewish Community paid high rent in the Orczy House, and it really wanted a plot of land to call its own. Twice already, in 1812 and 1825, the Community sought to purchase land for a synagogue and school. Both requests were denied. Individual Jews were prohibited from owning land, and there was no reason for the City Council to permit the Jewish Community to buy property either.

Finally, in 1837, the Jewish Community gave up its dream of land ownership and decided to rent the plot for a synagogue at the western end of Dohany Street. They paid forty-seven thousand silver florins and fifty imperial gold coins for a thirty-two-year use of the plot, owned by Baron Antal Baldacsy. As luck would have it, a law was issued in 1840 that permitted the Jews to purchase land. In 1844, the Israelite Community of Pest acquired deeds both to the Dohany site and to an extension of the property on Sip Street, on which they intended to build a school. (The area, at today's Sip Street 12, was a school from 1854 and later became the Jewish Community offices, a function it still serves today.) With these purchases, the Jewish Community controlled a sizeable chunk of land bordered by three roads. As could be expected, this made the City Council nervous. When it sanctioned the deal in 1844, the council stipulated that the land and the house that stood there must be used in a nonprofit manner. In the City Council's certificate, we can see the frantic energy with which it continued to fear Jewish trade competition over sixty years after the Jews were permitted to live and trade in Pest: "This house and its plot of land may be used by the buying Israelite Community only for religious service and school purposes, and the Community may not perform any activity producing profit in the building already existing there or in the one to be established later on, i.e. it may not practice any craft, or trade, butcher's trade, or keep a pub, and may not have the above crafts practiced, and no shop may be opened there . . ." (quoted in Alfred Schoner, *The Synagogue of Dohany Street*).

The funds to construct the synagogue were raised, of all places, from the auctioning off of seats in the temple. As it was considered the greatest status symbol to have a seat in the Dohany Street Synagogue, all the seats were sold, in three price categories, before the first brick was even laid.

Meanwhile, the two synagogues in the Orczy House eyed the gigantic plot of land with barely concealed longing. Tension was increasing over which congregation, the Large Synagogue or the Cultus-Temple, would have ritual authority in the new synagogue. The delicate negotiations that followed were a textbook example of political diplomacy. The Cultus-Templers had three things in their favor: money, growing numbers, and Ignaz Einhorn.

Ignaz Einhorn (1825–1875) was one of the most radical Jewish reformers of the age, a boyish preacher who officiated in splinter congregations first in Buda and then in Pest. In 1848 Einhorn founded and led the Israelite Reform Society of Pest, where he abolished circumcision among his followers, moved Shabbat to Sunday, lent his support to mixed marriages, and ejected the *kippah* and the *shofar* from Jewish life. Whether he sanctioned pork-fests on Yom Kippur has not yet been determined. He was too extreme for the Pest Jewish Community, which would have nothing to do with him. The Cultus-Temple, on the other hand, was a fully recognized and accepted branch of the Jewish Community. Einhorn was not involved with the Cultus-Temple, which he considered not progressive enough, and that was just the point: Einhorn was the nightmare of the Orthodox movement. By contrast, the Cultus-Temple, with its relatively innocuous choir and organ, was like a loyal, albeit adolescent, member of the family. By playing themselves against the radical Reformers, the Cultus-Templers filled the niche of the only safe alternative to Orthodoxy. Einhorn made the Cultus-Temple mainstream.

That's just what happened. Rabbi Low Schwab (1794–1857), the liberal-leaning chief rabbi of Pest, broke off contacts with the radical Reformers, distributed leaflets censuring the group, and even condemned the Reform Society's activities to the government. As a result, in 1852, only four years after it had begun, the Reform Society was disbanded by the state.

This was more than enough to placate the Orthodox, who were now ready to talk shop with the less-than-radical Cultus-Templers. One year later, in 1853, the Large Synagogue and Cultus-Temple agreed that the new synagogue would follow the tenets of the *Shulchan Aruch*. Other traditions, however—for instance, certain prayers in the service—could be altered. The Large Synagogue gave some ground when the Cultus-Temple wished to include an organ and male choir to make the service "festive." The Cultus-Temple, for its part, gave ground by agreeing to the building of an additional new synagogue for the worshippers of the Large Synagogue. After many years and much finagling, the Rumbach Synagogue was built for this purpose.

The Competition

A specially appointed building committee issued a request for design submissions from the leading architects of the age. For the competition, it was vital not only that the synagogue represent the Jews of the capital, but that it be cost-effective as well. After several years of deliberation and debate, final designs were submitted by three non-Jewish architects, Jozsef Hild (1789–1867), Frigyes Feszl (1821–1884), and Ludwig von Forster (1797–1863).

Hild was known throughout Hungary for his rural church designs and for his many neoclassicist buildings that redefined the landscape of Budapest in the nineteenth century. Appropriately, his plans for the Dohany Temple, submitted in 1848, were neoclassicist in style. Although he lost the design competition, Hild supervised much of the masonry and, for some time, the interior decoration of the synagogue. Feszl was known for his Romantic structures throughout the country. In Budapest, his most famous buildings were the Vigado concert hall and the Capuchin Church. The design he submitted in 1850 was a Byzantine structure topped by a spectacular dome. It was Feszl who designed the *aron hakodesh* of the Dohany synagogue.

The winning submission for the overall structure came from Forster. Of the three architects, Forster was the only one who did not hail from Budapest. He was born in Bayreuth, Germany, and was most active in the Vienna architectural scene, where he assisted in the designs for Vienna's Arsenal and Opera House. This Viennese pedigree could not have been lost on the Cultus-Templers, for whom the Viennese Jewish Reform movement was a model and a goal. In fact, Forster was in the process of constructing Vienna's Tempelgasse Synagogue (later destroyed on Kristallnacht) for the same Viennese Reformists who had inspired the creation of the Pest Cultus-Temple. Forster actually valued his Viennese design over the Dohany Street Synagogue because he had greater control over its execution. The main difference in the two structures is that the Dohany Street Synagogue was built on a larger plot of land, boldly announcing its presence to both Jew and Gentile. It was as if the Jews of Budapest were more sure of their social standing than their Viennese counterparts, whose synagogue was nearly hidden on a narrow street.

The unique design of the Dohany Street Synagogue was accepted by Pest's Jews: an expansive Moorish structure topped by two towers—Forster's trademark allusion to the two columns of the Old Temple.

It should be pointed out that none of the three competitors was Jewish. Although Jews were only beginning to make strides in the world of architecture, there was already no lack of experienced Jewish architects. It is possible that although the Jews of Pest were self-confident enough to build a grand, monumental synagogue, they felt a Jewish architect would be pushing things too far. People might think the huge building was "too Jewish." For the Reformers, it was a symbolic victory that a Jewish style of architecture was innovated by a Christian. It meant exactly what the Jews had been striving for: total equality with their Christian neighbors.

The Opening of the Synagogue

> On Tuesday, September 6, 1859, the Jews of Budapest basked in the glory of victory. No wars had been fought on the battlefield, no resolution had been passed in the Diet; nonetheless, the pomp and circumstance that attended that day was akin to the ecstasy of redemption. On that auspicious Tuesday, the gates of the Dohany Street Synagogue were opened for the first time.
>
> Never before in the modern Jewish history of Budapest had there been such a massive and unabashed turnout. From dawn of that morning, all the streets surrounding the synagogue were packed full of spectators dressed in their finest clothes. You would be hard put to find an open Jewish shop, not just near the synagogue but throughout the fourth, fifth, sixth, and seventh Districts. By 8:30 A.M., the synagogue was already pulsating with invited dignitaries and the Who's Who of Jewish Budapest. The most illustrious members of the Community had purchased seats to fund the construction. Outside, the streets were filled with the same jittery euphoria usually accorded a wedding or coronation—or, to use a more Jewish metaphor, the holiday of Yom Kippur. In fact, a contemporary chronicler recalled that no other date except Yom Kippur saw such a massive turnout and closing of stores in Pest.
>
> Some would even consider September 6, 1859, the high point in Hungarian Jewish history. When the Dohany Street Synagogue opened its doors, it was hailed as a victory for the three inseparable concerns of nineteenth-century European Jewish life: prosperity, Reform, and assimilation. Although the Jews had yet to be fully emancipated, sweeping changes were already on the horizon. Eighteen fifty-nine was the crowning peak of a decade in which Jews had made enormous strides in Hungarian commerce, art, and literature. The congressional schism that would rend the Jews into embattled Orthodox and Neolog camps was still a full decade away.

At 8:30 A.M., the ceremony began. Like a royal procession, every aspect of the service was endowed with multiple meanings. Texts from the Bible and Psalms were woven together to revel in Jewish prosperity as well as to mark the foundation of the Reform synagogue. Such a custom was not unique to the Neolog Community; for centuries, Orthodox synagogues had celebrated milestones with cut-and-paste pastiches from the *Tanach* and Talmud. Thus the Neologers followed a traditional form to chart their revolutionary course.

As soon as the Secretary of the Israelite Congregation of Pest finished reading the foundation certificate of the synagogue, the magnificent *aron hakodesh* was unveiled: its *parochet* was raised and its doors were opened to reveal an empty interior. That was the cue for the organ master, who began his melody for the choir. The choir broke into a lofty rendition of one of the most stirring psalms used in *zemirot* throughout the Jewish world: the *Odechah* (Psalms 118: 21–24). Awash in double entendre, they emphasized the verse, "The stone that the builders rejected has become the chief cornerstone." Thus the famous poem of redemption became a literal report of the building of the temple. As if to stress this point, the local, non-Jewish governor used the moment to place the final, symbolic stone of the Temple into place. The rabbi swung his hammer, the construction leader handed over the keys, and the games were ready to begin.

The chief cantor, Mor Friedmann, ascended the *bimah* and, to the accompaniment of an original composition by the organist, chanted the *Mah Tovu*. The *Mah Tovu* is the traditional start of the *shacharit*, or morning service. To begin with this prayer was a deliberate act of placation. One of the most contentious issues dividing the Orthodox and Neolog was the alteration and deletion of prayers. When the cantor sang the *Mah Tovu*, it was an olive branch of peace to his Orthodox detractors. Of course, this was not so much a service as a ceremony, and everything had its purpose. The *Mah Tovu* was thus also sung for its consecrating verses, "I, through Your abundant love, enter Your house; I bow down in awe at Your holy temple. O Lord, I love Your temple abode, the dwelling-place of Your glory" (Psalms 5:8 and 26:8).

All at once, dozens of children poured into the main sanctuary. They sprinkled flowers over the floor and waved burning torches in the air. Thus the Christian wedding and the Greek Olympics entered the motley crew of metaphors as the chief *machurs* in the Community seized a dozen Torah scrolls and prepared to march. Only the most prominent Jews in Pest— presumably the heavyweight temple donors—were given this honor. First in line was the chief cantor himself, who followed the prancing children to the *aron hakodesh* and sang the prayer of supplication *Ana Adon-i hosheah na, Ana Adon-i Hatzlichah na*, "O Lord, deliver us! O Lord, let us prosper!" (Psalms 118:25). Each of the dozen exquisitely dressed *machurs* walked the length of the sanctuary with freshly inked Torah scrolls as the organist worked himself into a frenzy of drama and anticipation. When they had climbed the *bimah*, the dozen men stopped just inside the gate. Using the gate as a metaphor, the choir, located just to the left of the *aron hakodesh*, broke into Psalms 24:9–10: "O gates, lift up your heads! Lift them up, you everlasting doors, so the King of glory may come in! Who is the King of glory? The Lord of hosts, He is the King of glory!" It was an original melody composed for the occasion by the organist himself. According to the synagogue's chronicler, "In the naves you could hear it reverberating throughout the Temple when Friedmann sang the *Adon-i tzvaot*" (Ede Vadasz, "*A Pesti zsido templom elso otven eve*"). Then the choir, in solemn recitation, sang the *Shema Yisrael*, the watchword prayer of unity for all the denominations of Judaism. "Hear, O Israel! The Lord is our God, the Lord is One." They must have sung it incredibly slowly, because before the prayer was finished each of the dozen *machurs* had placed his respective Torah in the open *aron hakodesh*. The *ner tamid*, or everlasting light, was kindled for the first time.

As the pomp crescendoed, the three thousand seated congregants prepared for the main speech of the day, delivered by Chief Rabbi Wolf Alois Meisel (1816–1867). It was notably delivered in German, beginning with "Gott, Vater, Herr!" Yiddish was out of the question in the Neolog temple, and it would be seven years before rabbis began to preach there in Hungarian. In his speech, Rabbi Meisel prayed for the Jews, the homeland Hungary, the emperor, and the synagogue itself. By many accounts, it was the greatest moment the Jews of Budapest had yet experienced.

The Dohany Temple of Solomon

The Dohany Street Synagogue epitomizes one of the most fascinating—and perplexing—currents in modern Jewish history: the Moorish style synagogue. Jews were so captivated by this style that many adopted it as their own. In fact, it is with the Moorish style that the synagogue made its first true innovation in architecture.

Jews weren't the first in Europe to use the style. At the end of the eighteenth century, the fruits of colonialism offered the average European an unbidden glimpse into relatively exotic locales. Faster than you could say, "Ali Baba and the forty thieves," armchair explorers were hooked by the wondrous, romantic aura of the Middle East and the Orient. Thus it was that, in the midst of all the "neo" movements in European architecture, the modern Moorish style was born. A hybrid of practically every trend that was in any way connected to the Orient, including Ottoman Turkish, Mameluk-Egyptian, Arabic, and Spanish-Moor, mixed with some Byzantine and Venetian Gothic, the specific term "Moor" was a bit of a misnomer. Nevertheless, the new buildings expressed the self-indulgent exoticism that hit Europe in the first half of the nineteenth century. In Hungary, to use one example, the Moorish style became part and parcel of the Hungarian national revival. The style was said to express the Asiatic origins of the Magyars.

At first, the style had nothing to do with synagogues. It was used in theaters, cafes, and other places of entertainment, as well as in Oriental-style chambers in the palaces of the nobility. In spite of its fetish for the Orient—or perhaps because of it—European society continued to perceive Arabic culture as sensuous and heathen. Thus the Moorish style was limited to nonsacred buildings—that is, until Christian scholars came along to adopt it for the Jews. Interestingly, it was German architects and historians, frustrated by the style's glass ceiling in the Christian world, who convinced the Jews that a Moorish design was ideally suited for the synagogues of an Arab-related people. It has to be said that these scholars were not always motivated by high ideals. Many considered the Jews to be an enigmatic, unspiritual group well-suited to Moorish exoticism and sensuousness. The style also permitted haughty architects to preserve their "pure" Christian styles from contamination in synagogues. In other words, it was better for a synagogue to resemble a theater than a holy church. Most of all, some argued, the style was a uniquely European way of branding the Jews as outsiders: They were outside the European architectural climate and outside mainstream life on the continent.

In spite of this, many Jews seeking to redefine Jewish identity and life were only too happy to appropriate the eastern aesthetic form. It was Jews, after all, who paid the architects; if they didn't like the style, they certainly would have found new designs.

In the 1830s, the Moorish style began to make itself felt on several synagogues in Germany. By the time the Moorish style crescendoed in the Dohany Street Synagogue, it had already become an accepted staple of synagogue architecture. At the same time, scholars were beginning to see connections between ancient Islamic and Gothic architecture. According to this view, the roots of Gothic architecture were found in the east. Imagine the aplomb this gave Jews in nineteenth-century Europe: They were returning not only to the east, but to an ancient architecture that had influenced all the architecture of Europe! It wasn't long before a new term was born: "Jewish Gothic."

It was a quintessentially Jewish dialectic. Just as they were excising entire swaths of their tradition, progressive Jews sought to return to their ancient roots. At the same time as they were assimilating at an unprecedented pace into European society, the Jews wished to declare themselves as distinct and unique from their neighbors. Perhaps the Moorish synagogue was a way for the Jews to say that they had their limits, that even though they wished to assimilate, they would not assimilate into oblivion.

In fact, the return to a pristine, primordial Jewishness was not limited to architecture. One of the most radical Jewish reformers in nineteenth-century Hungary was the scholar Moses Bruck (1812–1849). Bruck urged a return to a Mosaic form of Judaism unhindered by centuries of talmudic discourse. According to Bruck, a return to the pure origins of the Jewish people—its earliest expressions of faith—was the only way to resolve the crisis of Diaspora Jewry. Of course, Bruck went further and soon called for the abolishment of practically all Jewish law, but some of his early ideas were no different from those of the Moorish Jewish reformers: a return to the basic, eastern roots of Jewishness that united the people in their original homeland.

But the Moorish reformers weren't satisfied with a vague, generalized Orientalism in their architecture. Moorism for its own sake would have been looked upon as frivolous. After all, nobody would claim that Ashkenazi Jews were connected to Ottoman architecture. Instead, they wished to raise Moorish architecture to a level that was inseparably linked to the Jewish people. And what was a better symbol of the Jews than the ancient Temple of Solomon? This is how the Old Temple of Jerusalem, that most sacred symbol of both the origins and the destiny of the Jews, came to be (wrongly) remembered as a Moorish building. And of all the Moorish synagogues designed in nineteenth-century Europe, none was considered more Solomonesque than the Dohany Street Synagogue.

That was how Ludwig von Forster saw it. If fact, his own explanation of his Dohany design in 1854 is positively *obsessed* with the Temple of Solomon. Forster, one of a gaggle of Christian architects who converted the Jews into Moors, rhapsodized about the Old Temple's importance: "The architecture of [Arabs and Persians], as we know it today . . . accords with the fantastic and wondrous rites of the people of Israel and their prophets, clarifying the oft vague description of the Temple of Solomon which should form the archetype of all synagogues . . ." (Ludwig Forster, "Promemoria").

The Dohany Street Church

The punchline: Why, then, does the interior of the synagogue look so much like a church?

In spite of its Moorish decorations, the appearance of the interior, with its pulpits, altar-like *bimah*, and pews, is undeniably more Christian than Jewish. On the inside, it is perhaps the most church-like synagogue in the world. Forster claimed that the Christian church was influenced by Jewish architecture going back to the Temple of Solomon, but it does not necessarily follow that a synagogue must resemble a church. Some visitors whisper, "It looks so much like a church in here, and you know why? The architect was Christian." This is a misconception. Christians had always designed synagogues, since Jews were almost completely excluded from the field of architecture until the nineteenth century. Jewish communities, however, had repeatedly ensured that the designs were not overly church-like. On Dohany Street, though, the building committee—all of them prominent Jews in Pest—overwhelmingly approved of Forster's plans. Forster left the project before the interior was decorated, but the structural design of the interior was executed according to his plans.

What is doubly fascinating is that nineteenth-century synagogues often bore innocuous, Christian-influenced facades, saving the Moorish ornamentation for the interior. This stands to reason: in spite of the transformations in the nineteenth century, Jews were normally not so confident to declare, publicly and proudly, any pride in their heritage. In fact, contemporary European society encouraged the Jews to eliminate visible barriers. With the Dohany Street Synagogue, the situation is reversed: The uniquely ethnic characteristics are shown on the outside, while the overwhelmingly Christian elements are secreted within. It was as if the Jews of Budapest had so internalized the ways of the Christian majority that in their most private areas they had become Christian.

So why put up a Moorish facade at all? Perhaps, as mentioned earlier, the Jews wanted to show where their limits lay. By the middle of the nineteenth century, it was taken for granted that progressive synagogues followed church design. This caught the Jews in a vise: they wished to be more like their Christian neighbors, but not so Christian that all vestiges of their Jewishness would disappear. Realizing this, the Jews erected a Moorish facade to remind mainstream society that they would go only so far in their assimilation. They would drastically alter liturgy and law to be like Hungarians, but in the end they would maintain at least some reminder of their roots as "Hungarians of the Mosaic Faith." Evidently the Jews of Budapest felt secure enough in their status as Hungarians to be able to make such bold Mosaic claims, on the most enormous building in the vicinity, without fear of reprisal.

THE HUNGARIAN JEWISH MUSEUM

Address: Dohany Street 2
The Hungarian Jewish Museum is housed in the building to the left of the Dohany Street Synagogue. It is accessed from the same outside entrance, though.
Opening Hours: 10:00 A.M.–3:00 P.M. Weekdays
                 10:00 A.M.–1:00 P.M. Sundays
                 Closed on Jewish and Christian holidays.

The Dohany Street Synagogue, that triumph of both Hungarian Jewish assimilation and eastern Moorish architecture, stood just next door to the home in which Theodor Herzl (1860–1904) was born. In fact, Herzl, the father of modern Zionism, was born only one year after the synagogue was opened.

The plot was purchased by the Jewish Community in 1910, and in the 1920s a Community building was erected in place of the home, which had been previously demolished. The new building emulated the design of the synagogue, down to its diminutive cupolas, but perhaps the designers succeeded beyond their expectations. Situated as it is on the corner of a busy intersection, the new wing pulls one's attention away from the synagogue itself.

In 1931 the Hungarian Jewish Museum, created in 1916, moved into the building. Ironically, one of the earliest founders of the museum was Miksa Szabolcsi (1856–1915), editor-in-chief of the Jewish weekly *Egyenloseg* (Equality). Szabolcsi was a great Jewish leader and also a fierce Hungarian patriot; he believed the Jews of Hungary already lived in their true homeland. As such, he continually fought Herzl over the issue of a distinct Jewish nationality that needed its own state. When he met Herzl in 1903, Szabolcsi told him, "How can you reconcile a new nationalist idea with this deeply deep love of the fatherland?" (quoted in Raphael Patai, *The Jews of Hungary*). In any event, Szabolcsi might have enjoyed the irony of the Hungarian Jewish Museum, his own brainchild, moving into the birthplace of his Zionist ideological nemesis.

In the stairwell leading to the museum is a picture of Herzl that has become a pilgrimage stop for his spiritual descendants. Stones line the ledge beneath his picture.

The museum itself is small but filled with several gems of European Jewish life. Unfortunately, there is little in the way of explanation. Highlights include prayer books from the eighteenth and nineteenth centuries from all over Europe. There is also an ornate seder plate with the six dishes held by the Jewish slaves of Egypt in wheelbarrows and buckets. You will also see a sample seder plate made in the world famous Herend porcelain factory, founded by a Jewish man named Fischer (his portrait can be seen in the goblet). Also on view is a *mizrach* tablet from Transylvania that was very much influenced by Christian altars. *Mizrach* (east) tablets are customarily placed on the eastern walls of rooms, indicating the direction of Jerusalem. Another *mizrach* tablet contains painstaking papercutting from a single sheet of paper. There are also exquisite Italian *ketubbot*, or wedding contracts, handwritten in the eighteenth century. As in Prague, the most fascinating exhibit is probably that of the *Chevrah Kaddishah*, or Jewish Burial Society. On display is a late-eighteenth-century codex from Nagykanizsa with priceless illustrations, including one with a skeleton and the Hebrew caption, "Death comes in his window." Also on display are lots from a small village, circa 1860. The village was too small to organize a permanent *Chevrah Kaddishah*, so the duties of the society were assigned temporarily, based on the lot system. At this writing, the entire exhibition ends with an exhibit on the Holocaust and there is no depiction of postwar Jewish history and life.

The Hungarian Jewish Museum made international headlines in 1993, when its entire collection was stolen. The building was covered in scaffolding during the reconstruction of the Dohany Street Synagogue. Apparently the criminals climbed the scaffolding, opened the windows, and carried every last object out to a truck waiting nearby. Months later the collection was found unharmed in a small village in Romania. There are still unanswered questions concerning the theft, not least of which is how the items made their way into Romania. In any event, all the items were recovered with the exception of two Italian seder plates from the seventeenth century. In 1995, the exhibition of the Jewish Museum was reopened.

THE MARTYRS' CEMETERY

Address: Wesselenyi Street, in the garden between the Hungarian Jewish Museum and the Heroes' Temple.
As of this writing, the grounds are not open for visitors. It can be viewed through the arcade on Wesselenyi Street and near the entrance to the Jewish Museum.

The garden between the Hungarian Jewish Museum and the Heroes' Temple was originally connected with the Heroes' Temple itself, finished in 1931. Original plans were to dedicate a memorial garden remembering the ten thousand Jewish heroes who died for Hungary in World War I. The arcade surrounding the garden, in fact, is part of the Heroes' Temple complex, continuing the eastern imagery with references to town gates of ancient Babylonia. It was intended that a large pool of water be created inside the garden, but the plans were never realized.

The intended memorial became an actual graveyard during the Holocaust. After November 29, 1944, a ghetto was formed for the remaining Jews of Budapest and eventually even the dead could not be removed from the ghetto. Two areas became mass graves: one in the large square called Klauzal ter and the other in the garden of the Heroes' Temple. Twenty-four mass graves of 2,281 people eventually filled up the entire garden.

After the war, it was decided not to exhume the bodies but to preserve the area as a reminder of the atrocities of the Holocaust. Various plaques and tombstones were erected in memory of individuals and families buried here. Most names, however, are not marked.

When you look into the garden from the arcade of the Jewish Museum next to the synagogue, you'll see a piece of a brick wall with the Hebrew word *Zichor*, "Remember." This is a symbolic piece of the wall of the Budapest ghetto, not a genuine artifact; the ghetto was surrounded by wooden walls. It, too, serves as a memorial to the Jews murdered in the ghetto of Budapest.

THE HEROES' TEMPLE

Address: Wesselenyi Street, at the rear of the Dohany Street Synagogue
At the moment, the Heroes' Temple is not open for visitors, but this might change in the near future. The Heroes' Temple is open for services on Shabbat and festivals (*see page 476*).

When you see the Heroes' Temple for the first time, you might find yourself remembering Israel. This is partly because the simple geometry, color, and materials are strikingly reminiscent of the architectural style that dominated Israeli architecture throughout the twentieth century (think of the clean-cut cubes in the Jewish Quarter of Jerusalem's Old City, most of which was built after 1967). But there is something more specific about the Israeli association. If you have ever been to the Tomb of Rachel on the road to Bethlehem, you'll notice a definite connection.

Of all the bizarre eastern motifs in Budapest Jewish architecture, the connection of the Heroes' Temple with the Tomb of Rachel is perhaps the most appropriate. The Heroes' Temple was built in 1929–31 to memorialize the ten thousand Jews who died fighting for Hungary in World War I. As such, a memorial tomb of one of the matriarchs of the Jewish people is a fitting allusion for the building. Even more so because the Tomb of Rachel has become an archetype in Jewish tradition for the tears of a mother over her lost sons. When the First Jewish Temple was destroyed in 586 B.C.E., thousands of Jewish refugees filed by the Tomb of Rachel on their way into Babylonian exile. The prophet Jeremiah recorded the event in a classic verse:

> A cry is heard in Ramah—
> Wailing, bitter weeping—
> Rachel weeping for her children.
> She refuses to be comforted
> For her children, who are gone.
> Jeremiah 31:15

The ever flowing tears of Rachel, shed during an earlier catastrophe, thus resume their grief-stricken course in response to a latter-day tragedy. It is the most evocative allusion possible for the monument, one that links the biblical past with the historical present in a compelling continuum of grief and mourning. All of this is accomplished through the simple, timeless shape of Rachel's 3,500-year-old tomb.

The Jews had much to remember. World War I was considered the modern proving grounds on which the Jews had demonstrated their loyalty to the state. Twenty-three thousand five hundred Hungarian Jews fought in the Hungarian army and most of the army doctors were Jewish. King Charles IV repeatedly praised the heroism of Jewish soldiers. Jews contributed ten percent of the war costs although they formed less than five percent of the population. This was also the first war in which the army appointed rabbis to supervise the spiritual concerns of Jewish soldiers. Some ten thousand Hungarian Jews died fighting in the war. When the government asked various districts to erect monuments for their war dead, the Jewish Community chose to make an active temple-monument that would forever recall the sacrifice the Jewish people made for Hungary. (A separate memorial stands in the Kozma Street Cemetery—*see page 470.*) Designed and built by Ferenc Farago and Laszlo Vago, the structure was meant to recall the Middle Eastern and Moorish elements of the Dohany Street Synagogue, but with a decidedly Modernist edge. The International Modern avant-garde called for geometric simplicity; hence the cube of the synagogue structure, topped by a Byzantine dome. Original plans included a pool of water as well; that area is now the Martyrs' Cemetery (*see page 454*). The designers had intended this garden to be an open space offering a dramatic vista of the synagogue. Today, however, such a vantage point is impossible, as the garden is a series of mass graves.

The arcades that stretch from the synagogue back up Wesselenyi Street are said to recall traditional town gates of Babylonia—an interesting allusion, considering that during their Babylonian exile the Jews faced the constant pressure to assimilate. The entire Heroes' Temple, in fact, seems to be crying out to Hungarian Gentiles to accept the Jews as their equals. We fought with you, it seems to be saying. On the battlefield we died with you; our destinies are linked in an unbroken chain.

Since today we view our century, and indeed all of European history, through the retrospective lens of the Holocaust, it is easy to forget that during the interwar years, World War I—the "Great War"—was the most cataclysmic event Europe had yet experienced. The political, demographic, and social repercussions were felt throughout the continent; all the more so in Hungary, where ninety-three percent of its soldiers were killed or wounded and where the country lost seventy-one percent of its territory and sixty percent of its population in the postwar Trianon Peace Treaty. It was in this environment that the Jews built the Heroes' Temple. The synagogue was built not so much as a house of prayer, but as a testament of Jewish patriotism and loyalty. The question is, was this testament a proud celebration among the Jews themselves? Or was it meant as a display for the non-Jewish Magyar population?

From today's vantage point, the Heroes' Temple is a supreme symbol of the frantic, even desperate effort of the Jews to assimilate only decades before their destruction.

Above the entrance inside the synagogue, there is a Hebrew inscription in the form of a large Star of David that commemorates the wartime martyrs. As is the custom on Jewish tombstones, the inscription combines various passages from the *Tanach* to refer to the valor of those who died. The inscription reads:

> How have the mighty fallen in the thick of battle.
> (II Samuel 1:25)
> While the sun lasts, may their names endure.
> (Psalms 72:17)
> Their merit and beneficence lasts forever.
> (a variation of Psalms 111:3 and 112:3)
> Oh, let Your dead revive!
> Let corpses arise!
> Awake and shout for joy,
> You who dwell in the dust!—
> For Your dew is like the dew on fresh growth;
> You make the land of the shades come to life.
> (Isaiah 26:19)

THE HOLOCAUST MEMORIAL OF BUDAPEST

Address: Wesselenyi Street, in the courtyard behind the Heroes' Temple

The project to build a Holocaust memorial in the former Jewish ghetto of Budapest was spearheaded by the famous actor Tony Curtis. Remembering his Hungarian roots, Curtis established the Emanuel Foundation, named after his father, Emanuel Schwarz, who emigrated from Hungary after World War I.

In 1990, the Emanuel Foundation sponsored the construction of the Holocaust Memorial of Budapest by the sculptor Imre Varga. On each leaf of the tree is inscribed the name of a Hungarian Jew killed in the Holocaust. In this way the sculpture illustrates the traditional Jewish verse of mourning: "May their soul be bound in the bundle of life" (inspired by I Samuel 25:29).

There are several interpretations of the memorial. The broken weeping willow is said to represent the broken body of Hungarian Jewry. It is also an allusion to the image of a broken tree commonly depicted on Jewish gravestones. From the broken body of the tree, though, new shoots are emerging. These are often viewed as the generations of Hungarian Jewry born after the Holocaust. Still, the shoots are leadened down by the leaves, pointing to the grip the Holocaust continues to hold on subsequent generations. Nonetheless, the memorial offers offshoots of hope.

In addition, the bulk of the tree resembles an upside-down menorah, referring figuratively to the destruction of Jewish life, religion, and culture during the Holocaust. The menorah also points to an earlier image of Jewish tragedy: The Arch of Triumph in Rome, with its depiction of Roman soldiers carrying the menorah in celebration of the destruction of Jerusalem in the year 70 C.E.

Some people interpret the large granite centerpiece as the letter "M" for *Martyrok* (Martyr). A more subtle interpretation is that the negative space refers to the Two Tablets of the Law. Like the upturned menorah, the empty tablets remind us of the defiling of Jewish symbols in the Holocaust. More specifically, it refers to the Holocaust as a period in which the world lived in conscious neglect of the most basic commandments of humanity. In the chaos of the times, the Ten Commandments did not exist. On top of the granite is the Hebrew inscription, ". . . Is there any agony like mine, which was dealt out to me . . ." (Lamentations 1:12).

The plaque on the ground directly in front of the memorial says, "We remember." The plaque on the ground facing the Wesselenyi gate refers to a passage from the Talmud: "Whoever destroys one life is considered by the Torah as if he destroyed an entire world, and whoever saves one life is considered by the Torah as if he saved an entire world" (*Mishnah, Sanhedrin* 4:5).

It is possible to purchase leaves to memorialize additional Hungarian Jews killed in the Holocaust. The cost for one leaf, bearing one name, is $125. Orders can be placed at the offices of the World Jewish Congress on Sip Street 12.

Nearby the Holocaust Memorial

One block away from the Holocaust Memorial stands the Carl Lutz Memorial, next to Dob Street 12.

Carl Lutz was the Swiss Vice Consul in Budapest who helped save tens of thousands of Jews through so-called safe houses and emigration papers. He also helped to prevent the Arrow Cross Party from completely destroying the Budapest ghetto. The sculpture, erected by Tamas Szabo in 1991, depicts a golden angel of hope.

A more well-known European diplomat who assisted the Jews was Raoul Wallenberg, an attache to the Swedish embassy. Wallenberg saved thirty-three thousand Jews in an "international ghetto" in Budapest that was protected with the flags of neutral countries. He also provided Jews with protection papers, established hospitals in the Budapest ghetto, and saved hundreds of Jews from deportation trains and a death march. In 1945 he disappeared and is thought to have been placed in the Soviet Gulag. In the 1980s, a sculpture was erected by Imre Varga, who also designed the Holocaust Memorial of Budapest. Because the state authorities were uncomfortable with the topic of the monument, the sculpture was placed on Szilagyi Erzsebet fasor, far from the site of Wallenberg's work in downtown Budapest. In the 1990s, the memory of Wallenberg has been more publicly enshrined in a street name and a plaque (at the corner of Raoul Wallenberg Street and Pozsonyi Street in District XIII).

THE RUMBACH SYNAGOGUE

Address: Rumbach Sebestyen Street 11/13
As of this writing, the interior of the synagogue is closed.

If a yearbook of Budapest synagogues would ever be made, the Rumbach Synagogue would surely be listed under "Follows the Beat of a Different Drummer." Everything about this neglected, closed-down building smacks of a fierce iconoclasm that the Rumbach congregation had from the start. The first is its architect: The Rumbach Synagogue, built from 1870–73, was the first major work of the Viennese prodigy Otto Wagner, who submitted his design at the ripe age of twenty-eight.

The second idiosyncracy of the synagogue is its shape: This is one of the only *shuls* in the world deliberately planned in an octagonal style. In fact, among all the Moorish synagogues built in nineteenth-century Europe, the Rumbach is the only one featuring an octagon in both its floor and its roof. The others don't even have any multi-angled shapes, let alone an octagon. In Dresden in 1838–40, a synagogue was built with a daring octagonal roof, but its floor copped out with a rather unimpressive square. On Rumbach Street, the octagon motif took a giant leap forward: the eight sides are consistent both in the interior of the building and, in the back of the building, from the outside. If the synagogue is closed when you visit—as it has been, unfortunately, for years now—you won't be able to observe the brilliance of the geometric shape.

Whence comes this complex, unified design, a pattern so locomotive that the interior looks like a lithograph by M. C. Escher? Believe it or not, the octagon in the Rumbach is said to represent the third-holiest Islamic shrine, the Dome of the Rock in Jerusalem. Because the Dome of the Rock stands on the site of the Old Temple, it was an image as potent as the Moorish architecture in evoking the original house of worship for the Jews. In this regard, the Rumbach Synagogue beat the Dohany Temple at its own game of association. Both synagogues used Islamic motifs as symbolism for the Eastern origin of the Jews and for the Temple of Solomon, but only in the Rumbach Synagogue was the abstract Islamism visibly linked to the ancient Temple. Of course, the observant worshippers in the Rumbach did not wish their synagogue to resemble either a church or a mosque. In general, it was the progressive Jews who toyed with Eastern and Moorish styles, not the Orthodox. But the Rumbach congregation prided itself on a sense of tradition in tune with the times. This may be why they approved such a radical floorplan. It was neither typically Neolog nor traditionally Orthodox. The symbolic value of the Dome of Rock, in an age when the Arab-Jewish conflict had yet to appear on the horizon, was simply too tempting to refuse.

There is another way to explain the Dome of the Rock allusion. In Jewish tradition, Abraham's binding of his son Isaac took place on the Temple Mount, on the same spot where the Dome of the Rock was later built. It is with the non-sacrifice of Isaac that Abraham distinguished himself from contemporary religions that encouraged the sacrifice of children to gods. Later, when the Temple was built, animal sacrifice set the Jews apart from the practice of human sacrifice common in polytheistic religions. In Exile, synagogal prayer was introduced to replace the animal sacrifices of Old Temple days. Thus the Dome of the Rock enters an entirely new dimension. By referring to the site of the binding of Isaac, the Rumbach Synagogue draws a historical continuum from the origin of Jewish prayer all the way to the establishment of the Jewish synagogue. Indeed, the *bimah*, where the Torah is read, is situated in the exact center of the octagon, directly beneath the overhead dome.

Wagner's partner in construction was Mor Kallina, another child prodigy who was twenty-six years old when construction began in 1870. Following the innovations in the Dohany Street Synagogue, cast iron was employed as a cheap and effective medium for piers and arches. At the corners of the octagon Kallina erected eight iron pillars, extending from the level of the gallery into exquisite arches that define the perimeter of the octagonal dome. These, along with the intricate Moorish patterns painted throughout the interior, are the touches that transformed the synagogue into a mind-bending Escher landscape. Immense circular windows sunk into the sides of the octagon provide a dazzling display of light and color on various parts of the synagogue. Above them, rectangular windows make a ring around the octagon.

The women's gallery, based as it is around the octagon, twists and turns throughout the main sanctuary to create a funky spot for the ladies. It could be accessed not only from the main entrance, but from a side entrance as well. The Rumbach Synagogue held 786 seats for men and 474 for women. Unfortunately, the original wooden seats do not remain in the synagogue and if it is reconstructed it is unclear whether new ones will be put in. In accordance with Jewish tradition, the *bimah* was located in the center of the synagogue. An inscription on the *bimah* indicates that it was donated by a benefactor in 1878. The *aron hakodesh*, topped by its own cupola, was positioned so that it would be bathed in colored sunlight when the *Torot* were removed on Shabbat morning.

The synagogue also housed the rabbi's home and shops, which were later used for Community purposes. On either side of the main hall one could find, at various times, the Israelite Teacher Training Institute, the Jewish Community Talmud Torah Association, a *beit midrash*, and a school for Jewish girls.

The Rumbach Synagogue served as one of the three main synagogues of Budapest, along with the Dohany Street Synagogue and the Kazinczy Street Synagogue, until the Second

World War. In 1941, the synagogue was turned into a barracks for Slovak and Polish war refugees. During this time, much of the interior furnishing of the synagogue was destroyed. Nonetheless, the Rumbach congregation resumed services in the synagogue after the war. It was only in the 1980s that the Rumbach Synagogue was closed, though the few surviving members of the Rumbach continue to meet even today. They pray morning services in the *beit midrash* on Wesselenyi Street 7.

The most recent history of the Rumbach Synagogue throws a rather disturbing light on the post-communist restitution process, and, especially disconcertingly, on the Jewish Community in particular. In 1988, just a year before communism was to end, the Jewish Community sold the Rumbach Synagogue to the state for the paltry sum of six million forints. It is still unclear whether the "sale" was the result of state coercion or individual corruption. Regardless, the Jewish landmark fell into the hands of an agricultural association from a nearby town. It wished to restore the synagogue and sell it for a hefty profit, but after eighty percent of the synagogue was restored, the money ran out. The roof began to leak again, water returned to the walls, and the ceramic wall decorations began to deteriorate. Meanwhile the agricultural association demanded—and continues to demand, as of this writing—millions of dollars for the building. Parties interested in the building were rumored to include the Hungarian Stock Market, Israeli businessmen, international Jewish organizations, the Israeli consulate, and even Yoko Ono, who was rumored (rumored!) to be interested in turning the synagogue into an art gallery. At one point, Hungarian-born Israeli businessmen wished to buy the building and, with the help of Touro College, turn it into the main *yeshivah* of Central and Eastern Europe. It is said that they offered $5 million but the agricultural association refused, thinking it could get $6 million. The deal collapsed. The most optimistic scenario today, perhaps, is that the government will pay off the agricultural association as part of a larger restitution deal with the Jewish Community. The Rumbach will be returned to the Jews, and perhaps a museum will be installed in it, focusing either on the Holocaust or an earlier aspect of Hungarian Jewish history. This scenario is quite lofty; most Budapest Jews who have followed the story with any interest have become highly cynical about any future agreement. There is also a question of time: When will the issue be settled? It might take decades to bring the various parties to agreement. Meanwhile, one of the most vital relics of Budapest's Jewish history remains locked up, not owned by the Jews, and rapidly falling into further disrepair. It would seem that the Rumbach Synagogue, true to the association-laden octagon of its shape, has itself become a sacrifice.

History of the Rumbach Synagogue

The sale of the synagogue in the 1980s was consistent with the Jewish Community's treatment of the Rumbach congregation throughout its serpentine history.

The Rumbach Synagogue was the single voice of reason in Budapest during the Jewish religious battles of the nineteenth century. While the Neolog and Orthodox movements quarrelled to no end, the Rumbach congregation insisted on unity rather than fissure. Even as the Jewish Community of Budapest was dissolving into Neolog and Orthodox camps, the founders of the synagogue emphatically stated, "We are for peace, and have not followed the segregationist examples of other congregations. However, we must demand the construction of our synagogue, because this is the only way to maintain the peace, not to mention to strengthen it" (quoted in Zsigmond Groszmann, "*A pesti zsinagoga*").

It was a demand repeated throughout the middle of the nineteenth century. Before the age of monumental synagogues in Budapest, two main congregations convened in the Jewish tenement of the Orczy House: the Large Synagogue for ritually observant Jews, and the Cultus-Temple for progressive Jews (*see pages 442–447*). When the Dohany Street Synagogue was built under the supervision of the Cultus-Temple congregation, the Jewish Community promised to build an equally impressive synagogue for the Large Synagogue congregation.

It was about then that the two groups—the "Synagogue Party" and the "Temple Party"—broke their cold peace and engaged in increasingly disheartening hostilities. Just as the Dohany Street Synagogue opened its doors, the Jewish Community issued plans to move the Large Synagogue congregation into the smaller, vacated building of the Cultus-Temple. It was a pointless move that could only increase the tension. In August 1859, the Large Synagogue sent two dozen members to the Jewish Community with a petition asking for "equal rights" of religion. They requested the liberty to maintain their old synagogue until the Jewish Community could afford a new one: "We don't ask for anything else than to permit us to keep our own worship, undisturbed, in our habitual old synagogue" (quoted in Zsigmond Groszmann, "*A pesti zsinagoga*").

To the consternation of the Synagogue Party, their petition was ignored.

What followed was a decade-long struggle that foretold the collapse of Hungarian Jewish unity at the end of the 1860s. Chief Rabbi Wolf Alois Meisel, himself the leader of the Dohany Synagogue, sympathized with the Synagogue Party, and even threatened to resign if the Orthodox group was not treated with respect. Rabbi Meisel came to the Large Synagogue and spoke of his heart bleeding at the sight of the injustice. According to one account, he admonished the congregants to "Be men!" in the face of adversity.

The Large Synagogue would do anything to remain in its old house of worship, and in early 1860 offered the Jewish Community to pay the extra rent for their building. The Jewish Community acquiesced and permitted the Large Synagogue to remain in its site. Still in need of a new building, the Synagogue Party stopped short of nothing in their efforts to have their synagogue built. As it turned out, the members even purchased the land themselves. Twenty-four members of the Large Synagogue pooled their money and bought the Rumbach Street plot for forty-four thousand forints. The plot was donated to the Jewish Community on the condition that an Orthodox synagogue be built there. Since this occurred before the Jewish Congress of 1868–69, all synagogues were built and administered by the single Jewish Community of Pest.

However, as the Jewish Community was dominated by Neologers, they continued to drag their feet on the construction of the Orthodox synagogue. The Synagogue Party was losing its patience and tensions were visibly mounting. In 1867, almost a full decade after the opening of the Dohany Synagogue, the Synagogue Party demanded, in no uncertain terms, the construction of their synagogue. It was only when they began to hint at the possibility of seceding from the Jewish Community that their pleas were finally heard. On November 30, 1867, at the end of Shabbat services, Chief Rabbi Meisel marched into the Large Synagogue and declared, "Look what a change has occurred in just one decade! Back then, they . . . almost decided to close this house of prayer. But I—and now I can admit this to you—have saved this temple for you. Today, the leaders will happily satisfy your desires—you will receive a hall suitable for serving God" (quoted in Zsigmond Groszmann, "*A pesti zsinagoga*").

There were other problems: the fear that Rumbach Street was too narrow for a synagogue, the secession of six of the twenty-four property co-owners, and the threat by the remaining eighteen to pull out if the synagogue was not built at once. Nevertheless, construction of the Rumbach Synagogue began on the first of May, 1870. The ceremonial opening took place on the High Holidays of 1872. The congregation continued to pray in the Orczy House, however, until the synagogue was completed for Rosh Hashanah of 1873.

The largest Hungarian Jewish weekly, *Egyenloseg* (Equality), glowingly wrote about the Rumbach in 1915: "The entire Community felt pride in the construction of the monumental synagogue, mainly because it was a harbinger of badly needed peace as well as unity. . . . The members of the Synagogue Party did not allow themselves to be influenced [to secede from the Jewish Community], largely because they could see that the Community, even through great sacrifice, would satisfy all their legitimate desires. A magnificent new synagogue was built that does not exist anywhere in any Orthodox Community" (quoted in Zsigmond Groszmann, "*A pesti zsinagoga*").

The Rumbach and the Status Quo

As biased as the Neolog platform *Egyenloseg* might have been, the Rumbach Synagogue truly was an oasis of peace in Hungary. While traditional and progressive Jews fired off spiteful invectives at one another, the Rumbachers simply refused to get involved.

This became apparent after the defining moment in nineteenth-century Hungarian Jewish life: the Hungarian Jewish Congress in 1868–69 (*see page 434*). After the congress, Orthodox Jews were so enraged by Neolog domination that they seceded from the Jewish Community and formed their own. This act was unprecedented in European Jewish history, and it would define the nature and character of Hungarian Jewish life for generations to come.

In an effort to salvage some form of unity, the Status Quo movement emerged from the congressional debris. Status Quo congregations maintained the same balance of tradition and modernity that had existed prior to the congress. They did not join the Orthodox camp because they didn't want to be pushed into a corner, but there was also a quixotic hope: the Status Quoers wished to make the Neolog vs. Orthodox dispute obsolete by creating a nonpartisan organization of unity. In so doing, they thought they could hold Hungarian Jewry together.

The Status Quo movement did not count on three things: the fierce determination of the Orthodox to be autonomous, the backlash among the Orthodox at what they considered to be a betrayal by the Status Quo, and the fact that a third movement would only cause a further factionalization of Hungarian Jewry. To put it mildly, the dream of the Status Quo backfired. The Orthodox, insulted by the perceived desertion, labelled them traitors who were even worse than the Neologers. It got to the point that any person working for a Status Quo congregation, no matter how Orthodox or even hasidic he was, would be blacklisted from working for the Orthodox Community. A *shochet*, or ritual slaughterer, would be permitted out of financial need to work for a Status Quo congregation. But he would never find work in an Orthodox Community again, and he was even forbidden from eating from the meat he had butchered himself! When his children grew up, it would be difficult to marry them off.

This is where the strategy of the Rumbach Synagogue showed its brilliance. The congregation chose not to align itself with the Status Quo organization, because that would only add further friction to the Budapest Jewish life. Instead, the Rumbach remained in the rapidly organizing Neolog Jewish Community of Pest. This was one reason why the Status Quo movement, which claimed close to ten percent of Hungarian Jewry, had no official Community in Budapest. Nonetheless, in its prayers, its traditions, its behavior, and its philosophy, the Rumbach Synagogue was purely Status Quo. In this way they beat the Status Quo movement at its own game: By appropriating Status Quo philosophy but discarding its separatism, the Rumbach Synagogue became the most moderate, reasonable, and unifying congregation in Jewish Budapest. Instead of adding to the factional feud, the Rumbach sought the *true* course of the status quo: reconciliation and harmony. Thus, for all intents and purposes, the Rumbach Synagogue became the Status Quo synagogue of Budapest.

The Status Quo Traditions of the Synagogue

Differences between Rumbach worshippers and their Orthodox brethren arose not so much in worship but in their social lives. As the Budapest outlet of the Status Quo, the Rumbach congregation kept the Shabbos, kept strict *kashrut*, and prayed in a daily *minyan*—but also sent their children to secular schools, dressed no differently than Hungarians, went to the theater and opera, and read secular literature. This was what the Status Quo movement meant when it allowed for modernization. By contrast, the Orthodox Community isolated itself as much as possible from the secular world, in an effort to separate itself entirely from the assimilationists in the Neolog camp. A simple analogy to the Status Quo would be today's Modern Orthodox movement in America. In terms of their behavior if not their origins, both movements allowed the Jew to respect Jewish tradition while integrating himself into larger society.

Inside the synagogue, it was difficult to distinguish the Rumbach congregation from mainstream Orthodoxy. The *bimah* remained in the center and there was no organ. A choir sang in front of the *aron hakodesh*, but it was exclusively male: eight men and around thirty young boys who were mostly sopranos, to imitate women's voices. As in Neolog synagogues, though, members of the choir dressed in priestly vestments.

In its liturgy, the Rumbach Synagogue was almost identical to Orthodox synagogues. The congregation differed sharply with mainstream Neolog synagogues by using only the traditional melodies in prayer. Decorative and operatic ornamentation, quite the rage in Neolog services, was shunned in the Rumbach. "We had the real *nusach*, the true and pure melody, unadorned by the pomp of the cantor," one surviving member of the Rumbach congregation boasted to me.

The Rumbach Synagogue actually outdid the Orthodox liturgy in its steadfast devotion to complex prayer-poems known as *piyyutim*. In the Middle Ages, close to three thousand Jewish liturgical poets composed over thirty-five thousand *piyyutim* to channel the hopes, fears, and reverence of their people. Unfortunately, modern prayer books preserve only a tiny fraction of this poetry. The Rumbach was one of the few synagogues in the world that sought to bring as much of the poetic tradition as possible into the daily service. For instance, the congregation did not skimp on the traditional *piyyutim* known as *Yotserot*. *Yotserot*, a derivation of the phrase, "He forms light," are a series of *piyyutim* connected to the *Shema* prayers on holiday mornings. Because the *piyyutim* are not a codified part of the service, even Orthodox congregations will omit the melodies or recite them in a quick, hushed undertone. Not the Rumbach. They included all the *Yotserot* poems and sang the original melodies in unison. In addition, the congregation included special *selichot* prayers, or penitential hymns on suffering and redemption, which were recited almost nowhere else. With its sundry *piyyutim* and *selichot* added to the liturgy, the Rumbach congregation developed a service that was unique in the world.

The Rabbis of Rumbach

Even when it appointed its first rabbi in 1872, the Rumbach Synagogue showed its propensity for peace. The nascent congregation issued a request for a preacher, to which thirty-two rabbis responded. Lajos Pollak (1822–1905), the forty-nine-year-old leading contender among the applicants, wowed both the congregation and one hundred VIP guests during his trial sermons in 1871. When a paper was revealed in which Rabbi Pollak was found to agree with some stringent rulings of the Orthodox rabbinate was feared that the rabbi would alienate some of the congregants and push the synagogue into a confrontational pose. But since the congregation strove for a traditionalist outlook anyway, this obstacle was overcome. It helped that in his letters and speeches Rabbi Pollak had promised to fight the extreme Reformniks with the same gusto with which he would fight the intolerant Orthodox. The congregation was convinced, and elected Lajos Pollak to be its first rabbi with over ninety-nine percent of the vote.

Later rabbis of the Rumbach Synagogue also epitomized the moderate urge of the congregation. Dr. Illes Adler (1868–1924), the most famous rabbi and speaker of his time, dressed in the church-inspired vestments of the Neolog Community and preached in Hungarian. Afterwards, Rabbi Moses Feldmann (1859–1927), considered the greatest talmudic scholar of the day, shunned the Neolog vestments and gave sermons in Yiddish, but felt uncomfortable in the cynical religio-politics of Jewish Budapest. After he died, one pupil eulogized him as "a tame, naive soul, very loveable and kind, not familiar with worldly things . . . The Orthodox rabbis considered him Neolog, and the [Neolog] rabbis considered him Orthodox. So he felt uneasy in Pest . . ." (quoted in Gyorgy Haraszti, "A Rumbach utcai zsinagoga es hivei").

The last rabbi of the Rumbach was Dr. Benjamin Fischer (1878–1965). Rabbi Fischer also abandoned the wardrobe of the Neolog, but did wear a special hat that resembled those of Greek Orthodox priests. Dr. Fischer was influenced by the Frankfurt school of Orthodoxy and developed a wide traditionalist following in the Rumbach Synagogue. Although he normally preached in Hungarian, Dr. Fischer spoke in Yiddish during the two most important Shabbats of the year: *Shabbat Ha'gadol*, which precedes Pesach, and *Shabbat Shuvah*, which precedes Yom Kippur. Dr. Fischer was the longest standing rabbi of the Rumbach Synagogue, serving the congregation for fifty years before retiring to his family in England in 1950.

KAZINCZY STREET SYNAGOGUE

Address: Kazinczy Street 27

Until the synagogue is reconstructed, the interior is closed to visitors. However, there are sometimes helpful individuals in the courtyard who can contact the custodian to let you inside. You can also ask in the Orthodox Community Center, Dob Street 35, which is in the same enclave of buildings as the synagogue. In the summertime, the synagogue is usually opened for worship on Shabbat.

In response to the proliferation of Neolog synagogues throughout Hungary, some of the most prominent Orthodox rabbis of the country convened a *beit din*, or religious court, in Mihalovce in 1865. This would be a crucial forerunner of the Hungarian Jewish Congress of 1868–69, which rended Hungarian Jewry into three separate camps (*see page 434*). The Dohany Street Synagogue had recently been opened, and the Neologs spoke with gusto about creating a national rabbinical seminary to "modernize" rabbinical education in Hungary. When the *beit din* adjourned, it issued a declaration, the *Pshak Beit Din* of Mihalovce, that outlined the Orthodox position regarding the recent changes. It is one of the most important documents of the Orthodox-Neolog split of the nineteenth century. Almost all the points of the *pshak beit din* concentrate on synagogues: how they must be built, what is permitted, and so on. The *beit din* prohibited:

1. Foreign-language sermons other than Yiddish.
2. A *bimah* not placed in the center of the synagogue.
3. Towers on synagogues.
4. Vestments on the cantor and prayer leader.
5. Women's galleries not screened off from the main sanctuary.
6. Listening to a choir in a synagogue.
7. Entering a synagogue with a choir.
8. Weddings inside the synagogue.
9. Any alterations of Jewish custom or law.

Of the nine points expressed by the *beit din*, the first eight deal with the form of the synagogue and service. All Jews who defied the ruling were threatened with excommunication.

These eight points succinctly describe the differences between Orthodox and Neolog synagogues. It is with them in mind that one should view the Kazinczy Street Synagogue, built by the Autonomous Orthodox Community of Hungary in 1912–13. No towers adorn this building, the *bimah* is in the center, the women's galleries are sufficiently partitioned, and there is no place for either a choir or an organ. It should be noted that ever since the Jewish Congress of 1868–69, an Orthodox synagogue in Hungary is not only a traditional house of prayer but a conscious act of *withdrawal* from the Neolog Community. With the Kazinczy Street Synagogue, the segregation of Budapest Jewry into three distinct communities was complete. The Dohany Street Synagogue symbolized the Neolog, the Rumbach Synagogue symbolized the Status Quo movement, and the Kazinczy Street Synagogue stood for the Orthodox. The synagogue became the core not only of Orthodox Jewish worship, but of every conceivable aspect of traditional Jewish life.

More than anything else, the building of the Kazinczy Street Synagogue was a show of force. Orthodoxy in Hungary was mostly confined to the countryside, while in large cities such as Budapest, Neolog Jews predominated. From the nineteenth-century rise of Pest until the Holocaust, there was never a *yeshivah* in the city, though there were scores throughout the countryside. This was probably not a coincidence. Hungarian Orthodox leaders might have deliberately chosen not to lure *yeshivah bachurs* into Budapest, the den of assimilation. Still, by building the expansive synagogue on Kazinczy Street, the Budapest Orthodox establishment proved that even in the twentieth century, Orthodoxy was vibrant in the city. Before the war, the synagogue was filled to overflowing.

Unfortunately, the synagogue is today in a terrible state of disrepair. In the 1980s, three rows of windows in the roof fell apart. Rainwater leaked into the sanctuary until 1988, when the roof was covered with wood. The ceiling has not yet been fixed. The interior is used, though, in the summertime and on High Holidays. During the rest of the year, a *Shas Chevrah* next door is used for services.

On the top of the entrance facade, there is an inscription of Jacob's cry upon awaking from his angelic dream: "How awesome is this place! This is none other than the abode of God, and that is the gateway to heaven" (Genesis 28:17).

Inside, the size of the synagogue, with its double women's galleries, is startling. This is no *shtiebel*. The most famous seat in the synagogue stands to the left of the *aron hakodesh*. It was the seat of Koppel Reich (1838–1929), the most renowned rabbi in the Kazinczy Street Synagogue's short history. In 1905, Rabbi Reich led the convention that codified the rules of the Orthodox Community of Hungary. In 1927, at the age of 89, Rabbi Reich represented Hungarian Orthodox Judaism in the Upper House of Parliament. Like the chair of the Maharal in Prague, this seat is no longer in use; today's rabbi sits on the right side of the *aron hakodesh*. As for the *aron hakodesh*, it normally has two *parochets*, or draperies. Behind the main *parochet* is an older, white one used during the High Holidays as a symbol of repentance.

The most amazing feature of the synagogue is perhaps not the building itself, but its immediate surroundings. To step into the courtyard of the synagogue is to enter a Hungarian Jewish village in microcosm. Within the confines of the enclave on Kazinczy and Dob streets, there is a synagogue, a kosher restaurant, a kosher butcher, a kosher milkman, a wedding *chupah*, a Talmud Torah school, a Jewish burial society, a matzoh factory, and a *sukkah*. Since the Orthodox Jews seceded from the main Community in the nineteenth century, all the communal functions were organized along separate lines. In the bustling, Neolog-dominated metropolis of Budapest, the village-like atmosphere of the courtyard is startling. The enclave continues to be the heart of Orthodox Jewish life in Budapest even today. There is even an old tradition to do *tashlich* by the open water pipe beneath the stairs to the Hanna restaurant. *Tashlich* is a Rosh Hashanah custom in which Jews metaphorically cast their sins into the sea.

The centerpiece of the courtyard is the permanent area for the *chupah*, installed behind the synagogue like a graphic reminder of point #8 of the *Pshak Beit Din* of Mihalovce: "Weddings can be celebrated only under the open sky." During wedding ceremonies, the *chupah*, or wedding canopy, is attached to the top of the grillwork. On the grillwork is the Hebrew verse, "The sound of mirth and gladness, the voice of bridegroom and bride" (Jeremiah 7:34 and 33:11). The verse is repeated, referring to both the destruction of Jerusalem, when weddings ceased, and the promise of return, when weddings would again be celebrated. The context of the verse took on new meaning in 1945, during the first weddings after the Holocaust. Normally, Jewish weddings are not permitted for several weeks after Pesach, during the counting of the *Omer*. However, on the festive holiday of Lag Ba'Omer, weddings are not only permitted but encouraged. Thus on Lag Ba'Omer 1945, between forty and fifty Orthodox couples lined up in the courtyard of the Kazinczy Street Synagogue, waiting to be married. It was described as a "revolving door *chupah*," as couple after couple ascended the steps and became husband and wife. The scene was bursting with the energy of people eager to rebuild their lives, as well as to rebuild the Orthodox Jewish Community itself, after the Holocaust.

Unfortunately, such celebrations became far fewer in subsequent years. Today, the *chupah* platform is rarely used.

Elsewhere in Budapest

With the stunning array of synagogues spread throughout the city, one can experience the breadth of Jewish history in Budapest without once stepping foot inside a cemetery. What's more, Jewish cemeteries are either far from the city center or closed to the public. In some ways, this is a blessing: Elsewhere in Central Europe, the Jewish cemetery is often the single remaining testimony to the Community's former greatness. In this respect Budapest can be considered the opposite of Warsaw, whose cemetery is the largest Jewish landscape on that side of the Vistula to have survived the Nazis.

Nonetheless, Jewish cemeteries are worth a look in Budapest as well. In particular, the Kozma Street Cemetery is perfect for an afternoon stroll through generations of Jewish life in the city.

KOZMA STREET CEMETERY

Address: Kozma Street 6
Open: Sunday–Friday 8:00 A.M.–4:00 P.M.
The cemetery office—generally unhelpful unless you have a specific grave to find—closes at 1:00 P.M.

> Take tram 28 or 37 from Blaha Lujza Ter (the tram stop is on Nepszinhaz Street) to the final station. This is the New Public Cemetery. The Jewish cemetery adjoins it to the north; you can either walk or take bus 68 one stop, to the station "Izraelita temeto." The tram ride takes thirty-five minutes.

The Kozma Street Cemetery is also known as the Rakoskeresztur Cemetery, after the suburb in which it is located. Although today it is the largest Jewish cemetery in all of Hungary, the Kozma Street Cemetery was by no means the first Jewish cemetery in Pest. Two years after the Pest City Council acquiesced to the admission of Jews, in 1788, Jews were permitted to bury their dead in a cemetery known as Vaci. A century later, the Ferdinand Bridge (near the Nyugati train station) was built on the site. In 1808 the Lehel Street Cemetery was opened nearby, but by 1874, this cemetery was full. Eventually, in 1891, the Kozma Street Cemetery was established. It continues to be used today. Several funerals usually take place on Sundays. It is the main Neolog cemetery of Budapest.

The first thing to notice, of course, is the dazzling white ceremonial hall. Designed by Vilmos Freund in 1891, it has been acclaimed throughout Europe as one of the finest examples of the Jugenstil style. It is interesting because as stately and proud as it appears, it has no Hebrew inscriptions on its facade and no Jewish identifying marks save its diminutive Jewish stars.

Ohelim, *Budapest Style*

It is an ancient Jewish custom to bury the most outstanding members of the Community underneath rectangular or triangular *ohelim* (literally, "tents"). Resembling *sarcophagi* or little houses, the *ohelim* recognized the stature of the individual while offering more room for venerating text.

In the Neolog Community of Hungary, a different type of *ohel* was born. These were large and ornate chambers built not on the graves of important rabbis, but over the family plots of wealthy Jews. The most renowned and avant-garde designers of the day were commissioned to construct these Hungarian "houses," which could easily be termed "little temples." What made them unique was not their size—in Warsaw, for instance, *tzaddikim* were entitled to equally large *ohelim*—but the sculptural indulgence that turned the *ohelim* into secular shrines. They are art works in themselves, and in this they are no different from similar monuments in Christian cemeteries. Ranging from the neoclassical to the Jugenstil fringe, the little temples reflect the increased prosperity and assimilation of Hungary's Jews from the middle of the nineteenth century onwards.

You'll find these little temples hugging the inner wall of the Kozma Street Cemetery, as if guarding the grounds or perhaps yearning to escape. If you enter the cemetery through the main gate (to the right of the ceremonial hall), the row of little temples begins immediately to the right. The *ohel* of the Brull family ("Brull Csalad") is the third one down along the wall. It is an impressive example of neoclassicism, with lions, an eagle, a funeral urn, and rich mosaics on the inside. Don't miss the ceiling, which acts as a foil to the *ohel*'s otherwise Hellenistic imagery.

Four *ohelim* down from the Brull family lies the most unforgettable monument in the cemetery, a spectacular example of Art Nouveau that alone is worth the thirty-five-minute trip. It stands over the grave of the spice merchant Sandor Schmidl (d. 1899) and his wife Roza Hollander (d. 1904). The *ohel* was built in 1904 by Bela Leitersdorfer, who later Magyarized his name to Bela Lajta. Like Ostrzega in the Warsaw Jewish Cemetery, Lajta was renowned for his sculptural monuments. There are over two dozen Lajta sculptures in this cemetery alone. The retina-bending turquoise ceramic was made in the southern Hungarian city of Pecs. The monument was under heavy restoration in 1997; hopefully it will be finished when you visit.

Unfortunately, practically all the *ohelim* here are in desperate need of restoration. If you continue along the wall, after it turns right you'll see the neglected monument to the Wellisch and Adler family. The distinguished architects buried here are memorialized with a rich mosaic of a "family tree."

After the cemetery wall turns left you'll see the mausoleum of Baron Zsigmon Kornfeld (1852–1909). The *ohel* is not particularly distinguished, but it stands over the grave of the most powerful Hungarian banker of the nineteenth century. This early George Soros was actually not Hungarian. Born destitute in Bohemia, Kornfeld became the head of the Hungarian General Credit Bank at the age of twenty-six. He soon revitalized not only the bank but the entire Hungarian economy, basing the state budget on the gold standard and creating ports, factories, and refineries all over Hungary. Kornfeld played the financial markets with adroit skill, eventually becoming president of the Budapest Stock Exchange in 1899. He remained a devoted Jew. In 1904, after he orchestrated a large loan on behalf of the Austro-Hungarian government to Russia, he refused to accept a medal in protest of the Kishniev pogrom of 1903. He was made a baron before he died.

Eleven *ohelim* away from Baron Kornfeld is something best described as a spaceship. This is the Griesz family *ohel*, a conical tent-pod that expresses more than anything else in the cemetery the Oriental gaze of Budapest Jewry. Defiantly Jugenstil, the exotic pod looks set to take off at any minute. The interior looks like the work of Gustav Klimt in Egypt, with funky mosaic lions, stained glass, and enough gold to start a national currency.

The World War I Memorial

At the entrance of the cemetery just in front of the ceremonial hall, there is a cleared area with white benches and a large monument featuring an eagle and an obelisk. This memorial was erected after the First World War to remember the ten thousand Jews who died for Hungary.

The Heroes' Temple (*page 454*) wasn't the only monument established to remember Jewish participation in the war. The Jews, ever uncertain of their standing in the eyes of the Magyars, wanted to show their countrymen just how patriotic they were. The monument would prove they were no different from their countrymen, and thus deserving of full equality. Emphasizing this, the Hebrew inscription on the back of the memorial reads, *li'zacher olam*, "to remind the world," of the contributions the Jews gave to their adopted homeland Hungary.

The Holocaust Memorial

Beyond the World War I memorial and across the path is the large *Yizkor* wall, and nine smaller walls covered with names. This is the Holocaust memorial built in 1949. Tens of thousands of names cover the walls, but unlike the Pinchas Synagogue memorial in Prague, the list does not include all or nearly all of Hungary's or even of Budapest's Jewish martyrs. For this reason, many people have pencilled in the names of relatives hitherto missing from the walls. By now, parts of the walls are covered with these scrawled names. Because the new names are never washed off, the memorial is a growing, fluid monument in a constant state of recollection, as if its own symbolic memory is powerless to contain the enormity of the crime. Perhaps most importantly, the handwritten names transform the monument from a silent stone into a living scroll of torment, as idiosyncratic as each of the lives that were lost.

The large, monumental wall bears an inscription in Hebrew and Hungarian. They actually have different meanings. The Hebrew text reads, "Our brothers, the children of Israel, who sacrificed their lives on the holiness of God's Name." The Hungarian text reads, "They were killed with hatred, we shall keep their memory with love."

To the right of the monumental *Yizkor* wall, just behind the memorial, there are two gravestones inscribed in Hebrew. One is a memorial for an earlier destruction of Hungarian Jewry that occurred two and a half centuries before the Holocaust: the bloodbath perpetrated by Austrian and Hungarian soldiers in the Great Synagogue of Buda when the Turks were defeated in 1686 *(see page 421)*. During excavations of the synagogue in the 1960s, burnt skeletons of men, women, and children were found among fallen debris and cannonballs. This corroborated ancient accounts of the slaughter, which described the Jews of Buda being killed in the Great Synagogue and their bodies placed in the *genizah*. When the synagogue burned down during the night, the bodies remained trapped under the rubble for centuries. In the 1960s, when the remains were found they were buried in the grave on the left. The tombstone reads, "Here are buried the bones of the holy people of Israel who were killed in the synagogue in the year 5446 [1686], who were found in the same place and brought here to their rest in the year 5728 [1968]. May God avenge their blood."

The text on the tomb on the right reads, "Here are buried in the year 5729 [1969] ten Torah scrolls that were burnt in the great synagogue in Budapest." According to the inscription, it seems that the Torah scrolls were destroyed in the Dohany Street Synagogue during the Holocaust, and later buried here one year after the bones were buried in the adjacent grave.

Placed side by side, the two graves reinforce the Jewish view that God's word, embodied in the Torah, is intractably linked to His creations. It also links the two catastrophes of Hungarian Jewry into a single historical continuum.

Not as prominent as the large Holocaust memorial, but perhaps even more moving, are the memorials established for various communities outside Budapest. These are placed over mass graves that were exhumed throughout Hungary and brought to the Kozma Street Cemetery. From the *Yizkor* wall, take the first left (between Plots B and A) away from the center of the cemetery. You'll find these graves starting in the ninth row of Plot A and interspersed throughout the plot.

On each memorial tablet, there are two numbers. The first refers to the total number of martyrs from the town and the second is the number of unidentified individuals. The difference between the two numbers is the number of identified Jews who were killed, each of whom is listed on the small tombstones or plaques that extend from the main one. In the city of Koszegi, for example, 2,500 Jews were murdered, 1,220 of whom were not identified at the time these memorials were made. Thus there are 1,280 names alphabetically listed on the stones. When they are listed on small tombstones, each stone carries four names. Sometimes relatives tend to the names of loved ones, cleaning the area around the name to make sure the individual is not forgotten.

The Rabbinical Row

From the end of the large Holocaust memorial closer to the ceremonial hall, head one plot into the cemetery to the path dividing Plot 5 on the left and Plot 4 on the right. Plot 4 is unmistakable because the tombstones in the first row are almost exclusively written in Hebrew.

At the left-hand corner of Plot 4 is the grave of the first chief rabbi of Pest, Israel Wahrmann (1725–1826). His grave, as well as those of other individuals who were buried before the Kozma Street Cemetery was opened, was brought from the Lehel Street Cemetery to this cemetery. Although Rabbi Wahrmann presided over the traditionalist Large Synagogue in the Orczy House (*see page 443*), he nonetheless initiated certain modernizing programs, such as opening the first Jewish elementary school in Pest in 1814.

Across the path between Plots 4 and 5 is the grave of the next chief rabbi of Pest, Low Schwab (1794–1857). The tombstone is adorned by a drowsy-looking lion, symbolizing the name "low," German for "lion." The path between Rabbi Wahrmann and Rabbi Schwab symbolizes the time it took the Jews of Pest to choose a new chief rabbi: Rabbi Wahrmann died in 1826, but Rabbi Schwab was not chosen until 1836. Schwab stood as a great mediator during the cataclysmic shifts that were beginning to rend the Hungarian Jewish Community. He sympathized with the reformers, but fought against reforms that were too radical. It was Rabbi Schwab who orchestrated the compromise that led to the construction of the Dohany Street Synagogue. His deal allowed for vernacular sermons, a choir and an organ in exchange for a promise on the part of the progressive Jews not to stray from the tenets of traditional Jewish liturgy and law. Like his fellow Budapest Jew Theodor Herzl, he died before he could see his dream become a reality. Two years after the death of Rabbi Schwab, the Dohany Street Synagogue was opened.

Budapest's most famous Neolog rabbis are buried in Rabbi Wahrmann's row. It should be mentioned that the rabbis here are not as important to world Judaism as to Budapest Jewish history. There are very few pilgrimages to these rabbinical graves, in contrast to the frequent pilgrimages to Orthodox cemeteries.

THE UJPEST SYNAGOGUE

Address: Berzeviczy Street 8
Take the M3 (blue) metro line to the Ujpest-Varoskapu stop. Berzeviczy Street begins on the other side of Arpad Street.

The story of the Ujpest Synagogue is intertwined with the story of this distinct district in Budapest. Perhaps more than anywhere else in the city, the Ujpest district reveals the uncanny adaptability of the Jews to overcome racist legislation and, in a word, succeed.

At the age of thirty, Isaac Lowy (1793–1847) took over his father's leather factory. The factory was in Nagysurany and he sold the leather in neighboring Ersekujvar. But Lowy found the job onerous. The merchants and townspeople of Ersekujvar could not accept a Jew as their chief leather supplier. They taunted him, harassed him, and often refused to buy his products on the grounds that he was a Jew. Lowy wanted to move to Pest, but because of the anti-Semitic legislation there, it was very difficult for a Jew to settle in the city, let alone to establish a factory. So Lowy did things his own way.

He built a town.

In 1835, Lowy bought an empty tract of land north of Pest from the family of Count Karolyi. He settled there with several other Jewish families, and immediately set to work building his leather factory. In the deed to the land, Lowy included provisions concerning religious and industrial freedom as well as self-government. It was probably the most progressive land deed in all of Hungary. Lowy formed a Jewish Community and served as its first leader. In 1838, there were thirteen Jewish families living in his town, called Ujpest (meaning, somewhat spitefully perhaps, "New Pest"). Christians soon settled in Ujpest, and in 1840 the inhabitants elected Lowy to serve as the first town judge.

Ujpest wasn't just a haven for a rejected industrialist; it also featured, from its inception, a burgeoning religious Community. In 1840 the Jews chose their first rabbi, Markus Stern. In 1842 they established a Jewish school, and in 1844 the *Chevrah Kaddishah*, or Burial Society, was established. The first *shtiebel* was built on land donated by the Count Karolyi family, and in 1886 the majestic, Romantic-style Ujpest Synagogue was built. It was the crowning achievement of a Jewish Community that had built itself, quite literally, out of nothing. The one thousand seats in the synagogue show just how big—and wealthy—was the Jewish Community at the time.

From its start, it was a Neolog house of prayer. In fact, the Ujpest Orthodox were so incensed that they split from the official Jewish Community, following the model of their counterparts in Pest. The Ujpest congregation was indeed progressive, and invited Sander Rosenberg, a rabbi from Arad, to officiate the opening ceremony. (Rosenberg went down in Hungarian history as the first rabbi to give his blessing to a Jewish-Christian intermarriage.) The newspapers referred to the opening of the synagogue as a "great holiday" for both the Jews and Christians of Ujpest.

Until 1914, prayers were sung in Hebrew and sermons were delivered in German. After 1914, perhaps as a patriotic response to the First World War, sermons were given in Hungarian. The interior of the synagogue resembles the average Neolog synagogue of the nineteenth century: there are three naves, the *bimah* is situated in the front, the organ is in back, and balconies on the sides serve as women's galleries. An interesting addition to the Ujpest Synagogue is the deep blue embedded mural above the *aron hakodesh* that depicts a starry sky. Stained glass windows memorialize the departed, often those who were murdered in the Holocaust.

The house next to the synagogue, which serves as a small prayer room for the congregation today, was originally built in 1912 as a rabbi's house. The Jewish retirement home next to the synagogue was built in 1926.

In 1870, there were seven hundred Jews in Ujpest. By 1920, the number had increased to 11,300 and in 1940 there were twenty thousand Jews in Ujpest. The Neolog Community was particularly flourishing. Two famous rabbis of the Ujpest Synagogue were Lajos Venetianer, who wrote one of the major histories of Hungarian Jews, and Denes Friedmann, also a well-known writer. In 1871, the Israelite Women's Association was formed in Ujpest.

From 1899 there was a special society for orphaned Jewish girls. All told, by 1914 there were seventeen Jewish associations in Ujpest.

Because Ujpest was not annexed to Budapest until after the war, the Jews of Ujpest shared the fate of the Jews from outside the capital. Almost all the Jews of Ujpest were murdered after June 3, 1944, when the Nazi-created Ujpest ghetto was liquidated and the Jews were sent to death camps. The Germans looted and partially destroyed the synagogue. Of the twenty thousand Jews in Ujpest before the war, approximately seventeen thousand were murdered.

After the Russian army liberated Ujpest on January 10, 1945, the indomitable Jewish Community set itself the task of renewal. The second postwar rabbi of Ujpest, Miklos Muranyi, restored the Ujpest Synagogue and directed the construction of the Holocaust memorial next to the synagogue. The arcaded wall of names was unveiled by Hungarian President Zoltan Tildy in 1948. Like the Pinchas Synagogue Holocaust Memorial in Prague, the Ujpest memorial delineates the names of each victim of Nazi genocide who came from Ujpest. But where the Prague memorial lists the dates of birth and deportation, the Ujpest memorial is less circumspect: next to each name is the person's age, from one-year-old babies to people in their nineties. In this way the memorial freezes the mosaic of human life at the moment it was cut off. On the other side of the wall, facing the street, there is a bas relief sculpture depicting the deportations.

Ujpest was eventually annexed to Budapest and there is no longer a frontier feel to the district, as the approximately eight hundred Jews living in Ujpest are part of the Budapest Jewish Community. Still, if you walk around the empty streets of Ujpest today, you can imagine that it was once a booming refuge for Jews faced with the anti-Semitism of a European metropolis.

The Living Synagogue:
Budapest's Special Treasure

Of all the cities in Central and Eastern Europe, only in Budapest is it conceivable to provide a list of synagogues open to prayer. It is thus with great pleasure that I present a diverse catalog, with descriptions and times of prayer, of the various synagogue options in the capital of Hungary. This is not a comprehensive list of the roughly twenty active synagogues in Budapest, but rather a selection of the most popular, vibrant, and intriguing sites of prayer. Included here are the famous as well as the little-known.

I strongly encourage you to visit at least one of the synagogues off the beaten track in Budapest. There are several reasons for this. The major congregations on Dohany Street and Kazinczy Street are somewhat jaded with respect to visitors: Because they expect them, they often ignore them. The lesser-known synagogues, by contrast, are more intimate affairs; the congregants are pleased and often excited to meet people from around the world. You have a good chance of hearing some fascinating stories from the local worshippers in these small synagogues. It is there that you will find a secret corner of Jewish life in Budapest not even hinted at anywhere else.

Another reason to attend services at the smaller synagogues is that this is the only time you'll be able to see the synagogue interior—at other times it's closed to the public. Even though many of these congregations pray in small chapels adjacent to the main sanctuary (except for on holidays), the rabbis will usually be happy to give you a peak at the interior.

Practically all the synagogues are named after their streets, and many are built inside apartment blocks.

> Note: *"According to sunset"* means the congregation prays at the official time Shabbat or the holidays begin, i.e. when the sun goes down. If you don't have a sunset-calendar, the rough rule is to arrive at synagogue around twenty minutes prior to twilight. Or you can buy Uj Elet ("New Life"), the biweekly Jewish newsletter, which lists all active synagogues and their current times of prayer. This is particularly recommended if you visit during seasonal changes, when synagogues with fixed schedules will be changing their times of prayer. Uj Elet *is on sale in the Jewish Community building on Sip Street 12.*

A visit to services in the Dohany Street Synagogue, the largest synagogue in Europe, is considered by many to be the peak of their visit to Budapest. The Dohany congregation is an eclectic combination of tourists, locals, and, interestingly, the surviving fragment of worshippers from the closed-down Rumbach Synagogue. Unfortunately, the synagogue is not always open for worship. For reasons of dwindling congregations, tourist waves in the summertime and heating logistics in the wintertime, the Dohany Street Synagogue congregation meets in the Heroes' Temple in the winter. In addition, although the Rumbach Synagogue itself has been closed for years, a few surviving congregants meet mornings and evenings in a small chapel in Wesselenyi Street 7. There they are joined by the Dohany congregation for weekday services. Shabbat is the only day in which the congregations diverge into two separate services.

The three locations make the service schedule a tad confusing. If you keep in mind that one site is used in the winter, one in the summer, and one during weekday services, the system becomes simpler. What follows is the yearly schedule of the hybrid congregation of Dohany-Heroes'-Rumbach:

THE DOHANY STREET SYNAGOGUE

Address: Dohany Street 2, District VII
The Dohany Street Synagogue is used only in the SUMMER.
Kabbalat Shabbat: 6:00 P.M.
Shabbat and Holiday Mornings: 9:00 A.M., Torah reading at 10:00 A.M. From 9:45–10:00, there is a 15-minute break between the morning service and the Torah reading.
Rosh Hashanah and Yom Kippur: Evening services begin according to sunset.
Rosh Hashanah morning services begin at 9:00 A.M.; Yom Kippur morning services start at 8:00 A.M.
For weekday services and for Saturday evening services, see the Rumbach Congregation on page 477.

THE HEROES' TEMPLE

Address: Wesselenyi Street, District VII
The Heroes' Temple is used only in the WINTERTIME (approximately from the holiday of Sukkot until the end of Pesach).
Kabbalat Shabbat: 5:00 P.M.
Shabbat and Holiday Mornings: 9:00 A.M., Torah reading at 10:00 A.M. As in the summertime Dohany services, there is a 15-minute break from 9:45–10:00 before the Torah is read.

"RUMBACH" CONGREGATION

Address: Wesselenyi Street 7, District VII
Shacharit: 7:30 A.M., 8:00 A.M. Sundays and state holidays
Minchah/Maariv: 7:00 P.M. in the summertime. According to sunset in the fall and winter seasons. In the winter, for instance, services meet at the same time as that week's *Shabbat*.
Kabbalat Shabbat: 7:00 P.M. in the summertime. According to sunset in the fall and winter seasons.
Shabbat Morning: 7:00 A.M.
Shabbat Minchah/Maariv: 7:00 P.M. in the summertime. One hour before *motzaei Shabbat* in the fall and winter seasons.

On *Shabbat*, the Rumbach congregation holds separate services from the Dohany/Heroes' services. On Saturday evening, the Dohany/Heroes' congregation convenes with the Rumbach congregation in Wesselenyi Street 7.

THE KAZINCZY STREET SYNAGOGUE

Address: Kazinczy Street 27 District VII
Shacharit: 6:30 A.M. During the winter, when daylight comes after 6:30, services begin at 6:45.
Minchah/Maariv: According to sunset
Kabbalat Shabbat: According to sunset
Shabbat and Holiday Mornings: 8:00 A.M.
Shabbat Minchah/Maariv: Approximately one and a half hours before Shabbat ends.

The Kazinczy Street Synagogue has been a symbol of Orthodox autonomy in Budapest throughout the twentieth century (*see pages 465–467*). Although there are other Orthodox synagogues still in use in Budapest, the Kazinczy Street Synagogue, located in the village-like complex of Orthodox Community buildings, holds the tacit claim to the crown of Orthodox Jewish Budapest. It was actually built several generations after the infamous Hungarian Jewish Congress and the rending of Hungarian Jewry into Orthodox and Neolog camps. Nonetheless, the Kazinczy Street Synagogue stands for the fierce independence that marked Orthodox Jewry in Budapest from the middle of the nineteenth century.

The synagogue itself is in a highly deteriorated state. For this reason, the congregation often prays in the *beit midrash* adjacent to the main sanctuary. The women's section in the *beit midrash* is an impermeable cubicle; in the main synagogue, women sit in strictly separated, double-tiered balconies. In the summertime and on the High Holidays, the main synagogue is used, sometimes filling up with 400 worshippers during *Shabbats* in the summer. Several of the leading Orthodox Jews of Budapest make the Kazinczy Street Synagogue their favored place of prayer. It should be mentioned, though, that the large numbers of worshippers in the synagogue does not indicate the strength of the Orthodox Jewish

Community of Budapest. Most of the congregants are tourists. Still, praying in the Kazinczy Street Synagogue can feel like participation in history.

THE RABBINICAL SEMINARY

Address: Jozsef korut 27, District VIII
Kabbalat Shabbat: 6:00 P.M.
Shabbat and Holiday Mornings: 8:45 A.M.

Services in the Rabbinical Seminary of Budapest are probably the best bet for young people. The Seminary's synagogue has become the most popular place of worship for students in Budapest. Often, the sanctuary is used as a meeting place before a Friday night on the town. Seating is separate but equal for men and women. The service is much like that of an American Conservative synagogue, but with a Neolog touch: A rather jolting organ will remind any American visitor that he or she is in Budapest. After services, there is a large and lengthy *kiddush* headed by the director of the Seminary. Homilies are delivered in Hungarian.

The Rabbinical Seminary is worth visiting not only for its popular *Shabbat* services, but for its historical prominence in the city: The Seminary, which symbolizes the massive upheavals of nineteenth-century Jewry, is also famous for its role as the only rabbinical training school in all of communist-controlled Central Eastern Europe.

The struggle to establish a Rabbinical Seminary in Hungary was the centerpiece in the tug-of-war between Orthodox Judaism and the growing Neolog movement. As was the case elsewhere in Europe, the creation of a Rabbinical Seminary was lauded by progressive Jews and by government ministers, both of whom were eager to orient the Jewish religion toward secular society. The goals of the Seminary were indeed revolutionary: All students would be required to complete a doctoral thesis at the local university; the director would be proficient in secular studies and would be fluent in Hungarian; and all teachers would be approved by the emperor. Meanwhile, a windfall of cash made the dream of a Rabbinical Seminary much closer to a reality. In the Hungarian Revolution against Austrian rule in 1848, Jews had contributed far beyond their numbers as soldiers, financiers, doctors, and demonstrators. As a punishment, the victorious Austrians had imposed an outlandish fine of 2,300,000 forins on the Jews of Hungary. It was impossible to pay this fine, and so in 1850 the emperor reduced it to one million forins on the condition that the money went to the establishment of a rabbinical seminary and other Jewish schools and welfare institutions.

But Orthodox Jews in Hungary perceived the Seminary as the first step toward the dilution, and eventual disappearance, of the Jewish religion. In their view, a centralized and government-controlled Seminary would spell the destruction of the traditional rabbinical training grounds of the yeshivah. In addition, the notion of mixing secular and sacred studies was unthinkable among the Orthodox. Of all the battles over Jewish religion in the nineteenth century, the controversy over the Rabbinical Seminary of Budapest was perhaps the most incendiary. In April of 1864, a delegation of Orthodox rabbis even obtained an audience with Emperor Franz Josef himself.

In spite of Orthodox opposition, the Rabbinical Seminary and Teachers Institute of Budapest opened in 1877 in the presence of the most prestigious politicians in Hungary. Chief Rabbi Samuel Kohn delivered a charged address that encapsulated the Neolog battle with Orthodoxy. He spoke of "pure religiosity, free of narrow-minded zealotry and dark fanaticism," and predicted that the Seminary's teachers "will liberate their followers from the iron yoke of self-isolation and prejudice . . ." (quoted in Raphael Patai, *The Jews of Hungary*).

Over the course of the next sixty years, the Rabbinical Seminary of Budapest graduated an amazing array of scholars, rabbis, and teachers, becoming one of the most prestigious rabbinical academies in Europe. During the communist era the Seminary, however diminished of its former glory, trudged through as the single rabbinical academy in all of communist-controlled Europe. After 1947, it was no longer necessary for Seminary students to obtain Ph.D.'s in secular studies.

The Rabbinical Seminary continues to function today. In 1997, there were sixty pedagogical students and eight rabbinical students. The Seminary is no longer a symbol of the strife between Neolog and Orthodoxy. Because it is the single institution of its kind, the Rabbinical Seminary educates students of all Jewish affiliations, from progressive to traditionally Orthodox. The background of its students is also varied. There are students who were observant from birth, as well as students who learned the Hebrew alphabet in their late teens. People joke that the Seminary is today the opposite of the Hungarian Jewish Congress of 1868–69, since it actually unifies the formerly antagonistic strands of Hungarian Jewry.

NAGYFUVAROS SYNAGOGUE

Address: Nagy Fuvaros Street 4, District VIII
From Blaha Lujza ter, walk up Nepszinhaz Street—or take tram 28, 29, or 37 one stop— to Nagy Fuvaros Street on the right.
Kabbalat Shabbat: 7:00 P.M. in the summer. According to sunset in the winter.
Shabbat and Holiday Mornings: 8:00 A.M.
Shabbat Minchah/Maariv: According to sunset.
Shacharit: Aside from *Shabbat*, *Shacharit* is held only on Mondays, Thursdays, and Fridays, at 7:00 A.M.

> *Note: Apart from its other attractions, the Nagyfuvaros Synagogue is heated in winter. This allows the congregation to use the main sanctuary year-round. Wintertime travellers should take note that most of the other synagogues in the city do not use their main sanctuaries during the winter months. They use adjacent prayer rooms instead.*

The Nagyfuvaros Synagogue is one of the most popular *shuls* in Budapest. Unlike most other synagogues in the city, which are mainly attended by elderly men, Nagyfuvaros attracts its share of younger worshippers. This is partly due to the weekly Talmud Torah and

Hebrew language classes organized by the synagogue. The relatively youthful feel gives one the impression that Nagyfuvaros will be the Budapest congregation to reckon with fifty years from now.

Perhaps the vitality of the synagogue is a bequest from the building's former use as a casino and entertainment hall of District VIII, called the Jozsefvaros Casino. It served such a function until 1922, when the Jewish Community purchased the site and had the designer Dezso Freund transform the entire courtyard into a synagogue that would hold eight hundred. Like the Csaky Synagogue (see Bet Smuel, below), Nagyfuvaros falls at the more traditional end of the Neolog Community. The *bimah* remains in the center of the synagogue and there never was an organ in use here (at this, the former proprietors would have been appalled). As was the case in the Csaky Synagogue and the Bethlen Ter Synagogue, the worshippers in Nagyfuvaros behaved much like the congregations of the Status Quo movement, although neither of these synagogues ever broke officially with the Neolog Community.

This legacy continues today. Nagyfuvaros is still known as one of the most tradition-oriented Neolog synagogues in Budapest. In recent years, the congregation became somewhat lenient and allowed, among other things, mixed seating of men and women. In the mid-1990s, however, a new rabbi began turning the congregation back to its quasi-Orthodox tradition. He posted a sign in the main sanctuary gently prodding women to "remember the tradition" and to sit either in the balcony or in a special area he reserved in the back of the synagogue for them. Since many of the women are elderly and had difficulty climbing the steps to the balcony, the area in the back of the synagogue has become the *de facto* women's section. (On the High Holidays, the balconies are opened for women as well.) There was a small problem with two young women, aged 20 and 21, who had come to Shabbat services with their father since they were old enough to walk. They had no intention of sitting away from their father and breaking the family tradition. Smiling sympathetically, the rabbi confessed, "They're the ones we allow to sit together. They're a family together, and it's more important to encourage families to come than to force them apart." For their part, the girls promised that when they get older, they'll sit in the back. The rabbi agreed to wait.

It's that spirit of tradition with a touch of compromise that characterizes both the Nagyfuvaros Synagogue and the entire conservative wing of the Hungarian Neolog movement.

Before the war, there used to be an Orthodox prayer room just across the street from the Nagyfuvaros Synagogue. In Nagy Fuvaros Street 3, an apartment was remodelled to serve the prayer needs of the *Etz Chayim* ("Tree of Life") Society. It no longer exists today.

BET SMUEL ("CSAKY")

Address: Hegedus Gyula Street 3, District XIII

Metro to Nyugati station or tram 4 or 6 to Nyugati station
Walk two blocks up Szent Istvan Krt. Hegedus Gyula Street is on the right. The synagogue is the second building in on the right.

Shacharit: 6:30 A.M. weekdays, 8:00 A.M. Sundays.
Minchah/Maariv: According to sunset.
Kabbalat Shabbat: According to sunset.
Shabbat and Holiday Mornings: 9:30 A.M.
Shabbat Minchah/Maariv: According to sunset.

Services in this synagogue are highly recommended. Bet Smuel is situated in an apartment building in the thirteenth district of Budapest, in an area that was predominately Jewish before the war. It was predominately Jews who built the district, from the end of the nineteenth century up to the Second World War. Even today, there is a small Community of mostly elderly Jews who live in the district.

If you mention Bet Smuel in Budapest, most people won't understand. The synagogue is known—particularly among the older generations—simply as "Csaky" (pronounced "Chaky"), after the former name of the street. If you drop the name Csaky Synagogue into conversation, Budapest's Jews in the know will consider you a veteran.

The building was originally an apartment building without any official Jewish relevance; in 1927 the Jewish Community purchased space on the inside and built the synagogue. With its Two Tablets above the portal, it is a rare synagogue-in-apartment-building that refers to Jewish worship on the building's facade.

Officially, the synagogue is Neolog, but don't let the name fool you. There is no organ, women sit in a gallery (for those who cannot climb the stairs, there is a separate women's section on the side of the main sanctuary), and the *bimah* is positioned in the center. A two-man choir accompanies the *chazan*, and in certain prayers like the *L'chah Dodi*, a young boy joins the *chazan* to sing in a shrill soprano. Other than the makeshift choir, the service differs in no way from traditional Orthodox liturgy. In its routine, Bet Smuel has more in common with the Status Quo movement (*see pages 435–436*) than anything else. In fact, Bet Smuel shows how inane are such differentiations of "Neolog," "Orthodox," or "Status Quo." As the rabbi at Bet Smuel likes to say, "Dividing names are destructive; the people who pray in this synagogue are simply Jews."

The main sanctuary is used only from Pesach until winter begins. During the winter months, a smaller sanctuary adjacent to the main one is in use. The fifty or so congregants—mostly elderly men—make up a highly enthusiastic service. On Saturday evenings, the congregation eats the traditional "*se'udah shelishit*," or "third meal," between the afternoon and evening prayers in the synagogue itself.

There is also a group of Georgian-Israeli Jews who hold separate services in Bet Smuel, usually before the main services begin.

BET AHARON SYNAGOGUE

Address: Thokoly Street 83, District XIV
Kabbalat Shabbat: 6:30 P.M.
Shabbat and Holiday Mornings: 9:00 A.M.

For those who dismiss Eastern European synagogues as the catacombs of elderly men, Friday night at the Bet Aharon synagogue will be a refreshing experience. The congregation defies regional stereotypes by attracting Jewish families. This means a typical Friday evening service includes boys and girls of pre-*Bar Mitzvah* ages, young parents, middle-aged men and women, and older congregants. The trans-generational success of the service is due, in part, to the synagogue's two Talmud Torah Jewish schools. The synagogue reasoned that if classes were held on Friday afternoons instead of Sunday mornings, the students would bring their parents to services after class. The plan worked. At the Friday evening *Kiddush*, the festive atmosphere among the children has made several parents into active members of the synagogue. (The Talmud Torah, which draws around 20 children, is divided into two classes: 5-6 year-olds, and 8-13 year-olds. The synagogue's president invites visitors for a glimpse of the Talmud Torah classes before services begin.)

More than any other synagogue in Budapest—or, for that matter, anywhere in Central Eastern Europe—Bet Aharon resembles a small American Conservative synagogue. For many American visitors, Bet Aharon will be like a home away from home. Although the *bimah* is situated in the middle of the synagogue and the women sit separately from the men, all the accoutrements of a suburban American synagogue are here. You'll even find neon blue Stars of David on the eastern wall. Everything from the family atmosphere to the modern furnishings to the *Kiddush* following the service will be familiar to most Jews reared in the Conservative Jewish tradition in America. Like its American counterparts, Bet Aharon (or simply "Thokoly," named after its street) calls up the children to the *bimah* at the end of the service to lead a prayer. The difference here, of course, is that the children sing in a typically Eastern European Ashkenazi accent.

But the most charming aspect to Bet Aharon is the father-son cantorial tag team. The rabbi, Peter Kardos, doubles as the synagogue's cantor. For much of the service, however, his teenage son takes the pulpit with a vibrant singing voice.

If you have a choice between Friday evening or Shabbat morning services, Friday evening is the more popular service. Women are separated from men by the *bimah*, but it is a rather mild *mechitzah*; there is no curtain separating the two seating areas.

DESSEWFFY STREET SYNAGOGUE

Address: Dessewffy Street 23, District VI
Shacharit: 6:45 A.M. weekdays, 7:00 A.M. Sundays and national holidays.
Minchah/Maariv: According to sunset (until Shavuot), 7:15 or 7:30 P.M. from Shavuot through the summer.
Kabbalat Shabbat: According to sunset.
Shabbat and Holiday Mornings: 8:30 A.M.
Shabbat Minchah/Maariv: Approximately one and a half hours before *Shabbat* ends.

Visiting tourists will often ask, "Where's the *Bikkur Cholim* Synagogue?" That was the name of the Dessewffy Synagogue before the war, because at one time it was where the *Bikkur Cholim* Society (Society for Visiting the Sick) went to *shul*. Built in the eclectic style in 1870, the Dessewffy Synagogue is one of several Budapest synagogues located inside an apartment block. In this case, it was built at the same time as the building itself.

From the outside, the quaint red bricks and yellow walls combined with its diminutive size make for a much more home-style, personable atmosphere than you'll find in a synagogue like the Dohany Street Synagogue. The congregation has the same vibes: pleasant, amicable, and unassuming. The Dessewffy Synagogue is an official member of the Orthodox Jewish Community of Budapest, and among those in the know, it has become a favorite alternative to the main synagogue of Kazinczy Street. Although most of the congregants are elderly men, young people—either Orthodox or interested in Orthodoxy—often make Dessewffy their Jewish spiritual center. It is also the place to find a few visiting Israeli university students. In 1989, the synagogue reached out to Israelis studying in Budapest (usually medicine and law students) who had no connection to the Jewish Community. Since then it's been the traditional *shul* for Israeli students. You won't find dozens of youth, but two to five students in one synagogue is something here.

The main sanctuary is used about ninety percent of the time in the winter. On the rare occasion that the *minyan* is small (they always get a *minyan*), they pray in the adjacent prayer room. This is good to keep in mind, because most synagogues in Budapest pray in smaller prayer rooms during the entire winter. During the summer and on holidays, the interior is always used. With the sky-blue tint scattered throughout the interior, including the ceiling, you'll think you're in a synagogue in Tsfat, Israel. Women sit in balconies on the right and left sides of the main sanctuary. When the smaller room is used, women sit behind a transparent curtain in the back of the room.

The leader of the congregation is Laszlo Herczog, a reserved but friendly man who welcomes visitors to his synagogue. There is no rabbi in Dessewffy because, as Mr. Herczog jokes, "When there isn't a rabbi, there isn't a *maklochet* [disagreement]." Mr. Herczog is also the General Secretary of the Orthodox Community, so if you have any questions (e.g., *mikveh*, Pesach matzoh, etc.), it's wise to speak with him. If you happen to need a circumcision, Mr. Herczog's your man, too. Mr. Herczog is the only *mohel* in Hungary. In 1978 the Memorial Foundation for Jewish Culture paid for a plane ticket to London, where Mr. Herczog studied the trade. Today he travels throughout Hungary, Romania, SubCarpathian Ruthenia, and elsewhere to perform circumcisions. Unfortunately, the demand has been decreasing every year since the burst of interest in 1989. Feel free to have a chat with him; Mr. Herczog speaks very good English.

BETHLEN TER SYNAGOGUE

Address: Istvan Street 17 (off Bethlen Gabor ter), District VII
Kabbalat Shabbat: 7:15 P.M. in the summer. According to sunset in the winter.
Shabbat and Holiday Mornings: 9:30 A.M.
Shacharit: 7:15 A.M. weekdays, 8:00 A.M. Sundays.
Minchah/Maariv: There is no *minchah/maariv* service except on *Shabbat*, which begins according to sunset, and on Sundays (the rabbi explains that on Sundays, people have more time). The Sunday *minchah* begins at 7:00 P.M.

The Bethlen Ter Synagogue was built in 1923 into the site of a Jewish elementary school and high school. Today, the building is no longer owned by the Jewish Community. A school continues to function in the building, but it is not a Jewish school.

Like the "Csaky" Synagogue (*see* Bet Smuel, *page 480*), the Bethlen Ter Synagogue is officially affiliated with the Neolog Community. However, in its customs and liturgy, the congregation is basically Orthodox. There has never been an organ in the Bethlen Ter Synagogue. Even before the war, the orientation of the synagogue was very close to the Status Quo movement (*see pages 435–436*). It affiliated with the Neolog Community, though, in order to avoid further fissures in Budapest Jewry. Today, the rabbi and congregation are Orthodox in outlook.

The Bethlen Ter Synagogue is noted for the several young, observant families that make up its congregation. On Shabbat, a diverse crowd of around 35 worshippers gather in the synagogue for prayer. On holidays such as Purim, the chapel fills with young parents and their toddlers. The main sanctuary is used for *Shabbat* and holiday services from Pesach to Sukkot. The women's section is a gallery. During the rest of the year and in the mornings, services are held in the chapel next door. Women sit in a smaller alcove just off the chapel.

THE UJPEST SYNAGOGUE

Address: Berzeviczy Street 8, District IV

By metro, take the blue line (M3) to the Ujpest-Varoskapu station. Berzeviczy Street begins just across Arpad Street.

Kabbalat Shabbat: 6:00 P.M. in the spring and summer (until around Sukkot). According to sunset in the winter.
Shabbat and Holiday Mornings: 9:00 A.M. year-round.

The synagogue holds prayers only on Shabbat and the holidays. There is no daily *minyan*; even on Shabbat, there is no *minyan* for *minchah/maariv* on *motzaei Shabbat* (Saturday evening).

This Romantic-styled building is one of the most stunning synagogues in all of Budapest and a testament to Jewish perseverance in the face of government-sanctioned anti-Semitism. (For a discussion of the synagogue and its district, *see page 472*.)

The main synagogue is in use only on major holidays and during the warm season. During the rest of the year, the congregation gathers in a smaller prayer hall situated in the white residential complex to the right of the synagogue building. The complex serves as one of the Budapest Jewish Community's retirement centers (built in 1926; modernized in 1995) and as a home for the mentally disabled. Nowadays, much of the congregation is comprised of people living in the complex.

It isn't the most spirited service you'll find in Central Europe, but what the congregation lacks in *ruach* it more than makes up for in affability and warmth. The rabbi, too, is extremely helpful: a recent graduate of the Budapest Rabbinical Seminary, Rabbi Zoltan

Radnoti is an intriguing character with whom you may speak in English, although he prefers Hebrew. The congregation is Neolog, but the liturgy is basically traditional and no organ or choir are used. In fact, the organ in the main synagogue is under repair. After the repair is finished, it will be in use during the High Holidays.

Although the main synagogue is usually closed, it is worth seeing from the outside. You might wish to come fifteen minutes prior to services in order to view the Holocaust memorial, next to the synagogue, which lists the names of all the martyred Jews of Ujpest.

THE BUDA SYNAGOGUE

Address: Frankel Leo Street 49, District II

Take tram 4 or 6 to the first stop on the Buda side of Margit Hid (Margaret Bridge). Then either walk up Frankel Leo Street (it takes about fifteen minutes) or take tram 17 two stops north to the Kavics Street stop. The Buda Synagogue is not to be confused with the medieval "Small Synagogue" in the Buda Castle District [*see page 414*], which does not hold services.

The Buda Synagogue holds services only on Shabbat.
Kabbalat Shabbat: 5:30 P.M. in the winter, 6:30 P.M. in the spring and summer.
Shabbat and Holiday Mornings: 9:00 A.M.

As with the other synagogues, the Buda Synagogue has its own, play-it-by-ear interpretation of when the seasons change. If you arrive at the end of the winter or summer, it's best to check *Uj Elet* for the exact times for *Kabbalat Shabbat*.

During the winter months, and whenever it is too cold to pray in the unheated synagogue, the congregation gathers in an elongated room of the synagogue offices. When you enter the building's courtyard, take the apartment entrance on the left side and go up two flights of stairs; the chapel is through the door on the right side.

The Buda Synagogue is a pearl hidden inside an apartment block just next to the Danube River. On the facade of the apartment block, the depiction of a menorah and a Star of David are the only clues as to the synagogue secreted within. Only once you step inside the courtyard will you see the lush neo-Gothic facade of the synagogue. This has led several tour guides to explain that the Jewish Community rented out the entire apartment building, and only afterwards built the synagogue in the courtyard. This explanation, however, is wrong. The synagogue actually predates the apartment building by four decades. In 1888, the synagogue was opened; later, in 1928, the apartment building was built around the synagogue. From the time it was built, the apartment building included offices of the Jewish Community, a winter prayer hall, as well as classrooms, cultural spaces and a Jewish youth group center.

The synagogue seats 300 people, including the women's galleries. The service is carried out in its entirety at a relaxing pace by a mixture of observant and non-observant Jews.

In its tradition and rites, the synagogue bears much in common with the Conservative movement in American Judaism. *Shabbat* morning services are followed by a *kiddush* of light refreshments—a perfect time for schmoozing.

Ironically, the synagogue is located just below the verdant hills of Buda, which have become the favored neighborhoods of a new class of Jewish yuppies in Budapest. The synagogue itself, by contrast, is filled almost entirely with elderly Jews.

TELEKI TER SYNAGOGUE

Address: Teleki ter 22, District VIII

Take tram 28, 29, or 37 two stops on Nepszinhaz Street from Blaha Lujza ter to Teleki Laszlo ter. Bear in mind that this neighborhood is not the safest part of town.

Shabbat Morning: 8:00 A.M.

This synagogue is neither particularly impressive (it's a little prayer hall in an apartment courtyard) nor vibrant (*Shabbat* mornings are the only services they hold). But it deserves mention as the single congregation in Budapest that prays *nusach Sephardi*. In Judaism, there are two strains of origin and tradition: Ashkenazi and Sephardi. Ashkenazi Jews have origins in Europe, whereas Sephardi Jews have origins specifically in Spain and spread out after the Spanish Expulsion of 1492. There are also two styles of ritual and liturgy, Ashkenazi and Sephardi. These styles, which originally developed in the separate regions of Ashkanazi and Sephardi Jews, are not necessarily linked to one's place of origin. Many hasidic sects, for instance, whose origin was in Eastern Europe, pray according to the Sephardic liturgy.

This is noted so that you don't come to the Teleki Synagogue expecting to find Jews from Morocco or Syria. All the congregants are European Jews from Budapest, but they prefer the wording of the prayers in *nusach Sephardi* prayer books. In this case, the word Sephardi is a question of custom, not of origin.

There used to be another Sephardi *shtiebel* on Kiraly Street, but it closed in the 1970s. The remaining *shul* here on Teleki ter is not very strong, composed of a few elderly men and funded by the Orthodox Community, but if the Sephardi liturgy is your style, then you might want to give Teleki Ter a try.

SASZ CHEVRA

(English spelling "Shas Chevrah")
Address: Vasvari Pal Street 5, District VI
Kabbalat Shabbat: 7:30 P.M. in the summer, 5:30 P.M. in the winter.
Shabbat and Holiday Mornings: 9:00 A.M.

For a couple of weeks during seasonal changes, the time for *Kabbalat Shabbat* shifts to 6:00 P.M., 6:30 P.M., etc. If you arrive during one of these transitions, it's best to check *Uj Elet* for the exact time. Or call Rabbi Baruch Oberlander, who officiates at the synagogue, at (36–1) 268 0183. Rabbi Oberlander, an American Lubavitcher rabbi, speaks perfect English.

The roots of Shas Chevrah extend far beyond all other working synagogues in Budapest today. The society—more of a study group than a synagogue—began meeting as early as the 1830s in a building roughly one block away from its current site. This was a full quarter-century before the Dohany Street Synagogue was built, and long before the Jewish Congress would rend Hungarian Jewish life into three opposing camps.

"Shas Chevrah" roughly translates to "Talmud Society;" it's a generic term indicating a study and prayer hall. In this case, the Shas Chevrah functioned primarily as a *beit midrash*, or study hall. In the bylaws of the society from the first half of the nineteenth century, two rabbis were required to teach in the Shas Chevrah. The main rabbi would teach Jewish law every day between the afternoon and evening service. The second rabbi, for his part, taught Bible and Bible commentary every day. By emphasizing teaching and learning, the Shas Chevrah nimbly avoided being pigeonholed as either "Orthodox," "Neolog," or "Status Quo" when those labels emerged in the latter half of the nineteenth century.

In 1890, the Shas Chevrah moved to its current site on Vasvari Pal Street. The synagogue was not permitted to face the street front. Later, the Jewish Community erected a building around the synagogue. Throughout this time, the Shas Chevrah was composed of ritually observant Jews who did not wish to align themselves with either the Orthodox or the Status Quo movements. The society maintained its independence until 1950. In that year, the communist government forced the Orthodox and Neolog wings to merge into a single unit, with a degree of internal autonomy granted the Orthodox. Shas Chevrah wished to be grouped in this Orthodox sub-category, but the government felt it was too complicated. As a result, Shas Chevrah was classified as part of the larger Neolog Community. In its ritual and observance, however, the society continued to be de facto Orthodox.

In 1992, Rabbi Baruch Oberlander, the leader of Chabad Lubavitch in Budapest, agreed to officiate in the synagogue on one condition: it would continue to be a ritually Orthodox synagogue. And thus emerged a paradox: a Neolog synagogue run by the Orthodox Chabad movement.

Today, Shas Chevrah continues to be the Chabad synagogue of Budapest. Approximately 30 people come to services on Shabbat. Women sit in the second half of the synagogue, separated from the men by a transparent curtain. In the winter, the congregation prays in a chapel adjacent to the synagogue.

Appendix

The focus of this book has been the centuries of Jewish life in Central Eastern Europe that preceded the Holocaust. What follows is a brief description of three places that are also a vital part of many trips to the region. Only three sites of the Nazi killing machine are included here because these are often parts of visits to Prague, Warsaw, and Cracow.

TEREZIN

Seventy kilometers north of Prague

Terezin was built in 1780 by Emperor Josef II as a garrison against any Prussian advances into Bohemia. It was named Theresienstadt after the emperor's mother, Empress Maria Theresa. The fortification was complemented by a second garrison, called the Small Fortress, on the other side of the Ohre River.

After the Germans occupied Bohemia and Moravia in 1939, they made the Small Fortress into an S.S. prison and stationed S.S. officers in the town. In October 1941, the Nazis chose Terezin as a Jewish ghetto and detainment center while they organized transports to death camps in the east. With its pre-existing barracks and only 3,700 inhabitants to be evacuated, Terezin was seen as the ideal site for the containment of Jews from throughout Europe. Similar to other ghettos in Nazi-occupied Europe, the Terezin ghetto was run by a Jewish council that was strangulated by the demands of the S.S. The first chairman of the "Council of Jewish Elders" in Terezin was Jakub Edelstein, who was murdered in Auschwitz in 1944.

On November 24, 1941, the first transport arrived consisting of 342 Jewish men from Prague. Until June 1943, the closest railway stop was three kilometers away, in Bohusovice. From there, the Jews were marched into Terezin. Jews from the first two transports were actually a construction unit required to transform the town into a ghetto capable of receiving and accommodating mass transports. Even before they had finished, more deportations to Terezin had begun. By the end of the war, 150,000 prisoners had been sent to Terezin from Czechoslovakia, Germany, Austria, Holland, Hungary, Denmark, and elsewhere.

Eventually Terezin was transformed into what resembled a concentration camp, with segregated-sex barracks and buildings, forced labor, lack of proper food, and rampant disease. In the face of terrible conditions and the constant threat of deportations to the east, the Jews of Terezin consoled themselves with a relatively thriving cultural life. The S.S. generally tolerated these activities. Thus there were frequent concerts, plays, and lectures in Terezin. Some of the art and writing produced in the ghetto would become world-renowned in postwar years.

Execution in Terezin began in January of 1942, when nine men were murdered for offenses such as trying to purchase items in "Aryan" stores. Later, to quell public discontent, public executions were replaced by sentences in the Small Fortress and deportation to death camps. The first deportation to the east left for Riga on January 9, 1942. Over the course of the next six months, 16,000 Czech Jews, all under sixty-five years of age, were deported to camps in the east. A total of 87,000 Jews would be sent from Terezin to concentration and death camps in the east by October 1944.

During this time, social and health conditions in Terezin continued to deteriorate. From July to September 1942, the number of Jews in Terezin grew from 20,000 to 60,000. Transports of elderly Jews from Germany and Austria, combined with deportations from Terezin of young men, led to a health crisis the ghetto was not equipped to remedy. Between July and September 1942, 70,000 Jews died of disease in Terezin. Eventually, a crematorium would be used to dispose of the bodies. The ashes were later thrown into the Ohre River. To lessen the number of deaths on the streets of the ghetto, the S.S. began to transport thousands of elderly Jews to concentration and death camps.

In response to pressure from Denmark and other countries to permit the Red Cross to view Germany's treatment of the Jews, the Terezin ghetto was given a face-lift in the first half of 1944. This was accompanied by continuous transports to the east to lessen the overcrowding of the ghetto. On June 23, 1944, three Red Cross officials arrived and were given a tour of various staged scenes, including exquisite cafes and pleasant accommodations, and shown items such as specially printed currency in the ghetto. The Red Cross left Terezin satisfied that no injustices were being committed there. A second visit by the Red Cross, on April 6, 1945, had equal results. In the end of April, thousands of Jews were evacuated from concentration and death camps and sent, by train or foot, to Terezin. This led to a typhus epidemic in Terezin that affected 3,000 people, 500 of whom died.

Terezin was liberated by the Russian army in May 1945. There were approximately 30,000 prisoners there when the Russians arrived.

TREBLINKA

One hundred kilometers northeast of Warsaw

Treblinka served as the second largest Nazi death camp. Located four kilometers from a railway station, the camp was divided into Treblinka I, a forced-labor camp of Jews and Poles, and Treblinka II, a secret camp designed as a death camp.

Treblinka II was one of four camps—the others were Belzec, Sobibor, and Chelmno—designed exclusively for mass murder. The staff of Treblinka was composed of approximately thirty S.S. officers, between two and three hundred Ukrainians, and over 1,000 Jewish prisoner workers. In Treblinka, unlike in Auschwitz, the method of gassing was carbon monoxide piped into the gas chambers from diesel engines located outside. Gas chambers were located in two buildings: The building erected first contained three gas chambers, while the later building contained ten gas chambers, each twice as large as those in the former building.

On July 23, 1942, after the first gas chambers were functioning, the death camp was put into operation. It was then that the Mass Aktion in the Warsaw Ghetto was perpetrated, when several thousand Jews were sent from Warsaw to Treblinka every day. Over 800,000 people, the overwhelming majority of them Jews, were murdered in Treblinka. Other victims included Poles and Gypsies. Of the Jews, close to 300,000 came from the Warsaw Ghetto. The remaining Jews came from elsewhere in Poland and from Germany, Austria, Bohemia and Moravia, Slovakia, Holland, Belgium, Luxembourg, Greece, Yugoslavia, Bulgaria, and elsewhere.

Jews were murdered immediately after arrival. When a train arrived, some of its cars would be uncoupled and brought to the unloading station. From here, people would disembark and were told to drop all heavy bags, after which they were led to a disrobing site. Women were taken to have their heads shaved (the hair was sent to various German industries to insulate motors). Disabled and weak people were ushered away into the "Infirmary," where they were shot individually and buried so as not to slow up the procession to the gas chambers. In the disrobing site, men were forced to pile up hand luggage and clothing. They were attacked viciously by S.S. officers and Ukrainians, according to one view in order to force the Jews to run and therefore to breathe deeply, making the subsequent time in the gas chambers shorter. Afterwards, all the people were forced into an alleyway alternately termed "Ascension" or the "Pipeline"—a narrow, curving passageway that led to the gas chambers. The curve in the passageway was evidently designed so that those entering it would not see what existed on the other side. Halfway through the Pipeline, Jews were required to deposit papers and valuables at a small shed. On the other side of the Pipeline was the second part of the death camp, where the gas chambers were located. The killing took fifteen to twenty minutes. Sometimes the motors malfunctioned in the middle of the killing, and the Jews imprisoned in the chambers were forced to wait while repairs were made.

After the killing was finished, the chambers were emptied and the so-called "dentists" removed all gold teeth and any hidden items from the bodies. Then the bodies were arranged in mass graves and covered in lime and soil. During this time, a subsequent group would be ushered through the Pipeline to the gas chambers.

In the beginning of 1943, when the tide in the war appeared to be shifting, German leaders decided to destroy all evidence of their crimes in Treblinka. Jewish prisoners were forced to exhume bodies from mass graves and burn them on iron grates. On August 2, 1943, the prisoners launched an uprising and attempted escape in which they succeeded in killing several guards and setting the barracks on fire. Between three and five hundred prisoners escaped, but most were caught and killed. By the time of liberation, there were only about fifty survivors.

After the uprising, the Germans and Ukrainians continued the process of destroying evidence of mass murders at Treblinka. Buildings were destroyed, graves were planted over, and pine trees were planted. By the time of liberation, there was little that remained to speak of what had been perpetrated.

For years, there was no memorial at Treblinka. Construction of a memorial was begun in 1961 and finished in 1964. It consists of a two-hundred-meter pathway of concrete railway ties leading to seventeen thousand granite rocks surrounding a giant cracked obelisk. One stone bears the name Janusz Korczak, the famous orphanage director who accompanied his wards to Treblinka. It is the only stone accompanied by a name. The entire memorial was designed by sculptor Franciszek Duszenko and architect Adam Haupt.

AUSCHWITZ

Fifty kilometers southwest of Cracow

Auschwitz (Oswiecim in Polish) was the largest Nazi death camp, concentration camp, and slave-labor camp. The Auschwitz camp eventually consisted of three parts: Auschwitz I, the main camp; Auschwitz II, Birkenau; and Auschwitz III, Monowitz.

Auschwitz was a town of 12,000 residents (including 5,000 Jews) when it was occupied by Germany in September 1939. In the spring of 1940, the Nazi S.S. decided to establish a concentration camp outside the town as a place to gather political prisoners and Polish resistance fighters. Rudolf Hoss was made the camp's commander. The immediate vicinity was evacuated; this area eventually comprised forty square kilometers. Three hundred Jews were brought in to build the camp, in an area that had included sixteen prewar army barracks. In May 1940, the first prisoners, thirty German criminals, were brought to the camp. On June 14, 1940, 728 Polish prisoners were brought to Auschwitz. In March 1941, most of the 10,900 prisoners were Poles.

It was then decided to expand Auschwitz to hold 30,000 inmates. In 1941, construction was begun on a new camp in nearby Birkenau. Barracks designed to hold fifty-two horses were built to hold over four hundred inmates. The expansion was linked to the expectation of hundreds of thousands of Russian prisoners of war, but such an influx never arrived.

Auschwitz was considered as a site to serve for the mass murder of European Jews since the summer of 1941. Its location by rail lines made it logistically one of the most feasible locations for such a purpose. S.S. chief Heinrich Himmler spoke with Hoss about this plan in Berlin, and soon afterwards Adolf Eichmann came to Auschwitz to explain the details of the operation.

On September 3–5, 1941, Zyklon B (prussic acid) was used as an experimental method of killing six hundred Soviet prisoners of war and two hundred fifty ill prisoners. The Auschwitz mortuary was converted into a gas chamber and, together with two huts in Birkenau, served the purpose of mass annihilation of Jews until March 1943. By this time, 280,000 Jews had been deported to Auschwitz from France, Holland, Poland, Slovakia, Belgium, Croatia, Germany, Austria, Bohemia and Moravia, Salonika, and Norway. Originally, bodies of Jews who had been murdered were buried, but in July 1942, special crematoria were planned that were attached to the gas chambers. These were operational within one year. From April 1943 through March 1944, around 160,000 Jews were deported to Auschwitz.

On March 19, 1944, with the German invasion of Hungary, the influx of Jews to Auschwitz increased dramatically. In a period of eight months, about 426,000 Hungarian Jews were brought to Auschwitz.

The overwhelming majority were murdered immediately after arrival in Auschwitz. In the *selektion* process, young, weak, and sick individuals, as well as many others, were murdered in the gas chambers and their bodies burned immediately thereafter. The remaining men and women were forced into slave labor amid inhuman conditions of the camp. These people, too, faced the constant threat of new *selektionen*.

All told, approximately 1.1 million people were murdered in Auschwitz. Ninety percent of them were Jews. The rest were Poles, Soviet prisoners of war, Gypsies, and other inmates.

Glossary

This is not meant to be a detailed glossary, but rather a series of concise definitions to supplement the text. For this reason, definitions are as brief as possible.

Aleph: First letter of the Hebrew alphabet
Aliyah: "Ascendance." The term refers to the act of a congregant being called to read a blessing before one of the seven installments of the weekly Torah portion
Amidah: The central prayer in the Jewish service, read while standing
Amud: Pulpit or stand
Aron hakodesh: "Holy Ark" in which *Torot* are kept. It faces Jerusalem (in European synagogues, it is found on the eastern wall)
Ashkenazim: Jews with ancestry in northern, central, or eastern Europe
Avodah zarah: Idolatry
Bachur: Young man
Badhan: Jester or humorist
Bar mitzvah: The passage into manhood at the age of thirteen, when a boy is called to the Torah for his first *aliyah*
Beit din: Court of law
Beit midrash: A study and prayer hall
Bimah: Raised platform in the synagogue where the Torah is read
Birkat hamazon: Grace after meals
Brit milah: Also *Bris*. Circumcision of eight-day-old male child
Bubbe meise: Folkloric anecdote or story
Bund: Yiddish based, socialist national autonomy movement among Jews in Eastern Europe, formed in Vilna in 1897
Challah: Twisted loaf of bread used on *Shabbat* and festivals
Chattan: Bridegroom
Chazan: Cantor
Cheder: Traditional Jewish elementary school; study hall
Cherem: Writ of excommunication (plural *cheremim*)
Chevrah Kaddishah: Jewish burial society
Cholent: All-night stew typically prepared for *Shabbat*
Chometz: Leavened bread

Chupah: Wedding canopy
Cohen: Jewish priest in Ancient Israel; one who is patrilineally descended from such priests (plural *Cohanim*)
Dayan: Rabbinical judge
Derashan: Rabbinical homily
D'var Torah: Commentary on the Torah
Dybbuk: Evil spirit, often known to enter and possess a person
Eruv: Specially demarcated area within which Jews may transport certain items on *Shabbat*
Ezrat Nashim: Women's section in the synagogue
Gabbai: Sexton; the person who distributes *aliyot* on *Shabbat*
Gemarah: The commentary on the *Mishnah* that forms the second part of the Talmud
Gematriah: Numerical equivelant of Hebrew letters, used in *midrash* and *Kabbalah*
Genizah: Chamber in which old holy books are stored before being buried in a cemetery
Gilgul: Metempsychosis
Haggadah: Guidebook to the Passover *seder* in which the order of ceremonies is delineated in tandem with the story of Passover, prayers, and song
Hakafah: On Simchat Torah, a synagogue's Torah scrolls are carried around the sanctuary seven times. Each circuit is called a *hakafah* (plural *hakafot*)
Halachah: Jewish law (adjective *halachic*)
Hanukkah: The Festival of Lights commemorating the triumph of the Maccabees over the Syrian Greek oppressors in ancient Israel
Hasid: Follower of Hasidism (plural *hasidim*)
Hasidism: Populist mystical movement originating in Eastern Europe in the eighteenth century
Haskalah: The Jewish Enlightenment
Havdallah: Ceremony marking the conclusion of *Shabbat*
Heksher: Rabbinical certification that kosher standards are maintained
Kabbalah: Jewish mysticism
Kabbalat Shabbat: The "Welcoming in the *Shabbat*" ceremony that begins the Friday evening service
Kaddish: Aramaic doxology recited by the prayer leader at certain points of religious service. The "Mourner's Kaddish" is recited by the mourners in the congregation
Kallah: Bride
Kapporet: Curtain or ornament above the *parochet* in front of the *aron hakodesh*
Kavanah: Devotion and concentration during prayer
Keter Torah: Crown of the Torah
Kettubah: Marriage contract (plural *kettubot*)
Kiddush: The ceremony over wine on *Shabbat* and festivals
Kinah: Elegy
Kippah: Yarmulke, male headcovering
Kittel: White robe worn by the cantor during High Holiday services
Klaus: Small prayer hall
Kugel: Baked noodle pudding

Kvittel: A written note left on the tombstone of a *tzaddik*
Lag Ba'Omer: Festive holiday on the thirty-third day of the Omer
Levi or Levite: Member of a priestly tribe; one who is patrilineally descended from this tribe
Lilith: Adam's first wife and later the queen of demons
Maariv: Evening prayer service
Macher: A powerful individual, a mover and shaker
Machzor: Prayer book for the festivals
Magen David: Shield of David, "Jewish Star"
Maklochet: Disagreement
Marrano: Widespread but derogatory term used for Spanish Jews who were forced to convert to Christianity but who practiced Jewish tradition in secret
Mashgiach: The person who supervises and inspects a kosher kitchen or factory for its compliance with kosher dietary laws
Matzoh: Unleavened bread eaten on Passover
Mechitzah: The barrier between men and women in a traditionally observant synagogue
Menorah: Seven-branched candelabra used in the Old Temple in Jerusalem
Mezuzah: Parchment containing passages from Deuteronomy, traditionally fastened to the doorposts of Jewish homes
Midrash: Allegorical, inspirational, and interpretive literature meant to explain the text of the Torah
Mikveh: Ritual bath
Minchah: Afternoon prayer service
Minhag: Jewish custom
Minyan: Ten men traditionally required for a Jewish prayer service
Mishnah: The first part of the Talmud containing Jewish law and ethics
Mitnaged: Observant Jews who opposed *hasidim* (plural *mitnagdim*)
Mitzvah: Divine commandment (plural *mitzvot*)
Mohel: Person who performs the *brit milah*
Motzaei Shabbat: The cessation of *Shabbat*
Ner Tamid: Eternal light lit in synagogues
Ohel: Literally a tent; large stone monument, often a small room, built atop the grave of a prestigious or wealthy individual (plural *ohelim*)
Omer: A sheaf of barley offered at the Old Temple on the second day of Passover; the method of counting the forty-nine days between Pesach and Shavuot
Parnas: Leader of a Jewish community
Parochet: Curtain covering the doors of the *aron hakodesh*
Pesach: Passover, the festival celebrating the liberation of Jews from slavery in Egypt
Piyyutim: Liturgical poems
Pogrom: A violent riot perpetrated against Jews
Purim: Joyous festival celebrating the deliverance of the Persian Jews from the genocidal designs of Haman
Rashei Tevot: Hebrew abbreviations, often acronyms

Rashi: Rabbi Shlomo ben Isaac (1040–1105), whose enormous body of commentary is one of the primary sources of explanation of the Bible
Rebbe: Leader of a hasidic court
Rebbetzin: Rabbi's wife
Rimonim: Decorative objects placed atop the wooden Torah scrolls
Rosh Hashanah: The Jewish New Year
Ruach: Wind, spirit
Sabbatian: Of or relating to the followers of the seventeenth-century false-Messiah Shabbetai Tzvi
Sandek: The person who holds the baby during the *brit milah*
Schnorrer: Literally a beggar, also a moocher
Seder: Passover evening ceremony involving symbolic foods, prayer, and the narration of the enslavement and Exodus from Egypt
Sefer Yetzirah: "The Book of Formations," an early kabbalistic work dealing with numerology, cosmology, and analyses of the Hebrew alphabet
Selichah: Penitential prayer or poem (plural *selichot*)
Semichah: Rabbinical ordination
Sephardim: Jews with ancestry in Spain or Portugal
Shabbat: Sundown Friday night through sundown Saturday night, the Jewish day of rest
Shabbat Hagadol: The "Great Shabbat" that precedes Pesach
Shabbat Shuvah: The "Shabbat of Return" that falls between Rosh Hashanah and Yom Kippur
Shacharit: Morning prayer service
Shamash: Synagogue sexton (plural *shamashim*)
Shavuot: The "Feast of Weeks" seven weeks after Pesach, celebrating the wheat harvest and, later, the giving of the Torah
Shem Hamefurash: The unpronounceable tetragrammaton
Shemini Atzeret: The eighth day of Sukkot
Shemurah Matzoh: Matzoh that is made under the most stringent ritual precepts, from the planting of the seed through the baking of the dough
Shivat Ha Minim: The "Seven Species" of Israel
Shochet: A ritual slaughterer
Shofar: Ram's horn blown on Rosh Hashanah and Yom Kippur
Shtiebel: Small prayer hall
Shul: Synagogue
Shulchan Aruch: Guide to Jewish law written by Rabbi Joseph Karo (1488–1575)
Sh'viti Tablet: Tablet with kabbalistic and inspirational inscriptions placed in front of the prayer leader during services
Siddur: Prayer book (plural *siddurim*)
Simchat Torah: Festival of the rejoicing over the Torah when the yearly cycle of Torah readings is finished and then begun again
Sukkah: Tabernacle built during Sukkot celebrations
Sukkot: The harvest festival; plural of *Sukkah*

Taharah: Ritual cleansing of the dead before burial
Tallis or Tallit: Prayer shawl
Talmud: The *Mishnah* and *Gemarah*, containing laws and ethics for every conceivable aspect of Jewish life
Teumah: Impurity
Tikkun chatzot: The midnight service
Tishe B'av: Day of mourning for the destruction of the First and Second Temples in Jerusalem
Torah—The five books of Moses; the scroll of this work (plural *Torot*); all of Jewish religious literature (broad sense)
Tosafot: Talmudic commentary from the twelfth through the fourteenth centuries that supplements the commentary of Rashi
Tsuris: Troubles
Tzaddik: Righteous person (plural *tzaddikim*)
Tzedakkah: Charity
Tzizit: Ritual undergarment with four corners and fringes, worn by men
Yad: Literally a hand; silver pointers used to read the Torah (plural *yadayim*)
Yahrzeit: The death anniversary of one's parents
Yeshivah: Traditional school of talmudic study for students who have finished *cheder*
Yizkor: Memorial service
Yom Kippur: The Day of Atonement, ten days after Rosh Hashanah
Zemirot: Hymns sung during *Shabbat*, especially at meals

Bibliography

To facilitate further reading, I have separated sources into their basic categories. There is, of course, some overlapping.

GENERAL WORKS AND REFERENCE WORKS

Ash, Timothy Garton. *The Magic Lantern: The Revolution of '89 Witnessed in Warsaw, Budapest, Berlin, and Prague.* New York: Random House, 1990.

Birnbaum, Philip. *Encyclopedia of Jewish Concepts.* New York: Sanhedrin Press, 1979.

Bloch, Abraham P. *The Biblical and Historical Background of Jewish Customs and Ceremonies.* New York: Ktav, 1980.

Braham, Randolph L., ed. *Anti-Semitism and the Treatment of the Holocaust in Postcommunist Eastern Europe.* New York: The Rosenthal Institute for Holocaust Studies, 1994.

Doblin, Alfred. *Journey to Poland.* Ed. Heinz Graber. Trans. Joachim Neugroschel. New York: Paragon House, 1991.

Heschel, Abraham Joshua. *The Earth Is the Lord's: The Inner World of the Jew in Eastern Europe.* Woodstock, Vermont: Jewish Lights, 1995.

Krinsky, Carol Herselle. *Synagogues of Europe: Architecture, History, Meaning.* Cambridge, Massachusetts: The MIT Press, 1985.

Kurlansky, Mark. *A Chosen Few: The Resurrection of European Jewry.* Reading, Massachusetts: Addison-Wesley, 1995.

Mendelsohn, Ezra: *The Jews of East Central Europe between the World Wars.* Bloomington: Indiana University Press, 1987.

Mendes-Flohr, Paul, and Jehuda Reinharz, eds. *The Jew in the Modern World: A Documentary History.* New York: Oxford University Press, 1995.

Roth, Cecil, ed. *Encyclopaedia Judaica.* Jerusalem: Keter Publishing House, 1971.

Rubin, Alexis P., ed. *Scattered among the Nations: Documents Affecting Jewish History 49 to 1975.* Northvale, New Jersey: Jason Aronson Inc., 1995.

Sachar, Howard M. *The Course of Modern Jewish History.* New York: Vintage, 1990.

Singer, Isidore, ed. *The Jewish Encyclopedia.* New York: Funk and Wagnalls, 1905.

Tanakh: A New Translation of the Holy Scriptures According to the Traditional Hebrew Text. Philadelphia: The Jewish Publication Society, 1985.

Telushkin, Joseph. *Jewish Literacy.* New York: William Morrow, 1991.

PRAGUE

Alter, Robert. "Jewish Dreams and Nightmares." In *After the Tradition: Essays on Modern Jewish Writing*. New York: E. P. Dutton, 1971, pp. 17–34.

Altshuler, David, ed. *The Precious Legacy: Judaic Treasures from the Czechoslovak State Collections*. New York: Summit Books, 1983.

Anderson, Mark, ed. *Reading Kafka: Prague, Politics, and the Fin de Siecle*. New York: Schocken Books, 1989.

Beckova, Katerina. *Langweiluv model Prahy*. Trans. Augustin Palat. Prague: The Prague Municipal Museum, 1986.

Benesova, Marie, and Rudolf Posva. *Prague's Ghetto Asanace*. Prague: Arch, 1993.

Berger, Natalia, ed. *Where Cultures Meet: The Story of the Jews of Czechoslovakia*. Tel Aviv: Beth Hatefutsoth and Ministry of Defense Publishing House, 1990.

Bernard, Paul P. "Joseph II and the Jews: The Origins of the Toleration Patent of 1782." *Austrian History Yearbook* 4–5 (1968–1969): pp. 101–119.

Bloch, Chayim. *The Golem: Mystical Tales from the Ghetto of Prague*. Trans. Harry Schneiderman. Blauvelt, New York: Rudolf Steinder Publications, 1972.

Bokser, Ben Zion. *The Maharal: The Mystical Philosophy of Rabbi Judah Loew of Prague*. Northvale, New Jersey: Jason Aronson Inc., 1994.

Brod, Max. *Franz Kafka: A Biography*. Trans. G. Humphreys Roberts and Richard Winston. New York: Da Capo Press, 1995.

———. *Zivot plny boju*. Trans. (from German to Czech) Bedrich Fucik. Prague: Nakladatelstvi Franze Kafky, 1994.

Cervinka, Frantisek. "The Hilsner Affair." In *The Blood Libel Legend: A Casebook in Anti-Semitic Folklore*, ed. Alan Dundes. Madison, Wisconsin: University of Wisconsin Press, 1991, pp. 135–161.

Dagan, Avigdor, ed. *The Jews of Czechoslovakia*. Three volumes. Philadelphia: The Jewish Publication Society and the Society for the History of Czechoslovak Jews, 1984.

Fiedler, Jiri. *Jewish Sights of Bohemia and Moravia*. Prague: Sefer, 1991.

Fischl, Viktor. "Hodiny v ghettu." *Ceskozidovsky almanach* 5755 (1994/1995): 85.

Gans, David. *Tzemach David*. Updated by Mordechai Brauer. Jerusalem: Magnus, 1983.

Gilman, Sander. *Franz Kafka, The Jewish Patient*. New York: Routledge, 1995.

Gottlieb, Freema. *Mystical Stonescapes of Prague Jewish Town and Czech Countryside*. Prague: Tvorba, 1997.

Grozinger, Karl Erich. *Kafka and Kabbalah*. Trans. Susan Hecker Ray. New York: Continuum, 1994.

Havel, Vaclav. *Toward a Civil Society: Selected Speeches and Writings 1990–1994*. Trans. Paul Wilson. Prague: Lidove Noviny, 1994.

Idel, Moshe. *Golem: Jewish Magical and Mystical Traditions on the Artificial Anthropoid*. Albany: State University of New York, 1990.

Iggers, Wilma Abeles, ed. *The Jews of Bohemia and Moravia: A Historical Reader*. Trans. Wilma Abeles Iggers, Kaca Polackova-Henley, and Kathrine Talbot. Detroit: Wayne State University Press, 1992.

Janouch, Gustav. *Conversations with Kafka*. Trans. Goronwy Rees. New York: New Directions, 1971.

Kafka, Frantisek. *Novy Zidovsky Krbitov*. Trans. Dusan Zbavitel. Prague: Marsyas, 1991.

Kafka, Franz. *The Castle*. Trans. Willa and Edwin Muir. New York: Schocken Books, 1982.

———. *The Complete Stories*. Ed. Nahum N. Glatzer. New York: Schocken Books, 1971.

———. *The Diaries 1910–1923*. Ed. Max Brod. Trans. Joseph Kresh and Martin Greenberg. New York: Schocken Books, 1976.

———. *Letters to Milena*, trans. Philip Boehm. New York: Schocken Books, 1990.
———. *The Sons*. New York: Schocken Books, 1989.
———. *The Trial*, trans. Willa and Edwin Muir. London: David Campbell Publishers, 1992.
Kara, Avigdor. "All of the Hardships That Befell Us." In *A Story of the Jewish Museum in Prague*, by Hana Volavkova. Prague: Artia, 1968, pp. 253–258.
Kieval, Hillel J. "In the Image of Hus: Refashioning Czech Judaism in Post-Emancipatory Prague." *Modern Judaism* 5:2 (May 1985): pp. 141–157.
———. *The Making of Czech Jewry: National Conflict and Jewish Society in Bohemia, 1870–1918*. New York: Oxford University Press, 1988.
Kisch, Egon Ervin. "Kde je pochovan Golem." In *Ceskozidovsky almanach 5755–1994/1995*. Prague: Apeiron, 1994, pp. 83–85.
Langer, Jiri. *Nine Gates to the Chasidic Mysteries*. Trans. Stephen Jolly. Northvale, New Jersey: Jason Aronson, Inc., 1993.
Lustig, Arnost. "The Wall." In *A Story of the Jewish Museum in Prague* by Hana Volavkova. Prague: Artia, 1968, p. 326.
Mairowitz, David Zane, and Robert Crumb. *Introducing Kafka*. Northampton, Massachusetts: Kitchen Sink Press, 1994.
McCagg Jr., William O. *A History of Habsburg Jews, 1670–1918*. Bloomington and Indianapolis: Indiana University Press, 1989.
Meyrink, Gustav. *The Golem*. Trans. Madge Pemberton (revised by E. F. Bleiler). New York: Dover, 1976.
Muneles, Otto. *Prague Ghetto in the Renaissance Period*. Trans. Iva Drapalova. Prague: Orbis, 1965.
Nosek, Bedrich. *Jewish Prague*. Trans. Jana Svabova. Prague: Asco, 1991.
Parik, Arno. *The Old Jewish Cemetery in Prague in the Works of Romantic Painters*. Prague: The State Jewish Museum in Prague, 1982.
———. *The Prague Synagogues in Paintings, Engravings and Old Photographs*. Trans. Slavos Kadecka. Prague: The State Jewish Museum in Prague, 1986.
———. "Znovuotevreni Vysoke synagogy." *Ros Chodes* 58:10 (October 1996): pp. 10–11.
Parik, Arno, and Pavel Stecha. *The Jewish Town of Prague*. Trans. Dusan Zbavitel and Gita Zbavitelova. Prague: Oswald, 1992.
Pawel, Ernst: *The Nightmare of Reason: A Life of Franz Kafka*. New York: The Noonday Press, 1992.
Perutz, Leo. *By Night under the Stone Bridge*. Trans. Eric Mosbacher. New York: Arcade, 1990.
Putik, Alexandr. "The Hebrew Inscription on the Crucifix at Charles Bridge in Prague. The Case of Elias Backoffen and Berl Tabor in the Appellation Court." Trans. J. Moss Kohoutova. *Judaica Bohemiae* XXXII (1996): pp. 26–103.
Ripellino, Angelo Maria. *Magic Prague*. Ed. Michael Henry Heim. Trans. David Newton Marinelli. London: Picador, 1995.
Rybar, Ctibor. *Jewish Prague*. Trans. Joy Turner-Kadeckova and Slavos Kadecka. Prague: TV Spektrum and Akropolis, 1991.
Sadek, Vladimir, and Jirina Sedinova. *The Old Jewish Cemetery and the Klausen Synagogue*. Trans. Slavos Kadecka. Prague: The State Jewish Museum in Prague, 1989.
Scholem, Gershom. "The Idea of the Golem," in *On the Kabbalah and Its Symbolism*, trans. Ralph Manheim. New York: Schocken Books, 1965, pp. 158–204.
———. *The Messianic Idea in Judaism*. New York: Schocken Books, 1971.
Sedinova, Jirina, and Eva Kosakova. *The Golem Walks through the Jewish Town*. Trans. Joy Moss Kohoutova. Prague: The Jewish Museum in Prague and Reag Prague, 1994.
Sherwin, Byron L. *Mystical Theology and Social Dissent: The Life and Works of Judah Loew of Prague*. East Brunswick: Associated University Presses, 1982.

Skvorecky, Josef. *Horkej svet*. Prague: Odeon, 1991.

Tomek, V. V. *Prazske Zidovske povesti a legendy*. Prague: Volvox Globator, 1995.

Vilimkova, Milada. *The Prague Ghetto*. Trans. Iris Urwin. Prague: Aventinum, 1993

Volavkova, Hana. *The Pinkas Synagogue: A Memorial of the Past and of Our Days*. Prague: Statni pedagogicke nakladatelstvi, 1955.

———. *A Story of the Jewish Museum in Prague*. Trans. K. E. Lichtenecker. Prague: Artia, 1968.

———. *Zmizele prazske ghetto*. Prague: Sportovni a Turisticke Nakladatelstvi, 1961.

Weil, Jiri. *Life with a Star*. Trans. Rita Klimova with Roslyn Schloss. Middlesex: Penguin Books, 1991.

———. *Mendelssohn Is on the Roof*. Trans. Marie Winn. Middlesex: Penguin Books, 1992.

Wiesel, Elie. *The Golem: The Story of a Legend*. Trans. Anne Borchardt. New York: Summit Books, 1983.

Winkler, Gershon. *The Golem of Prague*. New York: The Judaica Press, 1994.

WARSAW

Alfasi, Yitzchak. *Glimpses of Jewish Warsaw*. Trans. and ed. Avraham Yaakov Finkel. Lakewood, New Jersey: C.I.S. Publishers, 1992.

Bromberg, Avraham Yitzchak. *Rebbes of Ger: Sfas Emes and Imrei Emes*. Trans. Uri Kaploun. New York: Mesorah Publications, 1987.

Buber, Martin. *Tales of the Hasidim*. Trans. Olga Marx. New York: Schocken Books, 1991.

Dobroszycki, Lucjan, and Barbara Kirshenblatt-Gimblett. *Image before My Eyes: A Photographic History of Jewish Life in Poland before the Holocaust*. New York: Schocken Books, 1977.

Gebert, Konstanty. "The Dialectics of Memory in Poland: Holocaust Memorials in Warsaw." In *The Art of Memory: Holocaust Memorials in History*, ed. James E. Young. New York: Prestel-Verlag and The Jewish Museum, 1994, pp. 121–129.

———. "Jewish Identities in Poland: New, Old, and Imaginary." In *Jewish Identities in the New Europe*, ed. Jonathan Webber. London: Oxford Centre for Hebrew and Jewish Studies and Littman Library of Jewish Civilization, 1994, pp. 161–167.

Gutman, Yisrael. "Emanuel Ringelblum, the Chronicler of the Warsaw Ghetto." *Polin* 3 (1988): 5–16.

———. *The Jews of Warsaw 1939–1943: Ghetto, Underground, Revolt*. Trans. Ina Friedman. Bloomington and Indianapolis: Indiana University Press, 1989.

———. *Resistance: The Warsaw Ghetto Uprising*. New York: Houghton Mifflin, 1994.

Heller, Celia S. *On the Edge of Destruction: Jews of Poland between the Two World Wars*. Detroit: Wayne State University Press, 1994.

Howe, Irving and Greenberg, Eliezer, eds. *A Treasury of Yiddish Stories*. New York: Meridian Books, 1958.

Jagielski, Jan. *Przewodnik po cmentarzu zydowskim w Warszawie przy ul. Okopowej 49/51: Zeszyt II: Kwatera 20*. Warsaw: Towarzystwo Opieki nad Zabytkami, 1995.

Jagielski, Jan, and Robert Pasieczny. *A Guide to Jewish Warsaw*. Trans. Robert Pszczel. Warsaw: Our Roots, 1990.

Kaplan, Chaim A. *Scroll of Agony: The Warsaw Diary of Chaim A. Kaplan*. Trans. Abraham I. Katsh. New York: Collier Books, 1973.

Karmi, Abraham M. "The Jewish Cemetery in Occupied Warsaw." *Yad Vashem Bulletin* 16 (February 1965): 42–50.

Kasprzycki, Jerzy, ed. *Warsaw as It Was: Original City Maps before 1939 and In 1945*. Warsaw: Alfa, 1985.

Khayim, Ben. "The Jewish Porters of Warsaw." In *From a Ruined Garden: The Memorial Books of Polish Jewry*, ed. and trans. Jack Kugelmass and Jonathan Boyarin. New York: Schocken Books, 1983, pp. 53–59.

Kieniewicz, Stefan. "The Jews of Warsaw, Polish Society and the Partitioning Powers 1795–1861." Polin 3 (1988): 102–121.

Korczak, Janusz. *Ghetto Diary*. Trans. Jerzy Bachrach and Barbara Krzywicka. New York: Holocaust Library, 1978.

Krall, Hanna. *Shielding the Flame: An Intimate Conversation with Dr. Marek Edelman, the Last Surviving Leader of the Warsaw Ghetto Uprising*. Trans. Joanna Stasinska and Lawrence Weschler. New York: Henry Holt, 1986.

Lewin, Abraham. *A Cup of Tears: A Diary of the Warsaw Ghetto*. Trans. Christopher Hutton. Oxford: Basil Blackwell, 1989.

Lewin, Isaac. *A History of Polish Jewry during the Revival of Poland*. New York: Shengold Publishers, 1990.

Liptzin, Sol, ed. *Peretz*. Trans. Sol Liptzin. New York: YIVO, 1947.

Malkowska, Ewa. *Synagoga na Tlomackiem*. Warsaw: Wydawnictwo Naukowe PWN, 1991.

Niger, Shmuel, and Yakov Shatsky, eds. *Leksikon fun der Nayer Yidisher Literatur*. New York: Marstin Press, 1956.

Nomberg, Hersh D. "Isaac Leibush Peretz as We Knew Him." In *The Golden Tradition: Jewish Life and Thought in Eastern Europe*, ed. Lucy S. Dawidowicz. New York: Schocken Books, 1984, pp. 286–297.

Opalski, Magdalena, and Israel Bartal. *Poles and Jews: A Failed Brotherhood*. Hanover: University Press of New England, 1992.

Paszkiewiczowie, Hanna and Piotr, and Monika Krajewska. *Cmentarze zydowskie w Warszawie*. Warsaw: Wydawnictwo Naukowe PWN, 1992.

Pogonowski, Iwo Cyprian. *Jews in Poland: A Documentary History*. New York: Hippocrene Books, 1993.

Rapoport, Nathan. "Memoir of the *Warsaw Ghetto Monument*." In *The Art of Memory: Holocaust Memorials in History*, ed. James E. Young. New York: Prestel-Verlag and The Jewish Museum, 1994, pp. 103–107.

Roland, Charles G. *Courage under Siege: Starvation, Disease, and Death in the Warsaw Ghetto*. New York: Oxford University Press, 1992.

Scharf, Rafael F., ed. In *The Warsaw Ghetto Summer 1941: Photographs by Willy Georg with Passages from Warsaw Ghetto Diaries*. New York: Aperture, 1993.

Sieramska, Magdalena. *Salvaged from the Warsaw Ghetto: The Archives of E. Ringelblum*. Warsaw: The Jewish Historical Institute, 1993.

Singer, Bernard. *Moje Nalewki*. Warsaw: Czytelnik, 1993.

Singer, Isaac Bashevis. *The Certificate*. Trans. Leonard Wolf. New York: Farrar, Straus & Giroux, 1992.

———. *In My Father's Court*. Trans. Channah Kleinerman-Goldstein, Elaine Gottlieb, and Joseph Singer. New York: The New American Library, 1967.

———. *Old Love*. New York: Farrar, Straus & Giroux, 1979.

———. *Shosha*. New York: Fawcett Crest, 1978.

———. *Scum*. Trans. Rosaline Dukalsky Schwartz. Middlesex: Penguin Books, 1992.

———. *The Family Moskat*. Trans. A. H. Gross. Middlesex: Penguin Books, 1980.

Sloan, Jacob, ed. *Notes from the Warsaw Ghetto: The Journal of Emmanuel Ringelblum*. New York: Schocken Books, 1975.

Sokolow, Nahum. "Henri Bergson's Old-Warsaw Lineage." In *The Golden Tradition: Jewish Life and Thought in Eastern Europe*, ed. Lucy S. Dawidowicz. New York: Schocken Books, 1984, pp. 349–359.

Stiffel, Frank. *The Tale of the Ring: A Kaddish*. Wainscott, New York: Pushcart Press, 1984.

Sujecki, Janusz. *Prozna, ocalona ulica zydowskiej Warszawy*. Warsaw: Ortis, 1993.

Weschler, Lawrence. *The Passion of Poland: From Solidarity through the State of War*. New York: Pantheon Books, 1984.

Wiesel, Elie. *Somewhere a Master: Further Hasidic Portraits and Legends*. Trans. Marion Wiesel. New York: Summit Books, 1982.

Wrobel, Piotr. "Jewish Warsaw before the First World War." *Polin* 3 (1988): 156–187.

Young, James E. *The Texture of Memory: Holocaust Memorials and Meaning*. New Haven: Yale University Press, 1993.

Zeitlin, Aaron. "The Last Walk of Janusz Korczak." Trans. Hadassah Rosensaft and Gertrude Hirschler. In *Ghetto Diary* by Janusz Korczak, pp. 7–63. New York: Holocaust Library, 1978.

CRACOW

Balaban, Majer. *Historja zydow w Krakowie i na Kazimierzu, 1304–1868*. Two volumes. Cracow: Krajowa Agencja Wydawnicza, 1991.

———. *Przewodnik po zydowskich zabytkach Krakowa*. Cracow: Krajowa Agencja Wydawnicza, 1990.

Bauminger, Aryeh, et al. *Sefer Krako: ir ve-em be-Yisrael*. Jerusalem: Mosad ha'Rav Kuk, 1959.

Carlebach, Shlomo. *Shlomo's Stories: Selected Tales*. With Susan Yael Mesinai. Northvale, New Jersey: Jason Aronson Inc., 1994.

———. "The *Taz* and the *Bach*." Recorded, transcribed, and edited by Reuven Goldfarb. *Agada* 3:1 (Summer 1984): 14–17.

Dobrzycki, Jerzy. *Stara boznica Kazimierska*. Cracow: Museum Historyczne Miasta Krakowa, 1965.

Duda, Eugeniusz. *A Guide to Jewish Cracow*. Warsaw: Our Roots, 1990.

———. *Krakowskie judaica*. Trans. Ewa Dmyterko. Warsaw: PTTK "Kraj," 1991.

———. *Old Jewish Cemetery and Remuh Synagogue—Short Guide*. Trans. Ewa Basiura. Cracow: Argona—Jarden Art, 1996.

Gluckman, Ch. S. *Sefer Be-ohole Tsadikim*. New York: Mosad "Zekher Naftali," 1990.

Graf, Malvina. *The Krakow Ghetto and the Plaszow Camp Remembered*. Tallahassee: Florida State University Press, 1989.

Pioro, Anna, and Wieslawa Karlinska. *Krakow Getto Guide*. Cracow: Oficyna Konfraterni Poetow, 1995.

Scharf, Rafael F. *Poland, What Have I to Do with Thee: Essays without Prejudice*. Cracow: Universitas and Judaica Foundation in Cracow, 1996.

Shmeruk, Chone. *The Esterke Story in Yiddish and Polish Literature: A Case Study in the Mutual Relations of Two Cultural Traditions*. Jerusalem: Zalman Shazar Center for the Furtherance of the Study of Jewish History, 1985.

Shulman, Yaakov Dovid. *The Rema: The Story of Rabbi Moshe Isserles*. Lakewood, New Jersey: C.I.S. Publishers, 1991.

Taitz, Emily, and Sondra Henry. *Remarkable Jewish Women*. Philadelphia: The Jewish Publication Society, 1996.

Weiss, Moshe. *From Oswiecim to Auschwitz: Poland Revisited*. Oakville, Ontario: Mosaic Press, 1994.

Zgrzebnicki, Jacek. *Cracow's Kazimierz Jewish Town*. Trans. Magdalena Loska and Joanna Thompson. Cracow: Patchwork and Wiktor, 1994.

BUDAPEST

Barany, George. "'Magyar Jew or Jewish Magyar?' Reflections on the Question of Assimilation." In *Jews and Non-Jews in Eastern Europe 1918–1945*, ed. B. Vago and G. L. Mosse. New York and Jerusalem: John Wiley & Sons and Keter, 1974, pp. 51–98.

Budapest Negyed 8 (Summer 1995). [A special issue focusing on Jewish history in Budapest]

Carmilly-Weinberger, Moshe, ed. *The Rabbinical Seminary of Budapest 1877–1977*. New York: Sepher-Hermon, 1986.

Ferenc, Orban. *Jewish Life In Hungary 1996 / 5756*. Trans. Magdalena Seleanu. Budapest: Makkabi, 1995.

Forster, Ludwig. "Promemoria," February 1854. Hungarian Jewish Museum Archives *MZSML T.79.236*.

Frohlich, Robert, et al. *The Dohany Street Synagogue*. Trans. Ildiko Barna. Budapest: Red Raster, 1996.

Gazda, Aniko. *Magyarorszagi zsinagogak*. Budapest: Muszaki konyvkiado, 1989.

Groszmann, Zsigmond. "A pesti zsinagoga." *Egyenloseg* December 12 and 19, 1915: 12–17.

Grunvald, Fulop. "A buda-varhegyi zsinagoga es zsido temeto helye torok idokben." In *Jubilee Volume in Honour of Professor Bernhard Heller*, ed. Alexander Scheiber. Budapest: 1941, pp. 164–169.

Grunvald, Fulop, and Erno Namenyi. "Budapesti zsinagogak." In *A 90 eves Dohany-utcai templom* by Jozsef Katona. Budapest: Orszagos Magyar Zsido Muzeum, 1949, pp. 19–31.

Haraszti, Gyorgy. "A Rumbach utcai zsinagoga es hivei." In *A Rumbach Sebestyen utcai zsinagoga* by Ines Muller. Budapest: MTA Judaisztikai Kutatocsoport, 1993, pp. 103–119.

Hatvany-Deutsch, Ludwig. *Bondy Jr.*. Trans. Hannah Waller. New York: Knopf, 1931.

Herczl, Moshe Y. *Christianity and the Holocaust of Hungarian Jewry*. Trans. Joel Lerner. New York: New York University Press, 1993.

Hertzberg, Arthur, ed. *The Zionist Idea: A Historical Analysis and Reader*. New York and Philadelphia: Meridian Books and The Jewish Publication Society of America, 1960.

Kassowitz, J. H. "Memorandum," May 19, 1854. Hungarian Jewish Museum Archives *MZSML T.80.5*.

Katona, Jozsef. *A 90 eves Dohany-utcai templom*. Budapest: Orszagos Magyar Zsido Muzeum, 1949.

Katzburg, Nathaniel. "The Jewish Congress of Hungary, 1868–1869." In *Hungarian Jewish Studies*, ed. Randolph L. Braham, vol. 2. New York: World Federation of Hungarian Jews, 1969, pp. 1–33.

Komoroczy, Geza, ed. *A zsido Budapest: Emlekek, szertartasok, tortenelem*. Two volumes. Budapest: MTA Judaisztikai Kutatocsoport, 1995.

Kovacs, Andras. "Changes in Jewish Identity in Modern Hungary." In *Jewish Identities in the New Europe*, ed. Jonathan Webber. London: Oxford Centre for Hebrew and Jewish Studies and Littman Library of Jewish Civilization, 1994, pp. 150–160.

Meyer, Michael A. *Response to Modernity: A History of the Reform Movement in Judaism*. New York: Oxford University Press, 1988.

Muller, Ines. *A Rumbach Sebestyen utcai zsinagoga*. Budapest: MTA Judaisztikai Kutatocsoport, 1993.

Patai, Raphael. *The Jews of Hungary: History, Culture, Psychology*. Detroit: Wayne State University Press, 1996.

Pawel, Ernst. *The Labyrinth of Exile: A Life of Theodor Herzl*. New York: Farrar, Straus & Giroux, 1989.

Perlman, Robert. *Bridging Three Worlds: Hungarian-Jewish Americans 1848–1914*. Amherst: The University of Massachusetts Press, 1991.

Schoner, Alfred. *The Synagogue of Dohany Street*. Budapest: Miok, 1989.

Schulhof, Izsak. *Budai Kronika*. Trans. (from Hebrew to Hungarian) Laszlo Jolesz. Budapest: Magyar Helikon, 1981.

Sellyei, Anna. *The Jewish Face of Budapest*. Budapest: B'nai B'rith Budapest, 1996.
Temple Building Committee, "Report," June 23, 1854. Hungarian Jewish Museum Archives *MZSML T.80.11*.
Vadasz, Ede. "A Pesti zsido templom elso otven eve." *Magyar-Zsido Szemle* (1909): 193–227.
Zolnay, Laszlo. *Buda kozepkori zsidosaga*. Budapest: TIT, 1968.

HOLOCAUST

Blodig, Vojtech, et. al. *Ghetto Museum Terezin*. Trans. Dagmar Lieblova and Rita McLeod. Terezin: Memorial Terezin, 1995.
Bondy, Ruth. *"Elder of the Jews": Jakob Edelstein of Theresienstadt*. Trans. Evelyn Abel. New York: Grove Press, 1989.
Dawidowicz, Lucy S., ed. *A Holocaust Reader*. West Orange, New Jersey: Behrman House, 1976.
———. *The War against the Jews 1933–1945*. New York: Bantam Books, 1976,
Glatstein, Jacob, et al., eds. *Anthology of Holocaust Literature*. New York: Atheneum, 1980.
Glazar, Richard. *Trap with a Green Fence: Survival in Treblinka*. Trans. Roslyn Theobald. Evanston, Illinois: Northwestern University Press, 1995.
Gutman, Yisrael, and Michael Berenbaum, eds. *Anatomy of the Auschwitz Death Camp*. Bloomington and Indianapolis: Indiana University Press, 1994.
Langer, Lawrence. *Admitting the Holocaust: Collected Essays*. New York: Oxford University Press, 1995.

Index

Abeles, Lazar, 13, 144–145
Abeles, Simon, 144–145
Abraham, Golem legend and, 47
Abraham ben Azriel, 6
Abraham Danzig of Vilna, R., 73
Adam, Golem legend and, 45–46
Adler, R. Illes, 464
Agudath Israel, 161, 165, 192
Agunah/agunot, 335
Aharon, Reb, 359–360
Aktions. *See also* Mass deportations
    Podgorze ghetto, 273–274
    Warsaw Ghetto, 170–171, 214, 228–230
Aleje Jerozolimski, 151
Alexander II (czar), 159
Aliyah/aliyot, in Altschul (Cracow), 301–302
Alkalai, R. Yehudah, 396
Alter, R. Avraham Mordechai, 197
Alter, R. Yehudah Aryeh, 158, 197
Alter, R. Yitzchak Meir (Chiddushei HaRim), 158, 193, 197
Alter, Victor, 208–209
Altneuschul, 51
    Altschul (Cracow) and, 293, 294, 299
    antechamber, 66–68
    aron hakodesh, 66–67, 70–71
    bimah, 75–76
    description, 64–65
    Easter Pogrom, 79, 130
    Golem legend, 58–59, 64
    Gothic style and, 64, 68, 69
    history, 4, 6, 7, 8, 21, 22, 54, 66
    Holocaust and, 79–80
    Jewish Town Hall and, 85
    kapporet, 71–72
    legendary founding, 65
    main sanctuary, 68–78
    meaning of name, 65–66
    Rabbi Judah Loew and, 33
    services, 58–59
    Vaclav Havel and, 31
    visiting, 61–63
Altschul (Cracow), 265, 267, 291
    aron hakodesh, 302–303
    bimah, 301–302
    charity box, 298–299
    frescoes, 299, 300, 302
    history, 292–295
    Holocaust and, 296
    inscriptions, 298, 299
    keter Torah, 302
    main sanctuary, 298
    museum exhibits in, 303–304
    ner tamid, 303
    ownership of, 296
    religious customs in, 304–307
    vestibule, 297–298
    women's sections, 300–301
Altschul (Prague), 6, 65, 79, 129–131
American Foundation School, 395
American Jewish Joint Distribution Committee, 177

Amidah, 141
Amud. See Pulpits
Anielewicz, Mordecai, 171, 172, 173
Anne Frank High School, 394
An-ski. *See* Rapaport, Solomon Zainwil
Anti-Semitism. *See also* Expulsions;
   Pogroms
  Budapest, 379–381, 389, 394, 408
  Cracow, 263–264, 274
  Holocaust and, 80
  Prague, 6–8, 15–17, 19, 21–23, 144–145
  Tomas Masaryk and, 29
  Warsaw, 159–160, 164, 240
Apollinaire, Guillaume, 86
Appeasement, of Germany, 21
Apteka pod Orlem, 369
Aquincum, 3776
Architects
  Dohaney Street Synagogue and, 447–448
  Jewish, 90, 447–448
  Rumbach Synagogue and, 458, 459
Arch of Titus, 107
Ariel cafe, 288, 341
Arizal. *See* Luria, R. Yitzchak
Aron hakodesh (holy ark), 75
  Altneuschul, 66–67, 70–71
  Altschul (Cracow), 302–303
  Dohaney Street Synagogue, 439–440
  High Synagogue (Prague), 83
  Klausen Synagogue, 122–123
  Nozyk Synagogue, 250
  Pinchas Synagogue, 95
  Popper Synagogue, 342–343
  Rema Synagogue, 309
  Tempel Synagogue, 355
  Tlomackie Street Synagogue, 238
Arrow Cross Party, 391, 457
Artura Zawiszy, 151
Ashkenazi, R. Eliezer, 82, 318–321
Ashkenazi, Solomon, 268
Ashkenazi Judaism, 486

Assimilation
  in Budapest and Hungary, 386–389, 392, 393, 444–445, 456
  in Prague, 16–21, 131
Asterblum, Henryk, 213
Auerbach, Gittel bat Moshe, 316–317
Auerbach, R. Ze'ev, 108
Augustus Sulkowski, Prince (of Poland), 151
Auschwitz, 21, 274, 368, 492–493
Austria. *See also* Hapsburg monarchy
  conquest of Buda, 384, 413, 415–416, 421–422, 424–425
Austro-Hungarian monarchy, 131, 271
Autonomous Orthodox Community (Budapest), 399, 466
Azrylewicz, Henryk, 213

Babies, burial of, 116
(the) Bach. *See* Sirkes, R. Joel
Bach, Joszef, 443
Bachelors, in Reform Judaism, 443
Backoffen, Elias, 142–143
Badges. *See also* "Hat of Shame"
  worn by Hungarian Jews, 378, 411
Balaban, Majer, 198, 239, 264, 268, 294, 295, 309, 338
Balint Jewish Community Center, 395, 400
Banner, of Jewish sovereignty in Prague, 80–81
Bans, on Jewish settlement in Warsaw, 150–152, 154, 251
Baroque architecture, Jewish Town Hall (Prague), 86
Bashevi, Hendel, 114–115
Bashevi, Jacob (von Treuenberg), 12, 52, 114
Baths. *See* Mikveh
Baum, Oskar, 20
Baxa, Karel, 29
Bayit Chadash (Sirkes), 326, 327
Bazin, 384

Beakers, of Prague's Burial Society, 118
Beer, Peter, 136
Beis Yaakov school, 271–272
Beit din (rabbinical court), 16
  Altschul (Cracow), 297
  Kazinczy Street Synagogue, 465
Beit Josef (Karo), 276–277
Beit midrash (prayer/study halls)
  Cracow, 345, 359–360, 363–364, 365
  Praga, 255
  Warsaw, 162
Bejt Praha (House of Prague), 27, 59, 85
Bejt Simcha (House of Happiness), 26–27, 60
Bela IV (king of Hungary), 7, 378–379, 408–409, 410
Bella, Miriam, 316
Belzec death camp, 273, 367, 490
Bergson, Henri Louis, 196
Bergson, Michal, 196, 255
Berlin, R. Naphtali Tzvi Yehuhad (Netziv), 206
Berlinksi, Hirsch, 208
Bet Aharon Synagogue, 481–482
Bethlen Ter Synagogue, 480, 483–484
Bet Smuel (Csaky Synagogue), 480–481
Bezalel, R., 32
Biber, Shlomo, 210
Bible, Polish edition, 303
Bielinski, Pawel, 155
Bikkur Cholim Society, 482
Bimah
  Altneuschul, 75–76
  Altschul (Cracow), 301–302
  High Synagogue (Prague), 84
  Klausen Synagogue, 123
  Maisel Synagogue, 127
  Obuda Synagogue, 429
  Pinchas Synagogue, 95
  Rema Synagogue, 309
  Tempel Synagogue, 355
Birkenau, 21, 274, 368, 492

Black Death. *See also* Plague
  Cracow, 262, 270
  Prague, 13, 135
Blood libel
  Hungary, 381, 384, 389
  Prague, 8, 29, 32
"Bloody Thursday," 367, 368
Blue Building (Warsaw), 238
B'nei Emunah, 363–364
Bochenska Street (Cracow), 365
Bodleian Library, 108
Bohaterow Getta. *See* Nalewki Street (Warsaw)
Bohemia. *See also* Czechoslovakia; Prague
  Edict of Tolerance and, 16–17
  expulsions in, 9–10
  Familiants Laws and, 14
  history of rabbinate, 107
  Jewish emancipation and, 17–21
  Jewish emigration from, 266
  Land's Jewry and, 142
Bohemian Jews, conflicts in Cracow, 293–294, 308
Bohusovice, 489
Bonaparte, Napoleon. *See* Napoleon I
Bondy Jr. (Hatvany-Deutsch), 437
Borges, Jorge Luis, 49
Bozian. *See* Popper, Wolf
Brahe, Tycho, 12, 144
Bratislava, 384
Breker, Arno, 219
Bris (circumcision), 73
Brisker, R. Chaim. *See* Soloveitchik, R. Chaim
Brit milah (circumcision ceremony), 95
Brod, Max, 20, 108, 138
Brodnowska Street (Praga), 254
Bromberg, Avraham Yitzchack, 197
Bruck, Moses, 451
Brull family *ohel,* 469
Buda. *See also* Budapest
  anti-Semitism, expulsions, and pogroms, 408, 411

Buda (*continued*)
　cemeteries, 410, 417
　history of Jews in, 377–385, 386
　Mendel houses, 412–413
　New Jewish District (Tancsics Mihaly Street), 411–412
　Old Jewish District (Szent Gyorgy Street), 408–411
　synagogues, 409, 413
　　Great Synagogue, 384, 413, 417–425, 471
　　Small Synagogue, 383, 413, 414–417
Budapest. *See also* Buda; Pest
　anti-Semitism, expulsions, and pogroms, 379–381, 389, 394, 408, 411
　assimilation and emancipation, 385–389, 392, 393, 444–445, 456
　Autonomous Orthodox Jewish Community, 399
　Balint Jewish Community Center, 395, 400
　butchers, 402
　cemeteries
　　Kozma Street Cemetery, 468–472
　　Martyr's Cemetery, 454
　census figures, 391, 393–394, 3909
　Chabad House, 399
　grocery store, 402–403
　Heroes' Temple, 454–456
　history of Jews in, 376–395
　　Holocaust, 390–391
　　in Ujpest, 472–474
　　in World War I, 389, 455
　Holocaust memorials, 456–458, 470–471, 474
　hotels, 403
　Hungarian Jewish Congress, 434–436, 462, 465
　Hungarian Jewish Museum, 452–453
　Jewish Community, 399
　kosher food, 401–403
　mass graves, 471
　Mendel houses, 412–413
　mikveh, 403–404
　milk store, 402
　New Jewish District (Tancsics Mihaly Street), 411–412
　Obuda, 384–385, 426–430
　Old Jewish District (Szent Gyorgy Street), 408–411
　patisserie, 403
　prayer in, 475–487
　Rabbinical Seminary, 397, 478–479
　Reform Judaism. *See* Neolog movement
　restaurants, 401
　salami store, 402
　schools, 394–395
　synagogues, 375, 409, 413
　　Bet Aharon Synagogue, 481–482
　　Bethlen Ter Synagogue, 480, 483–484
　　Bet Smuel (Csaky Synagogue), 480–481
　　Buda Synagogue, 485–486
　　Dessewffy Street Synagogue, 482–483
　　Great Synagogue, 384, 413, 417–425, 471
　　Kazinczy Street Synagogue, 434, 436, 465–467, 477–478
　　Nagyfuvaros Synagogue, 479–480
　　Obuda Synagogue, 428–430
　　Rumbach Synagogue, 447, 458–465, 466, 476, 477
　　Sasz Chevra, 486–487
　　services, 475–487
　　Small Synagogue, 383, 413, 414–417
　　Teleki Ter Synagogue, 486
　　Ujpest Synagogue, 473–474, 484–485
　World War I memorials, 454–456, 470
　Yizkor wall, 470–471
Buda Synagogue, 485–486
Bund party, 160, 164, 165, 209, 222
Buonaccorsil, Filippo, 264

Burials
  as *mitzvot,* 110
  in Warsaw, 187, 193–195
Burial Society *(Chevrah Kaddishah)*
  Cracow, 358
  Pest, 433
  Prague, 12, 32, 116–120, 122, 319, 320
  Warsaw, 186
Butchers, Budapest, 402

Calahora, Mattathias, 270
Calahora, Michael, 332–333
Calahora, Solomon, 268
Calahora trial, 331, 332
Candles, Shabbat, 73
Capek, Josef, 49
Capistrano, Jan, 263–264
Carlebach, Shlomo, 288
Carl Lutz Memorial, 457
Casimir the Great, 259–260, 262, 265, 292
Cast-iron, in Dohaney Street Synagogue, 438
Castle District (Buda), 408–411
Castle District (Prague), 5
Catholic Church. *See also* Anti-Semitism; Expulsions; Pogroms
  antagonism to Isaac Synagogue, 347–348
  anti-Semitism and, 80, 144–145, 379
  "desecration of the Host," 78
  enforced conversions, 12
  influence on Dohaney Street Synagogue, 451–452
  influences on Judaism, 75
Cemeteries
  in Budapest, 410, 417, 468
    Kozma Street Cemetery, 468–472
  in Cracow, 261, 338
    New Jewish Cemetery, 313, 357–362
    Old Jewish Cemetery, 276, 291, 310–337
  in Praga, 185, 251, 253–254
  in Prague, 5, 13, 88
    Fibichova Street Cemetery, 99
    New Jewish Cemetery, 99
    New Olsany Cemetery, 117, 135, 137–139
    Old Jewish Cemetery, 61, 63, 95, 99–101, 103–117, 121
    Old Olsany Cemetery, 134–137
  in Warsaw, Jewish Cemetery
    history, 185–188
    location, 183–185
    religious disputes and, 193–195
    walking tour, 188–213
Cemetery Square (Cracow), 337–341
Census
  of Jews in Prague, 13, 14, 17, 21
  of Jews in Warsaw, 159, 161, 162, 173, 175
Center for Jewish Culture (Cracow), 287–288
Central Jewish Museum (Prague). *See* Jewish Museum of Prague
Ceremonial Hall, 54, 116–120
  inscription from, 137
  visiting, 61, 63
Cervena Street (Prague), 51
Chabad House (Budapest), 399
Chabad House (Prague), 56–57
Chair of Elijah, 73, 95, 123
Chair of the Maharal, Altneuschul, 70
Chandeliers
  Altneuschul, 69
  Altschul (Cracow), 303
Chanukkah menorah, High Synagogue (Cracow), 344
Charity box, 118, 123
  Altneuschul, 81
  Altschul (Cracow), 298–299
  Ceremonial Hall, 118
  High Synagogue (Cracow), 344
  Rema Synagogue, 309

Charles Bridge, 13, 64, 81, 141–143
Charles I (Emperor of Austria), 455
Charles IV (king of Bohemia), 7, 8, 80
Charles IV (king of Hungary), 455
Charles University, 8, 28
Charles VI (Holy Roman emperor), 14, 385
Chatam Sofer. *See* Sofer, R. Moses
Chayim ben Shabbetai, R., 420
Chelebi, Evilya, 416
Chelmno death camp, 490
Chemdat Shlomo. *See* Lipschitz, R. Solomon Zalman
Cherubim, Altneuschul, 71
Chessed Neurim, 443
Chevrah Kaddishah (Prague). *See* Burial Society
Chevrah Tehillim, 364
Chiddushei HaRim. *See* Alter, R. Yitzchak Meir
Children, Janusz Korczak and, 211–213
Chmielnicki massacres, 14
Chorin, R. Aaron, 427
Chorus-Temple. *See* Cultus-Temple
Christianity. *See also* Anti-Semitism; Catholic Church
  influences on Judaism, 75
Chupah (wedding canopy)
  Altneuschul, 76
  Dohaney Street Synagogue, 438
  Kazinczy Street Synagogue, 467
Churban of 1686, 421–422
Church of Saint Jindrich, 134
Church of St. Hedvik, 349
Church of the Holy Spirit (Prague), 129, 130
Circumcision, 73, 95
Clocks
  Altneuschul, 68
  Hebrew, in Prague, 4, 86
Cohanim (priests), graves in Prague, 113
Cohen area, New Jewish Cemetery (Cracow), 358

Communism
  in Hungary, 390, 392–393
  persecution of Czech Jews, 22–23
  in Poland, 164, 174
Computers, Golem legend and, 49
Congress Poland, 155–156
Convent of St. Agnes, 68, 74
Conversion, enforced, 12
Copernicus, 103
Corpus Christi (Cracow), 347, 364–365
Cossacks, pogroms and, 152
Council of Szabolcs, 377
Cracow. *See also* Kazimierz
  anti-Semitism, expulsions, and pogroms, 263–264, 269–270, 274, 298–299, 304–305, 332, 352
  beit midrash, 345, 363–364, 365
  Black Death, 262
  cemeteries, 261, 338
    New Jewish Cemetery, 313, 357–362
    Old Jewish Cemetery, 310–337
  Cemetery Square, 337–341
  Center for Jewish Culture, 287–288
  conflicts between Jewish groups, 293–294, 308
  gate to Kazimierz, 345–346
  hasidic prayer houses, 359–360
  hasidism, 270–271, 301, 333, 353, 359–360
  history of Jews in, 261–274
    Holocaust, 272–274, 366–371
  Holocaust memorials, 337, 359
  itinerary, 291–292
  Jewish commercial rights, 269
  Jewish Community, 287, 296.301, 312–214
  Jewish Fighting Organization, 369–370
  legends of, 259–260, 278–286
  mikveh, 261, 289, 341
  plague in, 262, 270, 307, 316
  Podgorze ghetto, 366–371

Progressive Judaism and, 352–355
restaurants, 288, 289
Ronald S. Lauder foundation, 287–288
schools, 271–272, 351
synagogues, 261
  High Synagogue, 266, 267, 291, 343–346
  Isaac Synagogue, 268, 269, 291, 346–349
  Kupa Synagogue, 268, 291, 349–351
  Popper Synagogue, 268, 269, 291, 341–343
  Rema Synagogue, 266, 267, 276, 288–289, 291, 307–310
  services, 288–289
  Tempel Synagogue, 291, 352–357
Yiddishkeit in, 271–272
Cracow Academy, 263, 264
Cracow Historical Museum, 296
Cracow Niggun (Carlebach), 288
Creation, Golem legend and, 45–46
Crucifix, on Charles Bridge, 64, 141–143
Crusades, 5, 377
Csaky Synagogue, 480–481
Cultus-Temple, 388, 443–444, 446–447, 461. *See also* Neolog movement
Curtis, Tony, 456–457
Cylkow, R. Isaac, 303
Czechoslovakia. *See also* Prague
  Holocaust in, 21–22
  Jewish emigration from, 22, 27
  military support of Israel, 22
  national movement, 19
  National Revival movement, 100
  "Prague Spring" and, 91
  Six Day War and, 91
  Tomas Masaryk and, 28–29
  Vaclav Havel and, 30–31
Czerniakow, Adam, 168, 186, 199–200, 226
Czyste Hospital, 202, 226–228

Dagan, Avigdor. *See* Fischl, Viktor
Darkei Moshe (Isserles), 276–277
Das judische Prag, 3
Davidsohn, R. Chaim, 193
Dawidowicz, Lucy, 167
Day of Atonement, at Altschul (Cracow), 305
Death anniversary, in Altneuschul, 77–78
Delmedigo, Joseph Shlomo, 82, 319
Demographics, effects of emancipation on, 18
Denhof, Karl, 443
de non tolerandis Judaeis, 150–152, 154, 251
"Desecration of the Host," 78
Dessewffy Street Synagogue, 482–483
Diamant, Dora, 139
Dinah, Malkah, 307, 316–318
Dineson, Jacob, 207
Dissidents. *See also* Opposition movements
  Judaism and, 23
Dlugosz, Jan, 259, 264, 299
Doblin, Alfred, 235, 237–238
Dohaney Street Synagogue, 388, 461
  architectural features, 436–439
  aron hakodesh, 439–440
  history, 436, 442–448
  Hungarian Jewish Congress and, 434–436
  interior, 451–452
  memorial to, 471
  Moorish style, 450–451, 452
  Neolog movement and, 466
  opening ceremonies, 448–450
  organ, 440–442
  pulpits, 439
  services, 476
  Theodor Herzl and, 396
Dome of the Rock, 458–459
Draizel bat Moshe (daughter of R. Moses Isserles), 318
Drawings. *See also* Frescoes; Murals; Paintings
  in Small Synagogue (Buda), 414
  from Terezin, 117

Dreyfus Affair, 397
Duchy of Warsaw, 155
Duszenko, Franciszek, 492
Dwa Izraele, 157

Easter Pogrom (1389), 78–79, 130, 293
Easter Pogrom (1407), 298–299
Eating. *See* Groceries; Kosher food; Restaurants
Eber, Edward Zacharia, 238
Edelman, Marek, 173, 209, 227, 229, 230
Edelstein, Jakub, 489
Edict of Olomouc, 10
Edict of Tolerance, 15–17, 386
Education. *See also* Schools
  Edict of Tolerance and, 16, 17
  in Prague, 25–26
Ehrlich, Eliyahu, 208
Ehrlich, Henryk, 208–209
Eichmann, Adolf, 21, 391, 492
Einhorn, David, 388
Einhorn, Ignaz, 388, 434, 446
Eisenbaum, Antoni, 193–194
Elberg, Yehuda, 168
Elef Ulfanim (Spira), 322
Elijah's seat, 73, 95, 123
Elster, Pola, 208
Emancipation. *See also* Assimilation
  Hungary, 385–389
  Poland, 153
  Prague, 16–21, 131
Emanuel Foundation, 457
Emigration, from Hungary, 391–392
Endre II (king of Hungary), 377–378
Enosh, Golem legend and, 46, 48
Epstein, Henrietta, 198
Epstein, Jacob, 156, 195, 198
Epstein, R. Kalonymus Kalman, 270, 333, 359
Eruv, 409–410
  Altneuschul, 76
Erzatei nashim (women's sections),
  Altschul (Cracow), 300–301

Esperanto, 200–201
Estates. *See Jurydyka*
Esterka legend, 259–260
Esztergom, 408
Everlasting light. *See Ner tamid*
Exhibitions. *See also* Museums
  Altschul (Cracow), 303–304
  Ceremonial Hall (Prague), 117–120
  Hungarian Jewish Museum, 452–453
  Klausen Synagogue, 123–125
  Maisel Synagogue, 127–128
  Spanish Synagogue, 132
Expulsions
  Budapest and Hungary, 379–380, 384, 411
  Cracow, 264
  Moravia and Bohemia, 9–10
  Prague, 14–15
  Russian cities, 159
  Warsaw, 155
Ezat nashim. See Women's gallery

Familiants Laws, 14, 16, 385
Family traditions, effects of emancipation on, 18
Farago, Ferenc, 455
Feldmann, R. Moses, 464
Ferdinand II (Holy Roman emperor), 13, 114
Ferdinand II (king of Bohemia), 334
Ferdindand I (king of Bohemia), 10, 11
Feszl, Frigyes, 439, 447
Fibichova Street Cemetery, 99
Fire, in Jewish Town (Prague), 13, 15, 63, 82, 83, 86, 121, 122, 130
First Crusade, 5
Fischer, Joseph, 355–356
Fischer, Otokar, 20
Fischer, R. Benjamin, 465
Fischer, R. Gyula, 439
Fischl, Viktor, 4, 86
Flag, of Jewish sovereignty in Prague, 80–81

Fleckeles, R. Eleazar, 136
Food. *See* Groceries; Kosher food
Forster, Ludwig von, 437, 438, 447, 451
Fourth Lateran Council, 6–7, 66, 68
France, Duchy of Warsaw and, 155
Franciszkanska Street (Warsaw), 155, 162, 236
Frank, Hans, 166–167, 272, 303, 344
Frescoes. *See also* Drawings; Murals; Paintings
    Altschul (Cracow), 299, 300, 302
Freud, Sigmund, 20
Freund, Vilmos, 469
Friedmann, Mor, 449
Friedmann, R. Denes, 473
Frohlich Patisserie, 403
Frydberg, Abraham Shalom, 206
Fuchs, Scheindl Bina, 304

Gans, David, 12, 121, 128
    on death of King Sigismund August, 268
    Esterka legend and, 259
    grave, 102, 103
    on High Synagogue (Prague), 82
    on Maisel Synagogue, 125
    Tzemah David and, 103, 105
Gas chambers, 490–491
Gebirtig, Mordecai, 272, 273
Gematriah (numerical equivalents), 72
    R. Nathan Nata Spira and, 321–332
Genealogy, resources in Warsaw, 180, 239
Genizah
    Altneuschul, 67
    Great Synagogue (Buda), 421–422
Gepner, Abraham, 248
Gerer Hasidism, 158, 161, 162, 197
German (language), Prague Jews and, 16, 18, 19
German names, forced adoption of, 16, 93, 153
Germany (medieval), anti-Semitism in, 380
Germany (Nazi). *See also* Holocaust
    anti-Semitism and, 80
    destruction of Old Jewish Cemetery (Cracow), 312, 314
    invasion of Poland, 165
    Museum of an Extinct Race and, 53–55, 74, 123
    Museum of the Prague Ghetto and, 117
    occupation of Czechoslovakia, 21
    occupation of Prague, 140
    plunder of High Synagogue (Cracow), 344
"Gersonide" family, 10–11
Gesia cemetery. *See* Jewish Cemetery (Warsaw)
Gesia Street (Warsaw), 186
Ghetto. *See also* Jewish Town (Prague); Warsaw Ghetto
    in Budapest, 391
    meanings of term, 267
Ghettoization
    Old Jewish Cemetery and, 100–101
    in Prague, 66
Glasses, of Prague's Burial Society, 118
Glatstein, Jacob, 210
Glucksberg, Jan, 194
Goeth, Amon Leopold, 273, 274
Goethe, Johann Wolfgang von, 49
Goldberg, Abraham, 210
Goldschmied, Judah, 90
Goldszmit, Henryk. *See* Korczak, Janusz
Golem legend, 34–43, 44–49, 58–59, 64
Gora Kalwaria, 158, 197
Gothic style, Altneuschul and, 64, 68, 69
Gotthard, Wohler, 440
Gottlieb, Marcin, 303
Gottlieb, Maurycy, 271, 303, 361–362
Graf, Malvina, 367, 368–369, 370
Graniczna Street (Warsaw), 154
Gravestones
    from Buda, 417
    leaving pebbles on, 109–110, 211
    in Old Jewish Cemetery (Prague), 105–106, 107

Gravestones (continued)
  Roman, 376
  styles of, 108
  in Warsaw's Jewish Cemetery, 187,
    193–194, 196–197, 198
    Ostrzega monuments, 201–202,
      205, 207, 208, 210
Great Court Synagogue (Prague), 133
Great Synagogue (Buda), 384, 413
  destruction of, 421–422
  excavation, 422–423
  history, 417–421
  Megillat Buda and, 423–425
  memorial to, 471
Great Synagogue (Warsaw). *See*
  Tlomackie Street Synagogue
Griesz family *ohel*, 470
Grimm, Jakob, 49
Groceries. *See also* Kosher food
  Budapest, 402–403
  Prague, 57
Grunbaum, Yitzchak, 163
Grzyb, Balbina, 213
Grzyb, Felix, 213
Grzybowski Square (Warsaw), 244, 245
Gucci, Matteo, 295
Guilds, Jewish, in Prague, 14
Gunther, Hans, 124
Guterman, R. Yaakov Aryeh, 205
Gutman, Yisrael, 167, 172

Ha'am, Ahad, 29
HaCohen, Gershon, 10
Ha'Cohen, R. Ephraim ben Jacob, 383,
  420–421, 423
Hadarim. *See* Schools
Haggadah, of Prague (1526), 10
Haidamaks, pogroms and, 152
HaKohen, R. Akiva ben Menahem, 381
Ha'levi, R. David (Taz), 327–329
Halevi, R. Isaac ben Mordechai, 301, 331,
  333
Halkowski, Henryk, 292

Ha'Maggid, 356
Hanna Restaurant, 401
Hapsburg Empire, 10, 12, 13, 114. *See
  also* Josef II; Rudolf II
  Edict of Tolerance, 15–16, 386
  toleration tax and, 14–15
Hapsburg monarchy. *See also* Austria
  Jewish emancipation and, 385–387
  rule of Hungary, 384–385
Harburg (Germany), Holocaust memorial
  in, 94
Haselbauer, Franciscus, 108
Hasidism
  Cracow, 270–271, 301, 333, 353,
    359–360
  prayer houses, 359–360
  Rabbi Judah Loew and, 33
  Warsaw, 155, 158, 161, 162, 197
Haskalah. *See* Jewish Enlightenment
"Hat of Shame," 81, 128
Hatvany-Deutsch, Ludwig, 437
Hatzadik, R. Shmuel, 47
Haupt, Adam, 492
Havdallah, at Altschul (Cracow), 305–306
Havel, Vaclav, 30–31, 92
Haynt newspaper, 210
Hebrew, Edict of Tolerance and, 16
Hebrew clock, in Jewish Town Hall
  (Prague), 4, 86
Hebrew Grammar School (Cracow), 362–
  363
Hebrew newspapers, 356
Hebrew printing press, 10, 125
Hebrew publishers, 355–356
Hehalutz movement, 161
Heller, R. Yomtov Lippman (Tosefot
  Yomtov), 13, 121, 268, 301, 330,
  331
  grave, 333–334, 335
  legends of, 336–337, 348–349
  life, 334–335
Hendel, Zygmunt, 295
Hendela bat Gershon, 313

Herczog, R. Laszlo, 483
Heroes' Temple, 454–456, 476
Herz, Judah Tsoref de, 90, 126
Herzl, Theodor, 396–398, 436, 452, 453
Heschel, R. Abraham Joshua, 207, 331, 332
Hevesi, R. Simon, 439
Heydrich, Reinhard, 21, 140
High Synagogue (Cracow), 266, 267, 291, 343–345
High Synagogue (Prague), 12, 54, 82–85, 343
  visiting, 61, 63
  worship in, 84–85
Hild, Jozsef, 447
Himmler, Heinrich, 170, 171, 492
"Hislner Affair," 29
History of the Jewish Sermon (Zunz), 130
Hochman, Henryk, 365
Holesovice, 21
Hollander, Roza, 469
Holocaust
  antecedents of, 80
  in Budapest and Hungary, 390–391, 454
  in Cracow, 272–274, 296
    Podgorze ghetto, 366–371
  in Prague and Czechoslovakia, 21–22, 79–80
    High Synagogue and, 84
    Jewish Museum of Prague and, 53–55
    Oneg Shabbat and, 177–178
    Vaclav Havel on, 31
  in Warsaw, 165–173. *See also* Warsaw Ghetto
Holocaust memorials
  Budapest, 456–458, 470–471, 474
  Cracow, 337, 359
  criticism of, 93–94
  Prague (Pinchas Synagogue), 31, 91–94, 95, 96
  Treblinka, 492
Warsaw, 183
  Memorial Route of Jewish Martyrdom and Struggle, 214–231
  Umschlagplatz Memorial, 199
Holocaust survivors, Jewish identity and, 23, 393
Holy ark. *See Aron hakodesh*
Honorius III, 378
Horowitz, Aaron Meshulam, 11, 89, 94, 97
  grave, 106, 115
Horowitz, Israel, 106
Horowitz, Pinchas (of Cracow), 269
Horowitz, R. Pinchas (of Prague), 88, 97–99
Horowitz, Shabbatai, 90
Horowitz family, 10, 11, 89–90
Hospitals. *See* Jewish hospitals
Hoss, Rudolf, 492
Hotels, Budapest, 403
"House of Happiness," 26–27
House of Jacob school, 271–272
"House of Prague," 27
Hruzik, Jan Kanty, 299
Hungarian Jewish Congress, 434–436, 462, 465
Hungarian Jewish Museum, 452–453
Hungarian Revolution (1848–49), 389, 478
Hungarian Uprising (1956), 393
Hungary. *See also* Budapest
  history of Jews in, 376–395
Hus, Jan, 8–9, 141
Hussites, 8–9

Ibn Ezra, 47
Ibn Jakub, Ibrahim, 5, 261
Illiteracy, in Hungary, 378
Inscriptions
  along Memorial Route of Jewish Martyrdom and Struggle, 217
  Altneuschul, 76–77
  Altschul (Cracow), 298, 299

Inscriptions (*continued*)
  Ceremonial Hall, 137
  Dohaney Street Synagogue, 437, 440
  High Synagogue (Prague), 83
  Jewish Cemetery in Warsaw, 193–194
  Klausen Synagogue, 122–123
  Obuda Synagogue, 429
  on Old Jewish Cemetery gravestones, 105–106
  Pinchas Synagogue, 94–95
  Small Synagogue (Buda), 415
  Tempel Synagogue, 354
Iron, in Dohaney Street Synagogue, 438
Isaac ben Moses, R. *(Or Zaru'ah)*, 6, 378
Isaac Reb Jekeles, R. (Isaac Jacobowicz), 269, 321, 346–347, 348
Isaac Synagogue, 268, 269, 291, 346–349
Isaac the Rich, 316
Israelite Reform Society of Pest, 446
Israelite Women's Association, 473
Israel (state), 398
Isserl, Reb. *See* Lazars, R. Israel
Isserles, R. Moses (the Rema), 103, 194, 195, 267–268, 301, 307
  books of, 276–277
  family of, 316–318
  grave, 314–316
  legends of, 278–282, 315, 338–341
  life, 275–276
  Maimonides and, 315
  in Rema Synagogue, 310
Istvan I (king of Hungary), 377, 408

Jabotinsky, Zev, 164
Jacobowicz, Isaac (Reb Isaac Reb Jekeles), 269, 321
Jacob the Rich, 346
Jagiellonska Street (Praga), 255
Jail cells
  Altneuschul, 67
  Altschul (Cracow), 295
  Great Synagogue (Buda), 419
  Obuda, 430

Jakuba Street (Cracow), 313, 335–336
Jan Kazimierz (king of Poland), 349
Jan Olbracht (king of Poland), 264
January Uprising (Warsaw), 157
Javen School, 394–395
Jeitteles, Jonas, 119
Jekeles, Jacob, 269
Jekeles, Moses, 293
Jeremiah the prophet, Golem legend and, 47, 48
Jerusalem ("Jubilee") Synagogue, 59, 132–134
Jesuits
  anti-Semitism and, 144–145
  in Prague, 13
Jewish Cemetery (Warsaw)
  history, 185–188
  location, 183–185
  maps, 184, 189–191
  Ostrzega monuments, 201–202, 205, 207, 208, 210
  religious disputes and, 193–195
  walking tour, 188–213
Jewish Community
  Budapest, 399
    Dohaney Street Synagogue and, 445–446
    Rumbach Synagogue and, 460
  Cracow, 287
    Altschul and, 301
    Old Jewish Cemetery (Cracow) and, 312–314
    ownership of Altschul and, 296
  Prague, 24–27, 56, 61–63
  Warsaw, 154, 175, 179, 237, 244, 252
Jewish Congress, in Hungary, 434–436, 462, 465
Jewish court. *See* Rabbinical court
Jewish Crafts School (Cracow), 362
Jewish Enlightenment, Rabbi Landau and, 136

Jewish Fighting Organization (ZOB)
    Cracow, 273, 369–370
    Warsaw, 171–173, 178, 225, 248
Jewish Fighting Union (ZZW), 171
Jewish Flying University, 175
Jewish Historical Institute (Warsaw), 180, 238–240
Jewish hospitals, 116
    Cracow, 366
    Czyste Hospital, 202, 226–228
    Podgorze ghetto, 370
Jewish identity. *See also* Assimilation; Emancipation
    in modern Hungary, 392–395
    in post-war Warsaw, 173–176
    in Prague, 3–4
        effects of emancipation on, 17–21
        modern state of, 23–27
Jewish intellectuals, in Prague, 19–20
Jewish Museum of Prague, 15, 56, 117, 128
    history, 53–55
    parochets in, 71
    Spanish Synagogue and, 132
    visiting, 61, 63
Jewishness. *See* Jewish identity; Yiddishkeit
Jewish Prague, 3
"Jewish prefect," 381–382, 411–412, 419
Jewish Question, Zionism and, 398
Jewish revolutionaries, 153, 156–158, 208–210
Jewish Star. *See Magen David*
The Jewish State (Herzl), 397
Jewish Street (Buda). *See* Szent Gyorgy Street; Tancsics Mihaly Street
Jewish Theater (Warsaw), 249
Jewish Town Hall (Prague), 51, 85–88
    Czech attack on, 19
    Hebrew clock, 4
    High Synagogue and, 82
    modern condition, 25

Jewish Town (Prague)
    census figures, 13, 14
    early history, 5–6
    effects of slum clearance in, 51–52
    ghettoization, 7
    Golden Age of, 11–12, 101–102
    Hapsburgs and, 10, 12, 13
    Jewish emigration from, 50
    Jewish identity and, 3–4
    maps, 62, 104
    natural disasters and, 13, 15, 63, 82, 83, 86, 121, 122, 130
    population control in, 13–14
    slum conditions in, 50–51
    visiting, 61–64
Jew Judge, 380, 411
Jews Praying In The Old Synagogue in Cracow (Hruzik), 299
John of Luxembourg (king of Bohemia), 7
Joint Distribution Committee. *See* American Jewish Joint Distribution Committee
Josef II (Holy Roman emperor), 61, 99, 119, 128
    adoption of German names, 16, 93
    Edict of Tolerance, 15–16, 386
    Hungarian Jews and, 385–387, 427, 428
    Jubilee Synagogue and, 133
    Theresienstadt and, 489
Josefov district (Prague). *See* Jewish Town
Joselewicz, Berek, 153, 252, 298
Joseph II (Holy Roman emperor). *See* Josef II
Joshua ben Joseph, R. (Meginnei Shlomo), 268, 301, 329–331
Jozsefvaros Casino, 480
Jubilee Synagogue. *See* Jerusalem ("Jubilee") Synagogue
Judaism. *See also* Hasidism; Orthodox Judaism; Progressive Judaism; Reform Judaism
    Franz Kafka and, 138–139

Judenrat
  Cracow, 272
  Warsaw, 166, 199, 222–223
Jurydyka, 151

Kabbalah, R. Nathan Nata Spira and, 321–332
Kafka, Franz, 49, 128
  grave, 137
  Jewish assimilation and, 18, 19, 20
  Jewish Town (Prague) and, 4, 87
  Judaism and, 138–139
  manuscripts of, 108
  Yiddish and, 87–88
  Zigeuner Synagogue and, 51–52, 133
Kallina, Mor, 459
Kalman (king of Hungary), 377
Kalmush, Reb, 360
Kaminska, Esther Rachel, 163, 208
Kaminska, Ida, 208
Kaplan, Chaim, 239
Kapporet
  Altneuschul, 71–72
  High Synagogue (Prague), 83
  Maisel Synagogue, 127
Kara, R. Avigdor, 8, 9, 64
  Easter Pogrom and, 78, 79, 80, 130
  grave, 99, 115
  tombstone, 128
Karo, R. Josef, 275, 276–277, 319
Kassowitz, Jakab Hirsch, 438
Katz, R. Joseph, 316
Katzenellenbogen, R. Avraham, 155
Kavanah, 72
Kaviory Street (Cracow), 261
Kazimiercek, Stanislaw, 364
Kazimierz. *See also* Cracow
  anti-Semitism, expulsions, and pogroms, 269–270
  Bochenska Street, 365
  gate to, 345–346
  Hebrew Grammar School, 362–363
  history of Jews in, 264–271
  itinerary, 291–292
  Jewish commercial rights, 269
  Jewish Crafts School, 362
  Jewish hospital, 366
  mikveh, 265
  Plac Novy, 363
  synagogues, 266, 268, 269
  Town Hall, 365
Kazinczy Street Synagogue, 465–467
  Hungarian Jewish Congress and, 434, 436
  services, 477–478
Kepler, Johannes, 12, 103
Keter Torah (Torah crown), in Altschul (Cracow), 302
Kharkov, expulsions from, 159
Khazar Jews, 377
Kieval, Hillel J., 131
King's Hotel, 403
King's Hotel Restaurant, 401
Kisch, Egon Erwin, 20, 43, 144
Kisei Ha'Maharal (Chair of the Maharal), 70
Klamerus, Wladyslaw, 199, 216, 231
Klaus, 359–360
Klausen Synagogue, 51, 54, 121–125
  Nefele mound and, 115
  visiting, 61, 64
Klausen yeshivah, 121–122
Kleir Yakar. *See* Luntschitz, R. Shelomo Ephraim
Klementinum, 13
Klima, Ivan, 12
Klopotowskiego Street (Praga), 255
Kohn, R. Samuel, 479
Koplan, Chaim, 165, 166
Korczak, Janusz, 200–201, 211–213, 230, 492
Kornfeld, Zsigmon, 470
Kornitzer, R. Akiva, 361
Kornitzer, Shmul Shmulke, 360–361
Kornitzer, Yosef Nechemiah, 360–361
Kosciuszko, Thaddeus, 153, 292, 297, 301

Kosciuszko Insurrection, 153, 157, 297, 298
Kosher food
    Budapest, 401–403
    Cracow, 289
    Prague, 58
    Warsaw, 182
Kosher Shop (Prague), 57–58
Kossuth, Lajos, 389, 445
Kozma Street Cemetery, 468–472
Krasinski Gardens, 234, 240
Krieger, Ignac, 303, 349
Krisztinavaros, 417
Krochmalna Street (Warsaw), 240–244
Krzepicki, Maurycy, 301
Kun, Bela, 390
Kupa Synagogue, 268, 291, 350
    history, 350
    interior, 351
Kurtzhandl, Lobl, 144
Kvittel (notes left on gravestones), 100, 109

LaGuardia, Fiorello, 209
Lajos II (king of Hungary), 419
Lajos I (king of Hungary), 379–380, 411
Lajta, Bela, 469
Landau, Moshe Israel, 136
Landau, R. Ezekiel *(Nodeh Bi'Yehudah)*, 15, 17, 64, 70, 128, 135–136
Landau, R. Moses Halevi, 275, 316
Landau, Wilhelm, 205
Landherr, Andras, 429
Land's Jewry, 142
Landy, Michal, 157, 203
Langer, Frantisek, 20
Langer, Jiri, 20
Langweil, Antonin, 145
Langweil model of Prague, 145
Large Synagogue (Budapest), 443, 444, 461
Laszlo IV (king of Hungary), 410
Lateran Councils, 6–7, 66, 68
Lauder Foundation. *See* Ronald S. Lauder Foundation

Lavabo
    Altschul (Cracow), 297
    Rema Synagogue, 309
Law Book of Buda, 380, 411
Lazar (citizen of Prague), 8
Lazars, R. Israel ben Joseph (Reb Isserl), 266, 275
    grave, 316
    legends of, 278–279
    Old Jewish Cemetery and, 313
    Rema Synagogue and, 295, 307–308
League of Israel. *See* Agudath Israel
Lehel Street Cemetery, 468, 472
Lejserowicz, Sabina, 213
Leopold II (Holy Roman Emperor), 387
Lesser, Aleksander, 203
Lesser, Levi, 203
Letiersdorfer, Bela, 469
"Letter killing," 380
Levites, graves in Prague, 113
Lewin, Abraham, 214
Lewko ben Jordan, 262
Libuse (Libussa), 5
Libussa, 5
Lichtenstadt, Abraham Aron, 142–143
Lieberman, Helise, 179
Life With a Star (Weil), 22, 79–80, 137
Light, everlasting. *See Ner tamid*
Lipiec-Jakubowska, Roza, 213
Lipschitz, R. Solomon Zalman (Chemdat Shlomo), 157, 192
Liszt, Franz, 441–442
Lithuanian Jews, 159–160
Litvaks, 159–160
Lodz ghetto, 21
Loew, Pearl, 112, 114
Loew, R. Judah (Maharal of Prague), 11–12, 64, 65, 82, 128
    chair of, 70
    Chevrah Kaddishah and, 118
    elected Chief Rabbi of Prague, 122
    Emperor Rudolf II and, 103, 105
    Golem legend and, 34–43, 58–59

Loew, R. Judah (*continued*)
  grave, 102, 112
  Klausen Synagogue and, 121–122
  life, 32–33
  Mordechai Maisel and, 111
  R. E. Ashkenazi and, 319
  Rabbi Luntschitz and, 112–113
  statue of, 140–141
  on Torah study, 121–122
Lowy, Isaac, 472–473
Lubomirski Palace, 240
Luntschitz, R. Shelomo Ephraim (Kleir Yakar), 71, 112–113
Luria, R. Yitzchak (Arizal), 72, 90
Luriah, R. Isaac, 72, 90
Lurianic Kabbalah, 72
Luther, Martin, 9
Lutz, Charles, 391

Ma'asei Ha'Shem (Ashkenazi), 319
Machzike Hadas, 271
Magen David (Jewish Star, Star of David)
  on David Gans' gravestone, 103
  first heraldic use of, 64, 81
  in Holocaust, 166
  in Small Synagogue (Buda), 414–415
Magyars, 377, 408
Maharal of Prague. *See* Loew, R. Judah
Mahler, Gustav, 20, 135
Mah Tovu, 449
Maimonides, 81, 315
Maisel, Mordechai, 32, 116
  grave, 102, 111–112
  High Synagogue and, 12, 82
  Jewish Town Hall and, 12, 85–86
  Klausen Synagogue and, 121
  Maisel Synagogue and, 12, 125–126
  wealth and philanthropy of, 12, 110–111
Maisel Synagogue, 12, 71, 90, 117
  description, 125–129
  tombstone of Rabbi Avigodor Kara, 99, 115, 128
  visiting, 61, 64

Majdanke concentration camp, 274
Mala Strana, 5, 99, 101
Mala Street (Praga), 254–255
Manes, Antonin, 100
Mannheimer, R. Isaac Noah, 443
Mappah (Karo), 277
Marconi, Leandro, 237
Maria Theresa (Holy Roman empress), 14–15, 385
Marranos, 173
Masaryk, Tomas G., 21, 28–29
Mass deportations
  form Warsaw Ghetto, 170–171, 214, 228–230, 491
  from Podgorze ghetto, 367
  from Terezin, 490
Mass graves
  Budapest, 454, 471
  Warsaw, 187, 198–199, 213–214
Matthias Corvinus (king of Hungary), 381–382, 411–412, 419
Matzoh, 76
Maximillan II (king of Bohemia), 11, 86, 121
May Laws, 159
Mechir Yayin (Isserles), 276
Medigo, Joseph Shelomo del, 47, 115
Megalleh Amukkot. *See* Spira, R. Nathan Nata
Megalleh Amukkot (Spira), 322–323
Megillat Buda (Schulhof), 423–425
Megillat Eiva (Heller), 334
Meginnei Shlomo. *See* Joshua ben Joseph, R.
Meginnei Shlomo (Joshua ben Joseph), 330
Meisel, R. Wolf Alois, 449–450, 461, 462
Meisels, R. Dov Berush, 157, 192–193, 298, 301, 313
Meisels, R. Simchah Bunim, 318
Melling, R. Isaac, 122
Memorial Route of Jewish Martyrdom and Struggle
  inscriptions, 217
  Mila 18 memorial, 225

Stawki Street 5/7, 225
Stawki Street 6/8 (Czyste Hospital), 226–228
Szmul Zygielbojm memorial, 222–224
Umschlagplatz, 228–231
Warsaw Ghetto Monument, 218–221
Zegota memorial, 221–222
"Memory of the Destruction," in Altneuschul, 69
Mendel, Judah, 412, 419
Mendel, R. Menahcem, of Worke, 204–205
Mendel family, 382, 412
Mendelssohn, Felix, 140
Mendelssohn Is on the Roof (Weil), 140
Menorah, from High Synagogue (Cracow), 344
Meyrink, Gustav, 49
Miczynski, Sebastian, 341
Midnight prayer, at Altschul (Cracow), 306
Mihalovce, 465
Mikulov (Moravia), 32
Mikveh
  Budapest, 403–404
  Cracow, 261, 265, 289, 341
  Praga, 254
  Prague, 60, 96–97
  Warsaw, 182
Mila 18 memorial, 225
Milejkowski, Izrael, 226
Milk stores, Budapest, 402
Minorities' Treaty, 163
Mint (coinage), Buda, 410
Miodowa Street (Cracow), 352
Mirrors, Altneuschul, 69
Miscarriages, burial of, 116
Mitnagdim, Warsaw, 155
Mitzvah, of burial, 110
Mizrachi movement, 352
Mizrach tablet, Dohaney Street Synagogue, 440
Mlada Boleslav, 114

Moczar, Mieczyslaw, 174
Mohacs Disaster, 382–384
Moneylending, 66
  Fourth Lateran Council and, 6–7
Monuments. *See* Gravestones; Holocaust memorials
Moorish style
  Dohaney Street Synagogue, 437, 438, 450–451, 452
  Rumbach Synagogue, 458–459
  Spanish Synagogue, 131
Moravia
  Edict of Tolerance and, 16
  expulsions in, 9
  Familiants Laws and, 14
Mordechai, R. Moshe, of Pelcovizna, 207
Mordechaja Anielewicza Street (Warsaw), 186
Morning prayer, at Altschul (Cracow), 306
Moscicki, Ignacy, 298
Moscow, expulsions from, 159
Moses ben Maimon, R. *See* Maimonides
Muenz, R. Moses ben Isaac Halevi, 388, 427, 428, 429
Mugs, of Prague's Burial Society, 118
Muhlhausen, R. Yomtov Lippmann, 9
Munich Agreement, 21
Murals. *See also* Drawings; Frescoes; Paintings
  Popper Synagogue, 342
Museum of an Extinct Race, 53–55, 74, 127, 131
  High Synagogue (Prague) and, 84
  Klausen Synagogue and, 123
  Pinchas Synagogue and, 90
Museum of the Prague Ghetto, 117
Museums. *See also* Exhibitions; Jewish Museum of Prague
  Cracow Historical Museum, 296
  Hungarian Jewish Museum, 452–453
  Wolfsohn Museum, 343
Mushkat, Yeshayah, 192

My Father's Court (Singer), 242
Mysticism, numerical equivalents and, 72

Nagyfuvaros Synagogue, 479–480
Nagyszombat, 384
Naidus, Leib, 210
Nalewki Street (Warsaw), 155, 162, 234–236
Names, German, forced adoption of, 16, 93, 153
Napoleon I, 155
Natanson, Henryk, 158, 203
Natanson, Jakub, 203
Natanson, Ludwik, 158, 202, 237
Natanson, Zelig, 202
Naves, twin, 69, 418
Nazis. *See* Germany (Nazi)
Nebuchadnezzar, 109
Nefele mound, 115–116
Neo-Gothic style, Maisel Synagogue, 127
Neolog movement, 388. *See also* Cultus-Temple
  Bethlen Ter Synagogue and, 484
  Csaky Synagogue and, 480, 481
  Dohaney Street Synagogue and, 435–436, 444, 466
  ohelim and, 469
  Rabbinical Seminary and, 478–479
  Rumbach Synagogue and, 460–463
  Sasz Chevra and, 487
  Ujpest Synagogue and, 473
Neo-Romanesque style, Ceremonial Hall (Prague), 116
Nepauer, Matyas, 428
Ner tamid (everlasting light)
  Altneuschul, 72
  Altschul (Cracow), 303
The Netziv. *See* Berlin, R. Naphtali Tzvi Yehuhad
Neuschul (Cracow), 294–295, 308. *See also* Rema Synagogue

Neuschul (Prague), 79. *See also* Altneuschul
The New Ghetto (Herzl), 397
New Jewish Cemetery (Cracow)
  history, 357–358
  walking tour, 358–362
New Jewish Cemetery (Prague), 99
New Jewish District (Buda), 411–412
New Life, 475
New Olsany Cemetery, 117, 135, 137–139
New Synagogue (Cracow). *See* Rema Synagogue
New Synagogue (Prague), 133
New Town (Prague), 5, 99
Nicholas I (czar), 157, 195
Nifla'ot Maharal (Rosenberg), 48–49
Nikolsberg (Moravia), 32
Nimoy, Leonard, 113–114
Nissenbaum Family Foundation, 213, 214, 246, 337
Nissenbaum Kosher Restaurant, 289
Nodeh Bi'Yehudah. See Landau, R. Ezekiel
Nomberg, Hersh David, 211, 239
Non tolerandis Judaeis, 150–152, 154, 251
Notes. *See* Kvittel
November Uprising (Warsaw), 157, 195
Nove Mesto. *See* New Town (Prague)
Nozyk, Ryvka, 249–250
Nozyk, Zalman, 247, 249–250
Nozyk Synagogue, 179, 180–181, 247, 249–250
Numerical equivalents, 72
  R. Nathan Nata Spira and, 321–32
Numerus Clausus law, 390

Oberlander, R. Baruch, 487
Obuda, Jewish history in, 384–385, 426–430
Obuda Synagogue, 428–430
Offshoot of David (Gans), 103, 105

Ofyn Berg Shul, 293
Ogrod Saski, 234, 240
Ohel/ohelim
   Jewish Cemetery (Warsaw), 188
   Kozma Street Cemetery, 469
   Old Jewish Cemetery (Prague), 108, 112
Okopowa Street (Warsaw), 185
Old Jewish Cemetery (Cracow), 276, 291, 310–337
   destruction of, 312, 314
   famous individuals in, 314–337
   history, 312–314
   Jakuba Street gate, 313, 335–336
   legends of, 336–337
   map, 311
Old Jewish Cemetery (Prague), 95, 99–117, 121
   description, 99–100
   history, 100–101
   map, 104
   visiting, 61, 63
   walking tour, 103–116
Old Jewish District (Buda), 408–411
"Old New Synagogue." *See* Altneuschul
Old Olsany Cemetery, 134–137
Old Town (Prague), 5–6, 10, 11, 129–130
Olsany Cemetery, 99, 117, 134–139
Oneg Shabbat, 177–178, 239, 346
Oppenheim, R. David, 107–108
Oppenheim(er), Samuel, 108, 122, 422
Opposition movements, philo-Semitism and, 9
Oppression. *See* Anti-Semitism
Optima Building (Cracow), 370
Orczy House, 433, 442–443, 444, 445, 461
Organ
   Dohaney Street Synagogue, 440–442
   Maisel Synagogue, 127
Orgelbrand, Samuel, 158, 204

Orthodox Judaism
   in Budapest, 435–436, 446–447
      Bethlen Ter Synagogue and, 484
      Kazinczy Street Synagogue and, 466, 477–478
      Rabbinical Seminary and, 478–479
      Rumbach Synagogue and, 460–463
      Sasz Chevra and, 487
   in Cracow, 271, 361
   Mizrachi movement, 352
   in Prague, 26–27
   in Warsaw, 161, 162
Or Zaru'ah. *See* Isaac ben Moses
Osterreicher, Joseph Manes, 427
Ostrzega, Abraham, 201–202
Ostrzega monuments, 201–202, 205, 207, 208, 210
Otakar II (king of Bohemia), 7, 66, 68
Ottoman Empire, rule of Buda, 382–384, 412–413, 414
Oxford University, Bodleian Library and, 108
Ozick, Cynthia, 49

Paintings. *See also* Drawings; Frescoes; Murals
   Corpus Christi Church (Cracow), 364–365
   High Synagogue (Cracow), 345
   Kupa Synagogue, 351
   Small Synagogue (Buda), 414
Palestine, Polish Zionism and, 161, 164
Pankiewica, Tadeusz, 369
Pannonia, 376, 377
Parizska Street (Prague), 51, 73
Parochets
   Altneuschul, 71
   Maisel Synagogue, 126, 128
   Nozyk Synagogue, 250
Patai, Raphael, 378, 383
Patisseries, Budapest, 403
Pave, Ester, 208
Pebbles, left on gravestones, 109–110, 211
Pecaric, R. Sacha, 287, 288, 289

Peretz, Isaac Leib, 49, 162, 207, 239
Perl, Felix, 211
Perlasca, Giorgio, 391
Perlmutter, Abraham Tzvi, 192
Perutz, Leo, 51
Pest. *See also* Budapest
   census figures, 389, 434
   Heroes' Temple, 454–456
   history of Jews in, 385–389
   Holocaust memorials, 456–458, 470–471
   Hungarian Jewish Museum, 452–453
   Jewish history in, 431, 433–436, 444, 445
   Kazinczy Street Synagogue, 465–467
   Kozma Street Cemetery, 468–472
   map, 432
   Martyr's Cemetery, 454
   rabbis of, 472
   Rumbach Synagogue, 458–465
   World War I memorials, 470
   Yizkor wall, 470–471
Pharmacy, "Under The Eagle," 369
Philo-Semitism, Hussistes and, 9
Piekarska Street (Warsaw), 150
Pillars, in Altneuschul, 74–75
Pilpul, 33, 121
Pilsudski, Jozef, 164
Pinchas, R. Israel, 88
Pinchas Synagogue, 88–96, 101, 103, 117, 126
   cemetery, 88
   history, 6, 10, 11, 51, 89–90
   Holocaust memorial in, 31, 91–94, 95, 96
   interior, 94–96
   legend of Rabbi Pinchas Horowitz and, 97–99
   meaning of name, 88
   visiting, 61, 63
Pinkas Synagogue. *See* Pinchas Synagogue
Pires, Diogo, 89
Pius IV, 10
Piwna Street (Warsaw), 150

Piyyutim, 464
Plac Bohaterow Getta. *See* Plac Zgody
Plac Grzybowski (Warsaw), 244, 245
Plac Novy (Cracow), 363
Plac Zgody (Cracow), 367, 368–369
Plague
   Cracow, 262, 270, 307, 316
   Prague, 13, 135
Plaszow concentration camp, 273, 274, 358, 367–368, 371
Po'alei Zion party, 208
Podgorze ghetto, 273–274, 366–371
Pogroms
   Cracow, 263–264, 269–270, 298–299, 304–305, 332
   Hungary, 381, 389
   Prague, 8, 9, 21, 78–79, 130
   Russia, 159
   Warsaw, 152, 153, 154, 159, 164, 174
Polacek, Karel, 20
Polak, R. Jakob, 264
Poland. *See also* Cracow; Kazimierz; Praga; Warsaw
   anti-Semitism, expulsions, and pogroms, 152, 153, 154, 155, 159–160, 164, 174, 240
   under Czarist rule, 156–158
   under French rule, 155
   German invasion, 165
   interwar period, 163–165
   partitioning of, 15, 152–153
   pogroms, 152
   uprising (1944), 246
Polish-Swedish War, 304, 331
Pollack, Mihaly, 429
Pollak, R. Lajos, 464
Popper, Joachim, 95
Popper, Wolf (Bozian), 341–342
Popper Synagogue, 268, 269, 291
   history, 341–342
   interior, 342–343
Population control, in Jewish Town (Prague), 13–14

Portals
  Altneuschul, 68
  Pinchas Synagogue, 94–95
Portheim, Leopold Porges von, 137
Portheimka building (Prague), 137
Portrait of a Rabbi (Marcin Gottlieb), 303
Poz, Natalia, 213
Poznanski, R. Samuel Abraham, 198
Praga, 151–152, 183
  cemetery, 185, 251, 253–254
  history, 251–252
  visiting, 252–255
Praga Synagogue, 252
Prague. *See also* Jewish Town (Prague)
  anti-Semitism, expulsions, and pogroms, 6–8, 9, 14–15, 78–79
  assimilation and emancipation in, 16–21, 131
  Burial Society *(Chevrah Kaddishah)*, 32, 116–120, 319
  cemeteries, 5, 13, 88
    Fibichova Street Cemetery, 99
    New Jewish Cemetery, 99
    New Olsany Cemetery, 117, 135, 137–139
    Old Jewish Cemetery, 61, 63, 95, 99–101, 103–117, 121
    Old Olsany Cemetery, 134–137
  census figures, 13, 14, 17, 21
  Chabad House, 56–57
  Crucifix on Charles Bridge, 64, 141–143
  Edict of Tolerance and, 15–17
  flag of Jewish sovereignty, 80–81
  Gersonide logo, 11
  ghettoization in, 66
  Golem legend, 34–43, 48–49
  grocers, 57
  history of Jews in, 5–27
  Holocaust and, 21–22, 53–55, 79–80
  itinerary for, 61–64
  Jewish Community of, 24–27, 56, 61–63
  Jewish Golden Age in, 11–12, 101–102
  Jewish identity and, 3–4, 23–27
  Jewish symbol of, 94, 95
  Langweil model of, 145
  maps, 62, 104
  mikveh in, 60, 96–97
  museums. *See* Jewish Museum of Prague
  persecution of R. Yomtov Heller, 334
  plague in, 13, 135
  "Prague Spring," 23, 91
  Rabbi Judah Loew and, 32–33
    statue of, 140–141
  restaurants, 57, 85, 86
  Rudolfinum, 140
  schools, 25–26
  synagogues
    Great Court Synagogue, 133
    High Synagogue, 12, 54, 61, 63, 82–85
    Jerusalem ("Jubilee") Synagogue, 132–134
    Klausen Synagogue, 51, 54, 61, 64, 115, 121–125
    Maisel Synagogue, 12, 61, 64, 71, 90, 99, 115, 117, 125–129
    New Synagogue, 133
    Pinchas Synagogue, 6, 10, 11, 31, 51, 61, 63, 88–99, 101, 103, 117, 126
    services, 58–60
    Spanish Synagogue, 4, 6, 61, 64, 65, 89, 128, 129–132
    Vinohrady Synagogue, 89
    visiting, 61–64
    Zigeuner Synagogue, 51–52, 128, 133
  Tyn Church, 144–145
"Prague Spring," 23, 91
Prayer. *See also* Services; Worship
  Budapest synagogues, 475–487
  Cracow, 288–289, 306
  Prague, 57–60

Prayer halls
  Cracow, 345, 359–360, 363–364, 365
  Praga, 255
  Warsaw, 162
Prayer shawl, Umschlagplatz Monument, 231
Prefect. *See* "Jewish prefect"
Premysl Otakar II (king of Bohemia), 7, 66, 68
Press. *See* Printing press
Priests, graves in Prague, 113
Printing press, Hebrew, in Prague, 10, 125
Prisons. *See also* Jail cells
  in Obuda, 430
Privus, Shaja, 244
Progressive Judaism. *See also* Reform Judaism
  Budapest, 435–436
  Cracow, 352–355
Prozna Street (Warsaw), 244–249
Prussia, rule of Poland, 153–155
Prussic acid, 492
Psalms Society, 364
Pshak Beit Din, 465
Pulpits
  Altneuschul, 72
  Dohaney Street Synagogue, 439
Putik, Alexander, 132

Raba Bara Gavra, 44–45
Rabbinate, history in Bohemia, 107
Rabbinical court, 16
  Altschul (Cracow), 297
  Kazinczy Street Synagogue, 465
Rabbinical Seminary (Budapest), 397, 478–479
Rabbinical Seminary (Warsaw), 193
Rabbis, at Altschul (Cracow), 307
Rakosi, Matyas, 392–393
Rakoskeresztur Cemetery. *See* Kozma Street Cemetery
Rapaport, Solomon Zainwil (An-ski), 207–208

Rapoport, Nathan, 218–219, 220–221
Rapoport, R. Solomon Judah (Shlomo Jehudah), 18, 136
Rashi. *See* Shlomo ben Isaac, R.
Red Cross, Terezin and, 490
Reform Judaism. *See also* Progressive Judaism
  in Budapest, 388, 427, 435–436. *See also* Neolog movement
  Chessed Neurim and, 443
  Dohaney Street Synagogue and, 442–445, 446–447, 448–450
  in Prague, 26–27, 127, 131
Reich, R. Koppel, 439, 466
Reichmann Foundation, 395
Reisner, Yale, 180
(the) Rema. *See* Isserles, R. Moses
Rema Synagogue, 266, 267, 276, 291
  history, 307–309
  interior, 309–310
  services, 288–289
Remba, Nachum, 230
Renaissance, Prague in, 10–11
Renaissance architecture
  Altschul (Cracow), 295, 299
  High Synagogue (Prague), 82–83
Restaurants
  Budapest, 401
  Cracow, 288, 289
  Prague, 57, 85, 86
  Warsaw, 182, 247–248
The Revealing of the Depths (Spira), 322–323
Ringelblum, Emmanuel, 177–178, 228, 229, 230, 239, 243
Roder, Pancratius, 82, 86
Roland, Charles G., 228
Roman Empire, in Eastern Europe, 376, 377
Ronald S. Lauder Foundation
  Cracow, 274, 287–288, 346
  Hungary, 394–395
  Prague, 25

Warsaw, 175, 179–180, 249
  genealogy project, 180, 239
  Jewish Historical Institute and, 239
  meals and, 182
Rosenberg, R. Judel, 48–49
Rosh Hashanah, at Altschul (Cracow), 305
Rothschild Kosher Foodstore, 403
Rows of Gold (Ha'levi), 327
Royal Charter (Bohemia), 66, 67
Rudolf II (Holy Roman emperor), 11, 33, 109, 415
  Jewish Golden Age and, 102
  Mordechai Maisel and, 110–111, 126
  Rabbi Judah Loew and, 103, 105
Rudolfinum, 140
Rumbach Synagogue, 447
  history, 459–462
  Hungarian Jewish Congress and, 434, 436, 462
  interior, 459
  liturgical traditions, 463–464
  Moorish style, 458–459
  rabbis of, 464–465
  services, 476, 477
  Status Quo movement and, 462–464, 466
Russia
  emigration to Warsaw, 159
  expulsions from, 159
  pogroms, 153, 159
  rule of Poland, 156–158
Russian army, Jewish suppliers to, 156
Ruthenia, sub-Carpathian, 20, 22, 24, 29
Rycerska Street (Warsaw), 150

Sacrificial ceremony, 71–72
Saint-Saens, Camille, 442
Salami stores, in Budapest, 402
Saloun, Ladislav, 140, 141
Samuel Bar Meshulam, 268
Sanctuary
  Altneuschul, 68–78
  Altschul (Cracow), 298
  High Synagogue (Prague), 82

Sarcophagi. *See also* Ohel/ohelim
  Old Jewish Cemetery (Prague), 108
Sasz Chevra, 486–487
Saturday Gate (Buda), 409, 413
Saxon Gardens, 234, 240
Schenker, Leon, 342
Schindler, Oskar, 371
Schindler's List (Spielberg film), 366, 369, 371
Schmidl, Sandor, 469
Schnirer, Sarah, 271–272
Scholem, Gershom, 49, 81, 414–415
Schools
  Budapest, 394–395, 427
  Cracow, 271–272, 351, 362–363
  Edict of Tolerance and, 16, 17
  Praga, 255
  Prague, 16, 17, 25–26
  quotas and, 390
  Warsaw, 162, 175, 179
Schudrich, R. Michael, 180, 182
Schulhof, Isaac, 423–425
Schwab, R. Low, 444, 446–447, 472
Scroll of Hatred (Heller), 334
Scum (Singer), 242–243, 246
Second Temple, Warsaw Ghetto Monument and, 219–220
Sefer Yetzirah, Golem legend and, 47
Segre, R. Jacob, 125
Selichot, 464
Seminary, 18
  Budapest, 397, 478–479
  Warsaw, 193
Sephardism
  Altschul and, 129
  Budapest, 383, 414, 486
  Kazimierz, 266
  Prague, 75
"Servants of the royal chamber," 6–7, 66, 409
Servi camerae regiae (servants of the royal chamber), 6–7, 66

Services. *See also* Prayer; Worship
   Budapest, 475–487
   Cracow, 288–289, 306
   Prague, 58–60
"Seven Species," Altneuschul, 69
1794 Insurrection. *See* Kosciuszko Insurrection
Sfas Emes, 158
Shabbat candles, 73
Shachna, Golda bat Shalom, 307, 316–317
Shachna, R. Shalom, 275
Shalom (restaurant in Prague), 57, 85, 86
Shapiro, Yakov Yitzchak, of Balandov, 205
Shavuot, Altneuschul, 76
Shelley, Mary, 49
Shem, R. Elijah Baal, 48
Shemurah matzoh, 76
Shield of David, in gravestone carvings, 108
Shield of Solomon (Joshua ben Joseph), 330
Shivah Minim ("Seven Species"), Altneuschul, 69
Shlomo ben Isaac, R. (Rashi), 330
Shlomo Molcho, 89, 117, 128
Shmuel of Slonim, R., 207
Shofar/shofarim
   Altschul (Cracow), 307
   in gravestone carvings, 107, 108
Shosha (Singer), 241–242
Shtiebel, Warsaw, 162, 254
Shulchan Aruch (Karo), 277
Shulman, Baruch, 208, 244
Sh'viti Tablet
   Altneuschul, 72
   Rema Synagogue, 310
Shylock and Jessica (Maurycy Gottlieb), 303
Sicher, R. Gustav, 17
Sidon, R. Karol, 25–26, 84
Sierota, Jan, 201
Sigismund II Augustus (king of Poland), 151, 265, 266, 267, 268, 269, 308, 309

Sigismund III (king of Poland), 268
Sigismund I (king of Poland), 150, 308
Sigismund (king of Bohemia and Hungary), 381
Simchat Torah
   Altneuschul, 76
   Altschul (Cracow), 304–305
Singer, Bernard, 236
Singer, Isaac Bashevis, 162, 232, 241–243
Sirkes, R. Joel (the Bach), 268, 301
   Bayit Chadash, 326, 327
   grave, 326
   legends of, 283–286, 325–329
   R. Nathan Spira and, 327
Six Day War, Czechoslovakia and, 91
Skra Stadium, mass graves in, 199, 213–214
Skroup, Franktisek, 130
Slanksy, Rudolf, 22
Slansky Trial, 23
Slivenec, 105
Slonimski, Chain Zelig, 201
Slum clearance, Jewish Town (Prague), 51–52
Small Synagogue (Buda), 383, 413, 414–417
   image of arrow, 415–416
   star of David, 414–415
Smuggling, in Warsaw ghetto, 168–169, 186
Sobibor death camp, 490
Socialism, in Jewish Warsaw, 160–161
Socio-Cultural Society of Jews in Poland, 179, 249
Sofer, R. Moses (Chatam Sofer), 18
Sofer, R. Simeon, 271, 301, 320, 361
Sokolow, Nahum, 196
Solidarity, 209
Solnicka, Dora, 213
Solomon ibn Gabirol, 47
Solomon's Temple, 107
Soloveitchik, R. Chaim, 206

Sonnenberg, Berek, 156, 195–196, 255
Sonnenberg, Temerel, 196
Sony Building, 238
Sopron, 384
"The Sown Light." *See* Isaac ben Moses
Spanish Jews, in Buda, 414
Spanish Synagogue, 4, 6, 65, 89, 128
    Altschul and, 129–131
    history and description, 131–132
    visiting, 61, 64
Speech, Golem legend and, 36, 45
Spielberg, Steven, 366, 369, 371
Spira, R. Nathan Nata (Megalleh Amukkot), 268, 293, 301
    family of, 323–324
    grave, 321
    legends of, 282–285, 324–325
    life, 321–322
    R. Joel Sirkes and, 327
    The Revealing of the Depths, 322–323
Spira, Rosa, 323
St. Anne's Church (Cracow), 298–299
St. Petersburg, expulsions from, 159
Stained glass windows, Tempel Synagogue, 355
Stalin, Joseph, 209
Stalowa Street (Praga), 254
Stanislaw Augustus (king of Poland), 251, 252, 253
Star of David. *See Magen David*
Star Trek, 113–114
Status Quo movement, 435–436, 462–464
    Bethlen Ter Synagogue and, 484
    Rumbach Synagogue and, 466
Stawki Street (Warsaw), 225–228
Stefan Batory (king of Poland), 267, 268
Stephen I (king of Hungary). *See* Istvan I
Stern, Abraham, 253
Stern, R. Markus, 473
Stiassny, Wilhelm, 134
Stiffel, Frank, 227
Stiffelman, Henryk, 255

Stones, left on gravestones, 109–110, 211
Stroop, Jurgen, 172, 173, 232
Strzelecka Street (Praga), 254
Study halls. *See Beit midrash*
Sub-Carpathian Ruthenia, 20, 22, 24, 29
Sukkah, High Synagogue (Prague), 84
Sulzer, Solomon, 443
Surnames, German, forced adoption of, 16, 93, 153
Swaddling cloths, 125
Sweden, 81
    occupation of Cracow, 269–270, 349
    Polish-Swedish War, 304, 331
Symbolism, on tombstones, 107
"Synagogue On the Hill," 293
Synagogue Party, 461, 462
Synagogues
    architectural history, 294
    in Budapest, 375, 409, 413
        Bet Aharon Synagogue, 481–482
        Bethlen Ter Synagogue, 480, 483–484
        Bet Smuel (Csaky Synagogue), 480–481
        Buda Synagogue, 485–486
        Dessewffy Street Synagogue, 482–483
        Great Synagogue, 384, 413, 417–425, 471
        Kazinczy Street Synagogue, 434, 436, 465–467, 477–478
        Obuda Synagogue, 428–430
        Rumbach Synagogue, 447, 458–465, 466, 476, 477
        Sasz Chevra, 486–487
        services, 475–487
        Small Synagogue, 383, 413, 414–417
        Teleki Ter Synagogue, 486
        Ujpest Synagogue, 473–474, 484–485

Synagogues (*continued*)
  in Cracow, 261, 266
    High Synagogue, 266, 267, 291, 343–346
    Isaac Synagogue, 268, 269, 291, 346–349
    Kupa Synagogue, 268, 291, 349–351
    Popper Synagogue, 268, 269, 291, 341–343
    Rema Synagogue, 266, 267, 276, 288–289, 291, 307–310
    services, 288–289
    Tempel Synagogue, 291, 352–357
  in Jewish communities, 375
  in Prague
    Great Court Synagogue, 133
    High Synagogue, 12, 54, 61, 63, 82–85
    Jerusalem ("Jubilee") Synagogue, 132–134
    Klausen Synagogue, 51, 54, 61, 64, 115, 121–125
    Maisel Synagogue, 12, 61, 64, 71, 90, 99, 115, 117, 125–129
    New Synagogue, 133
    Pinchas Synagogue, 6, 10, 11, 31, 51, 61, 63, 88–99, 101, 103, 117, 126
    services, 58–60
    Spanish Synagogue, 4, 6, 61, 64, 65, 89, 128, 129–132
    Vinohrady Synagogue, 89
    visiting, 61–64
    Zigeuner Synagogue, 51–52, 128, 133
  in Warsaw, 154
    Nozyk Synagogue, 247, 249–250
    Praga Synagogue, 252
    services, 180–181
    Tlomackie Street Synagogue, 154, 158, 162, 173, 186, 202, 237–238, 239

Syrian Jews, in Buda, 414
Systematic Regulations of the Jewish Nation *(Systematica Gentis Judaicae Regulatio)*, 386–387, 427, 428, 433
Szabo, Tamas, 457
Szanto, Gabor, 394
Szbolcsi, Miksa, 453
Szenicer, Pinkus, 187
Szent Gyorgy Street (Buda), 408–411
Szeroka Street (Cracow), 291, 337–338, 341
Szinhaz Street (Buda), 409
Szmalenberg, Hanna, 199, 216, 231
Szmulewizna, 152, 195, 251, 253
Szmul Zygielbojm memorial, 222–224
Sztokman, Roza, 213
Szyc, Ania, 179

Taharah, 115, 116
Taitzak, Joseph, 318
Tallis, Umschlagplatz Monument, 231
Talmud instruction, Rabbi Judah Loew and, 33
Talmun Torah school, 351
Tancsics Mihaly Street (Buda), 411–412, 417
Tashlich, 467
Tausk, Sender, 422
Taxation. *See also* Toleration tax
  of Jews in Hungary, 382
  of Jews in Prague, 66, 67
Tax collectors, 7, 378, 379
Taz. *See* Ha'levi, R. David
Teha, Count, 377, 410
Teleki Ter Synagogue, 486
Teller, Issachar Baer, 115
Teller, Judah Loew, 115
Tempelgasse Synagogue, 447
Tempel Synagogue, 291
  history, 354, 356–357
  interior, 355
  religious disputes and, 352–355, 356–357

Temple of Solomon, 451
Terezin, 21, 489–490
  drawings from, 117
Terezvaros (Budapest), 433–434
Theater, Yiddish, 87
Theresienstadt. *See* Terezin
Third Lateran Council, 66, 68
Thirty Years' War, 13, 81, 334
Thon, R. Osias, 356, 358–359
A Thousand Ways (Spira), 322
"Times of Prayer," Altneuschul, 68
Tishe B'Av, 305
Tisza Eszlar, 389
Tlomackie Street Synagogue, 154, 158, 162, 173, 186, 202, 237–238, 239
Tlomackie Street (Warsaw), 239–240
Toleration tax, 14–15
  Hungary, 385
  Warsaw, 154
Tomb of Rachel, 454–455
Tombstones. *See* Gravestones
Torah crown, Altschul (Cracow), 302
Torah mantle, Maisel Synagogue, 126, 128
Torah study, Rabbi Judah Loew on, 121–122
Torat ha'Olah (Isserles), 276
Tosefot, 330
Tosefot Yomtov. *See* Heller, R. Yomtov Lippman
Tosefot Yomtov (Heller), 335
Towers, of Dohaney Street Synagogue, 437
Trawniki labor camp, 178
"Treasury Count," 377, 410
Treblinka death camp, 170, 178, 214, 228, 490–492
Treuenberg, Jacob Bashevi von, 12
Trianon Treaty, 390, 456
Tuberculosis, Warsaw ghetto, 169
Turei Zahav (Ha'levi), 327
Turks, rule of Buda, 382–384, 412–413, 414

Twin-naved synagogues. *See* Naves, twin
The Two Israels, 157
Tyn Church, 64, 144–145
Typhus, Warsaw ghetto, 168, 243
Tzedakkah box. *See* Charity box
Tzemah David (Gans), 103, 105
Tzvi, Shabbetai, 301

Uj Elet, 475
Ujpest, 4, 472–474
Ujpest Synagogue, 473–474, 484–485
Umschlagplatz, 170, 171, 199, 228–231
"Under The Eagle" pharmacy, 369
Universities, quotas and, 390
Urban IV, 379
Urban renewal, Jewish Town (Prague), 51–52
Usury, 6, 66
Utopianism, in Jewish Warsaw, 160–161

Vaci Cemetery, 468
Vaclav II (king of Bohemia), 7
Vaclav I (king of Bohemia), 6
Vaclav IV (king of Bohemia), 7
Vago, Laszlo, 455
Varga, Imre, 457, 458
Venetianer, R. Lajos, 473
Vestibule, in Altschul (Cracow), 297–298
Vieliopoler. *See* Yosef, R. Shlomo Zalman
Viennese Gate (Buda), 409, 413
Vietnam War Memorial, 94
Vigilantes, Warsaw, 246
Vinohrady Synagogue, 89
Vishniac, Roman, 364
Vladisolavova Street (Prague), 99
Vlaidslav Jagiello (king of Bohemia), 10
Vltava river, 96
Volavkova, Hana, 12
Volozhin, 206
Vysehrad, 5, 9, 101

Wagner, Otto, 458
Wahl, Saul, 269, 331

Wahrmann, R. Israel, 431, 443, 472
The Wailing Wall (Cracow), 314
Waldstein, Albrecht, 114
Wallenberg, Raoul, 391, 458
Warsaw. *See also* Praga; Warsaw Ghetto
   after World War II, 149
   anti-Semitism, expulsions, and pogroms, 152, 153, 154, 155, 159–160, 164, 174, 240
   census figures, 159, 161, 162, 173, 175
   de non tolerandis Judaeis, 150–152, 154, 251
   hasidism, 155, 158, 161, 162, 197
   history of Jews in, 150–176
      Holocaust, 165–173
      Holocaust memorials, 183
         Memorial Route of Jewish Martyrdom and Struggle, 214–231
         Warsaw Ghetto Monument, 218–221
   Jewish Cemetery
      history, 185–188
      location, 185
      religious disputes and, 193–195
      walking tour, 188–213
   Jewish Community, 154, 175, 179, 237, 244, 252
   Jewish Historical Institute, 180, 238–240
   Jewish identity and, 173–176
   Jewish Theater, 249
   Jewish vigilantes, 246
   kosher food, 182
   Krochmalna Street, 240–244
   maps, 184, 189–191, 233
   mikveh, 182
   Plac Grzybowski, 244, 245
   proposed museum site, 222
   Prozna Street, 244–249
   Rabbinical Seminary, 193
   restaurants, 182, 247–248
   Ronald S. Lauder Foundation, 175, 179–180, 182, 239, 249
   schools, 175, 179
   Socio-Cultural Society of Jews in Poland, 179, 249
   synagogues
      Nozyk Synagogue, 179, 180–181, 247, 249–250
      Praga Synagogue, 252
      services, 180–181
      Tlomackie Street Synagogue, 154, 158, 162, 173, 186, 202, 237–238, 239–240
   walking tour, 232–250
   Yiddish culture, 161, 162–163, 179, 207–208, 210
   Yiddishkeit, 149, 241–243
Warsaw Ghetto, 166–173
   Adam Czerniakow and, 199–200
   Emmanuel Ringelblum and, 177–178
   Janusz Korczak and, 211–213
   Krochmalna Street, 243–244
   mass deportations, 170–171, 214, 228–230, 491
   mass graves, 187, 198–199
   Memorial Route of Jewish Martyrdom and Struggle, 214–231
   Mila 18 bunker, 225
   Praga and, 252
   Prozna Street, 248
   Stawki Street 5/7, 225
   Stawki Street 6/8 (Czyste Hospital), 226–228
   Tlomackie Street Synagogue and, 238
   Tlomackie Street Synagogue library, 239
   Umschlagplatz, 170, 171, 199, 228–231
   uprising, 171–173, 186, 225
   Zegota and, 221–222
Warsaw Ghetto Monument, 218–221
Warsaw Ghetto Uprising, 171–173, 186, 225
Warsaw Rabbinical Seminary, 193
Warschauer, Jonatan, 350, 362

Warszauera Street (Cracow), 350, 351–352
Waski Dunaj Street (Warsaw), 150
Wawelberg, Henryk, 203
Wawelberg, Hipolit, 204
Wawel Castle, 303, 344
Wedding canopy
  Altneuschul, 76
  Dohaney Street Synagogue, 438
  Kazinczy Street Synagogue, 467
Weddings
  at Altschul (Cracow), 306
  in Dohaney Street Synagogue, 438
  in Kazinczy Street Synagogue, 467
Weil, Jiri, 22, 54, 79–80, 140
Weissenberg, Isaac Meir, 162, 211
Wells, Altschul (Cracow), 297
Weltsch, Robert, 3
Werfel, Franz, 20
Western Wall, 219
Wezyk, Aleksander, 156
White Mountain, battle of, 12, 13
"White Terror," 390
Wiesel, Elie, 205
Wilczynska, Stefania, 213
Windows
  Altneuschul, 74
  stained glass, Tempel Synagogue, 355
Wladyslaw II Jagiello (king of Poland), 263
Wladyslaw IV Vasa (king of Poland), 347
Wohl, Henryk, 209–210
Wolanowski, Majer, 210
Wolfsohn Museum, 343
Women, burial in Warsaw's Jewish Cemetery, 194–195, 205
Women's gallery
  Altneuschul, 74
  Dohaney Street Synagogue, 438
  Great Synagogue (Buda), 420
  High Synagogue (Prague), 83
  Pinchas Synagogue, 96

Women's service, Cultus-Temple and, 444
Wonders of the Maharal (Rosenberg), 48–49
Wood Square (Prague), 51, 65
World Monuments Fund, Prozna Street (Warsaw) and, 245
World War I, 456
  Hungarian Jews in, 389, 455
World War I memorials
  in Budapest, 454–456, 470
  Heroes' Temple, 454–456
World War II. *See* Holocaust
World Zionist Organization, 397–398
Worship. *See also* Prayer; Services
  Budapest synagogues, 475–487
  High Synagogue (Prague), 84–85
Writers' Society (Warsaw), 239

Yadayim, 128
Yad Vashem, 221
Yahrzeit (death anniversary) boards, Altneuschul, 77–78
Yechiel, R. Chaim Meir, of Mogelnice, 205
Yiddish
  abandonment of, 18
  Franz Kafka and, 87–88
Yiddish culture, Warsaw, 161, 162–163, 179, 207–208, 210
Yiddishkeit
  Cracow, 271–272
  Warsaw, 149, 241–243
Yiddish theater, 139, 163, 208, 365
Yisrael of Modzhitz, R., 206
Yitzchak, R. Levi, 155
Yizkor wall, 470–471
Yoko Ono, 460
Yom Hashoah Vehagvurah, 221
Yom Kippur
  Altneushcul, 8
  Altschul (Cracow), 305
Yosef, R. Shlomo Zalman (Vieliopoler), 360

Yoskowitz, R. Pinchas M., 180, 182
Yossef Sheida, 36
Yotserot, 464
Young, James, 219

Zalman, Shneur, 410
Zamenhof, Ludwik, 200–201
Zbitkower, Shmuel, 152, 153, 195, 251–252, 253, 254
Zecher Ha'Churban ("Memory of the Destruction"), Altneuschul, 69
Zegota, 221–222
Zemah, Mardocai, 10
Zichy family, 384–385, 426–427, 428

Zigeuner Synagogue, 51–52, 128, 133
Zionism
  Poland, 164
  Prague, 20
  Theodor Herzl and, 396, 397–398
  Tomas Masaryk and, 28–29
  Warsaw, 160–161
Z'Manei Ha'Tfilot (Times of Prayer), 68
ZOB. *See* Jewish Fighting Organization
Zogerke, Altschul (Cracow), 300–301
Zunz, Leopold, 130
Zygielbojm, Szmul, 222–224
Zyklon B, 492
ZZW. *See* Jewish Fighting Union

ABOUT THE AUTHOR

Eli Valley, the son of a New York City rabbi, moved to Prague after graduating from Cornell University in 1992. There he became the first American Jew to be fully integrated into the local Jewish community since the fall of communism. Over the course of the next five years, Eli Valley worked in sundry capacities for the Prague Jewish Community and served as the first program director of Bejt Praha, the nascent Jewish cultural and religious organization in Prague. His activities included organizing Jewish cultural events, planning religious services, lecturing on Jewish history, preparing children's carnivals, and participating in productions of the Jewish Community Theater. Mr. Valley worked with the younger generation of Czech Jews in events ranging from Passover seders to youth seminars in eastern Slovakia. He has written extensively on these experiences and has been published in newspapers and magazines in Central Europe and the United States. Throughout his years in Prague, Mr. Valley also worked as a guide and lecturer in the former Jewish Town for thousands of visitors from Europe, North America, and Israel. It was this experience that inspired Mr. Valley to write a comprehensive visitor's guide to the Jewish communities in the region.